C000241823

Text, topos and crag photography
by Chris Craggs and Alan James.
Action photography by Chris Craggs
or as credited.
Edited by Alan James.
Printed in Europe on
behalf of Latitude Press Ltd.
(ISO 14001 and EMAS certified printers).
Distributed by Cordee (www.cordee.co.uk).

All maps by ROCKFAX
Some maps based on original source data
from openstreetmap.org.

Published by ROCKFAX in April 2015
© ROCKFAX 2015
www.rockfax.com

This book is printed on FSC certified paper
made from 100% virgin fibre sourced
from sustainable forestry

FSC ®

ISBN 978 1 873341 08 7

Cover: Lucinda Whittaker on *The End of the Affair* (E8 6c)
- *page 414* - at Curbar. Photo: Adam Long
This page: Hazel Findlay finishing off *Usurper* (E4 6a)
- *page 433* - also at Curbar. Photo: Adam Long

In a back street in Liverpool a small wall was created in 1998 by a passion to prove to the world that climbing walls can be fun and inspiring places to climb and train. Awesome Walls Climbing Centres aim to provide frequent well set routes and boulder problems in a clean and friendly atmosphere!

Ryan Edwards on the short and anything but sweet *Jeepers Creepers* (HVS 5b) - *page 167* - at High Neb on Stanage North. Photo: David Bond

Sheffield Area

Ladybower Area

Stanage

Burbage Valley

Millstone Area

Derwent Edges

Chatsworth Area

Southern Crags

Sheffield Area
Ladybower Area
Stanage
Burbage Valley
Millstone Area
Derwent Edges
Chatsworth Area
Southern Crags

The Peak District was the UK's first National Park and it remains one of the most visited in the world, with 16 million people living within an hour's drive and around 25 million visitors a year squeezing into its 555 square miles. The central limestone core is ringed by a ragged edge of gritstone that generally faces towards the centre of the park. The eastern side of this ring of rock is formed by a 30 mile broken banner that runs from Wharncliffe, north of Sheffield, all the way down to Shining Cliff, south of Matlock. The nucleus of this consists of the classic edges, including the ever popular cliffs of Bamford, Stanage, Froggatt and Curbar. There are many lesser edges, plus a rather fine set of quarries, which are virtually all in west-facing hill-top situations. Escape from the city is easy and great sunsets are a given - there is little wonder that Sheffield has become the home of choice for so many climbers.

I first climbed on Stanage in 1968, waking early from a cold night's camping at North Lees and wandering up to gaze at the shadowy line of dark rock running off in both directions. I can still recall the joy of those first explorations almost 50 years on. We spent the first day doing classics such as *Martello Buttress* and *Inverted V*, dodging squally showers along the way. That was followed by a day whacking pegs into Millstone's hairline cracks and slipping off the start of *Great Slab*. I was smitten and moved to Sheffield in 1970 to start a long-term love affair with gritstone that continues to this day.

Even back then, these cliffs and their short, intense climbs had a bigger place in the mythology of UK climbing than their size might suggest. Easy access and perfect rock has created a playground for bold and talented climbers and a place for the rest of us to learn our trade and test our abilities. As time has passed ever more people have been introduced to the world of gritstone climbing and all its wonderful weirdness, at some of the most popular climbing venues on the planet. If the older pioneers could see the number of people who now regularly climb on the gritstone edges, they would doubtless be surprised.

My involvement with guidebooks goes back well over 20 years, meaning I have had the long-term pleasure of combining my two obsessions - climbing and writing. These fantastic cliffs now have another guidebook which I hope will give you as much pleasure and inspiration using it as it has given me while writing it.

Chris Craggs, March 2015

Chris Craggs, older and wiser - well maybe. To the left on *Right Unconquerable* (HVS 5a) - *page 214* - in 1974, and to the right on *Twin Chimneys Buttress* (VS 4c) - *page 238* - in 2014, both at Stanage.

Sheffield Area

Ladybower Area

Stanage

Burbage Valley

Millstone Area

Derwent Edges

Chatsworth Area

Southern Crags

The Book

The arrival of Peak Gritstone East back in 2001 changed climbing guidebooks forever. Marking lines on full-colour photographs of the cliffs on proved to be an approach breathtaking in both its simplicity and effectiveness. Bernard Newman described opening the book as "like looking out of the window at the cliffs". In 2006 we produced Eastern Grit which had a hundred extra pages and 900 more climbs. Amazingly we have managed a similar expansion so this time the book weighs in at a massive 560 pages, almost twice the thickness of the original 2001 book, and includes over 4000 routes.

Peak Gritstone East was photographed with a 3 megapixel camera, which limited the size and quality of the topos that we could produce. This time round the photography was done using 24 megapixel cameras allowing for much larger and clearer photo-topos. Every cliff has been re-photographed in stunning detail and all the photo-topos (okay, except for two owing to tree growth) are new. The extra space has also allowed for a more lavish layout and the cliffs have never looked so good.

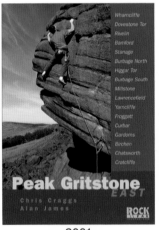

2001

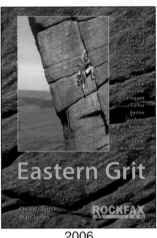

2006

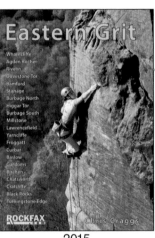

2015

Other Guides

There are some other guides by different publishers which complement the Rockfax series of books. Most are produced by the British Mountaineering Council and contain in-depth listings of routes for all the crags covered.

Froggatt to Black Rocks (BMC 2010)
Froggatt, Curbar, Birchen, Cratcliffe, Black Rocks and lots of minor stuff around Matlock.

Stanage (BMC 2007)
A single book for Stanage with all the routes and bouldering.

Burbage, Millstone and Beyond (BMC 2005)
Burbage Valley, Millstone, Lawrencefield, Rivelin, Derwent, Bamford, Wharncliffe. Includes bouldering.

Peak District Bouldering (Vertebrate Graphics 2011)
Bouldering throughout the Peak area including Western Edges and the Limestone.

Rockfax Guides

There are three Rockfax books that complement the coverage in this one. With all four books you will have all the best climbing over the whole Peak area (gritstone, limestone and bouldering) plus you get Lancashire and Merseyside thrown in!

Peak Bouldering (2014)

The Peak Bouldering Rockfax is a massive book covering a huge area, including all the main bouldering venues of the Peak District. Some have said that if you wrapped a bit of padding around it, you would have an extra bouldering mat! It includes many more low-grade problems than have ever been documented before, including 17 circuits with problems at *f4+* and under, and a further 21 circuits with problems at *f5+* and below. The book uses 'V' grades and Font grades, plus UK technical grades for easier problems.

There is some overlap with this Eastern Grit book for the bouldering which is on, or very close to, the main edges. In these cases the problems are covered in both books. In other places references have been included this book pointing to bouldering areas given full coverage in the Peak Bouldering book.

Peak Limestone (2012)

The first single-volume guidebook to Peak Limestone to have hit the shelves since 1992. The book includes detailed coverage of the classic venues of Stoney, Cheedale and Water-cum-Jolly and the southern crags around Matlock, Dovedale and the Manifold, plus the ever popular sport climbs in the many bolted quarries.

Western Grit (2009)

The most recent edition of the original award-winning 2003 Western Grit guidebook. It ranges from the popular Staffordshire gritstone edges of the Roaches, Hen Cloud and Ramshaw up onto the remote Kinder and Bleaklow moorland crags. Also included are the superb Chew Valley edges, the best of the Lancashire crags and the fine sandstone buttress of Helsby, Pex Hill and Frodsham in Merseyside.

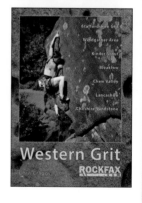

For more information on all Rockfax publications visit
www.rockfax.com

Guidebook Footnote

Sheffield Area · Ladybower Area · Stanage · Burbage Valley · Millstone Area · Derwent Edges · Chatsworth Area · Southern Crags

This book brings together the best climbing on Eastern Grit. Our aim is that you should never have to turn more than a few pages to first get to the crag, then get to the buttress and finally locate the start of your chosen route. All route descriptions are on the same page as their topo and listed from left-to-right. There are many features to help choose suitable crags depending on specific weather conditions or your ability level. You can select a crag from the crag tables on page 42. Each topo also has crag symbols so you can check its suitability at a glance - see key to the right.

The Rockfax App

There is an 'app' version of this guidebook (available in 2015) which contains all the crags and routes. You can purchase each crag individually, or the whole book. The main data on the app is downloaded and stored on your device so you don't need any signal to be able to read the descriptions and see the topos and maps.

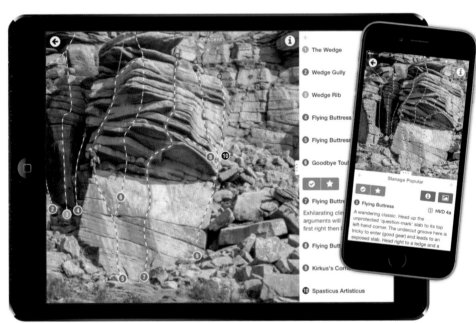

UKC Logbooks

An incredibly popular method of logging your climbing is to use the **UKClimbing.com** logbooks system. To date this database lists more than 312,000 routes, over 19,100 crags and, so far, more than 25,800 users have recorded over 3.8 million ascents! To set up your own logbook all you need to do is register at **UKClimbing.com** and click on the logbook tab. Once set up you will be able to record every ascent you make, when you did it, what style you climbed it in, who you did it with and each entry has a place for your own notes. You can also add your vote to the grade/star system linked to a database on the Rockfax site used by the guidebook writers. The logbook can be private, public or restricted to your own climbing partners only.

The Rockfax App can be linked to your **UKClimbing.com** user account and logbook so that you can record your activity as you progress and look at photos, comments and votes on the routes, although this does require a 3G/4G data connection. You can also look at the UKC logbooks to see if anyone has climbed your chosen route recently to check on conditions, and see any comments they made about it.

Sheffield Area   Ladybower Area   Stanage   Burbage Valley   Millstone Area   Derwent Edges   Chatsworth Area   Southern Crags

Topo Key

Descent — Belay — Height indicator

16m

Boulder problem

6 7 8 9 10 11

Route featured more prominently on a different topo

Alternative for same route

Map Key

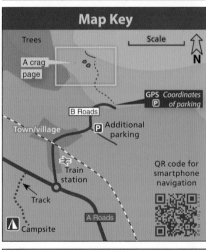

Trees

Scale

N

A crag page

GPS Coordinates of parking

B Roads

Town/village

Additional parking

Train station

QR code for smartphone navigation

Track

A Roads

Campsite

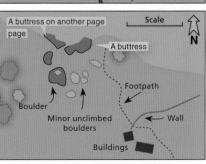

A buttress on another page

Scale

N

A buttress

Footpath

Boulder

Minor unclimbed boulders

Wall

Buildings

Route Symbols

 A good route which is well worth the effort.

 A very good route, one of the best on the crag.

 A brilliant route, one of the best on Eastern Grit.

 A significant route which is one of the most iconic of its type in the book.

 Technical climbing requiring good balance and technique, or complex and tricky moves.

 Powerful climbing; roofs, steep rock, low lock-offs or long moves off small holds.

 Sustained climbing; either lots of hard moves or steep rock giving pumpy climbing.

 Fingery climbing with significant small holds on the hard sections.

 Fluttery climbing with big fall potential and scary run-outs.

 A long reach is helpful, or even essential, for one or more of the moves.

 Graunchy climbing, wide cracks or awkward thrutchy moves.

 Some loose rock may be encountered.

 Typical rounded gritstone holds and sloping breaks.

 A dynamic move ('dyno') may be required.

 A sit-down start for a boulder problem.

Crag Symbols

 Angle of the approach walk to the crag with approximate time.

 Approximate time that the crag is in the direct sun (when it is shining).

 The crag is exposed to bad weather and will catch the wind if it is blowing.

 The crag can offer shelter from cold winds and it may be a good suntrap in colder weather.

 The crag suffers from seepage. It may well be wet and unclimbable in winter and early spring.

 The rock can be green and dirty after prolonged rain.

Deserted - Currently under-used and usually quiet. Fewer good routes or remote and smaller areas.

Quiet - Less popular sections on major crags, or good buttresses with awkward approaches.

Busy - Places you will seldom be alone, especially at weekends. Good routes and easy access.

Crowded - The most popular sections of the most popular crags which are always busy.

Sheffield Area

Ladybower Area

Stanage

Burbage Valley

Millstone Area

Derwent Edges

Chatsworth Area

Southern Crags

The largest ever Rockfax crown was briefly held by the recent Peak Bouldering book, but this has been handed over now to this new massive tome. Working on this for the past two years has been a real pleasure; visiting old favourite venues as well as a few that had fallen off the radar a bit over the years. I have been accompanied by many of the usual suspects, in particular Graham and Dan Parkes, Steve Cunnington, Dave Gregory, Colin Binks, Dave Clay, Martin Veale and Brian Rossiter. There were a few mutterings when I kept suggesting venues like Turningstone Edge and Shining Cliff instead of the usual Froggatt/Stanage/Bamford circuit but, in the event, we had some great days on some out-of-the-way crags.

The combined skills of the Rockfax/UKC team have made the production of the book a breeze - Alan James has bought his layout skills and eagle eye to bear with stunning results. Also Stephen (FB) Horne has come up with some superb scripts that have automated many of the more onerous tasks associated with writing guidebooks.

As ever Sherri Davy has been my rock; helping and supporting me at every stage of the production, from the early days tramping about in the fog checking stuff all the way through adding the finishing touches - a huge thank you is in order.

Chris Craggs, March 2015

We owe a huge debt of thanks to all those who have contributed to the documentation of climbing on the Eastern Edges over the years. Whether this be through work on older guidebooks, or diligent crag moderators on UKClimbing, your efforts are very much appreciated.

For this book we have once again worked with a number of superb photographers. Thanks go to Mike Hutton and Adam Long especially for their many fine contributions. We are also grateful to David Bond, Chris Fox, Graham Parkes, Guy Van Greuning, Jamie Moss, Dan Arkle, Jonathon Percival, Franco Cookson, Calum Muskett, Owen Hughes, Michael Watson and Rob Greenwood for their photographs.

Thanks also to Mark Rankine, Pete Whittaker, Paul Phillips (*497 ticks on the Eastern Grit Top 500*) and Rob Greenwood.

I would like to make a special mention for our two excellent proof readers. Jaimella Espley and Rebecca Ting have done an amazing job and continue to be great people to work with.

Once again Chris Craggs has come through with the goods, 14 years on since our first collaboration. I am very grateful to both Chris and Sherri for their excellent work making this third edition of Eastern Grit the biggest and best ever.

Alan James, March 2015

We are grateful to the following for their support of this guidebook.

Equipment Manufacturers

Black Diamond - *Outside back cover*
blackdiamondequipment.com

Beta Climbing Designs - *Page 33*
Tenaya, climbOn, Snap, Sterling Rope
betaclimbingdesigns.com

Beyond Hope - *Page 19*
Prana, Metolius, Evolv, AustriAlpin
beyondhope.co.uk

DMM - *Page 29*
dmmclimbing.com

Rab - *Page 31*
equipuk.com

Mammut - *Inside front cover*
mammut.ch

Marmot - *Page 15*
www.marmot.com

Wild Country - *Page 27*
wildcountry.com

Climbing Walls

Awesome Walls - *Page 2*
Liverpool, Stockport, Stoke-on-Trent, Sheffield, Dublin
awesomewalls.co.uk

Shops

Rock On - *Back flap*
London, Guildford, Birmingham
rockonclimbing.co.uk

Outside - *Inside Back Cover*
Hathersage
outside.co.uk

Guiding

Expedition Hot Rock - *Page 21*
expeditionhotrock.com

Sheffield Area

Ladybower Area

Stanage

Burbage Valley

Millstone Area

Derwent Edges

Chatsworth Area

Southern Crags

Merlin Andrew taking flight off *The Link* (E1 5b) - *page 233* - on Stanage Popular. Photo: Jonathon Percival.

Sheffield Area

Ladybower Area

Stanage

Burbage Valley

Millstone Area

Derwent Edges

Chatsworth Area

Southern Crags

Eastern Grit
Logistics

Heading homeward after a mid-winter's day on Curbar; tingling fingers and happy hearts as the hard frost starts to bite again.

Mountain Rescue
In the event of an accident requiring the assistance of Mountain Rescue:
Dial 112 and ask for 'POLICE - MOUNTAIN RESCUE'
This is very important since just asking for 'Police' will redirect you to a switchboard which could be a long way from your current location. This can cause delays in the rescue procedure as the authorities try and track down where the injured party is. Asking for 'Mountain Rescue' will immediately redirect you to people who know the area well.

Mobile Phones
Most of the crags described in this book have reasonable mobile phone coverage across the major networks. Possible exceptions are the remote moorland crags to the north and some of the deeper quarries where coverage can be intermittent or not available at all. In an emergency scramble up to higher ground to try to access a decent signal.

Tourist Information Offices
If you are short of ideas of what to do on a wet day, need some accommodation, want information on walks or are just interested in local history, take a look at the **Tourist Information Offices**. They will be able to provide much more information than is possible to include on these pages.

Sheffield - The Winter Gardens. Tel: 0114 273 4672
Chesterfield - Rykneld Square, Chesterfield. Tel: 01246 345777
Buxton - The Pavilion Gardens. Tel: 01298 25106
Bakewell - Old Market Hall, Bridge Street. Tel: 01629 813227
Leek - 1 Market Place, Leek. Tel: 01538 483741

More information and other travel tips are available at **www.visitpeakdistrict.com**

When to Go
Eastern Grit can offer something for the diligent explorer on most days of the year; there is nearly always a vehicle or two parked at the Popular End of Stanage even on the most miserable of days. Crisp winter conditions are ideal for the harder routes, whereas spring can offer perfect conditions when the crags and ground dry out and it isn't too hot. Once the summer arrives, shade can usually be found by making an early start. Alternatively consider heading up to the higher edges where there is often a cooling breeze, although midges can be a problem. In the autumn the rain causes the greening of the lower cliffs but good conditions can often be found on the more exposed edges. A cloud inversion filling the Derwent Valley is quite a common experience with the long cold nights of late autumn and into the winter, making for superb conditions on Froggatt and Curbar.
On cold winter days Rivelin is a good bet. During wetter weather crags such as Wharncliffe and Agden are worth considering - not only are they both quick to dry but they also lie to the east of the main hills so benefit from a rain-shadow effect.

Temperature °C	Jan	Feb	Mar	Apr	May	Jun	Jul	Aug	Sep	Oct	Nov	Dec
Average Max Temp (°C)	6	6	9	10	14	17	20	19	15	12	8	5
Average Min Temp (°C)	1	1	3	3	6	9	11	11	8	6	3	1
Average Rain Days/Month	9	10	8	6	6	5	6	6	7	7	8	6

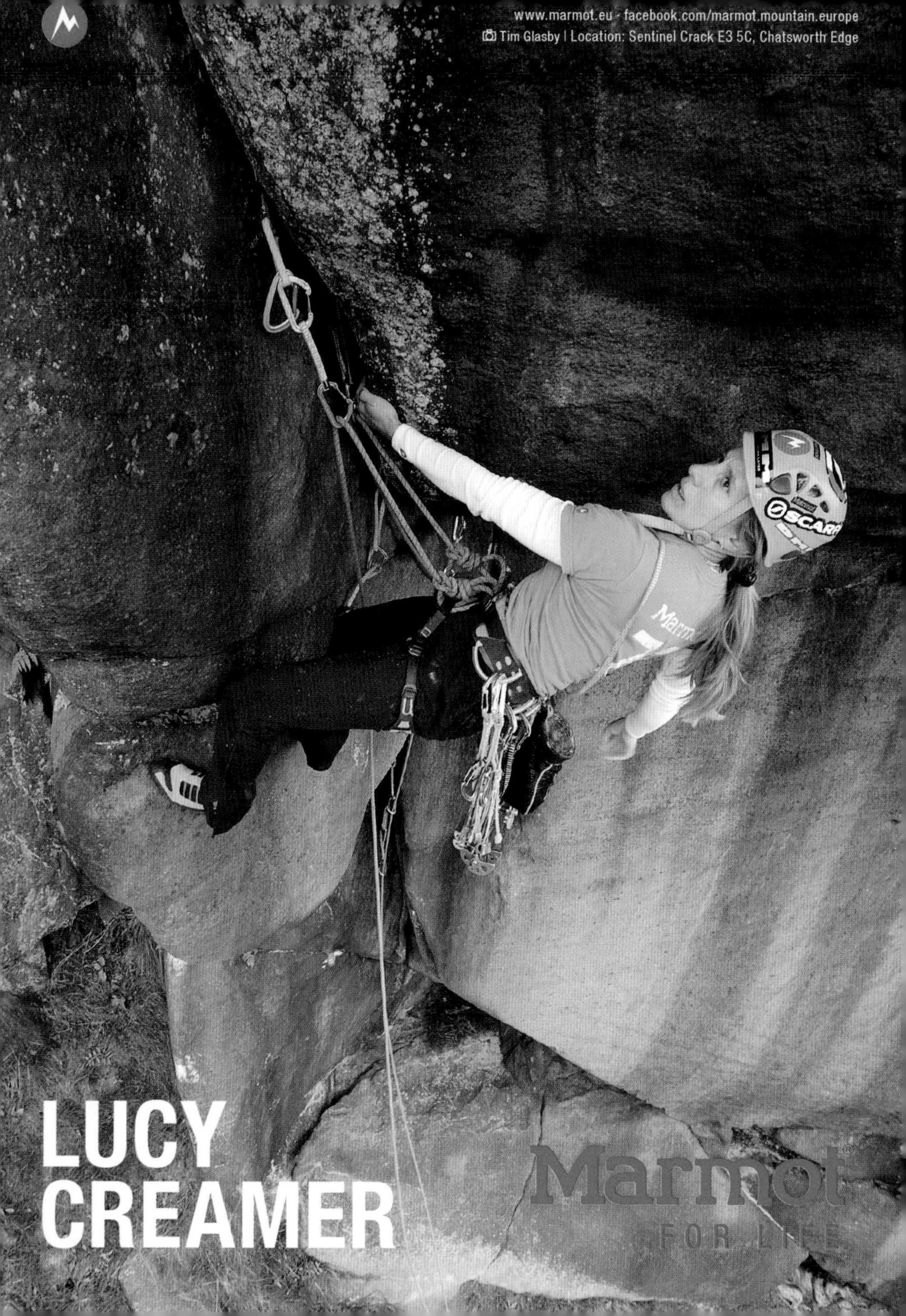
www.marmot.eu - facebook.com/marmot.mountain.europe
Tim Glasby | Location: Sentinel Crack E3 5C, Chatsworth Edge
LUCY
CREAMER
Marmot
FOR LIFE

The easiest way to access most of the crags in this book is by car and the approaches are written assuming you are using one.

Parking Locations

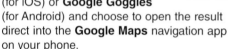 All the parking spots are indicated with a precise GPS location. This is in the form of two decimal numbers as in the sample blue box. Different SatNav devices accept these numbers in alternative formats.

QR codes have also been included. You can scan the QR code using an app such as **Scan** (for iOS) or **Google Goggles** (for Android) and choose to open the result direct into the **Google Maps** navigation app on your phone.

Trains ≽

There is a regular service from Sheffield and Manchester to Grindleford. A long but pleasant walk leads up the Padley Gorge to Burbage South, Millstone and Lawrencefield, or south to Tegness and Froggatt. Some trains also stop at Bamford station which again allows a longish walk (1.5 miles) through the village and on to Bamford Edge. The same distance again will reach Stanage. The best website for finding train information is **thetrainline.com**.

Buses

Bus coverage for the Peak District is reasonable. The best website for finding bus information is **traveline.info**. Also very useful is **travelsouthyorkshire.com** for buses in and around Sheffield.

From Sheffield
Wharncliffe - No. 57 to Stocksbridge.
Rivelin, Dovestone Tor, Stanage North and Bamford - No. 244/273/274 via Crosspool, Rivelin Dams and Bamford.
Stanage Plantation - No. 51 to Lodge Moor (a 1 hour walk, but it's a frequent bus service).
Burbage Valley, Millstone and Lawrencefield - No. 272 to Castleton via Fox House and No. 65 to Buxton via Fox House and Grindleford.
Burbage Valley, Yarncliffe, Froggatt - No. 240 to Bakewell.
Baslow and Gardom's - No. 218 to Buxton via Bakewell.

From Chesterfield
Birchen, Chatsworth - No. 170 to Bakewell.

From Matlock
Cratcliffe - No. 172 to Bakewell.

From Derby
Black Rocks - No. 6.1 to Wirksworth and Matlock.

Stanage Edge Popular End in the summer - arrive early if you want a prime parking space.

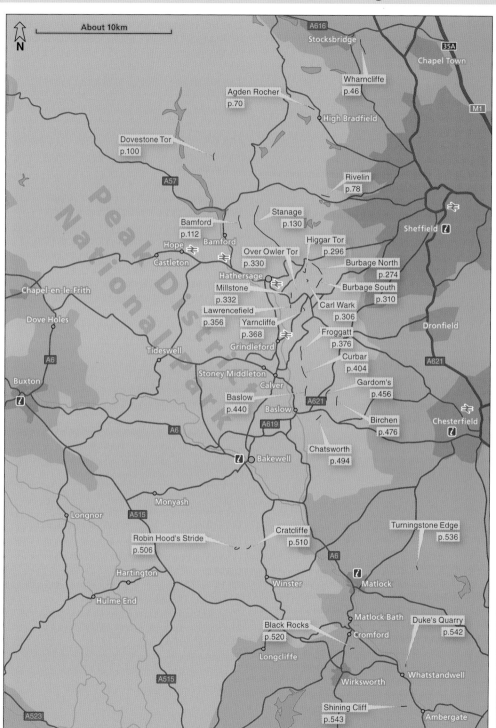

Peak District National Park

- Stocksbridge
- A616
- 35A
- Chapel Town
- M1
- Wharncliffe p.46
- Agden Rocher p.70
- High Bradfield
- Dovestone Tor p.100
- A57
- Rivelin p.78
- Stanage p.130
- Sheffield
- Bamford p.112
- Bamford
- Hope
- Castleton
- Over Owler Tor p.330
- Higgar Tor p.296
- Burbage North p.274
- Hathersage
- Millstone p.332
- Burbage South p.310
- Chapel-en-le-Frith
- Lawrencefield p.356
- Carl Wark p.306
- Dove Holes
- Yarncliffe p.368
- Froggatt p.376
- Dronfield
- Tideswell
- Grindleford
- Curbar p.404
- A6
- Stoney Middleton
- A621
- Buxton
- Calver
- Gardom's p.456
- Baslow p.440
- Baslow
- Birchen p.476
- Chesterfield
- A619
- A6
- Chatsworth p.494
- Bakewell
- Monyash
- Longnor
- A515
- Turningstone Edge p.536
- Cratcliffe p.510
- Robin Hood's Stride p.506
- A6
- Hartington
- Winster
- Matlock
- Hulme End
- Matlock Bath
- Black Rocks p.520
- Cromford
- Duke's Quarry p.542
- Longcliffe
- Whatstandwell
- A515
- Wirksworth
- A523
- Shining Cliff p.543
- Ambergate

Sheffield Area · Ladybower Area · Stanage · Burbage Valley · Millstone Area · Derwent Edges · Chatsworth Area · Southern Crags

About 10km
N

Accommodation
Useful websites for different types of accommodation are:
peakdistrictonline.co.uk
ukclimbing.com/listings
Youth Hostels - There are numerous Youth Hostels in the Peak District, check out **yha.org.uk**

Camping
There are many more campsites than these two popular ones here.

Stanage - North Lees Camp Site
Birley Lane, Hathersage (p.130).
Tel: 01433 650838
The most popular climbers' campsite in the area - booking will be needed at busy times.

Baslow - Eric Byne Memorial Campsite
Below Birchen Edge, off the A619 (p.477). This is a rudimentary site (no vehicles allowed) but it is in a central (and very quiet) location.

There are many other campsites scattered throughout the area, from small and basic to very plush - **ukcampsite.co.uk**

Pubs
Pubs are an integral part of the climbing experience for many. The Peak District is blessed with many fine hostelries which make great locations for an après-climb pint where you can discuss the highs and lows of your day. A few are listed below as recommended by readers of the **UKClimbing.com** forums.

The Strines Inn (p.100) - A very old pub. Decent food and good for Dovestone Tor.

The Anglers Rest - At Bamford. Owned by members of the local community. A good variety of beers, and excellent food.

The Norfolk Arms - Ringinglow, for homeward-bound Sheffielders. Good food, good beer, and well-used to smelly climbers.

The Scotsmans Pack - Hathersage, good for Stanage. Within walking distance of the North Lees campsite. Good beer and food.

The Millstone - Below Millstone! Friendly staff and well-kept ale. Overnight parking allowed if you have a pint and a breakfast.

The Grouse Inn (p.376) - Above the parking area for Froggatt. Good food and popular with climbers.

Chequers Inn (p.376) - Below Froggatt. Good food and ale plus a beer garden.

The Sportsman - Lodge Moor, Sheffield. Handy if you access Stanage from Redmires.

The Cheshire Cheese Inn - Hope. Great atmosphere, food and beer. Often very busy.

The Druid Inn (p.506) - In Birchover, handy for Cratcliffe. Very good food.

Climbing Shops
More shops listed at -
ukclimbing.com/listings

Outside - *Inside back cover*
Main Road, Hathersage
Tel: 01433 651936
outside.co.uk

Crag X - 45 Mowbray Street, Sheffield.
Go Outdoors - Hill Street, Sheffield.
Go Outdoors - Main Road, Hathersage.
Hitch 'n' Hike - Mytham Bridge, Hope Valley.

Cafes
There are plenty of tea shops and cafes but three used by climbers are:
Grindleford Station Cafe - (p.368) Just off the B6001 through Grindleford. Popular with climbers and walkers.
Outside Cafe - Above Outside in the centre of Hathersage. Excellent cafe with good food.
Palmers Cafe - By the traffic lights at Calver crossroads. Popular with cyclists and climbers. Nice and central for the Derwent Valley section of Eastern Grit.

www.prana.com

www.metoliusclimbing.com

www.evolvsports.com

The main wall at Awesome Walls in Sheffield - opened in 2013.

If you are rained off in the Peak, or if you just want to top up your power in the winter months, the climbing walls listed here are well worth considering.

- Lead routes
- Bouldering
- Cafe
- Major shop

More information and more walls are on the UKClimbing website at
ukclimbing.com/walls/

The Climbing Works
Little London Road, Sheffield.
Tel. 0114 250 9990
climbingworks.com

The Matrix
Goodwin Sports Centre,
Northumberland Road, Sheffield,
Tel. 0114 222 6999
sport-sheffield.com

The Foundry, Sheffield
45 Mowbray Street, Sheffield.
Tel. 0114 244 6622
foundryclimbing.com

Awesome Walls Sheffield
Garter Street, Sheffield.
Tel: 0114 244 6622
Large dedicated climbing centre.

Awesome Walls Stockport
The Engine House, Stockport.
Tel: 0161 494 9949
Large dedicated climbing centre.

Awesome Walls Stoke
Sefton Road, Stoke-on-Trent.
Tel: 01782 341919
Bouldering wall with some leading lines.

awesomewalls.co.uk
See advert on page 2

Wirksworth Leisure Centre
Hannage Way, Wirksworth.
Tel. 01629 824 717

Sheffield Area

Ladybower Area

Stanage

Burbage Valley

Millstone Area

Derwent Edges

Chatsworth Area

Southern Crags

Eastern Grit
Climbing Information

Dan Parkes placing the crucial runner before the crux of *Billy Whizz* (E2 5c) - *page 362*
- at Lawrencefield, while unseen monsters lurk in the watery depths of the pool below.

Sheffield Area

Ladybower Area

Stanage

Burbage Valley

Millstone Area

Derwent Edges

Chatsworth Area

Southern Crags

General Behaviour

Rock climbing has become ever more popular, increasing numbers of people want access to the cliffs and the pressures on the crag environment have never been greater. Complying with simple requests such as: no fires, leave no litter, close gates after you, park sensibly and avoid disturbing farm animals should be obvious to everyone.

Access

The majority of crags in this book have been climbed on for many years and we are lucky to enjoy largely unrestricted access to them. In a few cases there may be temporary restrictions because of nesting birds, or high fire risk. These are detailed in the text, and/or should be indicated by signs on the approach to the crags.

A contribution from the Rockfax web sales of this guidebook is made to the **BMC Access and Conservation Trust** - *see opposite for more information on the ACT*.

The BMC

Access arrangements can change and we recommend that, when unsure, you use the BMC Regional Access Database to check what the current situation is. You can check RAD here - **thebmc.co.uk/modules/RAD/**

or install the BMC RAD app from your iOS or Android app store. If you do encounter problems, contact the BMC Access and Conservation representative. They are always happy to discuss problems,

BMC RAD app

and often their involvement at an early stage can defuse a situation before it escalates into a serious access dispute.

**British Mountaineering Council,
177-179 Burton Road,
Manchester, M20 2BB.**
Tel: 0870 010 4878
Web: thebmc.co.uk
Email: office@thebmc.co.uk

The ring ouzels have fledged - thank you.

Parking

All the crags in this book have parking areas which are indicated with GPS coordinates and QR codes on the maps. Please use these parking areas! If there is one thing above all others that annoys landowners, it is having their drive/field blocked by someone's car. In some cases parking may involve you spending some money in one of the Pay and Display parking areas.

Dogs

All the moorland areas in this book are grazed by sheep and as such make an unsuitable destination for domestic dogs. If you do take your best friend on a climbing trip, please make sure it is tied up and on good behaviour.

A busy day at Dover's Wall.

Erosion

The increased popularity of climbing has caused erosion problems, especially under crags are used by lots of groups, and with a proliferation of paths at popular venues. Overuse of chalk also has impact on the rock and looks unsightly, as does needless wire brushing. Littering has also become an issue and this includes using the crag environs as a toilet.

Some general guidelines:
- Don't stray from the popular paths
- Use less chalk
- Don't use wire brushes
- Take your litter home
- Go before you go!

Rock Damage

There is no reason to try to improve holds on any of the routes on grit, if you think otherwise then you are wrong.
Cams are very effective at levering loose flakes - please think before you place them. Damage to routes sometimes happens when attempting to retrieve stuck gear. Runners that get stuck are usually poorly placed, so think before you place it. If a runner does get properly jammed it may be better leaving it for someone who can get it out without wrecking the rock.

Group Usage

The nationwide network of indoor walls has introduced a new generation to climbing. As these climbers develop, many look to move outdoors which has resulted in a significant increase in courses offered by instructors, schools and outdoor centres. This is a good thing but it has lead to some problems on the popular edges.
- Monopolisation of popular classic routes at busy times.
- The use of inappropriate and dirty footwear leading to much more damage to holds.
- Putting people on climbs that are too hard for them leading rock being damaged while they scrabble around on the rope.
- Sending a convoy of folks abseiling down popular lines causing significant erosion.
- Repeated use of the same venues. Places like the left-hand end of the Black Rocks and the first bay at Yarncliffe Quarry are showing serious signs of environmental degradation.

The effects of overuse need to be considered by all visitors to the crags. If you must visit the cliffs in a large group, please consider other climbers.
- Keep your kit in one area and avoid monopolising popular routes for long periods.
- Arrange yourselves into several small groups rather than one large one.
- Pull your ropes down when they are not being used so that others can climb.

Good group practice at Stanage - using less popular routes, keeping to a compact area and protecting the cliff edge.

Almost all the routes in this guide have no fixed gear so everything you need has to be carried with you. It is always worth taking a bit of time to scan a route to envisage the runner placements that might be available. It may seem obvious but wide cracks need big runners so starting up an off-width with a bunch of small wires doesn't make any more sense than setting off up a blank slab with a set of big cams, "just in case"!

Runners
Many old routes which were bold and unprotected leads in their day are now relatively safe with modern protection. A typical general gritstone rack will consist of a set of wires and a range of cams; the wide breaks and many cracks make gritstone ideal for camming devices. Hexes are a cheaper alternative though they are less versatile and are much noisier! Wires are useful for the narrow cracks plus a couple of slings for threads and for lassoing blocks and boulders at the cliff-top belays. For harder routes, micro-wires, tiny cams and other more advanced devices may be essential.

Ropes
Most grit routes are short enough to be climbed on a single rope, either 10mm or a triple-rated thinner rope. The only exceptions are routes which wander around in which case you need two half-ropes, or you can use one rope doubled up - colour confusion guaranteed.

Laced up!

Other Gear
Beyond these essentials you may also find useful: a poker for (gently) removing stubborn gear; tape for bandaging your hands before, or after, they are wrecked by some savage crack; a toothbrush for brushing smaller holds on hard routes. A bouldering mat can be very welcome on unprotected starts. The only other thing you need is in your hands now!

Dave Clay and Steve Cunnington away from it all on *Sneaking Sally Through the Alley* (VS 4c) - *page 169* - at Stanage North. Dave's gear matches the route well - a short climb up a thin crack = single rope, wires and small cams.

Sheffield Area

Ladybower Area

Stanage

Burbage Valley

Millstone Area

Derwent Edges

Chatsworth Area

Southern Crags

Sheffield Area

Ladybower Area

Stanage

Burbage Valley

Millstone Area

Derwent Edges

Chatsworth Area

Southern Crags

The British Trad Grade is probably never more appropriately used than it is on gritstone. Here the subtleties and versatility of the Trad Grade can be appreciated to their maximum and, because of its place at the heart of climbing in the UK, many of the routes are perceived as 'yard-sticks' for their respective grades.

Bold Routes - Some gritstone routes have limited protection and you can find yourself in some very serious situations, especially on the harder climbs. This should be clear from the text, but please make sure you use your own skill and judgment as to whether you will be able to safely complete a chosen climb. A bold E2 may only feel like a sport grade 6a on a top-rope but it is a very different proposition as a lead or solo.

Trad Grade

1) Adjectival grade (Diff, VD, HVD, Severe, Hard Severe (HS), Very Severe (VS), Hard Very Severe (HVS), E1 to E10).
An overall picture of the route including how well protected it is, how sustained, and a general indication of the level of difficulty of the whole route.

2) UK Technical grade (4a, 4b, 4c to 7b).
The difficulty of the hardest single move, or short section.

Colour Coding

The routes are all given a colour-coded dot corresponding to a grade band.
Green Routes - Everything at grade Severe and under. Good for beginners and those looking for an easy life.
Orange Routes - Hard Severe to HVS inclusive. General ticking routes for those with more experience. A large range of excellent routes is available across this band.
Red Routes - E1 to E3 inclusive. Routes for the experienced and keen climber. A grade band which includes many of the Peak's great classics.
Black Routes - E4 and above. A grade band for the talented and/or dedicated.

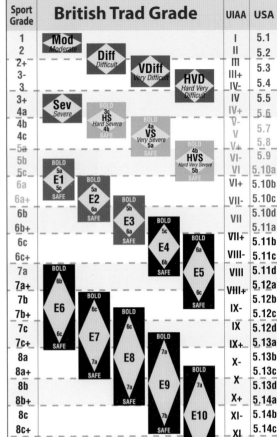

Bouldering Grades

The boulder problems in this book are given a Font Grade, which is the system established in Fontainebleau in France. This is now regarded by most British climbers as the best system for grading boulder problems and routes climbed using a 'highball approach' (see next page). The table below shows the approximate conversion between Font grades, V grades (the alternative bouldering grade system) and UK Technical grades which are mentioned above and used in this book for the routes.

Font Grade	f2	f2+	f3	f3+	f4	f4+	f5	f5+	f6A	f6A+	f6B	f6B+	f6C	f6C+	f7A	f7A+	f7B	f7B+	f7C	f7C+	f8A	f8A+	f8B	f8B+	f8C
V Grade		VB		V0-	V0	V0+	V1	V2		V3		V4		V5		V6	V7		V8		V9	V10	V11	V12	V13	V14	V15
UK Tech Grade		3b	3c	4a	4b	4c	5a	5b	5c	6a		6b				6c				7a					

Jules Littlefair high on Predator (8b), Malham Cove
Image ©Stu Littlefair

Bouldering pads have changed the way people approach hard gritstone routes. What used to be a bold solo, sometimes practised on a top-rope, is now more often done ground-up above a stack of pads with spotters gathered around. This has led to a significant increase in the number of ascents some routes get. Bold climbs that used to get two or three leads/solos a year can now receive ten ascents in an afternoon when the conditions (and number of pads and spotters) are right.

Highball Grades

This change in approach has led to a debate as to which is the correct style, and what grade is appropriate. This is a routes book so, in general, we have given route grades. For routes which tend to see a lot of bouldering style 'highball' ascents, we have mentioned the accepted Font grade in the route description. In other places, shorter routes, which are virtually exclusively soloed or bouldered above pads, are given straight Font grades (see previous page for a conversion table for Font grades).

As a further complication, there is also the 'snowball' grade. After heavy snow huge drifts build up under the edges and some very bold routes become much more amenable challenges with levelled out snow platforms covered with bouldering pads underneath them. There are some routes which only get highball ascents under these conditions and this is also mentioned in the descriptions.

Olivier Coenen 'highballing' *Ulysses Bow* (E6/*f6C*) - *page 191* - above pads and two spotters. Photo: David Bond

TENAYA®

Oasi

Extreme Climbing,
Total Connection

Working your way through a ticklist is one of climbing's esoteric spin-off activities that is great fun. It is a good indicator of your progress through the grades, or how well you are getting to know an area. Ticklists also give you an excuse (if one was ever needed) to visit new and varied areas.

Rockfax books have had a long history of high-quality ticklists with Top 50 and Top 500 routes lists always proving very popular. These ticklists, and many more, appear in the UKC logbooks so you can tick them in the books and log them online.

This time, in addition to the Top 50 symbol and Top 500 Graded List, we have also included 26 individual Ticklists spread across the full spectrum of Eastern Grit, geographically and grade-wise. There is even a Ticklist of Ticklists - so that is 27 to go at! Finish that lot and you can consider yourself and true aficionado and a damn good climber too!

TICKLIST
Peaks and Pinnacles

There are a surprising number of mini peaks and decent-sized pinnacles scattered along the Eastern edges, varying from simple scrambles, to summits that need climbing ability of up to VS. Here is a baker's dozen of some of the most interesting in roughly ascending order of difficulty.

☐ **The Promontory** *(525)*
Black Rocks - only a walk but super-exposed.

☐ **Three Ships** *(477)*
Birchen - three easy ticks for the price of one.

☐ **Over Owler Tor** *(330)*
A great viewpoint over the Burbage arena.

☐ **Higgar Tor** *(301)*
Mantel up the northeast corner - short and easy but leads to a great island in the sky.

☐ **Mother Cap** *(329)*
A tricky rounded scramble.

☐ **Bel Ami** *(433)*
Curbar - best as a mini summit finish to the VS route.

☐ **Prow Rock** *(48)*
Wharncliffe - *Inside Route, Diff* is the easiest line

☐ **Tegness Pinnacle** *(378)*
Tegness Quarry - *Original Route, Diff* is the way.

☐ **Weasel Pinnacle** *(508)*
Robin Hood's Stride - *Letter Route, Diff.*

☐ **Stonnis Pinnacle** *(524)*
Black Rocks - invariably done with *Central Buttress, VD.*

☐ **Inaccessible Pinnacle** *(508)*
Robin Hood's Stride - *Short Climb, VD.*

☐ **Rivelin Needle** *(86)*
Spiral Route, VS is the easiest option, abseil off.

☐ **Froggatt Pinnacle** *(394)*
Valkyrie, HVS is the choice route although you can get up the back on *Route One, VS 5a*. Abseil descent.

Inaccessible Pinnacle at Robin Hood's Stride, not living up to its name for Steve Cunnington and Dave Gregory. One of the harder ticks on the Peaks and Pinnacles Ticklist but still relatively amenable via *Boulder Climb* (HS 4c) - *page 508.*

TICKLIST
A Graded List of the Ticklists

Is it possible to have too many ticklists? If you think not, here is a real challenge; try working your way through this lot.

☐ Stanage Green Spot Starters: Mod - S *(133)*. 24 routes.

☐ Lawrencefield Taster: VD - VS *(360)*. 5 routes.

☐ Wharncliffe Hoary Classics: S - VS *(61)*. 6 routes.

☐ Peaks and Pinnacles: up to VS *(opposite)*. 13 routes.

☐ Stanage Orange Spot Heaven: HS - HVS *(261)*. 12 routes.

☐ Baslow Bits and Bobs: Diff - HVS *(449)*. 7 routes.

☐ Bamford Brilliance: HS - HVS *(113)*. 5 routes.

☐ Dovestone Summer Sampler: VS - HVS *(108)*. 5 routes.

☐ Best of Birchen: Mod - HVS *(476)*. 12 routes.

☐ Crack School Part: 1 VD - HVS *(36)*. 25 routes.

☐ Rivelin Mid-grade Gems: VS - E1 *(89)*. 6 routes.

☐ Gardom's Classics: HVD - E1 *(456)*. 6 routes.

☐ Never Been to Agden: S - E1 *(72)*. 7 routes.

☐ Black Rocks Historic Classics: HVD - E1 *(521)*. 8 routes.

☐ Rivelin Cracks: VD - E2 *(97)*. 6 routes.

☐ Burbage North Belles: HS - E2 *(287)*. 6 routes.

☐ Higgar Tor Abrasive Testers: VS - E2 *(299)*. 2 routes.

☐ Cratcliffe Classics: HVS - E3 *(511)*. 6 routes.

☐ Chatsworth Choice Cuts: VD - E3 *(495)*. 11 routes.

☐ Froggatt - the Cracks: HVD - E3 *(403)*. 14 routes.

☐ Stanage Original and Best Top Ten: E1 - E3 *(173)*. 10 routes.

☐ Gardom's E3s: E3 *(465)*. 4 routes.

☐ Millstone Crackers: VS - E5 *(355)*. 11 routes.

☐ Crack School Part 2: E1 - E5 *(37)*. 25 routes.

☐ Froggatt - the Slabs: Diff - E7 *(387)*. 14 routes.

☐ Curbar Crush: HS - E9 *(427)*. 16 routes.

☐ Burbage South Stoppers: E7 - E10 *(327)*. 9 routes ... so far.

Climbers on *The Rasp* (E2 5b) - *page 300* - at Higgar Tor. The Higgar Tor Abrasive Testers Ticklist may have only two routes but it is probably harder to complete for most climbers than the 25-route Crack School - Part 1 described on the next page.

Sheffield Area

Ladybower Area

Stanage

Burbage Valley

Millstone Area

Derwent Edges

Chatsworth Area

Southern Crags

TICKLIST
Crack School - Part 1

Jamming - favourite technique or bugbear - whichever way you feel you can't ignore the classics listed below. These should give you a good grounding in the technique, though you can always try laybacking them.

- [ ] **Kelly's Crack, VD** *(152)*. Mild but neat.
- [ ] **Trafalgar Crack, VD** *(485)*. The start is tricky.
- [ ] **Heather Wall, HVD** *(390)*. Just beautiful.
- [ ] **N.M.C. Crack, HVD** *(472)*. Often green but tasty.
- [ ] **Twisting Crack, S** *(164)*. Steep and juggy.
- [ ] **Christmas Crack, HS** *(249)*. An Xmas cracker.
- [ ] **Brooks' Layback, HS** *(291)*. Don't you dare layback.
- [ ] **Paradise Wall, HS** *(206)*. Paradise? Probably.
- [ ] **Amazon Crack, HS** *(292)*. Sweet and superb.
- [ ] **Stonnis Crack, HS** *(529)*. Some solid jamming moves.
- [ ] **Brown's Crack, HS** *(115)*. Best of its grade on Grit?
- [ ] **Mutiny Crack, HS** *(281)*. The start is perplexing.
- [ ] **Byne's Crack, VS** *(317)*. The best VS on Burbage.
- [ ] **Hell Crack, VS** *(230)*. The initial bulge is steep.
- [ ] **Cardinal's Crack, VS** *(371)*. Big fists help.
- [ ] **Fern Crack, VS** *(188)*. The start is a slippery pig.
- [ ] **Great Harry, VS** *(361)*. Wide and awkward at the top.
- [ ] **The File, VS** *(301)*. A true test of your skill.
- [ ] **Altar Crack, VS** *(96)*. Okay, you can layback this one.
- [ ] **Birch Tree Wall Direct, VS** *(532)*. Thin and technical.
- [ ] **Great Crack, HVS** *(542)*. Passing the lip is perplexing.
- [ ] **Sorrell's Sorrow, HVS** *(413)*. Wide and withering.
- [ ] **Terrazza Crack, HVS** *(148)*. A real HVS jamming crack.
- [ ] **Zapple, HVS** *(373)*. Fingers to hands.
- [ ] **Bond Street, HVS** *(350)*. A perfect quarry crack.

Exiting the pod is the crux for many on *The Peapod* (HVS 5b) - *page 436* - as big a classic as any crack in the Peak. Once ticked, it is eyes right for the chunkier challenge of *The Right Eliminate*. Photo: Mike Hutton

Sheffield Area Ladybower Area Stanage Burbage Valley Millstone Area Derwent Edges Chatsworth Area Southern Crags

TICKLIST
Crack School - Part 2

Okay, so you have should have made a good start by ticking a selection from Crack School - Part 1, now down to business with some real testers.

☐ **Goliath's Groove, HVS** *(191)*.The start is a struggle.

☐ **Avalanche Wall, HVS** *(430)*. Feels like a Millstone route.

☐ **Puppet Crack, HVS** *(497)*. The start needs a stiff pull.

☐ **The Peapod, HVS** *(436)*. Which way to face, left or right?

☐ **Tower Crack, HVS** *(198)*. Tough, though bridging helps.

☐ **Dexterity, E1** *(388)*. Go direct for the true pump.

☐ **Embankment 3, E1** *(349)*. A real ankle wrecker.

☐ **The Vice, E1** *(139)*. A jamming crack with teeth.

☐ **Castor, E1** *(74)*. The best on this neglected crag?

☐ **Deadbay Crack, E1** *(410)*. Usually a greasy battle.

☐ **The Unprintable, E1** *(256)*. A right ****ing struggle.

☐ **The Big Crack, E2** *(401)*. Not quite as fierce as it looks.

☐ **Regent Street, E2** *(353)*. Finger-locking glory.

☐ **Zeus, E2** *(324)*. Sustained and pushy.

☐ **Insanity, E2** *(434)*. A tottering layback for most.

☐ **Synopsis, E2** *(399)*. Very unFroggatty.

☐ **Elder Crack, E2** *(432)*. Don't get stuck in too deep.

☐ **The Dangler, E2** *(257)*. Steep, wide, awkward - yummy.

☐ **Billy Whizz, E2** *(362)*. Skinny fingers help ... a lot!

☐ **Gates of Mordor, E3** *(334)*. Off-fingers and very steep.

☐ **The Right Eliminate, E3** *(436)*. 5.10a is about right.

☐ **Sentinel Crack, E3** *(497)*. Put your best fist forward.

☐ **Saville Street, E3** *(337)*. Save some 'umph' for the bulge.

☐ **Goliath, E4** *(323)*. Only short but such hard work.

☐ **London Wall, E5** *(351)*. The best crack climb in the UK!

Sheffield Area

Ladybower Area

Stanage

Burbage Valley

Millstone Area

Derwent Edges

Chatsworth Area

Southern Crags

Sheffield Area

Ladybower Area

Stanage

Burbage Valley

Millstone Area

Derwent Edges

Chatsworth Area

Southern Crags

The last edition of this guidebook from 2006 had an extensive graded list of 343 routes which was added to from the Rockfax web site to create a list known as the '*ROCKFAX Eastern Grit: Top 500*'. This has become one of the most popular Ticklists on UKC Logbooks with over 300 subscribers yet no-one has yet completed it, although some are very close.

This new list below contains a full 500 routes this time. These have been assembled from the votes on UKClimbing which numbered over 200,000 separate grade votes at the time of writing. Every route in this list has had over 30 votes and most have had many more. This might make it very accurate, however you may disagree. What we do know is that it will be a while before anyone ticks all these!

Michele Caminati tackling the lower blank groove of Gaia (E8 6c) - *page 532* - at Black Rocks. Photo Mike Hutton

E 4

- Profit of Doom 431
- Old Friends 167
- Downhill Racer 397
- *** Peaches 483
- *** Chameleon 257
- *** The Knock 317
- *** Usurper 433
- ** Oedipus Ring Your Mother . . . 395
- *** Indoor Fisherman 380
- ** High Plains Drifter 362
- ** The Hathersage Trip 202
- Moon Walk 413
- *** Auto da Fe 93
- ** High Street 362
- The Brush Off 91
- *** Goliath 323
- ** I'm Back 88
- ** Comus 206
- *** The Strangler 200
- ** Above and Beyond 323
- Calvary 212
- *** Autumn Wall 66
- ** Jetrunner 116

E 3

- ** Demon Rib 533
- *** Saville Street 337
- ** Ontos 125
- *** Twikker 342
- Sentinel Crack 497
- ** Finger Distance 429
- The Archangel 191
- ** Boulevard 362
- ** Banana Wall 63
- *** Cave Wall 386
- ** Moribund 210
- ** Brown's Eliminate Direct 400
- ** The Guillotine 226
- ** Crocodile 469
- *** Censor 256
- *** Great West Road 345
- *** The Right Eliminate 436
- *** Tippler Direct 257
- ** King Kong 165
- ** Angst 87
- *** The Asp 240
- ** Exit 82
- ** Ashes 229
- *** Impossible Slab 165
- ** Gates of Mordor 334
- *** Escape/Boot Hill 514
- Great Slab 398
- *** Waterloo Sunset 471
- ** The Unreachable Star 414
- ** Golden Days 534
- ** Dextrous Hare 338
- ** Telli 212
- ** Black Hawk Bastion 258
- *** Time For Tea 349
- ** Cave Crack 386
- ** Long John's Slab 396
- ** Silica 206

E 2

- ** March Hare 338
- ** Synopsis 399
- ** Embankment 1 348
- *** Zeus 324
- ** Scroach 437
- ** Apollo 416
- Five Finger Exercise 515
- ** Tom Thumb 512
- ** Saddy 425
- The Rasp 300
- ** Insanity 434
- ** Cave Eliminate 242
- ** Undercut Crack 119
- Fern Hill 514
- ** Easy Picking 90
- Billy Whizz 362
- *** Suspense 361
- *** The Dangler 257
- ** Midshipman 481
- ** Fern Groove 188
- *** Elder Crack 432
- ** Sorb 320
- ** Regent Street 353
- ** Wall End Slab Direct 189
- *** Knightsbridge 347
- Quietus 165
- ** Mad Hatter 421
- ** Pearls 499
- ** Savage Messiah 517
- *** Orang-outang 149
- ** Piccadilly Circus 353
- ** Bean Stalk 512
- ** Dirty Stop Out 124
- *** Erb 342
- Brown's Eliminate 400
- *** The Sentinel 285
- ** Brimstone 334
- ** Yosemite Wall 251
- ** Fate 163
- Tower Face Direct 198
- ** Auricle 124
- ** Pot Black 207
- *** Wuthering 240
- ** Cinturato 196
- ** Soyuz 416
- *** Count's Buttress 181
- ** Nightmare Slab 180
- *** The Big Crack 401

E 1

- Left-hand Pillar Crack 474
- L'Horla 434
- *** Dark Continent 233
- ** The Wobbler 142
- *** Time For Tea Original 349
- ** Pig's Ear 159
- ** Pollux 74
- ** Now or Never 284
- ** Smoke ont' Watter 425
- ** The Left Eliminate 436
- ** Great Peter 361
- Moyer's Buttress 463
- *** Millwheel Wall 325
- The Tippler 257
- ** Vibrio 500
- ** Kayak 428
- ** Wrong Hand Route 122
- ** Wild and Woolly 151
- ** The Irrepressible Urge 291
- *** Promontory Traverse 526
- *** Embankment 3 349
- ** The Unprintable 256
- *** Desperation 242
- *** The Toy 435
- *** The Eye of Faith 464
- *** Tower Chimney 198
- ** Goodbye Toulouse 254
- ** Embankment 4 349
- ** Nonsuch 96
- ** White Out 84
- *** Great Buttress Arete 56
- ** Motorcade 391
- Flying Buttress Direct 254
- ** Nemmes Pas Harry 115
- ** Autumn Day 108
- ** Strapiombante 382
- ** Hugo de Vries 541
- ** The Vice 139
- Long Tall Sally 292
- ** Billingsgate 343
- ** Delectable Direct 367
- ** Lamebrain 422
- ** Mississippi Variant Direct . . . 233
- ** Strapiombo 382
- ** Anniversary Arete 170
- ** Eros 341
- ** Fringe Benefit 91
- ** Saliva 229
- The Left Unconquerable 214
- ** Kirkus's Corner 255
- ** Pedlar's Rib 225
- ** Tom-cat Slab 184
- The Link 233
- ** Morrison's Redoubt 233
- ** Easter Rib 249
- ** Surform 300
- Millsom's Minion 207
- ** Hearse Arete 466
- ** Hades 324
- ** Dexterity 338
- ** Thread Flintstone 105
- ** Biven's Crack 463

Sheffield Area

Ladybower Area

Stanage

Burbage Valley

Millstone Area

Derwent Edges

Chatsworth Area

Southern Crags

Margin tabs: Sheffield Area · Ladybower Area · Stanage · Burbage Valley · Millstone Area · Derwent Edges · Chatsworth Area · Southern Crags

HVS

- ** Sepulchrave . . . 517
- ** [T50] Valkyrie . . . 394
- ** [T50] Suicide Wall . . . 517
- ** [T50] The Peapod . . . 436
- *** [T50] Tower Crack . . . 198
- ** [T50] Terrazza Crack . . . 148
- ** Lancaster Flyby . . . 107
- ** Nowanda . . . 460
- *** Surgeon's Saunter . . . 140
- ** Kelly's Overhang . . . 164
- *** Brooks' Crack . . . 317
- ** Good Friday . . . 244
- ** Cue . . . 207
- ** Orpheus Wall . . . 483
- ** Titanic Direct . . . 168
- ** Deuteronomy . . . 156
- *** Zapple . . . 373
- *** The Scoop . . . 229
- *** Eliminator . . . 258
- ** Puppet Crack . . . 497
- *** Neb Buttress Direct . . . 124
- *** Sorrell's Sorrow . . . 413
- ** Cave Gully Wall . . . 241
- ** Fina . . . 196
- ** Roof Route . . . 95
- ** Green Crack . . . 433
- ** [T50] The Right Unconquerable . . . 214
- ** Travesties . . . 159
- *** The Blurter . . . 161
- *** Right-hand Tower . . . 150
- ** Overton Arete . . . 541
- ** [T50] Goliath's Groove . . . 191
- ** Amber Buttress . . . 539
- ** Great North Road . . . 347
- ** Whitehall . . . 349
- ** Chequers Crack . . . 401
- ** [T50] Great Buttress . . . 105
- ** Rugosity Crack . . . 264
- ** Tree Wall . . . 411
- ** Cold Turkey . . . 246
- *** Plexity . . . 337
- *** Queersville . . . 251
- ** [T50] Great Portland Street . . . 350
- ** Billiard Buttress . . . 207
- ** Blizzard Ridge . . . 84
- ** The Rainmaker . . . 286
- ** Overhanging Wall . . . 205
- ** The Flange . . . 249
- ** [T50] Maupassant . . . 434
- ** Tower Crack . . . 316
- ** Pedlar's Slab . . . 225
- ** Neb Buttress . . . 124
- *** Whillans' P./Black Magic . . . 249
- ** Kremlin Krack . . . 82
- ** Estremo . . . 336
- ** [T50] Congo Corner . . . 233
- ** Charlie's Crack . . . 316
- ** The Happy Wanderer . . . 125
- ** Avalanche Wall . . . 430
- ** Paucity . . . 241
- ** The Knutter . . . 159
- ** Jeepers Creepers . . . 167
- ** The Line . . . 409
- ** Namenlos . . . 210
- ** [T50] Three Pebble Slab . . . 392
- ** [T50] Bond Street . . . 350

- ** Cave Arete . . . 242
- ** Ratline . . . 482
- ** Butcher Crack . . . 227
- ** Harding's Super Direct Finish 241
- ** Microbe . . . 143
- ** Pedestal Crack . . . 400
- ** [T50] Chequers Buttress . . . 402
- ** Robin Hood's/Harding's . . . 241
- ** Mort Wall . . . 496
- ** Tower Face . . . 198
- ** Mississippi Variant . . . 233
- ** Leaning Buttress Direct . . . 252
- ** [T50] Croton Oil . . . 86
- ** Old Salt . . . 142
- ** Townsend's Variation . . . 255
- ** Centre Stage . . . 236
- ** Retroversion . . . 246
- ** Birch Tree Wall Variations . . . 532
- ** [T50] Great Crack . . . 542
- ** Claw Climb . . . 107
- ** August Arete . . . 212
- ** April Arete . . . 338
- ** Cioch Crack . . . 411
- ** Agony Crack . . . 237
- ** Dover's Wall, Route 2 . . . 222
- ** [T50] Sunset Slab . . . 384
- ** Bamford Rib . . . 124
- *** BAW's Crawl . . . 224
- ** Tody's Wall . . . 390
- *** David . . . 323
- ** Doctor's Saunter . . . 140
- ** [T50] Knight's Move . . . 286
- ** Right Fin . . . 293
- ** Quantum Crack . . . 158
- ** Randy's Wall . . . 128
- ** The Groper . . . 217

VS

- ** Chequers Climb . . . 402
- ** Robin Hood's Cave Innom . . . 241
- *** Altar Crack . . . 96
- *** Step-ladder Crack . . . 230
- *** Fern Crack . . . 188
- ** First Sister . . . 151
- ** The Spiral Route . . . 86
- ** Great Harry . . . 361
- *** Hawk's Nest Crack . . . 386
- ** Embankment 2 . . . 349
- ** Roof Route . . . 315
- ** [T50] Birch Tree Wall . . . 532
- ** Two Pitch Route . . . 417
- ** [T50] The Mall . . . 351
- ** Curving Crack . . . 116
- *** Gardom's Unconquerable . . . 468
- *** Sand Buttress . . . 529
- *** Excalibur . . . 362
- ** Great Crack . . . 286
- *** Saul's Arete . . . 191
- *** Left Edge . . . 83
- ** Obscenity . . . 292
- ** Gable Route . . . 315
- *** Grammarian's Progress . . . 67
- ** [T50] The File . . . 301
- ** Gunpowder Crack . . . 128
- ** Amber Arete . . . 539
- ** Broken Crack . . . 396
- ** The Shylock Finish . . . 107

- ** Count's Crack . . . 181
- *** Ellis's Eliminate . . . 244
- *** Twin Chimneys Buttress . . . 238
- ** The Brain . . . 418
- ** Central Buttress . . . 176
- ** High Neb Buttress Variations . . . 166
- *** Titanic . . . 168
- ** Peter's Progress . . . 286
- ** Lorica . . . 341
- ** Paradise Arete . . . 206
- ** Undertaker's Buttress . . . 466
- ** Oread . . . 466
- *** Lean Man's Climb . . . 529
- ** [T50] Mississippi Buttress Direct . . . 233
- ** Typhoon . . . 161
- ** Crewcut . . . 344
- *** Route 1 . . . 107
- *** The Delectable Variation . . . 367
- ** Narrow Buttress . . . 251
- ** Bilberry Crack . . . 115
- *** Quien Sabe? . . . 115
- ** [T50] High Neb Buttress . . . 166
- ** Remembrance Day . . . 337
- ** [T50] Hargreaves' Original . . . 249
- ** [T50] Titanic . . . 102
- ** Richard's Revenge . . . 67
- *** Hell Crack . . . 230
- ** The Louisiana Rib . . . 232
- *** Inaccessible Crack . . . 164
- ** Porthole Direct . . . 480
- ** Hollyash Crack . . . 286
- ** Barney Rubble . . . 105
- ** Macleod's Variation . . . 249
- ** Parallel Cracks . . . 170
- *** Wrinkled Wall . . . 123
- ** Inaccessible Crack Direct . . . 164
- ** Lone Tree Groove . . . 533
- ** [T50] Himmelswillen . . . 62
- ** The Crow's Nest . . . 478
- ** Greeny Crack . . . 292
- ** Zig-zag Flake Crack . . . 247
- ** Wall End Flake Crack . . . 190
- ** Central Trinity . . . 249
- ** Titania . . . 103
- *** Bel Ami . . . 433
- ** Straight Crack . . . 246
- ** Jonathan's Chimney . . . 84
- *** Wall End Slab . . . 189
- ** Rubber Band . . . 243
- ** Queen's Parlour Slab . . . 523
- ** Via Media . . . 250
- *** Gargoyle Flake . . . 120
- ** Covent Garden . . . 350
- ** Crab Crawl Arete . . . 139
- ** [T50] Martello Buttress . . . 229
- ** [T50] Inverted V . . . 246
- ** The Whittler . . . 74
- ** The Nose . . . 228
- ** Dunkley's Eliminate . . . 325
- ** Fairy Steps . . . 192
- ** [T50] Apple Arete . . . 473
- ** Gargoyle Buttress . . . 259
- *** Nelson's Nemesis . . . 493
- ** Topsail . . . 482
- ** Reginald . . . 320
- ** Fox House Flake . . . 325
- ** Cosmic Crack . . . 158

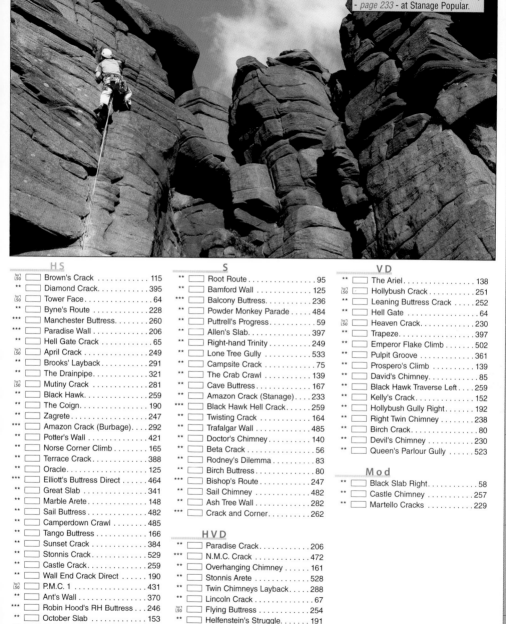

The delightful _Amazon Crack_ (S 4a) - _page 233_ - at Stanage Popular.

Sheffield Area
Ladybower Area
Stanage
Burbage Valley
Millstone Area
Derwent Edges
Chatsworth Area
Southern Crags

	Routes	up to S	HS to HVS	E1 to E3	E4 upwards
Sheffield Area					
Wharncliffe	197	58	62	57	20
Agden Rocher	50	12	24	11	3
Rivelin	137	28	46	33	30
Ladybower					
Dovestone Tor	117	39	53	20	5
Bamford	186	71	65	35	15
Stanage					
Stanage North	451	114	219	86	32
Stanage Plantation	416	80	148	116	72
Stanage Popular	470	123	200	100	47
Burbage Valley					
Burbage North	221	87	84	30	20
Higgar Tor	87	28	32	16	11
Carl Wark	29	15	8	4	2
Burbage South	170	35	49	36	50
Millstone Area					
Over Owler Tor	21	6	10	5	
Millstone	155	11	62	43	39
Lawrencefield	67	13	27	20	7
Yarncliffe Quarry	32	5	20	4	3
Derwent Edges					
Froggatt	179	24	49	43	63
Curbar	289	39	101	76	73
Baslow	115	42	47	20	6
Chatsworth					
Gardom's	159	28	65	43	23
Birchen	195	92	61	29	13
Chatsworth	69	22	18	24	5
Southern Crags					
Robin Hood's Stride	17	6	7	1	3
Cratcliffe	51	8	15	15	13
Black Rocks	101	24	22	22	33
Turningstone Edge	44	7	16	14	7
Duke's Quarry	2		1		1
Shining Cliff	23	3	4	11	5

Sheffield Area | Ladybower Area | Stanage | Burbage Valley | Millstone Area | Derwent Edges | Chatsworth Area | Southern Crags

Approach	Sun	Shelter	Green	Summary	Page
20 - 40 min	Afternoon	Sheltered	Green	A short outcrop overlooking Stocksbridge. Routes tend to be steep, fingery and hard. Bad landings are common.	46
6 - 10 min	From mid morning	Sheltered	Green	A large and rather unstable cliff that adds something a little different into the local mix. GREAT CARE is needed when climbing here.	70
10 - 15 min	Lots of sun	Sheltered	Green	A crag within the Sheffield city boundary. South facing and quite low so a good bet for cold sunny days. Can be green after rain.	78
40 min	Afternoon	Windy	Green	A wild and remote-feeling crag reached by the longest walk-in in the book. A superb setting makes it well worth a summer visit.	100
15 - 22 min	From mid morning	Windy	Green	A lovely setting above the Ladybower Reservoir with a great set of routes on a series of quality buttresses. Often busy.	112
12 - 25 min	From mid morning	Windy	Green	The northern chunk of Stanage provides a neat contrast to the rest of the cliff with remote-feeling climbs that can be green in winter.	134
12 - 18 min	From mid morning	Windy	Green	The Plantation provides many and varied routes in a charming setting above the trees. Very popular with both boulderers and route climbers.	178
5 - 15 min	From mid morning	Windy	Green	The most popular crag in the Peak/UK/World - you will need to share it with others, but there is plenty to go round.	218
2 - 20 min	From mid morning	Windy	Green	Plenty of short but good quality routes scattered along the edge. The left end can be very busy but walking right will ease the crowding.	274
5 - 6 min	Sun and shade	Windy	Green	Only a small crag but the Leaning Block has a brilliant set of rough, tough and steep climbs. The shorter walls are worth a visit.	296
20 min	Morning	Windy	Green	A minor outcrop with some morning sun which is rare for Eastern Grit. The more impressive northern sector is always dirty.	306
8 - 20 min	Evening	Windy	Green	A set of generally short and shady buttresses and a couple of dingy quarries. Oddly it is home to many of grit's hardest offerings.	310
10 min	Evening	Windy	Green	Only a small outcrop with a minor selection of climbs in a lovely breezy setting. A great spot to watch the sun go down.	330
5 - 12 min	Afternoon	Sheltered	Green	The finest quarry in the UK with superb walls and soaring crack-lines. Once an aid venue, now home to a great set of free climbs.	332
4 - 8 min	Afternoon	Sheltered	Green	Millstone's little sister, a tree-filled quarry with a fine set of steep routes around a green pond. Quite good for beginners.	356
1 - 2 min	From mid morning	Sheltered	Green	Another hole in the ground. The popular easy climbs in the first bay are very tired although there are better routes to the right.	368
5 - 18 min	Afternoon	Windy	Green	Some excellent cracks and the best set of slabby routes in the Eastern Peak. The cracks are safe, the slabs aren't.	376
3 - 20 min	Afternoon	Windy	Green	Curbar's reputation is well known; beefy cracks and serious face climbs means that visits here often involve memorable struggles.	404
5 - 20 min	Afternoon	Windy	Green	A small rambling crag which is often very quiet. Not much in the way of classics but a decent set of easier climbs.	440
10 - 25 min	Afternoon	Sheltered	Green	Some jutting buttresses poking from a wooded bouldery hillside. Can be green and midgy when humid. Best after a dry spell.	456
10 - 15 min	From mid morning	Windy	Green	A popular spot with beginners and groups and often very busy. Some routes are polished, especially the starts.	476
8 - 10 min	Evening	Sheltered	Green	A crag with a similar feel to Gardom's, neglected and a bit overgrown, although nice when the conditions are right.	494
6 min	Sun and shade	Sheltered	Green	Twin pinnacles in a superb rural setting. Popular with boulderers and walkers, but there is a pleasant set of climbs here too.	506
10 min	Sun and shade	Sheltered	Green	Some superb soaring walls and classic routes. The removal of the trees means the place can now be viewed in all its glory.	510
5 - 8 min	Sun and shade	Sheltered	Green	A dark crag with a contrasting set of climbs, some great historical challenges and a fine set of modern desperates. Often green.	520
10 - 12 min	Morning	Sheltered	Green	A rhododendron-cloaked crag overlooking the Amber Valley. The main buttresses stick proud of the shrubs and are worth a look. Very sheltered.	536
5 min	Sun and shade	Sheltered	Green	An extensive and gloomy quarry, though most of the routes are neglected and overgrown. We include the two classics.	542
10 - 12 min	Sun and shade	Sheltered	Green	Another very sheltered crag, a good bet on windy days and you will probably have the whole place to yourself.	543

Faded symbol means that only some of the routes are green or the crag doesn't always offer shelter.

Sheffield Area

Sheffield Area

Ladybower Area

Stanage

Burbage Valley

Millstone Area

Derwent Edges

Chatsworth Area

Southern Crags

About 2km

N

Stocksbridge

A616

M1

29

A629

Wharncliffe
p.46

Chapeltown

Wharncliffe
Side

A61

A6102

Agden Rocher
p.70

Oughtibridge

High Bradfield

A57

Sheffield

Rivelin
p.78

Steve Cunnington involved with *Scarlett's Climb*
(HS 4c) - *page 50* - in a typical Wharncliffe setting.

	No star	✪	✪✪	✪✪✪
Mod to S	27	25	6	-
HS to HVS	22	34	4	2
E1 to E3	21	31	4	1
E4 and up	5	12	1	2

Tucked away northeast of the mainstream of Peak climbing, Wharncliffe used to have a rogue reputation owing to tough grades and its rather industrial location. The main section of cliff has routes across the grade spectrum and, although only up to 14m high, they are usually action-packed. The climbing tends to be steep and fingery, with many small sharp holds rather than the roundedness usually associated with gritstone. Many of the landings are awful, so make a point of getting an early runner in - small cams are especially useful here. Wharncliffe was significant at the birth of British outcrop climbing with Jimmy Puttrell first scratching the rock here with his nailed boots in 1885. By 1900, Wharncliffe was probably the most popular cliff in the country, due to the nearby railway line. An article published in 1910 described 110 routes here. Nowadays Wharncliffe is a place to escape the crowds found elsewhere in the Peak. Strange to think that it is one of the few venues in the UK that is less popular now than it was 100 years ago.

Conditions

Set 200m lower than Stanage, Wharncliffe is sheltered enough to miss much of the bad weather that hits the Peak. Being northeast of the main range of hills, a rain shadow often occurs here. The rocky base of the cliff plus the incut holds and the fact that the cliff dries rapidly means it is a viable option in poor weather. Sunny winter afternoons, can be very pleasant here. It is also relatively midge-free in warm weather compared to other Peak crags.

Steve Cunnington balancing his way up the lovely *Tower Face* (HS 4b) - *page 64* - the best route of its grade on the cliff featuring varied moves and good runners.

Sheffield Area

Ladybower Area

Stanage

Burbage Valley

Millstone Area

Derwent Edges

Chatsworth Area

Southern Crags

Cycle track

A616

Junction 29
on M1

Woodhead
Pass   Tunnels

GPS 53.47895
P   -1.56101

A629

Stocksbridge

Prow Rock Area
p.48

GPS 53.47325
P   -1.53367

Stone yard

Great Buttress
p.56

Hell Gate Area
p.64

Bridleway
with 2 small
boulders

Long John's Stride
p.66

Wharncliffe
Heath

Cascade Buttress
p.68

Outlook Boulders
Peak Bouldering

Grenoside

Bass Rock
p.68

Private road
- DO NOT GO
DOWN HERE

Lodge/Ewden Buttresses
p.69

N
About 500m

Sheffield

Wharncliffe
Lodge

Side tabs: Sheffield Area · Ladybower Area · Stanage · Burbage Valley · Millstone Area · Derwent Edges · Chatsworth Area · Southern Crags

Approach   Also see map on page 45

The cliff flanks the eastern side of the Don Valley 10km north of Sheffield.

The **Main Edge** is most easily approached from the A616 Stocksbridge bypass taking the turning for Deepcar. The first left on entering the town from the north is Station Road and 400m down here is a steep left turn best accessed by turning around. A short distance up here is parking on the left. Parking on Station Road is also possible as the main spot is known for car crime. From either parking follow the track uphill through two tunnels (often muddy) under the railway line and across a cycle track. Continue to a large pool and turn right. The path rises out of the trees to arrive above the first buttress on the cliff. Alternatively turn right along the cycle track to a pylon where a steep path joins the other approach.

Long John's Stride, Cascade Buttress, The Bass Rock and **Lodge/Ewden Buttresses** are best approached from a minor road that connects the A61 and Grenoside to the A616/A629. Park at a small lay-by almost opposite a stone yard, about 1km south of the A616/A629 junction. From the parking, walk back up the road towards Grenoside to a bridleway on the right by two boulders. Go down here, keeping the wall and Wharncliffe Heath just on your left and ignoring any tracks veering off to the right. After about 1km you arrive at the edge. Turn south (left - looking out) and walk along the edge for about 200m to the top of Long John's Stride.

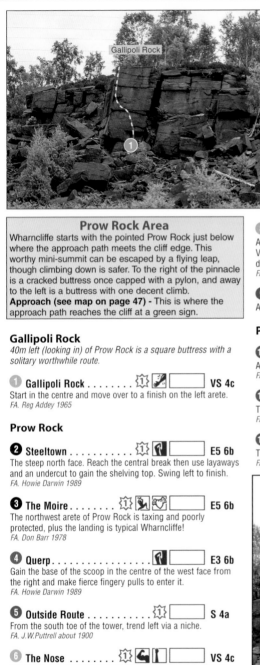

Gallipoli Rock

Prow Rock Area

Wharncliffe starts with the pointed Prow Rock just below where the approach path meets the cliff edge. This worthy mini-summit can be escaped by a flying leap, though climbing down is safer. To the right of the pinnacle is a cracked buttress once capped with a pylon, and away to the left is a buttress with one decent climb.
Approach (see map on page 47) - This is where the approach path reaches the cliff at a green sign.

Gallipoli Rock

40m left (looking in) of Prow Rock is a square buttress with a solitary worthwhile route.

① Gallipoli Rock . . . . VS 4c
Start in the centre and move over to a finish on the left arete.
FA. Reg Addey 1965

Prow Rock

❷ Steeltown E5 6b
The steep north face. Reach the central break then use layaways and an undercut to gain the shelving top. Swing left to finish.
FA. Howie Darwin 1989

❸ The Moire E5 6b
The northwest arete of Prow Rock is taxing and poorly protected, plus the landing is typical Wharncliffe!
FA. Don Barr 1978

❹ Querp E3 6b
Gain the base of the scoop in the centre of the west face from the right and make fierce fingery pulls to enter it.
FA. Howie Darwin 1989

❺ Outside Route . . . . S 4a
From the south toe of the tower, trend left via a niche.
FA. J.W.Puttrell about 1900

❻ The Nose . . . . VS 4c
The juggy and worthwhile prow-like south arete of the tower.
FA. Fred Jones 1933

❼ Inside Route . . . . Diff
The gloomy face is the easiest way up (and off) the tower.
FA. J.W.Puttrell 1885

❽ Exonian's Return . . . . HVS 5c
A fingery rightward traverse of the wall behind the Prow. Variations are available; the green left arete is **VS 4c** and a more direct start to the traverse is **5b**.
FA. Reg Addey early 1960s

❾ Teresa's Slab . . . . HVD 4a
A tricky start gains the easier right side of the face.

Pylon Buttress

❿ Pylon Corner . . . . Diff
A short angular groove on the left has its moments.
FA. J.W.Puttrell and friends about 1900

⓫ Pylon Crack . . . . VD
The steep narrow crack in the centre of the north face.
FA. J.W.Puttrell and friends about 1900

⓬ Quern Crack . . . . S 4a
The steeper fissure just to the right to an awkward exit.
FA. J.W.Puttrell and friends about 1900

Prow Rock

Descent

10m

Afternoon 20 min

Approach path

Scarlett's Wall, Tensile Test and Mantelshelf Pillar

p.50

Prow Rock

Pylon Buttress

13 **Jimmy Puttrell is a Legend** . . . . ◻ **VS 4c**
The arete leads to the direct finish to *Hamlet's Climb*. The name is new though the climbing isn't.

14 **Hamlet's Climb** . . . . ◻◻ ◻ **HVD 4a**
Climb the steep crack in the left-hand side of the buttress to a notch then escape leftwards across to *Pylon Crack*. A rightward variation is harder - **Hamlet's Traverse**, a pumpy **HS 4b**.
FA. J.W.Puttrell and friends about 1900

15 **Requiem of Hamlet's Ghost**. . ◻◻ ◻ **E1 5b**
Steeply up the face between the cracks past a set of overlaps.
FA. Terry Hirst 1976

16 **The Crack of Doom**. . . . . ◻◻ 🧍 ◻ **HS 4b**
The steep awkward off-width was a great effort for its day.
FA. J.W.Puttrell and friends about 1900

17 **Despair** . . . . ◻ **E2 5c**
Climb the steep pillar on the right-hand side of the buttress, passing a low roof.
FA. Nick White 1982

18 **The Zig-zag Climb** . . . . ◻ **Diff**
Follow the easy groove on the right then move left to the kinked and chockstone-filled crack.
FA. J.W.Puttrell and friends about 1900. Also known as Chockstone Climb.

19 **The Crack of Delight**. . . . . ◻ **Mod**
The pleasant easy groove on the right.
FA. J.W.Puttrell and friends about 1900

Pylon Buttress

Descent

10m

Afternoon 20 min

Sheffield Area

Ladybower Area

Stanage

Burbage Valley

Millstone Area

Derwent Edges

Chatsworth Area

Southern Crags

The Zig-zag Climb - p.49

Crack of Doom - p.49

Scarlett's Wall

A fine square pillar home to one of Harry Scarlett's original bold (pumped in pumps!) offerings from the 1930s and a few more modern routes. The climbs tend to be reachy and fingery, plus as is often the case with Wharncliffe, protection is not especially generous and the landings are worrying.

Approach (see map on page 47) - This is just beyond Prow Rock which is where the approach path reaches the cliff.

❶ Earth Blues **E5 6b**
The tough side-wall is climbed trending left to the break. Move left again and layback the arete.
FA. Roger Doherty 1985

❷ Scarlett's Wall Arete . . . **VS 4c**
The left arete is reachy and not too well protected.
FA. Reg Addey 1965

❸ Scarlett's Climb . . . . . . **HS 4c**
Climb the centre of the wall on flaky holds to a stretchy finish. Harder for the short. *Photo on page 46.*
FA. Harry Scarlett 1931

❹ Scarlett's Edge . . . . **VS 4b**
The arete eases with height. This route was previously known as *The Scarlett Letter.*

❺ Scarlett's Chimney . . . . . . **Diff**
The chimney starts off okay then fizzles out a bit.

Tensile Test

A short wall with a slightly quarried feel about it and a flattish base - a rarity at Wharncliffe. The routes are usually soloed or done above a bouldering mat.
Approach (see map on page 47) - This is just beyond Prow Rock and Scarlett's Wall.

❻ Suspense . . . . **VS 5b**
The left edge of the wall soon eases.
FA. Pete Crew late 1950s

❼ Mellicious. **E1 5c**
Up the wall between the arete and a shallow groove.
FA. John Camateras 2000

❽ Tensile Test. **E1 5c**
The technical slab and beckoning shallow groove above is the best offering here. Balance up to it then sprint.
FA. Terry Hirst 1977

❾ Elastic Limit **E1 5c**
Climb the middle of the slab to the horizontal crease then step left to a good pocket foothold and finish direct.
FA. Michael Anderson 1977

❿ Forget-me-not . . . . **HS 4a**
Swing onto a finger ledge left of the gully then climb the wall above, stepping left to finish with a mantel. Unprotected.

⓫ Abair **E1 5b**
Finger traverse the thin break that cuts the wall from right to left, to a finish on the arete.
FA. Don Barr 1978

⓬ Blocky Corner . . . . **Mod**
The main angle is included for completeness.

Sheffield Area

Ladybower Area

Stanage

Burbage Valley

Millstone Area

Derwent Edges

Chatsworth Area

Southern Crags

13 **Handover Arete** . . . . . . 🔧📙⬜ **VS 4c**
Climb the arete to the block overhang and pull over this with a
long reach for a distant jug and quick sprint.
FA. Frank Fitzgerald 1955

14 **Cracked Arete** . . . . 📙⬜ **VD**
The wide crack in the next arete is less taxing than it looks.

15 **Legover Arete** . . . . 🧗⬜ **VS 4c**
The next arete is a bit artificial but has some good moves.

16 **Monolith Crack** . . . . 📙⬜ **HVD 4a**
The narrowing chimney has a tricky exit for the long of leg.
FA. J.W.Puttrell and friends about 1900. Also known as 'Foot and Back'.

Mantelshelf Pillar

Next comes a squat square-cut pillar that is actually
detached from the edge. It has a couple of aretes and a
couple of chimney routes that are of interest.
Approach (see map on page 47) - Continue a little way
from the Tensile Test Wall over blocks at the crag base.

17 **Mantelshelf Pillar** . . . . . 🔧📙⬜ **VS 4c**
Mantel the left-hand arete of the pillar. Quite a bit harder (HVS?)
for the short.
FA. John Fearon late 1950s

18 **The Mantelshelf.** . . . . 🔧📙⬜ **HS 4b**
The right arete of the pillar via a tough mantelshelf move.
FA. J.W.Puttrell and friends about 1900

19 **Back and Foot** . . . . 📙⬜ **VD**
A bit wide to practice the suggested technique. Instead tackle
either of the awkward green corners.
FA. J.W.Puttrell and friends about 1900

Sheffield Area
Ladybower Area
Stanage
Burbage Valley
Millstone Area
Derwent Edges
Chatsworth Area
Southern Crags

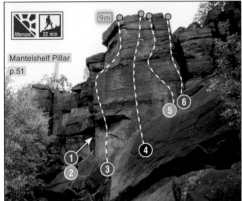

Mantelshelf Pillar
p.51

❶ Rook Chimney . . . . 🎔▐ ⬛ **Diff**
The steep rift in the side-wall is easier and better than it looks.
FA. J.W.Puttrell and friends about 1900

❷ Post Horn . . . . 🎔🎔 ⬛ **HVS 4c**
Climb the bold green wall and rib just right to a finish out on the right arete. A **Direct Finish - HVS 5a** is a better option really.
FA. Reg Addey early 1960s

❸ Tears Before Bedtime . . . . . .🎔 ⬛ **E3 5c**
The angular arete has hard moves to pass the roof.
FA. John Darwin 1987

❹ Reveille . . . . 🎔🎔 ⬛ **E4 6a**
The technical and bold wall on the right to an easier upper face.

❺ Curved Balls . . . . ⬛ **HS 4c**
The curved flake and short crack above make a bit of a filler-in.
FA. David Simmonite 2001

❻ Letter Box Arete . . . . ⬛ **VD**
This is the pleasant right arete of the face.

Around to the right is an attractive slabby buttress with a huge boulder on its crest that is supposed to rock in a high wind. Just to the left are a couple of isolated routes.

❼ Mantelshelf Slab Right . . . . . . ⬛ **S 4a**
The slabby buttress. A left-hand variation is a little easier.

❽ Addey's Addition . . . . 🎔 ⬛ **HVS 5c**
The green and narrow wall past a niche and overlap.
FA. Reg Addey early 1960s

❾ The Corner . . . . . . 🎔▐🎔 ⬛ **VS 5a**
From the left balance up the arete to a finish up the groove.
FA. John Henry Fearon 1955

❿ Slab and Corner . . . . 🎔🎔 ⬛ **HS 4b**
From the centre of the slab trend left by neat footwork and a mantel to the shallow groove in the arete. Not much gear!
FA. Fred Jones 1933

⓫ Photo Finish . . . . 🎔🎔 ⬛ **E1 5b**
Climb *The Corner* then step right and climb the slab rightwards to a jug. Pull up to the overhang, traverse right and finish up the short face of the rocking block. A finish on the left is harder.
FA. Terry Hirst 1979

⓬ Dead Heat . . . . 🎔🎔🎔 ⬛ **E5 6a**
The slab just right of centre is technical, tenuous and unprotected, with crucial moves to pass the end of the overlap.
FA. Nick White 1985

⓭ Renrock . . . . 🎔🎔 ⬛ **E1 5a**
The right-hand edge of the slab is balancy and protection is lacking. Escape into the gully is not easy once committed!
FA. Rod Wilson late 1950s

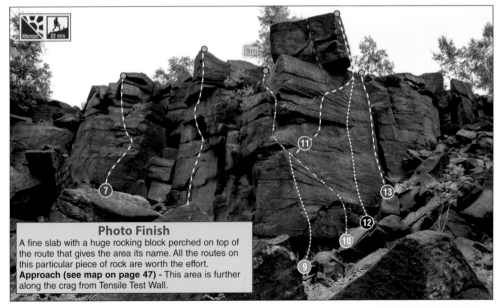

Photo Finish
A fine slab with a huge rocking block perched on top of the route that gives the area its name. All the routes on this particular piece of rock are worth the effort.
Approach (see map on page 47) - This area is further along the crag from Tensile Test Wall.

Cheese Block Area
This isolated blocky buttress is split by a series of cracks and grooves. It is a great area for beginners and those in search of an easier time. In general, the routes are not at all cheesy!
Approach (see map on page 47) - Continue along the crag-top path until just past some trees.

50m to the right is a buttress split by a series of vertical cracks of various widths. There are several decent easier routes here.

14 Black Wall . . . . HS 4b
The north-facing wall is climbed by a trio of tricky mantelshelves.

15 Hard Cheese E1 5b
The narrow wall and flying arete.
FA. David Simmonite 2000

16 Cheese Cut . . . . Diff
The angular groove gives pleasant bridging at a very amenable grade and includes at least one loose hold.
FA. J.W.Puttrell and friends about 1900

17 Cheese Cut Crack . . . . VD
The crack in the right-hand wall of the groove starts steeply but soon leads to easier ground.
FA. J.W.Puttrell and friends about 1900

18 Cheese Block . . . . . HS 4b
Just to the right, reach the arete over the jutting nose and follow it steeply. A side-runner may ease the strain a little.

19 Cheese Cut Groove . . . . Mod
The mild central rift.

20 Cheese Cut Flake Left . . . . . . HVD
Up the centre of the tricky wall then tackle the roof on the left.

21 Cheese Cut Flake . . . . . . HVD
Climb the wide crack past an awkward overhang then continue up the twisting crack above.
FA. J.W.Puttrell and friends about 1900

Imaginary Boulder
To the right, past a few oddities, is a square jutting buttress.

22 Owen's Dilemma . . . . . . HVS 4c
The valley face on rounded holds to a high crux. Indifferent gear.
FA. Mick Owen late 1950s

23 Imaginary Boulder Climb . . . VS 4c
The steep crack right of the arete was a fair effort for its day.
FA. J.W.Puttrell and friends about 1900

Imaginary Boulder

Pete's Sake

The main challenge on this fine tall tower was unlocked by local legend Pete Crew before he move on to greater things in Wales. Up and right are a series of short walls with a few interesting problems that you will doubtless have to yourself.

Approach (see map on page 47) - Continue along the crag-top path until just past some trees.

①　Railway Wall . . . . 🔲 ▨ ▭　**VS 4c**
Climb the hand and fist crack to the break, scoot left and finish up the well-positioned final arete.
FA. Fred Jones 1933

②　Chimney Groove . . . . . . 🔲 🖐 ▭　**VD**
The chimney leads to the top of a tower/block. Move right to the crack just left of the corner. A direct finish is harder.

③　Easy Groove . . . . 🖐 ▭　**Diff**
Pleasant bridging up the long groove past a ledge.

④　Pinnacle Arete . . . . 🔲 ▨ ▭　**E1 5b**
Climb a couple of shallow grooves in the wall to reach the block of the pinnacle on the left, then finish up the exposed arete. Upgraded from VS to HVS to E1 in three editions of the guide.
FA. Pete Crew late 1950s

⑤　Cumberland Groove . . . . . . 🔲 ▭　**VD**
Steep climbing on good holds and with good gear.
FA. J.W.Puttrell and friends about 1900

⑥　V Groove . . . . ▭　**VD**
The angular groove just before the edge of the buttress.
FA. J.W.Puttrell and friends about 1900

⑦　North Side Route . . . . . . 🚶 ▨ ▭　**HVS 5a**
Start up the arete then move left across the north face to gain a ledge by a tricky sequence, then finish more easily.
FA. Reg Addey 1965

⑧　Baal . . . . ▭　**E2 5c**
Finish straight up the arete.
FA. Gary Gibson 1981

⑨　Pete's Sake . . . . 🔲 ▨ ▨ ▭　**E1 5b**
The fine tower across the gully is climbed via its valley face to the notch. Move right along the break and finish up the arete.
FA. Pete Crew early 1960s

⑩　Thin Chimney . . . . 🔲 🖐 ▭　**VD**
The widening rift is easier the deeper you go.
FA. J.W.Puttrell about 1900

⑪　Overhanging Chimney . . . . ▭　**HVD 4a**
The next chimney narrows to an awkward exit.
FA. J.W.Puttrell about 1900

⑫　Ma'son . . . . ▨ ▭　**E2 5b**
Climb the narrow and fingery north-facing wall direct.
FA. Robert Taylor 1971

10m

🌇 Afternoon　🚶 22 min

Descent

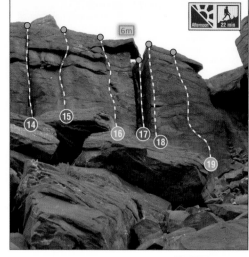

The rest of the routes start from a ledge up and right. This can be reached from either end. The routes are short.

13 Drums and Kicks . . . . . . 🧗🪨 ⬜ **HVS 5b**
The groove and roof to the right of the arete.
FA. Gary Gibson 1982

14 Overhanging Crack . . . . . 🔟📋 ⬜ **S 4b**
The next rift has some good jamming. The pumpy traverse that links this with *Split Chimney* is **The By-Pass, VS 4c**.
FA. J.W.Puttrell about 1900. The By-Pass Fred Jones 1933.

15 En Passant . . . . 🧗 ⬜ **E1 6b**
The wall is technical but short-lived.
FA. Jon Darwin 1987

16 Pass By . . . . ⬜ **HVS 5b**
Climb the weakness in the wall to the left of the chimney.
FA. Fred Jones 1933

17 Split Chimney . . . . 📐 ⬜ **VD**
The chimney with its flake is awkward and tricky to protect.
FA. J.W.Puttrell about 1900

18 Splitter . . . . 🔟🧗🖼️ ⬜ **E1 5b**
The compelling angular arete on its right-hand side is bold.
FA. Paul Harrison 2001

19 Split Chimney Wall . . . . 🔟 ⬜ **HVS 5b**
Sprint up the centre of the wall.

Descent

Sheffield Area
Ladybower Area
Stanage
Burbage Valley
Millstone Area
Derwent Edges
Chatsworth Area
Southern Crags

Great Buttress

One of the best buttresses on the cliff with a good set of worthwhile routes on the main piece of rock and some milder offerings on its slumped neighbour to the left.
Approach (see map on page 47) - From the green sign above Prow Rock, take the cliff-top path for 250m to where the path approaches the edge for the second time. Here you can see a triangular slab which stands in front of the Great Buttress.

❶ Alpha Crack. . . . . 🔄 ☐ **Diff**
A good beginner's climb following flakes up the left-hand side of the buttress to ledges, finishing on the left-hand arete.
FA. J.W.Puttrell and friends about 1900

❷ Beta Crack . . . . 🔄 ☐ **S 4a**
The long flake running up the right-hand side of the slab; a fine pitch with exciting moves rightwards over a small overhang. It is also possible to escape left as a worthwhile **VD**.
FA. J.W.Puttrell and friends about 1900

❸ Trapeze . . . . 🔄 🔧 ☐ **HS 4b**
A swinging traverse of the break high on the right is a bit wild.

❹ Trapezium. . . . . 🔄 🔧 ☐ **E1 5b**
Climb the wide crack to a notch and then the steep wall above on a surprisingly good set of holds.
FA. Don Barr 1978

❺ The Great Chimney . . . . 🔄 📷 ☐ **Diff**
The cleft is a good line - pity it is a bit dirty and loose!
FA. J.W.Puttrell and friends, about 1900

❻ Great Chimney Crack . . . 📷 📷 ☐ **S 4a**
In the right wall of the cleft a steep left-trending crack is followed on good (and creaky) holds until it is possible to stride into the chimney to finish. Or finish direct - a little harder.
FA. J.W.Puttrell and friends about 1900

❼ Thrown Away. . . . . 🔄 📷 ☐ **E2 5c**
The right-hand wall of the chimney starting up a thin crack and trending left towards the top. Escapable but with some good stretchy moves, especially the one off the undercut!
FA. Gary Gibson 1981

❽ Great Buttress Arete. . . . 🔄 📷 ☐ **E1 5b**
A fine climb up the long arete. A tape can be placed over a flake early on for protection, and above this the route gives sustained and interesting climbing.
FA. Pete Crew early 1960s

❾ Great Buttress . . . . 🔄 ☐ **VS 4c**
Start up the arete to the flake then traverse right just above the pruned sapling to the right edge of the face. Climb to a small cave then finish direct on broken flakes. Sadly escapable.
FA. Fred Jones 1933

Pete's Sake
p.54

Split Chimney
- p.55

10m

10 Just a Minute . . . . 🌣 🖼 ☐ **E1 5b**
Start direct to the sapling, then climb the centre of the face
(hard) to the edge of the cave. Step left and make steep moves
to the block. Finish direct or exit rapidly right.
FA. Frank Horsman 2000

11 Romulus . . . . 🌣 ☐ **VD**
The pleasant straight crack by some mild jamming.
FA. J.W.Puttrell and friends, about 1900

12 Remus . . . . 🌣 ☐ **S 4a**
A thin crack leads to a tiny shallow groove; sustained.
FA. J.W.Puttrell and friends, about 1900

13 Fly Wall . . . . 🖼 ☐ **HS 4a**
The centre of the short wall gives a mild, poorly protected pitch.
FA. Frank Fitzgerald 1955

To the right is the jutting flake of the Leaf.

14 Gold Leaf . . . . 🌣 ☐ **HVS 5b**
Climb the arete of the Leaf, starting up its edge and then at
half-height up its left-hand side via a useful slot.
FA. David Simmonite 1992

15 Leaf Buttress . . . . 🌣 ☐ **VS 4c**
The front face of the Leaf trending left via a flake and tiny
groove. Poorly protected, so it needs a steady head.
FA. Pete Crew late 1950s

Sheffield Area

Ladybower Area

Stanage

Burbage Valley

Millstone Area

Derwent Edges

Chatsworth Area

Southern Crags

Black Slab

1 Black Slab Left . . . . **HVD 4a**
The left-hand line on the slab trending slightly right then back left to finish. Not too well protected.

2 Black Slab Centre . . . . **VD**
The central line has a tricky start. Pull over the overlap in the centre of the slab and finish up a slim groove.

3 Black Slab Right . . . . **Mod**
A fine beginner's climb. Start from a block, pass a flake, and finish with a steeper section. A direct start is harder - **4a**.
FA. All variations probably climbed by J.W.Puttrell and friends, late 1800s

4 Black Finger **E3 5c**
Climb the tower that supports the buttress then a series of thin spidery cracks leftwards to a finish up the short arete.
FA. John Allen 1973

5 Diamond White **E3 5c**
From above the roof trend right to the blunt arete.
FA. David Simmonite 1992

6 Anzio Breakout/Pilgrimage . . **E5 6b**
Take *Black Finger* to the roof, reach right for tiny holds and make a fierce pull to reach the break on *Puttrell's Progress*. Pull through the centre of the roof and finish up the wall above.
FA. (Anzio Breakout) Jon Darwin 1987. FA. (Pilgrimage) Don Barr 1978

Puttrell's Progress
A proud buttress that has lost bits and pieces over the years. Probably best to get the classic *Puttrell's Progress* done before the whole thing goes! Over on the left *Black Slab* is always popular with its decent collection of easier routes.
Approach (see map on page 47) - From the green sign above Prow Rock, take the cliff-top path for 250m to where the path approaches the edge for the second time. Continue a little further for Puttrells's Progress buttress.

Sheffield Area

Ladybower Area

Stanage

Burbage Valley

Millstone Area

Derwent Edges

Chatsworth Area

Southern Crags

7 Puttrell's Progress . . S 4a
A fine mini-expedition. Climb the right arete of the big cave and enter the vertical slot with difficulty. Make a bold-feeling traverse left and finish up the steep juggy crack.
FA. J.W.Puttrell and friends, about 1900

8 The Flue . . . . 🗝 📖 HVD
Start up *Puttrell's Progress* but head through the cliff.
FA. J.W.Puttrell and friends, about 1900

9 Helping Hand . . . . 🗝 E1 5c
The right-hand pillar leads to the hard wall above.
FA. John Allen 1973

10 As You Like It . . . . 🗝 VD
The left crack in the right wall of the gully is a bit escapable.
FA. J.W.Puttrell and friends, about 1900. It used to have an adjustable hold, hence the name.

11 Black Crack . . . . 🗝 HVD
The right-hand crack has some huge holds.
FA. J.W.Puttrell and friends, about 1900

12 Black Cap . . . . 🗝 E2 6a
The short sharp arete of the gully.
FA. Roger Doherty 1985

Twin Pillars

These are more like a couple of squat blocks; 20m to the right of *Puttrell's Progress,* they are home to a few interesting offerings, generally in the short but serious category. The first pillar has a prominent roof at half-height, the original routes here from the 1960s took devious lines that avoided this. More recent offerings have straightened things out a bit to give arguably better routes (though via a bit of historical mangling).

Approach (see map on page 47) - From the green sign above Prow Rock, take the cliff-top path for 250m to where the path approaches the edge for the second time. Continue a little further for the Twin Pillars.

❶ Little Fellow E2 5b
The left arete of the face is bold and precarious.
FA. Nick Taylor 1999. Only the finish was new.

❷ Bolster E1 5b
The centre of the face and the roof leftwards to easier climbing.
FA. Terry Hirst 1982

❸ First Pillar Route 2 . . . . E1 5a
Up the face to a ledge then teeter out left to find better holds on the previous climb.
FA. Reg Addey 1965

❹ Summer Lightening E1 5b
The direct finish is bold.
FA. Roger Doherty 1985

❺ Flake Climb . . . . VS 4c
A good line on the second pillar. Ape up the flake then finish up the tricky arete.
FA. John Fearon 1950s

❻ Schard E2 5b
This follows the centre of the face to a high crux. There are runners but sadly not where they are much use.

❼ The Elf . . . . HVS 5a
May still contain a loose block - care needed.

The Blue Defile

A taller buttress with a wide central crack of the *Blue Defile* which was first climbed by Tom Stobbart in 1933 who had to resort to some choice language before the route would "submit to his authority".

❽ Dilemma . . . . VS 4c
The short arete high on the left, swapping sides at half-height.
FA. Barry Clarke 1969

❾ Defile Left . . . . HS 4b
The wall is climbed on some suspect flakes to the break. Move left and finish up the arete.
FA. Robert Taylor c1970

❿ Brand New Nothing E4 6a
The true finish to the *Defile Left* up the sketchy flake.
FA. Paul Harrison 2001

⓫ The Blue Defile . . . . VS 4b
The wide crack is quite intimidating but easier than it looks. A monster cam may be of considerable help. Exit left.
Photo opposite.
FA. Tom Stobbart 1933. He described it as Bloody Vile - get it?

⓬ Blasphemy E4 6b
The lower wall is hard, fingery and bold. If you reach the ledge the upper arete is (a little) easier.
FA. Ian Hirst 1981

⓭ Duplicate E1 5b
Climb the buttress across the gully via a shallow groove to a finish up thin cracks in the left arete.
FA. Terry Hirst 1978

The Blue Defile - 20m

10m

Descent

Sheffield Area
Ladybower Area
Stanage
Burbage Valley
Millstone Area
Derwent Edges
Chatsworth Area
Southern Crags

TICKLIST

Wharncliffe Hoary Classics

A nice set of routes that offer an indication as to how good the old guys were. Leave the runners, chalk and fancy footwear at home for the full effect.

- [ ] **Puttrell's Progress, S** *(59)*. FA. 1900
- [ ] **Scarlett's Crack, VS** *(69)*. FA. 1931
- [ ] **The Blue Defile, VS** *(60)*. FA. 1933
- [ ] **Himmelswillen, VS** *(62)*. FA. 1933
- [ ] **Tower Face, HS** *(64)*. FA. 1933
- [ ] **Grammarian's Face, VS** *(67)*. FA. 1944

Steve Cunnington on the easier final section of *The Blue Defile* (VS 4b) having done the wide and awkward lower section- *opposite* - no swearing was involved.

Descent

Himmelswillen

An impressive tower and wall with a fine set of routes. *Himmelswillen* is a true classic, while *Banana Wall* is the easiest and best of the harder routes.
Approach (see map on page 47) - From the green sign continue on the cliff-top path for 500m until you reach a wall. Descend to the right to reach the Hell Gate Area with Himmelswillen just beyond.

1 **Sidewinder** . . . . **HS 4b**
The steep north-facing wall is climbed leftwards on good finger-holds, finishing with a long reach above the ledge.

2 **Frigging Saw** **E3 6a**
The roof and blunt arete.
FA. Nick MacFarlane 1983

3 **Himmelswillen** . . . . Top 50 **VS 4c**
The classic of the crag, surprisingly steep and pumpy for its time. Climb the left arete to ledges then step right and layback into the finger-crack that splits the centre of the tower. Finish on the left arete. Starting up the right arete is an option at the same grade. *Photo opposite.*
FA. Tom Stobbart 1933. The name translates as 'Good Heavens'.

4 **Serrated Edge** **E1 5b**
The right-hand arete can be followed throughout. It is too close to *Himmelswillen* in its central section (runners but no holds allowed) but features good climbing with a worrying finale. High in the grade.
FA. Gary Gibson 1981

5 **Teufelsweg** . . . . **Diff**
The historical rift that splits the face.
FA. Hans Teufel (of Tryfan's Munich Climb peg-placing infamy) 1936

6 **Y.M.C.A. Crack** . . . . **VD**
The crack that forks right from the chimney is pleasant.
FA. Barnsley YMCA 1970

Sheffield Area · Ladybower Area · Stanage · Burbage Valley · Millstone Area · Derwent Edges · Chatsworth Area · Southern Crags

Graham Parkes strikes *the* classic pose on the final exposed moves of *Himmelswillen* (VS 4c) - *opposite* - one of the most popular climbs across the whole of Wharncliffe and with good reasons - a striking line, steep pushy moves and good gear. The exposed exit is the icing on the cake.

Sheffield Area
Ladybower Area
Stanage
Burbage Valley
Millstone Area
Derwent Edges
Chatsworth Area
Southern Crags

❼ Dragon's Hoard **E6 6b**
From the right side of the block, tiny cracks lead up the centre of the face to a desperate, grasping final sequence.
FA. Simon Jones 1993

❽ Cardinal's Treasure . **E4 6b**
Climb *Dragon's Hoard* until it is possible (or even essential?) to swing right to finish up *Banana Wall*.
FA. John Allen 1984

❾ Banana Wall **E3 6a**
Climb the small wall right of centre using undercuts (good cam) and poor holds to reach easier ground by a long stretch. Finish rapidly up the final wall. Much harder for the short.
FA. Don Barr 1977

Hell Gate Area

The finest set of hard climbs on the cliff based around a trio of jutting aretes. Half a dozen routes weigh in at E4 and above and all are steep, fingery and bold. Those in search of something less serious should enjoy *Tower Face* on the left and the *Hell Gate* routes on the right.
Approach (see map on page 47) - From the green sign continue on the cliff-top path for 500m until you reach a wall. Descend to the right to reach the Hell Gate Area.

1 Tower Face . . . . Top 50 **HS 4b**
The left-hand facet of the square buttress is split by a thin crack. Approach this via a short slab (awkward for the short and with poor protection), then climb it using the arete on the right as and when needed. A finish to the left extends the pleasure a bit.
See photo on page 46.
FA. Eric Byne 1933

2 Down to Earth . . **E4 5c**
The right-hand face of the buttress is fingery, sustained and unprotected where it matters - the landing is unfriendly too! Using side-runners drops the grade a notch or two.
FA. Roger Doherty 1985

3 On the Air **E5 6a**
The right-hand arete of the face is climbed on its right side until it is possible to teeter around onto the front face to finish. Bold and precarious though a little escapable.
FA. Terry Hirst 1978

4 Journey into Freedom . . . **E7 6b**
Bridge out of the wide cleft in the left wall and climb leftwards using undercuts to slap for the arete. After a couple of moves up this, swing back right and climb the wall to join the last few moves of *On the Air*.
FA. Simon Jones 1993

5 Seconds Out **E5 6b**
Ding, ding! Mantel onto the jutting block, then move up and finger traverse the thin break all the way to the arete and a finish as for the last couple of routes.
FA. Don Barr 1978

6 Hell Gate Gully . . . . **Mod**
The blocky central gully provides light relief from the more august outings that surround it. Climb a slab then bridge past blocks to reach easier ground above. All very historical.
FA. J.W.Puttrell and friends about 1900

7 News at Zen **E3 5c**
The right wall of the gully is climbed centrally passing a useful black pocket. A side-runner in the gully to the left lowers the grade to around **E1**.
FA. Simon Jones 1993

8 Desolation Angel **E6 6b**
The central arete gives a fine route, climbed on its left-hand side throughout. A distant side-runner is often used at **E5**, though the upper section remains bold.
FA. Terry Hirst (with side-runner) 1978. FA. Simon Jones (solo) 1992

9 Hell Gate . . . . **VD**
The deep groove has an awkward bulge early on and more tricky moves to leave the half-height niche. Not a bad effort for a century ago. An exposed exit up the arete to the right is a worthwhile variation.
FA. J.W.Puttrell and friends about 1900

10 Gavel Neese **E2 5b**
The blunt arete has a height-dependent start (at least 6a for shorties) and no runners before the break (which takes a very big cam). The short upper arete is much easier, plus it has runners and great positions.
FA. Reg Addey early 1960s

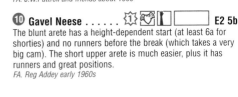

14m

14m

Descent

⓫ Lucifer E2 5c
Climb *Hell Gate Crack* to the first overhang (avoiding it via the crack just left is possible but artificial), then step left and climb a thin crack to the roof. Pull blindly over this and climb the open groove by difficult and fingery moves.
FA. Terry Hirst 1984

⓬ Hell Gate Crack . . . . . . HS 4b
The steep flake-crack splitting the face leads to the large overhang - the central section is both pumpy and awkward to protect. Step right for an easier finish.

⓭ Joie-de-Vivre . . . . . HVS 5c
The right arete of the wall to the break then extend-a-way to the top. Safe but taxing, if all else fails, escape to the left.
FA. Pete Crew late 1950s

⓮ Primal Void . . . . HVS 5a
Starting round to the right climb the arete then traverse left under the roofs, crossing *Hell Gate Crack* to finish up the last moves of *Gavel Neese*. The start is quite bold and pumpy too.
FA. Frank Horsman 1998

⓯ Ce ne Fait Rien . . . . HVS 5b
Start right of the arete where a wide crack leads to bulges then escape leftwards under the roofs to *Hell Gate Crack*.
FA. Pete Crew early 1960s

⓰ Well Now It Is E2 6a
A dynamic direct finish through the bulges.
FA. Andy Barker 1991

⓱ Wheelbrace . . . . VS 4c
Start as for the last route but follow the juggy crack right then back left. Short and steep.
FA. George Kitchen early 1960s

To the right is a short wall with two prominent crack-lines.

⓲ Green Groove . . . . Diff
The deeper left-hand one is a green groove.
FA. Fred Jones 1933

⓳ Obscenity . . . . HS 4b
This is the thinner right-hand one.

There are various small buttresses to the right but the next area of interest is Long John's Stride - a ten minute walk south (right) via the cliff-top path.

Sheffield Area

Ladybower Area

Stanage

Burbage Valley

Millstone Area

Derwent Edges

Chatsworth Area

Southern Crags

Long John's Stride

An isolated set of quiet buttresses with a good selection of climbs. It can be very green here in winter or after rain, and the trees make it midgy in summer.

Approach (see map on page 47) - There are two approaches. If on the main edge, follow the cliff-top path from above the Hell Gate Area for 10 mins until the towers appear on the right - scramble down the slope north of them. If you wish to go direct to this area then use the shorter eastern approach described on page 47. Escape from the top of the two main towers involves The Stride and/or a tricky down-climb.

① October Climb . . . .   **S 4a**
Climb a crack passing a tall jammed block to ledges then finish up the left-hand side of the face above.
FA. John Fearon 1955

② October Arete Original . .   **HVS 5a**
Start up *October Climb* to the jammed block then make tricky moves out to the arete. Finish on the right with difficulty.
FA. John Fearon 1955

③ October Arete **E2 5c**
The left-hand arete of the tower has a hard, reachy and poorly protected start until it joins the *Original* and eases to romping.
FA. Pete Crew early 1960s

④ Autumn Wall **E4 6a**
The face of the tower is climbed past an overlap early on with thin moves on poor holds at half-height. A great outing.
FA. Terry Hirst 1978

⑤ A Deepcar Named Desire . . .   **E5 6b**
A narrow eliminate up the wall.
FA. Bill Birch 1999

⑥ Equinox **E3 6a**
The right-hand arete features escalating difficulties.
FA. (by a left-hand finish) Terry Hirst 1978. FA. (Direct) John Hesketh 1988

The next routes are in the cleft behind the tower and can't be seen on the topo. In poor conditions they can be greener than a really green thing that is feeling a bit seasick.

⑦ Chockstone Chimney . . .   **VD**
Climb the blocky crack on the left inside the alcove to a tricky final section, which includes a belly-flop exit.
FA. J.W.Puttrell late 1800s

⑧ V-Chimney . . . .   **VD**
Bridge the right-hand cleft, recognisable by its angular form.
FA. J.W.Puttrell late 1800s

⑨ The Candle Snuffer . . . . . .   **S 4b**
In the back right side of the alcove is a narrowing chimney. Climb this to its closure then escape out right. Make sure you don't get snuffed.
FA. J.W.Puttrell late 1800s

Sheffield Area | Ladybower Area | Stanage | Burbage Valley | Millstone Area | Derwent Edges | Chatsworth Area | Southern Crags

⑩ Spider Cracks . . . . 🔲 VS 5a
The left-leaning thin cracks to a deeper continuation.
FA. John Fearon late 1950s

⑪ Grammarian's Progress . 🔲🔲 VS 4c
Worthwhile but bold. Starting at the tunnel, climb the arete on its left before pulling round onto the front face. A poorly-protected mantelshelf reaches better holds, then traverse right to a wide crack to finish. High in the grade, bizarrely it used to be VD!
FA. R.A.Brown 1944

⑫ Grammarian's Direct . . . 🔲🔲 HVS 5a
Balance up the lower arete to join the original then finish direct with an awkward mantelshelf.

⑬ Gwyn . . . . 🔲🔲🔲 E3 5c
The centre of the north-facing wall of the central tower has taxing moves to start, a tricky mantel and scant gear.
FA. Reg Addey early 1960s

⑭ Grammarian's Face . . . . 🔲🔲 E1 5b
Start up the right arete (runners to the left) then make awkward moves out left to access the mantel on *Gwyn*.
FA. Rodney Wilson late 1950s

⑮ Grammarian's Face Direct . . 🔲 E2 5b
The right-hand arete is tackled direct with bold and precarious moves at half-height that will concentrate the mind.
FA. Gary Gibson 1982

⑯ Long John's Eliminate . . 🔲🔲 E2 5b
A fine bold pitch that meanders up the valley face. Climb the arete as for the previous climb but traverse the face on the right to reach a groove in the far side of the wall. Climb this awkwardly then move back left to a short crack.
FA. Pete Crew early 1960s

⑰ Long John's Superdirect . . . . 🔲 E3 5c
A direct line up the face via a flake and scoop, crossing *Long John's Eliminate* and finishing close to the top right-hand arete.
FA. Bill Birch 1999

⑱ Cannae . . . . 🔲🔲 E2 5b
The wall left of the tunnel leads to the groove on the *Eliminate*.
FA. Gary Gibson 1982

⑲ Long John's Ordinary . . . . . . 🔲 S 4a
The easiest way up the tower. Tackle the left-hand of a pair of chimneys to the notch then continue up the inside arete of the tower - usually green - via a crack to tricky moves onto the summit. Now try and escape!
FA. J.W.Puttrell late 1800s

⑳ Impish . . . . 🔲🔲🔲 f6C
The undercut arete gets quite high.
FA. Simon Jones 1994

㉑ Imp Wall . . . . 🔲 f6A+
Climb the wall using some slopers.

㉒ Long Chimney . . . . 🔲🔲 Diff
The prominent tall narrowing cleft. The wall just left gives a variation at a slightly harder grade.
FA. J.W.Puttrell and friends about 1900

㉓ Inclusion . . . . 🔲🔲 E1 5b
Shin up the awkward arete on its right-hand side.
FA. Terry Hirst 1980

㉔ Richard's Revenge . . . . . 🔲🔲 VS 4c
The thin crack is awkward to start (almost 5a), passing an ancient peg scar (tut, tut!) and features excellent jamming above.
FA. Dick Brown (one naughty peg) late 1940s

㉕ Lincoln Crack . . . . 🔲🔲 HVD 4a
The lovely clean-cut crack on the right often looks green though the holds are usually clean. A neat little pitch.
FA. Dick Brown late 1940s

㉖ Long John's Arete . . 🔲🔲🔲 f6B
The sharp arete above a poor landing.

Sheffield Area

Ladybower Area

Stanage

Burbage Valley

Millstone Area

Derwent Edges

Chatsworth Area

Southern Crags

Cascade Buttress

Far South

Beyond Long John's Stride the edge continues as a scattered set of small buttresses, many of which are worth a look. Linking several of these together can make for a decent day out with a fair bit of walking involved too. **Approach (see map on page 47)** - The usual approach is to head south from Long John's Stride (see page 66 for approaches to here) following a good path though the trees. After 50m the path forks and the right-hand branch (heading gently downhill) reaches Cascade Buttress (on the left) in just over 100m. 350m further on The Bass Rock is hidden in the trees below the path - some careful pacing should help locate it. Beyond The Bass Rock the path heads up towards the crest of the escarpment. The final two buttresses are located below the path about 300m from The Bass Rock and are most easily reached by walking over the top and doubling back. If you reach the buildings of Wharncliffe Lodge you have overshot the rocks by about 200m.

Cascade Buttress

❶ Cascade Climb . . . . 🗒️🚹⬜ **VS 5b**
Boulder up the slabby arete then grovel-a-way leftwards to access a ledge. Brush yourself down then finish up the wall. The route can also be started from the next climb by an exciting swing at around 4a/b to access the stomach-traverse.
FA. Jon Fearon/Dave Gregory 1955

❷ Flying Angel . . . . 🗒️🚹⬜ **E1 5b**
The compelling bell-shaped central fissure only succumbs to a stout effort. Huge cams and ham fists might be of help too.
FA. Hugh Banner early 1960s

❸ Spring Tide . . . . 🚶🏋️⬜ **E2 6b**
The blunt central arete gives a technical pitch. Side-runners are used at this grade for the balancy upper section.
FA. John Hesketh 1988

❹ Watson's Crack . . . . 🗒️🚹⬜ **VS 4c**
The steep slanting crack is still a bit of a stout test piece over a century on; it still requires elementary jamming/laybacking skills.
FA. W.J.Watson late 1800s

❺ Bedrock . . . . 🖐️⬜ **E6 6b**
This is the long right arete of the crack giving bold and technical laybacking; a side-runner drops the grade.
FA. John Hesketh 1987

❻ Puttrell's Crack . . . . ⬜ **VD**
The big corner gives bridging to a tricky outside exit. Thin people with no sense of history can avoid the crux by burrowing.
FA. J.W.Puttrell late 1800s

❼ Pocket Buttress . . . . 🗒️⬜ **VS 4b**
Trend right to twin pockets (direct is harder) then move out right to the arete and finish up this. Nice stuff.
FA. Jon Fearon/Dave Gregory 1955

❽ Pocket Buttress Direct . . 🗒️🚹⬜ **E5 6a**
The wall above the pockets is hard and bold.
FA. Terry Hirst 1984

❾ Stinkpit . . . . 🖐️⬜ **E2 6a**
Climb the arete on its right-hand side until it eases.

❿ Cadence . . . . 🗒️⬜ **E1 5b**
From *Deep Chimney* swing left to access the neat hanging groove then sprint up this to easier ground.
FA. Terry Hirst 1980

⓫ Deep Chimney . . . . . 🗒️🚹🖐️⬜ **Diff**
The deep rift manages to feel bold; sadly cams that big haven't been invented yet.
FA. J.W.Puttrell and co. About 1900

Up and right is the lost Upper Tier with 20 neglected routes - not described here.

The Bass Rock

The Bass Rock

12 Byne's Route . . . . 🏆 ☐ **S 4a**
From the left arete move up and right to climb the face just left
of the crack. A nice pitch.
FA. Eric Byne (on a top rope) 1933. The first lead isn't recorded.

13 Rossiter's Route . . . . 🏃 ☐ **HVS 5b**
Boulder up the wall to the right of the arete then move left and
continue up its right side delicately.
FA. Brian Rossiter (ably managed by Chris Craggs) 2000

14 Scarlett's Crack . . . . 🏆 🏃 🏔 ☐ **VS 5a**
Start up the tricky green groove then follow the thin crack
throughout. Well worth calling in for if you are over this way.
FA. Harry Scarlett 1931. An impressive solo for the day.

15 Brooks' Route . . . . . 🏆 🐾 🏔 ☐ **HVS 5a**
The right arete in its entirety. Bold towards the top.
FA. John Fearon 1955. Originally top roped by Rupert Brooks in 1933.

Lodge Buttress

16 Ogilvie's Corner . . . . 🏆 🏃 ☐ **HVS 5c**
A thin traverse across the pockety seam leads to easier climbing
up the groove left of the main arete
FA. Alan Clarke early 1960s

17 Ogilvie's Direct . . . . 🏆 🏔 ☐ **f6B**
The finger-crack. Traverse left to get off or continue upwards.
FA. Terry Hirst 1978

18 Curvaceous . . . . 🏆 ☐ **f7A+**
The blunt arete to a sloper. Good and very technical.
FA. Jon Fullwood

19 Nightjar . . . . 🏆 🏔 🐾 ☐ **E3 5c**
The right-hand side of the arete is gained by a rising traverse
from the right. To the sloping hold is a 5c boulder problem.
FA. Howie Darwi 1991

20 Lodge Buttress Direct . . . 🏆 🔧 ☐ **VS 4b**
Climb into the sentry-box in the roof then swing left (a bit
creaky) to access the easier upper wall.
FA. Dave Gregory 1955

Ewden Buttress

21 Windfall . . . . 🏆 🔧 ☐ **E2 5c**
The left-hand side-wall gives a steep and powerful pitch through
the roofs keeping just left of the arete.
FA. Terry Hirst 1978

22 Ewden Edge . . . . 🏆 ☐ **VS 4c**
Climb the disjointed arete with nice positions along the way.
FA. David Simmonite 2002. Almost certainly climbed (long) before.

23 Ewden Wall . . . . 🏆 🐾 ☐ **VS 4c**
The centre of the face gives another fine climb, though the
protection requires a bit of care/thought.

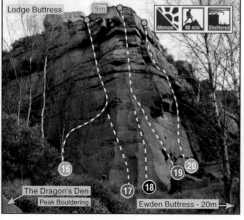

Lodge Buttress

The Dragon's Den
Peak Bouldering

Ewden Buttress - 20m →

Ewden Buttress

Sheffield Area | Ladybower Area | Stanage | Burbage Valley | Millstone Area | Derwent Edges | Chatsworth Area | Southern Crags

	No star	⚂	⚂	⚂
Mod to S	9	2	1	-
HS to HVS	8	15	1	-
E1 to E3	3	4	4	-
E4 and up	1	2	-	-

Esoteric is the best adjective to use for Agden. The cliff isn't composed of gritstone but a coal measures sandstone formed by a landslip in the geologically recent past, which accounts for the blocky, loose and unweathered nature of much of the cliff. On the plus side, the setting is sublime and the cliff is almost always quiet. There are over 100 recorded climbs here but many of them are poor; loose, vegetated or downright dangerous. We have included a selection of the best and most popular. The routes have a big feel, which makes a nice change from much of the climbing on offer in the Peak, though be warned that you WILL encounter vegetation and dubious rock - so come prepared - some care is required to climb safely here.

Approach   Also see map on page 45

Agden Rocher is close to the hustle and bustle of Sheffield, just northwest of High Bradfield. Follow the minor road of Brown House Lane north out of High Bradfield keeping left at the only junction. A short distance after this is a narrow lane on the left with restricted roadside parking - try to get as close to the wall as possible. Follow the lane round the top of a steep-sided valley and down through the woods to locate the right-hand end of the crag up in the trees on the right - 5 minutes from the car. A right branching path that runs along the top of the cliff

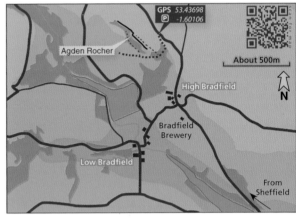

is a good option for getting to the far reaches of the crag (*Great Wall*, *The Whittler* etc) more quickly, descending a wide grassy gully located just before the point where a fence with a stile cuts across the path.

Conditions

The edge faces southwest and catches the sun from the mid-morning onwards. This means it can get very hot here. It is exposed to any bad weather but dries quite quickly after rain although the trees slow this in summer. The many trees also make route identification tricky, especially at the right-hand side of the cliff and, although they offer shade in the summer, they encourage lichen growth and promote humidity.

Sheffield Area

Ladybower Area

Stanage

Burbage Valley

Millstone Area

Derwent Edges

Chatsworth Area

Southern Crags

Dan Parkes eyeing up the thin crux moves on the classic *Castor* (E1 5c) - *page 74* - Agden Rocher. Photo: Graham Parkes

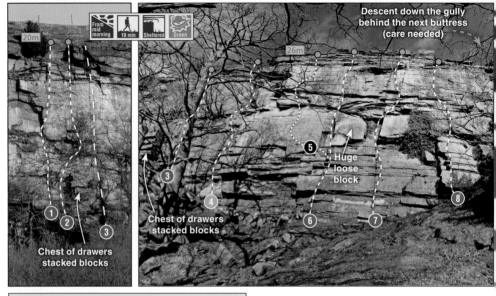

Descent down the gully behind the next buttress (care needed)

Chest of drawers stacked blocks

Chest of drawers stacked blocks

Huge loose block

Great Wall

The most impressive section of the cliff has a reasonable set of climbs BUT, like elsewhere, there is vegetation and loose rock to be handled - care is needed. Beyond the Great Wall there are a few routes though they see little interest. A series of stacked blocks resembling a chest of drawers is a useful reference point on the left-hand side. **Approach (see map on page 70) -** Follow the normal approach but branch right along the top of the cliff to reach a grassy gully just before a stile.

❶ The Snip E2 5b
The wall 2m left of the stacked blocks. Climb the wall to a ledge at a hanging groove. Step right and finish up the arete.
FA. Paul Harrison 1998

❷ Jaffa E1 5b
Climb just left of the stacked blocks to trees on the ledge on the right. Climb the wall above on spaced holds.
FA. Paul Harrison 1999

❸ Ardua E1 5b
Start just right of the stacked blocks and climb the continuous crack past a tree on a ledge. The upper section is good climbing.
FA. Mike White (5pts) 1963. FFA. Keith Myhill 1969

❹ S.O.S. . . . . VS 4b
A decent line though the tree gets in the way! Climb into, and up, the groove at the left edge of the wall then head up right to a big tree (possible stance). Continue above the tree until a short leftwards traverse leads to a steep groove. Up this to finish.
FA. Roy Briggs 1952

❺ Monster Munch . E4 6a
Powerful and bold climbing, protected in part by some old pegs; the first one in particular should be treated with suspicion. Move left out of *Asteris* onto the wall then climb direct to the break. Climb steeply left then back right before finishing direct.
FA. Paul Harrison 1996

❻ Asteris E1 5c
The long thin crack passing left of the massive perched block has a short hard crux section through the bulge. Make sure you don't put too much trust in the old pegs!
FA. Neil Mather (some aid) 1963. FFA. Keith Myhill 1969

❼ Conjunctus Viribus . . E1 5b
"With Combined Powers". Low in the grade but some of the rock is a bit suspect and you have to pull hard on it! Climb the crack and the shrubby groove then move right and power though the bulge to the parallel cracks. Up these to ledges and the top. *Photo opposite.*
FA. Al Evans 1967

❽ Ignis Fatuus E3 5c
The lower arete and thin crack lead to the bold upper wall.
FA. Roger Brookes 1983

TICKLIST
Never been to Agden?
The least popular large cliff in the book; is it actually worth a visit? Well there is only one way you will find out. On the plus side you should have the place to yourself.

☐ **Campsite Crack, S** *(75)*. A long and engaging line.

☐ **Oak Tree Walk, VS** *(76)*. Got any monkey skills?

☐ **The Whittler, VS** *(74)*. Stop whittling and get on it.

☐ **Conjunctus Viribus, E1** *(72)*. The best on Great Wall.

☐ **Pollux, E1** *(74)*. Sustained and really rather good.

☐ **Castor, E1** *(74)*. The right-hand twin - so thin.

☐ **Asteris, E1** *(72)*. Good but back-up the old pegs.

Sheffield Area

Ladybower Area

Stanage

Burbage Valley

Millstone Area

Derwent Edges

Chatsworth Area

Southern Crags

Graham Parkes setting up for the steep crux moves on *Conjunctus Viribus* (E1 5b) - *opposite* - Great Wall, Agden Rocher.

Descent and
approach gully

20m

Battered fence

The Whittler

An interesting buttress with a small selection of decent
routes; the twins of *Castor* and *Pollux* are especially
worthwhile, as is *The Whittler* at a more amenable grade.
Approach (see map on page 70) - Follow the normal
approach but branch right along the top of the cliff to
reach a grassy gully just before a stile. Turn right (looking
out) at the bottom of the gully.

① Pollux. . . . . 🏵🗝📷 [____] **E1 5b**
Worth seeking out. Climb the sustained crack to ledges and a
tree then move up left for a well-positioned finish up the arete.
Well protected and a good bet for a first E1.
FFA. Al Evans 1969 - previously aided

② Wheat Thin . . . . 🏵🗝📷🗝 [____] **E4 6a**
Serious. Climb the wall 3m left of the tree to a dubious old blade
peg, step right then continue direct to better holds. Easier and
safer climbing then leads to the top.
FA. Paul Harrison 1984

③ Castor . . . . 🏵🗝📷🗝📷 [____] **E1 5c**
The hairline crack just left of the tree has a couple of very
thin moves (small wires) to reach a niche and easier ground.
Continue past the holly keeping left of a well-wedged hanging-
death block. *Photo on page 71.*
FA. Keith Myhill 1969

④ The Whittler . . . . . . 🏵📷🗝 [____] **VS 4c**
A fine climb up the left-hand side of the smoother face. Exiting
the niche at the start is tricky, especially for the short, and gives
access to the fine sustained climbing above. From the oak tree
in the niche, finish up the arete on the right or the groove on
the left.
FA. Colin Whittle 1952

⑤ Briggs' and Titterton's . . 🏵🗝 [____] **HVS 5b**
A thin crack (small wires) leads with difficulty to the tree stump
and a good break. Step right and finish up the wider crack.
FA. Colin Whittle 1952

⑥ Cock o' the North . . . . [____] **S 4a**
The thin cracks on the right lead to a huge tree and a finish up
a groove. The original finish was up the face to the left - this is
better but a bit harder and more exposed.
FA. John Gordon 1952

Descent and approach gully

20m

Sheffield Area

Ladybower Area

Stanage

Burbage Valley

Millstone Area

Derwent Edges

Chatsworth Area

Southern Crags

Campsite Crack

A tall grooved buttress with the main attraction being the long groove of *Campsite Crack*. The pioneers used to camp on the flat ground below this part of the crag, hence the name.

Approach (see map on page 70) - Follow the normal approach but branch right along the top of the cliff to reach a grassy gully just before a stile. Turn left (looking out) at the bottom of the gully.

7 Mike's Route . . . . � □ HVS 5a
Climb the slab and hanging arete.
FA. Mike Snell 1999

8 Gemini . . . . 🔒 □ VS 4c
Climb up the thin crack and steep twin cracks in the right wall of the tottery groove.
FA. Keith Myhill 1968

9 Campsite Crack . . . . 🌟 □ S 4a
Nice climbing up the long groove with a jig right at half-height. Care is required with some of the rock but the positions are excellent.
FA. Eric Byne 1952

10 Scouting for Boys . . . . . . 🌟🔒 □ E3 5c
You won't find any round here. Climb the bold arete to the break, continue through the roof to a groove then move out right to access the square arete. Finish up this and the wall above.
FA. Paul Harrison 1997. The lower arete was done back in the 1960s.

11 Indirect Start . . . . 🔒 □ S 4a
The steep angle to the right is well-named.

12 Man of God . . . . 🌟👤 □ VS 4b
25m right of *Campsite Crack* is a left-facing groove with a wide crack in the back. Climb this (big gear needed) to the tree and an abseil descent.
FA. Dick Brown 1952. One of the first routes on the cliff.

13 Artifax Arete . . . . 🌟🔒 □ E3 5c
Another bold square-cut arete to a huggable tree.
FA. Dennis Orwin 1968 at VS!

Right-hand Walls

A wide section of rock with a broad selection of climbs, generally in the mid grades. Loose rock and vegetation will be encountered on all of the routes here. A helmet is essential and take care at all times.

Approach (see map on page 70) - The approach path levels out just to the right of the end of the cliff, a small branch path reaches the first buttress.

1 Flamingo Wall . .   **HVS 5a**
A couple of metres left of the crack of *Oak Tree Walk*, climb the bold slab to a reachy groove. Up this then through a small crack in a bulge before making an extended reach for the top.
FA. Al Evans 1968

2 Oak Tree Walk . . . . .   **VS 4b**
A climb with exciting shenanigans on the upper wall. Climb the wide crack to the tree, then access the wall above with difficulty using the rotting woodwork. Finish direct or a little more easily, over to the right.
FA. Albert Heath 1944

3 E.N. 24 . . . .   **VS 5a**
Climb the wall to the right to a bulge split by a thin crack - old peg. Pass this by fingery moves to gain the final groove.
FA. Al Evans 1968

4 Koh-I-Noor . . . .   **HVS 5a**
The wall is bound on the right by a jutting arete which is climbed on its left-hand side throughout.
FA. David Law 1999

5 The Resurrection . . .   **E2 5b**
The same arete, on its right-hand side this time, is harder and bolder. At two-thirds height, either climb the shallow groove on the right or continue up the arete - both ways are spooky.
FA. Mike Hunt 1980

6 Extra Tasty **E4 6a**
Bold, technical, devious and often dirty too! Climb the thin crack to the upper break, move right to a niche then head left up the final wall by hard and pushy climbing.
FA. Paul Harrison 1996

7 Derision . . . .   **S 4a**
The grubby main groove improves with height to a steep finish.
FA. Dick Brown 1952

8 Filth . . . .   **HVD 4a**
The twin cracks in the right wall of the main groove are a bit far apart to be climbed in tandem so choose just one - or the other.
FA. Dick Brown 1952

9 Bianco . . . .   **VS 4b**
The jutting left arete of the white slab/wall gives a fine pitch.
FA. Bob Hassel 1962

The wall to the right has a large tree at half-height (don't they all here) and a couple of fallen flakes/blocks at its foot.

10 Martini Crack . . . .   **VS 4b**
From the left-hand block trend right to the tree. The crack behind it gives a worrying blocky finish. Moving left to the arete is better and maybe worth an extra star.
FA. Pete Titterton, John Gordon (alts) 1952

11 Martini . . . .   **VS 4b**
From the right-hand block a fingery and bold start gains the wall then a tree. Move out left for a good finish up the cracked arete.
FA. Roy Briggs 1952

12 White Rose Flake . . .   **VS 4c**
The long crack/groove gives a fine varied pitch with a bit of loose rock and a fine steep finish.
FA. John Gordon 1952

13 Numenorean . . . .   **VS 4c**
Start up the groove but pull over the roof to access the arete. Move right to finish up the shallow corner.

Huge flake/block

Campsite Crack - 80m

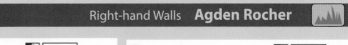
14 Painter's Climb . . . . S 4a
A flaky crack just left of the huge flake is followed to the tree.
The shallow corner above leads to the top - a bit of loose rock.
FA. Terry Lee 1952

*A couple of routes climb the flake/block and the wall above; they
see even less traffic than the rest of the cliff. The cracks in the
steep side-wall are (a bit) more popular.*

15 Baker Street . . . . . . VS 4c
A worthwhile and pumpy pitch that wouldn't be out of place in
one of the hidden bays at the far end of Millstone.
FA. Paul Baker 1979

16 Scarred Climb . . . . HS 4a
The slabby face using stuck-on holds leads to the tree. Move
left to the cracks right of the arete for a nice finish. Mild at the
grade.
FA. Roy Briggs 1952

17 Jericho Wall . . . . HS 4a
A good line and not quite as unstable as the name suggests
though a brittle band requires care. Follow the long crack as it
develops into a groove.
FA. Peter Biven 1955

18 Grey Wall . . . . VS 4b
Beyond the next arete, climb the centre of the lower wall to
tricky moves to access a tree on a ledge. Continue up the steep
wall behind into a pleasant groove.
FA. Roy Briggs 1952

19 Funeral Crack . . . . S 4a
The long crack system to the right has a poor start but the upper
section is much better.
FA. Eric Byne 1952

20 Aberration . . . . HVS 5a
Another worthwhile pitch up the wall to the right. From the
ubiquitous tree finish up the thin crack - take care with the rock.
FA. Al Evans 1966

21 Oak Tree Saunter . . . . VD
Start up the long corner (**Disappointment, VD** - a good line but
loose towards the top) then wander left to the tree. Use the tree
to gain the wall behind to finish.
FA. George Kitchin 1956

22 Double De-Clutch . . HVS 5a
The long arete gives a bold but worthwhile pitch.
FA. David Price 1963 He fell off it - twice!

23 Hagg . . . . S 4a
Another long blocky corner - care with the rock is needed,
especially the scary stuff at 3/4 height.
FA. Nat Allen 1955

24 Iceni . . . . VS 4c
Wanders up the wall to the left of the next long corner.
FA. Pete Scott 1966

25 Boadicea's Wall . . . . S 4b
Start as for *Agden Arete* but finish on the left.
FA. John Gordon 1952

26 Agden Arete . . . . S 4b
The arete has a tough start and some decent climbing above.
FA. Terry Lee 1952

27 Tartan Slab . . . . . . VS 4c
Climb the orange groove right of the arete to a small roof. Move
right across the slab to access a juggy roof to finish.
FA. John Gordon 1952

28 Protozoan . . . . HS 4a
An exciting left-hand finish to the next route. Traverse left from
the tree and pull over into a groove. Up this to a leftward exit.
FA. Ernie Marshall 1953

29 Deadnettle Crack . . . S 4a
This is the wide crack splitting the yellow wall. The start is tricky.
FA. Geoffrey Pigott 1958

Crag-top approach
to other areas

20m

**Loose even by
Agden's standards**

	No star	⚹	⚹⚹	⚹⚹⚹
Mod to S	9	13	6	-
HS to HVS	14	24	5	3
E1 to E3	11	14	8	-
E4 and up	9	12	7	2

The low-level, south-facing outcrop of Rivelin Edge was once ignored because of its reputation for midges and tree-shrouded greenery. It is now widely known that it is sheltered enough to be a great venue in the winter and the quick and easy approach (it is inside the Sheffield city boundary) makes it popular when time is short. It is possibe to finish work and nip out for an ascent of the Needle before the sun sets. Alternatively grab the opportunity on a beautiful winter's day to have a go at one of the big aretes or blank walls whilst the friction is good. The central area of the cliff, near the Rivelin Needle, has the highest quality concentration of good routes but hidden away to either side are some gems across the grades. The place is well worth several trips; Rivelin no longer plays second fiddle to some of its more illustrious brethren.

Approach   Also see map on page 45

The crag looks south over the Rivelin Valley, above the A57, on the west side of Sheffield. Parking is in the free car park on the south side of the dam at Rivelin Reservoir. Walk back to the main road and take the path opposite that runs up towards the cliff and then veers right through a

damp area, rising gently. Take a left fork which rises towards the crag, ignoring any paths leading off right, and you should emerge by the Rivelin Needle. This is easier to follow in the summer when the vegetation covers many of the minor paths here.

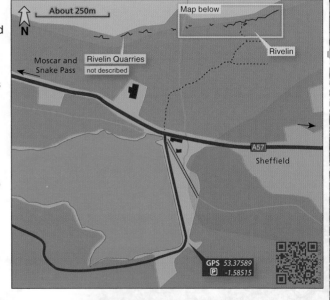

Conditions

Originally the slope below the cliff was open heath but woodland has grown up and now silver birch grow almost up to the cliff face. This tree cover gives shelter on windy days but makes the place green in the winter, although the Rivelin Needle itself stands proud of the trees and is seldom green. The whole crag is a south-facing sun-trap.

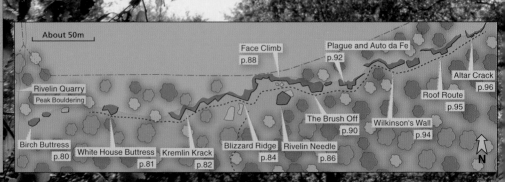

Dave Clay getting stuck into the meaty *Roof Route* (HVS 5b) - *page 95* - on the far right-hand end of Rivelin.

Sheffield Area

Ladybower Area

Stanage

Burbage Valley

Millstone Area

Derwent Edges

Chatsworth Area

Southern Crags

Rivelin Quarry
Peak Bouldering
10m
Descent
Cool Running - 10m

6m

Birch Buttress

Tucked away on the far left-hand side of the natural edge is a pleasant slabby buttress and a smaller and steeper buttress. These tend to be green early in the year.
Approach (see map on page 78) - Follow a very vague, undulating path leftwards from White House Buttress. Tricky in high summer when everything can be very overgrown.

① Birch Bark . . . . **HS 4a**
The left arete of the face - the start is usually a bit dirty. At the level of the ledge, traverse right for a tricky finish. Climbing the arete on its left-hand side is: **Birch Side, VS 5a.**

② Birch Buttress . . . . . **S 4a**
The centre of the slab is pleasant though awkward for the short and a bit bold. From the ledge finish up the stepped arete.

③ Don't Birch the Doc . **VS 5a**
The blunt rib is balancy and leads to an awkward finish that is a grade harder if the crack on the right is ignored!
FA. Graham Hulley 1994

④ Birch Crack . . . . **VD**
The compelling wide crack has useful holds on the face. Large gear is needed to protect it well. The finish is awkward.

⑤ Silver and White . . . . . . **HVS 5b**
A poor eliminate up the narrow face. There are runners on the right at half-height. The route is more like **E2** without these.
FA. Brian Middleton 1994

⑥ Birch . . . . **HVS 5b**
The balancy arete has a tricky upper section. Finish up a fluting.
FA. Al Wright 1964

Up and right is a short buttress in the trees with some highball bouldering.

⑦ Cool Running Left-hand . **f6B**
The left side of the wall trending to the right until leftwards escape becomes a possibility.

⑧ Cool Running . . . . . **f6B+**
Climb to the undercut then trend left up the slab.

⑨ Faze Action . . . . **f7B+**
The centre of the wall. From the undercut on *Cool Running* make a technical sequence upwards. Finish here or continue at **E2** via an undercut move for the top.
FA. Andy Chrome 1997

⑩ Uncle Buck . . . . **VS 5b**
The right arete is climbed mainly on its left-hand side and offers a couple of interesting moves. To the break is **Hot Dog, 5b.**
FA. Doug Kerr 2000

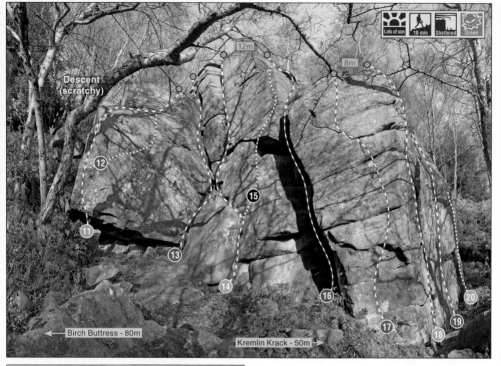

Descent (scratchy)

Birch Buttress - 80m

Kremlin Krack - 50m

White House Buttress

A secluded buttress with a mixture of old fashioned crack climbs and more modern stuff up the blank faces and aretes in between. Currently the routes don't see much traffic so everything tends to be rather green. This is one of the most sheltered buttresses on the whole cliff.
Approach (see map on page 78) - From Kremlin Krack area, a vague path leads leftwards though the trees to the buttress which is well hidden in the trees.

⑪ Red's Slab . . . . **VS 4c**
Climb the awkward lower arete to ledges then move right and balance up the centre of the face. Sticking with the arete is easier but just as bold. A sling on an old stump up and left (if it is still there) is the only possible runner, lowering the grade and grip factor. Both versions are usually dirty.
FA. R.A.Brown 1952

⑫ We're Only Here for the Smear
. . . . **E3 5b**
Start up the arete then balance out right along the lip to a finger-hold and friction up to the midway ledge. Finish easily. Technically easy enough but often green.
FA. Paul Harrison 1984

⑬ White House Crack . . . . . **S 4a**
Climb onto the ledge then continue via a good old fashioned thrash. A worthwhile route that would benefit from more traffic.

⑭ The President's Crack . . . **HVS 5a**
The wide and widening crack is an awkward and precarious struggle, though a chockstone thread offers protection. Not bad for a long-standing Severe!

⑮ Milena **E6 6b**
Above *Senator's Gully* is this wild hanging arete. Climb it by desperate pebble pulling and smearing to a grim mantel.
FA. Andy Healey 1998

⑯ Senator's Gully . . . . **S 4a**
The deep, gloomy rift leads to a ledge. From the ledge (possible stance) a tricky move on small footholds leads to easy ground.

⑰ Money For Old Rope **E2 6b**
The narrow wall to the right. From the left arete link a sloping break, a left-trending seam and the obvious ramp. Reachy.
FA. Percy Bishton 1999

⑱ Ray Crack . . . . **VS 5a**
The short crack past a creaky flake is more awkward than it looks. The blunt arete just left is **Stealing the Misanthrope's Wallet, HVS 6a**. It starts okay but it isn't long before *Ray Crack* is unavoidable.
FA. Al Wright 1956

⑲ Parallel Universe **E3 6b**
The wall on blind pockets and poor slopers. *f6B+* above pads.
FA. John Allen 1984

⑳ Ukase . . . . **VS 4c**
The tiny rib on the right is almost always dirty.

Sheffield Area | Ladybower Area | Stanage | Burbage Valley | Millstone Area | Derwent Edges | Chatsworth Area | Southern Crags

1 Seville Flake . . . . VS 4c
The flake on the side-wall is worth seeking out. Gain it from the left and finish out right. More direct variations are harder.
FA. Al Wright 1956

2 Ausfahrt E3 5c
The arete of the wall is gained from the left via a bulge and leads to a bold finish up the rib. Poor wires can be placed over on *Exit*.
FA. Chris Craggs 1983

3 Exit E3 5c
Climb the crack through the bulge to a ledge on the left then the delicate wall via a thin seam trending rightwards. Tiny wires offer some protection.
FA. Roger Greatrick 1983

4 Der Kommissar E4 6a
The original route of the wall has been neglected but is worthwhile. Up the wall to the break, move right and use the flake to pass the roof and start the wall, before moving left to find a finish.
FA. Roger Greatrick 1983

5 Jaded E4 6b
Cut out the loop on *Der Kommissar* via some fierce moves through the bulge.
FA. Graham Hoey 1989

Kremlin Krack
The left end of the main section of the cliff is a steep bay bounded on the right by a pleasant slab and rib a little further right. The hard, fingery routes here are sheltered, staying dry in light rain.
Approach - From the point where the path arrives at the crag, scramble up some blocks under the base of *Blizzard Ridge* and walk left for 50m.

6 Moontan E5 6c
The right-hand side of the wall has a desperate start to the break. Finish direct for the full route tick. A popular *f7A+* boulder problem as far as the first break.
FA. John Allen 1987

7 Kremlin Krack . . HVS 5a
A fine and intimidating route that would not be out of place on *Curbar*. The upper section is hard to enter, although fortunately good protection is available even without giant cams.

8 Scarlett's Chimney . . VS 4b
The chimney on the right of the hanging rib is an easier affair than its neighbour, though its still a struggle to get established.
FA. Harry Scarlett late 1920s

9 Left Under . . . . HVS 5a
A groove to the left of *Left Edge* leads awkwardly to a position below the flake of *Left Edge*. Layback up and right to join and finish as for that route.
FA. Bruce Goodwin 1992

Descent - 30m

15m

White House Buttress - 50m

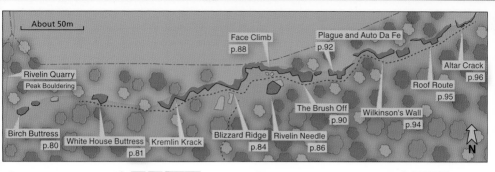

About 50m

Face Climb p.88 | Plague and Auto Da Fe p.92

Altar Crack p.96

Rivelin Quarry
Peak Bouldering

Roof Route p.95

The Brush Off p.90 | Wilkinson's Wall p.94

Birch Buttress p.80 | White House Buttress p.81 | Kremlin Krack | Blizzard Ridge p.84 | Rivelin Needle p.86

N

10 Left Edge .... VS 4c
The arete of the slab is fine climb, delicate with an interesting and bold-feeling detour out left onto a hanging flange. HVS for the faint of heart maybe?
FA. Pete Crew early 1960

11 Better Late than Never .. E1 5a
The slab direct on friction. It is delicate and protection is limited.
FA. Phil Baker 1984

*The right side of the slab is **Rivelin Slab**, an easy **Mod** or more usually a descent route for the competent.*

12 Angle Rib .... HVS 5a
Up the thin crack, then access the awkward hanging arete above by a loop to the right. More like **5b** if done direct.

13 Angle Crack............. Diff
The main groove improves once the vegetation is passed.

14 Solitaire .... HVD
The right-trending crack to a move right below the top passing a rickety flake on the way.

15 Isolation............ S 4a
The wide crack is more pleasant than it looks. Tricky at the top.

16 Rodney's Dilemma........ S 4a
The arete gives airy moves past fiddly runners in the breaks.
FA. Rodney Wilson early 1960s

Easier descent - 80m | Descent (tricky down-climb) | 15m | Blizzard Ridge | 10m

Lots of sun | 10 min | Sheltered

Descent - 80m

Rodney's Dilemma - p.83

Rivelin Needle

Ghostly guidebook writer

Blizzard Ridge

A fine arete gives one of the cliff's classic HVS routes, though it is a bit of a bold one. There are several worthwhile easier crack climbs here too, both to left and right of *Blizzard Ridge*. The cluster of easier climbs around *Rodney's Dilemma* is popular although the rock is less clean.

Approach (see map on page 83) - The area is just left of the point where the path arrives at the crag.

❶ Clinker **E5 6c**
Easy climbing leads to a ledge, then make a weird move on a small pebble in the middle of the scoop and rock right to the top. Easier for the tall and desperate for the short. Finishing using the left arete is the minor **End of the Road, E1 5c**.
FA. Percy Bishton 1998

❷ Temple Crack . . . . **HVD 4a**
The groove and steep crack has good holds and runners.

❸ Crafty Cockney **E2 5c**
An eliminate up the narrow wall passing a thin overlap.
FA. John Allen 1984

❹ Pious Flake . . . . **S 4b**
Steep but short-lived. Finish up the grubby groove.

❺ Tree Crack . . . . **VD**
Good climbing to the woodwork and a tricky little finish up the continuation crack above.

❻ Ulex . . . . **HS 4b**
The left-hand of the near parallel cracks is an adventure - a huge cam or two will be found useful by most. The shrubbery is cleaned out periodically.
FA. Byron Connelly 1933

❼ Gardener's Pleasure . . . . **HS 4b**
The widening right-hand crack is better. Large gear is needed for the middle section and the finish is a bit of a grovel - luuverly! If the tree ever goes it will be really tough.

❽ White Out **E1 5c**
The centre of the left-hand wall avoiding the tendency to drift towards the arete as much as possible. Follow the cracks leftwards for the best finish. Gentle for 5c especially for the tall.
FA. Bob Bradley 1983

❾ Blizzard Ridge . . . . **HVS 5a**
The juggy lower wall leads left to the fine bold upper arete, which is both superb and photogenic. The central section is bold putting the route at the upper end of the grade. It can also be started direct (strenuous) up the lower arete for a full **E1 5b** tick.
FA. Allan Austin 1958

❿ The Tempest . . . **E5 6a**
The centre of the face has a big rattling flake, a hand-placed peg runner and hard moves on rounded breaks. It is slightly escapable and also easier for the tall.
FA. Graham Hoey 1983

⓫ Jonathan's Chimney . . . . **VS 4c**
The angular rift is more of groove and is awkward to enter - try laybacking facing right. Once established it eases a little.
FA. Harry Scarlett late 1920s

⑫ Jonad Rib . . . . 🔺🐾◣ ▭ **VS 4c**
The rib between the chimneys is climbed on rounded holds and is poorly protected where it matters.
FA. Glyn Owen 1955

⑬ David's Chimney . . . . 🔺 ▭ **VD**
Another chimney that isn't one! A slightly awkward tussle early on and a stretch near the top (though there is plenty of gear available). A good one to learn on perhaps.
FA. Harry Scarlett late 1920s

⑭ Mad as Cows . . . . 🔺 ▭ **E1 5c**
Climb the narrow wall between *Layback Crack* and *David's Chimney* without deviation. Technical and just a bit blinkered.
FA. Matthew Hill 1990

⑮ Layback Crack . . . . 🔺 ▭ **Diff**
The clean-cut crack left of the groove bounding the wall can be laybacked. It was popular once, hence the polish. Used as a descent by the competent.
FA. Eric Byne 1933

⑯ Corner Crack . . . . 🔺 ▭ **HVD**
The main angle of the bay is surprisingly sustained, and leads to a sneaky exit out to the left to avoid the prickles.
FA. D.White 1951

⑰ Twin Hole . . . . 🔺 ▭ **HVS 5a**
From the ledge behind the gorse, climb the sketchy slab on spaced holds (bold) to reach the thin crack. Up this more easily.

⑱ Acid Reign . . . . 🔺🔺 ▭ **f6C**
The short arete has a high crux, though rightward escape is possible for the harassed.
FA. Greg Griffith 1985

South Face 18m

North Face Not much sun

8m

West Face 12m

rickety flake

The Notch

Rivelin Needle

Standing proudly in front of the cliff is the fine obelisk of the Rivelin Needle, one of grit's more inaccessible summits. All the routes on the pinnacle are worthwhile, and *Croton Oil* is a classic. Several climbs arrive at the small ledge of the Notch where the rickety flake leads to the summit. This flake needs handling with care and placing runners behind it is a bad idea.

Approach (see map on page 83) - The area is above where the path arrives at the crag.

Descent - A chipped notch or some rather rusty old chains (or both) provide the anchors for an abseil.

① Croton Oil . . . . **Top 50** ☐ **HVS 5a**

A great classic featuring fine climbing and good protection. At the lowest toe of the pinnacle, climb a wide crack (often damp) to ledges then the wall trending left via a series of finger-cracks. Finish up the rickety flake with care. *Photo opposite.*
FA. Dick Brown (5 pegs) 1953. FFA. Pete Crew 1963

② Only Human . . . . . . ☐ ☐ ☐ ☐ **E5 6c**

The right-hand side of the south face leads to desperate moves up the final steep wall.
FA. Roger Greatrick (with peg runner) 1983. FA. John Allen (without) 1988

③ The Spiral Route . . . . . . ☐ ☐ ☐ **VS 4c**

A tough little expedition - the easiest way to the summit, but not that easy. Follow *Croton Oil* then move right to a crack, which leads to escapable ledges behind the tower. From the right end of these, hand traverse the break strenuously out right (crux) to the rickety flake to finish. Potential for rope-work nightmares!
FA. Don Wooler 1950

Croton Oil (HVS 5a) - *opposite* - possibly the best route at Rivelin. Most people treat the rickety flake with bit more caution than the climber is doing here.

Sheffield Area
Ladybower Area
Stanage
Burbage Valley
Millstone Area
Derwent Edges
Chatsworth Area
Southern Crags

❹ Jumpey Wooller . . . 　　　　　　　 **E6 6c**
The left arete is sustained and slappy, use a layaway high on the right. A small Hex in a sandy pocket offers doubtful protection.
FA. Niall Grimes 1998

❺ The Eye . . . . 　　　　　　　 **E2 6a**
The right arete on the short side of the Needle is only a couple of moves long, but one of those is a bit of a beast. If you can't reach the holds, try stretching from a leg-lock in the break.
FA. Bill Briggs 1976

❻ Declaration . . . . 　　　　　　 **E5 6c**
The centre of the west face is extremely technical. Climb a crack (gear) then slap up the blunt arete to the break. Finish direct.
FA. Dave Pegg 1986

❼ Angst . . . . 　　　　　　 **E3 5c**
Climb the groove in the arete to the flat roof then step left to a grasping exit. Fortunately large cams in the final break (hard for the short to place) reduce the stress levels.
FA. Ian Riddington or Keith Sharples 1984

❽ The Original Route . . 　　　　　　 **E2 5c**
Climb the groove to the roof then exit right (crux) to *Croton Oil* and a finish up the rickety flake. Low in the grade but pumpy.
FA. Eric Byne (2 pegs) 1935. FFA. Joe Brown 1954

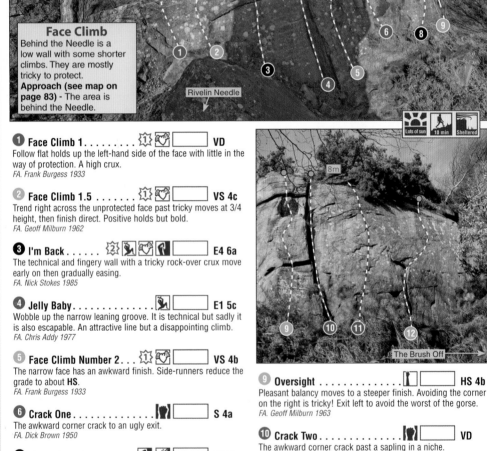

Descent (awkward downclimb)

8m

Face Climb
Behind the Needle is a low wall with some shorter climbs. They are mostly tricky to protect.
Approach (see map on page 83) - The area is behind the Needle.

Rivelin Needle

Lots of sun | 10 min | Sheltered

❶ **Face Climb 1** . . . . 🌣 💿 ☐ **VD**
Follow flat holds up the left-hand side of the face with little in the way of protection. A high crux.
FA. Frank Burgess 1933

❷ **Face Climb 1.5** . . . . 🌣 💿 ☐ **VS 4c**
Trend right across the unprotected face past tricky moves at 3/4 height, then finish direct. Positive holds but bold.
FA. Geoff Milburn 1962

❸ **I'm Back** . . . . . . 🌣 🏋 💿 🧗 ☐ **E4 6a**
The technical and fingery wall with a tricky rock-over crux move early on then gradually easing.
FA. Nick Stokes 1985

❹ **Jelly Baby** . . . . 🏋 ☐ **E1 5c**
Wobble up the narrow leaning groove. It is technical but sadly it is also escapable. An attractive line but a disappointing climb.
FA. Chris Addy 1977

❺ **Face Climb Number 2** . . . 🌣 💿 ☐ **VS 4b**
The narrow face has an awkward finish. Side-runners reduce the grade to about **HS**.
FA. Frank Burgess 1933

❻ **Crack One** . . . . 🧗 ☐ **S 4a**
The awkward corner crack to an ugly exit.
FA. Dick Brown 1950

❼ **Garibaldi Twins** . . . . 🧗 📷 ☐ **E4 6b**
The fingery and technical traverse along the break.
FA. Paul Mitchell, John Allen 1988

❽ **Takes the Biscuit** . . . . . . 🏋 💿 ☐ **E4 6b**
The technical blunt rib gives an extended boulder problem.
FA. Pete Robins 2000ish

The Brush Off ➡

❾ **Oversight** . . . . 🚪 ☐ **HS 4b**
Pleasant balancy moves to a steeper finish. Avoiding the corner on the right is tricky! Exit left to avoid the worst of the gorse.
FA. Geoff Milburn 1963

❿ **Crack Two** . . . . 🧗 ☐ **VD**
The awkward corner crack past a sapling in a niche.
FA. Dick Brown 1950

⓫ **Where Bulldykes Daren't** 🧗 🏋 ☐ **f6B+**
A technical problem up the blunt rib.
FA. Andy Pollitt 1985

⓬ **Shelf Wall** . . . . 🌣 ☐ **VS 4c**
Mantel-a-way up the wall to the right to a grotty mantel exit, or escape down and right.
FA. Dick Brown 1950

TICKLIST
Rivelin Mid-grade Gems

A sweet selection of fine climbs scattered along the edge in the VS/E1 range. Left to right we have:

- [ ] **Left Edge, VS** *(83)*. Feels bold and oddly balancy.
- [ ] **Blizzard Ridge, HVS** *(84)*. Features an airy crux.
- [ ] **Croton Oil, HVS** *(86)*. Classic - the best route here.
- [ ] **Fringe Benefit, E1** *(91)*. Another bold and balancy one.
- [ ] **Roof Route, HVS** *(95)*. Short but really quite brutal.
- [ ] **Altar Crack, VS** *(96)*. So pumpy if you try laybacking.

Sheffield Area

Ladybower Area

Stanage

Burbage Valley

Millstone Area

Derwent Edges

Chatsworth Area

Southern Crags

Graham Parkes enjoying his own discovery, the delightful *Fringe Benefit* (E1 5b) - *page 91* - 30+ years after making the first ascent. At the time he worked at one of the local secondary schools in the area and nipped out in his lunch break with another well-known climber, Nigel Baker, to grab the first ascent - the name alludes to working so close to some great climbing.

The Brush Off

To the right of the clean, quarried wall behind the Rivelin Needle is the fine slabby face of The Brush Off buttress, home to some bold offerings, including the magnificent *Brush Off* and the pleasant *Fringe Benefit*. Those who prefer their sport short and sharp should find *Easy Picking* more to their liking.

Approach (see map on page 83) - The buttress is 20m right of where the path arrives at the crag.

❶ Birth of Venus . . . . 　　　　　　 E2 6b
The left arete reached from the ledge around the corner. A side-runner protects the start.
FA. John Allen 1984

❷ Easy Picking . . . . 　　　　　 E2 6b
The thin crack splitting the wall has a desperate start and even more desperate moves to reach the wider upper section. The start is a good *f6B*.
FA. Don Wooller (8 pegs) 1953. FFA. Steve Bancroft 1976

❸ Holly Gut . . . . 　　　　 VS 4c
The main angle of the bay is another struggle, normally green.
FA. Dick Brown 1953

❹ Oliver's Twist . . . . . 　　　　　 VS 4c
The wider crack of the pair (or both) just right of the main corner gives a couple of good fist-jamming moves to a steep dirty exit. The thin crack on its own is **Short but Thick, HVS 5b**.
FA. Oliver Woolcock 1963

5 The Terminator . 🔲🔲🔲🔲 E5 6c
The centre of the steep wall to the right. A high side-runner
protects the tough lower section but not the easier finish.
FA. John Allen 1985

6 I'll Be Back . . . . 🔲🔲🔲 E5 6b
A counter line to *The Terminator*.
FA. James Ibbertson 2003

7 Grim Fandango . . . . . . 🔲🔲🔲 E5 6a
The long-overlooked left-hand side of the arete has a bouldery
start, bold moves right at the top and not much in the way of
gear - just the few poor runners on *The Brush Off*.
FA. Dave Law 1999

8 The Brush Off . . . . [50]🔲 E4 5c
The slabby left arete is sweetly delicate and remains effectively
unprotected - a couple of dubious small cams are available but
you wouldn't want to trust them! Despite being low in the grade,
it was a superb effort for its day and still requires a cool head.
FA. Pete Crew 1963

9 Party Animal . . . . . . 🔲🔲🔲 E3 5c
The centre of the slab has bold moves to the midway break
(small cams) and then turns technical and reachy above. A bit
escapable but the climbing is good enough to ignore that fact.
FA. John Allen 1985

10 Fringe Benefit . . . . 🔲🔲 E1 5b
The right-hand side of the slab is delicate to a finish at a perched
block. Low in the grade though protection is poor on the lower
crucial section - there have been a few nasty falls here.
Photo on page 89.
FA. Graham Parkes 1980

Around the corner is a short wall.

11 Ebenezer's Staircase . . . . 🔲 VD
A tricky move gains a ledge, a flake and a leftwards exit. A
technical **Direct Start, 5b,** is possible up the lower wall.
FA. Dick Brown late 1940s

12 Deep Chimney . . . . 🔲🔲 HVD
The wide crack is a thrash; exit right to avoid the ugly slot.

13 Fumf . . . . 🔲🔲 VS 5b
The arete has a funny starting sequence and bold exit.

14 Wobbly Wall . . . . 🔲🔲 HVS 5b
Small holds allow the shallow seam to the right to be climbed.
FA. Ed Drummond 1969

15 Europe After Rain. . . 🔲🔲🔲 f7A
The right-hand side of the wall to a hairy exit. Short but intense.
FA. John Allen 1984

Sheffield Area · Ladybower Area · Stanage · Burbage Valley · Millstone Area · Derwent Edges · Chatsworth Area · Southern Crags

Plague and Auto da Fe

A couple of good buttresses; the left-hand one has a pair of highly technical outings both protected by one of the last bolts on natural grit. Despite vows over the years from various souls to do away with the bolt, it is still there! Over to the right is a fine tower with one of Rivelin's best routes, *Auto da Fe*, plus some easier offerings.
Approach (see map on page 83) - From the point where the path arrives at the crag, follow the path rightwards for 70m.

❶ Caravaggio . . . . 🎌 📷 ☐ **E3 6b**
The side-wall of the buttress, on sloping holds to a fierce undercutting move and an easier finale.
FA. Mark Stokes 1979

❷ Outsider . . . . 🎌 📷 ☐ **E2 5c**
Climb the left wall to the break. Traverse round the arete on jams where a powerful move gains the arete - then sprint. Low in the grade but intense for a moment or two. A good but bold **Direct Start, E3 5c**, laybacks the unprotected lower arete.
FA. Bill Briggs 1976

❸ Ring of Roses . . . . 🎌 📷 ☐ **HVS 5b**
Start as for *Outsider* but traverse the break on good jams but not many footholds; a pumpy little number.
FA. Chris Craggs 1981

❹ Big Al . . . . 🎌 📷 ☐ **E7 7a**
The left side of the face with great difficulty. Originally it was started on the right, with the bolt pre-clipped, at **E5 6c**.
FA. Neil Stokes 1986. FA. Nick Jennings (Direct without the bolt) 2000

❺ Plague . . . . 🎌 📷 ☐ **E4 6b**
The centre of the overlapping wall past an ancient, naughty and unwelded bolt. The move to pass the overlap containing the bolt is hideous for all but the very tall.
FFA. Jonny Woodward 1981

❻ The Crevice . . . . 🎌 ☐ **HVD**
Bridge the short steep corner just to the right to a tricky exit.

❼ The Slot . . . . 📷 ☐ **HVD**
The wide and mucky crack in the wall just to the right.

Left Holly
Pillar Crack
- p.94

Roof Route - 50m

8 Moss Side . . . . **HS 4b**
The left arete of the jutting slab from some fat chips. Lichenous.
FA. David Simmonite 1991

9 Lichen Slab . . . . **VS 4a**
The scoop and overlap around to the right climbed centrally.
This one is cleaner than you might expect. An eliminate variation
goes through the bulge on the right at **HVS 5b**.

10 Lichen Slab II . . . . **S 4a**
The right arete of the slab is pleasant enough - and clean too.

11 Sparks **f7B**
Scratch up the fierce arete. Originally finished up the next route.
FA. Adrian Berry 1993

12 Palm Charmer **E3 5c**
The thin crack in the front of the buttress is awkward, then step
left and layback the tricky and reachy arete to finish.
FA. Paul Harrison 1985

13 Auto da Fe **E4 6a**
Rivelin's second classic E4 arete - technically harder than *The
Brush Off* but with much better gear. Climb the short crack
to the break, arrange a few wires and cams whilst getting
ever more pumped, then sprint for the top via some tough
laybacking.
FA. Andy Parkin 1976

14 Reprieve **E3 5c**
The bold face with hard moves just before it eases.
FA. Dave Mithen 1976

Reprieve
- p.93

Wilkinson's Wall

A small set of indifferent routes and a bit of bouldering just round from the impressive arete of *Auto da Fe*. The trees offer a bit of shade in summer.

Approach (see map on page 83) - This is the shady bay just round right of the jutting arete of *Auto da Fe*, 160m right of the Needle.

1 Left Holly Pillar Crack . . S 4a
A right-slanting crack in the wall has good gear.

2 Right Holly Pillar Crack . . S 4a
The deep, wide crack.

3 Kellog Corner . . . . S 4a
The flaky corner on some suspect rock.
FA. Al Wright 1956

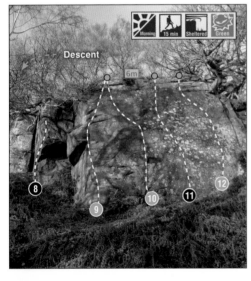

Descent

4 Double Decker. E4 6a
A technical wall climb.
FA. Jonny Woodward 1981

5 Caveman's Caper. . . HS 4b
The awkward slanting rift leads to a recess and easy ground.
FA. J.Lakey 1951

6 Bob Phlegming . . . . HS 4b
The thin slanting crack to an exit as for *Caveman's Caper*

A short distance right is a small slab with horizontal break.

7 Boulder Club . . . . f6C+
More fiercely technical climbing, via a thin slot.
FA. Greg Griffith 1985

20m further right is a small face with a couple of prominent square roofs on its left-hand side.

8 Chimp A . . . . f7A+
The hanging arete above the left-hand roof.
FA. John Allen 1998

9 Cocaine Place . . . . HVS 5a
The left edge of the wall has a move of interest and runners too.
FA. Dave Mirfin 1979

10 Wilkinson's Wall . . . VS 4b
Climb the wall leftwards on razor holds to reach the arete, then finish direct. Unprotected.
FA. Peter Wilkinson 1951

11 Of Mice and Men E5 6b
The blank centre of the slab has the crux at the top. Escapable.
FA. Adrian Berry 1992

12 Mount Krusty. . . . . VS 4c
Makes the most of the right edge of the face.
FA. Kirsty Raine 2000

Roof Route

The edge continues with an impressive buttress offering some great challenges which are rarely busy. The jutting jamming crack of *Roof Route* is the main attraction, though the corners of *Groove Route* and *Root Route* are also excellent.

Approach (see map on page 83) - From the point where the path arrives at the crag, follow the undulating path rightwards for 200m.

⑬ Summertime E3 5c
Climb boldly through the bulge to gain the undercut left arete of the large slab. It eases once established. Often green.
FA. Dave Morgan 1976

⑭ Small Time E2 6b
The centre of the slab is tough, though a side-runner on the right eases the strain a little.
FA. John Allen 1985

⑮ Renshaw's Remedy . . . . HVD
The fine angular corner left of the slab has a tricky start and great climbing above - bridging or jamming, or a bit of both.
FA. J.Renshaw c1950

⑯ Regular Route . . . . HVS 5a
The centre of the slab left of the big overhang of *Roof Route* was a late discovery. The final rib is the crux. Keep left and be aware of the closeness of the ledge; it will break your fall!
FA. John Allen 1988

⑰ Groove Route . . . . HVS 5b
Climb the pleasant shallow groove left of the jutting roof via a short boulder problem sequence. Despite its brevity, it is hard for HVS and hard for 5b!
FA. Bill Briggs 1976

⑱ Roof Route . . . . . . HVS 5b
A traditional grit HVS, the enticing roof crack is as good and as hard as it looks. Getting your hands round the lip is okay, then the problems begin. Not one to learn the mystical art on!
Photo on page 79.
FA. Joe Brown late 1950s

⑲ The Bush Off . . . . HS 4b
Link *Roof Route* with the right arete via a sideways ramble.
FA. Sarah Smart 2004

⑳ Root Route . . . . S 4a
An excellent sustained route up the groove to the right of the roof. Gaining the ledges early on is the crux for most.

㉑ Dynasty E4 6a
The cramped wall has fiddly wires under the roof that protect the hardest moves.
FA. Keith Sharples 1984

㉒ April Fool E2 5b
The wall and overhang to the left of the arete are bold but not too technical - or are they?
FA. Andy Parkin 1976

㉓ Steph . . . . HVS 5a
The wall just right of the arete has good holds - mild but bold.
FA. Bill Briggs 1976

Sheffield Area | Ladybower Area | Stanage | Burbage Valley | Millstone Area | Derwent Edges | Chatsworth Area | Southern Crags

Sheffield Area

Ladybower Area

Stanage

Burbage Valley

Millstone Area

Derwent Edges

Chatsworth Area

Southern Crags

10m

Descent

The Altar

Roof Route

① **Altercation** . . . . **HVS 5b**
The left arete of the face is accessed from the flakes on the gloomy side-wall and leads to a bit of a tussle at the finish.
FA. Bill Briggs 1976

② **Reredos** **E1 5b**
Pump along the break from the previous route until a welcome escape is possible. Have a good look at the non-existent holds on the E5 routes below you along the way.
FA. Johnny Woodward 1981

③ **New Mediterranean** . **E5 6c**
The left-hand line on the smooth wall is technical, fingery and reachy. Runners are normally placed in the next route first.
FA. John Allen 1985

④ **Moolah** **E5 6b**
The right-hand line on the wall is another arduous outing. If all else fails, try a right-facing egyptian to avoid the huge reach.
FA. John Allen 1988

⑤ **Altar Crack** . . . . **VS 4c**
The clean-cut corner crack is a VS with attitude. With gear placed as high as possible, layback and jam with conviction and try not to pump out before the sanctuary of the horizontal break. A 'go for it' approach is a poor idea here. Move right a short distance and belly-flop over the top. For those who are not pumped senseless a direct exit is not much harder.
FA. Dick Brown late 1940s

⑥ **Nonsuch** **E1 5b**
The thin crack has perfect protection and superb finger-jams but still manages to be shockingly hard work considering its length. A long-term hard HVS. *Photo opposite.*
FA. Alan Clarke early 1960s

Altar Crack
Rivelin winds up with this fine little buttress. *Altar Crack* and *Nonsuch* are great crack climbs, short but action packed and solid at their respective grades, whereas *New Mediterranean* and *Moolah* are a couple of excellent and hard face routes.
Approach (see map on page 83) - The area is the last significant buttress 250m right of the Needle and approach path.

⑦ **Grimace** **E5 6c**
Head up the narrow wall by super-sketchy moves, trending right to a hanging flake. Finish up the arete. Side-runners used.

⑧ **Gettin' Kinda Squirrelly** . **E6 6b**
The left arete of *Vestry Chimney*, climbed on its left-hand side, finishing via the flake on the left wall.
FA. Mark Hundleby 1999

⑨ **Vestry Chimney** . . . . **VD**
The tricky chimney with a worrying wobbling chockstone.

⑩ **Too Much** **E2 6a**
The thin crack in the slab has small wires protecting the mid-height crux followed by a quick blast for the top. *f6A+* as a highball problem to half-height
FA. Andy Parkin 1976

⑪ **Altered** . . . . **f6A+**
The wall right of *Too Much* is **E1 6a** if you carry a rack up it.

TICKLIST
Rivelin Cracks
A short list of some great cracks.

☐ **Birch Crack, VD** *(80)*
A grovel - suits big boots.

☐ **Root Route, S** *(95)*
A lovely line with loads of gear.

☐ **Altar Crack, VS** *(96)*
Good enough to be in two lists.

☐ **Kremlin Krack, HVS** *(82)*
Easier than it looks.

☐ **Nonsuch, E1** *(96)*
Innocuous but very uphill.

☐ **Easy Picking, E2** *(90)*
So tough it is untrue.

Dave Clay sprinting up the sustained and tricky *Nonsuch* (E1 5b) - *opposite* - on Altar Crack buttress at Rivelin. The climb is a classic example of one of those that looks innocuous enough from the ground but proves to be more of a challenge once you get on it; off-balance moves and poor holds combine to make it a bit of a struggle.

Sheffield Area

Ladybower Area

Stanage

Burbage Valley

Millstone Area

Derwent Edges

Chatsworth Area

Southern Crags

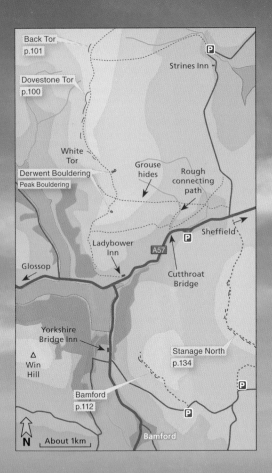

Back Tor
p.101

Strines Inn

Dovestone Tor
p.100

White
Tor

Grouse
hides

Rough
connecting
path

Derwent Bouldering
Peak Bouldering

Sheffield

Ladybower
Inn

A57

Glossop

Cutthroat
Bridge

Yorkshire
Bridge Inn

Stanage North
p.134

Win
Hill

Bamford
p.112

Bamford

N

About 1km

Ladybower Area

Sheffield Area

Ladybower Area

Stanage

Burbage Valley

Millstone Area

Derwent Edges

Chatsworth Area

Southern Crags

Graham Parkes on the excellent *Nemmes Pas Harry* (E1 5b) - *page 115* - on the Lower Tier, at Bamford, with what is probably the finest backdrop in the Peak. The dam holding back the Ladybower Reservoir was built between 1935 and 1943. The water collected here flows south to supply Derby and Leicester while a side tunnel runs under Stanage to top-up the Rivelin Reservoirs for Sheffield.

	No star	☆	☆☆	☆☆☆
Mod to S	25	13	1	-
HS to HVS	25	19	7	2
E1 to E3	10	8	2	-
E4 and up	1	3	1	-

Dovestone Tor is the most significant of a series of outcrops overlooking the flooded Derwent valley. It is well worth a visit if you want to escape the crowds. Having said that, nice summer weekends can be surprisingly busy up here nowadays. The cliff is a long west-facing wall riddled with many circular holes. The rock can be dirty, especially after rain, but the outlook is as fine as any cliff in the Peak and sunny afternoons spent here can be enthralling with superb views out into the wilderness of Bleaklow. Developments in the 1990s increased the number of routes listed here markedly, though many of the climbs done at this time will have been climbed in the past but were never recorded.

Approaches
Dovestone Tor is situated high above Ladybower Reservoir. There are two main approaches:
1) Cutthroat Bridge (50 mins walk). Park in the lay-by on the A57 above Cutthroat Bridge, or the bigger pull-off further up the hill if this is full. From the bridge, pick up one of two paths up to the crest of the moor, where a right turn leads past some good bouldering, to the Tor.
2) Foulstone Delf near the Strines Inn (40 mins walk). Park on the bend opposite the gated track and follow it past the shooting lodge and up to the crest of the ridge, then turn left (south) onto the flagged path which leads to Dovestone Tor, Back Tor is to the right at the junction. WARNING - Both parking areas, especially Foulstone Delf, are visited regularly by thieves. Leave nothing in your car.

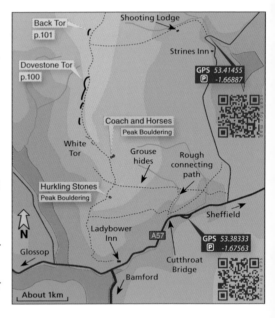

Access
Much of the moor to either side of Dovestone Tor and Back Tor is controlled to promote the grouse population. Access is freely given but on shooting days (notices posted) you need to stay on the main paths.

Conditions
The cliff is set at an altitude of 600m and facing due west it will catch any bad weather going. It can be green and is at its best on summer afternoons when the grassy base to the crag can be utilised to the full. In the winter or any poor weather it can be very wet and wild up here.

Bouldering
There is bouldering on the rocks below the main edge. Also two of the formations passed on the Cutthroat Bridge approach have some fine bouldering on some of the most rounded grit anywhere. Check the Rockfax Peak Bouldering guidebook for more details.

Back Tor

To the north of Dovestone Tor, the flagged path rises steadily up toward the conspicuous trig point on the rocky crest of Back Tor at 538m - a magnificent view point. There is worthwhile scrambling and bouldering all over the summit area, though the recognised routes are on a small west-facing outcrop just to the south. The rock is of good quality though it is green after rain. Also, extensive pools form under the crag, forming a potential SWS spot.

Approach - Follow the Dovestone approach from the Strines/Foulstone Delf parking, but at the crest of the moor, turn right. The crag is hidden a short way up the path, over to the left, facing away from the path.

① Mertle . . . . **VS 5b**
The left side of the wall on green slopers.

② Voice of the Turtle . . . . **HVS 5b**
The centre of the north-facing wall on rounded green holds.
FA. Chris Craggs 1982

③ Broggin Wall . . . . **S 4a**
The pleasant flake near the right edge of the face.

④ Turtle Rib . . . . **HVS 5a**
Climb the front face of the blunt rib using an array of pockets. The bulge is tricky.

⑤ Turtle Chimney . . . . **VD**
The awkward narrowing black gritty rift.
FA. John Tout 1976

⑥ Terrapin . . . . **HS 4c**
A worthwhile pitch heading right up the side-wall via a short crack and rounded holds. Exit to the right.
FA. Stuart Gasgoyne 1981

⑦ The Bone Cruncher . . **f7B**
The low level traverse is stern test of stamina. Hands go in the holes and on the crimps, keep your feet off anything large.

⑧ ET . . . . **f6A+**
With hands in the holes, pull up the bulge.

⑨ Hoplite **E4 6b**
Climb the blunt rib to the break, graunch right then do battle with the hanging nose - grotesque! The start is a *f5+* problem.
FA. Simon Cundy 1993

⑩ Hueco Wall **f6C**
Using two holes right of the arete, pull desperately up the face.

⑪ Eyes Without a Face **f7A**
Climb the wall past some pockets.

⑫ Spartan **E1 5c**
The main roof crack is a mini-classic and a tough tussle for most. Fortunately the landing is soft, even without a mat. Swinging along the line of crimps on the lower lip then up is **Rainbow**, *f6A+*.
FA. Con Carey 1976

⑬ Tortoise . . . . **HS 5b**
The right-hand roof crack is easier - but not much!
FA. Stuart Gasgoyne 1981

⑭ Hare . . . . **HS 4b**
The short wall to the right starting from a block. The low start is **Codfinger**, *f6C* starting from the back and reaching out.

⑮ Grouse Related Nonsense . . . . . **VS 4c**
The short arete that bounds the wall.

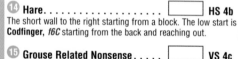

8m

Approach from flagged path

Sheffield Area · Ladybower Area · Stanage · Burbage Valley · Millstone Area · Derwent Edges · Chatsworth Area · Southern Crags

Dovestone Tor Bouldering
Peak Bouldering

Titania Area

The left side of the crag has a collection of shorter climbs. Although none of these are outstanding, they are usually quiet and there are a few easier climbs - a good spot for a bit of soloing or learning the ropes.

Approach (see map on page 100) - Drop rightwards off the flagged path as it starts to rise to locate the left-hand side of the cliff.

① Squawk . . . . HVS 5b
The arete leads to a stretch for the break and a tricky mantel. *f6B* from sitting.
FA. Chris Craggs 1996

② Sick as a Parrot . . . . HVS 5a
Start by a big pocket at ground level and climb straight up the wall before heading right to a precarious exit.
FA. Chris Craggs 1996

③ Sick Bay . . . . VS 4b
From just left of a groove, stretch left then traverse on solid jams to a rounded exit on the far left, above the overhangs.
FA. Ted Howard and friends 1957

④ Handy Wall Hole . . . . S 4a
Climb the easy groove to a ledge and then the wall on the right, passing the hand pocket.
FA. Dave Gregory 1996

⑤ Thunderbirds . . . . S 4a
From the centre of the wall climb awkwardly to a ledge, through a bulge and diagonally left across the final wall.
FA. Jim Rubery 1996

⑥ Woodentops . . . . S 4a
The left-hand crack to ledges then move left to another crack.
FA. Jim Rubery 1996

⑦ Stingray . . . . HVD 4a
The mild hand-jamming crack just left of the arete leads steeply to ledges. Finish around to the right.
FA. Ted Howard and friends 1957

⑧ Stingray Arete . . . . f5+
The arete, climbed on its right-hand side, is excellent. There is some more much harder bouldering to the right.

⑨ Windblasted . . . . Diff
The short wall 4m left of the chimney is climbed direct.

⑩ Windblown . . . . VD
The juggy wall 3m left of the chimney. Not much gear.
FA. Ted Howard and friends 1957

⑪ Domusnovas E2 5c
Climb up to and enter the hanging groove. A one-move-wonder.
FA. Paul Harrison 2002

⑫ Jonah . . . . Diff
The wriggly, giggly cleft. Finish up the inside though the detritus for the full Jonah experience!
FA. Ted Howard and friends 1957

⑬ Tight 'uns . . . . VS 5a
Climb the tricky slab just right of the chimney to a ledge. A short awkward wall leads to easier ground.
FA. Chris Craggs 1995

⑭ Titanium . . . . VS 5a
The technical centre of the slab from a gravel patch, and then the bulging wall above keeping left of the blunt central rib.
FA. Chris Craggs 1994

⑮ Titanic . . . . VS 4c
Climb past a wide pocket in the right-hand side of the slab and then up a short slanting crack. Some tasty moves along the way.
FA. Chris Craggs 1996

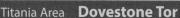

Descent

16 Titania . . . . **VS 4c**
Climb the left arete of the slab and the leaning wall on spaced and hidden jugs. Graded VD for years and upgraded again!
FA. Ted Howard and friends 1957

17 Iltis . . . . **HS 4b**
Climb the steepening right side of the arete to a tricky landing onto a shelf using a huge hidden bucket.
FA. Ted Howard and friends 1957

18 Outflanked . . . . **HVS 5b**
Climb the leaning wall just left of the corner (low crux) to a pocket and a sloping ledge. Take the tower above by worrying climbing, noting the way that the huge final block rocks easily!
FA. Chris Craggs 1996

19 Outfoxed . . . . **VS 4c**
Climb the front of the flake to its top then step right and climb the centre of the wall delicately to a large rocking block.
FA. Chris Craggs 1996

20 Fox's Chimney . . . . **Mod**
Amble up the diagonal flake and steeper corner beyond.
FA. Ted Howard and friends 1957

21 Foulstone Wall . . . . **VD**
The steep pocketed wall above the start of the last route.
FA. Ted Howard and friends 1957

22 Finerock Rib . . . . **HS 4b**
Misnamed; grassy and broken. Up a thin rib on the left side of the slab, step left and continue to a ledge. Finish up the arete.
FA. Dave Gregory 1996

23 Scrapyard Slab . . . . **S 4a**
The centre of the slabby face of the block is pleasant and leads to a steep tricky finish through the roof.
FA. Dave Gregory 1996

24 Boneyard Buttress . . . . **VD**
Climb the arete to ledges then pass the roof on the left.
FA. Ted Howard and friends 1957

Descent

Polecat - p.104

The Great Buttress

A well-named piece of rock - the main feature of the crag. The long routes here mostly provide absorbing climbing with the *Great Buttress* being a fine example of a reasonably-graded route weaving through territory usually reserved for much harder climbs. The whole buttress is often green.

Approach (see map on page 100) - Wander down and right from *Titania* to below a much more impressive face.

1 Polecat . . . . **VS 4b**
Head into and up a shallow groove part way up the face, then trend left to climb the roof via the flake-crack.
FA. Tony Howard, 1957

2 Poll Taxed . . . . **S 4a**
Climb just left of the central rib of the bay, through the mid-height bulge, then side-step the upper one.
FA. Chris Craggs 1996

3 Pole-axed . . . . **S 4a**
Climb just right of the centre of the bay on large pockets, then pull through the bulge at a flake. Trend left up the slab.
FA. Chris Craggs 1996

4 Jacobite's Route . . . . **Diff**
Climb a slab and groove to a step right. Climb to the bulge and finish up a flake crack. A VD direct version is less satisfying.
FA. Albert Shutt 1949

5 Slow Cooker . . . . **S 4a**
Climb the shallow central groove of the projecting buttress to join *Jacobite's Route*. Follow this then make a tricky move up the steep scoop just left of the capping overhang.
FA. Chris Craggs 1996

6 Slocum . . . . **S 4a**
Devious. Trend out right to a flake. Follow this then more broken rock to the bulges. A short loop left, then right, is needed to get onto the ledge below these. Finish out right or go direct at 4c.
FA. Ted Howard and friends 1957

7 First Come . . . . **HVS 5a**
A variation on *Slocum*. Pull over the centre of the low roof then keep right, avoiding *Slocum*. Mantel onto the large ledge below the top then finish out left with difficulty. Hard for the short.
FA. Chris Craggs 1996

8 Gruyère . . . . **VS 4c**
From the toe of the gully, climb the pocked wall to bulges. Step left, then pull back right onto the nose (tricky) and finish easily.
FA. Dave Gregory 1996

9 Dovestone Gully . . . . **Diff**
The interesting deep chimney. Climb the debris, cross the right wall to the front face of the buttress, up this, then cross a giant jammed boulder to an exit on the left.
FA. Ted Howard and friends 1957

10 Dovestone Edge . . . . **S 4a**
Climb the bulges right of the gully (odd rock) and then the face right of the arete to short slab that is taken centrally. Often dirty.
FA. Chris Craggs 1996

11 Dovestone Wall . . . . **VD**
Worthwhile with a steep start and inclined to be dirty after rain. Protection is well spaced. Begin 2m right of the gully and climb holey rock to the slab. Head right until below the overhangs, then back left to finish above *Dovestone Gully*.
FA. Albert Shutt 1949

12 A Little Green Eyed God . . . . **VS 4c**
Starting 3m right of the gully, climb past a jammed block and up the juggy wall to a break. Pull awkwardly onto the slab between the eyes, then up this before moving left to the exposed arete.
FA. Chris Craggs 1996

14m

Descent

11

9

Titania Area

1

2 3 4 5 6 7 8 10

The Dovestone
Peak Bouldering

13 Barney Rubble . . . . . 🖼️ 📷 □ **VS 4c**
Jugtastic, and a bit bold too. Start 5m right of the gully, just right of a block on the ground. Climb into the left-hand sandy cave then continue up juggy rock above. Pull through the prominent notch in the flat roof, to an easy finish.
Photo on page 111.
FA. Paul Harrison 1984

14 Thread Flintstone . . . . . . 📷 📷 □ **E1 5b**
Cross the roof directly below the rib between the twin caves and head straight up the bulging wall (thread out left) to the roof. Power over this 1.5m right of *Barney Rubble's* notch.
FA. Mike Appleton 1996

15 Brown Windsor . . . . 📷 □ **VS 4b**
Devious. Starting at a soft orange thread at the centre of the wall trend right to a square block. Step left and power over the bulge to below the big roof. Traverse away left until past the end of the roof and pull onto the slab for an easy finish, trending right.
FA. Ted Howard and friends 1957

16 Mock Turtle . . . . 📷 □ **E1 5b**
An eliminate but with good moves. From a spike pull over the roof and head straight up the rib between *Brown Windsor* and *Great Buttress Eliminate*. Climb up a scoop then hand traverse 3m to the right and pull over the right edge of the capping roof.
FA. Mike Appleton 1996

17 Great Buttress Eliminate . 📷 □ **HVS 5a**
Good climbing but deffo an eliminate. Start under a blunt arete, below a patch of orange rock, and pull strenuously over the roof. Continue directly, through bulges, and up a steep crack, until it is possible to traverse right to join *Great Buttress*.
FA. Stuart Gascoyne 1981

18 Great Buttress . . . . Top 50 📷 □ **HVS 5a**
A moorland classic; worth the hike up. High in the grade. Start in a green corner below the roof and trend left past the arete. Climb straight up the steep wall then trend strenuously rightwards through the bulges, keeping just above the lip of the overhang, to a tricky pull to ledges (possible stance). From here finish up and left via a final delicate slab or sneak off up *Central Climb*.
FA. Ted Howard and friends 1957

19 Sforzando . . . . 📷 📷 📷 □ **E5 6a**
The large roof that hangs over the bay is tackled via up left edge using are a couple of small flakes. Wild!
FA. Alan Monks 1985

20 Central Climb . . . . 📷 □ **VS 5a**
1) 4c, 12m. Up the floral groove under the big roof and trend right, gaining a groove with difficulty. Climb to a large ledge.
2) 5a, 12m. From the belay ledge, move left and make one tricky move to gain the undercut crack. Finish up this.
FA. Albert Shutt, Robert Gratton 1949

21 Fennario . . . . 📷 📷 □ **VS 4c**
1) 4b, 12m. Climb the left-slanting crack left of stepped overhangs to a grassy vertical crack and then a terrace stance.
2) 4c, 12m. Climb up the wall to a sloping ledge, then head up the steep crack and bulge above. The crack direct is harder.
FA. Ted Howard and friends 1957

22 Nippon, Nippoff . . . . □ **E3 6a**
Follow the break that runs out left of the second pitch of *Fennario* to the exposed arete.
FA. Andy Bailey 1983

twin caves

22m

Gargoyle Buttress Area

Sheffield Area
Ladybower Area
Stanage
Burbage Valley
Millstone Area
Derwent Edges
Chatsworth Area
Southern Crags

Gargoyle Buttress Area

Gargoyle Buttress features a slab on its left, a crenellated tower in the centre, and a walled-in bivvy cave at its foot. It has a collection of routes of which *Stony Faced* and *Gargoyle Buttress* are the pick. The taller buttress to the right is home to a classic VS and some other routes in the middle grades. *Route 1* is a real gem and would be a polished horror on a more popular cliff. *Lancaster Flyby* is the best of the rest here.

Approach (see map on page 100) - Drop right off the flagged path where it starts to rise and walk down under all of the rest of the routes.

① Gargoyle Traverse .... 🔄 [____] S 4a
Begin up the slab on the left and climb to its top right-hand corner. Traverse right around the buttress, with exposed moves midway, to finish up a block-filled chimney.
FA. Albert Shutt 1949

② Caveman .... 🚶 [____] S 4b
Start in the roofed recess on the left side of the buttress. Climb to the roof and struggle out left. Follow the easy crack then climb the tower above starting at its right corner.
FA. Chris Craggs 1996

③ Dead on a Rival ...... 🔄 🏃 [____] E5 6b
Neglected. The arete to the left of the bivvy cave leads to the break, then traverse right into the middle of the wall. Climb directly up this to a ledge and finish easily through the bulges.
FA. Nick White 1985

④ Woodhouse's Wandering Way 🐾 [____] E2 5c
Unbalanced. Boulder up the wall 1.5m right of the arete (suspect flakes) then traverse the break to the arete. Climb the slab and the bulges above.
FA. Stuart Gasgoyne 1981

⑤ Stony Faced ..... 🔄 🏃 🧗 [____] E1 5b
Take the left arete of the leaning wall to a slab then the bulging wall left of a crack to a baffling (heel-hooking?) exit.
FA. Mike Appleton 1996

⑥ Gargoyle Buttress ..... 🔄 🐾 [____] VS 4c
Tough! Climb the corner to a landing on a smelly shelf on the left. Continue on jams to a finish swinging by the gargoyles.
FA. Geoffrey Sutton 1957

⑦ Barker's Got a Sweat On .... 🐾 [____] HVS 5a
The wall and right-slanting flakes to a finish over a roof.
FA. Martin Veale 1996. Barker (the dog) was suffering with the heat.

⑧ Conservative Tendencies ..... [____] HS 4b
Climb the lower wall past a large pocket and the awkward right-trending groove above.
FA. Chris Craggs 1996

⑨ Canker .... 🚶 [____] HVD
Climb the wall 3m left of the chimney slightly rightwards. Step left onto a ledge then trend right to finish in a bay.
FA. Ted Howard and friends 1957

⑩ Back Blast .... 🚶 [____] HVS 5b
Start just left of the foot of the gully of *Wind Tunnel* and climb the steep wall rightwards via long reaches. Finish up a short slab avoiding easy escape out to the left.
FA. Chris Craggs 1996

⑪ Wind Tunnel .... 🔄 🚶 [____] Mod
The dark chimney often lives up to its name and is often used as a way down by the competent.
FA. J.W.Puttrell 1890s

The Great Buttress

12 Hurricane .... 🎯 ☐ **VD**
Nice moves up the gloomy arete on the right of the chimney, before stepping left and heading up the centre of the steep wall on good holds. A pleasant pitch considering its setting.
FA. Ted Howard and friends 1957

13 Typhoon .... 🖐☐ **HVS 5b**
A bit of an eliminate. Climb centrally up the wall between the two aretes (reachy) then cross bulges to an overhang. Mantel over this on the right, then weave through the final bulges.
FA. Mike Appleton 1996

14 Route 1 .... 🎯🐾🖐☐ **VS 4c**
A classic. Start up the outer arete of the buttress and mantel awkwardly onto a ledge. Step left and make a second mantel over a bulge onto a sloping shelf, then step right and mantel (again!) past an undercut crack. Finish easily out to the right.
FA. Albert Shutt 1949

15 The Shylock Finish .. 🎯💚💪☐ **VS 5a**
From above the crux on *Route 1*, follow the lowest break awkwardly out to the left. Finish easily in a dramatic position, always being careful not to lose a pound of flesh. Wild!
FA. Stuart Gascoyne 1981

16 Blue Velvet .... 🎯🖐☐ **E1 6a**
From just right of the arete make hard moves to and up a thin crack, then pull through the bulges to a ledge. Move left then right through bulges and mantelshelf awkwardly onto a ledge just below the cliff top.
FA. Chris Craggs 1996

17 Claw Climb ...... 🎯↰📋☐ **HVS 5a**
Start under the roof and trend left to pass it strenuously using a large jammed block just above the lip with care. Once above the bulges, step back right and finish more easily up the slabby face and groove.
FA. Ted Howard and friends 1957

18 Talon .... 🎯☐ **VS 4c**
Climb the deeply-recessed V-groove until forced to step right onto the rib at the level of the roof. Pull straight up into a thin crack just above and use this to reach easier ground.
FA. Ted Howard and friends 1957

19 Lancaster Flyby ...... 🎯🐾☐ **HVS 5b**
Pleasant climbing throughout. Begin just right of the arete and climb the wall to a deep horizontal break (good gear). A difficult pull on small holds reaches another break. Continue trending right up the interesting wall, with one last tricky move where things steepen. The arete is out-of-bounds really!
FA. Chris Craggs 1996

20 Route 2 .... 🖐🔧☐ **VS 4c**
Climb onto the large grass ledge on the right then follow the diagonal break out left, it is strenuous and awkward until past the arete. Finish up easier rock.
FA. Albert Shutt 1949

21 Grindle Crack .... 🖐☐ **HVD**
The gritty fissure above the back of the ledge.
FA. Albert Shutt 1949

22 A'rete Do .... ☐ **VD**
The slabby arete is pleasant enough.

23 Another Flaky Wall .... ☐ **VD**
The flaky crack up the wall just right.

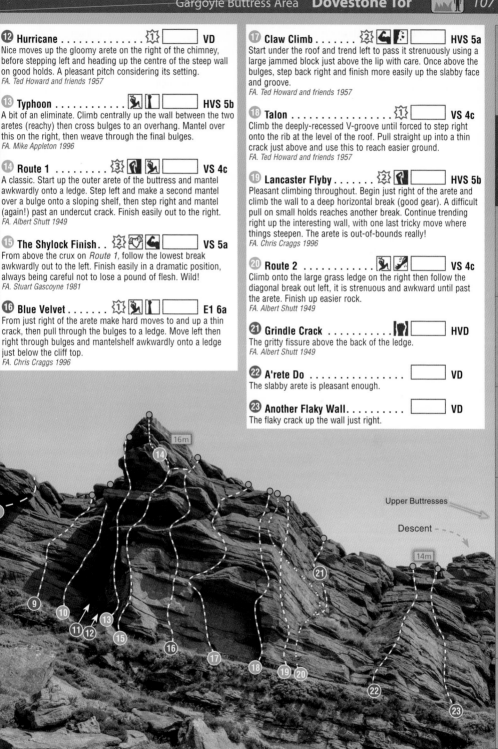

Upper Buttresses

Above and right of the main edge is a smaller cliff of nice quality rock. This has a maximum height of 8m and forms a series of fine buttresses that, although short, are generally cleaner than the main cliff.

Approach (see map on page 100) - Follow the flagged path over the cliff top then drop rightwards down a ramp to locate the routes.

1 Barefoot . . . . Diff
The left arete of the wall past a handy pocket.
FRA. Chris Craggs 1996. Though doubtless done before.

2 Slab Happy . . . . S 4a
The centre of the slab is pleasantly delicate.
FRA. Dave Gregory 1996. Though probably done before.

3 Step It Up . . . . S 4c
The slab left of the central groove. A tricky start leads to a crack.
FA. Dave Gregory 1996

4 Groovy Moves . . . . S 4b
A shallow groove leads to a bulge - pull through this on jams.
FA. Dave Gregory 1996

5 Jam On It . . . . HVS 5a
The left crack is gained from the left; avoiding *Squirm* is tricky.
FA. Chris Craggs 1996

6 Squirm . . . . HVS 5a
The right crack is also entered from the left - squirmtastic!
FA. Chris Craggs 1996

7 Hang 'em High . . . . HS 5b
The short hanging corner from a block eases instantly.
FA. Dave Gregory 1996

8 Chicken Head E2 5c
Gain the prow from the right (or left) by a swinging hand-traverse and make a couple of delicate moves to easy ground.
FA. Paul Mitchell 1991

9 Pleasant . . . . Diff
From blocks in the gully follow the slabby arete on the right.
FA. Dave Gregory 1996

10 Spring Night E1 5c
Trend left to the left edge of the steep wall and a reachy finish.
FA. Chris Craggs 1982

11 Autumn Day . . . E1 5c
A neat micro-route which includes a hard pull on small holds and a long reach for the distant edge.
FA. Graham Hoey 1981

12 Stretch Marks E1 6a
Gain the initial ledge from the right then climb the wall trending right passing a floral hole to a massive final reach.
FA. Chris Craggs (6' 3") 1996

Descent

Gargoyle Buttress Area

TICKLIST
Dovestone Summer Sampler

Generally this is a summer-only venue, a small selection of the very best climbs will repay the effort involved with getting here. This set of five routes along the edge will ensure you get a good look around.

☐ **Titania, VS** *(103)*. A nice slabby starter.

☐ **Route 1, VS** *(107)*. Super classic and a bit reachy.

☐ **Great Buttress, HVS** *(105)*. Steep and intimidating.

☐ **Lancaster Flyby, HVS** *(107)*. A nice balancy move or two.

☐ **Excel, HVS** *(109)*. A bit of a stopper move.

13 Razor Cut . . . . 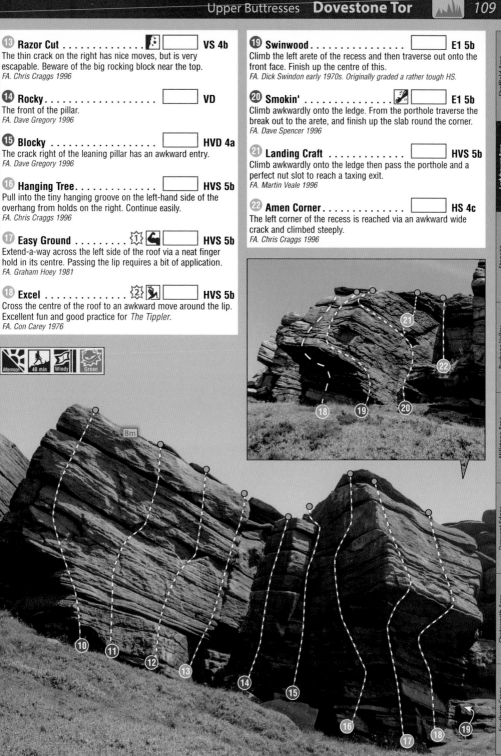 VS 4b
The thin crack on the right has nice moves, but is very
escapable. Beware of the big rocking block near the top.
FA. Chris Craggs 1996

14 Rocky . . . . VD
The front of the pillar.
FA. Dave Gregory 1996

15 Blocky . . . . HVD 4a
The crack right of the leaning pillar has an awkward entry.
FA. Dave Gregory 1996

16 Hanging Tree . . . . HVS 5b
Pull into the tiny hanging groove on the left-hand side of the
overhang from holds on the right. Continue easily.
FA. Chris Craggs 1996

17 Easy Ground . . . . HVS 5b
Extend-a-way across the left side of the roof via a neat finger
hold in its centre. Passing the lip requires a bit of application.
FA. Graham Hoey 1981

18 Excel . . . . HVS 5b
Cross the centre of the roof to an awkward move around the lip.
Excellent fun and good practice for *The Tippler*.
FA. Con Carey 1976

19 Swinwood E1 5b
Climb the left arete of the recess and then traverse out onto the
front face. Finish up the centre of this.
FA. Dick Swindon early 1970s. Originally graded a rather tough HS.

20 Smokin' E1 5b
Climb awkwardly onto the ledge. From the porthole traverse the
break out to the arete, and finish up the slab round the corner.
FA. Dave Spencer 1996

21 Landing Craft . . . . HVS 5b
Climb awkwardly onto the ledge then pass the porthole and a
perfect nut slot to reach a taxing exit.
FA. Martin Veale 1996

22 Amen Corner . . . . HS 4c
The left corner of the recess is reached via an awkward wide
crack and climbed steeply.
FA. Chris Craggs 1996

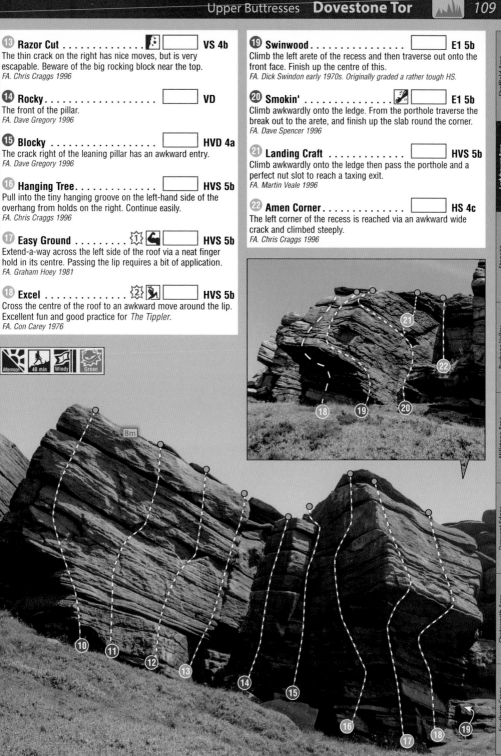

Sheffield Area
Ladybower Area
Stanage
Burbage Valley
Millstone Area
Derwent Edges
Chatsworth Area
Southern Crags

23 Old Man's Corner . . . . [ ] **VD**
The grotty right-hand corner of the recess in two stages.
FA. Dave Gregory 1996

24 Village Green . . . . [ ] **VS 5a**
Straight up the steep slab, finishing just left of a short crack.
Often as green as the name suggests.
FA. Chris Craggs 1996

25 Lambo . . . . [ ] **S 4b**
Follow the thin crack on surprising holds. North-facing and so inclined to be green except after a good dry spell.
FA. Oliver Woolcock 1960s

26 Bertie . . . . [ ] **E1 5c**
The leaning wall just right of the arete is climbed on good but spaced holds to a delicate finish where the angle eases. Tough.
FA. Martin Veale 1996

27 Blunt . . . . [ ] **HVS 5b**
The centre of the bulging wall via a blunt nose and tricky mantel.
FA. Chris Craggs 1982

28 Philby . . . . [ ] **HVS 5b**
The right side of the wall, passing a jammed block at 2/3 height.
FA. Paul Harrison 1984

29 Granny Smith . . . . [ ] **E1 5b**
The leaning arete has good holds, and is best climbed quickly.
FA. Graham Hoey 1981

30 Cox's Pippin . . . . [ ] **HVS 5b**
The roof crack to the right proves to be reachy.
FA. Oliver Woolcock 1960s

31 Ganges . . . . [ ] **VD**
The awkward block-filled chimney is tricky towards the top.
FA. Oliver Woolcock 1960s

32 Crackless Bottom . . . . [ ] **E1 5b**
The centre of the last buttress of the cliff. Pull into a hanging crack and exit awkwardly.
FA. Chris Craggs 1996

33 Soft Top . . . . [ ] **E1 5a**
Start at the right arete of the cliff and climb the flat wall on the right easily (small cams) to an awkward shelving exit.
FA. Martin Veale 1996

Descent

Sheffield Area

Ladybower Area

Stanage

Burbage Valley

Millstone Area

Derwent Edges

Chatsworth Area

Southern Crags

Dave Bankart and Mike Dowsett heading through the bevy of bulges on *Barney Rubble* (VS 4c) - *page 105* - on Great Buttress, Dovestone Tor.

	No star	🌣	🌣	🌣
Mod to S	55	14	2	-
HS to HVS	30	21	8	6
E1 to E3	10	18	7	-
E4 and up	4	4	6	1

Bamford Edge consists of a fine series of jutting buttresses in a spectacular situation above the upper reaches of the Derwent Valley and the Ladybower Reservoir. For many years restricted access meant that the edge became something of a backwater, though this changed with the introduction of CROW. The crag is now firmly on the circuit; it can get busy especially on fine summer weekends and is starting to look a little tired in places. The rock is a coarse form of gritstone, the pebbles forming crucial holds on some of the hardest climbs.

Approach   Also see map on page 98

A minor road (New Road) runs below the cliff from a point 1km north of the village of Bamford and just south of the Yorkshire Bridge pub. At the top of this is roadside parking for a dozen or more cars by a gate. Cross this then follow the track that heads left rising steadily to Gun Buttress, which is hidden just around the corner, about 15 mins from the road.

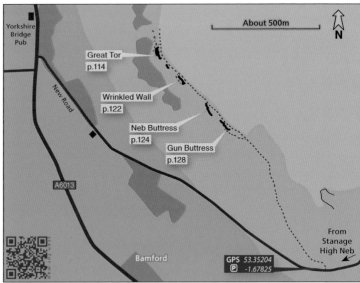

Access
Access is now possible year round except when there is grouse shooting or a risk of fire. Signs will be posted.

Conditions
The edge is exposed to the weather, though it can be delightful on summer evenings as the sun goes down over Ladybower.

TICKLIST

Bamford Brilliance
Such a great set of Orange
Spot Routes. These are the
best of the best (though
plenty of the rest are almost
as good!)

☐ **Brown's Crack, HS** *(115)*
A perfect mild jamming crack.

☐ **Quien Sabe?, VS** *(115)*
The crux is technical but safe.

☐ **Gargoyle Flake, VS** *(120)*
Don't forget the photo-op.

☐ **Wrinkled Wall, VS** *(123)*
A lovely airy arete.

☐ **Neb Buttress, HVS** *(124)*
Varied and superb.

Sheffield Area

Ladybower Area

Stanage

Burbage Valley

Millstone Area

Derwent Edges

Chatsworth Area

Southern Crags

Jordan Curry on *Gargoyle Flake* (VS 4c) - *page 120* -
possibly the most photographed (and most photogenic)
route in the Peak District. Photo: Mike Hutton

10m

Salmon Boulders
Peak Bouldering

Great Tor - Lower Tier

The best rock on the cliff, in a great setting and with a collection of excellent climbs. The well-protected *Bilberry Crack*, the superb jamming on *Brown's Crack* and the well-positioned *Quien Sabe?* are the classics in the Orange Zone. The Salmon Slab has a great collection of intense Black Zone routes.

Approach (see map on page 112) - Scramble down from below the overhang of the Upper Tier.

❶ Shallow Groove . . . . **S 4a**
The pleasant groove would benefit from a bit of traffic.

❷ Hasta La Vista . . . . **HVD 3c**
Climb the wide awkward crack (not much gear) to its top then traverse out right to escape the overhangs.
FA. Geoffrey Sutton 1957

❸ Back Flip **E1 5b**
The bold left arete, passing a tricky overlap, to the capstone. An odd off-balance move leads out left then finish direct. Originally graded a rather stiff VS!
FA. Gwyn Arnold 1991

❹ Benberry Wall **E3 5b**
The centre of the wall is strenuous, poorly protected and usually dirty. Just to cap it all, some of the flakes feel creaky.
FA. Gary Gibson 1982

❺ The Naked Eye **E2 5b**
Climb the right side of the wall using flakes and then the steep and worrying arete, eventually on its right-hand side. Scary.
FA. John Allen 1976

Great Tor - Upper Tier

Descent

p.118

10m

6 Bilberry Crack . . . . . VS 5a
The excellent and very protectable thin crack in the corner. It is possible to start round to the left up a gloomy corner.
FA. Dick Brown 1952

7 Recess Crack . . . . VD
The right-hand corner of the recess is a decent lower grade climb with mostly good holds and plenty of protection.
FA. Dick Brown 1952

8 Recess Groove . . . . HS 4b
Climb the V-groove, and short wall, just left of the arete. Try to avoid holds on the route to the left.
FA. Dave Gregory 2000

9 Nemmes Pas Harry . E1 5b
Climb the steep bulging wall on flexible flakes, then the delicate scoop above, moving right past a disappointing pocket.
Photo on page 98.
FA. Gary Gibson 1981

10 Nemmes Sabe . . . . HVS 5a
A neat and sustained combo, starting up the previous route and finishing up the next one. Heading left at a lower level is harder - **E1 5b**.

11 Quien Sabe? . . . . VS 4c
Classic. Start up *Brown's Crack*, but follow ramps left and tackle the crucial crack that splits the bulge. Well protected but quite taxing, it may be the best VS on the crag, who knows?
FA. Brian Evans 1958

12 Brown's Crack . . . . HS 4b
The straight fissure is a real cracker. Awkward moves gain the deepening crack/groove, protection is perfect throughout.
FA. Dick Brown 1951

There are two isolated routes 50m right across the steep hillside, at a scoop - see overview on the left for their location.

13 The Egg E4 6a
The elegant hanging scoop is entered from the left and exited rapidly to the right.
FA. Johnny Dawes 1984

14 High and Dry E6 6b
The scoop direct is technical to a harrowing exit. No sideways chicanery is allowed on this one though!
FA. John Dunne 1986

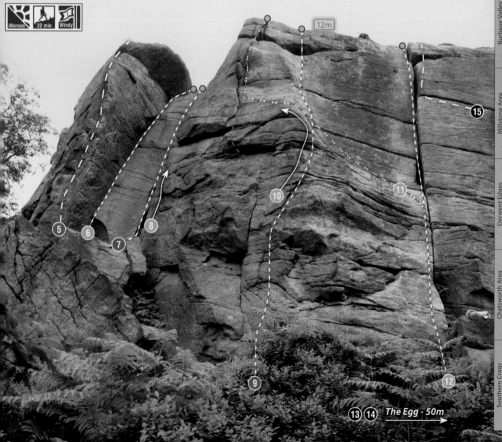

The Egg - 50m

Sheffield Area | Ladybower Area | Stanage | Burbage Valley | Millstone Area | Derwent Edges | Chatsworth Area | Southern Crags

Sheffield Area
Ladybower Area
Stanage
Burbage Valley
Millstone Area
Derwent Edges
Chatsworth Area
Southern Crags

⑮ Jetrunner **E4 6a**
Climb the wall to hard moves past a tiny pocket to the top break - micro-wires and tiny cams. Traverse left and sprint up the arete on its right. A **Direct Start** isn't much harder.
FA. Andy Bailey 1983

⑯ The Salmon. **E7 6c**
As for *Trout* until standing in the high pocket. Traverse right to the small group of poor pockets, and finish as for *Smoked Salmon*. Slightly artificial as it's easier to make the final move of *Salmon Direct* than to continue heading rightwards.
Photo opposite.
FA. Johnny Dawes 1984. Reclimbed by Dawes 1995 after loss of a pebble.

⑰ Trout **E6 6b**
The most popular of the shoal, also known as *Salmon Left-hand*. As for *Jetrunner* to the top break then make a high step into twin pockets, with the right foot in the high right pocket, smear left and reach the top. Can be combined with *Salmon Direct* by making a tricky left-foot cross-through in the high pocket.
FA. Nick Dixon 1995

⑱ Salmon Direct **E6 6c**
As for *Jetrunner* to the top break then move right and make some hard moves to gain a high pocket from the right (left foot in pocket). Smear high rightwards and reach for the sky.
FA. Jon Read 1998. In mistake for The Salmon.

⑲ Smoked Salmon **E7 7a**
Gain the top break direct then make three wild moves up to a poor edge and then a slightly better pocket to the right. Finish direct on pockets. Harder for the short, though that's no excuse!
FA. Johnny Dawes 1995

⑳ Curving Crack . . . . **VS 4c**
Loop along the curving crack then swing right on jams past the arete to finish up *Sandy Crack*, which some find to be the crux!
FA. Allan Austin 1958

㉑ Poached Salmon . . . **E5 6c**
Tackle the arete via a series of slaps to gain the break, reach up and left for a small flake (very hard for the short) to finish.
Photo opposite.
FA. Jon Read 1999

㉒ Sandy Crack . . . . **HS 4b**
The steep, widening crack in the corner has a tricky exit passing a large threadable chockstone.
FA. Eric Byne 1930

㉓ Quebec City. . . . . . . **VS 4c**
From *Sandy Crack*, follow the inviting horizontal break through hard-man's territory, all the way to *Quien Sabe?*
FA. Chris Craggs 1981

㉔ Greydon Boddington . . . . **HVS 5b**
The left-hand line in the short wall, passing a shelf, and finishing up a short crack. The crack is slow to dry.
FA. Martin Veale 1977

㉕ Fizz **E1 5c**
The right-hand line with two pairs of strange pockets that provide both holds and awkward-to-thread runners.
FA. Martin Veale 1980

Afternoon | 22 min | Windy

12m 8m

⑰ ⑯ ⑱ ㉓ ㉕ ㉑ ㉒ ㉔ ㉓ ⑳ ⑲ ⑮

The Egg - p.115

Salmon Slab
Johnny Dawes climbed this fine face in 1984 as *The Salmon*, E6 6c. The loss of a crucial pebble left the wall 'unclimbable' so he called in again in 1995 finding two even harder ways up it! There are now six recognisable outings. For those looking for milder sport *Curving Crack* and *Sandy Crack* are worthwhile.

Sheffield Area

Ladybower Area

Stanage

Burbage Valley

Millstone Area

Derwent Edges

Chatsworth Area

Southern Crags

Two photos showing the commitment required for the intense slab moves at the top of the Salmon Slab. On the left Mark Rankine runs it out above the bomber gear in the break on *The Salmon* (E7 6c) - *opposite*. On the right he deadpoints for the flake on *Poached Salmon* (E5 6c) - *opposite*.
Photos: Franco Cookson on his phone (hence the photo quality isn't great).

Great Tor - Upper Tier

Great Tor - Lower Tier

p.114

Great Tor - Upper Tier

Great Tor Upper Tier has some decent climbs, *Undercut Crack* is the best, although it isn't everyone's style. There are also a collection of neglected easier climbs and some bold little face climbs. It is less popular than the rest of the cliff.

Approach (see map on page 112) - To go straight to Great Tor, follow the cliff-top path above the other buttresses and drop down just before the Upper Tier.

① End Face. . . . . VS 5b
The north-facing wall on a poor selection of holds.

② WRoEF . . . . HS 4c
Follow the crack up the face right of the arete.

③ WLoEC . . . . HVD 4a
The wide zig-zag crack leads to a tricky leftward exit.

④ Easy Chimney . . . . Mod
The deep, easy and often midgy rift leads to a through cave.
FA. J.W.Puttrell 1900

⑤ Palpitation . . . . HS 4c
Gain the crack above the arete from a block round to the left.
FA. Eric Byne 1930

⑥ Thumping . . . . . HVS 5c
A direct start via the undercut left arete of the buttress.

On the front of the buttress to the right are three steeper lines, all are poorly protected and have hard rounded exits.

⑦ Thin on Top E2 5b
The left-hand line past a hole to a tough exit on shelving holds.
FA. Colin Binks 1981

⑧ Green and Nasty E2 5c
The right-hand line starts up a flake. It also has a taxing exit.
FA. Chris Craggs 1981

⑨ In my Pocket E1 5b
Climb the wall left of the arete - another bold and rounded one. The arete right again is a short **5a** problem with a dodgy landing.
FA. Paul Harrison 1999

⑩ Initiation. . . . . S 4a
The tiny green groove and flake in the back right side of the bay.

⑪ Introduction. . . . . S 4a
This is the short arete and shorter crack above.

⑫ Beer Matters . . . . VS 5a
Layback the arete to a finish up the large and rather suspect-looking jutting flake.
FA. Paul Harrison 1987

17 Astronaut's Wall ⛺ 🔲 🖊 📷 ⬜ **HVS 5b**
The steep centre of the undercut buttress is strenuous through the roofs to a delicate mantelshelf reaching easier ground and some fine flaky jugs. Be aware of suspect rock under the roof.
FA. Pete Hatton 1963

18 Possibility . . . . ⛺ ⬜ **S 4a**
Tackle the cracks in the south-facing side-wall and make an exit round to the left. Neglected but quite pleasant.
FA. Bob Downes 1957

19 Primitive Chimney . . . . 👊 ⬜ **VD**
The deep chimney separating the buttresses. The start is tricky and at least one of the chocks is a wobbler.
FA. J.W.Puttrell 1901

To the right, an impressive roof runs right across the crag. There are three imposing lines through this, plus the possibility of one more on the left. A belay on the ledges under the roof is sensible if the leader requires a bit of moral support!

20 Undercut Crack . ⛺ 🖊 🤚 👊 ⬜ **E2 5c**
The short crack through the left-hand side of the great roof is a real gritstoner's glory, where subtlety is definitely not required. Be prepared for a brutal battle is the best advice!
FA. Allan Austin 1958

21 MAy35 . . . . ⛺ 🤚 ⬜ **E6 6c**
The vague break in the roof to the right of the overhanging crack via a short powerful sequence. Originally known as *A35*.
FA. Joe Brown (with one sling for aid) 1958. FFA. John Allen or Jim Reading or Jim Campbell about 1975. Reclimbed by Steve Allen in 1984 after most of the crucial flake disappeared and again in 2006 by Ben Bransby after the rest of the flake had gone.

22 Avoiding the Traitors ⛺ 🖊 🤚 ⬜ **E7 6c**
The inverted scoop and hanging flutings in the roof to the right of MAy35 are the substance of this brilliant little micro-route.
FA. Johnny Dawes 1995

23 Overhang Traverse . . . . 🔲 ⬜ **Mod**
A right to left (or left to right) trip under the roof. Mild though with impressive views and not for timid seconds.

13 Fat Cat . . . . 🔲 ⬜ **VS 5b**
The short green tilted wall. The nearby boulder interferes a bit.
FA. Paul Harrison 1987

14 Deep Chimney . . . . ⬜ **Mod**
Another historical cleft for aficionados of the dark and dingy. Approach over ledges and squirm to the cliff top.
FA. J.W.Puttrell 1900

15 Kelly . . . . ⛺ 👊 ⬜ **HS 4b**
The left arete via a tough groove to the shelf, an awkward wide crack, and a rightward exit.
FA. Harry Kelly 1918

16 Deaf Raspberry Climb . . 🤚 🔲 ⬜ **E1 5c**
Swing over the nose and continue easily.
FA. Andy Barker 1982

24 Bad Wind . . . . `[  ]` **S 4a**
The crack behind the block (crux) and wall left of the corner give
the line. A direct finish is the best, though an easy escape out
left is an option.

25 Claim to Fame . . . . `[  ]` **HVS 5a**
Climb to the ledge then up the steeper face - tricky to start.
FA. Dave Spencer 1981

26 Terrace Rib . . . . `[img][img][  ]` **VS 4c**
Climb the tricky rib to a scruffy landing left of the tree. Continue
up the rib above on its left-hand side. Artificial and a bit bold.
FA. Steve Clark 2003

27 Terrace Wall . . . . `[img][img][  ]` **VS 4b**
A block and short crack lead to the ledge. Trend right up the face
to a flake and a steep finish.
FA. Pete Hatton (the upper part) 1963

28 Terrace Trog . . . . `[img][  ]` **Mod**
A decent easy route up the diagonal break, to a steep finale.

29 Old Wall . . . . `[img][img][  ]` **HVS 5b**
Climb onto the tip of the perched flake at the base of the wall,
then through a notch and up the face on poor holds. Rather
neglected but with some good moves.

30 Gargoyle Flake . . . . `[img][img][  ]` **VS 4c**
The delicate slabby arete, or the face just left, leads to a ledge.
Access the flake and a dramatic finish that will find you swinging
by the gargoyles. Variations are inferior. Photographed a
thousand times, almost aways from the cliff top to the right with
the reservoir in the background. *Photo on page 112.*
FA. Pete Hatton 1963

31 Gargoyle Gully Left . . . . `[  ]` **Diff**
Round to the right is a wide rift climbed via its left-hand corner.

32 Gargoyle Gully Right . . . . `[  ]` **Diff**
The more open right-hand side involves grassy scrambling and
some loose rock. A more **Direct Finish** to this is **VD**.

33 Sunset . . . . `[img][  ]` **S 4a**
A line up the scoop, wide crack and wall above. The start is bold.

34 Beelzebugger . . . . `[img][  ]` **HVS 5b**
Fills a gap. Gain a projection then the break. Stand in this then
another tricky move gains the slab. Finish up the juggy wall.
FA. Nick Taylor 2005

35 Bum Deal . . . . `[img][img][  ]` **E1 5c**
The bottom-shaped crack leads powerfully to a ledge. Romp on
up the crack and wall above.
FA. Chris Craggs 1981

36 Clean, Squeaky and Scented . `[img][  ]` **E1 6a**
The rough, tough bulge is short and sharp.
FA. Mark Stokes 1985

*Right is a descent gully and beyond this a striated buttress
which has routes that all involve steep climbing on green holds.*

37 Hard Rain . . . . `[img][img][  ]` **E2 5c**
The left neglected left arete of the face.

38 Left Wing . . . . `[img][  ]` **S 4a**
The grassy crack is short, steep and awkward.

39 Almost Granite . . . . `[img][img][img][  ]` **E1 5b**
The crack and bulge above give a bold and worrying pitch.
FA. Paul Harrison 1999

Great Tor - Upper Tier
The right-hand side of Great Tor Upper Tier is neglected with the exception of the photogenic *Gargoyle Flake*.
Approach (see map on page 112) - To go straight to Great Tor, follow the cliff-top path above the other buttresses and drop down just before the Upper Tier.

Descent

40 Tinner .... HVS 5b
The left side of the wall up a flake to a ledge. Then climb right with a tricky stretch for better holds and a bolder finale.
FA. Allan Austin 1958

41 Right-hand Twin ...... HVS 5a
The centre of the wall via a crack and right-trending ramp is easier and better protected than its left-hand twin.
FA. Allan Austin 1958

42 Private Practice E1 5b
Use a pocket to reach the flake, then climb up and left to finish. A right-hand finish has been claimed but it is an eliminate.
FA. John Allen c1990

43 Solstice Arete .... VS 4c
Climb the crack then the narrow arete and rounded bulges. Escapable but with good moves and a bold central section.
FA. Peter Stone 1997

Descent

Wrinkled Wall - 80m

Descent

8m

Great Tor - 80m

Wrinkled Wall Area

A small collection of short but interesting buttresses with the projecting fin of *Wrinkled Wall* being the most significant piece of rock here. The grassy base to much of the cliff makes for a pleasant setting. There is also some bouldering on the collection of blocks, aretes and boulders to the left of the fin.

Approach (see map on page 112) - The crag-top path is the best approach. Drop steeply down just before the prow of *Wrinkled Wall*.

❶ Que? Slab . . . . ☐ **Diff**
The left-hand line on the slab. Not much gear.

❷ Que? Slab Direct . . . . ☆ ☐ **Diff**
The central line is also poorly protected.

❸ K Buttress Slab . . . . ☆ ☐ **VD**
Climb the right-hand side of the slab.
FA. Dick Brown early 1950s

❹ K Kole Arete . . . . ☆ 🔲 ☐ **f6B+**
Climb the arete starting at the big hole. Traversing in from the right is *f6B* unless you use the back wall.

❺ K Buttress Crack . . ☆☆ 🔲🔲 ☐ **S 4a**
The deep slanting cleft to a taxing exit. A perverse affair. A steep direct start is **4c** and misses out on some of the fun.
FA. Dick Brown early 1950s

❻ Wrong Hand Route . . . . . ☆☆ 🔲 ☐ **E1 5c**
The leaning crack has a useful pocket and is well named. A technical gem where forward planning will help.
FA. John Gosling 1971

❼ Skarlati . . . . ☆ 🔲🔲 ☐ **E2 5b**
Gain the ledge from the right then commit to the rounded bulges, trending rightwards. More interesting than it looks.
FA. Martin Boysen 1969

❽ Fern Chimney . . . . 🔲 ☐ **Diff**
The ferny chimney leads to an interesting exit.

❾ Bracken Crack . . . . ☆ ☐ **VD**
Pleasant with a tricky start. Move right at the final bulge.
FA. Pete Hatton 1963

❿ The Bookend . . . . ☆ 🔲 ☐ **f6B**
The jutting book-end is climbed on its narrow face. It is *f6C+* if done on its right-hand side.

⓫ The Plumber Has Landed ☆ 🔲 ☐ **f6B**
The thin seam passing left of the small hanging roof.

⓬ Down to Earth . . . . ☆☆ 🔲 ☐ **f6A+**
The elegant arete is tricky though the landing is fairly soft and there are runners if you need them (E3 6a).
FA. Al Rouse 1985

⓭ Deb . . . . 🔲 ☐ **VS 5a**
The square-cut arete of the boulder - watch the exit.
FA. Peter Stone 1997. Also known as Crunchy Nuts.

The next three routes are short interesting offerings, starting from a terrace which is most easily reached from the right.

⓮ Wee Lassie . . . . 🔲🔲 ☐ **VS 5b**
The left side of the face on spaced holds from a creaky flake.
FA. David Simmonite 2000

⓯ Special K . . . . ☆ 🔲 ☐ **HVS 5b**
The short left-hand crack in the side-wall passing the blank section using a fortuitous good jug.
FA. Arthur Robinson 1971

⓰ Dead Mouse Crack . . . . 🔲 ☐ **HS 4c**
The steep, left-slanting central crack in the front face feels pushy and is rather exposed.
FA. Allan Austin 1958

⓱ Hanging Crack . . . . 🔲 ☐ **HS 4b**
The right-hand crack is approached steeply from the right.
FA. Allan Austin 1958

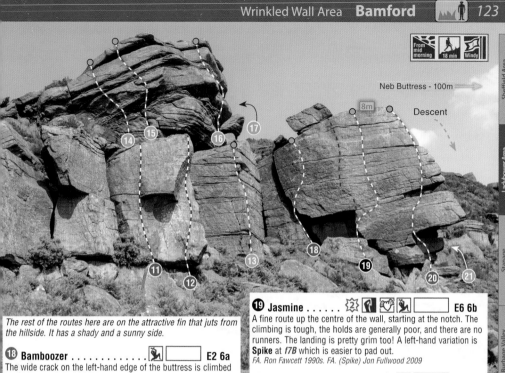

Neb Buttress - 100m

Descent

The rest of the routes here are on the attractive fin that juts from the hillside. It has a shady and a sunny side.

⑱ Bamboozer . . . . 🧗 ▭ **E2 6a**
The wide crack on the left-hand edge of the buttress is climbed until it is possible to swing right to access the hard upper left-hand section of the face.
FA. Andy Popp 1993

⑲ Jasmine . . . . . . ②🧗🤸🧗 ▭ **E6 6b**
A fine route up the centre of the wall, starting at the notch. The climbing is tough, the holds are generally poor, and there are no runners. The landing is pretty grim too! A left-hand variation is **Spike** at *f7B* which is easier to pad out.
FA. Ron Fawcett 1990s. FA. (Spike) Jon Fullwood 2009

⑳ Access Account . . . . ①🧗 ▭ **E3 6a**
Hard moves past the overhang on the right-hand side of the face gain the break. Then step right to climb the arete on its left-hand side. Gear is minimal.
FA. Al Rouse 1985

The rest of the routes are on the sunnier face of the fin.

㉑ Wrinkled Wall . . . . ③🧗 ▭ **VS 4c**
From a short crack/slot climb diagonally left along the break to gain the easier arete by a tricky move. A very photogenic pitch.
FA. Allan Austin 1958

㉒ Old and Wrinkled . . . ①🤸🧗 ▭ **HVS 5a**
Start as for *Wrinkled Wall*, but climb the face just to the left of centre and keeping to the right of the arete. Delicate.

㉓ The Crease . . . . ①🤸🧗 ▭ **E1 5a**
Precarious climbing, on sloping holds, up the right side of the wall, starting up the short crack/slot and continuing in the same line. Avoid the arete for the full effect.
FA. Mark Davies 1979

㉔ Sinuous Crack . . . . 🧗 ▭ **VD**
The mildy wriggly crack on the right-hand side of the face has a useful chockstone at about half-height.

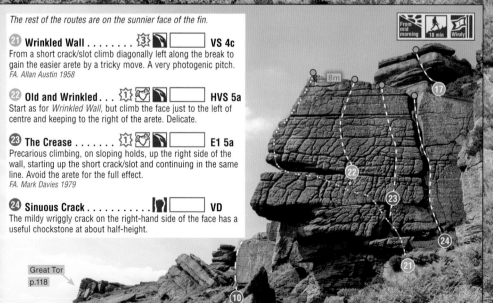

Great Tor
p.118

Sheffield Area

Ladybower Area

Stanage

Burbage Valley

Millstone Area

Derwent Edges

Chatsworth Area

Southern Crags

1 Cleopatra . . . . VS 4c
Approach the hanging crack by a steep groove. Short-lived but strenuous climbing.

2 Samson's Delight. . . . . . VS 4c
The cracked arete is another short 'n' steep one.
FA. Pete Hatton 1963

3 Dirty Stop Out . . E2 5c
Tackle the thin crack and bulging wall. A bit of a fist-fight!
FA. Chris Lawson 1981

4 Delilah . . . . HS 4b
The crack is awkward to climb and protect.

5 Short Curve. . . . . HVD
Make a tricky start up the short curving crack, which then eases to give a few pleasant moves above.

6 The Business Boy. f6B
Bound up the short wall to the left of the deep corner.
FA. Martin Veale 1987

7 N.B. Corner. . . . . Diff
The deep angle eases with height.

8 Big Ben . . . . VS 4b
Starting up *N.B. Corner*, climb the steep left-hand crack on jams and jugs leading to a high crux.

9 Parliament E1 5c
The thin right-hand crack in the north-facing wall is offset and climbs best on the right; sustained and hard work.
FA. Chris Craggs 1981

10 Neb Buttress Direct . . . . HVS 5a
Starting up the lower arete is a popular way of doing this classic and only a little harder than the original version. It also causes fewer problems with the ropes.

11 Auricle E2 5c
Low in the grade, though the loss of a hold has made it even harder for the short than it used to be. The face right of the arete has hard moves above the roof to the ear. Escape right below the roofs or throw yourself at the next offering.
FA. John Gosling 1971

12 Jumping Jack Longland . E3 5c
A good left-hand finish to *Auricle*. Span left along the lip, from where the ordinary exits rightwards, to reach the jugs and a spectacular finale out in space.
FA. Steve Bancroft 1979

13 Neb Buttress . . . . HVS 5a
Classy - the original and best! Climb the crack to its top then traverse left past the arete, where a crack and short wall lead to an escape out right. Double ropes and some attention to their organisation is a sensible idea.
FA. Allan Austin 1958

14 Bamford Rib . . . . HVS 5a
The rounded rib to the right of the crack leads steeply to a ledge where a holly competes for space. Lean awkwardly left to access good lumpy holds on the final wall and a short layback to finish.
FA. John Allen 1973

15 Bramble Crack. . . . . VD
The long groove is approached by bridging past the worst of the greenery and then gives a couple of tricky mantels to an escape left. A direct finish is a bit harder.

← Wrinkled Wall Area - 100m

Descent

From mid morning | 17 min | Windy

16m

8m

Neb Buttress
The finest section of the cliff has an excellent collection of climbs on a series of fine jutting buttresses and undercut walls. Once the preserve of the few in the know, crowds are not uncommon nowadays and the crag base is starting to show signs of wear.
Approach (see map on page 112) - There is a lower path running across the slope from near Gun Buttress, otherwise use the crag-top path and drop steeply down just before the buttress.

16 The Happy Wanderer . . . 🏴 HVS 5a
A steep arete but at an amenable grade and with good protection
- the crux is easiest on the left. Excellent and elegant climbing
up a rather unlikely looking line for the grade.
FA. Geoff Morgan 1967

17 Reach. . . . . VS 4c
A direct line 2m right of the arete with the expected long
stretches (or more technical manoeuvres for the short) to a
tricky exit. Beware the loose block in the last break.
FA. Chris Craggs 1991

18 Bamford Wall . . . . S 4a
Climb the slanting flake then move right to a crack. Up this to a
niche then follow a thin crack to ledges. Move back out left for a
reachy exposed finale if required. Some care is needed with the
protection as wires in the niche tend to lift out.
FA. Hugh Banner 1960

19 Bamford Buttress . . . . . . S 4a
From an ochre-coloured hole, climb to top of the flake and trend
right up scoops to reach the top of *Twin Cracks*.
FA. Brian Evans 1958

20 Busy Day at Bamford . . . . . . VS 5a
The blunt arete is followed through a series of bulges to easier-
angled ground above.
FA. Chris Craggs 1991

21 Twin Cracks. . . . . VS 4b
From the cave, bridge the steep cracks, left then right.
FA. Hugh Banner 1960

22 Custard's Last Stand . . . . . . HVS 5b
The hanging rib just right of the last route.
FA. Paul Evans 1983

23 Oracle . . . . HS 4b
Climb near the outside of the cleft until the front of the fine
exposed arete on the right can be gained by a bold swing. Wild!
FA. Paul Nunn 1971

24 Deep Cleft. . . . . Mod
Almost always a windy trip. Exiting outside the chock is **Diff**.
FA. Probably JWP about 1900

25 Sterling Moss E4 6b
The wall and flat roof right of the hanging arete have baffling
moves to pass the bulge.
FA. Johnny Dawes 1984

26 Ontos E3 6b
The centre of the huge wall is approached by an easy rib and
has a desperate reach/pull move at the bulge.
FA. John Allen 1975

27 Fatal Inheritance . . . E4 6a
The wall to the right requires a huge reach. Sometimes dirty.
FA. Gary Gibson 1982

28 Purgamentum E4 6b
The wall can be a little dirty.
FA. James Pearson 2004

29 Trouble with Lichen . . . . HVS 5b
A superbly positioned girdle of the buttress. There is a crucial
stride onto the jug of *Ontos*, then head for the arete.
FA. John Allen 1973

30 Slanting Slab . . . . Mod
The easy slab on the right-hand side of the face is mild and a bit
shrubby, but still worthwhile at the grade.

31 Grey Days E2 5c
The short-lived roof on the far right.
FA. Colin Binks 1981

16m

Christmas Buttresses

Descent

Cold Turkey - 20m →

Christmas Buttresses

A small set of short easier routes on the rock to the left of Gun Buttress. The rocks here have been scrambled on for years, but have always been regarded as too small to be worthy of description. Then the routes were named, graded and described around 2010.

Approach (see map on page 112) - Continue just beyond Gun Buttress, which is where the path arrives at the crag.

1 Dream . . . . ▢ Diff
The left arete.

2 Quince . . . . ▢ VD
This is the steep left wall of the groove.

3 Snug . . . . ▯▢ VD

4 Midsummer Madness . . . . ▢ HS 4b
Tackle the overhang on the right arete.

5 Dawn and Dusk . . . . ▯▢ S 4b
Stretch up the face right of the arete.

6 The Curse . . . . ▢ S 4b

7 Midsummer Wall . . . . ▢ VD
The wall left of the arete.

8 Bilberry Arete . . . . ▢ VD
Balance up the arete itself.

The next routes are 20m further right where there is a trio of short buttresses.

9 Cold Turkey . . . . ▢ S 4a
The blunt arete left of a prominent roof to a tricky last move.

10 Stuffing . . . . ▢ VD

11 Santa's Pants . . . . ▢ VD
An awkward (4a?) line up the narrow buttress.

12 Overindulgence Arete . . . . ▢ HS 4b
The long arete is pleasant.

13 Troglodyte's Route . . . . ▯▢ Diff
Trend left to reach the wide crack and a caving exit.

Just left of Gun Buttress is a more continuous section of rock, it has a some decent mini-routes.

14 Christmas Pudding . . . . ▢ VD
The juggy (and heathery) wall on the left.

15 Christmas Present . . . . ▣▢ VD
This is the blunt rib.

16 Christmas Cracker . . . . ▣▢ Diff
The central scoop via a tricky start and creaky hold.

17 A Traditional Christmas . . . . . . ▢ HS 4b
From a short crack, climb the wall and final roof.

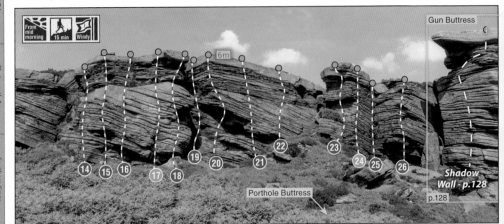

18 Paxo Arete . . . . `[ ]` S 4a
The arete on its left, side then the roof on its right.

19 Chestnut Chimney . . . . `[ ]` Diff
Pleasant and easy bridging up the rift.

20 Mistletoe . . . . `[⌐]` `[ ]` S 4c
The juggy arete just right is pleasant.

21 Ivy . . . . `[⬛]` `[ ]` VD
Climb the centre of the face on rounded breaks.

22 Holly . . . . `[ ]` VD
Follow a ramp rightwards.

23 Bellyflop Extravaganza . . . . . `[👤]` `[ ]` HVD 4a
The narrow buttress to the right has some inelegant moves.

24 Feast of Stephen . . . . `[ ]` HS 4c
Tricky moves lead up the left side of the crinkly wall.

25 Wenceslas . . . . `[ ]` Diff
The green corner.

26 Ebenezer . . . . `[ ]` S 4c
The final offering pulls over the roof to access the rib.

Descent

8m

From mid morning | 15 min | Windy

Porthole Buttress
In front of and below Gun Buttress (see next page) is a pleasant face with a small collection of climbs in the lower grades. It is usually quiet and is always worth a short visit, especially if the Upper Tier is busy. The rock can be a bit green and gritty.
Approach (see map on page 112) - The area is in front of and below Gun Buttress which is where the path arrives at the crag.

27 Slab and Crack Arete . . . . . . `[⬛]` `[ ]` Diff
The short left arete of the face.

28 Slab and Crack . . . . `[☆1]` `[ ]` Diff
The features left of the slanting chimney have a tricky start.

29 Möglichkeit . . . . `[👤]` `[ ]` HS 4b
The narrow chimney is a grovel, especially at the top.
FA. Allan Austin 1958

30 Plimsoll Line . . . . `[⬛]` `[ ]` HVS 5b
Gain the porthole from the cave and finish up the wall above on a disappointing selection of holds.
FA. Colin Binks 1981

31 Porthole . . . . `[☆]` `[⬛]` `[⬛]` `[ ]` HVS 5b
Climb to the hole then head portwards to an arete finish.

32 Portside . . . . `[ ]` S 4a
The right edge of the slab to steeper rock and a third porthole.
FA. Steve Clarke 2003

33 A Treat for the Gimp . . . . `[ ]` f4
The centre of the short slab.

34 Leaning Slab . . . . `[☆1]` `[🔖]` `[ ]` VD
The slab on the right and the steeper wall above.

35 Trango 2 . . . . `[⬛]` `[🔖]` `[ ]` E3 5c
The centre of the tiny face of the block, to a high crux.
FA. Martin Boysen 1987

Sheffield Area

Ladybower Area

Stanage

Burbage Valley

Millstone Area

Derwent Edges

Chatsworth Area

Southern Crags

1 Shadow Wall . . . . VS 4b
The north-facing side-wall of the buttress has a long reach. Exit to the right under the gun and mantelshelf to finish.
FA. Chris Craggs 1981

2 Life During Wartime E2 5c
The bulging left arete of the buttress is short-lived but manages to be a pumpy little number despite this.
FA. Keith Ashton 1985

3 Randy's Wall . . . . . . HVS 5a
From under the arete trend right past the bulge to the centre of the wall and a poor rest. Finish delicately up the face.
FA. John Robson early 1960s

4 Magnum Force . . . . HVS 5a
Pull through the centre of the bulges to the rest on *Randy's Wall*, then traverse left to climb close to the arete.
FA. Chris Craggs 1981

5 Gunpowder Crack . . . . . . VS 5b
The enticing hand-jamming crack is a swine to enter (can be done from left or right) but is much more pleasant above.
FA. Hugh Banner 1961

6 Master Blaster E1 5c
The right-hand side-wall on poor sloping holds, to a final long reach for a shallow crack. A solo but escapable.
FA. Chris Craggs 1981

7 Loader's Bay . . . . Diff
The deep and ferny groove gives easy bridging or a grovel.

8 Ammo . . . . S 4a
The short arete and wall above.

9 Long John . . . . VS 5b
The jutting snout is gained by a leap and brief struggle. The short may have to use lateral thinking.

10 Three Real Men Dancing E2 6a
The undercut wall is short, sharp and difficult to access.
FA. Martin Veale 1982

11 Green Chimney . . . . Diff
As the name suggests, this fissure is often verdant.

12 Artillery Corner . . . . Diff
Another lurid feature.

13 Gangway . . . . VD
Amble up the ramp on the right wall. It can also be reached by a swift pull and finished direct, at about **S 4b**.
FA. (Direct Start) Chris Craggs 1981

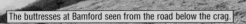

The buttresses at Bamford seen from the road below the crag.

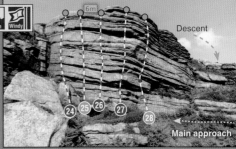

⑳ Opposite . . . . ☐ **S 4a**
Head straight up the juggy wall just right of the open corner.
FA. Chris Craggs 1991

㉑ Vertigo . . . . ⛏️ 🧗 ☐ **HS 4c**
The undercut left-hand arete of the jutting buttress has a steep
start on jams and pleasant jug-hauling above.
FA. Pete Hatton 1963

㉒ Armed and Dangerous . . ⛏️ 🧗 ☐ **E4 6a**
The roof is crossed at its widest point with trepidation.
FA. Mark Stokes 1987

㉓ Dynamite Groove . . . . 🧗 ☐ **HVS 5b**
From a convenient boulder, pull into the hanging groove then
continue direct.
FA. Martin Veale 1981

---

⑭ Green Parrot . . . . ⛏️ 🧗 ☐ **VS 5b**
Gaining the hanging beak is a touch butch. *f5* with mats.
FA. Martin Veale 1981

⑮ Bosun's Slab . . . . ⛏️ ☐ **Mod**
The mild slab on the right-hand side of the prow.

⑯ Concave Slab . . . . ☐ **Diff**
The scooped slab is also pretty straightforward.

⑰ Convex or Perplexed . . . . . . 🔺 ☐ **VS 5b**
Pull awkwardly over the nose then finish easily.
FA. Chris Craggs 1991

⑱ Adjacent Slab . . . . ☐ **VD**
The narrow slab is easy enough. A direct start is **4c**.

⑲ Hypotenuse . . . . ⛏️ ☐ **Mod**
The open corner by utra-mild bridging and jamming.

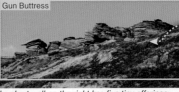

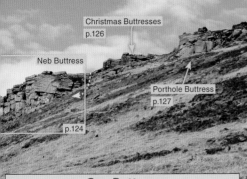

Christmas Buttresses
p.126

Neb Buttress

Porthole Buttress
p.127

p.124

Gun Buttress
The buttress nearest the road has a good collection of
easier routes on rough rock. With the added attraction
of a delightful grassy base, the place is worth half a
day - consider bringing a picnic.
Approach (see map on page 112) - This is the first bit of
rock you come to on the usual approach. You can't miss
the characteristic jutting beak of the gun on the top of the
main buttress.

The short wall on the right has five tiny offerings.

㉔ Funny Side . . . . ☐ **S 4a**
The wall on the far left.
FA. Keith Ashton 1987

㉕ Topside . . . . ⛏️ 🚪 ☐ **HS 4b**
Stretch up the wall.

㉖ Sunny Side . . . . ⛏️ ☐ **S 4a**
The centre line here is the original one.
FA. Chris Craggs 1981

㉗ Right Side . . . . ☐ **S 4a**
Just left of the rounded arete.
FA. Keith Ashton 1987

㉘ Slopy Side . . . . 🔺 ☐ **HVS 5b**
The right-hand side of the final face, starting at a hole.
FA. Colin Binks 1991

Sheffield Area | Ladybower Area | Stanage | Burbage Valley | Millstone Area | Derwent Edges | Chatsworth Area | Southern Crags

N

About 1km

A57

Moscar

Stanage North
p.134

Stanage Plantation
p.178

Bamford
p.112

Dennis Knoll

Stanage Popular
p.218

Bamford

Plantation

North Lees
Campsite

Popular End
(Hook's Car)

Stanage Edge

The beautiful slabby sweep of *Wall End Slab* (VS 5a) - *page 189* - at Stanage Plantation. The route is great and varied trip, but is also rather unbalanced with a very sketchy start using some ancient tiny chipped holds, leading to a bulge then a long traverse. The final section, shown in the photo, is poorly protected which focuses the mind nicely. Photo: Adam Long

Stanage has to be the most popular climbing destination in the country and perhaps that means anywhere; the finest of all the gritstone edges and by a margin, with over 4km of exposed rock, in a wild setting. The cliff has routes of every grade from the easiest of scrambles to routes at the limit of human ability. It has become popular to dismiss climbing on Stanage as a crowded circus of incompetent top-ropers, though this level of disdain points to an ignorance of this magnificent cliff, even on the busiest weekends of the year there are plenty of hidden gems hidden far away from the crowds! Stanage has climbing of almost every style and there is enough here to keep most climbers busy for at least half a lifetime. The rock is of impeccable quality and climbing is possible throughout the year, with much of the crag drying rapidly and all of it facing the afternoon sun. Some sections of the cliff have been quarried in the distant past for the production of millstones, most notably the Marble Wall and Wobbler areas. The climbing here is characterised by clean-cut grooves and aretes, whereas the rest of the cliff has the more usual rounded breaks and sloping tops that gritstone climbers grow to love.

Most people's first encounter with Stanage is at the Popular End where there are enough classics for many months of superb climbing at almost any grade. Next a visit to the magical arena of the Plantation Area is a must, usually followed by a trip up the long bracken-covered slopes to sample the delights of High Neb. Once you have climbed on each of these three main areas a few times your true Stanage apprenticeship can begin by calling in at a few of the more out-of-the-way locations. Try checking out *End Slab, Surgeon's Saunter, Marble Wall, The Blurter, Count's Buttress, Tower Face, The Unconquerables* and *Millsom's Minion*; by then you will begin to get a feel for the place.

The popularity of the cliff can make it very busy on nice summer weekends, especially at the Popular End, though a 10 minute walk to the left will leave the crowds behind. Whatever your aspirations are, welcome to Stanage - this is one place you will enjoy.

Conditions

The cliff is almost always climbable if the weather is kind. Days when the bracken glows like burnished gold in the low winter sun can be just as memorable as those long summer evenings. Short crisp winter days can be magical, with superb friction and a quiet cliff, and the first spring evening after the clocks go forward is always a very special time too.

Most of Stanage comes into condition rapidly after poor weather, although the northern end of the cliff is usually green in winter or after periods of rain. Midges can make life unbearable on calm days between June and August.

Set at an altitude of 450 metres and facing southwest, conditions on the Edge are often bracing, the almost ever-present west wind is equally good at drying the cliff and blasting away the cobwebs. On the rare occasions when an easterly is blowing, especially in the winter, conditions on the Edge can be warm and calm at the foot of the cliff, but wild and freezing up on the belay. Facing west, the cliff receives the afternoon sun until it sets and the sunsets here are often magnificent.

Sheffield Area

Ladybower Area

Stanage

Burbage Valley

Millstone Area

Derwent Edges

Chatsworth Area

Southern Crags

TICKLIST
Stanage Green Spot Starters

Grit is often regarded as a tricky medium to learn to climb on - there are not enough holds, and the ones that do exist are too far apart. Here is a good varied sampler to get you started. If you can manage all 24 of these, you will be well on your way to grit competence.

☐ **Castle Chimney, Mod** *(257)*. The perfect intro.

☐ **Black Hawk Traverse Right, Diff** *(259)*. Mild but lovely.

☐ **October Crack, Diff** *(153)*. One of several good easier routes at Crow Chin.

☐ **Prospero's Climb, VD** *(139)*. A neat slab and flake tucked away near the northern extremity of the crag.

☐ **Black Hawk Traverse Left, VD** *(259)*. A cunning way up this fine face.

☐ **Hollybush Gully Right, VD** *(192)*. A tricky start leads to enclosed rambling.

☐ **Kelly's Crack, VD** *(152)*. Good gear, nice climbing - what's not to like?

☐ **Heaven Crack. VD** *(230)*. As good as easier grit gets.

☐ **Hollybush Crack, VD** *(251)*. Superb steep bridging.

☐ **Helfenstein's Struggle, HVD** *(191)*. For skinny types.

☐ **Broken Buttress, HVD** *(175)*. A great line in the middle of nowhere.

☐ **Robin Hood's Crack, HVD** *(241)*. Visits the classic cave.

☐ **Paradise Crack, HVD** *(206)*. A proper struggle.

☐ **Flying Buttress, HVD** *(254)*. The most popular route in the UK with the most ticks on UKC Logbooks.

☐ **Crack and Cave, HVD** *(238)*. Trickier than you expected?

☐ **Verandah Buttress, HVD 5b** *(227)*. The grade must be a joke, surely?

☐ **Doctor's Chimney, S** *(140)*. You can't avoid all of these if you are concentrating on lower-grade grit.

☐ **Bishop's Route, S** *(247)*. Long and excellent, you can even belay along the way.

☐ **Twisting Crack, S** *(164)*. Steep and exhilarating.

☐ **Cave Buttress, S** *(167)*. A sneaky trip up the right edge of the High Neb Area.

☐ **Black Hawk Hell Crack, S** *(259)*. Steep and imposing but with great gear.

☐ **Crack and Corner, S** *(262)*. A great line but the start will test your footwork and perseverance.

☐ **Balcony Buttress, S** *(236)*. A superb open climb that manages to feel quite long.

☐ **Right-hand Trinity, S** *(249)*. A great intro to jamming.

The popular and tricky *Crack and Cave* (HVD 4a) is as good an introduction as any to gritstone, with its fair share of sloping, polished holds and a wide, awkward cracks - *page 238* - Stanage Popular.

	No star	☆	☆☆	☆☆☆
Mod to S	72	32	10	-
HS to HVS	125	64	21	9
E1 to E3	38	30	14	4
E4 and up	4	12	8	8

Stanage North is the first section of the cliff to be described, and is the least popular of the three main sections. It runs from the Long Causeway all the way out to End Slab, and apart from High Neb and Crow Chin the whole area is normally pretty quiet. It lacks the ranked classics of the Plantation and the Popular End but there is plenty of good climbing here, in a remoter feeling setting than the rest of the cliff, and with a greater chance of solitude.

The Blurter (HVS 5b) - *page 161* - on Blurter Buttress, Stanage North. Occasionally you get those evenings on the eastern edges where everything comes together. Perfect conditions, pleasantly warm without being baking, enough breeze to keep the midges away, and a glorious sunset. When that happens you know there is no better place to climb! Photo: Jamie Moss

Sheffield Area

Ladybower Area

Stanage

Burbage Valley

Millstone Area

Derwent Edges

Chatsworth Area

Southern Crags

Approach Also
see map on page 130
The High Neb
parking is the usual
starting place - it
is rarely full except
on sunny summer
weekends. The Long
Causeway leads
towards the cliff
then bears away
rightwards towards
western Sheffield. A
couple of stiles on
the left lead steeply
to a good horizontal
track that runs below
the whole of this
section of the cliff.
It is also possible to
approach from the
A57 - there is limited
parking just west of
the crest of the road.
This is the quickest
approach for the
crags at Stanage
End.

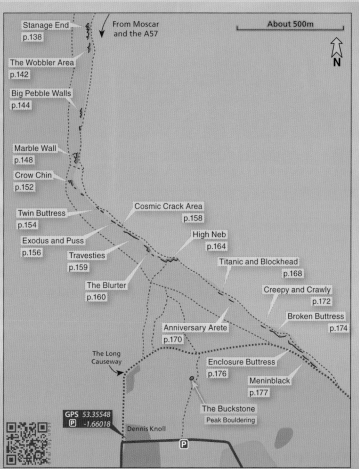

Stanage End
p.138

From Moscar
and the A57

About 500m

N

The Wobbler Area
p.142

Big Pebble Walls
p.144

Marble Wall
p.148

Crow Chin
p.152

Cosmic Crack Area
p.158

Twin Buttress
p.154

High Neb
p.164

Exodus and Puss
p.156

Travesties
p.159

Titanic and Blockhead
p.168

Creepy and Crawly
p.172

The Blurter
p.160

Broken Buttress
p.174

Anniversary Arete
p.170

The Long
Causeway

Enclosure Buttress
p.176

Meninblack
p.177

GPS 53.35548
Ⓟ -1.66018

Dennis Knoll

The Buckstone
Peak Bouldering

Ⓟ

Conditions
The right-hand half of this section of the
edge faces southwest and catches the sun
from mid-morning onwards. It is exposed to
any bad weather but dries quickly after rain,
although a few routes can be a bit green and
sandy. Further left the cliff swings round to
face due west - it gets the sun later in the day
and is greener in the winter. Midges can be a
problem in the late spring and summer when
the wind drops.

Sheffield Area

Ladybower Area

Stanage

Burbage Valley

Millstone Area

Derwent Edges

Chatsworth Area

Southern Crags

Start Area
The first (or is it last?) bits of rock on the whole of the mighty edge that is Stanage are a couple of relatively insignificant buttresses with a small set of routes that wouldn't be out of place tucked away on Burbage.
Approach (see map on page 135) - The slabs are reached in 20-25 minutes from Moscar (limited parking) and in about 30 minutes from the High Neb parking.

❶ **Start.** . . . . HVS 5b
Stretch up the face on the left to a hard finish up the arete.
FA. Bruce Goodwin 1992

❷ **Move** . . . . Diff
The flaky central crack.
FA. Bruce Goodwin 1992

❸ **Faster.** . . . . VS 5a
Another short face climb just right of the crack has a tricky start.
FA. Gordon Mason 1992

❹ **Slow Down** . . . . HVD 4a
Climb the wide corner-crack then pass the overhang to reach easier ground.
FA. C.Drinkwater 1992

55m to the right is another small buttress just left of the more impressive green sheet of rock of End Slab.

❺ **Goodtime** . . . . HS 4b
The steep and pumpy flake-crack in the side-wall.
FA. David Simmonite 1989

❻ **Splashing** . . . . HVS 5a
Start up the chimney then move right onto the leaning rib.
FA. David Simmonite 1989

❼ **Bathtime for Two** . . . . VS 5a
A short tricky wall leads to juggy bulges.
FA. David Simmonite 1989

❽ **You** . . . . VS 4c
Starting up a groove on the right, move left to a hanging crack.
FA. Bruce Middleton 1992

Start

Bathtime for Two

Stanage End
p.138

Surgeon's Saunter
p.140

The Wobbler Area
p.142

For much of the year, the routes on the two attractive slumped slabs at Stanage End tend to be green and unpleasant. However late summer often finds the crag in great condition and it is especially pleasant later in the evening when the sun hits the rock. Here a climber is enjoying *Crab Crawl Arete* (VS 4c) - *page 139*.

Sheffield Area

Ladybower Area

Stanage

Burbage Valley

Millstone Area

Derwent Edges

Chatsworth Area

Southern Crags

Stanage End

A fine secluded pair of slabs has some good but poorly protected lower-grade routes. The area is best visited late on summer evenings when it gets the sun - it tends to be VERY green in winter.

Approach (see map on page 135) - The slabs are reached in 20-25 minutes from Moscar (limited parking) and in about 30 minutes from the extensive High Neb parking.

1 Green Party . . . . **VS 5b**
Across the gully, this is the oft-luminous slab on the left.
FA. David Simmonite 1989

2 The Rack . . . . **Diff**
The wide green crack in the groove on the far left.

3 Another Turn . . . . **VS 4a**
Delicate and unprotected up the central section. The steeper upper part is easier and safer.

4 Steamin' **E1 5b**
Start just right of the arete and climb delicately, passing the right-hand edge of a thin overlap. From the ledge, climb a short crack, a wall and the final roof centrally.
FA. Chris Craggs 1983

5 The Pinion . . . . **HVD**
Begin as for *Steamin'* and but trend rightwards to a ledge - the Corbel. Move right then up to the break, then right and up to finish. A varied selection of cams is useful.
FA. Harry Kelly 1921

6 End of the Line . . . . **HS 4b**
Overlooked but pleasant enough. Climb straight up the slab to a tiny ramp and finger traverse up this to finish.
FA. Chris Craggs 2013. Probably done before but never recorded.

7 The Ariel . . . . **VD**
Start just left of the overhang and trend diagonally leftwards to join *The Pinion* on the Corbel. Climb to the break and then left to the arete and finish in a nice position as for *Another Turn*.
FA. Fred Pigott and friends 1920s

8 The Green Streak . . . . **VS 4c**
Climb the slab left of the overhang with good delicate moves on spaced pockets. There is more gear than appears from below.
FA. Fred Pigott and friends 1920s

9 Slight Second **E1 5b**
An eliminate up the slab just left of *Incursion*.
FA. Bill McKee 1979

10 Incursion **E1 5b**
Climb *The Green Streak* to a delicate traverse out right onto the hanging slab. The crux follows - a low cam in a pocket may protect the start of the difficulties.
FA. Paul Nunn 1962. FA. Johnny Dawes (one-legged, no hands) 1990s

11 That Floating Fatman . . . **E1 5c**
Another eliminate following *Incursion* but stepping right and squeezing in a line, avoiding *High Flier* further right. The direct start is **R.I.P O.D.B.**, *f7C*.
FA. Darren Stephenson 1999

12 Incursion Direct *f6A*
The centre of the overhang is crossed rightwards to pockets before joining the original. Not helped by the perennial puddle.
FA. Andy Parkin 1976

Descent

12m

Start Area

13 Low Rider . . . . ⚅ 🎫 🎴 ⬜ *f7C+*
Start on the arete below the roof and traverse the lip before
moving up to a jug to finish. Linking this into *Chip Shop Brawl* is
a very sustained *f8A+*.
FA. Jon Fullwood

14 High Flyer . . . . ⚅ 💔 ⬜ **E4 6a**
From a boulder under the right arete of the slab, swing left to a
good hold, pull around and follow the right-hand edge of the slab
to an unnerving, semi-mantelshelf move to easy ground.
FA. Lee Bower 1979

15 Chip Shop Brawl . . . ⚅ 💔 🎫 ⬜ *f7A+*
From the tip of the block leap on to the hanging arete and power
up it. Short-lived but tough, it may leave you a bit battered.
FA. John Allen 1987

16 Caliban's Cave . . . . ⚅ 👊 ⬜ **HS 4b**
The dark chimney gives awkward back-and-footing to a ledge on
the left. Tricky moves are needed to pass the roof. Often green.
FA. Harry Kelly 1921

17 The Tempest . . . . ⚅ 🦎 ⬜ **VS 5a**
Right of the chimney, climb to a thin pocket (green) then make
harder moves up and right. Continue by pleasant climbing.
FA. Chris Craggs 1996

Evening	25 min	Windy	Green

18 Prospero's Climb . . . . ⚅ ⬜ **VD**
Climb the centre of the slab to a ledge, then move left to reach
and climb the prominent and mild layback flake.
FA. Harry Kelly 1921

19 Miranda's Variation . . . . . . ⚅ ⬜ **S 4a**
An oddity that moves right out of *Prospero's Climb*, makes a
tricky step up then traverses back left again to finish.
FA. Rice Kemper Evans c.1921

20 The Crab Crawl . . . . ⚅ ⬜ **S 4a**
Start under the edge an overlap at 3m. Climb past the overlap
then continue up the slab in a direct line to a tricky finale.
FA. Fred Pigott and friends early 1920s

21 Crab Crawl Arete . . . . . . ⚅ 👊 ⬜ **VS 4c**
Start at the right edge of the slab and follow the arete
throughout by lovely balancy (and slightly reachy) climbing.
Photo on page 137.
FA. Andy Parkin 1976

22 The Vice . . . . ⚅ 🎫 👊 ⬜ **E1 5b**
The leaning widening crack is climbed by strenuous jamming
to a gruesome shelving exit where the crack flares. Gritstone
brutality at its best, it can be a hideous affair, unless you are a
proficient jammer with big leathery hands!
FA. Clive Rowland (with single threaded chockstone runner) 1962

12m

Surgeon's Saunter ➤

Sheffield Area

Ladybower Area

Stanage

Burbage Valley

Millstone Area

Derwent Edges

Chatsworth Area

Southern Crags

Surgeon's Saunter

A fine, tall and isolated buttress which is rarely busy. The classic crack of *Surgeon's Saunter* is well worth calling in for and there are several other minor things of interest hereabouts. The north-facing routes can be green but the rest of the climbs are usually in condition.

Approach (see map on page 135) - The buttress can be reached in 20 minutes from Moscar (limited parking) and in 30 minutes from the High Neb parking.

❶ Kerb . . . . **Diff**
The slabby arete and short groove.
FA. Dave Gregory 1992

❷ Paved Vacuum . . . . **HVS 5b**
Tackle the tricky flake-crack and bulge in the front-face.
FA. Gary Gibson 1979

❸ Pie Face . . . . **VS 5a**
Climb the centre of the short green face with surprising difficulty.

❹ And There's More . . . . **VS 5a**
The right arete of the face.

❺ Kindergarten . . . . **VS 4b**
Another short, green, north-facing wall. Play nicely now.

❻ Child's Play . . . . **HVS 5a**
Balance up the rounded arete finishing to the left.
FA. Paul Harrison 1984

❼ Nursery Crack . . . . **VS 5b**
Tough to grade (it was Diff for years) and tougher to climb. Jamming is the traditional and torrid approach, laybacking is a more modern way of doing it. Monster cams are sensible.

❽ Doctored . . . . **HVS 5c**
The short wall left of the crack requires one long reach.
FA. Colin Binks 1983

❾ Cripple's Crack . . . . **S 4a**
An awkward customer up the wide right-slanting crack.
FA. Fred Pigott and friends early 1920s

❿ Physician's Wall **E1 6a**
The wall right of the crack has a short sharp crux.
FA. Andy Parkin 1976

⓫ Which Doctor **E5 6a**
Climb a flake, then the face above, until a horizontal break can be followed out right to the arete (small cams). Finish up this.
FA. Martin Veale 1991

⓬ Doctor's Chimney . . . . . . **S 4a**
Climb the crack up the left side of the pillar to reach the impressive chimney system. Tricky moves are then needed to enter the main fissure before following it with pleasure.
FA. Fred Pigott 1919

⓭ Doctor's Saunter . . . . **HVS 5a**
The original way of accessing the twin cracks. Start up the crack to the right of *Doctor's Chimney* then hand-traverse the lowest break to reach the cracks a short distance below the jammed block. Finish steeply up the left-hand crack. Good hard work.
FA. Fred Pigott, Morley Wood 1929. Named after Dr. Rice Kemper Evans

⓮ Surgeon's Saunter . . . . . **HVS 5b**
A great route with a hard, but safe start and excellent jamming above. The dubious looking jammed tooth at half-height has resisted many years of efforts to wrench it from its socket. Finish up the right-hand crack for the full effect.
FA. Peter Biven 1953

15 Kelly's Corner . . . . 🖾 [____] HVD
The awkward groove in the corner leads, via a tricky start, into a rocky bay. Escape, or try *Niche Climb*.
FA. Harry Kelly 1915-ish

16 Heath Robinson. . . . 🎊🖾❤ [____] E6 6b
Direct up the bulging right arete of the tower. The sloping exit requires some skill to avoid slithering off backwards. Try undercutting the break to reach the slopers, then go!
FA. Johnny Dawes 1984

17 Niche Climb . . . . 🎯 [____] S 4b
From the mid-height ledge, climb the narrowing groove in the left-hand corner of the bay - it usually proves a gritty and awkward struggle.
FA. Fred Pigott 1919

18 Niche Wall . . . . 🎯 [____] VS 5a
The short green wall on small holds.

19 Manhattan Arete . . . . ❤ [____] VD
The jutting arete of the buttress on shelving holds.

20 Wilbur's Wall . . . . 🎲 [____] f5+
Climb the wall starting from a low break.

21 Wilbur's Rib . . . . ❤ [____] f5
The prominent hanging arete, finishing slightly left.

22 Wilbur's Corner . . . . 🎲 [____] f5
Tackle the corner.

23 Manhattan Chimney . . . . 🎲 [____] S 4a
A short chimney capped by a flat block. Classic back-and-footing leads to the well-protected crux at the capstone.
FA. Fred Pigott 1919

24 New York, New York. . . . . . . 🎲 [____] f6B
A short arete - nicely technical.
FA. John Allen 1986

25 Sir Chilled . . . . 🎲 [____] E5 6b
The scritty extension arete above the previous climb gives a good exercise in dynamic climbing.
FA. Richard Heap 1999

26 Manhattan Crack . . . . 🎋 [____] VS 4c
The hard short-lived, layback crack in the angle with a steep and strenuous upper section.

27 Rib Tickler . . . . 🎋 [____] VS 5a
Nip up the short crack and bulging rib above.

Descent

18m

13

16 17   6m

15

14

11   12

18   19   20 21 22   23   24

25

27

26

The Wobbler - 60m

Sheffield Area

Ladybower Area

Stanage

Burbage Valley

Millstone Area

Derwent Edges

Chatsworth Area

Southern Crags

The Wobbler Area

Short, steep walls and some decent cracks alternate. The area was once quarried, which explains the angular nature of the rock and the piles of rubble in front of the cliff. The right-hand side offers some extended problems for the boulderer/soloist and a few easier offerings for quick-ticking.

Approach (see map on page 135) - The area can be reached in 20 minutes from Moscar (limited parking) and in 30 minutes from the High Neb parking.

① Concept of Kinky ... 🔲 **E6 6b**
The hanging flakes are tough and protection is minimal.
FA. John Allen 1989

② Good Clean Fun .... 🔲 **E4 6b**
From a couple of moves up *The Wobbler*, stride out left (side-runner above) to access the face and climb it by fierce pulls.
The Iain Farrar Experience, E5 7a goes direct, no side-runners.
FA. John Allen 1984

③ The Wobbler .... 🔲 **E1 5c**
Climb the well-named fierce left-hand crack by finger-jamming, then layback the cluster of cracks above, usually with a quiver.
FA. Pete Crew 1962

④ Gameo .... 🔲 **E2 5b**
Trend right to climb the rounded arete. Starting up the arete direct is **Marathonette, E1 5b**.
FA. John Allen 1986

⑤ Avril .... 🔲 **HS 4b**
Climb the pleasant jamming crack on good lockers.

⑥ Mai .... 🔲 **VS 4b**
The thinner cracks just to the right of an easy groove. A left-hand exit is harder and a bit artificial.
FA. Dave Gregory 1992

⑦ Tupperware .... 🔲 **E2 6a**
Climb to a thin flake and a decent pocket then access the right trending groove to finish
FA. Miles Gibson 1997

⑧ Mars .... 🔲 **S 4a**
The diagonal flake left of the groove has a tricky start.

⑨ 7% Soln .... 🔲 **HVS 5b**
The short wall left of the angle.
FA. Gary Gibson 1981

⑩ February Crack .... 🔲 **HS 4b**
Short-lived but steep moves up the main angle.

⑪ Acute Amnesia .... 🔲 **HVS 5b**
The dirty thin crack just to the right develops independence.
FA. Gary Gibson 1981

⑫ Exaltation .... 🔲 **E5 6c**
Fierce climbing and a good target for a hot day since it is in the shade. The original line, *Saltation*, finished by scuttling off to join *Old Salt*. The first crux can be protected by a hand-placed peg in a slot; without this the grade is **E6 6c**. Small cams and wires protect the stretch at the top.
FA. Paul Smith 1989. FA. (Saltation) Johnny Dawes 1984
FA. Pete Robins (without peg) 2000

⑬ Old Salt .... 🔲 **HVS 5a**
Climb the front arete of the buttress using the curving crack to gain a small ledge (5b for shorties). Move leftwards to follow flakes out onto the face and finish with some urgency.
Photo on page 147.
FA. Paul Nunn 1963

⑭ Rimmington Place ..... 🔲 **E2 5c**
A taxing finish to *Old Salt* up the flying right arete.
FA. Shaun Ainley 1987

15 Valediction . . . .  HVS 5a
Climb this through overhangs on jams and hidden jugs. Short-lived but quite intense and very worthwhile.
FA. Geoff Sutton 1959

16 Monad . . . . f6C+
The wall left of the chimney has a desperate start on a tiny, polished hold (a jump?). Bridging back to the opposite wall is an easier solution but there is still a hard move.
FA. Steve Bancroft 1979

17 Boomerang Chimney . . . . . . S 4a
The banana-shaped rift is often a slippery struggle.

To the right is a short slabby face of good rock. Most of these routes are usually done as highball boulder problems. We have only given boulder grades for the harder ones.

18 Twin Cracks. . . . . VD
Awkwardly up the parallel cracks just right of the chimney.

19 Quiver . . . . HVS 5c
The short crack ends in the middle of the wall. Undercut for the break and wobble up the final move on rounded holds.
FA. Graham Hoey 1981

20 Arrow Crack . . . . VS 5a
The crack right of *Quiver* doesn't run out halfway up the wall hence it proves to be a bit less demanding.

21 Blinkers . . . . VS 5b
A well-named narrow face with rounded holds.

22 Balance . . . . Diff
The left-trending ramp is a worthwhile easy climb.

The next routes are on the short quarried wall.

23 Problem Crack. . . . . VS 5b
The thin crack has one taxing layback/finger-jam move.

24 Microbe Left f6B
The wall is very crimpy.

25 Microbe . . . . HVS 5c
Climb the thin crack with a useful pocket, passing a narrow overlap early on.
FA. Steve Bancroft 1975

26 Germ f6B
A short wall with a taxing finale.
FA. Chris Sowden 1980

27 Crumbling Crack . . . . HS 4b
A bit better than appearances (and the name) might suggest!

28 Problem Corner . . . . VS 5a
Bridge the blank groove which bounds the wall on its right. Short and sweet.

29 Love Handles f6A
The wall right of the corner is less well-endowed than you might be expecting!
FA. Mark Stokes 1983

30 Mr M'Quod and the Anti-rock Squad
. . . . HVS 5c
The short-lived arete that bounds the wall.
FA. Mark Stokes 1983

Descent

Descent

8m

Descent

Big Pebble Walls - 400m

Sheffield Area
Ladybower Area
Stanage
Burbage Valley
Millstone Area
Derwent Edges
Chatsworth Area
Southern Crags

The Wobbler - 400m

Big Pebble Walls

The least popular part of Stanage and with good reason. The area is just about the most distant from any parking and the routes really aren't all that good, being short, usually green and with many snappy pebbles to contend with. It is normally quiet here!

Approach (see map on page 135) - The area is reached in 25 minutes from Moscar (limited parking) and in about the same from the more extensive High Neb parking.

1 Brown Wall . . . . VS 4c
The north-facing side-wall is climbed from a block to a break. Move left and finish direct. Rounded.
FA. Bruce Goodwin 1997

2 Bamboozled E1 5c
The scritty arete is a tricky monkey to start.
FA. Graham Parkes 1997

3 Ram Jam Full . . . . HS 4c
The short jamming crack is surprisingly pleasant.
FA. Chris Craggs 1997

4 Overhung E1 5c
Pull around the bulge via reachy moves on poor slopers.
FA. Graham Parkes 1997

5 Chippendale . . . . VD
The tiny corner.
FA. Alfie Conn 2003

6 Wedgewood . . . . S 4b
This is the awkward recessed crack.
FA. Chris Craggs 1997

7 Nosey Parkers . . . . VS 4c
The left arete passing a tricky bulge.
FA. Chris Craggs 1997

8 Slab Happy . . . . VS 5a
The centre of the slab is reachy/tricky, especially the last move.
FA. Chris Craggs 1997

9 Hueco Heaven . . . . HVS 5a
Slant left up the side-wall to a break with a jammed block then stretch for the hueco. Possibly the best route hereabouts.
FA. Graham Parkes 1997

10 Hard Nosed . . . . HS 5b
Climb the tough rounded nose then the easy corner.
FA. Chris Craggs 1997

11 Flaked Out . . . . HVS 5a
The flake in the arete leads to a bilberry ledge on the left and a steep finish.
FA. Chris Craggs 1997

12 Progressive Wall E2 5c
From blocks climb the wall to a tough exit.
FA. Bruce Goodwin 1997

13 Reptilian . . . . VD
Wander up the bouldery ridge and access the top block awkwardly from the left - scary. The descent off the back is also a little tricky.
FA. Chris Craggs 2007

14 Front Face . . . . VS 5a
Climb direct via a tricky start and a worrying finish.
FA. Chris Craggs 2007

Lonely Crag - 60m ➡

15 It's Scary Mary . . . . 🗝 [ ] **S 4a**
The groove and blocky ledges lead to the right-hand side of the top block. Another one with slightly worrying finish.
FA. Dave Gregory 1997

The next routes are 20m further right on a short arete.

16 Itchy. . . . . 🦎 [ ] **HVS 5c**
The left-hand of the arete is the easier option here.
FA. Mike Hayes 2003

17 Scratch Arete . . . . 🦎 [ ] **E1 5c**
The pebbly arete on its right-hand side. Not much for the feet.
FA. Bruce Goodwin 1997

18 Scratch Wall . . . . 🤸 [ ] **VS 5a**
A poor line up a steep crack and breaks on the right of the wall.
FA. Bruce Goodwin 1997

19 Ferret's Crack . . . . [ ] **S 4a**
The short crack in the side-wall of the next small buttress.
FA. Bruce Goodwin 1997

20 Ramps . . . . ◤ [ ] **HS 4c**
Trend left to access the right-trending ramp and a tricky exit.
FA. Dave Gregory 1997

21 Two Pitch Climb. . . . . [ ] **S 4a**
The dirty groove and short steep side-wall.
FA. Dave Gregory 1997

22 Natura Sanat. . . . . ◤ [ ] **HVS 5a**
The left-hand side of the wall starting at a waist-height pocket.
FA. Bruce Goodwin 1997

23 Medicus Curat. . . . . ◤ [ ] **HVS 5b**
The right-hand side of the wall from just left of a pointed block.
FA. Bruce Goodwin 1997

24 Dennis's Harp . . . . ◣ [ ] **HS 4b**
From the block, climb the left-hand side of the arete throughout.
FA. Bruce Goodwin 1997

25 Flake Chimney Arete . . . . [ ] **S 4a**
Climb the narrow front face of the arete. Blinkers required.
FA. Chris Craggs 2006

26 Flake Chimney. . . . . 🧍 [ ] **Diff**
The amiable rift is almost worth a star.
FA. Dave Gregory 1997

27 Drewitt, Drewitt. . . . . ◣ [ ] **VS 4c**
The next arete has some decent moves on shelving holds.
FA. Bruce Goodwin 1997

28 Greenman's Route . . . . [ ] **HVD 4a**
The next shallow angle to a tricky exit.
FA. Dave Gregory 1997

29 Pillar Route. . . . . [ ] **VS 5a**
The front of the narrow pillar.
FA. Bruce Goodwin 1997

30 Algol Corner . . . . [ ] **S 4b**
The short green groove right of the pillar is stubborn.
FA. Bruce Goodwin 1997

31 Shining Jewel . . . . ◣ [ ] **HS 4c**
Climb the wall on pockets trending right for the easiest exit.
FA. Bruce Goodwin 1997

32 Fall Guy . . . . [ ] **VD**
The flake crack 10m right.
FA. Mike Hayes 2003

33 Plucking Pebbles . . . . [ ] **HS 4b**
The next arete via a tiny groove.
FA. Barry Clarke 2003

← Big Pebble Walls - 60m

Marble Wall - 60m →

Lonely Crag

A small, isolated and well-named buttress midway between Marble Wall and Big Pebble Walls. It is rare to see any one here except for the odd soloist.
Approach (see map on page 135) - The area is roughly midway between the Moscar parking and the High Neb parking - around 25 minutes walk from either direction.

❶ **Wetness Wall** . . . . ☐☐ VD
The left side of the north wall. Often damp, always lacking in protection and a bit reachy.

❷ **God of Straw** . . . . ☐ E2 5c
Start just left of *Brittle Bones*, pull through the weakness in the overlap and continue direct. A bit scritty and on flat holds.
FA. Nick Taylor 2000

❸ **Brittle Bones** . . . . . . ☐☐☐ E2 5c
The left arete on its left side with a hard start.
FA. Gary Gibson 1982

❹ **Missing Link** . . . . ☐☐ E2 5c
The right-hand side of the left arete is accessed via a boulder and a notch in the roof to a precarious finale.
FA. Al Parker 1978

❺ **Clubbing** . . . . . . ①☐☐☐ E3 6b
The centre of the front face is taxing to start and scary to finish.
FA. Paul Mitchell 1979-80

❻ **Mr Pemphigoid** . . . . ☐ HVS 5c
Just like all the other routes here, accessing the arete is hard and the continuation is shelving and green.
FA. Gary Gibson 1982

❼ **Canine Canute** . . . . ☐☐ E1 5b
The centre of the right wall is sustained to a shelving finish.
FA. Nick Taylor 2009

❽ **Lonely Crag** . . . . ☐ HVD 4a
The angle is pleasant enough.

❾ **Flesh and Blood** . . . . ☐ HVS 5b
The final short wall has a tough start.
FA. Gary Gibson 1982

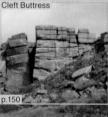

Big Pebble Walls
p.144

Lonely Crag

Marble Wall

Cleft Buttress

p.148

p.150

Sheffield Area

Ladybower Area

Stanage

Burbage Valley

Millstone Area

Derwent Edges

Chatsworth Area

Southern Crags

Great friction and no crowds at Stanage North, the cloaking bracken has died back for the year and midges are a distant memory. Here Graham Parkes is cruising up *Old Salt* (HVS 5a) - *page 142* - on a chilly winter's day when we had Stanage North to ourselves.

Marble Wall

A place where the quarry-men displayed their skills, leaving us a fine set of routes. Green in the winter but superb for the rest of the year, perhaps the most surprising thing about Marble Wall is that despite its quality, the place is rarely busy.

Approach (see map on page 135) - The buttress is roughly midway between the Moscar parking and the High Neb parking - around 20/25 minutes walk.

❶ Bifurcated Headplate Max..... ☐ **VS 4c**
The arete on the far left behind the blocks. Worth seeking out.
FA. Colin Banton 1970s

❷ Spock Out .... ☐ **VS 5a**
The central cracks in the wall.

❸ Green Crack .... ☐ **HVD 4a**
The angular groove is usually as green as expected.

❹ Marble Tower Flake .... ☼1 ☐ **S 4c**
Reach the good ledge on the arete from the left (a jump or a move of 4c) then traverse left finish up the tall flake.
FA. Eric Byne 1950

❺ Marble Arete .... ☼2 ☐ **HS 4c**
Start as for the previous route and follow the arete throughout. A little bold but with good moves and situations.
FA. Paul Nunn 1960s. Reclimbed and named by Chris Craggs 1970s.

❻ Sceptic .... ☼1 ☐ **HVS 5b**
From a block, step out right and climb the unprotected wall on flat holds to a spectacular finale over the juggy roof.
FA. Al Parker 1970s. Reclimbed and named by Chris Craggs 1970s.

❼ The Lamia .... ☼3 ☐ **E3 5c**
A superb girdle, the best of several on the cliff.
1) 5b, 12m. From *Sceptic* swing along the break to *Nectar*. Continue to an awkward hanging-stance on *Orang-outang*.
2) 5c, 16m. Continue swinging to an awkward move up a diagonal overlap to the break. Finish up the hard roof crack.
FA. Steve Bancroft, John Allen 1975

❽ Terrazza Crack........ Top 50 ☐ **HVS 5a**
The superb straight crack is a classic product of the Rock and Ice years. Well-protected and good honest hard work.
FA. Joe Brown 1952

9 Harvest. E4 6b
The short brutal roof crack has a good jam at the lip but above that it all gets very flared. One E-point per metre is good value!
FA. John Allen 1975

10 Nectar E4 6b
A blank corner and desperate roof crack give a 70s classic.
1) E3 6b. Hard bridging moves (loads of small wires) lead up the corner to a belay below the roof. Often climbed on its own.
2) 6b. Stretch into the roof-crack, shuffle towards the lip with your feet on the side-wall then levitate the final moves.
FA. John Allen, Steve Bancroft (alts) 1976

11 Spinach Slab. E6 6c
The non-slab above the initial roof on *Orang-outang*.
FA. Andy Popp 1990s

12 Orang-outang E2 5c
Another great route and low in the grade, which is always nice. Climb a small corner to a narrow stepped-overhang. Layback onto the front face to a poor rest, then follow the thin technical crack, using the left arete as required.
FA. John Allen 1973

13 Meisner's Link-up E3 5c
This one has no independent climbing but is a great pitch for bringing on the pump. From *Orang-outang* link into *Lamia*.
FA. Mike Meisner 1990s

14 Mother of Pearl . E8 7a
The left-hand start to *Marbellous* requires a desperate dyno (*f7C*) then the crux of the regular route. An awesome effort.
FA. John Welford 2004

15 Marbellous E8 7a
One of the last 'last great problems'. Start up the ramp then place small cams in the horizontal slot out to the left. The upper section succumbs to a desperate move on tiny undercuts.
FA. Robin Barker 1997

16 Goosey Goosey Gander. . Top L50 E5 6a
An action-packed pitch follows the thin crack splitting the bulges, it is often green. Protection is good but hard to place hence it is worth E5 for effort. Access the crack by a series of left-facing layback moves and sprint through the bulges. Things ease above, as long as you have a little puff left.
FA. Gabe Regan 1976

17 Don's Delight E1 5b
A short slab is climbed rightwards to where tricky balancy moves gain a shallow groove and easier climbing. Unprotected.
FA. Don Whillans 1962

18 Short 'n' Gritty. . . . . HS 4b
The short gritty green groove must have been done in the past.
FA. Chris Craggs 2012

19 Ledges, Edges. . . . . VS 4b
The ledgy face right then left to a tricky final mantel. No gear.
FA. Dan Parkes 2012

20 Hidden Delights. E2 5c
Climb the slab just left of the chimney trending right to the base of a groove. Stretch up this to a break (tiny cams - hard to place) swing left and layback the right side of the short arete.
FA. Graham Parkes 2012

21 Back Door. . . . . VS 4c
Bridge the wide cleft to a tricky exit round a capstone.
FA. Chris Craggs 1985

22 The Reach Card. . . . . S 4b
Bridge the gloomy cleft on the right of the rift to the top of the block, stretch up the wall on the left (very hard for the short) and finish up the corner.
FA. Chris Craggs 2012

Sheffield Area
Ladybower Area
Stanage
Burbage Valley
Millstone Area
Derwent Edges
Chatsworth Area
Southern Crags

Descent

Cleft Buttress

Cleft Buttress

To the right of Marble Wall, a large squat tower stands in front of the edge; it is possible to scramble all the way round behind it. Right again is a south-facing wall riven by a series of cracks. Almost all the routes here manage to feel a bit tough for their grade.

Approach (see map on page 135) - Marble Wall is roughly midway between the Moscar parking and the High Neb parking.

① Malc's Left-hand Slabs . . . VS 5a
An odd but amiable and entertaining amble up the slabby fallen blocks and short arete/groove above.
FA. Malc Baxter early 1960s

② Hideous Hidare f6C
Climb the rib of the block on slopers then step right and mantelshelf back left with considerable difficulty. A teaser.
FA. Paul Mitchell 1993

③ Left-hand Tower . . . . . . HVS 5a
The arduous wide crack leads to the tip of the block on the left. Step back onto the tower, traverse the wide break across to the arete and finish round the corner as for *The Jitters*.

④ Turtle Power E6 6c
The fierce centre of the concave wall, with hard moves to (micro wires protect) and from the break. May not have been repeated since the loss of pebbles.
FA. Neal Travers 1990

⑤ Slap 'n' Spittle E3 6a
The right arete of the concave wall is tackled on its left side. This used to be a soft E4 but don't be fooled, there is still a hard move before the gear arrives. Finish on the right.
FA. Andy Lewondowski 1983

⑥ The Jitters . . . . VS 4b
Bridge the entrance to the cleft then hop onto the left wall and climb this using the arete along the way, to reach the top.

⑦ Easy Cleft . . . . Mod
The green angle in the gloom. Can be used as a slippy descent.

⑧ Pacemaker . . . . HVS 5b
Bridge up the widening chimney until forced to hop onto the right wall, just above the crux of *Vena Cave-in.*
FA. Colin Binks 1983

⑨ Vena Cave-in E3 5c
A trip up the right-hand wall of the cleft with good protection from big cams, the closeness of the opposite wall detracts. Start up *Right-hand Tower* but trend left up well-separated and rounded breaks, to some particularly stretchy moves.
FA. Gary Gibson 1981

⑩ Right-hand Tower . . . . . . HVS 5a
A rounded classic that used to be given VS. Climb a thin crack left of the arete and head straight up to the final break. Move right round the arete to find a precarious final couple of moves. Can be well protected with large cams.

Descent

Marble Wall

⓫ Wild and Woolly . . . . . . 🔆 ◤ ▭ **E1 5b**
From the remains of a wall, move left to good holds in the break. Climb straight up, keeping just right of the arete, to the final ledge of *Right-hand Tower*. The original finish is up the left side of the nose using a small flake at **E2 5c** though topping out as for *Right-hand Tower* is more in keeping with the lower section.
FA. Chris Craggs 1995

⓬ Tempskya . . . . 🔆 ◤ ▭ **E3 5c**
Start as for the previous climb and head up the bulging face on spaced and rounded holds to a short crack. Finish as for *Right-hand Tower*. Protection is poor.
FA. Clive Jones 1978

⓭ First Sister . . . . 🔆 ⚒ ▭ **VS 5a**
The left-hand of the continuous cracks. Climb the thin lower section to good jams in the deeper upper section, then up this awkwardly to the top. Tricky but well protected.

⓮ Keep it in the Family . . . . . . ⚒ ▭ **E1 5b**
An eliminate up the shallow groove and bulging crack above.
FA. Graham Parkes 1997

⓯ Second Sister . . . . 🔆 ▭ **VS 4c**
The next continuous thin crack is a deceptive little trickster and the first decent runner is higher than you might wish for.
FA. Alan McHardy 1961

⓰ Richard's Sister . . . . . . 🔆 ✊ ▭ **HS 4b**
The widening crack in the right-hand side of the wall.
FA. Alan McHardy 1961

⓱ Not Richard's Sister Direct . . 🔆 ▭ **E1 6a**
A shallow right-facing groove leads to the crucial bulge.
FA. John Allen 1989

⓲ Sister Blister . . . . ▮ ▭ **HVS 5a**
The right arete of the wall has its moments and a reachy finale.
FA. Chris Craggs 1997

⓳ Difficult Sister . . . . ▭ **Diff**
The easy crack and groove on the right is nothing special but is an extra easy route hereabouts.

[Lots of sun] [18 min] [Windy]

Marble Wall
p.148

12m

Descent

Crow Chin - 120m

Crow Chin

A fine collection of lower grade climbs near the high point of the moor and with a superb outlook. This always used to be a great place to escape the crowds, though in recent years its reputation has spread and it can be quite busy.

Approach (see map on page 135) - Crow Chin is usually approached from the High Neb in about 20 mins.

❶ So Many Classics, So Little Time ☐ **E4 6b**
The hard wall on the left has poor holds and not much gear.
FA. John Allen 1984

❷ Rabbit's Crack . . . . ☐ **VS 5a**
A small roof and thin green cracks lead to an open groove.
FA. Chris Astill 1979

❸ Jim Crow . . . . ☐ ☐ ☐ **HVS 5a**
Start at a notch in the overhang. Pull through the roof - hard - then climb the face above, a good challenge at the grade.
FA. Terry Bolger 1979

❹ Perforation . . . . ☐ ☐ ☐ **HVS 5a**
From a block, pull over the overlap and stand in the horizontal break awkwardly. The slab and wall above are easier.
FA. Chris Craggs 1985. Up a misplaced dotted line in one of the old guides.

❺ Feathered Friends . . . . . ☐ ☐ ☐ **VS 4b**
Start at a blunt rib just left of *Kelly's Crack* and trend left to climb the slab passing a loose perched flake at half-height. Micro cams can help reduce the grip on the upper section.
FA. Terry Bolger 1979

❻ Kelly's Crack . . . . ☐ ☐ **VD**
The well-protected cleft has tricky moves at mid-height. The loose chockstone was removed by some do-gooder around 2012 having survived 100 years of being heaved on.
FA. Harry Kelly late 1910s

❼ Kelly's Eye . . . . ☐ ☐ ☐ **HS 4b**
The left-hand side of the front face leads to a shallow groove. Gain the flake above with difficulty and finish direct.
FA. John Street 1993

❽ Kelly's Eliminate . . . ☐ ☐ ☐ ☐ **HS 4b**
Excellent climbing up the centre of the buttress. The start is steep and strenuous, although on good holds. The upper section is delicate and poorly protected.
FA. Harry Kelly late 1910s. An eliminate from the time before eliminates.

Large suspect flake

12m

Cleft Buttress - 120m

9 Spring Sunshine . . . . 🔲 **VS 4c**
A proper eliminate up the right edge of the buttress. Avoiding the arete altogether is artificial and 5a.
FA. John Street 1993

10 October Crack . . . . 🔲 **Diff**
The worthwhile and well protected wide crack that splits the centre of the face.

11 May Crack . . . . 🔲 **VS 4b**
From the left edge of a triangular recess, follow the thin crack that splits the diagonal overlap above. Artificial and bold too.
FA. Chris Craggs 1985

12 October Slab . . . . 🔲 **HS 4b**
From the triangular niche, follow the thin seam above (small wires) finishing through a stepped overlap.

13 Big Al . . . . 🔲 **HVS 5a**
The fingery lower wall soon leads to wandering easier ground.
FA. John Street 1993

14 Bent Crack . . . . 🔲 **HVD**
The left-facing groove. Climb the steep awkward initial corner to ledges then onto the capping roof above. Traverse left to finish.

15 New Year's Eve . . . . 🔲 **S 4b**
Start up the fingery, square arete right of *Bent Crack*, to reach a short angular groove. Finish up the crack, or better, the arete.
FA. John Street 1993

16 The Marmoset . . . . 🔲 **HS 5a**
A one-pull-wonder. Power through the centre of the roof of the cave using the jammed blocks gently. Easy climbing remains.

17 Autumn Gold . . . . 🔲 **HS 4a**
Take the flat face to the right of *The Marmoset* cave and then the easing crack above.
FA. D.Leversidge 1983

18 Clare . . . . 🔲 **S 4b**
From a recess, pull through the roof awkwardly then head up the heathery cracks above.

19 Bright Eyed . . . . 🔲 **HS 4b**
The pleasant slab at the right side of the buttress is climbed centrally and is rather lacking in gear, though tiny cams help.
FA. Chris Craggs 1985

Twin Buttress

A neglected buttress with some interesting climbs. None of them are outstanding but together with the adjacent Meson Buttress they offer something for the connoisseur. The out-of-the-way nature explains why the grades here have always been stiff and the routes remain a bit gritty.

Approach (see map on page 135) - The area is usually approached from the High Neb parking - around 20 minutes walk.

1 Pull and Step . . . . ☐ VD
The left arete is awkward to access. Probably a move of 4a.
FA. Bruce Goodwin 1993

2 Undercut Crack . . . . ☐ VS 5a
The hanging right-hand crack requires a heave-ho or two. The left one gives an easier option - **Straight Variation, S 4b.**
FA. Bill Birch 1972

3 Bottomless Crack . . . . . . ☐ HVS 5a
The central crack is reached by a short hand-traverse.
FA. Al Parker 1972

4 Cutunder Crack . . . . ☐ f5
A boulder problem just right.

5 Bottomless Crack Direct . . . . . . ☐ f5
Reach the hanging crack by a hard double mantel.

6 Lysteria Hysteria . . . . . . ☐ E3 6a
A reachy and rounded route that was originally started from the right. The start is a **f5+** problem.
FA. Mike Lea 1990

7 Certainly Parakeratosis . . . . . ☐ E1 5b
The right arete of the buttress leads to a slanting crack.
FA. Gary Gibson 1982

8 Bow Crack . . . . ☐ VD
An awkward lower corner and jamming cracks above.

9 Frank Sinatra . . . . ☐ HS 4c
The steep cracks lead to a ledge. Move round right to finish.
FA. Chris Craggs 1999

10 Seranata . . . . ☐ E2 5c
The centre of the right-hand buttress has a tricky start leading to a taxing rounded finish. The start is a **f5+** problem.
FA. Al Parker 1958

11 Hardly Hyperkeratosis . . ☐ E2 5c
The right arete of the right twin offers more rounded reachy fun.
FA. Gary Gibson 1982

12 Quadrille . . . . ☐ S 4a
The narrow awkward groove just round the arete.
FA. Al Parker 1972

13 Twin Set . . . . ☐ VD
The short crack just right.

14 Th'ickle Buttress . . . . ☐ VS 5b
The neat 'ickle buttress across the gully, climbed left then right.
FA. Malc Baxter 1997

Descent

Crow Chin - 450m

Meson

A quiet companion to Twin Buttress with a few things of interest. The routes don't see many ascents and the rock can be gritty.

Approach (see map on page 135) - The area is usually approached from the High Neb parking - around 20 minutes walk.

15 Ventured Point. . . . . VS 5a
Access a ledge then weave up the arete above via mantelshelves.
FA. D.Leversidge 1983

16 Quark . . . . HVS 5b
Mantel twice up the left-hand side of the face then wander right along the ledge to a steep finishing move.
FA. Chris Craggs 1983

17 Graviton . . . . HVS 5c
Tackle the centre of the face via a couple of well protected but monstrous mantels.
FA. Colin Binks 2004

18 Meson . . . . VD
From a tricky 4b mantel (avoidable on the right) weave up the line of least resistance to a steep exit above the ledge.
FA. Peter Bamfield 1960

19 Lepton . . . . HS 4b
Hop onto the slab, climb the arete and the ensuing crack.
FA. Mike Snell 1989

20 Bandits in the Woods . . . . . . HVS 5a
Follow the thin crack to a roof and tough (avoidable) exit.
FA. D.Leversidge 1983

21 Spectacle . . . . S 4c
Mantel onto the slab and bridge the dirty groove to a choice of exits, outside or in.
FA. Mike Snell 1989

22 Side Effect E1 5b
The right arete of the recess leads to a tough exit.
FA. Bill Mckee 1978

23 Thalidomide E2 5c
The centre of the small buttress is another one that needs care.
FA. Paul Mitchell 1983

24 The Other Effect. E1 5c
The final offering here is the right arete of the buttress. Green holds and mediocre protection combine to cause stress.
FA. Simon Royston 1997

Descent

Descent

Beauty Slab
Peak Bouldering

Exodus - 50m

Sheffield Area
Ladybower Area
Stanage
Burbage Valley
Millstone Area
Derwent Edges
Chatsworth Area
Southern Crags

Exodus

An isolated buttresses which is well worth a look if you are after Orange Spot routes. The challenges are provided by some fine crack climbs. Easily combined with the adjacent Puss Buttress.

Approach (see map on page 135) - Best approached from the High Neb parking - 15 mins.

❶ Cheeky Little Number E2 5b
The left arete of the face sees little attention.
FA. Gary Gibson 1982

❷ Exodus . . . . HVS 5a
The left-hand crack from a niche gives steep jamming with a feeling of urgency despite its brevity.
FA. Alan McHardy 1959

❸ Deuteronomy . . . . HVS 5b
From the lowest point of the wall, climb the jamming crack then step left and take a brace of cracks. Hard work!
FA. John Allen 1974

❹ Leviticus . . . . HVS 5b
The best defined crack, just to the right of the centre of the wall, gives more steep and well-protected jamming.

❺ Missing Numbers . . . . HVS 5a
The rightmost crack in the wall is short but still steep.
FA. Graham Hoey 1981

❻ E.M.F. . . . . HVS 5a
The right arete of the face is not without interest.
FA. Gary Gibson 1979

Next is a square-cut tower with a trio of offerings.

❼ Treatment . . . . VS 5a
The left edge of the square-fronted tower across the gully is approached up easy rock and has one long reach.
FA. Gary Gibson 1979

❽ Sudoxe . . . . HVS 5b
The centre of the square-fronted tower is climbed pleasantly using some blisters. Avoid sneaking off right for the full effect.

❾ Radox . . . . S 4b
The right arete of the tower is the weakest of the trio.
FA. Dave Gregory 1992

From mid morning | 15 min | Windy

10m

Descent

← Meson - 50m

Sheffield Area | Ladybower Area | Stanage | Burbage Valley | Millstone Area | Derwent Edges | Chatsworth Area | Southern Crags

Twin Buttress and Meson
p.154

Cosmic Crack
p.158

Birthday Buttress
p.158

Travesties

p.159

Exodus

Puss

Puss

Pleasant fingery problems which are worth looking at if you have ticked the routes on the neighbour Exodus buttress.

Approach (see map on page 135) - Best approached from the High Neb parking - 15 mins.

10 Jam Good . . . . ☐ VD
The short crack on the left via some good jams.

11 Pup . . . . 🧗🪨 ☐ HVS 6a
The blunt left arete of the wall passing a couple of useful flakes.

12 Puss . . . . 🔄🧗 ☐ HVS 5c
The centre of the face has moves based around a bumpy boil!
FA. John Allen 1974

13 Kitten . . . . 🧗 ☐ VS 5b
Trend right and climb the right-hand side of the face.
FA. Al Parker 1959

14 Lucky . . . . 🧍 ☐ VS 5b
The right arete of the wall.
FA. David Simmonite 1991

15 The Cat Crawl . . . . ☐ S 4a
From a pedestal, hop onto the face and wander across to the left arete.

16 Ginger Tom . . . . . . 🪨🧗🧗 ☐ HVS 5b
The centre of the shorter wall. Blinkers help.

From mid morning | 15 min | Windy

Birthday Buttress

Cosmic Crack Area

A steep overhang-peppered buttress with a good collection of routes. Although short, most of them manage to feel quite hard for the grade. To the right, Birthday Buttress has a few of neglected outings.
Approach (see map on page 135) - The buttress is about 250m north (left - looking in) of High Neb.

❶ Pulse . . . . VS 4c
A short-lived crack on the far left is quite tricky if you are pure.
FA. Dave Gregory 1992

❷ Beanpod . . . . S 4a
The pod-shaped crack, then exit left or finish up the arete.
FA. Al Parker 1959

❸ X-ray . . . . HS 4b
A thin technical crack splitting the centre of the wall.
FA. Al Parker 1961

❹ Electron . . . . VS 5a
Bridge the groove and crack just left of the central roofs to a perplexing exit to easy ground.
FA. Alan Clarke 1964

❺ Quantum Crack . . . . HVS 5a
Climb the buttress, passing an overhang early on, to an awkward leftwards exit under the final roof. Intimidating but not too bad.
FA. Alan Clarke 1964

❻ Cosmic Crack . . . . VS 4c
The crack on the right gives good laybacking to a neat finale and is pleasantly low in the grade.
FA. Al Parker 1959

❼ Hale-Bopp E1 6a
Plugs a gap though not in a hugely satisfying way.
FA. Malc Baxter 1997

❽ Cosmos . . . . S 4a
The right arete, started from the right. Nothing special!
FA. Mike Snell 1989

Birthday Buttress
To the right is a small buttress.

❾ Birthday Buttress . . . . . . VS 4c
Hand-traverse out to the arete, climb to the ledge, then sneak around the left-hand end of the capping roof - spooky!
FA. Al Parker 1959

❿ Going Grey . . . . HVS 5a
A more direct version of *Birthday Buttress*.
FA. Paul Harrison 1996

⓫ 21 Today . . . . HVS 5c
The right arete of the buttress has a tricky start and finish. The sit-down start is a quality *f7A*.
FA. Martin Veale 1983

⓬ Angel in the Stars E1 5c
The side-wall is hard for the short.
FA. David Simmonite 1997

⓭ Life Begins at 40 . . . . HVS 5a
The next buttress, right of a big holly, is climbed rightwards.
FA. John Allen 1987

Sheffield Area · Ladybower Area · Stanage · Burbage Valley · Millstone Area · Derwent Edges · Chatsworth Area · Southern Crags

The Blurter - 30m ➞

Travesties

A pair walls of split by a deep chimney. The similarity between the two facets, especially the lines of *Travesties* and *The Knutter* is quite striking. The routes are short but intense and the area is usually pretty quiet - if High Neb is busy consider wandering over here.
Approach (see map on page 135) - The buttress is about 220m north (left looking in) of High Neb.

⑭ Little Things . . . . VS 6a
The tiny hanging roof crack. The grade is traditional and silly!
FA. Martin Boysen 1970s. Reclimbed and named by Chris Craggs 1980s

⑮ The Long and the Short. . . . . VS 5b
Boulder up the wall to a ledge and finish on the right.
FA. Chris Craggs (the long) Martin Veale (the short) 1996

⑯ Erica Micra . . . . S 4b
A micro-line just right of an easy flake.

⑰ Lamia Antics . . . . HVS 5b
Another short wall just left of a flake-crack.

⑱ Heather Crack . . . . HVD 4a
The pleasant, short-lived and long de-heathered crack.
FA. Barry Platt 1958

⑲ Flipside E4 6a
A bit of an eliminate with steady climbing to the break, a harrowing finish and not much in the way of gear. Fortunately escape is an easy option.
FA. Gabe Regan 1984

⑳ Travesties . . . . HVS 5b
Good moves lead into and up the shallow left-slanting groove in the centre of the wall.
FA. Robin Miller 1976

㉑ Timothy Twinkletoes E2 6a
Sketchy moves up the left-hand side of the face.
FA. Chris Hardy 1984

㉒ Pig's Ear E1 6a
Worthwhile, technical and tough on the tips. Use a series of tiny edges to sketch up the line just right of centre. *f6A+* above pads.
FA. Jonny Woodward 1978

㉓ Deep Chimney . . . . VD
The wide rift has tricky moves to pass the overhang.

㉔ Crew Pegs Diffs E3 6a
Climb the arete of *Deep Chimney* then move right to the hanging groove - hard. Improving holds are used to reach a wide break and an easy finish. A direct version straight over the bulging nose via a brittle flake is the neglected **Suitored, E4 6a**.
FA. Steve Bancroft 1977

㉕ An Embarrasment of Riches . f6B+
A direct start to *Crew Pegs Diffs*. E3 at least if you continue.
FA. Jon Fullwood 2010

㉖ No More Excuses . . . E4 6b
The centre of the fine wall gives a fine testing pitch. Difficult moves on poor footholds gain the thin overlap and a long reach from this (crux) gains a trio of pockets. Use these (hand-placed peg runner?) to make one more difficult move.
FA. Graham Hoey 1982

㉗ The Knutter . . . . HVS 5b
The blunt central arete of the wall has a thin flake crack running up it. Tricky moves (wires) lead to the beckoning holds, above which things rapidly ease off.
FA. Don Whillans 1962

㉘ Hearsay Crack E1 5a
Follow the right-slanting crack to its end and then continue up the bulging wall rightwards on green sloping holds. Protection is poor though it is possible (and sensible) to move left at the break to get good cams.

㉙ Pure Gossip . . . . HS 4b
The right-hand side of the face on shelving green holds.
FA. Gary Gibson 1979

The Blurter

The classic devious trip of *The Blurter* is the main attraction of this area but there are a couple of other gems to be found. *Overhanging Chimney* is a good one for those who think grit VDs are always a pushover.
Approach (see map on page 135) - The buttress is about 100m north (left - looking in) of High Neb.

❶ Emily May . . . . ☐ **S 4a**
The short leaning pillar away on the left.

❷ Undercoat . . . . ☐ **HS 4b**
The left arete of the pillar and a short wall on the right lead to a ledge. Shuffle round onto the north face and finish up the wall.
FA. Al Parker 1997. Nearly 40 years after he put up The Blurter!

❸ Overcoat . . . . ☐ **HVS 5c**
The left-hand pillar and parallel cracks splitting the roof.
FA. Chris Calow 1981

❹ Lucy's Slab . . . . ⟨1⟩ ☐ **HVS 5b**
The right-hand pillar and tricky scoop in the overhang.
FA. Al Parker 1978

❺ Stairway Crack . . . . ☐ **Mod**
The wide rift past a big chockstone.

❻ Jean's Route . . . . ☐ **VS 4c**
The right-hand crack leads to the slab - thread to the left. The slab is green and has a tricky move.
FA. Graham Fyffe 1978

❼ Meddle . . . . ⟨1⟩ ☐ **E2 5c**
Climb the arete on its right-hand side, until level with the base of *The Blurter* groove. Swing left around the arete and sprint to a large ledge, taking care with a loose block. Finish direct up steep rock. Other variations on the arete section are inferior.
FA. Jon de Montjoye 1976. Long credited to the 2nd man by mistake.

❽ Youth Meat . . . . ☐ **E4 6b**
The slab right of the arete and bulge above are taken by this counter-diagonal to *The Blurter*. Seldom climbed.
FA. Johnny Dawes 2000

From mid morning | 14 min | Windy

← Travesties - 30m

Sheffield Area · Ladybower Area · Stanage · Burbage Valley · Millstone Area · Derwent Edges · Chatsworth Area · Southern Crags

9 The Blurter . . . . HVS 5b
A fine but devious pitch - care with rope-work is required. Climb the chimney to an awkward traverse left under the roof. Gain the groove awkwardly and climb it to a step right. Pull over a bulge then trend left past the arete to the juggy north-facing wall.
Photo on page 134.
FA. Al Parker 1959

10 Overhanging Chimney . . HVD
The central chimney is a bit of a struggle. Easy climbing leads to the constricted central portion. This is most easily climbed facing left (or maybe right?) before things ease off.
FA. Harry Kelly 1915

11 Wolf Solent E4 5c
Rounded and bold. Start on the right and teeter leftwards up the slab until just right of the chimney. Pull through the overlap, rightwards (good runners at last) then back left, with difficulty and a poor pocket. Continue delicately up the slab to a large ledge and easy finish. A direct start is a bolder **5c**.
FA. Martin Berzins 1978

12 Typhoon Direct E3 6a
Link *Wolf Solent* with *Typhoon* by a short taxing sequence.
FA. Paul Clark 1982

13 Typhoon . . . . VS 4c
Follow the square groove just left of the arete to half-height then step left around the arete and climb a curving crack to a sloping ledge. Finish up rounded rock above.
FA. Al Parker 1959

14 Aries . . . . S 4b
Start as for *Typhoon* but continue up the groove to an airy and tricky, bulging exit. There is good gear where it matters.
FA. Al Parker 1957

15 Three Calm Men E1 5b
The delicate right arete of the buttress. A side-runner lowers the grade and the grip factor by a notch.
FA. Malc Baxter 1997

18m

Descent

Fate - 20m

Sheffield Area | Ladybower Area | Stanage | Burbage Valley | Millstone Area | Derwent Edges | Chatsworth Area | Southern Crags

Sheffield Area

Ladybower Area

Stanage

Burbage Valley

Millstone Area

Derwent Edges

Chatsworth Area

Southern Crags

Fate and Youth

A pair of pleasant slabby faces that are always popular, mainly because of easy-angled rock and a reasonable collection of lower-grade climbs on really great rock.
Approach (see map on page 135) - The area is less than a one minute walk to the left of the ever-popular High Neb section of the cliff.

The epitome of Stanage for many - you, a piece of rock and solitude. Will Birkett balances up *Rinty* (VS 5a) - *opposite* - typical of the superb micro-routes scattered along this part of the edge.

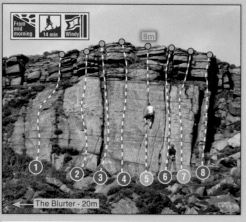

The Blurter - 20m →

1 Pleasant Slab . . . . [ ] VD
The (almost) pleasant slab on the left.
FA. Bruce Goodwin 1993

2 Ono . . . . [ ] S 4a
The left-hand slab and juggy bulge.
FA. Brian Cropper 1976

3 Uno Cracks . . . . [ ] Diff
The main crack splitting the left-hand side of the slab.

4 Fate . . . . [ ] E2 5c
The centre of the pocketed slab is especially taxing for the
short - beware the final reachy moves. Gear is minimal!
FA. Gary Gibson 1978

5 Rinty . . . . [ ] VS 5a
The thin cracks. Gear is a fiddle. *Photo opposite.*
FA. Clive Rowland 1961

6 Duo Crack Climb . . . . [ ] VD
The parallel cracks on the right-hand side of the slab.
FA. Harry Kelly 1921

7 Solo Slab . . . . [ ] VS 5a
Good moves up the slab. There are easily-placed side-runners.
FA. Dave Gregory 1992

8 Staircase Rib . . . . [ ] Diff
Wobble up the jutting fin on the far right.
FA. Dave Gregory 1992

10m across the slope to the right is a similar slab.

9 Side Plate . . . . [ ] S 4a
Pull over the small roof and balance up the rib.
FA. Dave Gregory 1992

10 Ice Cream Flakes . . . . [ ] HVD
The flakes on the right-hand side of the buttress are awkward.
FA. Dave Gregory 1992

11 Warm Afternoon . . . . [ ] VD
Start up the left arete then move right to the centre of the wall.
FA. Dave Gregory 1992

12 Frosty . . . . [ ] Diff
The cracks and open groove running up the left-hand side of the
right-hand slab.

13 Icy Crack. . . . . [ ] VS 4c
Good climbing up the shallow cracks in the centre of the slab.
FA. Bill McKee 1978

14 Point Five Crack . . . . [ ] VS 5a
Thin cracks right of centre are best with blinkers.
FA. James Thomas 1989

15 Youth . . . . [ ] VD
The deepening cracks in the right-hand side of the slab.

16 Mirror Hopping Days . . . . . . [ ] Diff
The ramp and slab on the far right conclude this section.
FA. Lee Bower 1978. Also claimed as Old Man in 2000.

High Neb - 30m →

1 Way Fruitsome Experience . . 🖐 ☐ HVS 5c
The short tough wall on the far left.
FA. John Allen 1986

2 Gunter . . . . 🖐 ☐ VS 4c
The bent crack is nice enough, but over too soon.
FA. T.Norcliffe 1966

3 Straight Crack . . . . 🏃1🏃 👐 ☐ HS 4b
Follow the straight crack as it gradually widens. Difficulties escalate to a wide and awkward exit. Big gear is useful.

4 Eric's Eliminate . . . . 🏃1🏃 ☐ S 4a
Take the short crack in the flat face and the continuation above. Only spoilt by its proximity to *Twisting Crack*.

5 Twisting Crack . . . . 🏃2🏃 🖐 ☐ S 4a
A fine climb, steep and intimidating, but on good holds. Climb the deep groove to the left edge of the roof (thread). Step left onto the arete and pull hard to gain the juggy cracks above.
FA. Harry Kelly 1915

6 Kelly's Overhang . . . 🏃3🏃 💪 🖐 ☐ HVS 5b
An amazing ascent for its day - it still sees much floundering. From *Twisting Crack*, make awkward moves to a poor rest on the block under the roof. Bridge right along the lip and make a hard move up and right to reach holds on the wall. Finish easily.
FA. Morley Wood 1926

7 Inaccessible Slab . . . . 🖐 ☐ S 4c
Climb the short slab with a tricky move to stand in the horizontal break. The green groove just to the left is the easiest way off.
FA. Henry Bishop and friends 1912

High Neb

High Neb offers superb climbing in a majestic location and is rarely as busy as the Popular End of the crag. There are classics of all grades to go at here.
Approach (see map on page 135) - From the High Neb (Dennis Knoll) parking, walk up the gravel track then cross either of two stiles on the left before flogging up through the heather to the crag.

8 Mouthpiece . . . . 🏃🏃 💪 ☐ E1 5c
An excellent counter-diagonal that is often overlooked. From the top of *Inaccessible Slab* monkey leftwards across the roof to rest on *Kelly's* block then finish direct with difficulty.
FA. Steve Bancroft 1973

9 Smelly Roof . . . . . 🏃1🏃 💪 🖐 ☐ E4 6a
A tough line hugging the right edge of the big roof - creaky!
FA. Paul Mitchell 2005

10 Inaccessible Crack Direct 🏃2🏃 💪 ☐ VS 4c
Climb the left arete of the recess and the crack to the foot of a groove which gives a steep and exciting finish. Traversing left along the prominent break is the exciting **Overflow, E1 5b**.

11 The Beautician . . . . 🏃2🏃 🖐 ☐ E3 5c
From *Inaccessible Crack*, step left above the roof and climb to the break. Finish up the precarious right-trending scoop.
FA. Steve Bancroft 1984

12 Inaccessible Crack . . . . 🏃3🏃 ☐ VS 4c
Devious but also excellent. Follow the crack sprouting from the right edge of the recess to its end then traverse left to finish as for the *Direct* variation.
FA. Harry Kelly 1915

Descent

16m

Youth - 30m

Sheffield Area | Ladybower Area | Stanage | Burbage Valley | Millstone Area | Derwent Edges | Chatsworth Area | Southern Crags

13 Impossible Slab.... E3 5c
A fine climb with a worrying finale. Start up the short crack and make hard moves (especially for the short) to easier ground. Lace the break, then teeter up the final slab by ever more committing moves. Side-runners lower the E-grade.

14 Eckhard's Arete .... HS 4b
The left arete of the chimney is a polished eliminate.

15 Eckhard's Chimney..... VD
Squirm the tight chimney. Things ease once past the blocks.
FA. Ms Eckhard, early 1910s

16 Zen Boy E7 6c
The left arete of *Quietus*. A long leap from the chimney gains poor holds near the lip where a desperate mantel/layaway sequence lurks.
FA. Johnny Dawes 2003

17 Quietus............. E2 5c
A superb roof climb; high in the grade. Climb a shallow groove to below the roof. Place solid runners then head out via good flakes to the lip. Getting established round the lip is the crux. Linking this with the *Right-hand* is **Quietus Middle Leg, E3 6a**.
Photo on page 173.
FA. Joe Brown 1954. It had previously been aided/top-roped by Pete Biven.

18 Norse Corner Climb .... HS 4c
An ancient tester. Pull onto the slab at a big pocket, head right to delicate moves to the flat ledge. Finish up the polished corner.
FA. Henry Bishop and friends, early 1910s

19 Silence............. HVS 5b
Weave around the line of the previous climb, devious and varied.
FA. Ed Wood 1980

20 Quietus Right-hand E4 6a
From the large ledge on *Norse Corner Climb*, make a committing move to the hand-traverse leading out to the arete. Scary but all over in a flash - or a blur - if you get it right!
FA. Ian Maisey 1981

21 Kelly's Variation .... S 4a
A variation start to *Norse Corner Climb*. Begin at a shallow scoop and climb to the first horizontal break, then move left to a shallow groove and up this to a good flat ledge. Finish up the slippery corner.
FA. Harry Kelly late 1910s

22 King Kong........... E3 6a
Bridge the shallow scoop up to the overhang, and reach over for a good hold. Then flick into the crucial mantelshelf, though the tall will probably just topple over backwards.
FA. Al Parker 1978

23 The Logic Book . E3 5c
The blunt arete is fingery and bold, especially for the short who will find it more like E4 6a, or even harder.
FA. Gary Gibson 1981

24 Sogines .... HVS 5b
The flakes just left of the corner give a quick sprint to a cave - beware loose blocks here. Finish to the left.
FA. Gary Gibson 1981

From mid morning | 12 min | Windy

16m

25 Neb Corner . . . . ☐ VD
The big angle on awkward polished holds leads to meadows.
FA. Henry Bishop and friends, about 1910

26 Cent . . . . ☐ E1 5b
Solo the narrow slab right of the corner. HVS with a side-runner.
FA. Gary Gibson 1978

27 Boyd's Crack . . . . ☐ VD
The crack right of the corner eases with height but becomes awkward to protect. A bit of a big boot route.
FA. W.A.Boyd early 1910s

28 Following On . . . . ☐ VS 5a
A tricky and often green line 1m right of the crack.
FA. W.A.Boyd early 1910s

29 Limbo . . . . ☐ S 4a
Start right of the easy break and climb to it, then step left to finish via the poorly-protected slab and ramp.
FA. Chris Craggs 1978

30 Lost Soul . . . . ☐ S 4a
The slab just left of *Tango Crack* soon eases after a tricky start.

31 Tango Crack . . . . ☐ VD
The straight crack; an awkward initial section but it eases above.
FA. F.C.Aldous, early 1910s

32 Tango Buttress . . . . ☐ HS 5a
A good slab with thin initial moves. Continue past another delicate section, which leads to the curving finishing flake. Not too well protected in its upper reaches.
FA. Fred Pigott and friends, early 1920s

33 Where did my Tan Go? . . ☐ HVS 5a
Climb just left of the arete to a break, move right and layback the arete. Low in the grade though harder for the short.
FA. Chris Craggs 1989

34 High Neb Buttress Arete . . . . ☐ S 4a
Bridge up and left out of the gloomy recess then move up and out right to access the arete. Finish up this.
FA. Bill Birch 2003

35 High Neb Buttress . . . . . Top 50 ☐ VS 4c
An ancient classic. Climb the rib under the centre of the buttress to a ledge (hard for the short). Up then right to climb the centre of the slab by a crucial mantel. Continue up the airy arete.
FA. Ivar Berg 1914

36 High Neb Buttress Variations . ☐ VS 5a
Climb the tough thin crack then continue in the same line to the crux of the original. Move left (good small cams) then mantel to better holds and continue up the left-hand side of the face.

37 High Neb Edge . . . . . ☐ HVS 5c
Climb the shallow groove just right of the arete to the horizontal break on the left. Continue up the flake until forced onto the front face. Finish easily.

38 The Crypt Trip . . . . . ☐ E6 6c
Fingery and bold. Start under the right end of a thin overlap, climb up and left through the notch by a big reach, or undercuts and thin flakes, to the first break. Safer, but difficult moves, lead past a pocket to the main horizontal break and an easier finish.
FA. Ron Fawcett 1983

Scramble descent

18m

24 25 26 27 28 29 30 31 32 33 34 35 36 37 38 39 40

39 Old Friends . . . . Top 50 E4 6a
A classic Stanage E4 giving a bold outing. From the bottom right-hand corner of the face, climb a tiny groove to a poor rest. Swing left and pull up with difficulty (a small cam in the base of the flake is hard to place) then make the crucial layback/stretch to reach the deep horizontal break. Move right and use a good pocket to gain the easier final wall.
FA. John Allen 1973

40 The Dalesman . . . . HVS 5a
The beckoning break gives a good pump with runners galore.
FA. Roger Greatrick 1983

41 Ami . . . . Mod
The amiable corner-crack is okay for an easy one.

42 Mantelshelf Climb . . . . . VD
Climb the slabby face just right of the corner by a series of mild mantel moves. Finish up the shallow groove.
FA. Fred Pigott and friends, early 1920s

43 It's a Cracker . . . . S 4b
The centre of the slabby face has an awkward well-protected move to enter the thin crack. Finish up steeper rock.
FA. Jim Rubery 1997

44 Sneezy . . . . HS 5a
The right-hand arete has a tricky little move passing the nose.
FA. Chris Craggs 1996

45 Little Slab . . . . VD
The narrow slab in the back left corner of the next recess.

46 Typical Grit . . . . S 4a
Climb the delicate narrow slab on the right-hand side of the bay to easier rock. Poorly protected and quite sketchy.
FA. Fred Pigott and friends, early 1920s

47 Cave Buttress . . . . S 4b
Start just to the left of the cave and climb, passing perched flakes with care, to below the overhang. Move right past the arete and finish up the juggy face a little further to the right.
FA. Fred Pigott and friends, early 1920s

48 High and Wild E3 5c
Follow *Cave Buttress* to ledges then launch across the roof by a long reach and a ladder of jugs. Harder for the short.
FA. Chris Craggs 1985

49 Jeepers Creepers . . . . . . HVS 5b
Follow *Cave Buttress* to the roof then attack the short-lived hanging jamming crack. A lot harder for wall-bred climbers!
Photo on page 3.
FA. Joe Brown 1958

50 Caved In . . . . VS 4c
A direct line up the right side of the arete to an awkward finish.
FA. Chris Craggs 1996

51 Cave Buttress Right-hand . . . S 4b
Start right of the large fallen blocks and climb the wide crack and final steep wall on generally good holds.

52 Teenage Lobotomy E1 5b
Harrowing climbing up the wall via wide breaks and slopers.
FA. Gary Gibson 1981

53 Fallen Archangel f6C
Situated on a block in front of the crag. From sitting, pull up leftwards along the fallen arete and heave onto the top slab.

Descent

Titanic - 180m

Sheffield Area | *Ladybower Area* | *Stanage* | *Burbage Valley* | *Millstone Area* | *Derwent Edges* | *Chatsworth Area* | *Southern Crags*

Titanic and Blockhead

The first of a series of small but interesting buttresses lost in the wilderness between High Neb and The Long Causeway, around 180m right of High Neb. Most of the routes are worth a look and you would be unlucky to have to queue at either of the buttresses covered here.

Approach (see map on page 135) - The crags are best approached from the High Neb parking, by walking up the Causeway to reach the good horizontal track that runs under the edge. Narrow paths lead up through the bracken to each buttress.

1 Barmy Brian's Flake Crack . . 🖐️ VS 5a
The awkward flake crack on the left.
FA. Brian Rossiter 1996

2 Gnat's Slab . . . . ◤ Diff 3c
Use the crack to gain a heathery ledge then take the easiest line.
FA. Al Parker 1959

3 Gnat's Slab Direct . . . . . 🖐️ ◤ HS 4b
The centre of the slab is bold. The heather ledge is a nuisance.

4 Gnat's Slab Arete . . . . . . 🔆 🖐️ HS 4c
The rib is tricky low down and poorly protected throughout.

5 Marie Celeste . . . . 🖐️ ◤ E1 5b
Climb directly up the left-hand side of the face; a lonely experience and usually a bit dirty too.
FA. Gabe Reagan 1984

6 Lusitania . . . . 🔆 🏃 HS 4b
Climb the gloomy groove to pass the tricky bulge. The direct finish on sloping holds is best, though some of them are rather creaky. Otherwise head right, though this is also a bit loose.
FA. Al Parker 1958

7 QE2 . . . . 🔆 🧗 VS 5a
The angular arete leads to a hanging groove. Exit right from this.
FA. Bill Birch 1972

8 Titanic . . . . 🔆 🔧 VS 4b
A fine little route, varied, sustained and with an exiting finish. Climb the groove then traverse right to the arete. The moves to pass this are unlikely but soon lead to the final juggy crack.
FA. Al Parker 1958

9 Gypsy Moth . . . . 🔆 🗺️ ◤ E1 5b
The tricky pocketed slab leads to the bulges, head left from here.
FA. Malc Baxter 1997

10 Titanic Direct . . . . . 🔆 ◤ ✊ HVS 5a
Varied and excellent. Climb the right arete, then the groove of the regular route followed by the flying arete above. Spectacular.
Al Parker (the finish) 1967. FA. Gary Gibson (the start) 1979

Descent

14m

← High Neb - 180m

Across the slope is a squat buttress and jutting flake. These are the main attractions, though a slab to the right is worth a look.

11 Miss World . . . . **VS 4b**
The flaky left arete of the face leads to heather. No beauty!
FA. Doug Kerr 1985

12 Mr Universe **E3 6a**
The centre of the face has taxing moves on tiny holds.
FA. Gary Gibson 1979

13 Angus . . . . **S 4a**
The narrowing rift has hidden delights but helmets don't fit!
FA. Al Parker 1959

14 Sinew Stretch . . . . **HVS 5c**
Balance and stretch up the left arete of the block. Nice moves.
FA. Bill Sutton 1978

15 Blockhead Direct **E1 5b**
The right arete also has some lovely moves, the central crack helps with holds and maybe a runner too.
FA. Richard McHardy 1959

16 Kryton . . . . **HVS 5a**
The arete can also be climbed on its right-hand side.

17 Headbanger **E1 5c**
Access the hanging book-end from the right.
FA. Keith Ashton 1985

18 Solomon's Seal . . . . **f7C+**
The centre of the wall using a poor flake. The sit-down start is **Solomon Grundy**, *f8A*.

19 The Jester **f7B**
Grab edges and go for the top. A low start is a grade harder.

20 Prairie Dog . . . . . . **HVS 5b**
The left-hand crack has a good finger-jam and a good runner, though using both at the same time can be tricky.
FA. Jim Rubery 1992

21 Slabenger **f7A**
The thin slab, avoiding the cracks.

22 Scavenger . . . . **VS 4c**
The thin crack splitting the centre of the slab is neat.
FA. S.Thorpe 1977

23 Scraps . . . . **VS 5a**
The right-hand line on the slab starting up the dark streak.
FA. Chris Craggs 1985

24 Sneaking Sally Through the Alley
. . . . **VS 4c**
Take the diagonal seam leftwards across the slab to a late crux.
Photo on page 28.
FA. Keith Ashton 1985

Descent (awkward)

13m

8m

From mid morning — 14 min — Windy

Left and Right - 50m ➞

Sheffield Area

Ladybower Area

Stanage

Burbage Valley

Millstone Area

Derwent Edges

Chatsworth Area

Southern Crags

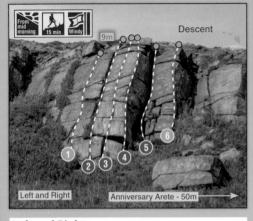

9m

Descent

Left and Right

Anniversary Arete - 50m

Anniversary Arete

The tower of Anniversary Arete has a small amount of good climbing in the middle of nowhere and one excellent headline route well worth calling in for.

Approach (see map on page 135) - Walk up the Long Causeway to a good horizontal track that runs back left under the edge at a stile. Narrow paths lead up through the bracken to each buttress - awkward in high summer.

7 49th Parallel . . . . VS 5b
Make hard moves out left to ledges then climb the thin crack.
FA. Bill Birch 1972

8 Parallel Cracks . . . . VS 4b
The converging parallel cracks give a pleasant pumpy pitch.
FA. Al Parker 1959

9 Beast of Endcliffe . . . E2 6a
The narrow wall has some intense moves.
FA. Percy Bishton 1985

10 Anniversary Arete E1 5b
The gem. Thin cracks lead to tricky moves to access the slab.
FA. Al Parker 1959

11 Grain of Truth E3 6b
Gaining and progressing up the hanging groove is hard work!
FA. Chris Calow 1981

Across the slope is a cracked face with a quarried feel.

12 Petazautte. . . . . VS 5a
The left line is poorly protected and vegetated - a bit rubbish really but as we had the space, at least you know what it is.
FA. Bruce Goodwin 1994

13 Genesis . . . . HVS 5a
Much better climbing up the central crack - nice.
FA. Paul Nunn 1959

14 Magazine . . . . VS 4c
Another decent little pitch up the right-hand crack.
FA. Gary Gibson 1979

15 Self-Propelled . . . . VS 5a
Aim yourself at the thin right-trending crack, then finish direct.
FA. Bruce Goodwin 1994

Left and Right

Roughly halfway between Blockhead Buttress and Anniversary Arete is a small buttress with a conspicuous central arete.

1 Sinister . . . . VS 4b
The pleasant slab on the left is a bit bold.
FA. Dave Gregory 1992

2 The Wide Crack . . . . Diff
Wide and shrubby - enough said!

3 Nice One. . . . . VD
Pleasant moves but a bit of an eliminate.
FA. Dave Gregory 1992

4 Left . . . . VD
Lovely. Pity it is so short.
FA. Doug Kerr 1985

5 Corner Crack . . . . VD
The awkward angle.
FA. Martin Whittaker 1989

6 Right . . . . HS 4b
The last line here has a couple of nice moves.
FA. Doug Kerr 1985

Descent 10m

10m

Fun in the Sun - 25m

Fun in the Sun

A series of short buttresses spread across the hillside. Many of these routes are being strangled by the holly trees and could do with a bit more traffic.

Approach (see map on page 135) - Walk up the Causeway to a good horizontal track that runs back left under the edge at a stile. Narrow paths lead up through the bracken to each buttress - awkward in high summer.

16 Hold Your Breath . . . . **S 4b**
Access the heathery ledge then climb the front of the slightly suspect flake to a tricky move accessing the final arete.
FA. Chris Craggs 1997

17 Flaked Out . . . . **Diff**
The flaky cracks are pleasant enough after the initial moves.
FA. Dave Gregory 1997

Across the slope is a narrow buttress with a tall holly tree on its right-hand side.

18 Heather Heaven . . . . **HS 4c**
The heathery crack and ledge lead to a better finish.
FA. Chris Craggs 1997

19 Reach for the Sky . . . . **HVS 5b**
The tricky lower wall (bloody tree) with a tricky reach for the break then nice moves up the thin cracks and arete above.
FA. Chris Craggs 1997

20 Shuffle . . . . **S 4a**
An awkward layback move gains a ledge on the arete. Shuffle round left and finish up the arete.
FA. Dave Gregory 1997

21 Deal . . . . **HVS 5c**
Start as for the last route but stick with the right-hand face.
FA. Bill Birch 2004

22 Short and Sweet . . . . **HVD**
The short slab on the left side of the face.
FA. Dave Gregory 1997

23 Fun in the Sun . . . . **HS 4b**
From a block gain a ledge, step left and balance up the arete. The battle with the tree is the main problem here.
FA. Chris Craggs 1997

24 D-Day Remembered **E2 5c**
The blunt arete by the holly is sketchy to start and then balancy.
FA. Bill Birch 2004

25 Grunt . . . . **VS 5a**
The awkward widening crack on the right.
FA. Chris Craggs 1997

26 Teeter . . . . **VS 4c**
Teeter up the arete to an overlap, then step right to finish. Rather spoilt by the tree.
FA. Chris Craggs 1997

27 Squash . . . . **VS 4c**
The central line on the slab - delicate.
FA. Bill Birch 2004

28 Squat . . . . **VS 5a**
The right arete with a tough move through the bulge.
FA. Chris Craggs 1997

Creepy and Crawly

Another tiny pair of buttresses between High Neb and the Long Causeway - this one is 20m left of the more recognisable Broken Buttress with its large rowan tree.
Approach (see map on page 135) - Walk up the Long Causeway as it bears away right to access the good horizontal track that runs back left under the edge at a stile. Narrow paths lead up through the bracken to each buttress, which can be awkward in high summer.

① Wall and Slab . . . . 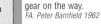 **HS 5a**
A long term VD with a baffling start, especially for the short. Climb past the overlap to the roof then swing left to access a ledge. The slab up and right is much easier.

② Dope Test **E3 6a**
The stacked overhangs of the tough nose are approached from right or left. The exit is tricky.
FA. Martin Veale 1990

③ Cracked Wall Direct . . . . **HVS 5a**
The cracks just right of the arete are climbed trending rightwards, generally on good holds and jams. Once the wider crack is reached it is in the bag.

④ Cracked Wall. . . . . **HS 4c**
A start up the wider crack to the right eases things, though it is a bit wide and awkward. Above this, amble up the arete.

⑤ Creepy . . . . **S 4a**
Creep up the narrow slab and don't expect much in the way of gear on the way.
FA. Peter Bamfield 1962

⑥ Cringe . . . . **VS 4c**
The left arete of the next slab has a high and delicate crux, fortunately next to a good wire.
FA. Gary Gibson 1979

⑦ Crawly . . . . **VD**
The centre of the slab leads pleasantly to a mild jamming crack.

⑧ Creepy Crawly . . . . **HS 4b**
Hop onto the arete from the right then follow it with balancy moves at half-height. A direct start over the bulge is *f5+*.
FA. Keith Ashton 1984

⑨ Meaty Bugs. . . . . **HS 4b**
Climb blocks and the arete above to reach the short jamming crack in the right wall.
FA. David Simmonite 1997

Sheffield Area

Ladybower Area

Stanage

Burbage Valley

Millstone Area

Derwent Edges

Chatsworth Area

Southern Crags

The classic roof climb of *Quietus* (E2 5c) - *page 165* - on High Neb, Stanage North, one of the original Top Ten Extremes on Stanage. Although not the serious undertaking it once was, it is still no pushover. Photo: Adam Long

TICKLIST
The Original and Best 'Top 10'

The 1964 Blue Stanage guidebook had 10 routes graded 'Extremely Severe' on Stanage; the highest available at the time. They were considered cutting edge routes often of great seriousness. Times change but doing them all in a day would be a nice outing for a competent team.

☐ **Impossible Slab, E3** *(165)*. A harrowing finish - a side-runner used to be the norm but isn't allowed nowadays!

☐ **Quietus, E2** *(165)*. Passing the lip is a real baffler. We could tell you how to do it, but where's the fun in that?

☐ **Count's Buttress, E2** *(181)*. Tricky for the short.

☐ **Fern Groove, E2** *(188)*. Described with a bit of aid originally, accessing the groove is still a tricky one.

☐ **Esso Extra, E1** *(196)*. Short but brutal. A meat grinder!

☐ **Left Unconquerable, E1** *(214)*. A great first Extreme. Hard enough but with no nasty surprises.

☐ **Millsom's Minion, E1** *(207)*. Now the easiest of this bunch. A good cam removes the mind-withering run-out.

☐ **Desperation, E1** *(242)*. The start has a real stopper move and that isn't even the real crux.

☐ **The Dangler, E2** *(257)*. A horizontal grovel for most though the lanky can yard past the nasty bit.

☐ **The Tippler, E1** *(257)*. Feels full-on at the grade, sustained and strenuous even before you reach the crux.

The Blurter
p.160

High Neb
p.164

Titanic
p.168

Blockhead
p.168

Anniversary Arete
p.170

Fun in the Sun
p.171

The Buckstone
Peak Bouldering

The Causeway track

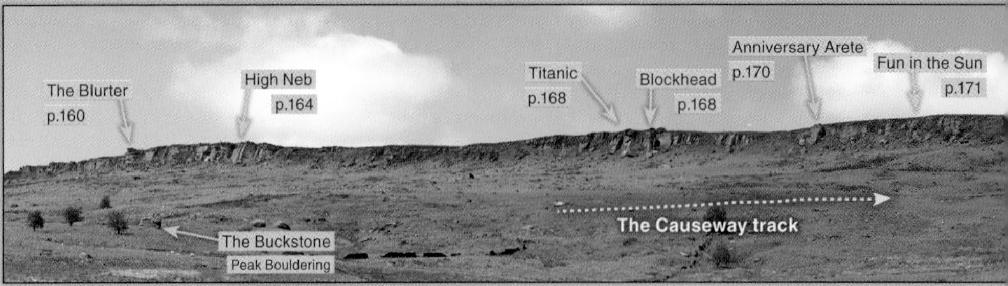

Broken Buttress

Broken Buttress is recognised by its prominent rowan tree. The crag is rather gritty, though a little more traffic has improved things.

Approach (see map on page 135) - The buttress is best approached from the High Neb parking, by walking up the Causeway past it, to access the good horizontal track the runs back north under the edge. Narrow paths lead up through the bracken to the buttress.

1 **Broken Arete** . . . . VS 4c
On the far left is a rib with heather fields. It is not as bad as it looks though it does look pretty poor!
FA. Paul Durkin 1997

2 **Dissuader** . . . . HS 4b
A green start (thread) leads to a ledge then on to better things.
FA. Dave Gregory 1992

3 **Darthuader** E1 6a
A bit of an eliminate, though with some good and escapable moves, up the narrow face.
FA. Simon Royston 1997

4 **Persuader** . . . . HVS 5a
The right arete is hardest at the bulge. Avoiding the boulder in the chimney is tricky, using it is more like **VS 4c**. Be aware of a loose block near the top.
FA. Al Parker 1972

5 **Burgess Crack** . . . . Diff
The bouldery rift by burrowing beneath the chockstones.

6 **Outside Exit.** . . . . HS 4b
Tackle all the jammed boulders by the outside route.
FA. Chris Craggs 1998

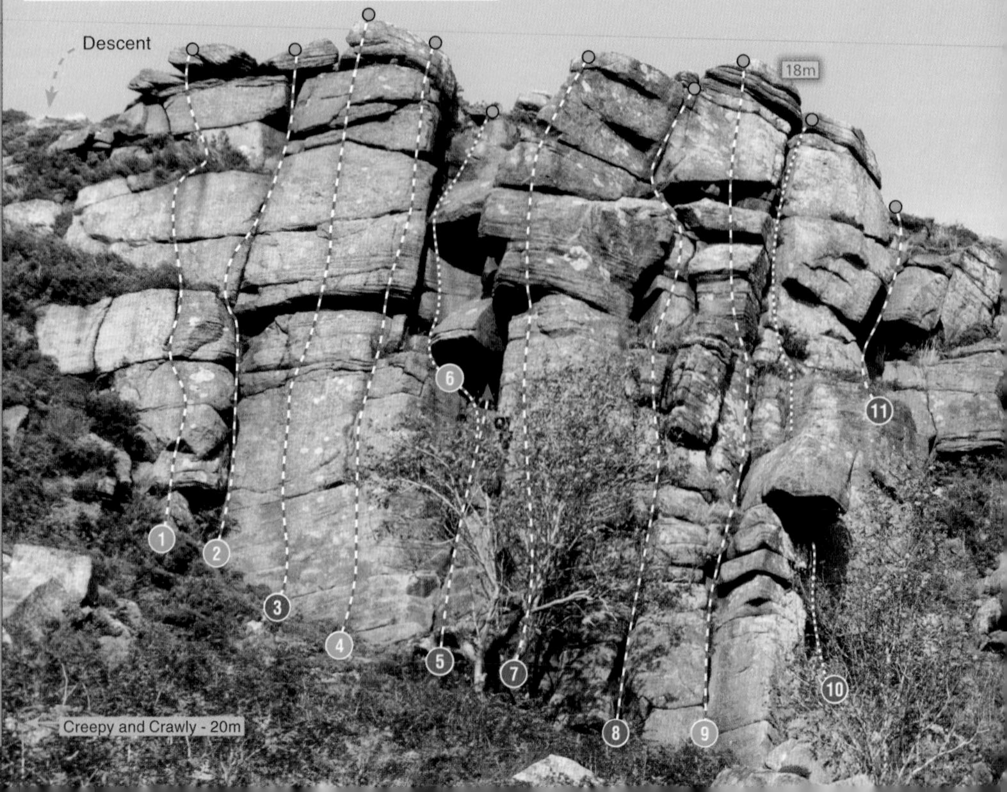

Descent

18m

Creepy and Crawly - 20m

Creepy and Crawly
p.172

Cock 'O The Rock
Peak Bouldering

Enclosure Buttress
p.176

Meninblack
p.177

Centurion's Slab - p.177

Broken Buttress

Causeway Slabs
Peak Bouldering

The Causeway track

7 **Pertinacious** . . . . ⬛🫀 [ ] **E2 5b**
The arete right of the chimney has a bold crux.

8 **Broken Buttress** . . . . 🔲23 [ ] **HVD 4a**
The long crack system is a fine climb, interesting and well protected. There are harder options at the start.

9 **Broken In** . . . . 🔲21 🖐 [ ] **HS 4c**
The groove and crack lead to a tough finale up the short steep headwall. Quite tricky if you stick rigorously to the line.
FA. Dave Gregory 1992

10 **Broken Groove**. . . . . 🔲 🖐 👐 [ ] **S 4b**
The right-hand groove leads to a taxing beached-whale landing on a ledge then better climbing above.

11 **Good Friday Corner** . . . . . . 👐 [ ] **S 4a**
On the far right-hand side of the buttress is a steep green groove. Another member of the 'bit better than it looks' club.
FA. Steve Clark 2003

12 **Pseudo-Intellectual Claptrap** . . . [ ] **HS 4a**
A tricky move to get going then steady away.
FA. Steve Clark 2003

13 **Jenny Wren**. . . . . [ ] **VD**
The short arete to a finish on the right.
FA. Ian Smith 1997

14 **Blown Away** . . . . 🖐 [ ] **HVS 5c**
The slab has a couple of tricky moves.
FA. Malc Baxter 1997

15 **Blow Out**. . . . . 🔲 🮲 [ ] **HVS 5c**
Yard, or more likely, leap the start then amble onwards. **5c** to the second break.
FA. Chris Craggs 1983

16 **Blow Peter** . . . . 🔲21 🖐 [ ] *f6C*
Start up *Blow Out* but move right along a break, then up a crack.

17 **Blown Drie** . . . . ⬛🖐 [ ] **E1 5c**
A line up the right edge of the face - delicate to a tricky mantel.
FA. Paul Durkin 1997

18 **Full Blown Finish**. . . . . . 🫀⬛ [ ] **E1 5b**
The tiny hanging slab is approached from the left. Don't fall!
FA. Warren Trippet 1995

19 **Prowler** . . . . ✊ [ ] **HVS 5a**
A very neglected line up the steep right wall of the prow high on the right edge of this area.
FA. Chris Calow 1981

Descent

10m

Enclosure Buttress - 100m ➡

From mid morning | 15 min | Windy

Enclosure Buttress

The iron fencing that gave the buttress its name has almost all gone now. The routes are not the best but it will certainly be quiet! Unfortunately the right-hand side is becoming smothered by the big holly tree.

Approach (see map on page 135) - The buttress is best approached from the High Neb parking, by walking up the Causeway until right under it. Narrow paths lead up steeply to the buttress.

❶ Bolt Buttress . . . . 🔲 S 4b
Climb the rib and wall to the left.
FA. Jim Rubery 1992

❷ Warm September . . . . . . 🔲 🐾 HVS 5a
Meander up the slabby face, left, right then left again. Bold.
FA. Dave Gregory 1992

❸ Enclosure Crack . . . . 🔲 Diff
A worthwhile easier route with good protection along the way.
FA. Al Parker 1959

❹ Mantelpiece . . . . 🔲 VS 5a
Mantel away up the buttress towards its left side - hard work.
FA. Bill Birch 1972

❺ Central Chimney . . . . 🔲 Diff
The chimney is entered awkwardly and followed more easily.
FA. Al Parker 1959

❻ Central Buttress . . . . 🔲 VS 5a
Nice and varied. Step up and trend out right to pass the roof then climb the bulge leftwards by a powerful pull to access the contrasting slab above. Pad up this paying homage to *Three Pebble Slab*.
FA. Al Parker 1959

❼ Central Buttress Direct . . 🔲 f6C
Tackle the bulge past hard moves at the lip.
FA. Gary Gibson 1981

❽ Iain's Prow . . . . 🔲 f6C
Jump to the lip, then finish out right, or left at *f7A+*.

❾ Centrepiece . . . . 🔲 VS 4c
Gain the right arete of the buttress from the green gully.
FA. Chris Calow 1981

❿ Holly Gully . . . . 🔲 Mod
The green block-filled gully to a steeper exit.
FA. Al Parker 1959

The next few routes have become ever more awkward to access as the holly has prospered. They are still worth a look, but only if you don't mind feeling a bit of a prick.

⓫ The Graduate . . . . 🔲 E1 5c
From behind the holly, climb to the deep break then balance into the scoop above. Finish direct.
FA. Chris Lawson 1977

⓬ Countess Buttress . . . . 🔲 VS 4c
Climb diagonally right all the way out to the arete and finish up this in a fine position.
FA. Al Parker 1960

⓭ Haze . . . . 🔲 HVS 4c
From right of the tree, pull through the roof and climb to the break. Continue carefully up the face above.
FA. Gary Gibson 1981

⓮ Four Winds, Eight Directions . 🔲 E4 6a
The main arete of the buttress gives a fine pitch where some power is useful.
FA. Gary Gibson 1981

Descent

14m

Cock 'O The Rock
Peak Bouldering

Broken Buttress - 100m

15 Slanting Chimney. . . . . HVD 4a
The shallow leaning groove in the right wall.
FA. Al Parker 1959

16 Keith's Crack . . . . VS 5a
The teasing thin crack splitting the left edge of the overlap.
FA. Keith Taylor 1959

17 Arsenic Poisoning . . . . HVS 5b
Another tester through the middle of the overlap.
FA. Gary Gibson 1981

18 Head over Heels E3 6a
Climb the hanging arete with difficulty, heels over head maybe?
FA. Doug Kerr 1985

19 Letter-box . . . . HVD 4a
The green groove then tricky moves left into the upper crack.
FA. Al Parker 1959

20 Europa E4 5c
The centre of the roof gives a powerful and worrying pitch.
FA. Chris Calow 1978

21 Turnover . . . . HS 4b
Tricky since the huge block that used to provide the footholds went. Traverse right under the roof, round the arete and up the side-wall on creaky jugs.
FA. Al Parker 1959

22 Block Buster . . . . VS 4c
The arete of the buttress to a leftward exit.
FA. Chris Craggs 1997. The huge block that now resides on the Causeway used to be perched precariously under the roof - and no, I didn't trundle it!

Meninblack
Just before the Long Causeway reaches the crest of the moor there is a series of small buttresses set at the top of a steep grass bank.
Approach (see map on page 135) - The buttress is best approached from the High Neb parking, by walking up the Causeway until right under it. Narrow paths lead up steeply to the buttress.

23 Meninblack II E2 5b
The left arete leads to a high and balancy crux.
FA. Gary Gibson 1981

24 Waiting for M.I.B. . . . E3 5c
Pull onto the centre of the face to a rest then a grasping exit.
FA. Gary Gibson 1981

25 Time and Tide . . . . HVS 5b
The right arete doesn't allow for any hanging around.
FA. Martin Veale 1983

26 High Tide . . . . HVS 5a
The arete has surprisingly tricky moves just below the top.
FA. Jim Rubery 1992

27 No Man . . . . S 4a
Pleasant moves up the scooped slab.
FA. Dave Gregory 1992

28 The Big C . . . . VS 5a
A puzzling high step gains the slab which eases after one more move. **The Big C Left-hand** has the same crux and a couple more moves heading out left.
FA. Jim Rubery 1992

29 Centurion's Slab . . . . . . Diff
40m right is a clean slab close to the Causeway which gives a pleasant easy pitch, though without much gear. Not on topo.

Sheffield Area
Ladybower Area
Stanage
Burbage Valley
Millstone Area
Derwent Edges
Chatsworth Area
Southern Crags

	No star	⚙	⚙⚙	⚙⚙⚙
Mod to S	48	27	5	-
HS to HVS	66	60	14	9
E1 to E3	34	55	15	10
E4 and up	16	24	18	15

Stanage Plantation has a superb array of routes, including many great classics across the grades, as well as lots of lovely discrete spots for a bit of peace and quiet. The area has a lovely ambience when you first pop out of the trees and, as it unfolds in front of you, it is obvious that this whole section of Stanage is somewhere rather special. The delights on offer here are displayed less extravagantly than the Popular End but there are enough high quality routes for a great many visits.

The Plantation Boulders are immensely popular and the area is almost always busy, often even more so than the main cliff. The Rockfax Peak Bouldering guidebook lists these in great detail but a small selection of the classics is included here.

Approach   Also see map on page 130

The Plantation Parking (often with tea wagon) is the usual starting place - the Pay and Display area has room for a hundred or so vehicles - it is rarely full. A flagged path leads up towards the trees. Stay with the path for everywhere between Count's Buttress and Calvary, branch right and cut through the trees for Paradise Wall, Millsom's Minion and the Unconquerables areas.

Conditions

The edge faces southwest and catches the sun from the mid-morning onwards. This means it can get very hot in summer. It is exposed to any bad weather but dries quickly after rain, although a few routes can be a bit green and sandy. Midges can be a problem in the late spring and summer when the wind drops.

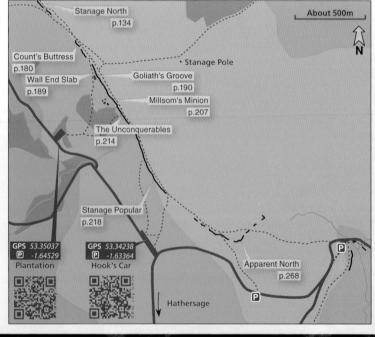

Stanage North
p.134

Count's Buttress
p.180

Wall End Slab
p.189

Goliath's Groove
p.190

Millsom's Minion
p.207

The Unconquerables
p.214

Stanage Popular
p.218

Apparent North
p.268

About 500m

N

Stanage Pole

GPS 53.35037
-1.64529
Plantation

GPS 53.34238
-1.63364
Hook's Car

Hathersage

Sheffield Area
Ladybower Area
Stanage
Burbage Valley
Millstone Area
Derwent Edges
Chatsworth Area
Southern Crags

Sheffield Area

Ladybower Area

Stanage

Burbage Valley

Millstone Area

Derwent Edges

Chatsworth Area

Southern Crags

Will Treasure on *Telli* (E3 6a) - *page 212* - a popular technical slab climb that always feels hard until you have done it. Photo: Mike Hutton

Count's Buttress

Below the gap in the edge, where the Long Causeway links the Hope Valley with Sheffield, is the fine undercut face of Count's Buttress. This neglected area is home to a good set of climbs all best suited to tall, bold climbers.
Approach (see map on page 178) - From the Plantation parking, follow the approach path past Wall End Slab to the top of the flagged section then cut left across the hillside for 200m.

The left-hand side of the face consists of a steep slab with a closely packed set of routes. These are usually bouldered (soloed) but be aware of the drop below the starting ledge.

❶ Eden Arete . . . . S 4a
The short angular arete on the left.
FA. Chris Calow 1977

❷ Nightmare Slab E2 5c
The left edge of the slab has a bold high step to reach a good break and gear. Pass the bulge by a long reach then finish direct, or stride out right - slightly easier.
FA. Al Parker 1959

❸ Dream Boat E3 6b
The slab between the two lines of poor holds. Highball *f6B*.
FA. Alan Doig 1986

❹ Daydreamer E2 6b
Start in the middle of the slab, at some sloping holds, and a short vertical flake. Make perplexing pebbly moves to gain the ledge and an easier finish. Highball *f6A+* but awkward to pad.
FA. Bob Brayshaw 1960. In plimsolls - an awesome achievement.

❺ Nightrider E3 6b
Pick a dry day to streak up the green line. Highball *f6B*.
FA. Chris Hamper 1980

❻ Sleepwalker E2 6a
Climb the slab passing a couple of tiny overlaps. Highball *f6A*.
FA. Chris Calow 1977

❼ Nightride Corner . . . . S 4a
The green and gruesome angle on the right of the slab.
FA. Henry Bishop and friends, about 1910

❽ Out For the Count E4 6a
The left arete of the main buttress has a bold move at half-height. A side-runner lowers the danger, and the E-grade.
FA. Chris Calow 1977

❾ The Cool Curl E6 6b
Climb the lower face to a ledge then step up and left to a precarious pull and crucial high step to get gain the central slab. Above this things ease dramatically - just keep cool.
FA. Johnny Dawes 1984. FA. Mike Lea (after loss of pebbles) 1987

❿ Touched . . . . HVS 5c
The left arete of the chimney is less good than most here.
FA. Gary Gibson 1981

⓫ Count's Chimney . . . . . . Diff
The rift that splits the face is vintage stuff. Once up the grubby lower section, nice back-and-foot work passes the chockstone.
FA. J.W.Puttrell late 1800s

⓬ Counterfeit E2 5b
The right-hand arete of the deep chimney is climbed on its right-hand side. Side-runners lower the grade to HVS.
FA. Graham Parkes 1997

⓭ Count's Wall . . . E1 5b
Climb the left-hand arete of the central cave to ledges, then the thin crack (poor small wires) to a bolder exit. Finish easily.
FA. Al Parker (1 nut aid) 1959. FFA. Dave Mithen 1976

⓮ Counterblast E2 5b
Climb the right-hand arete of the cave then move left to above its centre. Climb the slab using a small pocket and a crease - bold! Continue with one more stretch to easier ground.
FA. Gary Gibson 1981

10m

Sheffield Area

Ladybower Area

Stanage

Burbage Valley

Millstone Area

Derwent Edges

Chatsworth Area

Southern Crags

D.I.Y. Area ➤

⑮ Abacus E2 5c
Follow *Counterblast* to the first ledge, then climb straight up the
bold wall, directly above the right-hand edge of the cave. From
the horizontal break, things get easier and safer.
FA. Dave Mithen 1976

⑯ Count's Buttress. . . . E2 5c
A great route with a devious but logical line. Easier (E1 5b?)
for the tall. Climb the blunt arete on side-pulls to a small ledge
below the steep slab. Make an awkward traverse out right to the
arete then reach the horizontal break above with difficulty before
traversing back left to the short finishing crack.
FA. Joe Brown early 1950s

⑰ Count's Buttress Direct . . E3 6a
Cut out all the looping with delicate and reachy moves.
FA. Al Parker 1959. Also attributed to Eric Byne in the early 1930s

⑱ Count Me Out E2 5c
From the ledge on the traverse of *Count's Buttress,* pull up using
three small pockets, to reach the centre of the horizontal break.
Finish up the steep wall passing another pocket.
FA. John Allen 1985

⑲ The Count E2 5c
A great route with a bold start. Use a loose flake to reach the
break above the lip where cams protect the move to the ledge
on the arete. Climb up to jams under the bulge then follow the
upper arete in a fine position.
FA. Dave Morgan 1976

⑳ Count's Crack . . . . VS 4c
Gain the crack in the south-facing side-wall from the right by a
short traverse along the horizontal break. Once entered it gives
classic jamming. A **Direct Start** is **HVS 5c** and a **Left-hand
Finish** is a good solid **HVS 5a**, combine them for a good trip.
FA. Eric Byne early 1930s

㉑ B Crack. . . . . HVD 4b
The deep angle bounding the buttress has a hard start; above it
eases. The start can be avoided by sneaking round right.
FA. Henry Bishop and friends c1915

㉒ Anxiety Attack 2 . . . . . . E2 6a
The centre of the slab is tough and reachy.
FA. Mark Stokes 1984

㉓ Dracula . . . . HVS 5b
The arete is approached over a tricky bulge and climbed on its
left-hand side by laybacking. Markedly easier for the tall.
FA. John Gosling 1967

㉔ Scraped Crack . . . . VD
The awkward angle could do with a make-over!
FA. Henry Bishop and friends, c1910

㉕ Basil Brush . . . . HVS 5b
Scratch a way up the slab just right. No line but nice moves.
FA. Nigel Slater 1984

㉖ Mop Up E1 5c
A thinner move or two up the centre of the slab.
FA. Tony Nicholls 1994

㉗ Lino . . . . HS 4c
Technical moves left of the arete lead to jungle warfare.
FA. Al Parker 1959

㉘ Prickly Crack. . . . . VD
An oft damp start soon deteriorates into spiky nonsense .

㉙ Shirley's Shining Temple
. . . . f7C
A super-sketchy outing up the left edge of the blank slab. Start
at a small overlap and climb up and left before tackling the final
section direct.
FA. John Allen 1984. Initially started on the right, but later done direct.

㉚ Shock Horror Slab . . . f6C
Another technical teaser. Start below and right of a slight rib and
scrape up the lower bulges to an easier finish.
FA. Steve Bancroft 1980

Count's Buttress

p.180

D.I.Y. Area

Right of Count's Buttress are several short walls of lovely rock, though sadly with only a small collection of routes. Technicians who want to escape the crowds should enjoy the place, though don't forget the mat/spotter since there is some good bouldering.

Approach (see map on page 178) - From the Plantation parking, follow the path past Wall End Slab to the top of the flagged section, then cut left across the hillside.

1 **Flaked Crack** . . . . HS 4b
The left-slanting crack is harder than it looks especially if the grassy ledge to the left is avoided.

2 **Flaked Traverse** . . . . S 4a
From the same start, teeter away right to a short crack.

3 **The Trickledown Fairy** . . . E5 6a
The easy rib and sketchy upper slab. Bold and precarious.
FA. John Allen 1988

Descent

Shock Horror
Slab - p.181

From mid morning / 18 min / Windy

4 **The Stretcher** . . . . VS 4c
Climb directly into the base of the right-slanting groove and exit awkwardly from the top of this. Quite technical.
FA. R.Franklin 1973. FA. (Direct as described) Chris Craggs 1996

5 **Bon Ami** . . . . VS 5a
A shallow groove leads to a poor break, then take the left arete.
FA. Chris Calow 1981

6 **Amoeba on the Edge of Time.** VS 5b
The right arete of the block leads to an awkward exit.
FA. Paul Williams 1984

7 **Canton** . . . . Diff
Grubby and prickly work up the crack and groove.

8 **Have a Nice Day** . . . . . . HVS 5a
The pleasant arete just right. Small cams help protect.
FA. Chris Craggs 1991

9 **The Anomalous Snail** . . . HVS 5c
A tough start gains easier romping above.

10 **Sharpener** . . . . HVS 5a
Climb straight up the left-hand side of the face.
FA. Dave Gregory 1992

11 **Protractor** . . . . HVS 5b
A ramp leads to a break. Move left and finish direct - hard.
FA. Al Parker 1976

12 **Setsquare** . . . . S 4a
The right-hand side of the face to a break, then a mantel finish.
FA. Al Parker 1959

From mid morning / 18 min / Windy

Descent

Sheffield Area / Ladybower Area / Stanage / Burbage Valley / Millstone Area / Derwent Edges / Chatsworth Area / Southern Crags

13 Have a Break. E3 6a
The tough arete of the block set at a higher level.
FA. John Allen 1988

14 Kitkat. . . . . HVS 5c
The centre of the block has some decent moves.

15 Feeding the Pony. . . . . S 4a
The left arete of the short face.
FA. David Simmonite 1994

16 The Amazing Harry Greystoke II. VS 5b
Nice moves up the pocketed slab just right. Almost worth a star.
FA. Keith Ashton 1986

17 Leave Heather Alone . . . . . . HS 5a
A tricky finger-crack (with heather clump?) to the arete above.

18 Black and Decker. E2 6b
The technical left-hand side of the face. Highball *f6C+*.
FA. Greg Griffith 1985

19 D.I.Y.. . . . . E3 6a
A little gem up the centre of the wall linking pockets, slopers and the one useful flake. Highball *f6B*.
FA. Graham Hoey 1981

20 Torture Garden *f7A*
The face just left of the crack has a baffling extended reach for the beckoning pocket. No bouncing past the first move.
FA. Greg Griffith 1985

21 Grime. . . . . HS 4b
The central crack. Better than the name suggests when clean.

22 Sithee Direct. *f6C*
Boulder up the wall to the overlap where things ease.
FA. Graham Hoey 1981

23 Sithee *f5*
Start from the block on the right and swing left to reach the pockets then finish direct. Dragging a rope up it is worth E1 5b.
FA. Jim Lawrenson 1977

24 Committed . . . . VS 5a
The unremarkable short rounded arete.

25 Marmite. . . . . HS 4a
The short, wide and awkward crack in the side-wall. It is a bit of a love or hate affair.
FA. Chris Calow 1981

26 Toxic . . . . Diff
Zip up the flake, mantel right and exit up the cracks.

27 Cixot . . . . VS 5a
A counter-diagonal up the face and the arete.
FA. Chris Craggs 1997

Surprise

A complex and interesting area of slabs and walls. Despite the variety available here, the area sees little attention, probably because there are no mega-classics. Considering that it is only a five minute walk from the ever-popular Wall End Slab area, it should really see a bit more traffic, especially when the rest of the crag is busy.

Approach (see map on page 178) - From the Plantation parking, follow the approach path past Wall End Slab to top of the flagged section then cut left across the hillside (no real path usually) for 50m.

❶ Old Slob . . . . **VD**
Wander your way up the 'slobby' left arete of the slab.
FA. David Simmonite 1994

❷ Dot's Slab . . . . **Diff**
Hop onto the left-hand side of the slab then follow the break to the right-hand arete. Step round this to finish up an easy groove.
FA. Al Parker 1959

❸ Stumpy **E1 5a**
The bold centre of the slab, above the notch, on sloping holds.
FA. David Simmonite 1994

❹ Hard Head . . . . **VS 5a**
The bulge on the right (hard for the short, easy for the tall, 5a for the average) then the face left of the arete. An eliminate but with good climbing.
FA. David Simmonite 1994

❺ Dot's Arete . . . . **S 4a**
The arete gives a nice pitch climbed on the right then on the left.

The next set of routes are on the slabs above and behind *Dot's Slab*. They can be reached by scrambling round to the left, or up the awkward boulder-choked gully on the right.

❻ Pussy-Cat Slab . . . . **HVD 4a**
The narrowing slab leads to a crack round the corner.
FA. Alfie Conn 2003

❼ Basil Half-tail **E1 5c**
Pull over onto the slab, then head left to the hanging arete.
FA. John Allen 1988

❽ Tom-cat Slab . . **E1 5b**
The unprotected precarious centre of the slab past a loose flake.
FA. Alan Clarke early 1960s

❾ Skin Grafter **E3 5c**
The right arete of the slab leads to a worrying finale.
FA. Gary Gibson 1982

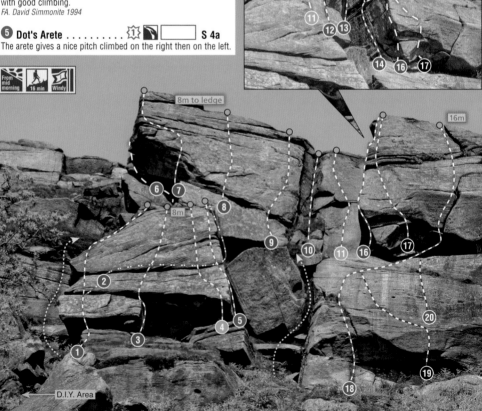

To the right in the back of the bay is a quartet of micro routes.

10 Short Crack . . . . [ ] **Mod**
The grassy rift on the left.

11 Non-Toxic . . . . [ ] **VS 4c**
The narrow dividing rib is tricky.

12 Dry Crack . . . . [ ] **Diff**
The main angle is the most popular of this quartet.

13 Flute Chimney . . . . [ ] **VD**
A chimney in the side-wall.

14 Ma's Retreat . . . . . . [ ] **E1 6a**
From the end of the thin crack in the right wall, head right.
FA. Al Parker 1977

15 Tram Eaters . . . . [ ] **E2 6a**
A direct finish to *Ma's Retreat* is reachy.
FA. Paul Mitchell 1983

16 Boobagram . . . . [ ] **E1 6a**
The short arete on the right with a side-runner. Rarely flashed!
FA. John Allen 1983

17 Feminist's Breakfast . . . . [ ] **E4 6b**
Start in an alcove right of the arete and climb leftwards to gain
the arete. Sprint up this. A tough and worrying pitch.
FA. John Allen 1985

The next routes are down and right, back on the main crag.

18 Surprise . . . . [ ] **E1 5c**
Worth the (considerable) effort. Struggle up the short crack on
the left then the wider one in the centre of the bulges on jams.
The start is a good **5c** problem.
FA. Al Parker 1959

19 Poundland . . . . [ ] **f7C**
From a poor pocket, follow slopers out left almost to a crack.

20 Surprise Direct . . . . [ ] **f6B+**
A hard mantel leads to the original line.

21 Mother's Day . . . . . . [ ] **VS 4c**
The crack in the right arete has a stopper move and good gear.
FA. Al Parker 1957

22 Warlock . . . . [ ] **HVS 5b**
A finger-crack and series of walls lead to a big ledge. Move left
climb the arete, then move right to pull through the bulge with
difficulty. Finish direct.
FA. Dennis Carr 1976

23 Afterthought . . . . [ ] **S 4a**
From a ledge, the left-hand crack, then the right one. Tricky.
FA. Clive Roland 1961

24 Forethought . . . . [ ] **HS 4b**
The counter ascent to *Afterthought*, right then left.
FA. Dave Gregory 1999. Cleaned by Chris Craggs and presented to Dave on
his 65th birthday.

25 Moments of Inertia . . . . . [ ] **E2 5b**
Climb the slab precariously. A long reach helps.
FA. Graham Parkes 1999

26 Zero Zero Sputnik . . . . [ ] **E2 5c**
Spiral up the blunt arete left of the holly.
FA. Steve Ashton 1984

27 Olly Wall . . . . [ ] **S 4a**
This is the short wall just to the right of the 'olly.
FA. Chris Craggs 1999

28 Waffti . . . . [ ] **VD**
Waft up the arete of the buttress, first on the left then the right.

10m

Descent

From the
flagged path
and Outlook
Buttress

Sheffield Area

Ladybower Area

Stanage

Burbage Valley

Millstone Area

Derwent Edges

Chatsworth Area

Southern Crags

10m

Descent

Descent

The Path Boulders
Peak Bouldering

The flagged path

1 The Introvert E2 5c
A retiring route on the shady wall climbing a crack then flakes trending left by long moves. Tough and always green.
FA. Johnny Dawes 1984

2 Outlook Buttress . . . . . . HVS 5b
Climb the left edge of the buttress then follow the rounded break rightwards to a steep finish on slopers.

3 Tying the Knot E3 6a
Use the flake to reach the break then finish direct.
FA. Mike Lea 1990

4 Look Before you Leap . . . E1 6b
The centre of the wall via a wild flying leap from undercuts.
FA. Chris Craggs 1981

5 Outlook Layback . . . . . . S 4b
The steep thrutchy corner crack at the back of the ledge.

6 A Thousand Natural Shocks . . E1 5c
From the ledge, climb the left side of the short-lived arete.
FA. Crispin Guest 1984

7 Weather Report E6 6c
Climb the centre of the face, trending left, with a crux slap over the bulge for slopers. Finish direct. A popular 'snow-ball' route.
FA. Johnny Dawes 1984

8 Nords with Attitude E4 6c
Traverse left from the crack and climb the desperate scoop.
FA. John Allen 1989

9 Outlook Crack . . . . . VS 4c
The thin crack in the left-hand side-wall of the gully has some good moves where you could do with knowing how to jam. Big cams can help and hinder.

To the right, a broken gully gives an awkward descent.

10 Outlook Chimney . . . VS 5a
The fissure behind the leaning flake is hard to enter and to exit from. Big cams help. The grade is up for debate!

11 I Didn't Get Where I am Today
. . . . E3 5c
Gain the front face of the flake, over the pocketed overhang, and climb it right then left. Technical and bold.
FA. Johnny Dawes 1984

12 Lookout Flake . . . . S 4b
A quick layback move gains the flake leading to a tricky exit.

13 Shard . . . . HVS 5b
Climb straight up the delicate slab to a mantelshelf finish.
FA. Chris Craggs 1997

Outlook Buttress

Above the upper section of flagged path that runs through the Plantation is a series of short walls with an interesting collection of routes. Several of the cracks provide great struggles at their respective grades.
Approach (see map on page 178) - From the Plantation parking, follow the approach path past Wall End Slab almost to the top of the flagged section. These walls are up on the right.

Sheffield Area

Ladybower Area

Stanage

Burbage Valley

Millstone Area

Derwent Edges

Chatsworth Area

Southern Crags

Descent

8m

Fern Crack

---

14 Splinter . . . . HVS 5b
Trend right to climb the blunt rib in the centre of the slab.
FA. Greg Griffith 1985

The next routes are on a short, square-fronted pillar. Despite its diminutive size almost all the routes manage to feel worrying.

15 Rebel Yell . . . . HS 4c
Mantel up the left arete of the block on its left-hand side then the upper arete left again. All feels bit aimless and escapable.
FA. Steve Clark 2003

16 Delicatessen . . . . HVS 5a
Balance up the arete on its right-hand side.
FA. Graham Parkes 2012

17 Tales of Yankee Power . . E1 5c
Climb the left-hand side of the front of the block, on small finger-holds. Reachy and easier for the tall.

18 Flaky Wall E1 5b
The flaky right side of the block leads to a swing left to reach its top. Finish easily. Unprotected where it matters.

19 Bastille E1 5b
The right arete of the face on its left-hand side is tough.
FA. Jim Rubery 1992

20 Shaky Gully . . . . S 4a
The awkward wide corner-crack and continuation behind.
FA. Dave Gregory 1992

21 Amphitheatre Face . . . . . VS 5a
Reach the wall right of the groove with a triple jump start, or some technical moves. If all else fails, traverse in from the left.

22 Ladder Cracks . . . . VD
The parallel cracks just left of the corner are awkward.

23 Ladder Corner . . . . Diff
The amiable corner that bounds the wall on its right

24 Tears and Guts E2 6a
The narrow but widening wall with overlaps just right.
FA. Stuart Lancashire 1990

25 Whimper . . . . S 4b
The thin layback and wider upper section right again.

26 Argus E1 5b
Climb the upper arete starting from a ledge on the left - a belayer is a good idea if you don't want to fall miles. Swing onto the arete and layback smartly, keeping on its left-hand side. Pulling around to the right is easier but feels a bit pointless.
FA. Tim Carruthers 1977

Fern Crack

Left of the slumped slab of Wall End is a fine tall buttress, tucked away in a recess. There are several worthwhile climbs here with the *Fern Crack/Groove* twins - the highlight of the area.

Approach (see map on page 178) - Walk up the flagged path from the Plantation parking.

❶ Silk **E5 6c**
An unprotected trip up the buttress left of *Fern Crack*. Starting left of the crack and swarm onto the bulge where slick friction moves lead left to rounded breaks. Some poor pockets enable a swift exit to be made. The start is a popular *f7A+* which can be extended into the whole route above snowdrifts. The sit-down start is *f7C*.
FA. Johnny Dawes 1984

❷ Fern Crack . . . . **VS 4c**
The long crack that is the major feature of the buttress proves to be an awkward customer and quite high in the grade. A slippery layback or awkward jamming start (5a?) leads to a tricky wide section off the ledge and another wide section to enter the upper crack. Escape out left at the top or move right for the extended reach of the short **Direct Finish, HVS 5a**.
FA. Probably Herbert Hartley or Albert Hargreaves 1930s Direct Finish Chris Craggs 2006

❸ Polished Bump . . . . **f7A+**
The bulge just right of the crack.

❹ Help the Aged . . . . . **f7A+**
The direct start to *Fern Groove* is very condition dependent.
FA. Johnny Dawes 1985

❺ Help Right-hand . . . **f7B**
A thinner start on the right.

❻ Fern Groove **E2 5c**
Climb the right-hand edge of the slab then reach the hanging groove by a traverse from the right. Enter it by a puzzling layback sequence then bung in some gear and sprint to safety. The hardest of the old Stanage Extremes!
FA. Pat Fearneough early 1960s

❼ Smash Your Glasses **E5 6b**
Follow *Fern Groove* to the first grassy ledge then tackle the taxing right arete of the buttress keeping on its left-hand side throughout. The crux is protected though the rounded and scary blunt upper arete is not. Accessing the arete from further up the gully is the poor **Spartacaid, E1 5b**.
FA. John Allen 1988

❽ Toothcomb . . . . **VS 4c**
The shrubby buttress to the right is tackled by one of John Allen's lesser known classics. Included for completeness.
FA. John Allen 1980s

Descent
18m

Outlook Buttress

Wall End Slab

An attractive slumped slab of rock with its eponymous venerable classic and some more recent offerings. All the routes here are bold to a greater or lesser extent.
Approach (see map on page 178) - Walk up the flagged path from the Plantation parking - the routes are on the right.

⑨ Wall End Slab . . . . 🔲🔲🔲 **VS 5a**
A devious classic with a bold - but easy - finish. The frustrating (and chipped) initial slab can be ascended in several places at **5a/b**. From the ledge, climb through the bulge just to the right of the arete, to another ledge. Step down (low runners) and traverse across the slab to reach its right arete. Follow the right side of this to the top; bold but mild. *Photo on page 130.*
FA. Fred Pigott and friends, early 1920s

⑩ Bridge's Variation . . . . . 🔲🔲🔲 **VS 5a**
A variation finish up the short slanting crack on the left is harder and safer, but less satisfying, than the original.
FA. Alf Bridge 1930s

⑪ Wall End Slab Super Duper Direct
. . . . 🔲🔲🔲🔲 **E3 5c**
Climb the centre of the lower slab and the bulge above on pockets. The final rib is the real challenge of the route with remote runners as well as scary, reachy climbing.
FA. Chris Craggs 1991

⑫ Wall End Slab Direct . . . 🔲🔲🔲 **E2 5b**
An amazing effort for its day. Climb the lower slab right of centre to a break and runners. Step right and balance up the slab, using an undercut ear to make a tricky mantel/high step well above the gear. Continue to the next break and escape right.
FA. Frank Elliott 1930

⑬ Wall End Slab Direct Finish
. . . . 🔲🔲🔲🔲🔲 **E3 5c**
A more fitting but more harrowing finish. Teeter warily up the scoop in the steepening wall to a reachy rounded exit miles above your gear. The edge is a surprising distance back!
FA. Chris Craggs 1983

⑭ Pure White and Deadly . . 🔲🔲🔲 **E2 5c**
Balance up the right arete of the slab until things ease.
FA. Tony Credland 1982

Up and right is a short wall with several unremarkable routes.

⑮ Narlavision . . . . 🔲🔲 **HVS 5b**
The wall finishing just to the right of the holly.
FA. John Allen 1984

⑯ Standing Around Trying . . . . 🔲🔲 **VS 5b**
The slightly artificial wall just left of the arete.
FA. David Simmonite 1993

⑰ Sittin' Here Drinkin' . . . . 🔲🔲 **VS 5b**
Climb the tricky left arete of the deep groove.
FA. David Simmonite 1993

1 Mate E1 5b
This takes the short buttress on the left. Climb the rib to the break, move round and finish with a flourish.
FA. Jim Rubery 1992

2 Cheque . . . . HVD 4a
The short steep corner to an awkward exit.
FA. Dave Gregory 1992

3 Giro E2 5c
The narrow tower left of the bouldery gully is climbed via the arete. At the roof, move right for an extended-reach finale. The wall just to the left is **Franklie Ferocious - E3 6a**.
FA. Martin Veale 1982

4 P.O. Crack . . . . HS 4b
The piggish orifice in the left side of the gully. Grunt away.

5 Jammed Stone Gully . . . . . . VD
The gully with jammed stones in it - innit?

6 Slanting Chimney . . . . HS 4b
The chimney in the right wall of the gully is flared and awkward.

7 The Coign . . . . HS 4b
The attractive angular arete. Climb the short crack and lower arete, then step awkwardly up onto the main arete which is followed past a couple of steeper moves at half-height.
FA. Geoffrey Sutton 1958

8 Outlook Slab . . . . . VS 5a
Climb the horizontally-cracked slab up its centre. The well protected crux move is at the steepening.
FA. Martin Veale 1978

9 Wall End Crack Direct. . . HS 4b
The widening upper crack is reached via a short action-packed jamming crack. The upper part is tricky to protect. The original left-hand start is a bit easier though gear is wanting. The face just right gives a smart *f6A* boulder problem start.
FA. Henry Bishop and friends, about 1914

10 Death, Night and Blood. . E1 5b
Start as for the last route, but step right and access the arete from the ramp. The final precarious section is reachy and harrowing, especially for the short. Wires in the creaky flake really shouldn't be relied upon.
FA. Gary Gibson 1978

11 Wall End Flake Crack . . . VS 4c
Climb the corner-crack of *Wall End Crack Direct* then take the sloping ramp to the foot of twin flakes. Climb the left-hand of these by laybacking and jamming. Big gear needed.
FA. Fred Pigott and friends, early 1920s

Descent

Wall End Slab

Goliath's Groove

An attractive set of aretes and walls that include some of the best offerings on the cliff. As might be expected, the area is always popular, though fortunately there is usually enough to go round! *Goliath's Groove* itself is the mega-classic (though folks not tuned-in to grit have been known to question this), and the trio of big aretes are also routes to aspire to, if you are up to them!

Approach (see map on page 178) - Walk up from the Plantation parking.

From mid morning | 12 min | Windy

20m

12 Wall End Holly Tree Crack... ☆ ▢ **HS 4b**
Reach the flake via the thin crack in the left wall of *Helfenstein's Struggle* (or better, start up the previous route, crowds permitting) and follow it by jamming and bridging. The closeness of the other crack makes it hard to ignore.

13 I Never Said It Was Any Good ▢ **E1 5b**
The short crack to a long reach then the wall above on slopers is actually not too bad if it is dry.
FA. Chris Craggs 1989

14 Helfenstein's Struggle ..... ☆ ▢ **HVD 4a**
The wide black rift is oddly alluring. A short polished corner leads to easier ground heading for the large boulder blocking the rift. Either squeeze through the rat-hole that gripped Helfenstein, or do the **Outside Exit** at an exposed **S 4a**.
FA. Helfenstein c1910. Only his top-half actually managed the route.

15 Saul's Arete .... ☆☆ ▢ **VS 4c**
Excellent and underrated with some great positions - an *Ellis's Eliminate* for grown-ups. Swing along the lowest break then climb the fine upper arete - bold to start.
FA. G.Dimmock 1965

16 Dark Angel .... ▢ **E4 6b**
From the break on *Helfenstein's*, continue up the left arete. The grade is a bit of a guess since it was originally given HVS, then E2 but that still seems to be rather wide of the mark.
FA. John Allen 1986

17 The Archangel .... Top50 ▢ **E3 5b**
A totally committing layback up the left side of the superb arete. Side-runners should be avoided at all costs. From the starting block, take a deep breath, and sprint for the midway break. Thankfully things are easier above.
FA. Ed-Ward Drummond 1972

18 Don .... ☆☆ ▢ **E4 5c**
The right-hand side is as good, longer and just as unprotected.
FA. Ed-Ward Drummond 1985

19 Goliath's Groove ...... Top50 ▢ **HVS 5a**
The fine twisting groove is one of the best routes on the crag though not all agree! The initial corner is the thrutchy crux for many, it is usually wedged and jammed facing right, though it can also be layback or even bridged, facing in or out! The midway ledge offers some respite then the upper bulging groove can be laybacked or bridged elegantly to easy ground.
FA. Peter Harding 1947

20 Doncaster's Route .... ☆ ▢ **HVS 5a**
Ascend *Goliath's Groove* to the midway ledge then go up the short slab on the right to another ledge. Finish up the thin crack in the wall. It is 4b after the *Goliath's* section.
FA. Michael Doncaster 1930s

21 Ulysses' Bow... Top50 ▢ **E6 6b**
The square-cut arete requires stacks of commitment and technique. Each move is harder than the one before, all the way to the ledge! Almost always done above a stack of pads at *f6C+* these days. It is a very different proposition without them!
Photos on page 32 and 193.
FA. Jerry Moffatt 1983

To the right is one of the biggest blank walls on Grit. Unlike most of them, this one really does look impossible.

Crescent Arete Bouldering

Routes 22 to 31 →

Sheffield Area | Ladybower Area | Stanage | Burbage Valley | Millstone Area | Derwent Edges | Chatsworth Area | Southern Crags

㉒ Hollybush Gully Left. . . . 🔲 HS 4b
The square-cut corner is climbed via the awkward left-hand crack to the top of the flakes. The right-hand crack is a good off-width problem. Continue up the groove passing the exposed chockstone to the easier upper gully and an exit. A finish out left as for *Doncaster's Route* is a more open and trickier option.
FA. Henry Bishop and friends c1914

㉓ White Wand . . . . 🔲 E5 6a
Another bald, bold and brilliant arete. Getting established on the sharp section of the arete is the crux - above this a traumatic layback leads quickly to the halfway break or even more quickly back to the ground. If successful, finish more easily. Very highball *f6B* above pads.
FA. John Allen 1975

㉔ Hollybush Gully Right Direct . 🔲 S 4a
A short direct start to the upper gully gives some good jamming.

㉕ Hollybush Gully Right. . . . . . 🔲 VD
A vintage outing from JWP. Climb blocks rightwards and make a hand-traverse back left (not much gear) to reach the gully. The upper section gives easier blocky rambling in the gloom.
FA. J.W.Puttrell late 1800s

㉖ Leaps and Bounds . . 🔲 E1 5b
From *Hollybush Gully,* move out left and climb the arete with tricky moves above the break.
FA. Simon Yearsley 1992

㉗ Last Arete . . . . 🔲 E5 6a
The left arete of the slab climbed on its right-hand side.
FA. Pete Whittaker 2008

㉘ Fairy Groove . . . . . . 🔲 *f6C*
The boulder problem groove leads to the ledge.

㉙ Gnome Man's Land . 🔲 E5 6b
Climb *Fairy Groove,* or scramble round and belay on the ledge below *Fairy Steps.* The wall above is bold, reachy and technical.
FA. John Arran 1984

㉚ Fairy Steps . . . . 🔲 VS 4a
An excellent and exciting route crossing the wide smooth wall - not a place for wobblers. From a grassy ledge, climb the steep slab just left of the corner to the start of a narrow ledge system. A delicate foot-traverse leads out left until better holds can be followed directly to the top.
FA. Alan Clarke early 1960s

㉛ Fairy Steps Escape. . . . . 🔲 VD
The corner in its entirety.

㉜ Double Act . . . . 🔲 HVS 5c
The short arete on the right in two stages is technically interesting. Tackle both section on the left by laybacking.
FA. Chris Craggs, Jim Rubery (alternate leads - honest) 1991

From mid morning | 12 min | Windy

Descent

Doncaster's Route - p.191

Satin →

Crescent Arete Bouldering

Ed Hamer nearing the crucial move on *Ulysses' Bow* (E6 6b/*f6C+*) - *page 191* - on the Goliath's Groove area. Photo: Mike Hutton.

Sheffield Area

Ladybower Area

Stanage

Burbage Valley

Millstone Area

Derwent Edges

Chatsworth Area

Southern Crags

❶ Ron's Slab . . . . *f7B+*
Starting at the arete, trend leftwards then back right to the arete at the top. It really needs properly straightening out.
FA. Ron Fawcett of course!

❷ Crescent Arete. . . . . *f5+*
The elegant arete succumbs to precarious laybacking then a sprint once it eases. Climbed exclusively on its right-hand side it is a scary but brilliant *f6B+*.
FA. Gabe Reagan 1976

❸ Crescent Slab *f7A*
The wall right of the arete, finishing up the arete.

❹ Mono Slab . . . . *f7A+*
The thin pebbly slab, with a mono.

❺ Crescent Groovelet. . . . . *f5+*
An excellent little groove which is harder than it looks. It is easier but not as good on the right.

The large block further back has a lot of highball problems and one of the shortest and weirdest routes on grit.

❻ Big Air *E6 6b*
Bizarre but a superb move. Leap the crevasse for the beckoning square hold and mantel a way to glory. Not a boulder problem but *f6C* when the snow is deep enough!
FA. Martin Veale 1987

❼ Careless Torque. *f8A*
The big jutting arete has a near impossible start coming in from the right. Above that it is barely any easier and often sees big falls onto pads from quite high.
FA. Ron Fawcett 1987

❽ Not to be Taken Away *f6C*
Boulder out the moves to access the ramp then hand-traverse up this to one more tricky move at a gap in the holds to gain the finishing jugs.
FA. John Allen 1976

Crescent Arete Bouldering

The blocks below the Goliath's Groove Area form one of the most popular bouldering spots in the Peak District. The following selection includes the best of the problems and a few routes. There are many more variations and lesser offerings. All these problems are described fully in the Rockfax Peak Bouldering guidebook which features *Not To Be Taken Away* on the cover.

❾ Brad Pit *f7C*
A famous problem situated in the pit behind one of the larger boulders. There are various cunning methods available depending on your body dimensions. If you are really tall then you may be able to contemplate the *f8B* sit-down start!
FA. Jason Myers 1995. FA. (Start) Thomas Willenberg 2000

There are several problems on the big rectangular block but, at the far right end, it gets a bit high and the climbing warrants using a rope.

❿ Video Nasty. *E1 6a*
This one only has a couple of precarious moves - you can slip but don't bounce!

⓫ The Photograph *E3 5c*
Traverse out right past a slot (runner?) to reach the arete. You definitely don't want to fall off this one! A direct finish is **Snap Shot, E3 5c.**
FA. Paul Mitchell 1982

⓬ Overexposed *E5 6b*
Traverse leftwards across the undercut end of the block to a frightening finish up the hanging arete. Very scary!
FA. Dan Honeyman 2000

From mid morning | 12 min | Windy

Goliath's Groove p.190

Fairy Steps p.192

Satin p.195

Satin

A collection of short buttresses squeezed between more popular areas. Although of a lesser stature, it is worth a visit, is usually quiet and has some good bouldering.
Approach (see map on page 178) - Walk up the flagged path from the Plantation parking. On exiting the trees the area is visible ahead, behind the main boulders

⑬ Spur Slab . . . . □ **Diff**
Mantelshelf onto the tip of the slab then climb to a shrubby ledge and finish up the crack above.

⑭ Spur Traverse . . . . . □⛰⛰ □ **f6C+**
Traverse the roof from left to right.

⑮ Left Spur. . . . . ⛰⛰ □ **f7A**
The left-hand side of the roof. Much harder than it used to be.
FA. John Allen 1986

⑯ Right Spur . . . . □⛰⛰ □ **f6C+**
Use the curving rib to pass the roof. A good problem.
FA. Adam Long 2000

⑰ Hot Spur. . . . . □ □ **HS 4b**
Stride the gap then climb the pleasant rib.
FA. Dave Gregory 1992

⑱ Stirrup . . . . □ **S 3c**
The right side of the slab leads to a wide crack and delicate finish. Not much gear apart from big cams in the break.
FA. Dave Gregory 1992

⑲ Ride Him Cowboy . . . . □ □ **VS 5a**
The recessed slab has a technical start, then climb the short arete and scoop in the final tower.
FA. Chris Craggs 1991

⑳ Corduroy. . . . . □ **VS 4c**
Climb the arete then cross to the other arete and finish up this.
FA. Dave Gregory 1992

㉑ Pressure Drop . . . . . □□□ □ **f7A+**
A piece of extremely blank slab climbing.
FA. Adam Long 2000

㉒ Satin . . . . □□□ □ **f7A**
The original problem on this slab offers very tenuous slab climbing on very poor holds. Traverse off.
FA. Johnny Dawes 1984

㉓ Living at the Speed . □□□ □ **E1 5b**
Trivial but popular. Climb the central chimney then traverse the break leftwards into the middle of the slab. Make a tricky mantelshelf move and continue delicately.
FA. Gary Gibson 1979

㉔ Central Reservation . . . . . . □ □ **S 4a**
The awkward chockstoned crack splitting the buttress.
FRA. Chris Craggs 1996

㉕ The Mark Devalued . . . . . . □ □ **VS 4b**
The left arete of the slab throughout.
FA. Dave Gregory 1992

㉖ Mark's Slab. . . . . □ **VS 5a**
Climb the chimney then hand-traverse the lowest break and climb the centre of the right-hand slab.
FA. Mark Whitfield 1978

㉗ Pullover . . . . □□□ □ **f5**
A flake under the lip of the overhang allows a tough pull up and left to a layaway - use this to gain a standing position. Finish direct much more easily. VS 5b if you take a rope up it!
FA. Allan Austin 1958

㉘ Woolly Pully . . . . □□ □ **f6A+**
From the right-hand flake heave over to easy ground.
FA. Chris Craggs 1991

㉙ Roll Neck . . . . □ **VS 5a**
From a block at the bottom right edge of the slab pull awkwardly leftwards, then follow the right-hand side of the slab.
FA. Dave Gregory 1992

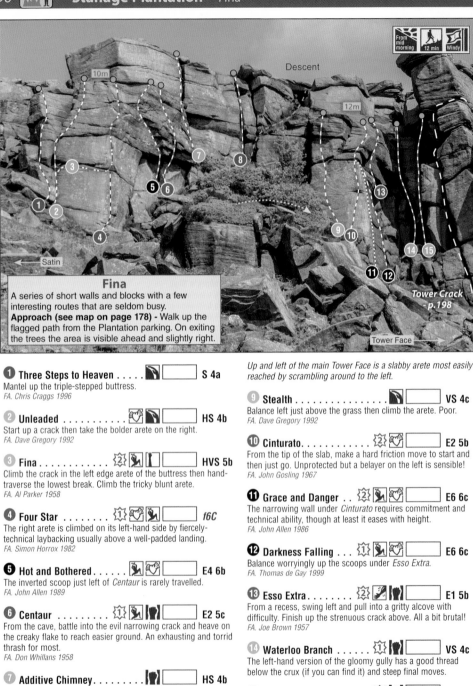

Descent

10m

12m

Fina

Fina
A series of short walls and blocks with a few
interesting routes that are seldom busy.
Approach (see map on page 178) - Walk up the
flagged path from the Plantation parking. On exiting
the trees the area is visible ahead and slightly right.

Satin

*Tower Crack
- p.198*

Tower Face

1 Three Steps to Heaven . . . . . 🗻⬜ **S 4a**
Mantel up the triple-stepped buttress.
FA. Chris Craggs 1996

2 Unleaded . . . . 💔🗻⬜ **HS 4b**
Start up a crack then take the bolder arete on the right.
FA. Dave Gregory 1992

3 Fina . . . . 🏋️🧗🚪⬜ **HVS 5b**
Climb the crack in the left edge arete of the buttress then hand-
traverse the lowest break. Climb the tricky blunt arete.
FA. Al Parker 1958

4 Four Star . . . . 🏋️💔🧗⬜ **f6C**
The right arete is climbed on its left-hand side by fiercely-
technical laybacking usually above a well-padded landing.
FA. Simon Horrox 1982

5 Hot and Bothered . . . . . . 🧗💔⬜ **E4 6b**
The inverted scoop just left of *Centaur* is rarely travelled.
FA. John Allen 1989

6 Centaur . . . . 🏋️🧗👤⬜ **E2 5c**
From the cave, battle into the evil narrowing crack and heave on
the creaky flake to reach easier ground. An exhausting and torrid
thrash for most.
FA. Don Whillans 1958

7 Additive Chimney . . . . 👤⬜ **HS 4b**
The short wide chimney is hard to enter, hard to make progress
on and not well protected. Graded VD for years.

8 Lead Free . . . . 👤⬜ **HVD**
Another narrow double rift. A real grovel.

*Up and left of the main Tower Face is a slabby arete most easily
reached by scrambling around to the left.*

9 Stealth . . . . 🗻⬜ **VS 4c**
Balance left just above the grass then climb the arete. Poor.
FA. Dave Gregory 1992

10 Cinturato . . . . 🏋️💔⬜ **E2 5b**
From the tip of the slab, make a hard friction move to start and
then just go. Unprotected but a belayer on the left is sensible!
FA. John Gosling 1967

11 Grace and Danger . . 🏋️🧗💔⬜ **E6 6c**
The narrowing wall under *Cinturato* requires commitment and
technical ability, though at least it eases with height.
FA. John Allen 1986

12 Darkness Falling . . . 🏋️🧗💔⬜ **E6 6c**
Balance worryingly up the scoops under *Esso Extra*.
FA. Thomas de Gay 1999

13 Esso Extra . . . . 🏋️📐👤⬜ **E1 5b**
From a recess, swing left and pull into a gritty alcove with
difficulty. Finish up the strenuous crack above. All a bit brutal!
FA. Joe Brown 1957

14 Waterloo Branch . . . . . . 🏋️👤⬜ **VS 4c**
The left-hand version of the gloomy gully has a good thread
below the crux (if you can find it) and steep final moves.

15 Tower Gully . . . . 🏋️👤⬜ **VS 4b**
The corner system tucked in the right side of the gully - an
imposing pitch. Bridge the initial groove to ledges then take the
steep but easier upper section to escape under the chockstone.

Sheffield Area

Ladybower Area

Stanage

Burbage Valley

Millstone Area

Derwent Edges

Chatsworth Area

Southern Crags

Sam Hamer setting off up the crucial section of the superb arete of *Flight of Ideas* (E6 7a) - *page 198* - on the Tower Face at Stanage. Photo: Mike Hutton

Tower Face

The tallest wall on the cliff with routes to match. *Tower Face Direct* and *Flight of Ideas* are great climbs and all the other routes described here are worth doing.
Approach (see map on page 178) - Walk up the flagged path from the Plantation parking. On exiting the trees the area is visible ahead and slightly right.

1 Tower Crack . . . . HVS 5b
A proper full-on jamming pitch. The central section is tough, although bridging helps, and the pull on to the ledge is tricky. Head up the corner on the right and then traverse awkwardly right to a ledge above *Tower Face*.
FA. Joe Brown early 1950s

2 Tower Chimney E1 5b
The soaring chimney is usually avoided! The bell-shaped upper section is the crux. Good gear is available in the depths of the rift, though it is hard to place, especially with a helmet on!
FA. Eric Byne 1933

3 Common Misconception . E6 6c
The end rib of the wall. Good gear in the half height break, then an airy finish to the top. Very spicy.
FA. Pete Whittaker 2010

4 Flight of Ideas E6 7a
A stunning route up the soaring arete, desperate though with good runners below the upper crux section. Climb past a curving sandy overlap to the break then move left. The blank upper section is climbed on its right-hand side with conviction.
Photo on page 197.
FA. Simon Jones 1994

5 Indian Summer E6 6c
Another desperate climb. Follow *Flight of Ideas* to the curving overlap, then use poor holds to reach the next break. Continue trending left up the crucial upper wall on tiny edges and smears.
FA. John Allen 1986

6 Tower Face Direct . . [Top 50] E2 5b
An excellent route which is mild but bold. Climb the centre of the face (creaky) to a rest out left. An odd sideways nut protects the moves up and right to the base of the superb upper flake.
Photo on page 203.
FA. Peter Biven 1956

7 Tower Face . . . . HVS 5a
Climb the *Direct* to good nuts then traverse right at one of two levels to a crusty flake just before the arete. Climb to the break then traverse left to gain the superb finishing flake.

8 Tower Face Indirect . . . . VS 4b
Wandering but with a good finale. Climb the easy chimney then step out left and make a short traverse to reach the base of the central flake-line. Romp up this.

9 Tower Face Gully/Terrace Gully . VD
The longest (straight up) route on Stanage and best done in two pitches. Climb the gully to ledges to a stance and belay, then take the green continuation just to the left.

10 Stretcher Case E2 5c
Climb the crack in the left-hand wall to its top, then swing right past the arete before making a mighty stretch for the top.
FA. Chris Jackson 1981

11 Scuppered E4 6a
From the left-hand end of the ledge, swing along the break and climb the arete on its right-hand side by difficult laybacking.
FA. John Allen 1988

12 Invisible Maniac E3 6b
A direct line up the centre of the wall to the crux of *Nuke the Midges*, with an arduous cheek-scouring mantelshelf.
FA. Richie Patterson 1996

13 Nuke the Midges E1 5b
Start up ledges on the right then head left for 5m (a dangle for the short) to a jug. A crux mantel on this may reach the top.
FA. Al Manson 1977

Above Tower Face is a short wall reached from the right.

14 Miserable Miracle . . E2 5b
A good extension to any of the *Tower Face* routes. The tiny but intense left-hand arete of the face feels bold and very exposed. The fall potential is daunting but remember it used to be HVS!
FA. John Allen 1976

15 Four Star, E10, 7b E5 6c
The wall left of centre is not quite as good or as hard it claims.
FA. Dan Honeyman 1999

16 Nihilistic Narl . . . . f7A+
The centre of the wall is the best of this bunch.
FA. John Allen 1984

17 The Descrittalizer...... E5 6b
Right of centre.
FA. Dan Honeyman 1999

18 Scrittalacious E4 6a
The final line on the right.
FA. Nick Jennings 1999

19 The Chute .... HS 4b
The wide crack just right is an arduous affair.

20 Scapa Flow E6 6c
From the left-hand end of the overhang, climb rightwards on pebbles towards the centre of the wall where the gripping and technical finale is located.
FA. Andy Barker 1992

21 Dreadnought ... E7 7a
The right-hand line is even harder. With runners in *Scapa Flow* cross the bulges, pebble pull, then dyno for the top.
FA. Mike Lea 1999

22 The Mangler E1 5c
The fearsome wide crack is traditionally climbed by squirming, though those with huge cams might try laybacking.
FA. Don Whillans 1959

23 Crescent............ VS 5a
The curving crack gives decent and well protected crux moves leading to easier bulges above.
FA. Don Whillans 1959

24 Foetus on the Eiger E1 6a
The bulging wall with some side-runners for protection.
FA. Paul Mitchell 1988

The Strangler Area

The Strangler Area

A secluded slab with a set of hard routes as well as a short Upper Tier above Tower Face which has a collection of easier lines. This area is rarely busy.
Approach (see map on page 178) - Walk up the flagged path from the Plantation parking. On exiting the trees the area is visible slightly to the right.

On the upper level is a jutting arete.

1 Grooved Arete . . . . S 4a
From the left, head out right to the arete. Next stop Tryfan?

2 Anji . . . . VS 5a
The bulge and face right of the arete. Pleasant.
FA. D.Constable 1970

A tall block in front of the upper edge has a fine arete.

3 Swooper E5 6b
The centre of the small slab, trending left near the top, is precarious and unprotected. Despite its size, it is a real gripper.
FA. Johnny Dawes 1984

4 Neutrons for Old E2 5c
Climb cracks in the north-facing wall to the arete then head right to the other arete and finish up this.
FA. Chris Jackson 1981

5 The Strangler E4 5c
The left arete of the tower features steady climbing leading to a high crux where you might need to get hold of yourself. A short and bold layback sprint above a good safety net is the spice.
FA. Gabe Regan 1977

6 Skidoo E6 6b
The slab, 2m right of the arete is climbed direct. It is a scary challenge requiring neat footwork and a degree of coolness.
FA. John Allen 1985

7 Skidoo Mk II E6 6c
Climb the right-hand line on the slab, from right to left, starting at an overlap and passing three small pockets.
FA. Niall Grimes 1997

Back up on the higher edge.

8 Slab and Crack . . . . VS 5a
Climb the slab to the overlap, move right and pull through via the wide crack, to a steep finish.
FA. Nat Allen 1958

9 Obstinance . . . . HVS 5a
The direct on *Slab and Crack* has a long reach and tough pull.
FA. Al Parker 1960

10 Sustenance . . . . HVS 5a
Trend left up the slab to the roof, a stretch gains easier ground.
FA. Chris Craggs 1996

11 Gardener's Groove . . . . HS 4c
A traditional green grovel once the evil holly is passed.
FA. Al Parker 1960

12 Compost Corner . . . . Diff
The recessed groove past some decaying vegetables.

13 Percy's Prow . . . . 🛅 ☐ **HVD**
The short arete has some pleasant moves.

14 Gardener's Crack . . . . 🛅 ☐ **Diff**
The pleasant crack has a tricky start.
FA. Al Parker 1960

15 Pizza Slab . . . . 🛅 🖼 ☐ **HS 4a**
The right-trending line across the slab is worthwhile but bold.

16 Pizza Cake . . . . 🛅 ☐ **VS 4c**
Climb the bulge on the right to join the previous route in the centre of the slab then move left to finish up the arete.
FA. Graham Parkes 2013

17 Cheapest Topping . . . . 🖼 ☐ **VS 4c**
Pull out of the recess and climb the gritty slab on slopers.
FA. Dave Gregory 1992

18 Poor Pizza . . . . ☐ **Diff**
The short crack on the right with hidden holds.

19 Nasty Green Dwarf . . . . ☐ **VS 4c**
The narrow slab.

20 Gothic Armpit . . . . . 🛅 🖼 🖼 ☐ **E5 6b**
Climb into the hanging niche, and escape right. Intense!
FA. Dave Thomas 1998

21 Small Dreams . . . . . 🛅 🖼 🖼 ☐ **E2 6a**
The undercut left arete is taxing to access, and delicate above.
FA. Chris Calow 1978

22 Big Screams . . . . . 🛅 🖼 🖼 ☐ **E1 5c**
Boulder the lower wall then pad up the centre of the easier slab.
FA. Chris Craggs 1991

23 Scorpion Slab . . . . 🛅 🖼 ☐ **HS 4a**
The right-hand edge of the tilted block is approached by an easy groove. Its upper part is precarious and unprotected.

24 Gripe Fruit Juice . . . . ☐ **HVS 5a**
Head up the blocky arete on the right of the gully to a high crux.
FA. Jim Rubery 1990

25 Hercules Crack . . . . 🛅 🖼 ☐ **HS 4b**
Climb the flake and continue up the wider crack above. It is about as strenuous as you might expect from its name.

26 Shelf Life . . . . 🛅 🖼 🖼 ☐ **E3 5c**
Just right of *Hercules Crack* climb a tricky wall, on tiny holds, to a bulge split by a crack. Head right on slopers to a ledge, then step back left to climb the upper wall. A direct version is E4.
FA. Chris Craggs 1991

27 Fruitcake . . . . 🛅 🖼 🖼 ☐ **HVS 5a**
A slab and flake lead to the shelf. Teeter left along this then pull boldly into the shallow groove above its left end. Approaching the crux from *Hercules Crack* is **Kinell, HVS 5a**.
FA. Phil Meats 1997

Hathersage Trip

A secluded area with a few interesting Orange Spot routes plus some harder stuff - typical out-of-the-way Stanage. **Approach (see map on page 178) -** Walk up the flagged path from the Plantation parking. From the gate at the exit from the trees the area is visible high up to the right.

① Squally Showers . . . . ☐ **VS 4c**
A slanting green groove leads to the pleasant upper arete.
FA. Chris Craggs 1991

② The Edale Trip . . . . 🔁 🖼 ☐ **E3 6a**
Lower meanderings lead to bulges then a ledge. The upper slab is the meat of the route, and is both bold and precarious.
FA. Colin Binks 1991. So named as he was 'beyond Hope'.

③ Mercury Crack . . . . 🔁 👤 ☐ **VD**
From the cave, struggle into the hanging crack.

④ My Herald of Free Enterprise. 🔁 ☐ **E6 6c**
A harrowing lead up the left arete. Gain it from the right and press on boldly! A dubious small cam is the only lifeline.
FA. Dave Thomas 1989

⑤ The Hathersage Trip . . . . 🔁 🖼 ☐ **E4 6a**
Climb the sustained centre of the wall to the left of the crack. Protection is adequate (small cams and wires) though fiddly.
FA. Bob Berzins 1982. So named because he thought he'd end up in Hathersage if he fell off.

⑥ Overhanging Crack. . 🔁 🔧 👤 ☐ **HVS 5a**
The wide crack splitting the wall is approached from the left up a thinner fissure. Awkward and thuggy climbing throughout.

⑦ Courtesy of Jonboy. . 🔁 🖼 🖼 ☐ **f7B+**
The undercut arete left of the crack.

⑧ Corner Crack . . . . 👤 ☐ **HVS 5a**
The leaning groove is thrutchy and feels bold despite the thread.

⑨ National Breakdown . 🔁 🖼 🖼 ☐ **f7B+**
The desperate bulging wall right of the corner.
FA. Greg Griffith 1987

⑩ Big Bob's Bazzer . . . . ☐ **E1 5b**
Use the thin flake to access the bulging arete.
FA. Bob Berzins early 1980s

Below the Upper Tier is a slab and to its left a big block.

⑪ Mr Twitch . . . . 🖼 ☐ **E6 6b**
The centre of the block is short and intense.
FA. Paul Mitchell 1996

⑫ Fulcrum . . . . 🔧 ☐ **HVS 5a**
The disjointed cracks in the north-facing wall.
FA. Chris Craggs early 1980s

⑬ Seesaw . . . . 🔁 ☐ **VS 4c**
Climb the left arete of the slab, starting from the left. The flake in the break that seesawed snapped years ago.
FA. Al Parker early 1960s

⑭ Margery Daw. . . . . . . 🔁 🖼 ▯ ☐ **HVS 5b**
Climb the scooped centre of the slab and the crucial overlap from a start on the left or on the right.
FA. Neil Stokes early 1970s

Fruitcake p.201

The Strangler Area ← | → Pegasus Wall Area

Sheffield Area

Ladybower Area

Stanage

Burbage Valley

Millstone Area

Derwent Edges

Chatsworth Area

Southern Crags

Once the huge flake is reached on *Tower Face Direct*
(E2 5b) - *page 198* - the difficulties are over. Here
Duncan Barrack is enjoying the feeling of knowing
this great classic is in the bag.

Sheffield Area
Ladybower Area
Stanage
Burbage Valley
Millstone Area
Derwent Edges
Chatsworth Area
Southern Crags

Pegasus Wall Area

This is a popular area with some good mid-grade routes. In addition to *Pegasus Wall*, *Overhanging Wall* is excellent and mild at the grade, and the *Taurus*, *Pegasus*, *Valhalla* trio offer good jamming. In front of the edge is a tall block with the desperate route of *Unfamiliar* up its front edge.

Approach (see map on page 178) Walk up the flagged path from the Plantation parking. At the gate exiting the trees, the area is visible up to the right, above the main Plantation Boulders.

5m left of the Unfamiliar tower is a fun slab not on the topo.

1 Fun Solo . . . . **HS 4b**
The blunt arete of the slab is short and sweet.

2 Solo Fun . . . . **HS 4b**
The centre of the slab just right.

The first route on the Unfamiliar pinnacle is round the back.

3 Crime **E4 6a**
The northeast arete of the block on its shady left-hand side.
FA. Martin Veale 1986

4 Punishment **E5 5b**
The right-hand side is longer, scarier and harder than its twin.
FA. John Allen 1986

5 Unfamiliar **E7 6c**
A great route up the frontal arete of the tower. It can be started direct by a jump, or by leaning in from the left from a pile of stones. Gear consists of a tiny cam or small wires in the diagonal crack at two-thirds height. Up to this point is *f7C*.
FA. Robin Barker 1992

6 Walking the Whippet . . . **E3 5c**
The delicate right side of the right-hand arete of the valley face is scary. Protection is poor but it is worth taking a rope along!
FA. John Allen 1984

7 Walking on Ice . . . . **S 4b**
Back on the edge there are V-cracks, take the left-hand one.

8 Horn . . . . **VS 5b**
This short wall with overlap and hard start.

9 Horn Corner . . . . **VD**
This is the rather green flaky corner.

10 Too Cold to be Bold **E1 6b**
The arete after starting up *Taurus Crack*, with a side-runner.

11 Taurus Crack . . . . **VS 4c**
The flake-crack in the left-hand edge of the smooth wall gives short-lived fun is but quite arduous and high in the grade.

12 Star Trek **E6 6b**
Start from a block, and trend right towards the middle of the face. Head up and right to reach a good hold (small cam) below the overlap then finish carefully on slopers. Can be highballed at *f7A+* but needs very careful spotting.
FA. Graham Parkes (side-runner) 1989. FA. Andy Popp (without) 1991

13 Klingon **E6 7a**
Spaced out holds and gear! Undercuts in the centre of the wall enable a wild leap to poor pockets, runners, and an easier finish. Also a possible highball with careful spotting at *f7C*.
FA. Mike Lea 2000

⑭ **Valhalla** . . . . VS 4c
Gain the prominent straight crack from the left, via a tricky wall and heathery ledge, then jam and layback it. Short but sweet.
FA. Wilf White 1948

⑮ **Pegasus Wall** . . . . VS 4c
Thin cracks run slightly leftwards up the wall, these are reached awkwardly, then followed as they kink right then left.

⑯ **Back to School** . . . . HVS 5b
The narrow pocketed wall above the start of the last route.
FA. Chris Craggs 1989. The day before the new term started.

⑰ **Pegasus Rib** . . . . HVS 5a
The right-hand arete of the buttress is bold and high in the grade. Climb the thin crack to the arete then balance round left and finish direct. The big black flake right of the arete and close to the crux is hollow and not a great spot to place runners.
FA. John Allen early 1970s

The next climbs are on a small slab below the main edge which used to be hidden behind a silver birch.

⑱ **265** . . . . VS 4c
The flaky left arete is pleasant though a bit scritty.
FA. Graham Parkes 2014. The name was the combined ages of the team.

⑲ **Old Enough to Know Better** . . HVS 5c
The centre of the slab to a high crux. A side-runner is placed from the route.
FA. Graham Parkes 2014

⑳ **Flake Gully** . . . . Diff
The gully is gained up a tricky slab and is easier above.

㉑ **Flake Chimney** . . . . HVD 4b
The constricted rift on the right is fun with a capital F!

㉒ **Overhanging Wall** . . . . . HVS 5a
Climb a tricky thin crack to a rest at a flake below the roof. Traverse away right and finish up the side-wall.
FA. Joe Brown early 1950s

㉓ **Crossover** E2 5c
Climb the slabby rib to the roof. Traverse left to a flake (last runners) then swing around the corner and finish up the scary wall on sloping holds. No sneaking off left, though many do!

㉔ **Passover** E1 5c
The pocketed rib on the right is soon over.
FA. Steve Bancroft 1986

㉕ **Flate** . . . . VS 5a
A thin flake leads rapidly to rounded holds.
FA. Gary Gibson 1979

㉖ **Unpredictable** . . . . f5+
The wall to the left side of the jutting block is hard and high.

㉗ **Zero Point** . . . . HVS 5a
The right side of the wall and the scoop in the boulder.
FA. Gary Gibson 1979

Plantation Boulders
Peak Bouldering

Paradise Wall →

Sheffield Area · Ladybower Area · Stanage · Burbage Valley · Millstone Area · Derwent Edges · Chatsworth Area · Southern Crags

Paradise Wall

A very popular area with a good collection of mid-grade routes including some classic cracks and a couple of testing wall pitches. Add the closeness of *Millsom's Minion* and you have a prime venue.

Approach (see map on page 178) - Take the flagged path from the Plantation parking. At the upper gate head up and right to above the Plantation boulders.

1 Paradise Lost . . . . **Diff**
Lost? Not really - it is the longish crack tucked round left of the arete and starting from a small alcove. Beware loose rock.

2 Parasite . . . . **HVS 5a**
Climb the tiny square groove in the arete then step out right and climb the narrow wall crossing a small overhang.
FA. Chris Craggs 1981

3 Paradise Arete. . . . . **VS 4c**
Up the flake-crack that starts 2m right of the arete, to its end. Shuffle up and left to a ledge then climb the arete. Connecting to *Parasite* is worth **HVS 5a** but is bit of an eliminate.

4 Paradise Wall . . . . **HS 4b**
Excellent stuff. Starting from left or right, climb the parallel cracks until they become one, then take the continuation to the top. A well protected and a popular climb for pushing the grade and honing the jamming.

5 Milton's Meander. . . . . **VS 4c**
Devious and worthwhile. Climb *Paradise Wall* to just below where the right-hand crack ends, then traverse right all the way to the exposed arete and finish up this.
FA. Alan Clarke 1960s

6 Comet **E3 5c**
A contrived start with (easily placed side-runner up the pockets), leads rapidly to easier climbing above.
FA. Jonathan Wyatt 1985

7 Comus **E4 6a**
The right-hand line of pockets in the face is bold to start involving fierce fingery climbing. The upper section is a little easier and much safer. Tiny cams are useful.
FA. Martin Berzins 1979

8 Paradise Crack . . . . **HVD 4a**
The crack is wide, sustained and has tricky finish. Big gear will be needed to back up the loose chockstones.

9 Sand Gully . . . . **Diff**
The main groove. Start to the left of a flake and climb the groove to a bilberry ledge. Continue using any combination of the diverging cracks. Tricky for the grade.

10 Quartz . . . . **HVS 5a**
This follows the shallow scoop in the slab left of *Silica*, gained by a short wide crack - delicate and poorly protected. A variation start up the arete of block in front of the route is also possible at about the same grade.
FA. Dave Gregory 1992

11 Silica **E3 5c**
Next is a thin flake in an undercut slab. Gain the slab by using the flake (wires) and then continue precariously up the flake also using the right arete to a harrowing final couple of moves. Harder and scarier than it looks.
FA. John Fleming 1977

12 Sand Crack . . . . **HS 4b**
Just to the right is a crack in a corner. Climb this by bridging to finish up a pleasant groove. Not normally especially sandy.

From mid morning | 14 min | Windy

14m

Descent

Pegasus Wall Area

13 Curved Crack... S 4b
The curving fissure that bounds the left side of the buttress
is novel. The start is awkward but the wide leaning section
provides the crux (not much gear) and is best tackled on your
back! Reckoned to be harder than *Billiard Buttress* by some!

14 Pot Black E2 5b
Climb the pocketed wall right of the arete then teeter up the
steep slab directly above, making a worrying high step to reach
a shallow groove. Mild for E2 but feels bold the first time.
FA. Giles Barker 1976

15 Billiard Buttress HVS 5a
A bold line up the left edge of the buttress. Climb the leaning
wall 3m right of the arete and head right to a flange. Mantelshelf
to reach the deep horizontal break then move left and head up
the delicate arete and the pleasant slab above.
FA. Al Parker 1959

16 Millsom's Minion E1 5b
A great classic, mild at the grade but thrilling. Start as for
Billiard Buttress to the deep break then move right for 3m. Step
up and right to reach the blunt arete. Balance up to reach a large
shallow pocket and use this to gain a scoop and easier rock
trending left. Originally led with a single chockstone runner in
the big break.
FA. Len Millsom 1962

17 In Off E3 5c
A worthwhile direct line. From under the left end of the overlap,
pull right on pockets and climb boldly to the break. Head
straight up the wall into the base of the scoop at the point where
Millsom's Minion comes in from the right. Finish easily.
FA. Steve Bancroft 1988

Millsom's Minion
A fine companion to Paradise Wall. Good for HVS to E3
routes offering hard starts on pockets with some bold
slabs above. The classic *Millsom's Minion* is the pick of
the routes although there is much of quality here.
Approach (see map on page 178) - Take the flagged
path from the Plantation parking. At the upper gate head
up and right to above the Plantation boulders.

18 Back in the Y.M.C.A f7B+
Round the arete, pull over the overlap and climb the desperate
pocketed wall to reach *Millsom's Minion*.
FA. Neal Travers 1991

19 Winner Stays On f7B
The arete on its left-hand side.

20 Cue HVS 5b
Hard work but oddly appealing and popular too. Thrash up the
slanting chimney-groove to reach a trough and possible stance.
Hand-traverse out left below the overhang until a steep pull
(good gear) gains the thin finishing crack - phew!
FA. Bob Brayshaw 1959

21 New Balls Please E1 5b
Climb the arete by a stretch and a mantel to reach the tip of the
flake. Finish up the wall just left of the nose. Solid at the grade.
FA. Graham Parkes, Wimbledon Week 1999

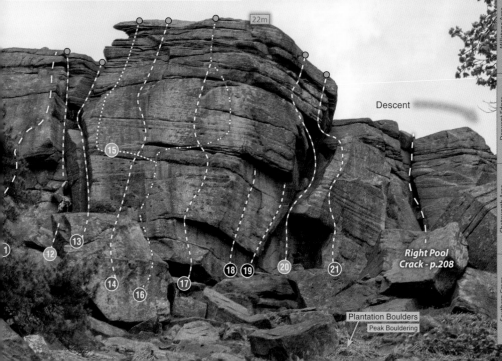

Pool Wall to Straight Ahead

A rambling section of the edge flanked on either side by more popular big hitters. An area to escape crowds without walking too far. For many years *Straight Ahead* was one of the cliff's biggest sandbags at Diff.

Approach (see map on page 178) - Walk up the flagged path from the Plantation parking. At the gate exiting the trees, follow the path up right through the boulders and on up to the edge.

❶ **Help the Young** . . . . 🔲 🔲 🔲 _____ *f7A+*
The leaning pocketed arete is superb. Jump start at this grade. The sit-start is *f7C+* and there is even a *f8A* version if you avoid using the foot block.
FA. Paul Mitchell 1996

❷ **Left Pool Crack** . . . . _____ Diff
The left-hand of a pair of cracks.

❸ **Right Pool Crack** . . . . 🔲 _____ VD
The thrutchy right-hand crack.

❹ **Between the Two** . . . . 🔲 _____ HVS 5b
Just to the right of *Pool Cracks*, (and not between the two) trending left.

❺ **Plug** . . . . 🔲 🔲 _____ *f6C*
The narrow rib is very eliminate in nature.

❻ **Pool Wall** . . . . 🔲 _____ VS 4c
The rib on the right with a pocketed start.

Next is a tiny slab below a diagonal path cutting across the edge.

❼ **Tridymite Slab** . . . . 🔲 🔲 _____ VS 5a
The left side of the slab via couple of interesting mantels.

❽ **Mitch Pitch** . . . . 🔲 🔲 🔲 _____ E1 5c
The right-hand side is harder and scarier to a tricky last move.
FA. John Allen 1984. Named after Paul Mitchell's 'eye for a line'.

❾ **Modesty** . . . . 🔲 _____ VS 4c
The short wall past decent gear to a rounded finish.
FA. Dave Gregory 1992

The Unconquerables   Away from it All

p.214   p.216

⑩ Elephant on the Dog House .. 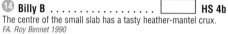 **E1 5b**
Creaky flakes allow the overlap to be reached. Finish rightwards.
FA. David Simmonite 1990

⑪ Cannonball . . . . **HS 4b**
The blunt arete past a useful pebble - pleasant.
FA. Chris Moor 2009

⑫ Cannon. . . . . **Diff**
The left leaning groove leads past the roof - worth a quick look.

⑬ Turnbull's Trajectory. . . . . . . **HS 4c**
Balance up the tricky arete and finish up a cracked scoop.
FA. Mark Turnbull 1989

⑭ Billy B . . . . **HS 4b**
The centre of the small slab has a tasty heather-mantel crux.
FA. Roy Bennet 1990

⑮ Slanting Crack. . . . . **HS 4b**
The slab leads to moves out right into the tricky steep crack.

⑯ Straight Ahead. . . . . **VS 4c**
The widening chockstoned crack is a battle! Once one the
toughest Diffs on the crag.

⑰ Blue Fluff **E4 5c**
Thin cracks lead to bold climbing up the wall and onto the
gripping rounded rib above.
FA. John Allen 1990

⑱ Don't Fluff It **E4 5c**
The wall above a block leads to a rest on the right. Finish
precariously up the rib above on poor holds.
FA. Brian Rossiter 1998

⑲ Symbiosis. . . . . **HVS 4c**
The slabby arete has little in the way of meaningful gear.
FA. Mark Scott 1974

⑳ Nephron . . . . **VS 4c**
The steeper face just right, passing the overlaps.
FA. Gary Gibson 1978

Descent

Namenlos

Namenlos

A fine hunk of rock with *Namenlos* and *Wall Buttress* as the popular ticks. The other climbs here see much less traffic despite there being some worthwhile offerings.
Approach (see map on page 178) - Walk up the flagged path from the Plantation parking. At the gate exiting the trees, the area is visible to the right and behind the Plantation. Alternatively branch right and wander up though the trees to pop out under the buttress.

❶ Men Only . . . . 🖐 ▢ **E1 5c**
Layback the rounded arete, then stride the gap and continue up the short upper arete, left then right.
FA. Brian Rossiter 1998

❷ O.D.G's Chimney . . . . 🖐 ▢ **VD**
The rift was missed by the old timers. Enter it awkwardly (4b?) and reach the top of the tall flake. Finish up the corner behind.
FA. Dave Gregory 1998

❸ Boys Will Be Boys . . ⛺ 🖐 ▥ ▢ **E6 6b**
The steep blank wall is an intense piece of climbing. Follow the vague line just left of centre. Most often done above snowdrifts!
FA. John Allen 1986

❹ Capstone Chimney . . . . . ⛺ 🖐 ▢ **S 4b**
The deep dark dank rift is okay as far as the blocking boulder. The thin can escape via a through-route past a trap-door rocking block, the rest face a taxing exit right at **VS 4c**-ish.

❺ Badly Bitten . . . . 🖐 🖐 ▢ **E4 6a**
Start up *Moribund* but swing left and climb the blunt rib on pebbles. Sadly stepping left to use the arete is nearer **E2 5c**.
FA. Paul Pepperday 1984

❻ Moribund . . . . ⛺ 🖐 ▥ ▢ **E3 6a**
Climb past the left edge of the overlap to a break, swing right and stretch past pockets to another break. A hard pull gains a flake on the left and easier ground. Probably 5c for the tall.
FA. Steve Bancroft 1980

❼ Wall Buttress . . . . . ⛺ 🖐 🖐 ▢ **HVS 5a**
A traditional grovel. Sprint up the right-slanting layback, then swing right to the base of a wider section. Alternatively, take the jamming crack in the centre of the face - better. Improvise a way up the wide bit then step left for the easiest finish or go direct.
FA. Frank Elliott 1930

❽ Direct Loss . . . . ⛺ 🖐 ▢ **E4 6a**
Climb the right-hand crack to its top, then a thinner one before stepping right onto the blunt arete (hand-placed blade-peg). Finish over the scary-looking capping block. An indirect start up the face to the left is **Walrus Buttress** which is a bit harder.
FA. John Allen 1986

❾ Improbability Drive . ⛺ 🖐 ▥ ▢ **E3 6b**
Start in the centre of the wall and climb a short crack and thin flakes to a good break. Use a small pebble to pull up the wall to a break. Finish more easily up right. E2 6a for technicians?
FA. John Hart 1978

❿ Namenlos . . . . ⛺ ▥ ▢ **HVS 5a**
Delicate and a bit bold but not E1. Climb the crack to a ledge then move left and balance up the ramp (tiny wires and cams out left). Finish up the chimney behind the huge perched block.
FA. Joe Brown 1950

⓫ Namelostit . . . . ⛺ ▢ **VS 4c**
An escape is possible by continuing up the wide cracks.

⓬ Memory Loss . . . . 🖐 ▢ **HVS 5b**
Disjointed. The short wall on the right has a long reach. Above this, move left and climb the blunt rib and final scoop.
FA. Chris Craggs 1991

⓭ Holly Crack . . . . 🖐 ▢ **S 4a**
To the right a stout holly bars access to the left-hand of a couple of fissures, a bit ugly. The right-hand finish up the fissure is **Straw Crack, VS 4c** - it is a bit of a beast.

Calvary ⟹

Descent

Straight Ahead ⟵

Sheffield Area

Ladybower Area

Stanage

Burbage Valley

Millstone Area

Derwent Edges

Chatsworth Area

Southern Crags

| From mid morning | 15 min | Windy |

Oddly the E1 grade is rather under-represented on Stanage though the great classic of *Left Unconquerable* (E1 5b) - *page 214* - makes up a little for this, as Andy Birtwistle finds out here.

100m below the edge is a lozenge-shaped block with a couple of short but memorable routes.

14 Editor's Vaseline . . . . **HVS 5b**
The left arete is approached by a traverse from the shady side. The sit-down start from the back is **Brass Monkeys**, *f7C*.
FA. Paul Mitchell 1979

15 Fear and Loathing . . **E3 5c**
The centre of the valley-face is unprotected and scary.
FA. Mark Stokes 1979

Calvary

A fine buttress with one of Stanage's best harder routes - *Calvary*. If that is too bland, *Defying Destiny* might be more to your liking. In the lower grades, there are several wide awkward cracks hereabouts.

Approach (see map on page 178) - Walk up the flagged path from the Plantation parking. At the gate exiting the trees, the area is over to the right, behind the Plantation. Alternatively branch right and wander up though the trees to locate the buttress on the right.

❶ Groovy **E2 5c**
The scoopy continuation of the initial crack. Precarious.
FA. Andy Healy 1999

❷ August Arete . . . . . . **HVS 5b**
Climb the crack to the right of the holly then move out right to reach the arete, which is climbed with difficulty.
FA. Al Parker 1959

❸ Telli **E3 6a**
Low in the grade and popular. The centre of the slab leads boldly to the break where a crucial mantel gains a standing position. A final difficult move up the pebbly slab remains. A right-hand variation is very inferior at **E2 5c/6a** depending on reach.
Photo on page 179.
FA. Steve Bancroft 1978

❹ The Spare Rib . . . . **VD**
Another awkward and dirty cleft - get in there!

❺ Traversty **E1 6a**
From a block, make bouldery moves to flakes and a break, pull up and right to the ledge then trend left up the final wall.
FA. Al Parker 1959

❻ Rib Chimney . . . . **VD**
The often-grubby cleft is climbed by skiddy back and footing to ledges and the dividing rib. Finish up its left side.

❼ Night Salt . . . . **f7A+**
The superb arete is brutal.

❽ Calvary Direct **E5 6a**
Swing round the arete and climb the wall to the deep break and runners, then move right into the regular route.
FA. Matt Carr 1989

❾ Calvary **E4 6a**
A great test of nerve and ability; protection is adequate. Start up a crack then swing out left and make a fierce mantel to reach a ledge (crucial small cams). Layback up and teeter right, or move right and climb the headwall direct - a bit harder.
FA. Gabe Regan 1976

Awkward descent

10m

Namenlos

10 Defying Destiny . . . . 🎿 ⬛ 🎣 ⬜ **E6 6b**
A tense and taxing line up the centre of the wall. Climb the initial
crack then move right and gain the next break with difficulty. Poor
cams away to the left protect a pull on some tiny flakes, then
sprint for the thin final crack. A direct start is a bouldery *f6C+*.
FA. Bill Turner 1982

11 Dark Reign . . . . 🕐 🛡 🎣 🔲 ⬜ **E5 6a**
The right arete of the buttress is climbed on its left side - gritty.
Protection is from poor cams and the crucial reach has a
potential ground fall. Better gear protects the finish.
FA. Mark Turnbull 1999

12 Chockstone Chimney . . . 🎿 ▥ ⬜ **HVD 3c**
The rift that cleaves the centre of the buttress, passing the chock
early on with difficulty. Safe but quite a battle.

13 Plugging the Gaps . . . . . 🕐 ⬛ ⬜ **E1 5b**
Climb the narrowing wall leftwards with the a long reach or two.
FA. Ian Riddington 1986

14 Cleft Wall Route 1 . . 🕐 🛡 ▥ ⬜ **HS 4b**
Take the zig-zag crack to the awkward final section.

15 Early Starter . . . . . . 🕐 ⬛ 🔲 ⬜ **E1 5b**
From the end of the wide crack, climb the wall direct.
FA. Chris Craggs 1988

16 Cleft Wall Route 2 . . 🕐 🎣 ▥ ⬜ **VS 5a**
A continuous crack running the full height of the buttress. It is
safe but awkward, especially towards the top.

17 Ritornel . . . . 🕐 🔲 🛡 ⬜ **E1 5b**
Climb the crack then move up and right to the arete. Bold.
FA. Al Parker 1972

18 Lucky Strike . . . . ▥ 🔲 ⬜ **E2 5b**
A short precarious direct finish to *Ritornel*.
FA. Andy Cave 1986

19 Strike it Lucky . . . . 🔲 🎣 ⬜ **E3 6a**
A bouldery direct start can be linked into *Lucky Strike*.

20 Three Lanky Sassenachs and one Wee Jock
. . . . ⬛ ⬜ **E1 5c**
The short crack and wee arete has a reachy move or two.
FA. Chris Craggs 1994

Descent

The Unconquerables ▶

The Unconquerables

Home to a trio of classic cracks including the peerless pitch of *The Right Unconquerable*, one of the most famous of all gritstone outings. Doing all three of the Unconquerable cracks in under an hour is a way of spicing up ascents when you have them wired.

Approach (see map on page 178) - Walk up the flagged path from the Plantation parking and branch right up though the trees to locate the buttress on the right. Alternatively wander left from the Popular End.

1 Little Unconquerable . . . HVS 5a
The left-hand crack is a mild and short test of fist-jamming. Thought by some to be the hardest of the three, though it isn't.
FA. Joe Brown 1953

2 The Left Unconquerable . E1 5b
The leaning crack is jammed to a poor rest at the break. Build a bomb-shelter then make the crucial precarious layback moves up and left to reach a ladder of jugs. A great contender for your first grit E1, as this one won't be down-graded.
Photo on page 211.
FA. Tom Probert 1949

3 Vanquished E4 6b
The upper wall between the diverging cracks has a stopper move using a really poor pocket, though the tall can reach past it.
FA. Tony Ryan 1988

4 The Right Unconquerable HVS 5a
One of gritstone's greatest classics which is sadly showing its age. Start up the polished central crack before shuffling right to the base of the flake. Layback the broken nose to reach easier though sustained climbing and a rest below the final roof. The belly-flop direct finish is best, though a sneaky traverse left is an easier option. A high stepping direct start is a polished *f6A* and is out of keeping with the rest of the climb. *Photo on page 5.*
FA. Joe Brown 1949

5 Monday Blue E2 5b
The right arete of the wall has runners just below the crux, but that is a fair way off the ground. Finish as for *The Right Unconquerable*. Low in the grade.
FA. Ernie Marshall 1981

6 The Vogon E2 5b
The inevitable girdle. Climb *Monday Blue* to the break then swing along this past *Right* and *Left* to finish up *Little*.

Descent

18m

Calvary

7 Curving Chimney Left Arete. . HVS 5a

It is possible, with considerable self-discipline and snug blinkers, to climb the narrow arete to the left of the chimney.

8 Curving Chimney . . . . . . VD

A good example of its type. Upward progress is a grind, slipping back down is a doddle. The upper section is easier.

9 Curving Buttress Direct. . E2 5b

From the left end of a ledge start up the blunt rib (poor micro wires to the left), then continue boldly and precariously straight up the rib to the sanctuary of a ledge. Finish over the roof.

FA. Pete O'Donovan 1993

10 Curving Buttress . . . E2 5b

Start as for the last route but make hard moves up and right to a ledge in the middle of the wall. Continue through a bulge to finish. Almost a full grade easier than the *Direct*.
The direct start is a very reachy *f6A*.

FA. Eric Byne 1930s

From mid morning — 15 min — Windy

Next is a set of short cracks and ribs with some easier routes. Nothing special here, except maybe a bit of peace and quiet.

11 Curving Buttress Corner . . . . . . Mod

The long shrubby corner is very mild. Suitable for the timid.

12 Chockstone Crack. . . . . HVD 4b

The short crack is a bit of thrash unless you layback it.

13 Pinch . . . . S 4b

The delicate arete then the small bulge up and right.

FA. Dave Gregory 1992

14 Greg's Retreat. . . . . HVS 5b

Spiral up the side-wall of the buttress.

FA. Mike Snell 1989

15 Pillar Arete . . . . VD

The pleasant undercut arete.

16 Jammy . . . . Diff

The central crack then the face on the right at the top.

FA. Dave Gregory 1992

17 Marmalade's Lost Start . E1 5c

The perplexing centre of the small wall to a bold finale.

FA. Tony Walker 1986

Sheffield Area · Ladybower Area · Stanage · Burbage Valley · Millstone Area · Derwent Edges · Chatsworth Area · Southern Crags

Straight Ahead
p.208

Namenlos
p.210

Calvary
p.212

The Unconquerables
p.214

Away from it All

Away from it All

Between the ever-popular *Unconquerables* and *Dover's Wall* is a series of short buttresses that used to be ignored. They are a fairly undistinguished set of routes BUT do offer a set of easier climbs in a quiet setting. Folks wishing to learn the ropes could do worse than spend a bit of time here.

Approach (see map on page 178) - Approach from either the Unconquerables or the Popular End in about 15 minutes.

❶ Delightful . . . . 🗲 [ ] **Mod**
The pleasant left-hand slab is well protected.
FA. Dave Gregory 1992

❷ Gabriel. . . . . [ ] **Mod**
The central crack is as mild as they come.
FA. Jean Carson 2001

❸ Delicious . . . . 🗲 🧗 [ ] **HVD 4b**
The right-hand of the pair of slabs.
FA. Dave Gregory 1992

❹ Little Side Line . . . . 🧗 [ ] **HS 4b**
The right side of the arete is awkward, especially the finish.
FA. Dave Gregory 1996

❺ Delicacy . . . . [ ] **HVD 4a**
Heathery ledges lead to the short layback flake. Poor.
FA. Steve Clarke 2001

❻ Delovely . . . . [ ] **S 4a**
Tricky moves access the slab which soon eases.
FA. Dave Gregory 1992

❼ Delirious. . . . . [ ] **Mod**
The crack with a - jammed flake is another easy one.
FA. Dave Gregory 1992

❽ Scoop and Corner . . . . 🗲 [ ] **Mod**
Up the rib then the right-trending scoop.
FA. Les Gillott and friends early 1960s

❾ Tumbledown . . . . 🗲 [ ] **VS 4c**
Climb up to and over an overlap. Finish up a short flake.
FA. Dave Gregory 1992

❿ One Two Eight . . . . 🧗 [ ] **HVS 5c**
Climb twin overlaps then pad to the top. Hard!
FA. Bruce Goodwin 2000

⓫ Tower Block . . . . . 🧗 ▯ 🧗 [ ] **E3 6b**
The left arete is hard to start then rounded and awkward.
FA. Al Rouse 1985

Descent

The Unconquerables - 30m

Stanage Plantation | Stanage Popular

Mounting Frustration

Pal

Dover's Wall p.222

Dover's Wall ➡

12 The Watch-Tower E2 5b
The right arete of the left-hand tower then move out left and gird yourself for gritty shelving holds and a grim exit. A long-time HVS that has caught a few folks out over the years.
FA. Gary Gibson 1981

13 Right Wall . . . . S 4a
The right wall of the widening rift is a bit contrived.

14 The Unthinkable E2 5b
Scratch past the tree then climb the centre of the wall.
FA. Paul Williams 1984

15 The Groper . . . . HVS 5a
Climb the front of the pillar then move right for an exposed and powerful finish via a crack that splits the nose.
FA. Les Gillott early 1960s

16 Accessory Chimney . . . . . . VD 4a
The groove to the right of the towers finishing up the back.

17 Accessory Wall . . . . HS 4b
The unremarkable short wall right of the chimney/groove.
FA. Steve Clark 2001

25m to the right, just beyond a break in the edge, is a short wall.

18 Older Still . . . . S 4b
The short crack and the left side of the wall.

19 Of Old f5
The short flake is tricky to get started on.
FA. Graham Hoey 1981

20 Mounting Frustration f6C
The tough centre of the wall, well named for the short.
FA. John Allen 1987

21 Pretty Petty . . . . . . f5+
Getting off the deck is the tricky bit.
FA. John Allen 1987

15m right is a tiny facet with some micro-routes.

22 Old Pals . . . . HS 4b
Up the left edge of the face.
FA. Paul Harrison 1984

23 Pal . . . . HS 4c
The wall just right is nice enough.

24 Palermo . . . . VD
A wide and wigglesome wift.

25 Pal Joey . . . . VD
A sweet little layback.

26 Kangaroo . . . . HS 4c
The pleasant blunt arete.
FA. Dave Gregory 1993

27 Skippy . . . . VS 4c
The flat wall on the right is the last route here before we head right to the delights of Dover's Wall and the Popular End.
FA. Chris Craggs 1996

	No star	☆	☆☆	☆☆☆
Mod to S	63	41	12	7
HS to HVS	77	69	36	17
E1 to E3	38	38	14	10
E4 and up	10	14	14	8

Stanage Popular - the name says it all really. The most popular section of the most popular crag in the UK - there is almost always someone climbing here, whatever the weather and whatever the time of year. Of course this popularity is with good reason, an abundance of classics across the grades, on perfect rock and in a stunning setting; a crag to return to again and again. Visit on a cold crisp winter day, or linger on into the twilight of a late summer evening, come alone or with good friends; however you do it, there is a lifetime of memories waiting to be harvested from the Queen of Grit.

Approach   Also see map on page 130

There is an elongated reinforced parking area below the right end of the cliff - a five minute walk away. This gets full fairly often on summer weekends - arriving early to bag a spot is an idea, or park at the Plantation and work left to right.

Conditions

The edge faces southwest and catches the sun from the mid-morning onwards. This means it can get very hot on calm summer days. It is exposed to any bad weather but dries very quickly after rain although a few routes can be a bit damp and sandy. Winter days can be mint, if the sun is out and the wind is absent or an easterly. Midges can make it unbearable here on calm days from May to September.

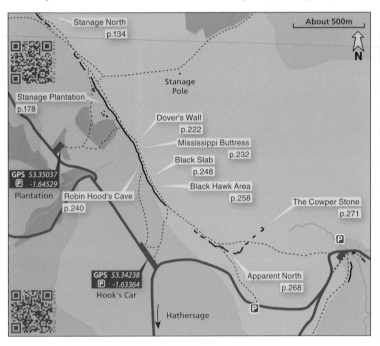

Stanage North p.134

Stanage Pole

Stanage Plantation p.178

Dover's Wall p.222

Mississippi Buttress p.232

Black Slab p.248

Black Hawk Area p.258

The Cowper Stone p.271

GPS 53.35037 ℗ -1.64529 Plantation

Robin Hood's Cave p.240

Apparent North p.268

GPS 53.34238 ℗ -1.63364 Hook's Car

Hathersage

About 500m   N

Sheffield Area

Ladybower Area

Stanage

Burbage Valley

Millstone Area

Derwent Edges

Chatsworth Area

Southern Crags

Dan Parkes powering through the bulges on the mega-classic of *The Link* (E1 5b) - *page 233* . I first did *Congo Corner* back in 1971 and spotted the direct line through the bulges, but was convinced it must have already been done. For three years it kept winking at me so in 1974 I led it anyway (inset: rope around the waist, red socks, minimal rack). In the event no earlier claims surfaced so I called it *The Link* and submitted a description - a three star route on the Queen of Grit!

Sheffield Area

Ladybower Area

Stanage

Burbage Valley

Millstone Area

Derwent Edges

Chatsworth Area

Southern Crags

Verandah Buttress
p.226

Martello Buttress
p.228

Twin Chimneys Buttress
p.238

Inverted V
p.244

Black Slab
p.248

ck
30

Mississippi Buttress
p.232

Balcony Buttress
p.236

Sheffield Area

Ladybower Area

Stanage

Robin Hood's Cave
p.240

Desperation Area
p.242

Burbage Valley

Millstone Area

The Last Day of Summer?

August 31st 2014, a fine sunny Sunday and Stanage Popular is packed with people making the most of the glorious weather before the schools restart and the autumn monsoon breaks. Maybe you were there and can spot yourself. If you can name all the routes that have climber on them, then you can consider yourself a true Stanage aficionado.

Leaning Buttress
p.252

Rusty Wall
p.250

Derwent Edges

Chatsworth Area

Southern Crags

Dover's Wall

At the northern extremity of the Popular End, the last gasp of the superb right-hand side of the cliff usually has a team or two in place. There is a bunch of good cracks here and strange goings-on around the Cleft Wing.
Approach (see map on page 218) - The usual approach is from the Hook's Car parking.

1 Bumbler's Arete . . . . [ ] **Mod**
Bumble up the teeny arete on the left.

2 A Black Ying . . . . [ ] **Mod**
This one is a titchy little groove route.

3 Beady Eye . . . . [ ] **VS 5a**
The arete can be climbed on either side at about the same grade.
FA. Dave Gregory 1993

4 Long Reaches . . . . [ ] **HVS 5c**
The centre of the wall. The grade is totally height dependant.
FA. Chris Craggs 1996

5 Newhaven . . . . [ ] **Diff**
The pleasant corner at the left-hand side of the wall.

6 Ramsgate . . . . [ ] **S 4b**
Romp up the face 1m right of the corner.
FA. Chris Craggs 1996

7 Dieppe . . . . [ ] **S 4b**
Use the thin diagonal crack to climb the wall
FA. Dave Gregory 1992

8 Falaise de Douvre . . . . [ ] **VS 4c**
Cross the ramp and head straight up the steep wall.
FA. Chris Craggs 1996

9 Dover's Wall, Route 3 . . . . . [ ] **VS 4c**
Follow the ramp, then the bulging crack, to a hard finish.
FA. Les Gillot, early 1960s

10 Nothing to do with Dover [ ] **HVS 5a**
The straightforward crack and the bulges above. Strenuous.
FA. Clive Jones 1978

11 Dover's Wall, Route 2 . . [ ] **HVS 5a**
Climb the thin crack (third from the right) to a steep thrilling finish. Beware the big wobbly spike on the right before the crux.

12 Dover's Wall Route 1.5 . . . . [ ] **HVS 5b**
Try to climb the narrow and narrowing face without recourse to the routes to either side.

13 Dover's Wall, Route 1 . . . . . [ ] **S 4b**
The thin crack (second from the right) leads past a useful horn.
FA. Harry Dover early 1930s

14 Dover's Wall, Route 4 . . . . . [ ] **VS 4b**
Climb the tricky crack left of the arete, to an awkward bulge.
FA. Dave Gregory 1970s

BAW's Crawl

Verandah Buttress

p.224

p.226

15 Wing Buttress Gully . . . . Diff
The deep cleft gives pleasant bridging when not too green.

Just to the right is a dingy recess formed by a huge flake.

16 On a Wing and a Prayer . E1 5c
Gain a small ledge 3m up the arete and continue over a nose. Climb the wall left of the roof to finish at a rocking stone.
FA. Graham Parkes 1996

17 Wing Buttress . . . . VS 5b
Start on the left wall of the cleft, at some polished footholds. Make delicate moves to better holds, swing left along the break to pass the arete, and climb the wide crack on the left.

18 5.9 Finish 5.10a
Follow either of the previous climbs, but cross the roof rightwards via a thin flake to a tough exit - **E1 5b** in English.
FA. Clive Jones 1977

19 Cleft Wing. . . . . VS 5b
Start as for *Wing Buttress* to the flake-crack that runs up to the overhang. About face, flop across the gap, and swing rapidly round the arete to easy ground. Weird and not recommended for the short who may end up with a cleft skull!
FA. Joe Brown 1953

20 Cleft Wing Superdirect . . . . . VS 4c
Climb up into the back of the gloomy recess, then hand traverse the overhanging right wall, swinging round the arete to finish easily. Feels bold, though the tall can make quite a bit of progress with their feet still on the slabby wall - cheaters.
FA. Joe Brown 1958

21 Trimming the Beard E3 6a
Layback the hairy leaning arete. *f6A* with mats.
FA. Chris Horsfall 1989

22 Spearing the Bearded Clam. . E2 5c
The tricky leaning arete on its right side is bold.
FA. Paul Mitchell 1983

23 Taking a Winger E1 5b
The centre of the front face of the wing on sloping holds eases after a tricky start.
FA. Graham Parkes 1996

24 Wing Wall. . . . . VD
The slabby rib on the right is tricky (useful holly) to a sloping ledge, then traverse left to an easy crack.

12m

Sheffield Area | Ladybower Area | Stanage | Burbage Valley | Millstone Area | Derwent Edges | Chatsworth Area | Southern Crags

BAW's Crawl

BAW's Crawl

Although only short, the quality routes on here make the area worth a visit. The contrast between the two pieces of rock is extreme; a smooth slab and a huge jutting nose - choose your poison. The slabs are usually soloed or bouldered though we have stuck with Trad Grades. There is no gear on most of them until you reach the easy upper sections anyway.

Approach (see map on page 218) - Walk up from the Hook's Car parking and head left for less than 10 mins.

❶ Bouldering Matt . . . . S 5a
The little arete starting on the right.
FA. Matt Stewart-Baker 2002

❷ Blue December Sky . . . . HS 5a
Up the right wall - short but quite pumpy.
FA. Steve Clark 2002

❸ The Nays . . . . Diff
A short arete with some breaks and ledges.
FA. Bruce Goodwin 1999

❹ Jon's Route . . . . S 5a
The pleasant centre of the face.
FA. John Street 1992

❺ Eyes . . . . HS 4b
Balance up the arete with a delicate move or two.
FA. Bruce Goodwin 1999

❻ Little Pete . . . . VS 5a
This is right side of the same arete.

❼ Obviously Done Before . . . . VD
The hanging groove just right again. Deeper in the chimney is **Probably Done Before, S 4a**, if you can avoid the opposite wall.

❽ The Punk . . . . VS 4c
The hanging crack in the north face is gained by a hand-traverse from the deep in the gully. Care with the rope-work is needed.
FA. Steve Bancroft 1973

❾ Cemetery Waits E7 6c
The hanging left arete is climbed on its left side if you can reach it. Taxing in the extreme and popular when the drifts are deep!
FA. Joe Brown (the younger) 1995

❿ Shine On E7 6c
Climb over the main overhang to reach the crack of *The Punk*. Cross the roof via a thin flake (small wires), then make difficult moves up using the very poor pockets. *f7A* above pads.
FA. Robin Barker 1992

⓫ BAW's Crawl . . . . HVS 5a
From the boulder below the overhang, swing your feet into the break (honest) then shuffle round to the front face. A couple of moves of proper climbing are needed to reach the top.
FA. Joe Brown, Nat Allen, Wilf White 1953

⓬ The Golden Path . . . f7C
The hanging arete gives a great problem.
FA. John Welford 2000s

⓭ Punklet E1 6a
Make a hard pull on tiny holds to reach the break and a hard finish on poor holds. *f6A+* if you sneak off right.
FA. Steve Bancroft 1976

⓮ Public Face . . . . VS 5a
Up the groove in the arete.

Dover's Wall

15 Public Image . . . . VS 5a
Traverse the top break leftwards all the way to *The Punk*.

16 Private Chimney . . . . Diff
The kinked left-hand rift in the open recess.

17 Green Chimney . . . . VD
The awkward narrow rift is best avoided when green.

18 Pedlar's Rib E1 5c
The neat blunt rib is climbed on fingery layaways (easier if you keep left) to a break and jams, swing right to easier ground. Unprotected until after the crux.
FA. Jim Perrin 1967

19 Non-stop Pedalling E2 5c
For more excitement, head left up the prow via strenuous pulls.
FA. Steve Bell 1985

20 Pedlar's Arete . . . . . HVS 5a
Climb the blunt arete using flakes (poor worn runners) to a spooky stretch right to finish up *Pedlar's Slab*.
FA. Don Morrison early 1960s

21 Keep Pedalling E2 5c
The blunt rib left of *Pedlar's Slab* on its right side directly to the ledge on the arete. Finish direct on more slopers.
FA. Chris Craggs 1991

22 Pedlar's Slab . . . . . HVS 5c
The centre of the slab has a tough start - hard unless you hop-it! Continue with care up pockets to easy ground.
FA. Barry Pedlar early 1960s

23 Top Block Rock . . . . VD
Up the angular rib to a rocky top block.

24 Elastic . . . . VS 4c
The very narrow pillar just right is stretching the point a bit.

25 Corner Crack . . . . Diff
The grassy corner steepens towards the top.

26 Recess Rib . . . . VD
The narrow rib forming the left edge of the gloomy recess.

27 Viridescent Corner . . . . HVD
This is the luminous green corner in the left side of the recess.

28 Pisa Pillar . . . . S 4a
A leaning pillar is reached via a small bulge and is soon over.
FA. Dave Gregory 1992

29 Hidden Crack . . . . VD
An odd trip behind the pillar, through a skylight and up the green corner beyond. Often very dirty.
FA. Dave Gregory 1992

30 Pisa Crack . . . . HS 4c
The leaning groove in the right-hand side of the recess leads to a tough exit round the roof at the top.

From mid morning | 14 min | Windy

10m

8m

Verandah Buttress

Sheffield Area
Ladybower Area
Stanage
Burbage Valley
Millstone Area
Derwent Edges
Chatsworth Area
Southern Crags

Verandah Buttress

Steep powerful routes attack the stacked bulges here, there isn't much for the slab climber. The routes on the right side of the buttress are (a bit) easier, but still feel quite intense. The shorter wall to the right offers a small selection of easier stuff, which is a nice change.

Approach (see map on page 218) - Walk up from the Hook's Car parking and head left.

❶ Plastic Dream **E3 6a**
The undercut left arete of the buttress is tricky to start, requiring flexibility and maybe a bit of ingenuity. Once established things ease.
FA. Ed Wood 1977

❷ Tarzan Boy **E3 6a**
A route to nowhere. Climb straight up to the dodgy looking hanging flake then shimmy left below this to finish up *Plastic Dream*. Rarely travelled.
FA. Andy Barker 1982

❸ Headless Chicken **E5 6b**
Climb left via a line of tiny flakes then stretch left to holds below the hanging 'guillotine'. Keep right of this to the roof, step left and pull over (hard) to gain the final wall.
FA. Neil Foster 1994

❹ Off With His Head . . **E4 6b**
Climb the centre of the face to a tiny ledge, step left and go up to the lip of the overhang, then trend left past a well-marked runner slot to hard moves over the nose. Another hard move using a pocket, leads through the final roof to an easy finish.
FA. Andy Barker 1982. Originally started via Tarzan Boy.

❺ Guillotine Direct **E4 6b**
Cut out the loop on the regular route by making a couple of fierce moves over the roof that it skirts round.
FA. John Allen 1987

❻ The Guillotine **E3 5c**
Devious, hard work and excellent. Start up the centre of the lower wall but swing right (poor wires) under the roofs to a rest on the right. Traverse the narrow hanging wall leftwards (gripping and hard for long legs) until past the arete. Cross the final overhang using the flake in the nose or the breaks just left.
FA. Ed Drummond (one fat aid peg) 1971. FFA. John Allen 1973

❼ The Old Dragon **E2 5b**
Climb the steep shallow groove on the right-hand side of the overhanging face to a good ledge. The holds are better than you might expect though the runners aren't. Finish up the short overhanging crack just to the left, or escape right - tut tut.
FA. Bill Birch (one nut) 1968. FFA. John Allen 1973

Dover's Wall

⑧ Mary Whitehouse...... 🛋️ 🧗 ☐ *f6A*
Follow then lip of the overhang rightwards then escape right.

⑨ Verandah Buttress Direct 🛋️ 🧗 ☐ *f7A+*
Climb direct over the roof.

⑩ Fit as a Butcher's Dog .. 🖐️ 🧗 ☐ **E1 5c**
Tackle the gruesome roof crack then finish up the open wall
directly above the shelf.
FA. Graham Parkes 1997

⑪ Verandah Buttress .. 🛋️ 🧗 🧗 ☐ **HVD 5b**
The polished sloping shelf of the Verandah is gained at its
bottom right-hand corner, usually by a torrid struggle -
combined tactics are frowned upon! From the scoop, traverse
left to finish up the exposed arete of the buttress. The climbing
is no harder then 4a once you get going and the start is
rumoured to be 4c for Masons and 6a for technical dunces.

⑫ Butcher Crack .... 🛋️ 🗜️ ☐ **HVS 5b**
Start as for *Verandah Buttress* to the shelf then continue direct
via a short crack and a final l-o-o-o-o-o-ng stretch.
FA. Peter Biven 1954

⑬ One Stop Shopping .... 🧗 🗜️ ☐ **E1 6a**
An eliminate straight up the wall has some decent moves.
FA. Graham Parkes 1997

⑭ Greengrocer Wall... 🛋️ 🧗 🧗 ☐ **HVS 5c**
The wall to the left of the corner cracks has a fingery start using
a thin diagonal crack. Continue up the wall passing a useful
lump to a reachy finish.
FA. Ray Burgess early 1950s

⑮ Verandah Cracks Left ...... 🧗 ☐ **VD**
The left twin crack is awkward where it widens.
FA. Don Morrison and friends, early 1960s

⑯ Verandah Cracks Right .... ☐ **Diff**
The right twin is milder giving pleasant bridging.
FA. Don Morrison and friends, early 1960s

⑰ Verandah Wall.......... 🧗 ☐ **VS 4c**
The centre of the wall to the right of the corner is short but
spirited, has some rounded holds and is surprisingly steep.
FA. Don Morrison early 1960s

⑱ Cocktails........... 🛋️ 🧗 ☐ **VS 4c**
From the small overhang, trend left through the bulge then finish
directly up the rib. Another short one with a bit of a bite.
FA. Dave Gregory 1993

⑲ Verandah Pillar .... 🛋️ ☐ **HS 4b**
Climb the left-facing flakes to a well protected finish.
FA. Dick Brown 1951

⑳ The Confectioner ...... 🛋️ 🧗 ☐ **VS 5a**
The rib on the right is approached from the right - sweet.

Sheffield Area

Ladybower Area

Stanage

Burbage Valley

Millstone Area

Derwent Edges

Chatsworth Area

Southern Crags

1 Intermediate Buttress... ▢▣▢ HVD 4a
Step in from the left then climb the left-hand edge of the north-facing wall via a series of good breaks, to a groping exit.

2 Jaygo's Pipe .... ▢▣▢ VS 4c
Straight up the centre of the buttress to a rounded exit.
FA. Bruce Goodwin 1994

3 The Nose .... ▢▣▣▢ VS 4c
Hand-traverse out right along the low break to the arete. Pumpy.
FA. Joe Brown 1954

4 Second Wind...... ▢▣▣▢ E1 5c
Hand-traverse left and pull into a short crack with difficulty. Continue up the right-hand side of the arete via a tricky bulge.
FA. Tony Ryan 1986

5 Swings .... ▢▣▢ E1 5c
Climb the centre of the buttress - tough - to jugs and runners. **Bail** out here if bouldering. Continue up the steep groove and overhang. Avoiding the crux by swinging in from the right is **Roundabout, HVS 5b**.
FA. Tony Walker 1983. FA. (Roundabout) Biven and Peck 1956

6 Turf Crack .... ▢▢ VD
The grass-less groove is a piece of well-protected bridging.
FA. Dick Brown 1951

7 Little Tower.......... ▢▣▢ VS 4c
The short arete avoiding the routes on either side. Tricky gear.
FA. Dick Brown 1951

8 49 Bikinis .... ▢▣▢ HVS 5a
Steeply up the centre of the face and then through the bulges.
FA. Bill Briggs 1993

Martello Buttress
Originally named because of a vague resemblance to the Martello Towers, set up on the south coast back in 1804, as protection against a possible invasion by Napoleon and his army. This buttress contains some fine routes with steep starts and rounded, airy finishes.
Approach (see map on page 218) - Walk up from the Hook's Car parking and head left for about 8 minutes.

9 Little Tower Chimney ...... ▣▢ Diff
The left-hand rift in the back of the bay.

10 Little Tower Chimney Right .. ▣▢ VD

11 Beads.................... ▢ S 4a
The thin green crack splitting the wall in the gloomy gully.

12 Trinket .... ▢ VD
This is the dinky arete just right.

13 Narrowing Chimney .... ▣▢ Diff

14 Byne's Route... ▢▣▣▢ HS 4b
Climb into a recess with a block. Exit rightwards to a short wide crack zigging up the wall and a rounded finish left of the arete.
Photo on page 231.
FA. Eric Byne early 1930s

15 Zel............. ▢▣▢ VS 4c
Climb *Byne's Route* to the top of the first crack then cross the wall leftwards to the arete and follow this on its right-hand side.
FA. Gary Gibson 1979

16 Choux . . . . 🔧☐ **E2 6a**
Pass the left edge of the roof then climb the centre of the wall.
FA. Brian Rossiter 1992

17 Choux Fleur. . . . . ▌☐ **E1 5c**
Struggle around the right edge of the overhang, reach left to a
block and use this to get onto the wall. Finish direct.
FA. Brian Rossiter 1992

18 Another Game of Bowls Sir Walter?
. . . . 🔆🔧☐ **E1 5b**
Up a short flake just right of the arete to where awkward moves
gain better holds. Continue steeply right of the arete - rounded.
FA. Chris Craggs 1992

19 Martello Buttress . . . . . . [Top⌐50]🔧☐ **VS 4c**
The original classic here. Climb either side of the left-hand
jammed block, then continue direct for 6m until a ledge on the
left can be reached. Move left to finish up the arete.
FA. Fergus Graham 1922

20 The Scoop. . . . . . 🔆▌🔧🔧☐ **HVS 5b**
Start to the right of *Martello Buttress* at a second jammed
block. Move up and left into an open shallow scoop where long
reaches and rounded breaks give excellent sustained climbing.
FA. Rodney Wilson 1959

21 Bloodshot . . . . . 🔆▌🔧🔆☐ **E3 5c**
Start up a leaning groove on the right moving left to a small
ledge. Step right and climb the bulge on sloping holds and with
long reaches.
FA. Gabriel Regan 1979

22 The Old Scoop. . . . . ☐ **VS 4c**
An earlier climb with the same name as route 20. Climb a tricky
slanting crack then trend back up the left edge of the scoop.

23 Martello Cracks . . . . 🔆☐ **Mod**
The parallel cracks in the slabby angle, a nice intro to grit.

24 Mistella . . . . 🔧▌🔧☐ **VS 5a**
Move right to the middle of the face and climb to a high crux.

25 Mistella Right . . . . 🔆☐ **S 4a**
Finishing up the arete is more logical and more pleasant.

26 Phlegethoa . . . . 🔆🔧☐ **E1 5c**
From under the nose, swing right onto the arete and make a
hard move to easier ground. Continue to the horizontal break
and the upper arete. A fingery direct start is *f6A*.
FA. Jim Perrin 1967

27 Fading Star . . . . . . 🔆▌🔧☐ **E2 6a**
The perplexing bulge - the tall will be able to mantelshelf it
but shorties may have to resort to pulling on the nonexistent
pebbles. A direct start up the lower wall is *f6B*.
FA. Gary Gibson 1979

28 Saliva. . . . . 🔆🔧☐ **E1 5b**
A thin crack gains a committing traverse to finish steeply up the
right-hand side of the arete. A dry-mouthed VS for many years!
FA. Peter Biven 1955

29 Ashes . . . . 🔆🔧▌🔆☐ **E3 5c**
From the thin crack of *Saliva*, continue boldly to a large
horizontal break, and runners. Finish up the steep wall above.
FA. John Fleming 1981

Heaven Crack

Devil's
Chimney
- p.230

Devil's Chimney - p.230

Sheffield Area
Ladybower Area
Stanage
Burbage Valley
Millstone Area
Derwent Edges
Chatsworth Area
Southern Crags

Heaven Crack

The fine fissures of *Heaven Crack* and *Hell Crack* are the easier ever-popular showpieces of this sector, though most of the routes see plenty of attention.
Approach (see map on page 218) - From the Hook's Car parking head up and left for 10 mins.

1 Devil's Chimney...... VD
The dark rift in traditional style to an awkward narrowing exit.

2 Stay in the Light...... HS 4b
Bridge the outer edge of *Devil's Chimney* for a different view of the world. Exposed but easier than the VD version?
FA. Steve Clark 1999

3 Step-ladder Crack........ VS 5a
From the pillar right of *Devil's Chimney*, pull right to access the hanging crack awkwardly. Climb this, via another hard move, then traverse rightwards to finish left of the top of *Hell Crack*.
FA. Ted Howard early 1950s. Once known as Styx.

4 Step-ladder Crack Direct. HVS 5c
Climb into the base of the crack with difficulty, then finish up the short wall by a final tough and rounded mantelshelf.

5 Dark Water......... E3 6b
The wall under the finish of *Step Ladder Crack* is gained from the right (highish side-runner) and climbed by a ludicrous dyno.
FA. Al Rouse 1983

6 Hell Crack.......... VS 4c
The bulging jamming crack is taken direct and is superb. The initial overhang is the crux and, although well protected, it will seek out any weakness in your jamming technique.

7 Still in Limbo.......... E1 5b
The groove, overhang and wall between *Heaven* and *Hell*.
FA. Chris Craggs 1993

8 Heaven Crack........ VD
The flake crack in the left-hand wall of the descent gully is an ever-popular mini-classic. Layback the flakes to a tricky exit always pausing to place a few runners along the way.

9 Lethe........... VS 4c
This is the green and reachy wall to the right of *Heaven Crack*.
FA. Jim Perrin 1967

10 Jean's Line.............. HS 4a
The undistinguished groove and crack at the top of the gully.
FA. Ron Kenyon 1977

12m

Descent

From mid morning   12 min   Windy

Acheron - p.232

Martello Buttress ◀

Mississippi Buttress ▶

Valerie Partington on the tricky but worthwhile
Byne's Route (HS 4b) - *page 228* - which makes
the most of the left side of Martello Buttress.
Photo: Mike Hutton

Sheffield Area

Ladybower Area

Stanage

Burbage Valley

Millstone Area

Derwent Edges

Chatsworth Area

Southern Crags

Mississippi Buttress

Perhaps the finest buttress on Stanage - a magnificent bastion of gritstone with a great set of climbs. *Mississippi Buttress Direct* is one of the best VS routes on grit and the nearby offerings of *Congo Corner* at HVS and *The Link* at soft E1 means that these ever-popular grades are well covered. Towards the lower end of the grade spectrum, *Mississippi Chimney* is a fair beginners' route and *Amazon Crack* is a good Severe.

Approach (see map on page 218) - Walk up from the Hook's Car parking and head left for about 10 mins to the tallest buttress in the area.

❶ Acheron . . . . 🔄 🗔 🗺 ☐ **E1 5b**
A worthwhile route up the left side of *The Louisiana Rib*. A reachy pull and delicate step from the break give a bold crux.
FA. Jim Perrin 1967

❷ The Louisiana Rib . . . . 🔄 ☐ **VS 4c**
Devious and worthwhile. Climb the crack on the left then traverse to the right arete. Up this awkwardly on its left-hand side then move left into the centre of the face to finish.
FA. Dick Brown 1950

❸ Finger Licking Good . 🔄 🗔 🗞 ☐ **E1 5b**
A fingery eliminate direct up the centre of the face with some neat moves along the way.
FA. Graham Parkes 1998

❹ The Levée . . . . 🔄 🗔 ☐ **HVS 5b**
Start just left of the *Chimney* and climb direct, through the crux of *The Louisiana Rib* to a finish on the right.
FA. Bill Briggs 1993

❺ Mississippi Chimney . . . . . . 🔄 ☐ **VD**
Enter the chimney by a steep blocky crack. Above this the main fissure is followed more easily. A decent beginners' climb.
FA. J.W. Puttrell late 1890s

❻ African Herbs . . . . 🗺 ☐ **E3 5c**
The bold rib high on the left sees very few visitors.
FA. Al Rouse 1985

Descent

22m

Heaven Crack

7 Dark Continent..... 🗝️ ▯ 🧗 □ **E1 5c**
A fine climb up the left-hand side of the face. Pull through the roof using a flake-crack then easier climbing leads to a blank section. This is climbed by a hard semi-mantelshelf (large cams) then move left to finish through the bulges with a flourish.
FA. Phil Burke 1978

8 Congo Corner..... Top50 ▯ 🧗 □ **HVS 5b**
A breathtaking pitch of outstanding quality. The technical thin crack leads to a rest below the overhang then traverse up and left until a good horizontal break is reached. Move back right and make a tricky move to gain a good ledge. From here a crucial precarious layaway move leads to the horn and a delicate finish.
FA. Peter Biven 1954

9 The Link........... Top50 🔗 □ **E1 5b**
A direct on *Congo Corner* with good rests between the hard moves and low in the grade. Climb *Congo Corner* to where it heads off left. Then go through the bulges, on creaky flakes, to where a swing left allows you to join *Congo Corner* again just below its upper crux. Finish up this. *Photos on page 219 and 11.*
FA. Chris Craggs 1974

10 The Mersey Variant.... 🗝️ ▯ □ **E2 5c**
A bit of a non-line but with some decent moves before it runs out of space and blinkers are needed.
FA. Trevor Pilling 1980

11 Mississippi Buttress Direct.. Top50 □ **VS 4c**
The flaky crack that splits the centre of buttress is one of Stanage's top VS routes, though some odd souls don't rate it. Start in a leaning groove and climb this steeply to a bridged rest below bulges. Pass this awkwardly and then follow the flake crack above which eases gradually.
FA. Roy Horsman 1927

12 Mississippi Variant.... 🗝️ 🔗 □ **HVS 5a**
Follow *Mississippi Buttress Direct* to half-height, then move right to reach the right-trending flake. Climb this steeply to an overhang and make difficult moves out right to gain a small ledge and an easier finish up the wall.
FA. Bernard Simonds 1930s

13 Orinoco Flow...... 🗝️ ▯ 🔗 □ **E2 5c**
An eliminate but worth doing. Climb through the centre of the big roof, do the crux of *Mississippi Variant Direct* then take the upper bulges by a flake, trending right up the head-wall.
FA. Graham Parkes 1996

14 Mississippi Variant Direct... 🗝️ □ **E1 5b**
Climb through the overhangs to a ledge then, from the left-hand end of this (low runners) step awkwardly up and left (much harder for the short who might claim an E2 5c) to reach a sloping ledge on the previous route. Finish up this.
FA. Bill Birch 1968

15 Stanleyville......... 🗝️ 🦅 □ **E4 5c**
Low in the grade but pretty damn scary. Climb the rib to a ledge then make worrying moves to a break and very poor cam runner. Make a hard mantel then finish easily or, if you haven't had enough yet, head left for a pumpier finale.
FA. John Allen 1973

16 Puzzlelock.......... 🦅 🔩 □ **E5 6a**
The blunt rib gives bold pitch on small holds and little gear until above the crux. A bit of an eliminate and low in the grade.
FA. Gary Gibson 1981

17 Morrison's Redoubt. 🗝️ 🦅 ▯ □ **E1 5b**
A good route, again low in the grade though the start is quite bold. From a block (low cam) climb the wall using tiny layaways to a good horizontal slot. Continue up a short vertical crack then a wider one, trending right to the top by great climbing.
FA. Don Morrison early 1960s

18 Melancholy Witness....... 🦅 □ **E3 5c**
Another eliminate, up the right arete. Start just right of *Morrison's Redoubt* and climb the left side of the arete to runners over on *Morrison's*. Move up right on flakes to finish.
FA. Gary Gibson 1981

19 Amazon Crack........ 🗝️ 🔗 □ **S 4a**
The undercut flaky crack is awkward to access (4b for the short) because of the undercut start. Once reached, the main crack soon eases to a steep but juggy romp. *Photo on page 41.*

20 Tributary............. 🔗 □ **E2 5b**
The blunt arete just right is rarely travelled and quite tough. A side-runner to the left lowers the grade and the grip a bit.
FA. Bruce Goodwin 1996

14m

Routes 21 to 28

Sheffield Area

Ladybower Area

Stanage

Burbage Valley

Millstone Area

Derwent Edges

Chatsworth Area

Southern Crags

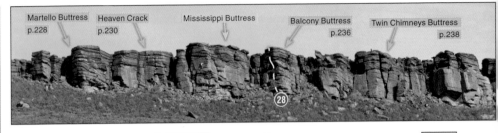

Martello Buttress p.228 Heaven Crack p.230 Mississippi Buttress Balcony Buttress p.236 Twin Chimneys Buttress p.238

㉑ Fallen Pillar Chimney . . . . . 🚻 ⬜ VD
The odious green rift in the gully leads to the slumped tower blocking the way. Bridge past this to easy ground.

㉒ Fairy Castle Crack . . . . ⬜ VD
The angular groove on the right leads past a small overhang and into the continuation groove.

㉓ Pixie . . . . ⬜ VS 4c
Climb the blocky pillar and finish up the thin left-slanting flake in the final tower. Decent moves but a bit of an eliminate.
FA. Dave Gregory 1992

㉔ Fairy Chimney . . . . ⚀ ⬜ Diff
The main groove on the left-hand side of the buttress leads past the right side of a jutting block and into a shallow chimney.
FA. Fred Pigott early 1920s

㉕ Polyfilla . . . . ⬜ VS 4c
Plugs a gap! The narrowing slab leads to the next route. A finish out right is possible but avoiding the routes either side is tricky.
FA. Chris Craggs 1996

㉖ Balcony Climb . . . . ⚀ ⬜ HS 4b
The leaning crack left of the niches in the north-facing wall is followed by well protected climbing on jugs 'n' jams.
FA. Fred Pigott early 1920s

㉗ Balcony Cracks . . . . . . ⚀ 🔨 ⬜ S 4a
Climb to the upper niche past a huge block, then the left arete until it is possible to pull right over the bulge to the final wall.

㉘ Nine-Eleven . . . . 💪 ⬜ E2 5c
A line keeping left of the arete to a tricky crux roof near the top.
FA. Bill Briggs 2003

Descent

Exit Stage
Left - p.236

Sheffield Area

Ladybower Area

Stanage

Burbage Valley

Millstone Area

Derwent Edges

Chatsworth Area

Southern Crags

Gordon MacNair showing that being three score years and ten is no excuse for not cruising the classic *Cave Arete* (HVS 5a) - *page 242* - Stanage Popular. Gordon set himself the challenge of 70 Extremes in his 70th year and stormed it.

1 Exit Stage Left ...... ☼ 🔲 HVS 5b
Start under the left edge of the face and climb the bulges to ledges. The next set of bulges is quite reachy. Move left to finish up the wall around the arete.
FA. Chris Craggs 1993

2 Centre Stage ...... ☼ 🔲 HVS 5a
Nice and steady at the grade. Start at ledges below the centre of the face, trend left then right through bulges. Stay left of *Balcony Buttress's* wide crack then, from the heather ledge, pull strenuously through the centre of the roof to finish at the notch.
FA. Chris Craggs 1993

3 Balcony Buttress ...... ☼ ◤ S 4a
A great classic. Trend left to a wide crack, climb this to a heathery ledge, then move left to an oddly-awkward flying-flake finish on the airy arete.
FA. Lewis Coxon 1922

4 Balcony Balustrade ...... ☼ VS 5a
Start just right and climb the thin slab to the roof and good gear. Launch through the overhang on surprisingly good holds.
FA. Chris Craggs 1993

5 The Flue ...... ☼ 🔲 HVD 4a
Climb the left-hand of a pair of parallel cracks then the wide left-trending rift to a narrow and exposed exit where helmets jam.

6 Big Yin ...... VS 4c
A pleasant line up the rib and scoop above.
FA. Chris Craggs 1993

7 Scoop Crack ...... ☼ 🔲 HS 4c
Climb the right-hand crack in a shallow groove and its continuation, passing the inverted V-shaped niche with difficulty.

8 Rib and Face ...... ☼ ◤ VS 4c
The angular rib then the centre of the flat face above.
FA. Mike Snell 1991

9 Balcony Corner ...... ☼ VD
Climb the short wall into a left-facing corner with a block overhang. Pass the left-hand side of this to reach easy ground.

10 Upanover ...... 🔲 VS 5b
The small square pillar is accessed via the notch in the roof.

11 Upandover Crack ...... S 4b
A tricky but safe move is needed to pass the bulge in the crack.

12 Twinkle Toes ...... Mod
The slab just right, and left of an awkward descent is usually green, though it gives a pleasant pitch when dry.

The buttress under the jutting spike of the Needle has some good beefy outings, though the first two are bolder affairs. On the Needle itself is one of the odder routes on Stanage.

13 Savage Amusement E1 5b
A dangling girdle of the break running round the Needle, in either direction. Bizarre and well named.

14 M Route . . . . VS 4c
The blunt arete on its left side is lacking in gear and reachy too. Not visible on the topo.
FA. Reg Pillinger 1952

15 Needle Crack. . . . . VS 4c
Start from a boulder and head right to a shallow groove. Climb this (again little in the way of gear) to an exit under the Needle.
FA. Nat Allen c1950. Also known as N Route.

16 Regret E4 6a
The wall to the right isn't popular mainly because it is hard and poorly protected, even with a side-runner in Agony Crack.
FA. Al Rouse (Finish) 1984. FA. (Start) Graham Parkes 1998.

17 Agony Crack . . . . HVS 5a
Climb the awkward thin crack in the blunt arete to a cramped ledge, then attack the crack that splits the overhang by jamming/ laybacking. Watch for the rope jamming in the crack.
FA. Len Chapman 1940

18 Thrombosis . . . . VS 5a
Climb the groove on the right to a ledge then the left-hand narrow crack above. Hard for the grade though the gear is good!
FA. Don Morrison early 1960s

19 Rigor Mortis . . . . VS 4c
Climb Thrombosis to the ledge then continue up the right-hand crack with a finish up the arete if required. Another tricky one.
FA. Don Morrison early 1960s

20 Paralysis . . . . VS 4b
From the gully climb the shallow groove (poor gear) to a steep but juggy exit via the horizontal breaks.
FA. Don Morrison early 1960s

21 Boris the Bold . . . . HVS 5a
The last route on the wall climbs the face on the right - it is fairly unremarkable but at least it plugs a gap.
FA. Chris Gilbert 1985

From mid morning | 12 min | Windy

The Needle

9m

8m

9

14

15   16   17   18   19   20   21

13

Twin Chimneys Buttress - p.238

Balcony Buttress
A tall buttress with a heathery ledge at half-height. The classic of Balcony Buttress always appears to have a team in place. There are other routes here worth doing such as Centre Stage. There are easier lines on the right.
Approach (see map on page 218) - Walk up from the Hook's Car parking and head left for 10 minutes.

Sheffield Area · Ladybower Area · Stanage · Burbage Valley · Millstone Area · Derwent Edges · Chatsworth Area · Southern Crags

Twin Chimneys Buttress

An area with an excellent collection of easier climbs including the delicate classic of *Twin Chimneys Buttress*. There are also several short climbs on the right which have proved to be much more popular since they were properly recorded.

Approach (see map on page 218) - Walk up from the Hook's Car parking and head left for 10 minutes.

① Via Roof Route .... 🗲 **HVS 5b**
Climb the tough thin crack into the cave (5c ?) pull up to the roof and swing right to access the easier wall.
FA. Eric Byne 1951

② Don't Bark, Bite .... 🗲 **E3 5c**
Climb the bold slab to the cave and then muscle along the cracks in the roof trending left to a finish up the hanging arete.
FA. Gary Gibson 1980

③ Crack and Cave .... **HVD 4a**
Climb the awkward wide crack to the right edge of the cave then move right to finish up the face. Well protected but hard work.
Photo on page 133.
FA. Eric Byne 1950

④ Bill and Ted's Lobotomy . 🗲 **E3 5c**
A bold eliminate up the narrow face. Nice moves but the escape routes along the way are just too tempting to ignore.
FA. Adrian Jones 1992

⑤ Twin Chimneys Buttress . 🗲 **VS 4c**
The blunt arete has a bit of a bold start. Slippery moves gain the arete, then a detached block. Another tricky move gains the upper section which soon eases. *Photo on page 5.*
FA. Lewis Coxon 1922

⑥ Lucy's Delight .... **VS 4b**
The narrow slab with a detour left towards the arete around the crucial central section.
FA. Al Parker 1978

⑦ Lucy's Joy............. **E1 5b**
A direct version of *Lucy's Delight* which tackles the roof.
FA. Bruce Goodwin 1995

⑧ Left Twin Chimney .... **Diff**
The left-hand fork of the prominent Y-shaped chimney is mild.
FA. J.W.Puttrell late 1800s

⑨ Right Twin Chimney ...... **VD**
Up the rib right of the chimney for 5m then the chimney. Finish up the wall behind. Starting direct is easier but can be green.
FA. J.W.Puttrell late 1800s

⑩ Triplet .... **VS 4b**
Meander up the airy widening wall between the chimneys.
FA. Bruce Goodwin 1992

⑪ Bobsnob **E1 5a**
The slab tucked behind the block is delicate and unprotected.
FA. Chris Craggs 1983

Balcony Buttress

Balcony Buttress
p.236

Twin Chimneys Buttress

Robin Hood's Cave
p.240

Desperation
p.242

Inverted V
p.244

⑫ Dave's Little Route. . . . . [   ] **S 4b**
Sprint up the left arete of the block, then step onto the wall
behind and access the rib via a tricky bulge.
FA. David Simmonite 1993

⑬ Little John's Step. . . . . 🔄 [   ] **S 4b**
A wanderer. Pull left through the initial overhang and climb to
the top of the block. Stride across on to the main face, move left
and climb just right of *Right Twin Chimney* then traverse left to
finish up the final easy section of *Crack and Cave*.

*For years the next bunch of climbs were ignored as being too
trivial to be recorded on Stanage. They have become popular
beginners' routes since being named and described.*

⑭ Little Slab. . . . . 📐 [   ] **S 4a**
The little slab behind the block
FRA. John Street 1992

⑮ Awl . . . . 🔄 [   ] **HVD 3c**
The delicate left arete and the face on the left of the final nose.

⑯ Bean . . . . 🔄 📐 [   ] **VS 4c**
The narrow slab gives delicate moves just below the ledge that
cuts across the buttress. Finish via a thin crack.
FA. Bruce Goodwin 1992

⑰ Dun . . . . 🔄 [   ] **HS 4b**
The blunt left arete of the central groove gives good
moves. Finish through the overhang as for the last route.
FA. John Street 1992

⑱ Bee . . . . 🔄 [   ] **VD**
A mild crack leads to an easier groove. A nice beginner's route.

⑲ Four. . . . . 🔄 [   ] **VS 4c**
Climb the right-hand face to a ledge. The upper arete is climbed
via a couple of small overlaps.
FA. Bruce Goodwin 1992

Descent

10m

The Asp
- p.240

⑭ ⑮ ⑯ ⑰ ⑱ ⑲

Sheffield Area
Ladybower Area
Stanage
Burbage Valley
Millstone Area
Derwent Edges
Chatsworth Area
Southern Crags

Robin Hood's Cave

Robin Hood's Cave is hidden on the left, halfway up Robin Hood's Cave Gully. This superb ever-dry bivi site has been used by generations of climbers; please respect it if you stop here and clean up after yourself. There are many fine climbs here across the grades with the combination of *Robin Hood's Cave Innominate* and *Harding's Super Direct Finish* the best.

Approach (see map on page 218) - Walk up from the Hook's Car parking and head left for 10 minutes.

① **Robin Hood's Cave Traverse** . ☆ [ ] **S 4b**
An expedition from above *Wuthering* all the way to the finish of *Robin Hood's Balcony Cave Direct*. It is mostly ledge shuffling but the 'bad step' between the two caves needs care as it is difficult to protect. Belay along the way.

② **The Asp** . . . . ☆☆☆ [ ] **E3 6a**
A fine and tenuous finger-crack. Gain the base of the crack from the left via the big pocket or (harder) from below. Perfect wires protect thin layback moves at two-thirds height and the awkward finishing crack which is less bold than it used to be.
FA. Ed Drummond 1975

③ **Boc No Buttress** . . . . ☆☆☆ [ ] **E5 6a**
An exciting climb with just enough protection. Climb *The Asp* to the good runners then make a difficult hand-traverse (easier for lanky types) to the arete, along a poor set of pockets. Continue boldly up the arete, past one good runner. The direct start, **6c**, is an astounding leap with a high side runner.
FA. Steve Bancroft 1979. FA. (direct) John Allen 1990

④ **Wuthering** . . . . ☆☆☆ [ ] **E2 5b**
A devious but classic solution to this fine buttress. Climb the chimney (a high sling runner is naughty but normal) until it is possible to bridge along a low line of pockets and bounce onto the left-hand arete. Traverse left and up to a slot in the centre of the face - small gear. When suitably sorted, trend left to a shallow groove just short of the arete. *Photo opposite.*
FA. Ed Drummond 1973

⑤ **Dithering Frights** . . . . . . ☆ [ ] **E2 5b**
Climbing straight up the face from the initial traverse gives this gap filler. A visit to the *Wuthering* slot for runners is a bit of pain but a sensible idea - more like E3 if you don't bother.
FA. Chris Craggs 1995

⑥ **Robin Hood's Chockstone Chimney**
. . . . ☆ [ ] **S 4a**
The deep chimney is an ancient classic, slick and awkward until the chockstone is passed. Protection is good throughout and the upper section is much easier.
FA. Fred Pigott and friends, early 1920s

⑦ **Connelly's Variation** . . . . [ ] **HS 4a**
From above the chockstone this is an exposed finish up the left arete. Traversing a couple of moves lower is **Premier, HVS 5a**.
FA. Byron Connelly 1930s. FA. (Premier) John Allen 1971

⑧ **Not Much Weak Stack Battered or What?**
. . . . [ ] **E4 6b**
The desperate undercut arete uses a side runner in the gully though the rope usually snags on the lip of the overhang!
FA. John Allen 1975

⑨ **Withered Thing** . . . . ☆ [ ] **E2 6a**
Climb the centre of the face, passing the overlap with difficulty. Side-runners are used at this grade.
FA. Chris Hamper 1978

Descent

Twin Chimneys Buttress

Desperation Area

10 Paucity . . . . HVS 5b
A fine and varied route. Climb an open groove to the left-hand side of a narrow roof, fiddle gear in here then step left and follow the delicate groove to ledges. Finish up the wall above.
FA. Don Morrison early 1960s

11 Robin Hood's Crack . . . . HVD 4a
Climb the crack in the groove to the roof, then move out right awkwardly to a ledge on the arete. From the bigger ledge above, ascend the slabby wall left of the cave.
FA. Eric Byne early 1930s

12 Little John . . . . VS 5a
The short arete by a tricky right-facing layback.
FA. Brian Rossiter 2010

13 Tea-leaf Crack . . . . HVD 4a
Climb the flake in the left wall of the gully to the ledges by the cave, then step left to join and finish as for *Robin Hood's Crack*.
FA. Alpha Club members 1959

14 Robin Hood's Cave Gully . . . . . Diff
The major rift that divides the buttress is awkward, gritty and polished. It provides access to Robin Hood's Cave.

The next two routes start near the top of the gully on the right-hand side, where a large hole provides a thread runner.

15 Last Ice Cream E2 5c
Thread the hole then head out left to climb the short but steep arete that hangs over the gully.
FA. Paul Mitchell 1982

16 Just One Cornetto E2 5c
Thread the hole then pull rightwards onto the wall. Climb it steeply on flat, spaced holds. Often dirty.
FA. Chris Craggs 1993

17 Cave Gully Wall . . . . HVS 5a
From the boulders climb the tricky slab to the left twin cave - tough (E1 5b?) in all but perfect conditions and often avoided by a traverse in. Move right and climb the rib between the caves and the shallow groove above on good flat holds - thrilling stuff.
FA. Alf Bridge 1932

18 Robin Hood's Cave Innominate
. . . . VS 4c
The thin crack is reached by a delicate traverse from the left or direct (5a) by a hard mantel. It provides finger-jams, runners and slippery footholds, and leads to the Right Twin Cave. Escape easily out right across the balcony or tackle the next route.
FA. Alf Bridge 1932

19 Harding's Super Direct Finish
. . . . HVS 5a
From the balcony, step left and make a long reach round the roof from undercuts to jugs, then sprint up the exposed final wall.
FA. Peter Harding 1946

20 Robin Hood's Cave Innominate/Harding's Finish
. . . . HVS 5a
A combination of the previous two routes is one of the best HVS routes on the edge and earns three ticks in one go. Miss out the stance to get the full effect but be sure to extend the runners.

Pete Whittaker, soloing *Wuthering* (E2 5b) - *opposite* - at Stanage. Photo: Mike Hutton

Sheffield Area

Ladybower Area

Stanage

Burbage Valley

Millstone Area

Derwent Edges

Chatsworth Area

Southern Crags

❶ Carpe Diem E6 6c
Climb the wall to a block and continue left to below the roof. Reach right for a pocket then make crux moves past the bulge.
FA. Neil Foster 1994

❷ Cave Eliminate E2 6a
Full on at the grade! A boulder problem start *f6A+* up a leaning rib leads to a ledge at 5m (or traverse from the left reducing the grade to 5c). Pull through the notch in the roof with difficulty and finish up the wall on sloping holds.
FA. John Allen 1973

❸ Cave Arete . . . . HVS 5a
Photogenic. The ledge on the arete is gained awkwardly from the right, then make long reaches (5b for the short) to gain better holds higher up the arete. The upper section is more delicate. Escape right across the chimney or through the cave.
Photo on page 235.
FA. Don Morrison early 1960s

❹ Robin Hood's Balcony Cave Direct
. . . . HVD
The imposing chimney is climbed on (very) polished holds to reach the balcony and a stance. Often green. Escape right across the top of the chimney or, better, finish through the overhang above the ledge by a couple of weird moves on jugs; **S 4b**.
FA. Fred Pigott and friends, early 1920s

❺ Broken Arrow E1 5b
The wide crack that hangs over the chimney requires an uphill udge to access, though it eases once past the first overhang.
FA. Graham Parkes 1999

❻ Constipation . . . E4 6a
A stiff problem. Climb the face just right of the arete (poor cam) using tiny holds away on the right and a scary slap for the break. The upper part is easier though reachy. It is possible to climb left of the arete at about **E2** (side-runner), but that just isn't the ticket!
FA. John Allen 1973

❼ Pacific Ocean Wall Direct E7 6b
Climb straight up the wall by sustained hard moves on tiny holds - with only a marginal cam for protection. Traditionally done with pre-placed side-runners in *Desperation* and starting from *Constipation* at around **E5**-ish.
FA. John Allen (with side-runners) 1983

❽ Desperation . . . E1 6a
The lower section of the smooth wall is climbed via a problem start at *f6A+* using a cruel finger-jam (desperate for short climbers). Swing left then gain a standing position in the break with difficulty. The upper section then follows the thin crack and gradually eases.
FA. Bob Brayshaw 1959

From mid morning | 10 min | Windy

Robin Hood's Cave Innominate - p.241

20m
16m
12m

Robin Hood's Cave

9 Robin Hood's Staircase Direct ☐ HS 4b
The short-lived thin crack leading into the easier shallow groove. Not much gear. Finish easily or head along the next route.

10 Rubber Band . . . . ☐ VS 4b
Follow either of the *Robin Hood's Staircase* starts until just below the cliff top then jam left along the horizontal break to a tricky finish up the left-hand arete. Slightly aimless but it gives easy climbing across an impressive wall.
FA. John Allen 1972

11 Robin Hood's Staircase . . . . ☐ VD
The weakness running diagonally leftwards up the wall is relatively straightforward but unprotected. Used as a way down by the competent.

12 Kenneth . . . . ☐ VS 4b
Mantel up the wall on poor holds.

13 Stringer . . . . ☐ HS 4c
The thin crack left of the corner to a tough direct finish. Escaping left or grovelling under the boulder will lower the grade and remove the point a bit.
FA. Bruce Goodwin 1992

14 Stringer Chimney . . . . ☐ VD
The green chimney in the back of the angle to an escape left or a tight exit rightwards under the boulder.

15 Titbit . . . . ☐ VS 4c
This tackles the hand-crack in the side-wall on solid jams and leads to an often-gritty exit.
FA. Don Morrison late 1950s

16 Muesli . . . . ☐ HS 4c
The blunt arete is awkward to start and then eases.
FA. Bruce Goodwin 1992

17 Cornflakes . . . . ☐ VS 5a
The face right of the arete has a tricky start.

18 Boot Crack . . . . ☐ HVD
The polished boot-wide crack that splits the centre of the short wall is an awkward little customer.

19 Soft Shoe . . . . ☐ HS 4c
Climb the centre of the wall using a shallow flake-crack.
FA. Bruce Goodwin 1992

20 Soft Shoe Arete . . . . ☐ HS 4b
If your blinkers are adjusted correctly you can climb the right arete without using too many holds on the routes to either side.

21 Shuffle . . . . ☐ VD
The wide crack above the base of the descent route.
FA. Bruce Goodwin 1992

To the right is the Porthole Descent - this is tricky, care needed as there have been accidents here.

'Porthole' descent - awkward

Inverted V

Desperation Area
Left of *Inverted V* is a series of short walls with a some easier climbs. Left again things become more impressive and the great classics of *Desperation* and *Cave Arete* await the enthusiast.
Approach (see map on page 218) - Walk up from the Hook's Car parking.

Sheffield Area | Ladybower Area | Stanage | Burbage Valley | Millstone Area | Derwent Area | Chatsworth Area | Southern Crags

Sheffield Area

Ladybower Area

Stanage

Burbage Valley

Millstone Area

Derwent Edges

Chatsworth Area

Southern Crags

1 Before Dunne . . . . ⚡ 🎒 ☐ HVS 5c
Monkey onto the hanging arete using a creaky jug.
FA. Bruce Goodwin 1992

2 Grovel? You Don't Know the Meaning of the Word!
. . . . ✊ ☐ HS 5a
Swim into and out of the black hanging cleft. Amusing stuff.
FA. Chris Craggs 1993

3 Madhouse . . . . 🗣️☐☐ E4 6a
The hanging rib on pockets to a ledge on the right. Step back left
and balance up the rounded arete to a final long reach.
FA. Paul Tattersall 1994

4 Twin Cracks . . . . ☐ VD
Climb the left-hand of a pair of cracks throughout. The awkward
start is often avoided by the first five metres of the next route,
with no change in grade.

5 Right Twin Crack . . . . . . ☐🎿☐ VS 4c
Follow the right-hand crack. It gives good finger-jamming and all
the difficulties are well protected. A good first VS, solid but safe
and full of interest.
FA. Rodney Wilson late 1950s

6 Ellis's Eliminate . . . . ☐🔧☐ VS 4c
A fair test of how the jamming is coming on! Traverse the
horizontal break on solid lockers (or by a gripping dangle) out to
the nose. Finish up the exposed juggy arete.
FA. Gilbert Ellis on a top rope 1950

Inverted V
Bishop's Route, *Inverted V* and *Robin Hood's Right-hand Buttress Direct* are a trio of great outings from the 1920s. They are as popular as any routes on the cliff though all the other routes hereabouts are well worth doing - glorious grit at its very best.
Approach (see map on page 218) - Walk up from the Hook's Car parking and head left to *Inverted V*.

7 Good Friday . . . ☐🏃☐☐ HVS 5b
Start along *Ellis's Eliminate* but make a long stretch and difficult pull on poor holds followed by a precarious high step to access the centre of the fine wall. Finish up this. *Photo opposite.*
FA. Pete Green 1977

8 Bob's Jolly Jape . . . . . . 🗣️☐☐ E4 6a
Climb the blunt rib then head up and right by long reaches between poor holds to the sanctuary of *Ellis's Eliminate*. Choose a way on, up or down.
FA. John Allen 1993. After Bob Berzins had decked from the crux.

From mid morning | 10 min | Windy

'Porthole' descent - awkward

18m

8m

Desperation Area

Sheffield Area
Ladybower Area
Stanage
Burbage Valley
Millstone Area
Derwent Edges
Chatsworth Area
Southern Crags

Making the critical long stretch on *Good Friday* (HVS 5b) - *opposite* - at Stanage. Photo: Mike Hutton

9 Inverted V . . . . ⎡Top⎤ ⎡____⎤ **VS 4b**
⎣50⎦
A polished crack (4c?) and deep groove lead to the niche under overhang - The Birdcage. Traverse right to the exposed crack that skirts the roof. Low in the grade and a good first VS lead. There are also leftward escapes - a mild low one and an exciting high one.
FA. Cyril Ward 1922

10 Retroversion . . . . . . ⟨2⟩ 🔲 🔲 ⎡____⎤ **HVS 5a**
Head up *Inverted V* for 5m then traverse right along the lowest break and make unlikely-looking pulls up the bulging arete. Once back in balance, finish up the exposed rounded rib - low in the grade. The direct start is the reachy **Our Version, E3 6a**.
FA. Don Morrison 1960s. FA. (Our Version) Graham Parkes 1985

11 Robin Hood's Right-hand Buttress Direct
. . . . ⟨3⟩ 🔲 🔲 ⎡____⎤ **HS 4a**
A great route up the wide crack splitting the centre of the face. Low in the grade but quite intimidating. Climb to the large overhang and shuffle out right to reach a small ledge below the main crack. Follow this with wide manoeuvres and big gear.
FA. Cyril Ward 1922. Also known as 'Button Hook' back then.

12 Thunder Road . . . . 🔲 🔲 ⎡____⎤ **E6 6b**
A fierce direct start to *Cold Turkey* through the wide roof.
FA. Gabe Regan (side-runners) 1979. FA. Mark Stokes (solo) 1980

13 Cold Turkey . . . . ⟨2⟩ 🔲 🔲 🔲 ⎡____⎤ **HVS 5a**
Climb the flake in the left rib of *Straight Crack*, step left and climb the fine face direct. Rounded and with less gear than you might like. An alternative to *Christmas Crack* on 25th December?
FA. John Allen, Christmas Day 1973

14 Straight Crack . . . . ⟨2⟩ ⎡____⎤ **VS 4b**
The central line. Climb the wide chimney to the roof and shuffle left. Easier climbing leads past the overhang to the final chimney. A few slings may be useful.

15 Robin Hood Zig-zag . . . . ⟨1⟩ ⎡____⎤ **S 4a**
A wanderer. Start up the chimney and exit awkwardly right to a good ledge, and possible stance. Continue up the crack left of the flake to a ledge and then the wall above this to a niche. Step right for a nicely exposed finish.
FA. Cyril Ward 1922

16 Spring into Action . . ⟨1⟩ 🔲 🔲 ⎡____⎤ **HVS 5b**
Bridge the wide chimney until you can swing onto the right arete. Continue to the ledge then climb the centre of the steep wall behind with long reaches between rounded breaks.
FA. Graham Parkes 1996

17 The Actress . . . . 🔲 ⎡____⎤ **E2 5c**
Tackle the centre of the overhang under *Bishop's Route*.
FA. Alan Clarke 1965

'Porthole' descent - awkward

18 Bishop's Route . . . . S 4a
An engaging romp. From the base of *Zig-zag Flake Crack* climb
the left-leaning crack to a ledge. Continue up the corner to a
higher ledge then make tricky moves to the flakes above. Climb
these to a horizontal break and finish direct with a stretch.
FA. Henry Bishop 1920s

19 Zagrete . . . . HS 4b
A bit aimless but pleasant and with only one tricky move. Follow
Bishop's Route to the ledge then step out right and climb
the well-positioned flake crack in the arete to a fine finish on
flutings.
FA. John Loy early 1960s

20 Zig-zag Flake Crack . . . . VS 4b
The tall straight flake is wide, awkward and slippery but cams in
the horizontal breaks make it safe enough. Swarm up the flake
to a high ledge with a huge wobbly block and finish up the short
wall behind, or step left onto the arete for more exposure.
FA. Herbert Hartley 1929. Known as 'The Great Flake' for years.

21 Coconut Ice E2 5b
A route with a good lower section but then it fizzles out. Climb
the wall via couple of long reaches (big cam to the left) to easier
terrain. As the wall gets ever-narrower make an escape.
FA. Gary Gibson 1981

22 Ice Boat E1 5c
A popular little eliminate with a harsh start. From a short crack
climb the wall to *The Little Flake Crack*. Trend right up the wall
past a couple of long reaches. Harder again for the short.
FA. John Allen 1983

23 The Little Flake Crack . . . VS 5a
Reach the hanging flake from the chimney by a hard traverse
(footholds scoured by nailed boots aeons ago), then layback to
easy ground. A short wall concludes things.
FA. Frank Elliott 1930

24 Flake Chimney . . . . HVD
The chimney in the left side of the bay can be climbed inside
or outside of the chockstones. The subterranean route is more
secure, and tight; the outer one is precarious and probably S 4b.

25 Hybrid E1 5b
Climb the rounded pillar between the two chimneys at the back
of the bay to its top. Then tackle the capping overhang with
difficulty using the flake on the right-hand tip of the nose.

20m

Huge loose
block

Wright's
Route - p.248

Black Slab

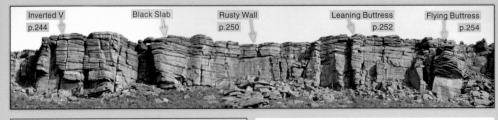

Inverted V
p.244

Black Slab

Rusty Wall
p.250

Leaning Buttress
p.252

Flying Buttress
p.254

Black Slab

Here are the superb Orange Spot offerings of *April Crack*, *Christmas Crack* and the *Trinities*, as well as the excellent *Hargreaves' Original* on Black Slab, the site of the famous leaping exploits of Alf Bridge.

Approach (see map on page 218) - From the Hook's Car parking walk up and left, continue for 90m past the prominent *Flying Buttress*.

❶ Pedestal Chimney . . . . . 🗲 🍴 ☐ **Diff**
Climb the slippery groove to the left of the pedestal then follow the deepening gully above to exit under the massive capstone.

❷ Wright's Route . . . . 🗲 ☐ **VS 4c**
The steep groove to the right of the pedestal is bridged and jammed to its top. Step up and make a short exposed swing out right to enter the final hanging corner.

❸ Wall of Sound . . 🗲 📱 🦎 🐾 ☐ **E6 6b**
A desperate line up the scooped wall. Climb the thin crack then move right via an enormous reach to a poor break. Continue slightly right using a pocket to gain the right arete and an easy finish. A more direct version is harder. Low poor wires protect.
FA. John Allen 1983

16m

Inverted V

4 Whillans' Pendulum/Black Magic
. . . . HVS 5b
A route of contrasts - the start is very hard for the short.
Swing out right to jugs and a ledge on the front face. Move up
awkwardly then step left on to the narrow side face and climb
this delicately by lovely moves in great positions.
FA. Don Whillans 1958. FA. (Black Magic) Giles Barker 1976

5 Macleod's Variation . . . . VS 4c
A decent variation finish from halfway up the slab feels like
a cop-out. Shuffle left to climb the shallow groove and short
crack.

6 Hargreaves' Original . . . VS 4c
One of Stanage's choice VS climbs. From a boulder, pull up
and left onto the slab, traverse left then move up and right to
a resting ledge. Continuing up the centre of the slab trending
slightly right. Well protected with enough cams, though it used
to be very bold.
FA. Albert Hargreaves 1928

7 The Flange . . . . . . HVS 5b
Powerful moves access the prominent niche at 4m (overhead
gear). Continue up the flake of 'the flange' then the steep slab on
rounded and sometimes green holds to a final short crack.
FA. Peter Biven 1956

8 April Crack . . . . HS 4b
The steep crack in the open corner is awkward to start (easiest
on the right) then gives fine sustained bridging and laybacking.
Protection is good throughout.
FA. Herbert Hartley 1928

9 Easter Rib E1 5b
Delicate and low in the grade - but precarious and scary! Climb
the shallow groove just to the left of the nose (technical crux),
then swing right and up to a deep break. From good runners,
teeter up the bold rib to the final easy but exposed arete.
FA. Peter Biven 1956

10 Christmas Crack . . . . . . HS 4a
This long straight crack is a must; mild for the grade, but
sustained. Climb a V-groove to the crack and follow it with
pleasure. The final leaning corner is awkward and there is also
an exposed alternative out left. The only route in the Peak where
you will be queuing every 25th December come hail or shine!
FA. George Bower 1926

11 Central Trinity . . . . VS 4c
Start at a vertical crack that ends at 6m. Climb this then traverse
left to the base of the continuation crack which is entered by
harder moves. Follow it more easily to finish up a right-facing
groove. The direct start is a boldish 5a problem.
FA. Herbert Hartley 1929

12 Twintrin E1 5c
Climb the reachy wall above *Central Trinity*'s initial crack.
FA. Gary Gibson late 1970s

13 Meiosis . . . . HVS 5b
The wall to the right is climbed direct via long reaches between
rounded breaks. Protection is good if you carry plenty of cams.
FA. Gary Gibson 1978

14 Right-hand Trinity . . . . . S 4b
Climb the right-hand continuous crack directly, initially up an
awkward right-facing corner. The crack is a good intro to the art
of hand-jamming being both mild and very protectable.
FA. Herbert Hartley 1928

15 Fergus Graham's Direct . HVS 4c
The wall immediately to the right of the crack. The route isn't
well protected, although it is easy to lean left to place runners,
reducing the grade to VS. The crux is accessing the final slab.
FA. Fergus Graham 1920s

16 Topaz E4 6a
Up the leaning arete on its right side by technical laybacking
and long reaches, until a grasping exit round the arete becomes
essential. Swinging around a couple of moves earlier reduces
the grade to a more sensible **E1 5b**.
FA. Gary Gibson 1979

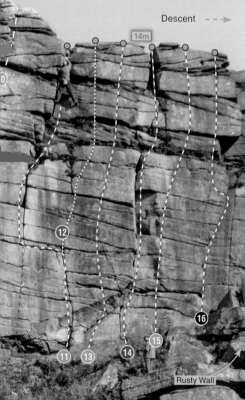

Descent - - -

Rusty Wall

Rusty Wall

The short wall decorated with a selection of rusty blobs is always popular. The cracks here are all well protected and make good introductions to their grades. Further right is the impressive wall of *Queersville* bounded on its left by the old classic *Hollybush Crack*. The routes are all good quality hereabouts and the area is always busy.
Approach (see map on page 218) - From the Hook's Car parking walk up and left, 60m past *Flying Buttress*.

① Green Crack . . . . VS 4c
The wide crack in the angular corner is fine when dry, though the final narrow chimney is always an awkward grovel.
FA. Herbert Hartley 1928

② Rugosity Wall . . . . HVS 5c
The wall 2m to the right of *Green Crack* has a technical start then easier-angled climbing which has one more tricky pull.
FA. Chuck Cook 1949. In nailed boots!

③ Rusty Wall . . . . HVS 6a
The wall left of the crack has hard starting moves. Once the first good hold (just a 4c hop away for the tall) is reached things ease. Most of the iron finger-jugs have long gone.
FA. Herbert Hartley 1928

④ Rusty Crack . . . . HVS 5c
The left-hand crack has a hard start using polished footholds and thin finger-jams. Although hard it takes good small wires.

⑤ Via Media . . . . VS 4c
The protectable and pleasant right-hand crack finishing up the short and easy chockstoned chimney above.
FA. Ron Townsend 1949

⑥ Via Dexter Direct E2 5c
The centre of the wall is quite technical and has no protection. Variations to the right are easier (**HVS 5a**) but inferior.
FA. Tony Moulam 1951

⑦ Oblique Crack . . . . S 4a
The crack that bounds the right-hand side of Rusty Wall. The lower section gives jamming past a wobbly chock. Finish easily.
FA. Herbert Hartley 1928

⑧ Oblique Buttress . . . . . . VS 5b
Teeter up the narrow buttress. Using either arete drops it to 4c.

⑨ Straight Chimney . . . . VD
The crack widens and has awkward moves past the closure.

⑩ Albert's Pillar . . . . VS 4c
The barrel-shaped buttress is tricky to start but soon eases.

⑪ Albert's Amble . . . . HVD
Another one that eases once you get going.

To the right is a blocky corner often used as a way down by the experienced. There have been accidents here so care is required.

Black Slab

Sheffield Area
Ladybower Area
Stanage
Burbage Valley
Millstone Area
Derwent Edges
Chatsworth Area
Southern Crags

12 Straight and Narrow . 〔〕🐾🗻▢ **HVS 5a**
A direct eliminate on the next route to a hard exit.
FA. Chris Craggs 1981

13 Narrow Buttress .... 🔭▢ **VS 4c**
Climb the right arete then move to the left edge briefly before
traversing back right again and going directly to a juggy finish.
FA. Ron Townsend 1949

14 Hollybush Crack .... Top⌐50▢ **VD**
The clean-cut corner-crack is steep and excellent. The lower
section has some polished footholds and is the crux, but the
imposing upper part is juggy and proves to be impressive at the
grade. Protection is excellent throughout.
FA. George Bower 1926

15 Straightsville .... 🐾🗻▢ **E2 5b**
The wall parallel to the crack has some good moves and no line.
FA. Bill Birch 1987

16 Queersville .... 🔭〖〗▢ **HVS 5a**
Start up a jutting rib on the right side of the bay, then stretch out
left to ledges. Climb to a broken flake under the roof and make a
long reach to the ledge above. Swing right to easy ground.
FA. Alan Clarke 1965

Hollybush Crack

A couple of popular routes on the left on the Leaning
Buttress and several routes that see much less action on
the wall just to the right.
Approach (see map on page 218) - From the Hook's
Car parking walk up and left, just past *Flying Buttress*.

17 The Nose .... 〔〕🐾🗻▢ **E3 5c**
Worthwhile but neglected with poor gear. The bulging arete
leads to a ledge. Step left and continue via bold laybacking.
FA. Andy Bailey 1985

18 Yosemite Wall ..... 🔭〖〗🗻▢ **E2 5b**
Climb into a small recess then make difficult moves to the ledge.
The thin crack on the left is well battered but a discreet wire to
the right protects moves on slopers to easy ground - varied.
FA. Alan Clarke 1965

19 Leaning Buttress Gully ..... 🧗▢ **VS 5a**
The left-hand crack in the square recess with hard moves past
the roof. Bridge direct or move right into the next climb to avoid
the hanging gardens, then exit right.
FA. Jim Lomas early 1930s

From mid morning | 8 min | Windy

Awkward descent

Alternative descent →

16m

12 13 14 15 16 17 18 19 20 21

20 Hangover . . . . 🖾 **VS 5a**
Climb the right-hand crack in the recess. OK - though avoiding the previous route completely can be problematic.
FA. Bob Brayshaw 1957

21 Leaning Buttress Direct . 🖾 **HVS 5b**
The pillar is climbed direct with tricky moves to leave the ground and a crux off the ledge. It is easier but a bit bolder above.
FA. Fergus Graham 1922

22 Leaning Buttress Crack . . 🖾 **VD**
The long groove on the right-hand side of the pillar is followed throughout. It is well protected, very pleasant and popular.

23 Leaning Buttress Indirect . . . 🖾 **VD**
A wandering route with an exposed finish. Climb the corner crack to ledges then traverse out onto the front of the buttress and climb its left-hand edge without much in the way of gear.

24 The Bishop's Move . . . . . 🖾 **VD**
Start up the previous route then squeeze through the gap behind the buttress to finish on the other side. A rope-work challenge.

25 Right On . . . . 🖾 **HS 4b**
The disjointed cracks right of the main groove give some decent moves, getting on top of a pedestal at half-height is the crux.
FA. Dave Gregory 1997

26 Garden Wall . . . . 🖾 **S 4a**
Climb the awkward angle to a ledge then move right to below the chimney (possible stance). Climb to the chock then step left onto the wall and finish up the crack just left again. Avoiding the loop out right is a bit harder - **Garden Fence, HS 4b**.
FA. Cyril Ward 1922

27 Space Junk . . . . 🖾 **HVS 5a**
Starting up the arete on the left of the jutting buttress and finish up the wall on the right of the upper crack. Often green.
FA. Gary Gibson 1979

28 Chockstone Direct . . . . . 🖾 **S 4a**
Climb the central crack to the ledge then continue direct passing the blocking boulder awkwardly.

29 Armchair Buccaneer . . . . 🖾 **HVS 5a**
Climb the centre of the wall aiming just left of the high holly bush. Often green.
FA. David Simmonite 1994

30 Beech Tree Wall . . . 🖾 **HS 4b**
A short crack leads to the right side of the ledge. Head right up the face (awkward to start) finishing just right of the holly. Tricky to protect and harder for the short.

31 Wild West Wind . . . . 🖾 **S 4a**
Go left then right making the most of the right side of the face.
FA. Chris Craggs 1997

32 Scrappy Corner . . . . 🖾 **Diff**
An initial groove leads to blocky ramblings above.

From mid morning | 7 min | Windy

Awkward descent

20m

15m

Easier descent

Flying Buttress

Sheffield Area

Ladybower Area

Stanage

Burbage Valley

Millstone Area

Derwent Edges

Chatsworth Area

Southern Crags

Andi Turner hanging out on *Flying Buttress Direct* (E1 5b) - *page 254* - at the Popular End of Stanage. The route was originally done as an aid climb (5 pegs) back in 1956 - ethics were a lot more lax back then but I suspect there were still a few misgivings. The grade of the route has bounced between HVS and E1 over the years, the latter seems fair enough for an on-sight lead. Photo: Adam Long

20m

Descent

Leaning Buttress

Flying Buttress

The stacked overhangs form one of the most recognisable pieces of gritstone - *Flying Buttress*; join the queue if you are after the classic HVD. The spectacular *Flying Buttress Direct* launches through the centre of the overhangs and is a real adrenaline trip, the grade of which always makes good pub-fodder. Across the descent gully are some milder though more serious adventures.

Approach (see map on page 218) - Walk up from the Hook's Car parking - about five minutes.

1 The Wedge . . . . **VS 5a**
The blunter of the twin buttresses has a tricky move before the angle drops back. Escape off left or finish up *Wedge Rib*.

2 Wedge Gully . . . . **Mod**
The deep rift leads through a tunnel to easier ground. Mild in the extreme though a bridging outside exit is harder - **VD**.

3 Wedge Rib . . . . **VS 5a**
The axe-edge rib in the gully has a delicate layback start (just worth a star) leading to easier climbing up the broad rib above.

4 Flying Buttress Gully . . . . **Diff**
The long blocky gully gives a neglected low-grade route.

5 Flying Buttress . . . . [Top 50] **HVD 4a**
A wandering classic. Head up the unprotected 'question-mark' slab to its top left-hand corner. The undercut groove here is tricky to enter (good gear) and leads to an exposed slab. Head right to a ledge and a finish on jugs. Walk off right or finish up the short wall behind to reach the cliff top and the moor.
FA. Fergus Graham 1922

6 Goodbye Toulouse . . . . . [2] **E1 5b**
An exciting route across the left-hand side of the roof. Climb the slab to the curving flake in the overhang, then using fat jams (large cam protection) trend to the right to finish just right of the nose on good holds.
FA. Gary Gibson 1978

7 Flying Buttress Direct . . . [Top 50] **E1 5b**
Exhilarating climbing on large holds. The grade is quite close to the HVS/E1 boundary so the arguments will go on. Climb the slab, build a safety net then head across the centre of the roof, first right then back left, with heel-hooks and some brute force.
Photo on page 253.
FA. D.Lomas (with 4 pegs - outrageous!) 1956. FFA. Paul Grey 1966

Descent

14m

Censor
- p.256

Tippler Buttress

❽ Flying Butt . . . . . . 🔲🔲🔲🔲 ▮ **E3 5c**
A bizarre route, said to be the longest roof pitch on grit and not
one for a busy day. From the start of *Kirkus's Corner* make an
awkward move out left then traverse the lip of the roof all the
way to a finish up the left arete.
FA. John Arran early 2000s

❾ Kirkus's Corner . 🔲🔲🔲🔲 ▮ **E1 5b**
A good varied route. Climb the edge of the slab to the right end
of the overhangs and pull through at a short vertical crack (good
wires). Step left into an open groove and bridge up this to a
rounded exit. HVS for those who don't mind exposed padding.
FA. Colin Kirkus 1934

❿ Spasticus Artisticus . . . . 🔲🔲 ▮ **E4 5c**
The right-hand face of *Flying Buttress* is climbed trending left by
pumpy moves on green and shelving holds. Harrowing.
FA. Paul Cropper 1982

⓫ Jitterbug Buttress . . . . . . 🔲🔲 ▮ **S 4a**
In the back of the gully is a narrow buttress. Climb the bold wall
to the capping overhang and then sneak off rightwards below
the final overhangs. The direct finish is **Malarete, VS 4c**.
FA. Eric Byne 1950. Malarete Finish, Falco Reche 1990

To the right is Avalanche Gully, an easy descent. The right-hand
side of this is a clean wall. All the routes here are poorly
protected and require a wary approach especially after rain.

⓬ The Kirkus Original . . . . 🔲🔲 ▮ **VS 5a**
Start from a block to the right of the base of the gully. Go up the
face to harder moves at half-height (holds to the right) which
lead to a scary mantelshelf and then easier ground. Despite what
you might expect from the grade, it is unprotected.
FA. Colin Kirkus 1930s

⓭ Jitter Face . . . . 🔲🔲🔲 ▮ **HS 4a**
Start below the centre of the face and climb until sloping holds
lead diagonally right towards the arete. After a couple of moves
up, traverse back left to join *The Kirkus Original*. Easy but
unprotected and a long way above a poor landing; care required.

⓮ Townsend's Variation . . . 🔲🔲 ▮ **HVS 4c**
Take the lowest possible line up the edge of the face on sloping
footholds and then move around onto the exposed face where
mild but bold moves up the rib reach superb finishing jugs. As
easy as it ever was but still completely lacking in protection.
FA. Ron Townsend 1949

Sheffield Area · Ladybower Area · Stanage · Burbage Valley · Millstone Area · Derwent Edges · Chatsworth Area · Southern Crags

Jitter Face
- p.255

Flying Buttress

16m

The big green corner

On the side-wall

Tippler Buttress

An impressive buttress, home to a fine set of strenuous routes, from the unnerving *Censor*, through the brutality of *The Unprintable* to the daunting roof of *The Dangler* and the technicality of *The Tippler*. The strong and proficient will love the place, others will probably move along. At the opposite end of the spectrum *Castle Chimney* is a great beginners' route.

Tippler Thread - There used to be a thread fixed in the lip of *The Tippler*, with modern protection this is not necessary. In line with 'no fixed gear on natural grit' please don't replace it.

Approach (see map on page 218) - Walk up from the Hook's Car parking - the area is easily recognised across the gully to the right of *Flying Buttress*.

❶ **Censor** **E3 5c**
Intimidating and memorable. From blocks, enter the leaning groove (poor wires) then climb to the roof. Swing right and scale the bulge - strenuous then delicate - to stand on the nose. Easier climbing remains - finishing up the centre of the face is the best option though the terminally harassed can escape left.
FA. Jim Perrin 1967. He is said to have top roped it 27 times.

❷ **The Unprintable** **E1 5b**
Chubbin' desperate! The left-hand crack leads to a cramped recess. The exit is difficult - swing into a layback on jams (knees!) before sprinting to safety. Only HVS for grit gurus.
FA. Don Whillans 1952

20m

Black Hawk Area

❻ The Tippler . . . . [Top 50] **E1 5b**
A devious classic and solid at the grade! Climb the right arete, past a tricky overlap, to the big roof. Traverse left then grope up and left for good jams. Swiftly make the crux moves to get established on the final wall then finish easily.
FA. Barry Webb 1964

❼ The 9 O'clock Watershed **E6 6c**
On the side-wall of *The Tippler*. Head up to a move out left to the arete where powerful use of an undercut accesses a good hold leaving a precarious finale.
FA. Neil Foster 1994

❽ The Muted Trumper **E6 6c**
The more direct version has a hard dynamic finish.
FA. Richard Heap 1999

❾ The Y Crack . . . . **VS 4c**
A good line up the long green groove to the right of *The Tippler*, best after a dry spell. The constricted lower section leads to a choice - both are awkward, though the right is better.

❿ The Z Crack . . . . . . **VS 5a**
The hanging crack that splits the jutting nose requires a bit of a tussle to access. Once established, things ease a lot.
FA. Joe Brown 1952

⓫ Castle Chimney . . . . **Mod**
The gloomy rift splitting the buttresses is a great beginners' route. Climb over blocks and into the gloom then bridge up to a large platform - possible stance. Choose a way to the cliff top.
FA. J.W.Puttrell 1904

⓬ Black Hawk Tower . . . . **VD 4a**
Devious - care with the rope needed. Climb the chimney to the exposed ledge on the tower and follow it all the way round past two aretes to the south face. Finish up a shallow groove.
FA. Eric Byne and friends, early 1930s

⓭ Master of Disguise . . **E6 6c**
Short and thrilling. Start left of *Chameleon* and climb the mottled wall then traverse out right to below the roof. Pull left (small wire above) gain the arete with difficulty, and finish wildly.
FA. Neil Foster 1994

⓮ Chameleon **E4 6a**
Intimidating climbing up the jutting prow. Climb the lower wall to jams below the overhang, up this with difficulty (good small wire up and left) to reach a ramp. Hand traverse rightwards up this to gain the arete and a sprint finale.
FA. Ed Drummond 1975

❸ The Dangler **E2 5c**
A thugtastic roof-crack. Climb the right-hand thin crack into a cave (threads) then head outwards. A long reach gains the break above the lip where hard pulls are needed to gain easy ground.
FA. Joe Brown 1954

❹ Tippler Direct **E3 6a**
A fine piece of roof climbing. Head through the stacked roof to a good hold where a massive lock-off or a short leap is needed to reach the break under the roof. The crux of *The Tippler* remains.
FA. Jim Reading 1976

❺ Paranoid **E6 6b**
Follow *Tippler Direct* to the roof, move right and make a desperate reach and fierce pull over. Shorties will need to traverse the lip.
FA. Johnny Woodward 1981

Sheffield Area

Ladybower Area

Stanage

Burbage Valley

Millstone Area

Derwent Edges

Chatsworth Area

Southern Crags

Tippler Buttress p.256

Black Hawk Area

Manchester Buttress p.260

Black Hawk Area

This may just be the most popular section of the most popular cliff in the country and with good reason. There are classics galore here especially in the lower grades. It is a place you will enjoy and keep returning to. If it is busy, consider walking a bit further down the edge to the delights of the Robin Hood and Mississippi Areas.

Approach (see map on page 218) - Walk straight up from the Hook's Car parking - about 6 minutes.

1 Black Hawk Bastion **E3 5c**
The capped groove is steady up to the big overhang where committing moves lead out left to a wild finish up the hanging left arete of the final groove. Low in the grade, but not that low!
FA. Dick Brown (1 peg for aid) 1952. FFA. John Allen 1975

2 Eliminator . . . . . **HVS 5b**
Elegant climbing up the arete left of the big corner. The lower part is technical as far as a short vertical crack. Beefy moves on spaced holds lead up the short wall to a final shallow groove.
FA. Alan Clarke 1965

Tippler Buttress

18m

Grotto Slab
p.262

Mantelpiece Buttress
p.264

5 Elliott's Eliminate . . . . 🔄 ☐ HS 4c
Linking the start of *Black Hawk* to the finish of *Black Hawk Tower* makes for a worthwhile trip.

6 Prudence . . . . 🔄 ☐ HVS 5b
Climb the V-groove to ledges, step right and follow the thin crack to just below its end. Go straight up the wall to finish.
FRA. Chris Craggs 1997 though probably done before.

7 Black Hawk Traverse Left . . . 🔄 ☐ VD
Up the polished groove then make the 'Bishop's Stride' around the bulge to the left. The short can go higher - **Burgess's Variation, S 4a**. Head up and left to the parapet, then choose a finish.
FA. Henry Bishop early 1910s

8 Providence . . . . 🔄 ☐ E1 5c
An eliminate up the wall with a couple of fierce fingery moves.
FA. Gary Gibson 1978

9 Tribute to Joy . . . . 🔄 ☐ E6 6c
Climb the shallow groove to the break and then access the slab with the greatest of difficulty. More pebbles may have popped.
FA. Mike Lea 1985

10 Black Hawk Hell Crack . . 🔄 ☐ S 4a
The crack in the right side of the wall is the line. It is juggy and well protected. A few slings for threads might be found useful.
FA. Eric Byne early 1930s. The resident hawk gave him Hell!

11 Black Hawk Traverse Right . . 🔄 ☐ Diff
Start left of the chimney and follow scratched footholds right to a crack and climb this to bulges. Step right and climb the main fissure to the capping overhang and escape out to the left.
FA. Henry Bishop early 1910s. Also known as Blizzard Chimney.

12 Ugly Mugs . . . . ☐ VS 4c
Bridge the groove under the chimney to a ledge then head onto the exposed juggy arete to the right.
FA. Chris Craggs 1987

13 Moriaty. . . . . 🔄 ☐ E3 6a
The jutting arete on its right side by a technical layback.
FA. Robin Barker 1989

14 Gargoyle Variant . . . 🔄 ☐ HS 4b
Start under the hanging left arete of the buttress and climb the awkward wide crack to the overhang. Traverse right to below the large perched block. Gain this carefully and finish up the arete directly above on good holds.

15 Gargoyle Buttress . . . . 🔄 ☐ VS 4b
Mild and excellent. Start at the right toe of the buttress and after a couple of moves, follow a horizontal break out to the left. Pull up on the suspect perched boulder with care then finish up the arete, or more in keeping with the lower section, the centre of the wall above trending slightly rightwards.
FA. Ron Townsend 1949

16 Dry Rot. . . . . 🔄 ☐ E2 5b
Start as for *Gargoyle Buttress* but climb the right-hand side of the upper slab precariously on poor holds and with scant gear.
FA. Gary Gibson 1982

3 Castle Crack . . . . . . 🔄 ☐ HS 4b
Up the slippery right-angled corner by laybacking or jamming. Finish direct easily, or up the steep arete just right - **VS 4c**.
FA. Henry Bishop and friends, early 1910s

4 Black Hawk . . . . 🔄 ☐ HS 4c
Climb the flake-crack right of the corner and the overhang to a ledge then step right and follow a shallow crack to a better ledge. Finish up the right-hand crack above.
FA. Eric Byne early 1930s

14m

Perched
block

Manchester Buttress

Manchester Buttress

Maurice Linnel's 1930s Mancunian classic is well worth doing, as is nearby *Gargoyle Buttress*. Despite their popularity the trio of routes in the back of the bay on the right are less worthwhile, although there is little doubt they are all better led than done on a tight top-rope. **Approach (see map on page 218)** - Walk up from the Hook's Car parking.

① **Physiology** . . . . 🎲 ☐ **VD**
The left-hand crack is arguably the best of the trio leading steeply, past plenty of runners, to an easy finishing groove.

② **Sociology** . . . . 🎲 ☐ **S 4a**
The centre of the narrow face is best climbed direct (poor protection on the line) to a finish up an easy groove.

③ **Anatomy** . . . . ☐ **VD**
The right-hand corner is climbed to a move left at the awkward overhang (mind your head) and a finish up the corner.

④ **Another Ology** . . . . 🚩 ☐ **HS 4b**
The awkward direct finish to the previous climb.
FA. Dave Gregory 2000

⑤ **Tinker's Crack** . . . . 🎲 ☐ **VS 4c**
A narrow wall split vertically in its upper part by a thin crack. Pull over a bulge to gain the crack and follow it to a stinker of a move where it disappears.
FA. Don Morrison and friends, early 1960s

⑥ **Beggar's Crack** . . . . 🚩 ☐ **VS 4c**
This wide crack starts off easily but has a hard move to pass the small overlap before easing again. Big cams are a great help.

⑦ **Tip Off** . . . . 🏴 ☐ **E2 5b**
A blunt rib leads to a flake oh so close to the previous route.
FA. Phil Burke 1978

⑧ **Tip Off Right** . . . . 🎲 ☐ **E1 5b**
This variation tackles the flake over right. Easier and better but still manages to feel a bit weedy.

⑨ **Moss Side** . . . . 🚩 ☐ **E3 6a**
Mantel up the polished scoop to the break then claw a way up the steep slab using a critical pebble.
FA. Bill Birch 1984

⑩ **Manchester Buttress** . . . . . . 🎲 ☐ **HS 4b**
A bit of proper class - how good is your rope-work? Start up the crack in the arete then head left to out-flank the first overhang. Move up to a deep break then make an awkward traverse back to the right to gain the ledge round the corner. Finish direct.
FA. Maurice Linnel early 1930s

⑪ **Manchester United** . . . . . 🏴 🚩 ☐ **HVS 5b**
A short eliminate up the slab and wall with one long reach/tricky move. Using the flakes on the right arete is the easier option.
FA. Chris Craggs 1988

⑫ **Tier Climb** . . . . ☐ **S 4b**
Disappointing work up the groove and crack just right.

To the right is a descent down the chimney behind a triangular chockstone. It wobbles and has done for years.

Descent behind loose chockstone

Gargoyle Buttress - p.259

Grotto Slab

Black Hawk Area

TICKLIST
The Popular End
Orange Spot Heaven

How much quality can you handle in one day out? A dozen routes, 36 stars - glorious grit at its marvellous best.

☐ **BAW's Crawl, HVS** *(224)*
Bizarre and brilliant, an upside-down oddity.

☐ **Martello Buttress, VS** *(229)*
A steep tricky start then rounded glory leading to an airy exit.

☐ **Congo Corner, HVS** *(233)*
Probably the hardest of this batch but, if you can do the first 3m, it should be in the bag.

☐ **Mississippi Buttress Direct, VS** *(233)*
Sustained and superb, bridging to heaven.

☐ **Robin Hood's Cave Innominate with Harding's Super Direct Finish, HVS** *(241)*
A brilliant combo with the crux at the top.

☐ **Inverted V, VS** *(246)*
Mild and a bit slippery but oozes class.

☐ **Robin Hood's RH Buttress Direct, HS** *(246)*
Wide and wonderful - another one that is soft at the grade but feels quite bold.

☐ **Hargreaves' Original, VS** *(249)*
Rounded, like palming up the side of an elephant. Must have been a real gripper before cams.

☐ **April Crack, HS** *(249)*
A great line, with a puzzling start then glorious bridging and jamming.

☐ **Christmas Crack, HS** *(249)*
Sustained, but well-protected and lovely throughout. A Christmas present to themselves for many.

☐ **Queersville, HVS** *(251)*
Devious and reachy climbing that just flows when you get it right.

☐ **Manchester Buttress, HS** *(260)*
A tester of rope technique. Devious and quite tricky for the grade.

Heather Wall (VS 4c) - *page 262* - at Stanage Popular. Almost good enough to have made the Orange Spot Heaven Ticklist - an indication of the quality of the routes that did make it.

Grotto Slab

A popular area with several worthwhile and well-travelled routes. For *Heather Wall* and *Crack and Corner* you will probably have to join the queue if here at a weekend. The rest of the climbs in this area see less attention than those just a little further left along the crag.

Approach (see map on page 218) - Walk up from the Hook's Car parking.

Descent - Experienced climbers use *Grotto Slab* as a way down, the easiest alternative is round the right-hand end of the cliff to the right (looking in).

① Two Tier Climb . . . . 🧗 📷 ☐ **VS 5a**
Climb a slabby pillar to a boulder-covered ledge. The upper wall gives one hard move above some low runners.

② Cakestand . . . . 🔄 ▯ 🎒 ☐ **S 4b**
The narrow pillar is followed with a couple of long reaches. The final tricky nose is easily avoidable. Beware the loose flake.

③ Cool Groove . . . . 🔄 ☐ **S 4a**
The open groove steepens as it rises giving steady bridging to a steep and tricky exit. The crack just right offers a rather harder alternative start - **4b**.

④ Lancashire Wall . . . . . 🔄 ▯ ☐ **HVS 5a**
The centre of the wall has a delicate start from a block and a good finish up the short leaning front face of the final block. Low in the grade and a good bet for a first HVS, always assuming the tilted summit block stays where it is!
FA. Dave Kenyon late 1970s

⑤ Crack and Corner . . . 🔄 🧗 ☐ **S 4b**
Set in the arete is this attractive groove. Enter this using an unhelpful set of scoured holds; frequently frustrating, though with good gear. Continue up the groove to a good ledge below an overhanging block. Overcome this at its left-hand corner by a short struggle or, if you have had enough, escape off to the left.

⑥ War Zone . . . . 🧗 🧗 ☐ **f6A**
The tricky right arete of *Crack and Corner* gives an extended boulder problem. There is an independent finish above, keeping out of the corner - **E1 6a** for the full route.

⑦ Heather Wall . . . . 🔄 🔧 ☐ **VS 4c**
Excellent climbing up the cracked face to a deeper vertical crack. Awkward moves gain a ledge then a right-trending scoop. From the large ledge above finish up the easy corner on the right.
Photo on page 261.

⑧ Heather Wall Variation . . 🔄 🔧 ☐ **VS 5a**
A right-hand start is also worthwhile, and less polished.

⑨ Chimp's Corner . . . . 🔄 ✊ ☐ **VS 5b**
Odd but amusing. Monkey up the steep blocky corner to its top then trend left up the wall to below the final large roof that caps the wall. Cross this via a superb curly jug to a belly-flop landing.

⑩ Grotto Slab . . . . 🔄 ☐ **Mod**
Often used as a descent route but also worthwhile as a beginners' route. Start at the toe of the slab and ascend to its tip - not much gear. A couple of short awkward corners complete the route. The right edge is even easier.
FA. Henry Bishop and friends, early 1910s

Descent behind rocking chockstone

16m

Manchester Buttress

11 Jersey Boys. . . . . 🪨🎨 ☐ **E1 5a**
Start right of the slumped flake in a pit. Climb the easy corner then a blunt rib on the right, and the final wall on slopers.
FA. Chris Craggs 1989. With Jersey locals Kevin Eloury and Phil Brown.

12 Grotto Wall . . . . 🎲🪨▐║🎨 ☐ **HVS 4c**
Start in the unsavoury pit and gain the shallow left-facing groove which is climbed boldly to a tricky exit and runners. Continue up the final wall, trending rightwards on better holds.

13 Reagent . . . . . . 🪨▐║🪨🎨 ☐ **E5 6a**
The right-hand side of the wall is rarely climbed. From a ledge trend left via fierce fingery moves and a huge span. The short will need to dyno the crucial move - probably worth E6.
FA. Al Rouse 1984

14 Green Wall . . . . 🎲🪨 ☐ **VS 4c**
The crack in the wall just left of the narrow chimney has a tricky landing on a green ledge. Best avoided when at all damp.

15 Capstone Chimney . . . . 🎲 ☐ **Diff**
The shallow open chimney is most easily climbed up its left-hand corner to a steep exit. Surprisingly popular.

16 Little Ernie . . . . 🎨 ☐ **S 4a**
Start on the left and trend right across the buttress via ledges to reach easy ground. Not well protected.

17 Big Chris. . . . . ☐ **HVS 5b**
The centre of the face starting down and right is followed via a thin crack to a tricky finale using the bum-crack.
FA. Chris Craggs 1993

18 In Earnest . . . . 🎲🎨 ☐ **HVS 5a**
The pleasant arete of the bay by boldish laybacking.
FA. Chris Craggs 1993

19 Recess Wall . . . . 🎲 ☐ **HVD**
The left-slanting groove in the recess using glossy holds and side-stepping a bevy of bulges to a tricky last move.

20 Right Wall Route . . . . 🎲 ☐ **HVD**
Start as for *Recess Wall* but follow the right-trending flakes to a crack that splits the right-hand edge of the capping overhang. Can you spot the ancient bolts on the left near the top?

21 Randolf Cheerleader . . . 🪨▐ ☐ **E3 6a**
Climb a blunt rib then make thin fingery moves up and left to a short crack which is much easier.
FA. Mark Stokes 1983

22 Gullible's Travels. . . 🎲🪨▐║ ☐ **E1 5b**
From the centre of the wall, trend delicately with hard moves to reach a shallow crack and then easier ground. Pleasantly technical climbing protected by small cams.
FA. Brian Pallet (1 point of aid) 1961. FFA. Alan Clarke 1963

23 Al . . . . . . 🪨🪨▐║▐🎨 ☐ **E5 6a**
From the prickly ledge, climb the vague scoop then the fingery wall trending rightwards. Usually dirty and rarely done.
FA. Al Rouse 1984

24 The 3-D Wall. . . . . 🪨▐║ ☐ **E2 6a**
The wall just left of the chimney has good moves (long reaches) though the option of rightward escape rather spoils the effect.
FA. Gary Gibson 1979

Descent at the end of the crag

10m

Mantelpiece Buttress

Sheffield Area · Ladybower Area · Stanage · Burbage Valley · Millstone Area · Derwent Edges · Chatsworth Area · Southern Crags

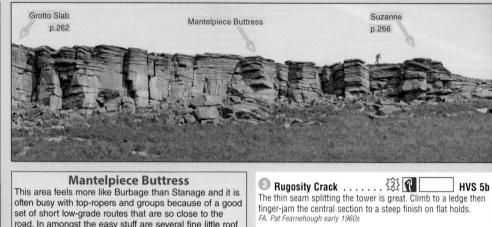

Grotto Slab
p.262

Mantelpiece Buttress

Suzanne
p.266

Mantelpiece Buttress

This area feels more like Burbage than Stanage and it is often busy with top-ropers and groups because of a good set of short low-grade routes that are so close to the road. In amongst the easy stuff are several fine little roof problems which are often soloed.

Approach (see map on page 218) - Walk up from the Hook's Car parking.

1 Black Chimney. . . . . . . 💥 🖐 ☐ **Diff**
The dark rift behind the tower is a struggle, especially for the fuller figure.

2 South Sea Charmer . . . . ☐ **HVS 5b**
The hanging left arete is gained from *Rugosity Crack*.
FA. Paul Williams 1978

3 Rugosity Crack . . . . 💥 🖐 ☐ **HVS 5b**
The thin seam splitting the tower is great. Climb to a ledge then finger-jam the central section to a steep finish on flat holds.
FA. Pat Fearnehough early 1960s

4 Niche Wall Direct. . . . . 💥 📏 ☐ **HS 4b**
Climb the awkward chimney crack to the niche, then take the steep continuation finger-crack above on mostly good holds.

5 The Cristiana Swing . . . . 💥 ☐ **S 4a**
Climb the wide central crack to the ledge then move right to finish up the next route.
Also known as 'Niche Wall'.

6 Nicheless Climb . . . . 🖐 ☐ **HS 4b**
Mantelshelf onto a flat ledge then climb the awkward wide crack above. Laybacking is probably the easiest way into it.

7 Nicheless Climb Direct . . . . ☐ **HS 4b**
The wall just right is a harder variant.

Grotto Slab

8 East Chimney . . . . [ ] **Mod**
The rift just right is pretty soft and mostly used as a descent.

9 Right Edge . . . . [ ] **S 4a**
The right edge leads to a ledge. Finish up the short wall.

10 Hoaxer's Crack . . . . [ ] **HS 4b**
The thin and fingery crack just right of the easy chimney.

11 Trivial Pursuit . . . . [ ] **VS 4b**
Climb the wall past a suspect flake to a tricky finish. Also known as *Blunt Arete*.

12 Small Crack . . . . [ ] **VD**
The short crack has solid jams and slippery footholds.

13 Ground Glass . . [ ] **VS 4c**
A shallow groove is climbed to the tricky wall above.

14 Plate Glass Slab [ ] **VS 4c**
The polished footholds in the centre of the slab lead past poor runners to easier climbing. Bold and harder for the short.

15 Carborundum . . . . [ ] **VS 5a**
The right side of the slab has a couple of long reaches but is less polished than the other routes here.
FA. Chris Craggs 1993

16 Mantelpiece Crack . . . . [ ] **Diff**
The right-slanting crack is nice enough.

17 Mantelpiece Buttress . . . . . . [ ] **Diff**
The left-slanting groove is reached from the right though a more technical direct start is also possible.

18 Mantelpiece Upper Traverse . [ ] **HVS 5a**
Traverse the central break right to easy ground round the arete.

19 Mantelpiece Hand-Traverse . . [ ] **HVS 5b**
Swing along the low break to the arete. Tricky for the long-legged.

20 Mental Peace . . . . [ ] **E2 5c**
Powerful moves through stacked roofs to a hard exit.
FA. David Simmonite 1993

21 Mantelpiece Buttress Direct . [ ] **HVS 5b**
Haul through the crack in the tip of the overhang. .

22 Fragile Mantel . . . . [ ] **HS 4c**
Stretch past the right edge of the narrow overhang. Finish easily.
FA. Chris Craggs 1993

23 Mantelpiece Right . . . . [ ] **HVD**
The shallow groove in the right edge of the wall is steep.

24 Zip Crack . . . . [ ] **Mod**
Easily up (or down) the short V-groove.

25 Button Wall . . . . [ ] **HVD**
Up the pleasant crack right of the nose of the buttress.
FA. Dave Gregory 1993

26 Toggle . . . . [ ] **VS 4b**
The centre of the face is steep to a tricky finish.
FA. Dave Gregory 1993

27 Velcro Arete . . . . [ ] **HS 4c**
The right arete to another rather sticky finish.
FA. Dave Gregory 1993

Descent

Square Buttress
Direct - p.266

Suzanne

Square Buttress Direct - p.266

Sheffield Area
Ladybower Area
Stanage
Burbage Valley
Millstone Area
Derwent Edges
Chatsworth Area
Southern Crags

Suzanne

The final pair of buttresses on the main section of Stanage have a pleasant collection of small routes and the classic bouldery roof of *Suzanne*.
Approach (see map on page 218) - Walk straight up to the right edge of the cliff from the Hook's Car parking.

1 Square Chimney Arete . . . . . 🪨 ☐ **S 4b**
The arete left of the chimney is a bit of an eliminate.
FA. Chris Craggs 1997

2 Square Chimney . . . . ☐ **Diff**
Climb the rift to an awkward exit leftwards.

3 Steve's Wall . . . . 🔦 ☐ **HVS 5b**
The tricky wall in the back of the recess.
FA. Steve Woolley 2013

4 Monkey Crack . . . . 🏵 🔦 ☐ **VD 4a**
The steep crack is a little tricky to access.

5 Square Buttress Direct . . 🏵 🪓 ☐ **HVS 5b**
Tackle the steep front face - worth having a spotter for.

6 Square Buttress Arete. . . . . . 🏵 ☐ **VS 4c**
Up the right-hand arete on its right-hand side.

7 Square Buttress Wall . . . . . . 🗺 ☐ **HS 4b**
The right wall of the buttress doesn't have much gear.

8 Square Buttress Corner. . . . . . . ☐ **Diff**
Bridge the angle. Maybe the shortest route on the cliff!

From mid morning | 6 min | Windy

9 Gashed Knee. . . . . 🔦 ☐ **VS 5a**
The bouldery hanging arete.
FA. Chris Craggs 1993

10 Gashed Crack . . . . 🖐 ☐ **HS 5a**
The awkward undercut crack in the last buttress.

11 Ding Dong. . . . . ☐ **f5**
Powerful moves up the arete right of the crack.

12 Suzanne . . . . 🏵 🪨 ▯ ☐ **f6A**
A classic problem. Reaching the large break above the overhang often involves a bit of a lunge. Continue up sloping rock.
FA. Reg Addey 1965

13 Finale Direct. . . . . . 🏵 🪨 ▯ ☐ **f6A+**
A tough start to *Finale*, over the right-hand side of the roof is a great problem for anyone who found *Suzanne* a bit easy.

14 Finale . . . . 🪨 ☐ **f5**
The right-hand arete is gained with difficulty. It is also possible to get at it from the right and continue for a **HVS 5b**.

15 Fire Curtain. . . . . ☐ **VD**
Bridge the angle which faces towards Millstone Quarry.
FRA. Dave Gregory 1992

16 The Be All and End All . . . . ☐ **VD**
Mantel into the triangular niche, step right and finish direct.
FRA. Chris Craggs 1997

17 The End of All Things . . . . ☐ **HVD**
The last gasp via the roofed niche.
FRA. Chris Craggs 1997

Sheffield Area

Ladybower Area

Stanage

Burbage Valley

Millstone Area

Derwent Edges

Chatsworth Area

Southern Crags

A blustery autumn day *Mating Toads* (*f5+*) - *page 269* - on the Apparent North Area of Stanage.

The Real 20-foot Crack

❶ Sleazy Jamming .... [ ] **S 4b**
A short crack on the left of the wall.

❷ Easy Walling .... [ ] **f5+**
The short narrow wall on the left has a tough start.

❸ Easy Jamming .... [ ] **HVD 4a**
A short-lived crack is worth the effort.

❹ Trainer Failure ..... [ ] **VS 5a**
The pumpy arete is technical and reachy.

❺ The Real 20-foot Crack .. [ ] **VS 4c**
The compelling crack is a decent test of your jamming.

❻ The Shiznit ..... [ ] **f7A**
Attack the left side of the face by a couple of unlikely dynos.
FA. Kim Leyland 2002

❼ Twin Cam .... [ ] **f7A**
Desperately climb the right side of the face via a chipped flake.
FA. Johnny Dawes 1984

❽ Scary Canary .... [ ] **HVS 5b**
Balance up the right arete of the wall.
FA. David Simmonite 1993

❾ Minah Variation ...... [ ] **f6C**
The right wall from the higher ledge.

Apparent North

The steep buttress seamed by diagonal overlaps is home to a concentration of hard routes. Recent new routers didn't follow Len Millsom's idea of creating finishing holds, so several of the climbs have desperate exits. Smaller walls to either side offer some short easy climbs.
Approach (see map on page 218) - Park on the side of the road leading down to the Hook's Car parking. A track leads to the prominent buttress and its photogenic millstones.

The next routes are on the big block below the trig point.

❿ My Crazy Head .... [ ] **f6B**
The superb little arete on its left-hand side. Easier on the right.

⓫ Frigid Witch .... [ ] **HVS 5b**
The steep wall on the left leads to a hard exit.
FA. Paul Mitchell (solo) 1983

⓬ Eminence Grise .... [ ] **E2 6a**
Climb the bottomless crack then tackle the jutting roof.
FA. Paul Mitchell 1983

⓭ Apparent North .... [ ] **HVS 5b**
Follow the short crack to its end then move round onto the front face. The expected belly-flop finish is made much easier by a surprising pair of ancient chipped finger jugs.
FA. Len Millsom early 1960s

⓮ Lead a Dance .... [ ] **E1 5b**
Start as for *Apparent North* but continue the pumpy traverse on jams all the way to the right arete - mega!
FA. Chris Plant, Brian Davidson, Alan Dance(!) 1984

⓯ Hamper's Hang .... [ ] **f7A**
A superb traverse starting at the back of the cut-away on the left and following the break and sloping ledge (the true *Hamper's Hang*) rightwards. Curiously it is only *f6C+* in reverse.
FA. Chris Hamper 1980s

The Real 20ft Crack • Apparent North • Trig Point (457m)

Huge Slab, Henge and Rim Areas
Peak Bouldering

Eeny, Meeny
p.270

10m

Lots of sun | 5 min | Windy

Sheffield Area
Ladybower Area
Stanage
Burbage Valley
Millstone Area
Derwent Edges
Chatsworth Area
Southern Crags

16 Skinless Wonder . . . E6 6c
Start up the small hanging arete and make a hard move on
undercuts to the break of *Apparent North*. A hideous shelving
exit awaits - chalk up your chest, move one metre right, then go!
The start is is *f7A+* above a pile of mats.
FA. Richie Patterson 1993

17 Stanage Without Oxygen. E5 6c
The easiest hard route here pre-dates the others by a decade - it
will still leave you breathless! Climb the left side of the capping roof
aiming for the right edge of the capping roof, to finish as for
Apparent North. Significantly easier in cool conditions. *f7A+*
above a (big!) pile of mats, and/or a snow drift.
FA. John Allen 1983

18 Little Women . . E7 7a
A high-quality modern desperate. Gain the shelf, place cams in
the highest break, then head up and right using a series of poor
holds linked by hard moves to reach a typically sloping finish.
FA. John Welford 1997

19 Hamper's Direct. f7A
Tackle the sloping roof from a low start, to a hard mantel.

20 Groove is in the Heart . . E7 7a
Technical and fingery moves through the stacked overlaps in the
scoop to another rounded finish. Only led with pre-placed RPs.
FA. Neil Bentley 1998

21 Black Car Burning . . E7 6c
An arduous climb up the vertical face on the right. Start under
the final scoop of *Groove is in the Heart* and trend right to poor
holds under the roof. Make a hard move to a good hold on the
lip and finish rapidly by a series of stretches. *f7A+* above pads
and a snow drift.
FA. Robin Barker 1993

22 Magnetic North E3 5c
Climb the arete (a nice problem) and move right to a jutting
ledge. At the roof swing back left to a difficult exit.
FA. Simon Horrox 1982

23 True North. . . . . VS 4c
From the large boulder jammed in the gully, climb up the
right-hand side of the blunt arete on the left, finishing up a short
wall by a long reach.
FA. Len Millsom early 1960s

24 Mating Toads . . . . . f5+
The delicate rib is more involving than first acquaintance might
suggest. *Photo on page 267.*
FA. Andy Barker 1982

25 Massacre E1 5b
A pumpy hand-traverse to a rapid exit.

The Cowper Stone - 300m

Grand Theft
p.270

Spare Rib
p.270

Eeny, Meeny

Spare Rib

Eeny, Meeny
30m to the right of Apparent North Buttress is a short wall with a tower 12m to its right. The routes have rounded holds and can feel tricky. They give good easy bouldering.

26 Eeny . . . . HVD 4a
The wall on the left with a tricky start.
FA. Dave Gregory 1992

27 Meeny . . . . HS 4b
The centre of the wall has an awkward rounded top-out.
FA. Dave Gregory 1992

28 Miny . . . . HS 4b
.. and so does the line just left of the arete.
FA. Dave Gregory 1992

29 Miny Arete . . . . HS 4b
The arete itself may still hold a loose flake in the break.

Spare Rib
12m to the right is a slabby tower.

30 Spare Rib . . . . VD 4a
The centre of the tower has an exciting pull on the top wall.
Avoiding the left arete makes it more like **4b**.
FA. Dave Gregory 1992

31 Scrag End . . . . HVD 4a
The crack on the right is beefy towards the top.
FA. Dave Gregory 1992

Grand Theft
After 60m there is a short wall with a well-chalked traverse line.

32 Sloper Traverse *f7A*
Traverse the slopy break and finish by moving up on crimps. The line through the traverse is a condition-dependent *f6C*.

20m further to the right is a prominent jutting overhang.

33 Petty Larceny . . . . *f5+*
Climb with difficulty round the overlap and then up the left arete.
Continue to the roof and mantel around it leftwards.
FA. Andy Barker 1982

34 Body Roll Finish E3 6a
The left-edge of the roof directly above the start.
FA. John Allen 1989

35 Almost a Hold . . . . . *f6C+*
A desperate traverse along the dog-leg break.

36 Small Time Crook E2 6b
The centre of the wall and the desperate roof above.
FA. John Boyle 2000

37 Grand Theft . . . . *f5+*
Trend right up the wall then reach left to a mantel finish (**E1!**).
FA. Andy Barker 1982

Grand Theft

The Cowper Stone - 300m

Flat and Long Walls
Peak Bouldering

32 20m left

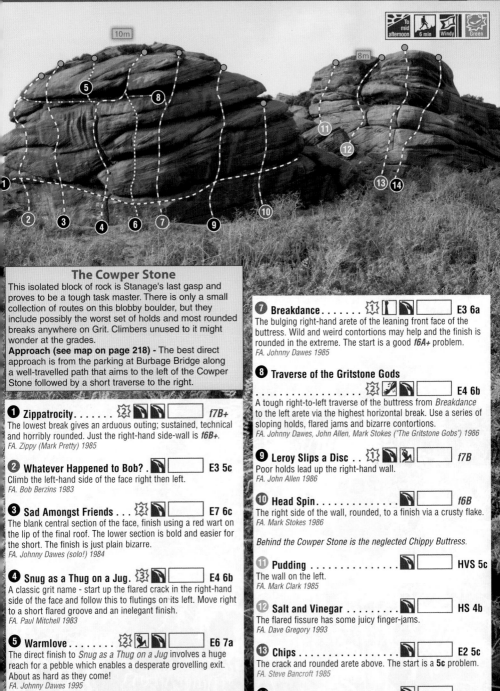

10m

8m

The Cowper Stone

This isolated block of rock is Stanage's last gasp and proves to be a tough task master. There is only a small collection of routes on this blobby boulder, but they include possibly the worst set of holds and most rounded breaks anywhere on Grit. Climbers unused to it might wonder at the grades.

Approach (see map on page 218) - The best direct approach is from the parking at Burbage Bridge along a well-travelled path that aims to the left of the Cowper Stone followed by a short traverse to the right.

❶ Zippatrocity. . . . . . .   *f7B+*
The lowest break gives an arduous outing; sustained, technical and horribly rounded. Just the right-hand side-wall is *f6B+*.
FA. Zippy (Mark Pretty) 1985

❷ Whatever Happened to Bob? .   E3 5c
Climb the left-hand side of the face right then left.
FA. Bob Berzins 1983

❸ Sad Amongst Friends . . .   E7 6c
The blank central section of the face, finish using a red wart on the lip of the final roof. The lower section is bold and easier for the short. The finish is just plain bizarre.
FA. Johnny Dawes (solo!) 1984

❹ Snug as a Thug on a Jug. .   E4 6b
A classic grit name - start up the flared crack in the right-hand side of the face and follow this to flutings on its left. Move right to a short flared groove and an inelegant finish.
FA. Paul Mitchell 1983

❺ Warmlove. E6 7a
The direct finish to *Snug as a Thug on a Jug* involves a huge reach for a pebble which enables a desperate grovelling exit. About as hard as they come!
FA. Johnny Dawes 1995

❻ Happy Amongst Friends .   E6 6c
The bulging wall just left of the arete is more of the same!
FA. Johnny Dawes (solo) 1996

❼ Breakdance E3 6a
The bulging right-hand arete of the leaning front face of the buttress. Wild and weird contortions may help and the finish is rounded in the extreme. The start is a good *f6A+* problem.
FA. Johnny Dawes 1985

❽ Traverse of the Gritstone Gods
. . . .   E4 6b
A tough right-to-left traverse of the buttress from *Breakdance* to the left arete via the highest horizontal break. Use a series of sloping holds, flared jams and bizarre contortions.
FA. Johnny Dawes, John Allen, Mark Stokes ("The Gritstone Gobs") 1986

❾ Leroy Slips a Disc . .   *f7B*
Poor holds lead up the right-hand wall.
FA. John Allen 1986

❿ Head Spin. *f6B*
The right side of the wall, rounded, to a finish via a crusty flake.
FA. Mark Stokes 1986

Behind the Cowper Stone is the neglected Chippy Buttress.

⓫ Pudding . . . .   HVS 5c
The wall on the left.
FA. Mark Clark 1985

⓬ Salt and Vinegar . . . .   HS 4b
The flared fissure has some juicy finger-jams.
FA. Dave Gregory 1993

⓭ Chips E2 5c
The crack and rounded arete above. The start is a **5c** problem.
FA. Steve Bancroft 1985

⓮ Peas E4 5c
Traverse in from the left and finish up the right-hand side of the wall. The direct start is a testing *f6C* mantel.
FA. Steve Bancroft 1985

Burbage Valley

Sheffield Area

Ladybower Area

Stanage

Burbage Valley

Millstone Area

Derwent Edges

Chatsworth Area

Southern Crags

Kevin Jorgeson making the first ground-up ascent of *Parthian Shot* (E10 6c) - *page 317* - on Burbage South. This route has had an eventful history much of which has been centred on the mythical flake halfway up the route that takes the key runners. Early ascents and attempts regarded this flake as unreliable but it was soon shown to be fairly solid after holding falls on a number of repeat ascents and the route settled at E9. Then the flake broke which probably came as a shock to some who had run it out over the previous decade. Ben Bransby has now taken the route full cycle by repeating it in its new state which is technically harder, more pumpy and with poorer gear, hence the grade has nudged up to E10. Photo: Adam Long

The Cowper Stone
p.271

About 1km

Sheffield

N

Stanage Popular
p.218

Apparent North
p.268

Burbage North
p.274

Carl Wark
p.306

Hathersage

Higgar Tor
p.296

Burbage South
p.310

Hathersage

Over Owler Tor
p.330

Millstone
p.332

A6187

Sheffield

B6521

Lawrencefield
p.356

A625

Sheffield Area

Ladybower Area

Stanage

Burbage Valley

Millstone Area

Derwent Edges

Chatsworth Area

Southern Crags

	No star	☆	☆☆	☆☆☆
Mod to S	46	38	3	-
HS to HVS	36	38	7	4
E1 to E3	10	12	5	2
E4 and up	6	8	5	1

Neil Foster nearing the top of *Now or Never* (E1 5b) - *page 284* - on The Sentinel area of Burbage North. Photo: Mike Hutton

Sheffield Area

Ladybower Area

Stanage

Burbage Valley

Millstone Area

Derwent Edges

Chatsworth Area

Southern Crags

Burbage North is a popular spot because its great accessibility makes it a regular haunt of many climbers. Unlike its darker sister, Burbage South, it has a reputation for friendly routes in a picturesque setting. Fine summer evenings will see the place swarming with locals grabbing a quick route or two before the sun goes down. Its accessibility and great supply of short and easy routes means that it is also popular with Outdoor Centres, although they tend to stick to the initial sections; a three minute extension to your approach walk will always reduce any crowds. Burbage North doesn't have any mega-classic climbs, though there is hardly a poor route on the whole cliff. The rock is the same quality as on the other edges, but overall the crag is on a smaller scale. Often you will only have time to place a couple of runners before topping out, which is why the place is so popular with boulderers and soloists.

Approach   Also see map on page 273

Burbage Bridge, at the north end of Burbage Valley, has two parking areas which usually have enough spaces except on the busiest of weekends when you may struggle to find a spot. An alternative is to park up at Higgar Tor and walk back (10 mins). From Burbage Bridge, there are three paths: the main one (the Green Drive) goes down the valley, a small path breaks left from this and runs along the base of the cliff. There is also the third option, a crag-top path, which is useful for reaching the more distant areas.

Conditions

The edge faces southwest and catches the sun from the mid-morning onwards. This means it can get very hot in summer. It is exposed to any bad weather but dries very quickly after rain, although a few routes can be a bit damp and sandy.

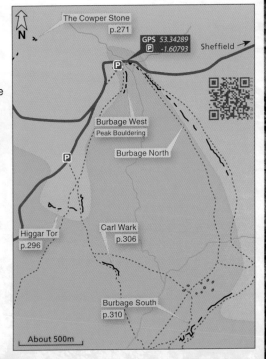

The Chant

The first part of Burbage offers bouldering and short routes and is always busy. The routes are packed in and feel quite tough for their grade, as is to be expected for short, roadside test-pieces. The proximity of the parking (and the city) means it is always a good bet for a quick-fix when time is tight.

Approach (see map on page 275) - Go through the gate and head left for 120m.

1 RT Wall . . . . *f5+*
The north-facing side-wall climbed centrally by a stretchy move.

2 Route 1 . . . . **HS 4b**
The left arete of the wall has a tricky last move.

3 Route 1.25 . . . . *f5+*
An eliminate just right of the arete. Around 5c.

4 Route 1.5 . . . . *f5*
The wall 2m right of the arete has a hard start. Around 5b.

5 Route 2 . . . . **S 4a**
Climb the steep wall and crack, 3m right of the arete, using ancient chipped and well-polished holds to start.

6 Route 2.5 . . . . *f5*
A fingery little number between the cracks eases above.

7 Route 3 . . . . **S 4a**
The zig-zag crack in the centre of the wall is another with a slippery start and jugs above.

8 Route 3.5 . . . . *f6A*
Plugs the non-gap. The crux is quite high. Worth 6a UK tech.

9 Route 4 . . . . *f5+*
Just left of the arete is a thin wall with tough finale.

10 Route 5 . . . . **HVD 4a**
The juggy right arete of the wall.

11 Cranberry Wall . . . . **VD**
This narrow face is a popular little outing.

12 Cranberry Crack . . . . **VD**
The widening, left-slanting crack is awkward. Large gear needed.
FA. Albert Shutt 1951

13 The Chant . . . . **HVS 5a**
The centre of the wall leads to tricky right-facing mantelshelf.
FA. Alan Clarke late 1950s

14 The Chant Direct Finish **E2 6a**
A left-hand finish is desperate!

15 The Chant Direct Start . . . . . **HVS 5b**
Tackle the wall right of the usual start on thin holds.

16 20-foot Crack . . . . **S 4b**
Too-thin jams and slippery footholds make this one feel tricky.

17 The Curse *f5*
A problem requiring some harsh crimping. Hard for the short.

18 Lost in France . . . . . *f5+*
A technical start on tiny holds, but fortunately easing rapidly.

Bouldering or Routes?

The first section of Burbage is very popular with boulderers. We have mostly used route grades in this book but for a bouldering approach, including a few more problems and many variations, check the Peak Bouldering Rockfax.

Triangle Buttress
The second section of the edge has a fair selection of lower-grade climbs and more good bouldering including a fine low-level traverse. The lower section of the wall under *Little White Jug* often seeps after rain.
Approach (see map on page 275) - The area is just right of The Chant area.

19 Little Plumb . . . . [ ] **Diff**
A straightforward blocky crack to a trickier finish.

20 Base Over Apex . . . . [ ] **VS 4c**
The wall right of the crack has one long reach. Finish up the short, hanging groove.
FA. Chris Craggs 1991

21 Baseless . . . . [ ] **HVD**
The straight crack left of the nose of the buttress to a steep exit.

22 Triangle Buttress Arete . . [ ] **VD**
Climb the arete with tricky moves onto a sloping shelf early on and then easier climbing above.
FA. Eric Byne 1932

23 Triangle Buttress Direct . [ ] **S 4a**
The wall just right of the arete is steep and juggy and has a couple of long reaches early on. A problem start just right is *f5* with a stiff pull to reach and the small overhang.

24 Triangle Crack . . . . [ ] **HVD 4a**
The awkward, narrowing corner can be a struggle; at least there is plenty of protection. A good spot to learn to bridge.

25 Leaning Wall . . . . [ ] **S 4b**
The hanging crack in the centre of the wall is best approached by a mildly bold traverse from the groove. It can also be reached from *Steptoe* rather more easily.

26 Leaning Wall Direct . . . . [ ] **HS 5a**
Fingery (often wet) moves on small sharp holds lead to the base of the easy upper crack. Many variations exist - the upper wall on the left is **VS 4c** if you use the arete and at least a couple of grades harder if you don't! A direct start to this is *f6A*.
FA. Ron Townsend 1957

27 Little White Jug . . . . [ ] **VS 4c**
The leaning and juggy wall to the right of the crack leads steeply to a grovelling mantelshelf exit on jams under a conveniently-placed block, or a crumbling little edge.
FA. Andy Hall 1977

28 Big Black 'un . . . . [ ] **HVS 5a**
Climb the juggy wall just right via a series of bulges to another mantelshelf exit.
FA. Graham Hoey 1987

29 Steptoe . . . . [ ] **Mod**
Easy cracks and blocks on the right-hand side of the wall give a pleasant beginners' outing.

30 . . . and Son . . . . [ ] **Diff**
Amble up the rock on the right. Another really easy one.

Banana Finger - 20m →

Triangle Buttress
p.277

The Chant
p.276

Banana Finger

Crag-top path

Lower path

Valley path

Overhanging Buttress

Banana Finger

This renowned buttress of tiered overhangs is home to the classic *Banana Finger* boulder problem and all its many derivatives. Bouldering mats are more common here than ropes! The two *Monkey* routes are nice beginners' climbs if the routes on the next buttress are occupied, but avoid using top-ropes if you can.

Approach (see map on page 275) - Walk 20m right from Triangle Buttress.

❶ Monkey Corner . . . . HVD
The steep and juggy groove on the left leads steeply to a swing right at the bulge to easy ground.

❷ Banana Finger Direct f6C
The best of several variations on the next route. A knee-bar is of help so avoid wearing shorts, and clean those boots well!

❸ Banana Finger f6A
A classic boulder problem. From the centre of the buttress piano-play left then stretch to cross the overlaps (knees usually help a bit) to easy ground.
FA. Ed Drummond 1971. Graded XS and given a detailed description!

❹ Monkey Wall . . . . Mod
The face, trending left via a series of ledges. About as mild as they come, much used in descent and a decent beginners' trip.

❺ Monkey Wall Direct . . . . Diff
Does what it says on the tin.

❻ Monk On . . . . HVS 5b
Pull through the roof just left of the arete. Escaping right is cheating!
FA. Steve Bancroft 1981

Triangle Buttress - 20m

All Quiet Area
p.280

Remergence Buttress
p.281

Ash Tree Wall - 200m

7 Ad Infinitum .... 🔲 S 4a
A pleasant and exposed left-to-right girdle following the line above the roofs and finishing up the far arete.

8 Wednesday Climb ..... 🔲 HVS 5b
The roof crack via a jam and jugs is easiest if you stay out from the crack as much as possible. A knee-bar might be of help.
FA. Pat Fearneough early 1960s

9 Life in a Radioactive Dustbin 🔲 f6C
The desperate roof is a good but highball problem.
FA. Paul Mitchell 1984

10 The Disposable Bubble..... 🔲 E4 6b
The right-hand side of the roof gives a hard problem which is low in the grade.
FA. Johnny Dawes 1984

11 Overhanging Buttress Direct . 🔲 S 4a
Use shiny holds to climb to the edge of the overhang, step right to pass this and finish more easily up the fine slab - nice.

12 Overhanging Buttress Variation . 🔲 VD 4a
An eliminate with a tough start which gets easier above.

Overhanging Buttress
A popular buttress with instructors because of a short approach march and some decent easy routes. If you find the classics unoccupied, then grab your chance to nip up them.
Approach (see map on page 275) - Direct from the valley path or by scrambling over the boulders under the Banana Finger buttress.

13 Overhanging Buttress Arete.. 🔲 Mod
The juggy arete is awkward to start - come in from the right.

14 Burgess Face .... 🔲 HS 4c
The face just left of the next arete.

15 Burgess Buttress .... 🔲 Diff
The flake crack is another popular beginners' climb. Starting left of the arete is a grade (or two) harder.

16 Burgess Street............ 🔲 Diff
The groove just to the right is another pleasant easy one. Exit left when the crack closes.

17 Union Street .... 🔲 S 4a
Nip up the short smooth wall on the far right.

All Quiet Area - 40m

All Quiet Area

Up the slope to the left from Remergence Buttress is a short wall split centrally by a wide crack. It is home to four interesting micro-routes plus bouldering variations.
Approach (see map on page 275) - This is the short wall between Overhanging Buttress and Remergence.

② The Busker . . . . VS 4c
The steep slab trending right has some nice moves.
FA. Steve Bancroft 1982

❸ Bracken Crack . . . . HVD 4a
The wide crack is awkward and harder for the short.

❹ Green Slab . . . . VS 5a
The juggy wall has an awkward start and is easier above.

❶ All Quiet on the Eastern Front
. . . . f6A+
Gain the left arete by a traverse from the left and then sprint. The direct start is f7A+ and a sit-down is even harder at f7B.
FA. Ed Drummond 1978

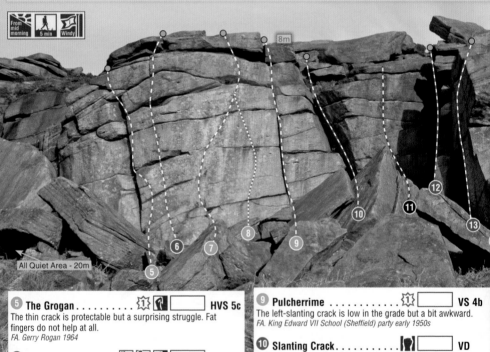

All Quiet Area - 20m

❺ The Grogan . . . . HVS 5c
The thin crack is protectable but a surprising struggle. Fat fingers do not help at all.
FA. Gerry Rogan 1964

❻ Groat E1 6b
The thin wall just right of the crack sees little attention.
FA. Al Rouse early 1980s

❼ Wollock . . . . HVS 4c
Trend right up the wall then finish direct. A bit reachy in its central section, to a high crux. Escaping right is only worth VS.
FA. Dave Gregory 1964

❽ Wollock Direct . . . . HVS 5c
A long stretch up the wall is interesting.

❾ Pulcherrime . . . . VS 4b
The left-slanting crack is low in the grade but a bit awkward.
FA. King Edward VII School (Sheffield) party early 1950s

❿ Slanting Crack . . . . VD
A short grovel up the wide crack just right.

⓫ Small is Beautiful f7A
The tiny wall to the right is climbed direct.
FA. John Allen 1985

⓬ Slanting Gully . . . . Diff
Polished holds lead to easier climbing above.

⓭ Chockstone Climb . . . . . VD
The deep chockstoned rift to a sloping or squeezy exit.

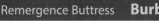
Remergence Buttress

An impressive buttress, the classics of *Mutiny Crack* and *Remergence* are test-pieces from two generations apart. The lower section of the buttress is very popular with boulderers and with the exception of *Mutiny Crack*, ropes are rarely used here. There are many more problems and eliminates described in the Peak Bouldering Rockfax.
Approach (see map on page 275) - It is best to approach direct from the valley path.

14 Stomach Traverse . . . . . HVS 4c
Muscle onto the arete and move up to the roof. Either crawl (historically correct but scary) or hand traverse to *Mutiny Crack*. Not too well protected and high in the grade.
FA. Eric Byne 1932

15 Tiptoe . . . . VS 4c
Start as for *Stomach Traverse* but step down and tiptoe to *Mutiny Crack*. Continue around the arete and back to base.
FA. Chris Craggs 1972

16 Gymnipodies E4 6b
From the ledge gain the break above then finish with difficulty.
FA. John Allen 1988

17 The Hanging Rib f6B
Climb the blunt arete using anything. It is slightly harder if you use the lip-pinch instead of the undercut.

18 Remergence E4 6b
The centre of the roof is passed with difficulty using chalked slots to gain a flatty above - a great *f6B* problem. The final roof is crossed via a strenuous stretch (good cams) and is well worth doing since it contains the E4 bit.
FA. Steve Bancroft 1977

19 Blind Date E4 7a
Usually done as a boulder problem over the first roof - *f7B+*. Continuing is well worth it though for the excellent top roof (6b).
FA. Al Rouse (start), Phil Burke (finish) 1984. Only Al could do the start, only Phil could do the finish. First complete ascent is unknown.

20 Mutiny Crack . . . . HS 4b
A mini-classic, and a great little route following the crack cleaving the bulges. It is jug-pulling once the initial awkward roof is passed but this is a real struggle for many.
FA. Eric Byrom 1934

21 Meddle . . . . HVS 5a
The arete is climbed on its right-hand side then take the short wall. Move left to finish up the perched slab. Low in the grade.
FA. Dennis Carr 1976

22 Detour . . . . S 4a
Climb the groove to a rapid escape left below the big overhang. A finish up the short hanging crack above is a grade harder.
FA. Ron Townsend 1950s

23 Diversion . . . . HVS 5a
The hanging crack reached with difficulty from the groove.
FA. Dave Gregory 1964

24 Dead Tree Crack . . . . . . HS 4b
25m to the right, this is the arduous wide and green leaning crack. Laybacking is easiest.

25 Side Face . . . . S 4a
The right-hand side face.

Ash Tree Wall

A good selection of lower grade routes with some mild cracks that make the area worth a visit for brushing up on your jamming. There is also plenty of bouldering hereabouts - see the Rockfax Peak Bouldering book.
Approach (see map on page 275) - Approach via the valley path and walk up through the bracken on a diagonal path. The crag-top path can also be used

① Sunlight Caller . . . . **VS 5b**
Awkward moves up the wall right of the arete.
FA. Michael Bridges 1985

② Oak Tree Face . . . . **HS 4b**
This is the short crack to an awkward exit.
FA. Dave Gregory 1977

③ Boggle Boothroyd . . . . **VS 4c**
Climb just left of the right arete.
FA. Michael Bridges 1985

④ The Last Great Problem . . . . **HVS 5c**
The left arete of the buttress is tricky but misnamed.
FA. Alex Thackway 1992

⑤ Striker . . . . **f7C+**
The centre of the blank wall has a desperate start. Slightly left, using the arete is an easier **f7A+**.
FA. Ben Moon 1990s

⑥ Beach Tea One . . . . **HVS 6a**
From the arete, move left then finish direct.

⑦ Ivy Tree . . . . **HVS 5b**
A tricky problem up the wall and arete. The roof direct is **E1 6a**.
FA. Dave Gregory 1977

⑧ All Star's Goal **E1 6a**
Climb the centre of the wall trending left to a deep horizontal break and finish direct with difficulty and/or a dyno.
FA. Colin Banton 1977

⑨ Evening Wall **E1 5b**
Trend right to finish just left of the arete.
FA. Dave Gregory 1964

⑩ Wall Chimney . . . . **S 4a**
The outrageous rift is a gradually-easing struggle. Tasty!

⑪ Happily Ever After **E6 6c**
Climbed direct past the nose to pockets with pre-placed runners.
FA. Richie Patterson 1995.

⑫ Nefertiti **E6 6c**
From the nose, move right and climb the scoop with difficulty. Pre-placed runners protect. Has been highballed at **f7A**.
FA. John Allen (from the chimney on the left) 1989

⑬ Wall Corner . . . . **HVD 4a**
Climb left of the arete steeply to reach a crack, which is then followed throughout. A direct finish is **VS 4c**.

⑭ Ash Tree Variations . . . . **VS 5c**
Climb the tricky wall (only 5b for the tall and talented) to the break, then step right and head up the slab to a tricky landing.

⑮ Ash Tree Wall . . . . . **S 4a**
Climb the grim fat-fist crack to its end then traverse left reach to the pleasant right-trending groove.

⑯ Ash Tree Wall Eliminate . . . . **VS 5b**
The narrow wall just right is, not surprisingly, an eliminate.

⑰ Ash Trees Forever . . . . . **HVS 5b**
The wall and arete right of the wide crack are nice enough.

⑱ Ash Tree Crack . . . . **VD**
The first continuous crack gives good jamming and good gear.

⑲ Artificial Stimulant **E2 5b**
The narrow slab has a couple of nice moves. No side-runners at this grade, or award yourself an HVS if you are tempted.

Sheffield Area
Ladybower Area
Stanage
Burbage Valley
Millstone Area
Derwent Edges
Chatsworth Area
Southern Crags

The Sentinel - 130m

The Terrace

Peak Bouldering

20 Bilberry Crack . . . . ⛬ [＿＿] **VD**
The next long crack is easier than those to the left but the finish up the slab is a little tricky.

21 Bilberry Face . . . . 🎔 [＿＿] **S 4a**
The next face. Using the (unavoidable?) crack drops the grade.

22 Bilberry Arete . . . . [＿＿] **Mod**
The slabby arete and easy flakes above.

23 Calvin Klimb . . . . 🦿🎔 [＿＿] **E4 6b**
Short-lived but desperate and sees few repeats. *f7B*ish maybe?
FA. Darren Thomas 1996

24 Puck . . . . ⛬🦿🎔 [＿＿] **f7B**
The arete using a pocket is highball.

25 A Phenomenological Problem . . [＿＿] **HVS 5b**
The tricky rib on the left-hand side of the descent gully.
FA. Clive Jones 1977

26 Leaning Block Crack . . . . . . 💪 [＿＿] **VD**
The dirty crack on the block right of the gully has a hard start.

27 Navana . . . . ⛬🦿 [＿＿] **E6 6b**
The side-wall is climbed diagonally to a dynamic finish.
FA. Darren Thomas 1994

28 Living in Oxford . . . . ⛬🦿🦿 [＿＿] **E7 7a**
The arete of the block sees few repeats. Follow its right-hand side with extreme difficulty and only mediocre protection.
FA. Johnny Dawes 1989

29 Superstition ⛬🦿🦿🎔🦿 [＿＿] **f8A**
The astounding blank wall is extremely technical. Better landing than its neighbour but still very highball.
FA. Miles Gibson 1999

30 The Promise . . . ⛬🦿🎔🦿 [＿＿] **f7C**
The arete is technical and bold. It had a single runner for a short time until the placement deteriorated. Now done above pads.
Photos on page 295.
FA. James Pearson 2007

31 Green Chimney . . . . ⛬💪 [＿＿] **VD**
The fissure to the right of the block is tricky with 3D moves.

Sheffield Area · Ladybower Area · Stanage · Burbage Valley · Millstone Area · Derwent Edges · Chatsworth Area · Southern Crags

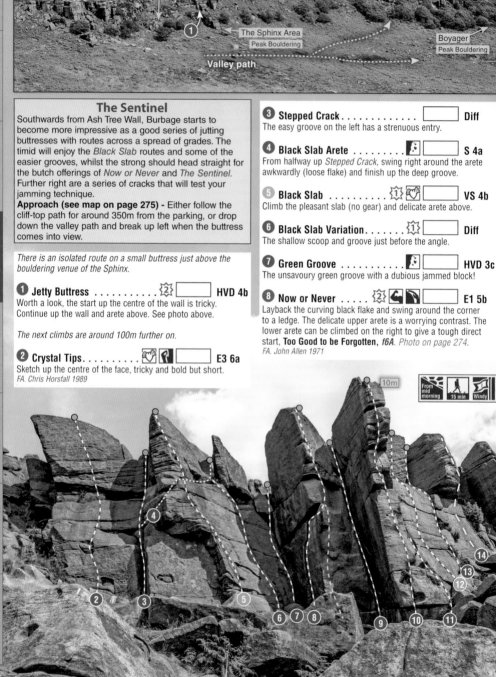

The Sentinel · Knight's Move p.286

Ash Tree Wall p.282 · The Terrace · Peak Bouldering · Boyager · Peak Bouldering · The Sphinx Area · Peak Bouldering · Valley path

The Sentinel

Southwards from Ash Tree Wall, Burbage starts to become more impressive as a good series of jutting buttresses with routes across a spread of grades. The timid will enjoy the *Black Slab* routes and some of the easier grooves, whilst the strong should head straight for the butch offerings of *Now or Never* and *The Sentinel*. Further right are a series of cracks that will test your jamming technique.

Approach (see map on page 275) - Either follow the cliff-top path for around 350m from the parking, or drop down the valley path and break up left when the buttress comes into view.

There is an isolated route on a small buttress just above the bouldering venue of the Sphinx.

1 Jetty Buttress . . . . **HVD 4b**
Worth a look, the start up the centre of the wall is tricky. Continue up the wall and arete above. See photo above.

The next climbs are around 100m further on.

2 Crystal Tips **E3 6a**
Sketch up the centre of the face, tricky and bold but short.
FA. Chris Horsfall 1989

3 Stepped Crack . . . . **Diff**
The easy groove on the left has a strenuous entry.

4 Black Slab Arete . . . . **S 4a**
From halfway up *Stepped Crack*, swing right around the arete awkwardly (loose flake) and finish up the deep groove.

5 Black Slab . . . . **VS 4b**
Climb the pleasant slab (no gear) and delicate arete above.

6 Black Slab Variation . . . . **Diff**
The shallow scoop and groove just before the angle.

7 Green Groove . . . . **HVD 3c**
The unsavoury green groove with a dubious jammed block!

8 Now or Never **E1 5b**
Layback the curving black flake and swing around the corner to a ledge. The delicate upper arete is a worrying contrast. The lower arete can be climbed on the right to give a tough direct start, **Too Good to be Forgotten, f6A**. *Photo on page 274.*
FA. John Allen 1971

10m

From mid morning · 15 min · Windy

9 Sentinel Chimney... 🎲🧗👥☐ **HVD 4a**
The sustained and awkward rift left of the imposing hanging arete has good gear throughout.

10 The Sentinel ...... 🎲🧗◣☐ **E2 5b**
The narrow projecting buttress has a couple of steep and powerful moves just below the top. *Photo on page 287.*
FA. Dennis Carr 1977

11 Sentinel Crack.......... 🎲☐ **Diff**
The crack on the right side of the prow is a good first lead and is heaps easier than its Chatsworth namesake. Finish with a short mild layback.

12 Present Arms .... ▯☐ **HS 4c**
Climb the slab to the large ledge then ascend the large block by embracing both aretes (long arms helpful!) with a final balancy long reach move for the top mantel.
FA. Mark Stephen Davies 2002

13 'armless................ ☐ **Diff**
The right-hand groove is ancient but has never been recorded.

14 High Flyer.......... 🎲👁☐ **E2 5b**
Climb the bold bulge from right to left, care needed.
FA. Gary Gibson 1978

15 The Grazer .... 🎲◣👥☐ **VS 5a**
The leaning jamming-crack gives a short-lived tussle. Good gear.
FA. Dave Gregory late 1950s

16 Lieback .... 🎲☐ **HS 4b**
A tricky shallow groove leads to a short layback flake.

17 Think of England .... ☐ **Mod**
The grassy groove makes a steady first lead.

18 Ring My Bell......... 🧗👁☐ **E4 6a**
The left arete of the wall to a serious finale up the hanging arete above the bulges.
FA. John Allen 1985

19 Ringo................. 🎲☐ **S 4a**
A straight crack with an awkward bulge passed by jamming.

20 Ring Piece .... 🧗🔲☐ **HVS 6a**
Climb the balancy wall with a side-runner.
FA. Jim Rubery 1991

21 Ring Climb .... 🎲☐ **S 4a**
The milder *Ringo* tackles the tricky central crack and short wall.

22 Ring Chimney .... ☐ **Diff**
The deep chimney and flake are fairly straightforward.

23 Agnostic's Arete.... 🎲🧗👁☐ **VS 5a**
The balancy arete eases with height, but there isn't much gear.
FA. Clive Jones 1977. Clive disappeared for a couple of minutes then announced to Dave Gregory that he had just done a new route, Dave declared that he didn't believe it.

24 Pickpocket .... 🎲☐ **VS 4c**
The south-facing wall with a low crux to a finish over a block.

Knight's Move

Knight's Move

Next is the tallest buttress on the edge, easily recognised by a large overhang on the right. There are several worthwhile routes here with the superb *Knight's Move* being especially memorable.
Approach (see map on page 275) - Walk along the cliff-top path for about 400m from the parking.

1 Seventy Niner . . . .  VS 4c
On the left the loss of the holly has revealed this crack and flake.
FA. Dave Gregory 2013. 57 years after Still Orange, aged 79.

2 The Keffer. . . . . VS 5a
The slabby face on the left. A finish up the bold arete is possible.
FA. Kevin Thaw 1986

3 Still Orange. . . . . S 4a
Climb the easy slanting ramp then step right to the short-lived but pleasant jamming crack.
FA. Dave Gregory 1956. His first new route, aged 22.

4 Rise 'n Shine. . . . . HVS 5a
The direct approach to the final crack of *Still Orange*.

5 Green Crack . . . . VD
The long blocky crack that leans to the right is awkward.

6 Dover's Progress . . . . . . HVS 5a
An ancient eliminate climbing the slim wall past the cannonball slots. Delicate and not well protected; micro-cams might help.
FA. Harry Dover 1932

7 Hollyash Crack . . . . VS 4b
The long crack is tricky in its central section. A good intro to off-widths, it can be face climbed too. Huge cams might help.
FA. Harry Dover 1932

8 Knight's Move . . . . HVS 5a
A Burbage classic. Climb past some holes then take the thin cracks (small wires) and the wall above, following the flakes rightwards to finish. Mild at the grade but some have to be!
FA. Gilbert Ellis 1933

9 Peter's Progress . . . . . . VS 4c
Climb *Knight's Move* to the break above the roof, follow this all the way to the arete passing a sapling, to an easy finish. A better finish is up the shallow crack above the sapling at **HVS 5a**.
FA. Peter Biven 1953

10 Arme Blanche . . E5 6a
Crawl past the left side of the overlap to easy ground. A side-runner is sensible though it has been done without.
FA. Gary Gibson 1981

11 Great Crack . . . . VS 5a
Climb the deep corner right of the holly to the overhang then shuffle right and make brutal moves past the lip to enter the easier upper crack. Jammed ropes are commonplace.
FA. Harry Dover 1932

12 The Big Chimney . . . HS 4b
The deep cleft is hard and bold to enter then eases to a capping-stone, which is most easily passed on the right, though a left-hand exit is more in keeping with the start.

13 Windjammer E1 5b
Pull through the roof and head for the left arete. The desperate direct start is **Enterprise**, a highball *f7C*.
FA. Gary Gibson 1980. F.A. (Enterprise) Adrian Berry 2006

14 The Rainmaker . . . . HVS 5b
Pull awkwardly up the rib to the roof then climb the face above, starting with a long reach, then easing.
FA. Keith Sharples 1977

15 Big Chimney Arete . . . . HS 4b
The arete on its right side by some mild laybacking and a tasty high step. Protected by small cams.

14m

Twin Chimneys

Martin Koscis on the superb finishing moves of *The Sentinel* (E2 5b) - *page 285* - at Burbage North. Photo: Mike Hutton

Sheffield Area

Ladybower Area

Stanage

Burbage Valley

Millstone Area

Derwent Edges

Chatsworth Area

Southern Crags

TICKLIST
Burbage North Belles
Some folks are rather dismissive of this low blocky edge, though it does have an excellent set of climbs scattered along its length.

☐ **Mutiny Crack, HS** *(281)*. The start may have you questioning the grade until you actually do it.

☐ **Amazon Crack, HS** *(292)*. A groovy little jammer.

☐ **Obscenity, VS** *(292)*. Thee stars but what a pig!

☐ **Knight's Move, HVS** *(286)*. Soft but bold to start.

☐ **Long Tall Sally, E1** *(292)*. Blank brilliance.

☐ **The Sentinel, E2** *(285)*. Steep with a pushy crux.

Twin Chimneys to Tharf Cake

The section of edge between Knight's Move and Long Tall Sally tends to be quiet, but tucked behind the trees are several decent climbs. None of these routes is exceptional but, if you want some solitude, then this area is worth a look. Many of the uncredited routes here were first climbed by Sheffield Climbing Club in the 1930s.
Approach (see map on page 275) - Walk along the cliff-top path for 400m, past the Knight's Move area. *Tharf Cake* is on an isolated buttress about 30m left of the more continuous section leading to Long Tall Sally. The other routes are scattered along to the north, often tucked behind battered birches.

Barry Manilow

20m south of The Knight's Move area is a narrow buttress with a prominent overhang.

❶ Barry Manilow........ VS 4c
Tackle the slabs and roof direct.
FA. Steve Bancroft 1985

Twin Chimneys Layback

20m up and right, and partly shrouded by trees, is a secluded bay with an attractive layback crack on the far left.

❷ Survivor's Syndrome . . . E2 5b
The squeezed-in left arete of the buttress needs care.
FA. Richard Davies 1984

❸ Twin Chimneys Layback .... HVD 4a
An excellent little pitch that is worth seeking out.
FA. Eric Byne 1932

❹ Left Twin Chimney .... VD
The sinister sister is awkward - large gear helps.

❺ Right Twin Chimney .... HVD
The dexter one is harder. A useful chock can be threaded.

❻ Happy Slapper........... HVS 5a
An escapable eliminate up the pocketed pillar on the right. Unobvious moves and lacking in gear.
FA. Chris Moor 1999

❼ Jimmy Riddle .... VS 4c
Committing moves up the right-hand pillar via a short crack.
FA. Chris Moor 1999

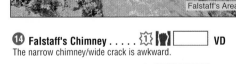

Grotto Slab
Just right of Twin Chimneys Layback *is a green slab.*

8 Split Slab Crack . . . . `[    ]` **S 4a**
The tricky thin crack is followed to a ledge. Continue direct.

9 Split Slab . . . . 🔄 👊 🔧 `[    ]` **HVD 4b**
The slippery slab leads to the wide awkward fissure above.

10 Slide-away . . . . 🔄 🔺 💚 `[    ]` **E1 5a**
Access the arete from below and teeter up it. Low gear.
FA. Gary Gibson 1978

11 Grotto Slab . . . . 🔺 `[    ]` **Mod**
Balance up the mild but unprotected slab and do battle with the holly. A more thrilling finish can be had up the exposed and unprotected hanging arete on the right (S 3c).

Falstaff's Area

12 Grotto Crack . . . . 👊 `[    ]` **VS 4b**
The hidden groove is normally green, though it is worth a quick visit during a dry spell. A couple of slings for threads may help.

13 Submission . . . . 🔄 💚 ⏸ `[    ]` **VS 5a**
From the crack balance out left and zip up the arete.
FA. Gary Gibson 1978

14 Falstaff's Chimney . . . . . 🔄 👊 `[    ]` **VD**
The narrow chimney/wide crack is awkward.

15 Falstaff's Innominate . . . 🔄 🔧 `[    ]` **S 4b**
Another eliminate from a time before eliminates. Be careful lest you tick three routes in one go.

16 Falstaff's Crack . . . . `[    ]` **Diff**
The right-hand fissure has an awkward entry.

17 Paleface . . . . 💚 🔺 `[    ]` **HVS 5a**
The pale face and arete across the gully.
FA. Simon Lockwood 2000

Sheffield Area · Ladybower Area · Stanage · Burbage Valley · Millstone Area · Derwent Edges · Chatsworth Area · Southern Crags

Bilberry Cake

18 Bilberry Cake . . . . 🔟 🔺 ☐ **VS 4c**
The left-hand side of the slabby face.
FA. Chris Hare late 1990s

19 Bilberry Wall . . . . 🔟 🔺 ☐ **VD**
Climb to the crack, then up this and the flakes above.

20 Bilberry Arete . . . . 🔟 🧗 ☐ **S 4a**
The tricky start then follow the arete to a ledge. Continue direct.

21 The Edging Machine . . . . . . 🧗 ☐ **HVS 5b**
Make technical moves up the left arete; minimal gear.
FA. Colin Banton 1978

22 Alpha Crack . . . . 🧍🧗 ☐ **HS 4b**
The first continuous crack is awkward to access.

23 Omega Crack . . . . 🧗 ☐ **VD**
Climb the shallow groove. Beware the wobbly blocks.

24 Scarred Buttress Climb . . . . . 🔟 ☐ **VD**
The right-hand face leads to the big flake and a layback move.

Tharf Cake
Across the slope to the right is a slabbier cracked buttress.

25 First Crack . . . . ☐ **S 4b**
A left-leaning crack has a tricky move or two.

26 Tharf Cake . . . . 🔟 🐢 🧗 ☐ **HVS 5a**
A two-move-wonder starting right of *First Crack*. It has small
holds and the odd useful pocket. Low in the grade but a bit bold.
FA. John Parkin 1977. Tharf cake is a north country name for parkin.

27 Left Twin Crack . . . . 🔟 ☐ **S 4a**
An awkward layback in its middle section.

28 Right Twin Crack . . . . 🔟 ☐ **HVD 4a**
Not to be left out, the right-hand crack is tricky in its middle
section. It is well protected where it matters.

29 Farcical Arete . . . . . 🔟 🐢 🧍 ☐ **HS 4b**
The arete is climbed on its left side throughout and is
unprotected. The start is the crux, and can be avoided on the
right at **4a**.

Brooks' Layback - 30m ➡

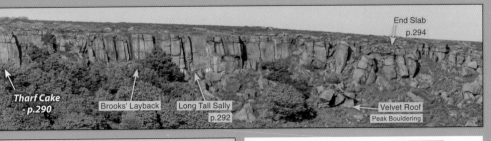

Tharf Cake
- p.290

Brooks' Layback

Long Tall Sally
p.292

End Slab
p.294

Velvet Roof
Peak Bouldering

Brooks' Layback

A fine area on the north end of the longest continuous section of the edge. It has a decent collection of short lower-grade routes. *Brooks' Layback* is a midget gem.
Approach (see map on page 275) - The quickest approach is along the crag-top path for 20 minutes from the parking. It can also be approached from the valley path. The direct approach from Knight's Move area is awkward, it is better is to use the crag-top path. The angular corner of area's headline route is a good marker.

1 The Irrepressible Urge . . E1 5b
The scary front face of the square buttress, trending right - neat.
FA. Colin Banton 1978

2 The Arctic Mammal E3 6a
An intense bouldery route up the arete. Originally done on the right side though the crack is too close for comfort - **Small Arctic Mammal, E1 6a**.
FA. Dave Musgrove 2001. FA. (SAM) Mark Millar late 1970s

3 Left Recess Crack . . . . S 3c
The short but pleasant crack in the left-hand angle.

4 Right Recess Crack . . . . . . HS 4a
The mirror image in the opposite angle has a bit of a stretch.

5 Ace . . . . VS 4b
A narrow, protruding arete which can be climbed first on the left and then up its crest. Delicate, sustained and gearless.

6 The Crack . . . . HS 4a
The wide fissure is good practice for *Goliath's Groove*.

7 The Chimney . . . . Diff
The narrow rift; often damp and dirty. Included for completeness.

8 Thrall's Thrutch . . . . S 4a
The wide corner-crack is well-named - you have been warned.

9 Brooks' Layback . . . . . . HS 4b
The short right-angled corner-crack starts from a ledge and many find it is just too thin for good jams.
FA. Rupert Brooks 1932

10 Wobblestone Crack . . . . HVD 4a
The crack with wobbling stones eases with height.

11 Red Shift E3 5c
The scary arete is gained from the right. Never gets done.
FA. Colin Banton 1978

Long Tall Sally

A great set of routes and well worth the walk. *Amazon Crack* gives superb jamming, the blank corner of *Long Tall Sally* is compelling, and there are others to delight.
Approach (see map on page 275) - Use the cliff-top path and continue to a significant section of edge about 20 minutes from the parking. The area can be busy. The valley path is also an option although there is a fair trog from the path up to the edge.

❶ Hollybush Gully . . . . ▢ **VD**
A green square-cut slot which is really more of a chimney.

❷ The Screamer . . . . ☆ 🔧 ▢ **E1 5c**
The rather dirty thin crack in the right wall of the gully/chimney.
FA. Colin Banton 1978

❸ Gazebo Watusi . . . . ☆ 🖐 🔧 ▢ **E6 6b**
From *Obscenity*, move left to layback boldly up the scary arete.
FA. Jonny Needham early 1990s

❹ Obscenity . . . . ☆☆☆ ✊ 🔧 ▢ **VS 4c**
A bit of a tussle especially at the bulge. Wearing a helmet tends to compound the difficulties and enrich the language.
FA. Nip Craven 1948

❺ Amazon Crack . . . . ☆☆☆ 🔧 ▢ **HS 4b**
A glorious fissure in the shallow corner which is quite superb and far too short. One of grit's better short 'n' sweet cracks.
FA. Jack Macleod 1932

❻ Amazon Gully . . . . ▢ **Mod**
The rift with a tall flake in its back is often used as a way down.

❼ Boney Moroney . . . . ☆ 🔧 🖐 ▢ **E2 5c**
The fierce thin crack is ultimately unsatisfying. Hard if done direct and a cop-out if not. Keep left for the best hidden holds.
FA. Jack Street 1969

❽ Long Tall Sally . . . . Top 50 🔧 🔧 ▢ **E1 5b**
A superb climb up the blank groove. Many people's first Extreme which is odd as it isn't that easy. Passing the bulge is awkward and leads to the tenuous crux; protection is good but fiddly.
FA. Alan Clarke early 1960s

❾ Three Blind Mice . . . ☆☆ 🔧 🔧 ▢ **E7 6c**
Fine technical climbing up the blank arching wall. Use a couple of chipped pockets on the right to climb the lower leaning wall leftwards, pass the bulge via wild mantel and finish direct. It gets popular when there is a snow drift and it can be highballed at *f7A*. There is even a left-hand version called **Snow Blind Mice**, *f7B* but this hasn't yet been done 'snow-less'.
FA. Dave Pegg 1994. FA. (Snow Blind Mice) Dan Varian 2013

❿ Greeny Crack. . . . . ☆☆ ▢ **VS 4b**
The steep right-hand corner is juggy, well protected and only occasionally green. Mild, with the crux right at the top.

⓫ Rhapsody in Green. . . . . 🖐 ▯ ▢ **HVS 5a**
A delicate lower arete leads to a grassy ledge. Continue up the bold lichenous and reachy upper arete.
FA. Colin Banton 1978

⓬ Left Studio Climb. . . . . ▢ **VD**
The left-hand crack leads to a high crux on the delicate arete.

⓭ The Artist . . . . 🔧 ▢ **VS 5a**
The disjointed slab between the two cracks has a thin start.

⓮ Right Studio Climb. . . . . ▢ **VD**
The right-hand crack leads to a ledge and groove - nice enough.

⓯ Rose Flake . . . . ☆ ▢ **VS 4b**
Steep and enjoyable crack climbing up the north-facing wall on jugs and jams, and with plenty of runners.

From mid morning | 20 min | Windy

10m

Brooks' Layback

16 The Fin . . . . 🎯 ✊ [ ] **E1 5b**
The hanging groove is a struggle to enter though at least it has overhead gear. It isn't much easier above either. Often frigged!
FA. Neil Stokes 1971

17 Ai No Corrida . . . . 🎯 👁 [ ] **E5 6b**
Layback boldly up the flying arete. A runner in the next route is only of limited help, but it is all you are going to get unless you come when the snow is deep.
FA. John Allen 1984

18 Right Fin . . . . 🎯 ▯ 👁 [ ] **HVS 5a**
An elegant curving flake with a layback move and long stretch before things ease. Low in the grade but bold.

19 Twenty Year Itch . . . . 🔊 [ ] **E4 6b**
The right-hand side of the wall. Highball *f6B*.
FA. Andy Barker (with a side runner)1993

20 The Enthusiast . . . . 🎯 🔊 [ ] **f6A+**
The tricky left arete can be very frustrating.
FA. Nick Hallam 1980s

21 Nicotine Stain . . . . 🎯 🔊 [ ] **f6B**
The seam is climbed on its left-hand side - thin! A very frustrating problem that sees many floundering attempts and much discussion about both line and grade.
FA. Al Rouse 1983

22 Nicarete . . . . 🎯 🔊 [ ] **f5**
The slab and arete just left of the wide crack.

23 April Fool . . . . ✊ [ ] **HVD**
Awkward climbing up the prominent wide crack

24 Approach . . . . 🎯 🔊 [ ] **f5+**
The thin pocketed wall just right has neat moves.
FA. Colin Banton 1978

25 Spider Crack . . . . 🎯 🔊 [ ] **VS 5b**
A pleasantly technical crack which even has runners.

26 The Be All . . . . [ ] **HVD 4a**
The left-hand crack is quite mild but often green.

27 The End All . . . . 🌙 ✊ [ ] **HS 4b**
Climb the last crack on the wall - it is a struggle.

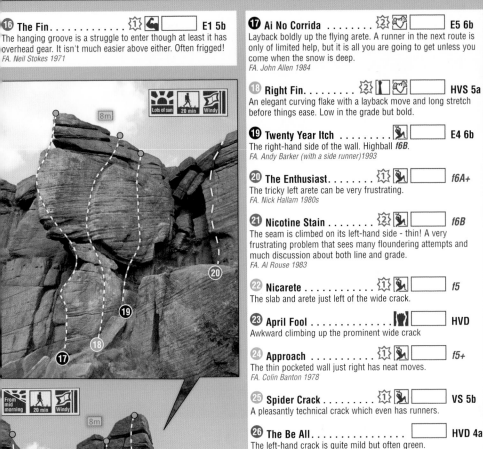

8m

Lots of sun | 20 min | Windy

From mid morning | 20 min | Windy

8m

Descent

End Slab

Sheffield Area

Ladybower Area

Stanage

Burbage Valley

Millstone Area

Derwent Edges

Chatsworth Area

Southern Crags

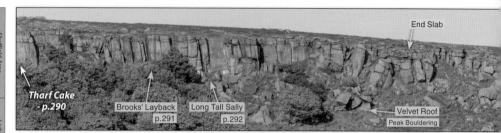

End Slab

Tharf Cake
- p.290

| Brooks' Layback
| p.291 |

| Long Tall Sally
| p.292 |

Velvet Roof
Peak Bouldering

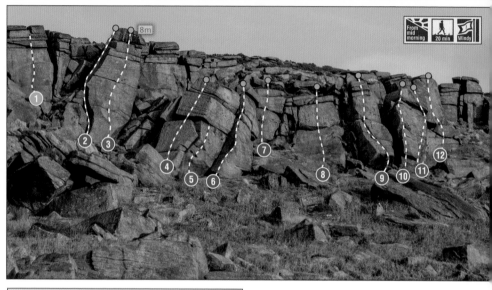

8m

From mid morning | 20 min | Windy

End Slab

Burbage North's last gasp has some pleasant slabs that might interest those in search of an easy time. It is normally quieter here than the rest of the cliff.
Approach (see map on page 275) - The best direct approach is to use the upper path from the parking for about 20 minutes.

❶ Shelf Wall . . . .   *f5+*
A short problem up and left.

❷ End Buttress . . . .   Diff
A wide crack and slab on the left-hand side of the arete.

❸ The Penultimate E1 5b
The pleasant narrow face has a technical start.
FA. Keith Sharples 1977

❹ End Slab . . . .   Diff
A nice easy slab. Climbing either arete is a tad harder.

❺ Two Pocket Sitter . . .   *f5+*
Steep moves past the two pockets. Slink off left or right.

❻ End Slab Ramp . . . .   Diff
Up the jutting rib just right of the slanting crack.

❼ Front End Slab . . . .   VD
A short slab round the back.

❽ Back End Slab . . . .   Diff
A nice easy slab with a steeper finish.

❾ Ender . . . .   Diff
The crack in the left-hand side of the face. Tricky to start.

❿ Endest Arete . . . .   VD
The left edge of the final slab has a steep start.

⓫ Endste . . . .   Diff
The wall and flake above.

⓬ Almost the Last Word E1 5c
The short rib accessed from the right really is the last word in terms of routes at Burbage North.
FA. Tom O'Rouke 2004

Contrary to the route names above, there is more climbing to be had; Beyond the End area is 100m further on at a series of aretes and slabs covered in the Peak Bouldering Rockfax.

Sheffield Area
Ladybower Area
Stanage
Burbage Valley
Millstone Area
Derwent Edges
Chatsworth Area
Southern Crags

Ben Bransby on an early repeat of the *The Promise* (E8/*f7C*)
- *page 283* - at Burbage North. The runner used on these early
ascents was a poor slider which is no longer reliable, so the
route is now usually done above some carefully placed pads.
Inset: This was part of the sequence that was used on the UKC
title bar for 6 years from 2008 to 2014. Photos: Alan James

	No star	☆	☆☆	☆☆☆
Mod to S	23	4	-	-
HS to HVS	16	16	-	-
E1 to E3	7	4	2	1
E4 and up	2	4	2	4

Higgar Tor is not an extensive venue but it manages to have a major impact courtesy of the Leaning Block. Steep and powerful climbing is the order of the day here and, in general, the routes only succumb to a forceful approach; hesitation will be punished with pumped forearms and a 'gritstone kiss'. The striking central line of *The Rasp* is the showpiece of the crag, a stunning outing that is typical of many of the routes - an overhanging crack with the odd good jam and plenty of jugs. Typically, protection is plentiful but placing it is tiring and the finishes may leave you breathless and battered. There is a theory that the routes feel under-graded because the block is slowly tipping.

The Leaning Block is the main event but the shorter walls to either side also have worthwhile offerings but don't expect any soft touches. There is plenty of bouldering to be found, some of which has been covered here, although it is quite highball and the landings are not very friendly. The abrasive-tool-themed names of the routes are an indication of the nature of the rock here.

Approach   Also see map on page 273

Higgar Tor is on the west side of the Burbage Valley, overlooking the minor road running down to Hathersage. There is roadside parking on the right-hand side as it starts to descend towards the valley. From the parking walk down the road for about 100m to a stile on the left. Cross the stile and contour the hillside to the right. The cliff appears as you round the ridge, less than 5 mins from the car.

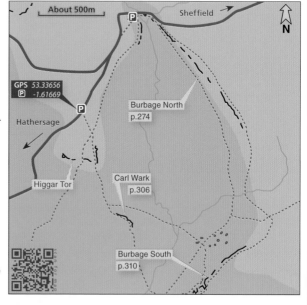

Conditions

Higgar Tor is exposed, catching any sun and wind going. Despite the steepness there is little to do here in wet weather apart from some ever-dry bouldering along the base of the Leaning Block - the water tends to run under the capping roofs and down the face. The almost ever-present wind means that this is one venue that is usable through the worst of the midge season.

Sheffield Area

Ladybower Area

Stanage

Burbage Valley

Millstone Area

Derwent Edges

Chatsworth Area

Southern Crags

So where do you get pumped exactly? Dan Arkle proving that *The Rasp* (E2 5b) - *page 300* - isn't pumpy at all, in fact there are hands-off rests all the way up it. Photo: Dan Arkle Collection

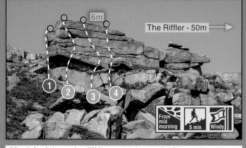

The Riffler - 50m →

50m left of the main cliff is a conspicuous jutting nose.

①Small Beginnings . . . . ▢ **S 4a**
The left-hand wall is climbed by this tiny offering.
FA. David Simmonite 1999

②Hathersage Climb . . . . . ▢ **VS 5a**
The left arete of the wall starting over the roof.

③All of a Quiver . . . . ▢ **HVS 5a**
An eliminate, with nice moves and gear to a mantel finale.
FA. David Simmonite 2004

④Tossing a Wobbler . . . . . ▢ **HVS 5a**
The groove and wall to the right to another difficult exit.
FA. Jim Rubery 1982

Next is the short wall left of the Leaning Block. Like the rest of the crag, it is steeper than it looks, and the routes pack a punch!

⑤The Warding . . . . ▢ **S 4b**
The shallow groove near the left edge of the wall. The crucial tricky start is avoidable on the left, dropping the grade a notch.

⑥Aceldama . . . . ▢ **E4 6a**
The wall is short, unprotected and has a harrowing exit.
FA. Gary Gibson (solo) 1980

The Riffler
The low wall left of the Leaning Block has a set of steep routes that have a similar reputation to those on its big brother to the right. Most of the routes follow cracks and proficiency in jamming is near essential. Once your technique is suitably honed, its time to head right!
Approach (see map on page 296) - Head left from the Leaning Block.

⑦Mighty Atom . . . . . . ▢ **E2 5c**
Thin cracks lead to good runners in the second break. The gritty and gripping exit is too far above them for comfort.
FA. Steve Bancroft 1975

⑧Brillo . . . . ▢ **E1 5c**
The left arete of the central recess and the thin cracks above are harder than they look. The cracks are often gritty after rain.
FA. Chris Craggs 1987

⑨The Riffler . . . . ▢ **HVS 5a**
Climb the roof of the cave, passing the jammed blocks with care and finish up the crack above. Juggy and pumpy too.

⑩The Cotter . . . . ▢ **HVS 5b**
Take the right arete of the central blocky recess and the thin crack directly above it on holds that are generally disappointing.

⑪The Rat's Tail . . . . ▢ **VS 5a**
The hand-crack in a shallow groove gives good climbing to a tough exit on jams.

⑫The Reamer . . . . ▢ **VS 4c**
Climb the left edge of the deep gully via ledges to a thin crack which gives a couple of good moves. The easiest of the bunch.
FA. Dave Gregory 1964

⑬Leaning Block Gully . . . . . . ▢ **VD**
Classic back and foot practice near the front, passing outside of the jammed block.

⑭Leaning Block Gully Inside Route ▢ **Mod**
The grubby gritty back of the gully is often used as a descent.

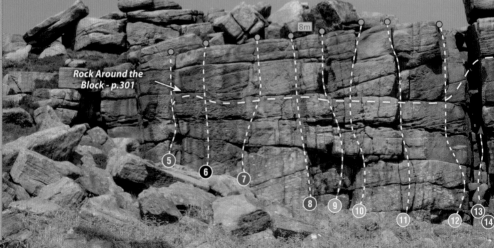

Rock Around the Block - p.301

Sheffield Area

Ladybower Area

Stanage

Burbage Valley

Millstone Area

Derwent Edges

Chatsworth Area

Southern Crags

TICKLIST
Higgar Tor Abrasive Testers

Higgar Tor has always had a reputation for steep routes and stiff grades. These are the best two routes here, making it the shortest ticklist in the book.

☐ **The File, VS** *(301)*. Possibly the best of its style and grade in the Peak. If you can't jam you will struggle.

☐ **The Rasp, E2** *(300)*. Regarded by many as the best route on grit. A relentless pitch that will search out any weakness, though its reputation for having no real rests may be a bit of yarn - see previous page.

Mike Hutton soloing *The File* (VS 4c) - *page 301* - on a fine winter's day, at Higgar Tor. Photo: Mike Hutton collection

❶ The Sander E4 6a
The side-wall is reached from across the gully (a direct start is possible but artificial). Make hard off-balance moves to reach the hanging crack. Low in the grade, providing you can do the crux!
FA. Jerry Peel 1972

❷ Block and Tackle . . . E6 6b
The arete is taxing. Start as for *The Sander* but swing on to the front at a jug. Move up to a good break and tackle the central section to reach a difficult layback finish up the final arete. The direct start is *f7B+*.
FA. Neil Foster 1994

❸ Surform E1 5b
Layback up the leaning flake quickly until a tricky traverse leads left to gain a small ledge. Bridge the corner then escape out left onto slabby rock, climbed rightwards to the summit.
FA. Joe Brown 1958

❹ The Rasp . . . . [Top 50] E2 5b
A contender for the best outing on grit! Sprint up the layback flakes trending right to a rest on jams at a break. Before courage and power flag more laybacking leads to unobvious jug-hauling and an ungainly rest in a niche. Escape out right awkwardly (rounded hand-traverse or ungainly grovel, using holds in the roof) to finish up a wide crack. A brilliant belay is located above. *Photos on page 35 and 297.*
FA. Joe Brown 1956

❺ Rasp Direct E3 6a
A sharp finger-crack and tough layback lead rapidly to the crux of the regular route and then its poor rest in the niche. Once recovered, pull straight over the roof to a belly-flop landing of the highest calibre. Action packed and high in the grade.
FA. Steve Bancroft 1975

❻ Flute of Hope . . E4 6a
A big butch diagonal that originally started by climbing the first 4m of *The File* creating a rope-work nightmare. Climb *Bat Out of Hell* to its second break. Now make a strength-sapping hand-traverse left to reach the crux of *The Rasp*. Up this to the niche then traverse left under the roofs to a finish through the exposed notch.
FA. Ed Drummond (2pts) 1971. FFA. Ron Fawcett 1977

❼ Bat Out of Hell . . E5 6a
An exciting direct line. Climb the blunt rib on the right-hand side of the crack. Follow this and, from the top of the crack, climb the wall via a long reach or short hop from the snapped flake. Finish with a flourish. Stopping to place a cam above the crux is pumpy but a good idea if you are struggling.
FA. Paul Bolger 1979

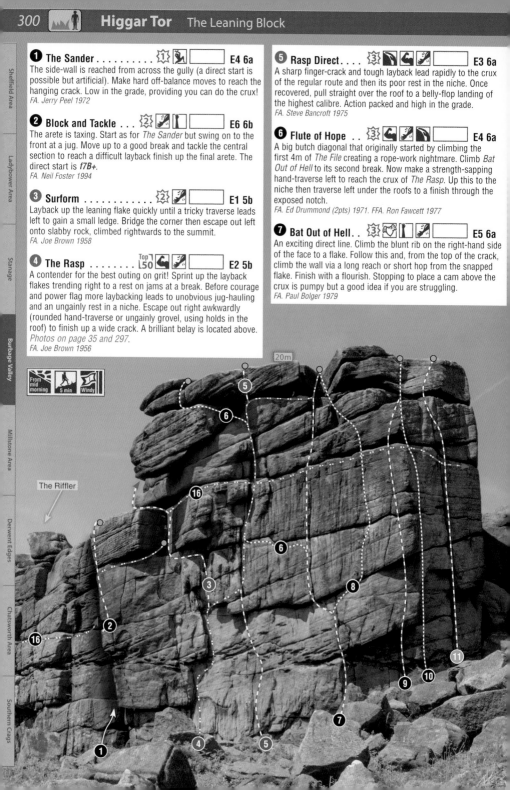

The Riffler

8 Linkline E5 6c
Follow *Bat Out of Hell* to the first break then step right to a large rugosity. Stand on this to reach the next break then continue direct via powerful moves to the niche at the end of *The Rasp*.
FA. Neil Foster 1993

9 Pulsar Direct E6 6b
The sustained and technical left side of the arete throughout. The original *Pulsar* started up *Rowley Birkin* and moved left to what is now *Linkline*, sharing little with this direct version.
FA. Ben Moon 1990s. FA. (Pulsar Original) Johnny Woodward 1980

10 Rowley Birkin QC . . . E6 6c
Follow the arete left of *The File* on its right side throughout. Precarious moves on tiny undercuts and pebbles are followed by a slap for a sloping break leading to easy ground.
FA. Percy Bishton 1998

11 The File . . . . VS 4c
Perhaps the Peak's pre-eminent jamming crack. A compelling crack in the south-facing wall gobbles cams and arguments about the grade continue. The initial roof is the crux, but interest is maintained to a superb, juggy finish. *Photo on page 299.*
FA. Don Whillans 1956

12 The Raven E2 6b
The right-arete of *The File* has a desperate lower section (runner up and right) but soon eases. **HVS 5b** if started on the right.
FA. (from the right) Gary Gibson 1980. FA. (start) Chris Plant 1990s

13 Paddock . . . . VD
From a block climb the zig-zag cracks.
FA. Dave Gregory 1964

14 Greymalkin . . . . S 4a
From the block, trend right up the face following a thin crack to a final (avoidable) long reach.
FA. Dave Gregory 1964

15 Hecate . . . . VD
The juggy groove and arete just to the right. A tough start up the crack (4b) is possible, otherwise step off the block.
FA. Dave Gregory 1964

16 Rock Around the Block . . E5 6a
The girdle of the Riffler wall and the Leaning Block is epic.
See page 299 for line of the first pitch.
1) 5a. Start up *The Warding* and follow the break to a belay on the arete of the gully.
2) 6a. Step up and stretch for a break on the side of the block. Follow this rightwards round the arete and continue (crux) to a belay in the niche of *Surform*.
3) 5c. Make a wild hand-traverse across *Bat Out of Hell* to the arete. Finish up *The File*, or (if persistent) belay and...
4) 4c. ...continue on the lower break, until you can step off at the back of the Block.
FA. Chris Craggs, Colin Binks (alt leads) 1982

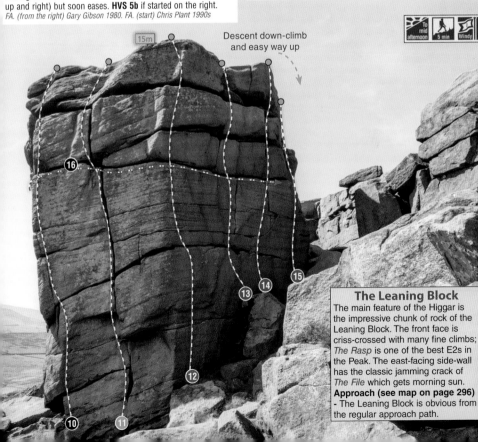

15m

Descent down-climb
and easy way up

The Leaning Block
The main feature of the Higgar is the impressive chunk of rock of the Leaning Block. The front face is criss-crossed with many fine climbs; *The Rasp* is one of the best E2s in the Peak. The east-facing side-wall has the classic jamming crack of *The File* which gets morning sun.
Approach (see map on page 296) - The Leaning Block is obvious from the regular approach path.

Sheffield Area

Ladybower Area

Stanage

Burbage Valley

Millstone Area

Derwent Edges

Chatsworth Area

Southern Crags

The Riffler
p.298

The Harvester
Peak Bouldering

The Leaning Block
p.300

Descent

Lots of sun | 5 min | Windy

6m

The Right Walls

To the right the crag continues as a collection of short buttresses and walls with a prominent tower capped by an overhang taken by *Achilles' Heel/Laze*. There is little here that is outstanding, but this is a good place to escape the crowds and most of the rock is superb. There are some interesting wide cracks scattered about the place if you like that kind of thing.

Approach (see map on page 296) - the area is immediately right of the Leaning Block, and is five minutes from the parking.

❶ Wotan's Corner . . . . Diff
The short blocky groove on the left.

❷ Wotan's Crack . . . . S 4b
Just right, the thin crack soon eases - pleasant.

❸ Chance Encounter . . . . VS 5a
Gain the slanting crack (hard) then meander up the arete.
FA. Dave Gregory 1982

❹ Rough Justice E3 6c
The short technical wall is a beast but it soon eases.
FA. Simon Jones 1995

❺ Sickle Overhang . . . . VS 4c
The wall and bulges on the right.

❻ Jupiter's Slab . . . . f5+
The short technical entry to the ledge, then trend right.
FA. Malc Baxter 1990

❼ Jupiter's Arete . . . . VS 4c
The pleasant grooved arete has a useful ledge on the left.
FA. Malc Baxter 1990

❽ Jupiter's Crack . . . . HS 4c
The narrowing fissure is tough at the overlap. A huge cam helps.

15m to the right are three wide and welcoming cracks.

9 Easy Peasy . . . . 🏃 [___] **E1 6a**
The sharp arete is hard to access.
FA. Dave Law 1999

10 Doddle . . . . 👐 [___] **S 4a**
It isn't! Wide and awkward, especially the bold start.

11 Lemon Squeezy . . . . 👤 ✊ [___] **HVS 5b**
A stretchy eliminate up the narrow face avoiding the aretes.

12 Walkover . . . . 👐 [___] **S 4a**
Another wide and awkward misnomer to a tricky exit.

13 Piece of Cake . . . . 👐 [___] **HVD 4a**
... at least when compared to its neighbours, but not really!

14 Achilles' Heel . . . . 🗡 [___] **E2 5b**
Climb flakes awkwardly to below the roof, then escape right
away to the arete and an easy finish.
FA. Gerry Rogan early 1960s.

15 Laze . . . . 🔩 [___] **E2 5c**
The powerful direct finish uses a useful flake on the lip - tough!
FA. John Allen 1975

16 Spirito di Onki . . . . ✊ 🏃 [___] **E3 6a**
Climb the dirty wall to a finish direct over the overhangs.
FA. James Pearson 2004

17 Daley Bulletin . . . . [___] **HVS 5a**
The shallow groove left of the gully then the bulge just left.
FA. David Simmonite 1990

18 Canyon Climb . . . . [___] **HVD 4a**
The crack leads to a tough exit. The skinny can head through the
vertical vice into mountain, the rest will be squeezed!

19 Zeus's Crack . . . . 👐 [___] **HS 4b**
The off-width crack is a bit of a battle, though the bold and
naughty might layback it.

20 Root Decay . . . . 🏃 [___] **E4 6b**
Boulder up the technical wall to runners (poor landing) then
trend right to finish.
FA. Mike Lea 1988

21 Stretcher Case . . . . . 🏕 🗡 👤 [___] **E2 5c**
The centre of the wall behind the holly is reachy and all the
holds slope horribly.
*FA. Chris Craggs 1979. Done just before being stretchered off an Austrian
ski slope having wiped out the instructor in spectacular fashion.*

22 Splint . . . . 🏕 🗡 [___] **HVS 5a**
The pleasant right arete of the wall on its left-hand side.
FA. Colin Binks 1979

23 Loki's Way . . . . 🏕 🗡 [___] **HS 4b**
Climb the crack right of the arete to a tricky finish up its
continuation just left. It is possible to exit further left along the
ledge reducing the grade to **S 4a**.
FA. Dave Gregory 1964

24 Fricka's Crack . . . . 🏕 [___] **VS 4c**
The thinner crack right again leads to an tough exit.
FA. Dave Gregory 1964

25 Jade Tiger . . . . 🏃 🗡 [___] **HVS 5b**
The narrow wall using the right arete where needed.
FA. Richard Davies 1984

26 Freya's Climb . . . . 🏕 [___] **VD**
The short corner-crack in the centre of the face to a tricky finish.
FA. Dave Gregory 1964

27 Freya's Wall . . . . [___] **HVD 4a**
The wall just right on mostly good holds.

28 Freya's Corner . . . . [___] **Diff**
This the final short groove on the right.

29 Pippin . . . . 👐 🗡 [___] **HVS 5b**
The roof split by a crack just right (off the topo) is a struggle.

The Trunk

7m

Higgar East

Looking out across the Burbage Valley is a small set of short routes, often soloed, though the biggest are quite high and the landings are often poor. The aspect offers afternoon shade so is a good option in the summer, though it will be green after any damp weather.
Approach (see map on page 296) - From the parking follow the path to the flat top of Higgar Tor - the crag is round to the left from here.

The Trunk

❶ Cherry's Crack . . . . 🔺☐ **S 4b**
The first real line is wide, undercut and tricky to start.

❷ Jason's Rib . . . . 🔅🔲☐ **HVS 5a**
The triple-blocked pillar is worthwhile despite the rounded holds.

❸ The Five Gs . . . . 🔳☐ **VD**
Chimney up the outer section of the giant gaping green grotty gash. The back of the rift can be used as a dirty descent route.

❹ The Tower of Power . . . . 🔅🔲☐ **HVS 5b**
The narrow rib right of the green gash.

❺ Golden Shower . . . . 🔳☐ **VD 4a**
The deep V-cleft is tricky to start.

❻ Independent . . . . ☐ **VS 5a**
The side-wall of the next buttress is a bit misnamed.

❼ Bigger Higgar . . . . 🔅☐ **VS 5a**
Wander up the front of the bulky buttress just right.

❽ Bigger Higgar Indirect . . . . ☐ **S 4a**
The short cleft to the left edge of the block then the rib above.

To the right the blocky gully has a few green bits and pieces best left for the diligent to discover, after a dry spell.

❾ Flake Chimney . . . . 🔅🔲☐ **VD**
Inclined to be green.

❿ The Trunk . . . . . 🔅🔲🔲🔲☐ **E2 5c**
The balancy broadening rib is one of the best here. The crux is a bold reach for the break and runners.

⓫ The Layback Crack . . . . . 🔅🔲☐ **VS 4c**
The wide green crack in the left side of the recess.

⓬ The Corner Crack . . . . . . 🔅🔲☐ **HS 4c**
The angle to a tricky finish.

⓭ Precarious Rib . . . . ☐ **HS 4c**
Balance up the rib to a high crux. Starting on the left is 5a.

⓮ Inset Flake Crack . . . . 🔲☐ **HVD 4a**
The short wide crack just right.

⓯ The Grassy Mantel . . . . ☐ **S 4b**
It is all in the name.

⓰ Wide Crack . . . . 🔲☐ **HVD 4a**

The Trunk

Black Choir

Black Choir

Black Choir

⑰ Cracked Rib . . . . 🫳🪜 ⬜ **E1 5a**
The rib starting on the right and trending left. Bold and reachy.

⑱ Open Thrutch. . . . . 🧍 ⬜ **S 4b**
The wide crack in the angle.

⑲ Black Choir . . . . 🔄🫳⬛🧗 ⬜ **E5 6b**
The bold and technical square face offers a route of substance -
unlike the rest of the stuff here.
FA. Joe Brown (the Younger) 1997

⑳ Wide Crack 2. . . . . ⬜ **HVD 4b**
This is the pleasant crack right of the smooth face.

㉑ Green Groove . . . . ⬜ **HVD 4b**
The greenish groove-shaped feature.

㉒ Tall Arete . . . . 🔄⬛🫳 ⬜ **HVS 5b**
Across the gully the short arete leads to a precarious finale.

Krush Regime

*Heading rightwards blocky rocks (plenty of bouldering) are
punctuated by four jutting aretes. These are worthwhile highballs
or short routes.*

㉓ Sharp Arete. . . . . ⬜ **VS 5a**
The arete features some nice moves and some rather dubious
and very thin flakes.

㉔ Toppled Block Arete . . . . ⬜ **HS 4c**
A nice little route finishing up the tilted drawbridge.

㉕ Triple Cracks Arete . . . . ⬜ **VS 5a**
The jutting left arete of the shady wall with three rather dirty
cracks in its right-hand side.

*This fine jutting angular buttress is the first decent sized piece
of rock reached on the approach from the parking, just after the
popular bouldering block of Excreta Buttress.*

㉖ Left Arete . . . . ⬜ **HS 4c**
Hop onto the left arete and climb it pleasantly.

㉗ Harry's Hole . . . 🔄🧗🪜🫳 ⬜ **f6C+**
The wall right of the arete usually requires a dyno.

㉘ Krush Regime . . 🔄🪨🧗🫳 ⬜ **f7A+**
From a sit-down start in the mucky little hole, use fingery holds
to claw your way up the wall. Highball.
FA. Greg Griffiths 1985

Krush Regime

Excreta Buttress
Peak Bouldering

Krush Regime

Sidebar tabs: Sheffield Area · Ladybower Area · Stanage · Burbage Valley · Millstone Area · Derwent Edges · Chatsworth Area · Southern Grags

	No star	{1}	{2}	{3}
Mod to S	12	2	1	-
HS to HVS	5	3	-	-
E1 to E3	-	3	-	-
E4 and up	-	1	2	-

Carl Wark is the lower of the two plateaux that sit in the heart of the Burbage Valley. Its flat crest is ringed, particularly to the northwest, by ancient fortifications. A fault line divides the two plateaux and explains the difference in height that can be seen running away between Burbage North and South edges. The crag is only a minor venue, but the routes on the Left-hand Buttresses give a decent collection of easier climbs which get morning sun and afternoon shade - unusual for Eastern Grit. The Right-hand Buttress is more impressive but is nearly always in poor condition.

Approach   Also see map on page 273

There is parking for about five cars at the southern end of Burbage Valley, where the Green Drive meets the main A6187 road. However this is often full and alternatives include the parking places for Burbage South (next nearest), then Millstone or Burbage North, leaving a 15-20 minute walk-in.

Conditions

The edge consists of two areas that face southeast and north. The southeast facing walls (Left-hand Buttress) are generally quite clean and quick drying - the north facing ones (Right-hand Buttress) are lichenous and grassy.

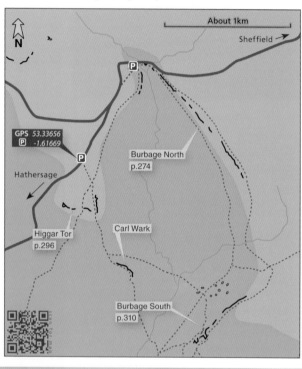

About 1km

Sheffield →

GPS 53.33656
P -1.61669

Burbage North p.274

Hathersage

Higgar Tor p.296

Carl Wark

Burbage South p.310

Steve Cunnington escaping the summer heat on the pleasant upper section of *Carl's Buttress* (S 5a) - *page 308* - at Carl Wark. There is nothing of any great quality here but its location in the valley and the fact that it is likely to be a lovely day when you come here mean that most will still have a pleasant day out (unless you decide to combine it with something savage at the nearby Higgar!).

Sheffield Area

Ladybower Area

Stanage

Burbage Valley

Millstone Area

Derwent Edges

Chatsworth Area

Southern Crags

Descent

8m

6m

13

12

10 11

1 2 3 4 5 6 7 8 9

Left-hand Buttress

A jumble of blocks that has a few things of minor interest. It catches the morning sun.

Approach (see map on page 306) - The area on the far east end of Carl Wark, best approached from the above.

❶ Lookout Ledge . . . . HVD 4b
Start on the right and balance up the arete to an awkward move onto the ledge. Mantel to the top.

❷ Sensory Overload E2 6a
The right arete of the buttress has some fine moves.

❸ Boulder Climb . . . . VD 4b
The wide crack is tricky to start. Finish up the left wall above.

❹ Ingle Nook . . . . VD 4a
An easy crack leads to a hard move to gain the final chimney.

❺ Lump Wall . . . . VD
An easy slanting crack leads to the leaning upper wall, which has good holds though the short may fail to reach them!

❻ Leaning Crack . . . . . S 4b
The steep thin crack leads past an ancient thread to the wide awkward upper section. A good thread is available below this.

❼ Boy Wonder E3 6a
The next arete to a spectacular finale.
FA. Andy Healy 1997

❽ Corner and Crack . . . . HS 4b
Easy bridging leads to a perplexing pull into the upper groove.

❾ Broken Buttress . . . . HVD 4a
A couple of mantelshelves trend right, then a short traverse back left past the heather gains a short crack which is tricky to start.

❿ Broken Buttress Crack . . . . HVD 4a
The short jamming crack in the left wall around the corner.

⓫ Broken Buttress Corner . . . . Diff

⓬ Broken Buttress Chimney . . . Diff

⓭ Broken Buttress Arete . . . HS 4a
The short right arete of the area is a solo.

Carl's Buttress

Across the boulder/heather slope to the right is the attractive Carl's Buttress, with one good route and a couple of variations.

⓮ Carl's Buttress Left-hand . . . . HS 4c
The left-hand side of the face (avoiding easy ground to the left) with moves right and left to pass the bulge.

⓯ Carl's Buttress . . . . S 5a
A tough mantel start (the 5a move) leads to nice ground above.
Photo on page 307.

⓰ Carl's Right Wall . . . . VD
Climb the right wall and a short crack via one long reach.

Descent

8m

Carl's Buttress

14 15 16

Right-hand Buttress

Although the most impressive part of the cliff, the wall faces north and sees precious little sun. There is much grass and lichen, only the better/cleaner routes are listed here. Save a visit for a long dry spell!

Approach (see map on page 306) - The routes are 100m right of the Left-hand Buttress and are most easily reached by crossing the moor and descending grassy ledges just to the west of the routes.

⑰ Layback Crack . . . . ▢ **S 4a**
The short clean corner under the oddly fluted boulder.

⑱ 2b or not 2b . . . . ▢ **HVS 5b**
Pump along the heathery break then pull up into the scoop.
FA. Nick White 1983

⑲ Chockstone Crack. . . . . ▢ **S 4b**
A tricky little number passing the blocks and into the scoop. A right-hand start up the chimney is much easier - **Diff**.

⑳ Carlos Warkos . . . .  ▢ **HVS 5b**
The tiny green arete above an unpleasant landing zone.

㉑ Orange Juice Wall . . . . ▢ **VS 4b**
A decent line that needs a cleaning, especially the crux mantel onto the overgrown ledge at the base of the final chimney. An even more neglected right-hand finish is **Six Pack, E3 6a**.
FA. Dave Gregory 1964

[icons: Not much sun | 20 min | Windy | Seepage | Green]

㉒ Lime Juice Chimney. . . . 🔲🔲 ▢ **HVD 4a**
The deep and green rift is 'a classic of its genre' - and we all know what that means! Best climbed outside the boulder.
FA. J.W.Puttrell early 1900s

㉓ Not Green Flag . . . . 🔲🔲 ▢ **f7A**
The left-hand side of the wall, on slopers, to the break.

㉔ Green Flag . . . . 🔲🔲 ▢ **f7B+**
The thin wall from a good hold and side-pulls to the mid-height break. Scramble off left.

㉕ Rugosity Dinks . . . . 🔲🔲 ▢ **f6C**
Climb the wall just left of the thin crack to the break.

㉖ Tower Wall . . . . 🔲 ▢ **HVS 5b**
Another decent route that would be popular in a more user-friendly situation. Climb the fingery initial crack to the break, traverse left along this and make tricky moves up and left to access a ledge and the final groove.

㉗ Lost World . . . . 🔲🔲🔲 ▢ **E6 6c**
An out-of-the-way gem, giving fierce, well-protected climbing to a hard sequence near the top.
FA. John Allen 1985

㉘ Tower Crack . . . . 🔲🔲 ▢ **HS 4b**
The widening fissure leads to a lie-down ledge (you may well need it). Finish up the awkward green corner behind.

㉙ Last Crack. . . . . 🔲 ▢ **S 4a**
The last offering in the form of two short awkward cracks.

Sheffield Area | Ladybower Area | Stanage | Burbage Valley | Millstone Area | Derwent Edges | Chatsworth Area | Southern Crags

	No star	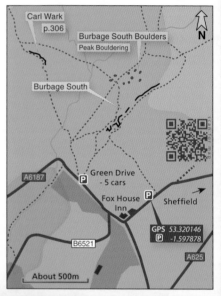★	★★	★★★
Mod to S	26	8	-	-
HS to HVS	17	21	8	3
E1 to E3	8	17	6	3
E4 and up	6	20	8	16

Burbage South has never really been as popular as its northern twin. While its shady aspect and greenness don't help, its popularity has been limited by the uncompromising appearance of its buttresses, which lack the lower grade classics that pepper most of the other edges in the area. It is something of a surprising fact that Burbage South is home to several of the hardest routes on gritstone which makes them amongst the hardest trad challenges anywhere. Don't be put off though, in amongst all the big names are plenty of other fine routes across the grade range as long as you choose a dry spell to visit. Summer shade is an added attraction on the hottest days of the year, as is evening sunshine on cooler summer evenings.

Approach   Also see map on page 273

The best approach is from the Fox House end of the valley. There is parking on the grass verge on the roadside 200m uphill from the entrance to the pub car park. A stile allows you to cross the wall and leads straight across the moor (splodgy after rain) for 550m to the reach the cliff-top path above the quarries. The rest of the crag is to the right (northeast) from here.

Green Drive - There is a very limited parking spot (about 5 cars) at the end of the main valley path. Walk up the Green Drive and head rightwards up the hill to reach the quarries.

Conditions

Burbage South faces northwest and only gets the sun late in the day from April to September. It can be a welcome retreat in hot weather. It tends to be green, lichenous and midgy after rain.

Sheffield Area

Ladybower Area

Stanage

Burbage Valley

Millstone Area

Derwent Edges

Chatsworth Area

Southern Crags

Bouldering
There is plenty of bouldering along the edge, some of which is covered in this book. However it is the boulders scattered across the hillside below the crag that form one of the most popular bouldering locations in the Peak with countless problems in a delightful setting. Check the Rockfax Peak Bouldering guidebook for details.

Olivier Coenen using the three varied pieces of protection on the magnificent *Braille Trail* (E7 6c) - *page 316* - at Burbage South. Photo: David Bond

Earl Area

The northern end of Burbage South continues as a series of small buttresses, gradually dwindling in height, with a few notable hard outings, some lower-grade cracks and lots of quality bouldering. The place is always quiet and is especially pleasant on warm spring evenings.

Approach (see map on page 310) - On arriving above the quarries, turn right and follow the cliff-top path northeast for 550m.

Pebble Crack

The Little Rascal

❶ **The Little Rascal** . . . . . 🔲 🔲 🔲 **E4 6c**
A technical gem. The starting groove is **Rascal Groove**, *f7A*. The direct start up the arete is **Dirty Rascal**, *f7A*.
FA. Johnny Dawes 1986

❷ **Ronnie's Rib** . . . . . 🔲 🔲 🔲 *f7A*
Climb the arete from a sitting start.

❸ **Flake 'n' Blob** . . . . 🔲 *f4*
Climb the flake and exit using the blob.

❹ **Standup Arete** . . . . 🔲 🔲 *f6B*
The arete on its right-hand side. On its left is *f6C*.

❺ **Rail Thing** . . . . 🔲 🔲 🔲 *f5+*
Dyno to the top ledge.

❻ **Pocket Wall** . . . . 🔲 🔲 🔲 *f6B*
Climb the centre of the wall via a pocket. To the left is *f7A*.

❼ **Pebble Crack** . . . . 🔲 🔲 **HVS 5a**
Thin jamming up the pebbled crack, reached from the right.

❽ **Footy Rib** . . . . 🔲 🔲 *f5+*
The rib on the right of the buttress. The dyno to the left is *f6C*.

Prow Crack

Impossible Groove

❾ **Snitch** . . . . 🔲 🔲 *f6A+*
The arete to the break.

❿ **Prow Crack** . . . . 🔲 **S 4b**
Awkward jams lead to steep pulls right of the jutting prow.

⓫ **The Rib** . . . . 🔲 🔲 *f7B+*
Thin climbing up the quarried face to a dynamic finish.

After a short gap is a smooth wall with cracks on either side.

⓬ **Fat Man's Misery** . . . . . . 🔲 🔲 **S 3c**
Thankfully the evil crack has a useful flake on its left.

⓭ **Brap Scallion** . . . . 🔲 🔲 *f6C*
The arete right of the chimney on its right.

⓮ **Impossible Groove** . . . . 🔲
The grade? Well your guess is as good as mine! One of three impossible projects on Burbage South.

⓯ **Desparete** . . . . 🔲 🔲 🔲 *f7B*
The classic desperate and yet appealing arete! **E4-ish**.
FA. Johnny Dawes 1990s

⓰ **No Name Crack** . . . . 🔲 **VD 4a**
A short-lived but very pleasant bit of jamming.

Approach easier on the crag-top path

The Little Rascal   Pebble Crack   Prow Crack   Impossible Groove   Big Bad Wolf   The Alliance

Big Bad Wolf   5m

Triangle Wall
Peak Bouldering

18 Sublime Indifference *f6A*
Climb past the right-hand end of the ramp via a long reach.
FA. John Allen 1984

19 Big Bad Wolf E5 6b
From the block climb the face up then right with difficulty.
FA. Paul Mitchell 1982

20 Home Cooking *f7A*
Make some fridge-lifting moves up the arete above a poor landing. The right-hand side on its own is an easier *f6C*.
FA. Johnny Dawes 1984

21 Chockstone Layback HVD 4a
Layback the left-hand side of the block then finish direct.

17 Clark's Route *f5*
The short and angular left arete.

22 Green S-Groove *f6A*
Sometimes a bit green as you might expect.

The Alliance   5m

23 Little Pig S 4b
The wide right-hand crack in the recess is a bit of a grunt.
FA. Dominic Lee 1977

24 The Alliance *f7A*
Bear-hug the jutting arete to the top. *f7B+* from sitting.
FA. Pete Oxley 1987

25 Friar's Wall *f3+*
The next arete on its green right-hand side. A VS for traddies.
FA. Dominic Lee 1977

26 Dominican HVD 4b
The next corner crack contains a good jamming crack.
FA. Dominic Lee 1977

27 Guppy Arete *f5+*
The left-hand side of the arete aiming for the big hold.

28 Classic Arete *f6C*
The right side of the arete, from low, to gain the good hold.

29 Slantside Mod
The slanting cleft is the mildest for miles.

30 Short Crack HVD 4a
The short-lived fissure on the left side of the next buttress.

31 Renobulous Bongetl E5 6a
The right arete is reachy, precarious and scary.
FA. Andy Barker 1982

32 Breathless HVS 5b
The left-hand side of the next arete leads to a final long stretch.

33 Lens Crack S 4a
The corner leads to good jamming up the short crack. The right-hand crack is a little easier.

Sheffield Area · Ladybower Area · Stanage · Burbage Valley · Millstone Area · Derwent Edges · Chatsworth Area · Southern Crags

9m

Split Nose

Just past the twin towers of *The Boggart* and *Byne's Crack* are some short walls with several interesting little pitches. The *Split Nose* buttress tends to be green. Like the rest of Burbage South the place is always quiet and is especially pleasant on warm spring/summer evenings.
Approach (see map on page 310) - On arriving above the quarries, turn right and follow the cliff-top path northeast for 450m, just beyond the tall buttress of *Brooks'* and *Byne's Cracks* .

❶ Split Nose Left. . . . . VS 4c
The short crack that is the other end of the split nose.

❷ Split Nose. . . . . HVS 5a
A split nose gained from a nearby boulder. Short and sassy.

❸ The Gnat. E1 5c
The left-hand crack gives a short and safe struggle.
FA. Neil Stokes 1972

❹ Midge. E2 6a
The right-hand crack is more than a gnat's harder.
FA. Neil Stokes 1972

❺ Kleg. . . . . HVS 5b
Climb the wall behind the boulder and escape right.
FA. John Allen 1972

❻ The Notorious B L G E7 6c
Teeter up the pebbled, but effectively holdless scoop, with a double dyno to finish!
FA. Pete Hurley 1990s

❼ Every Man's Misery . . . . VS 5a
The wide right-leaning off-width is a thrash. Usually well-named.

❽ Triglyph . . . . VS 4c
More graunchy climbing up the right-hand crack, or layback it!
FA. Dave Gregory 1964

Across the grassy bay are more short green walls.

❾ This Life . . . . VD
The green crack left of a narrow slab.

❿ Heidi-Boo E2 5c
The narrow slab with a quartet of breaks at two-thirds height.
FA. Darren Thomas 1995

⓫ Abu Simbel . . . . Diff
The green-looking groove is worthwhile when dry though it is usually green and skiddy, especially the start.
FA. Dave Gregory 1964

⓬ Bobby Dazzler E4 6a
Use edges to gain the grassy ledge and continue up the tilted wall above to good finishing holds.
FA. Darren Thomas 1995

⓭ The Connection . . . . HVD 4a
Mantel left out of *The Thistle Funnel* and head left delicately.

⓮ The Thistle Funnel . . . . VD 4a
The tricky crack splitting the arete leads to easier ground.
FA. Dave Gregory 1964

Sheffield Area

Ladybower Area

Stanage

Burbage Valley

Millstone Area

Derwent Edges

Chatsworth Area

Southern Crags

Roof Route

Just past the twin towers of *The Boggart* and *Byne's Crack* are some short walls with several interesting little pitches. *Roof Route* is bizarrely named but still an excellent tick. The area is always quiet and is especially pleasant on warm spring/summer evenings.

Approach (see map on page 310) - On arriving above the quarries, turn right and follow the cliff-top path northeast for 450m, to just beyond the tall buttress of *Brooks'* and *Byne's Cracks*.

⑮ Chimney Route . . . . . . 　　　　 **VD**
A thrutch up the wide flake-crack on the left. Safest and easiest if tackled in the ledgy depths.

⑯ Simba's Pride . . . . . 　　　　 **E8 6b**
The fearsome arete of the tower is climbed direct to a high and gripping final move. **Stampede, E8 6c** was a technically harder but less bold attempt on the arete, moving left to a crack.
FA. Toby Benham 2005. FA. (Stampede) Simon Jones 1995

⑰ Black Out . . . . 　　　　 **E9 6c**
The leaning arete was a well-known 'last great problem' when it was despatched by a 15 year old Toru on his first UK climbing trip - amazing stuff!
FA. Toru Nakajima 2009

⑱ Roof Route . . . . . . 　　　　 **VS 4c**
A oddly-named route up the wide crack in the slabby angle. Awkward but large gear, big feet and determination all help.
FA. Jack Macleod 1934

⑲ Daz Utra . . . . 　　　　 **E4 6a**
Sketch up the desperate and artificial slab. A sensible and easily-placed side-runner makes it more like **E2**.

⑳ Gable Route . . . . 　　　　 **VS 4c**
Climb the flake awkwardly then the balancy edge of the slab.
FA. Mark Vallance 1977

㉑ Rombald's Staircase . . . . . . 　　　　 **Mod**
A pleasant ramble up the giant steps.

㉒ The Gutter . . . . 　　　　 **HVS 5b**
Tackle the steep angular crack on gruesome grinding jams to a ledge. Thankfully the corner behind is easier.
FA. Dave Gregory 1977

㉓ Press On . . . . 　　　　 **E2 6a**
Hand traverse the mini-ramp on the tower to access the ledge on *The Gutter* and finish up the side-wall.
FA. John Allen 1987

9m

Lethargic Arete - p.316

The Boggart →

Sheffield Area · Ladybower · Stanage · Burbage Valley · Millstone Area · Derwent Edges · Chatsworth Area · Southern Crags

1 Mad Llehctim f6C
A good intense problem on the north-facing slab.
FA. Paul Mitchell 1984. Reverse the route name for a clue.

2 Lethargic Arete ...... S 4a
Climb the crack just left of the arete to reach the slabby upper section. Balance up this (poor gear) to the top.
FA. Joe Brown 1951

3 Charlie's Crack ...... HVS 5b
From the boulder lean right and pull into the curving crack then make a tricky layaway/pull to solid jams and easier ground. Step left to finish up slabbier rock.
FA. Charlie Curtis 1961

4 Life Assurance .. E6 6b
Thin smearing up the steepening slab. Runners in the crack become less useful as the sketchy two-move-wonder crux approaches. A popular first E6, though is it really E6 if you top-rope it first? Answers on a postcard to the Editor please.
FA. John Dunne 1988

5 Tower Climb ...... HS 4c
Climb awkward twin cracks (the left-hand two of three) to a chimney and an easier finish up the right-slanting crack.
FA. Byron Connelly 1934

Press On - p.315

Roof Route

6 Tower Crack ...... HVS 5a
The right-hand crack leads to a ledge. From here a short layback flake on the right gives the protectable crux. Nice.
FA. Geoff Sutton 1957

7 Boggart Left-hand .. E4 6a
Gain the thin hanging crack from the left by an extended reach (an oft used side-runner brings it down to **E2**) then sprint to the easier ground of the central crack system.
FA. Steve Bancroft 1976

8 Balance It Is E7 6c
The stunning left arete of the buttress is approached via *Boggart Left-hand* and gives short-lived but committing laybacking - it is all in the name! An RP4 might be found useful.
FA. Neil Foster 1995

9 The Boggart E2 6b
The thin (and anciently chipped) crack is technical as far as the first decent hold, and easier above. Often soloed as placing runners is hard work and blocks a semi-crucial finger-jam.
FA. Allen Clarke (2pts, a shoulder and a nut)1960s. FFA. John Allen 1975

10 Equilibrium E10 7a
Fifteen years on and it remains about as hard as they come. From runners below mid-height, climb the arete by a series of incredibly tenuous moves. Once committed, you are on your own. The lower arete to an escape left is **Yoghurt**, E3 6b.
FA. Neil Bentley 2000

11 Tower Chimney ...... VD
The long chimney starts with a thrutch then eases a lot.

12 Byne's Flake ...... VD
The short green flake across the gully.

13 The Braille Trail. E7 6c
The well-named line of pebbles and creases crossing the north face are followed to the arete (poor hand-placed blade peg and six-inch-nail runners). Climb desperately into the thin crack and finish easily out in the void. The direct line has been climbed as **Grandad's Slab**, E7 6c, but it has lost a crucial pebble.
Photo on page 311.
FA. Johnny Dawes 1984. FA. (Grandad's Slab) Pete Whittaker

⑭ Dynamics of Change 🔲🔲🔲 **E9 7a**
Bizarre climbing up the leaning face below *Braille Trail* includes a dyno and the world's hardest mantel. If successful wander up the easy slab above. The arete start was originally climbed as **Blinded by Science, E4 6a**.
FA. Pete Whittaker 2008

⑮ Parthian Shot . . . . . Top 50 🔲🔲🔲 **E10 6c**
An awesome route which is even harder than it used to be. Lurch left out of *Brooks' Crack* (side-runner up and right) to indifferent wires behind the broken flake which protect an increasingly harrowing set of moves up and left to the final gripping rock-over/foot change. A sport grade of 8b is found to be useful information by some. *Photo on page 272.*
FA. John Dunne 1989. In 2011 Canadian climber Will Stanhope broke the flake and took a ground-fall. Ben Bransby reclimbed the route in 2013.

⑯ Brooks' Crack . . 🔲🔲🔲🔲 **HVS 5a**
The left-hand crack is approached up a straightforward clean-cut groove to reach a recess. Steep and insecure moves gain the upper cave then good jamming leads to an awkward exit.
FA. Rupert Brooks 1934

⑰ Byne's Crack . . . . 🔲 **VS 4b**
The right-hand crack is juggy and excellent giving great jamming and bridging. Don't topple over the edge at the top.
FA. Eric Byne 1934

⑱ The Searing . . . . . . 🔲🔲🔲 **E3 6a**
Tricky climbing up the left edge of the wall.
FA. Pete Oxley 1987

⑲ Back Down Under. . . 🔲🔲🔲 **E6 6c**
The extension up the rounded arete and face above.
FA. Pete Whittaker 2007

⑳ The Knock. . . . . 🔲🔲🔲 **E4 6a**
A superb and committing arete with the crux, and some rather battered protection close to the top. Often done above pads at a scary *f6A+*.
FA. John Allen 1975

㉑ Wow! . . . . 🔲🔲🔲 **E4 6b**
The short but h'airy arete above *The Knock*.
FA. Johnny Dawes 1998

㉒ Keep Crack . . . . 🔲🔲🔲 **HVS 5a**
Hard work x2 and multi-pitch. The groove leads to a huge ledge and a steeper continuation corner which is bridged - hard work.
FA. Alan Clark early 1960s

The Boggart and Byne's Crack
These two superb blocky towers are the finest on the whole of Burbage. Home to a great set of routes from VD to E10, there is something for everyone. They receive late evening sun in the summer and can be a useful retreat on hot summer days. *Brooks'* and *Byne's Cracks* are sterling efforts from the 1930s and there is a whole selection of more modern test-pieces for the hard core to have a go at - the old guys could never have imagined what they started.
Approach (see map on page 310) - On arriving above the quarries, turn right and follow the cliff-top path northeast for 400m to the biggest buttresses on the cliff.

Dowel Crack

The central section of the cliff has a series of small walls split by some short and meaty cracks. It looks rather under-whelming but there are some decent climbs across the grades. The area is green after any rain and throughout any normal winter.

Approach (see map on page 310) - This is the area of lower rock just right of the tall tower of *Byne's Crack*.

❶ Captain Sensible . . . . 🔆1 ☐ **E1 5b**
Thin cracks in the north-facing slab - usually a bit green.
FA. Steve Webster 1977

❷ Fast Ledge . . . . 🏃 ☐ *f6B*
The wall past a sloping ledge

❸ Slow Ledge . . . . 🌂👤 ☐ **VS 4c**
Climb the tricky and bold arete to the shelf then escape left along it and up a short wall.

❹ Magog . . . . 🧗👋 ☐ **HVS 5b**
Up the left-hand angle of the recess then access the shelf with difficulty. Finish up the mean leaning fissure above.
FA. Joe Brown 1951

❺ Gog . . . . 🔆1 🏃 ☐ **HS 4c**
Reach the top of the arete from under the roof on the left and continue up slabby rock above.
FA. Joe Brown 1951

6 Gog Arete . . . . 　　　　 *f4+*
The short arete gives a nice little problem.

7 Ladder Rib . . . . 　　　　 *f6A+*
The left-hand side of the same slabby arete. It is slightly harder on its right-hand side.

8 Ladder Gully . . . . **Diff**
A slippery start to easy ground, often very green and gungy.

9 Connolly's Variation . . . . . . 　　 **Diff**
A left-hand exit grovel is possible though the cliff to a slab.

10 Recurring Nightmare . . . 　　　 **E5 6b**
The short rib to the right of the gully to a high scary crux.
FA. Andy Barker 1982

11 Macleod's Crack . . . . 　　 **HVD 4a**
The crack has an awkward slippery start but eases rapidly.

12 Lapwing Variation . . . . 　 **S 4a**
Once past the crux a nice finish up the right wall is possible.

13 Crikey! . . . . 　　　 **E5 6a**
Climb direct up the book-end aretes to a scary slap for a big hole. Finish up and left. **Fade Away, E1 6a** reaches the same hole starting from *Dowel Crack* and moving up and then left.
FA. Niall Grimes 2001. FA. (Fade Away) Paul Mitchell 1982

14 Dowel Crack . . . . . . 　　　　 **HVS 5a**
The tough crack to the right of the prow to a hard exit. The piece of dowel once used as a runner(!) has long gone.
FA. Dave Gregory 1964

15 The Iron Hand . . . . 　　 **S 4b**
Starting from a block, climb the short awkward crack/groove.

16 Vulcan . . . . 　　 **HVD 4a**
Access a ledge with difficulty then finish up the crack.

17 Pollux. . . . . 　 **HS 4c**
The left-hand crack-line is almost always dirty.

18 Castor . . . . 　　 **HS 4b**
The right-hand crack has some solid jamming.

19 Movie Star . . . . 　　　　 **E1 5b**
Swing onto the arete, then move left and right to finish.
FA. Colin Banton 1978

20 Surprise . . . . 　　 **S 4a**
The left-hand groove gets harder with height. Beware that the wobbly chockstone doesn't give you a surprise.

21 Pythagoras . . . . 　 **HS 4b**
The tricky right-hand groove is usually dirty.

22 The Big Dipper . . . . . . 　　　 **S 4a**
The rambling ridge is delicate and a little bold. From a tricky start ramble over blocks and up a rib to the moor.

Split Nose
p.314

Roof Route
p.315

The Boggart
- p.316

Byne's Crack
- p.317

Nosferatu Area

The tall buttress of *Nosferatu* is the main attraction here although there is some good bouldering in the vicinity as well, both on the edge, and amongst the blocks below. To the right are some short, action-packed easier routes.
Approach (see map on page 310) - The northern sections of the crag are best reached following the cliff-top path from the *Pebble Mill* area for 150m. The lower path is hard going.

1 Sorb . . . . `E2 5c`
Absorbing balancy climbing up the left arete of the buttress with a poor landing leads to a good horizontal break and runners. An immense reach is all that remains, or if over-reached, head left.
FA. Dennis Carr 1976

2 Nosferatu . . `E6 6b`
From the fallen block that used to belong to *Sorb* climb the right-hand arete with cunning (toe and heel hooking) and crimpy holds to a reach for a ledge. Finish up the arete or, more directly, via an extended but safe dyno. Quite a bit easier (**E5 6a**?) for the really tall.
FA. Andy Barker 1980

3 Reginald . . . . `VS 4b`
The narrow chimney gives quality thrutching to a rightwards exit - don't get stuck! Low in the grade.
FA. Nat Allen 1951

4 Bad Attitude . . . . `f6C`
Follow the flake to the ledge.

5 The Attitude Inspector `f7A`
The sharp arete by way of a dynamic leap. A great problem. The route continues to the top but nobody ever does.
FA. Derek Bolger (static!) 1979

6 Nathaniel . . . . `HVS 5b`
The right-hand chimney-crack gets harder with height. Big fists, big cams and a chockstone all help along the way.
FA. Nat Allen 1951

7 The Neck . . . . `f7B`
The crimpy wall, finishing at the break. Jump off.

8 The Knack . . . . `E1 5c`
The hanging groove is desperate to access unless you have the knack. Easier once the first decent hold has been latched.
FA. John Allen 1971

9 Nick Knack Paddywack . . `E2 6b`
From below a flake pull up to the break, traverse left and climb the wall to the top. The short but intense direct start is **Old MacDonald**, *f7A*.
FA. Andy Barker 1982

10m

Descent

Evening | 12 min | Windy | Green

Dowel Crack

Nosferatu Area Bouldering
Peak Bouldering

⑩ Less Bent . . . . **S 4a**
Climb the left-hand side arete to a big horizontal break then stretch for a finish, or move left if you can't reach. Often green.

⑪ Zig-zag . . . . **VS 4c**
Climb the crescent-shaped crack (tough) to the break then move left to the arete. Move round to finish as for *Less Bent*.

⑫ No Zag **E1 5b**
Climb the flake as *Zig-zag* to the break then move right to gain and battle up the widening hanging crack - a bit full-on!

⑬ Gib's Rib **f7A**
A super problem up the right arete to the break.

⑭ Unfinished Symphony . . . **HVS 5b**
Tackle the short hanging crack by leaping into it from the blocks on the right. A short but action-packed battle is assured.
FA. John Allen 1974

⑮ Ribbed Corner . . . . **Diff**
Take the stepped corner on the right to a short bridging groove.
FA. Joe Brown (no kidding) 1951

⑯ Left Bannister . . . . **HS 4a**
Mantel up the face just right of the shallow groove.

⑰ The Staircase . . . . **S 4a**
The steep stepped cracks just left of the arete are juggy with good runners and rests after a delicate start.

⑱ Confidence of Youth **E3 6a**
Layback the elegant angular arete.
FA. John Jeed 2000

⑲ The Drainpipe . . . . . **HS 4b**
The steep groove is a bit of a strenuous tussle - bridging helps.

⑳ Booby Prize **E3 6b**
The short cracked wall to the right has a stopper move.
FA. Andy Barker 1982

The final routes are on a small buttress beyond a blocky break.

㉑ Parson's Crack . . . . **HS 4b**
Climb the diagonal crack to reach the Pulpit. Finish direct via a mantel - much harder for the short.

㉒ Electrical Storm . . . . . . **f7A+**
Climb the rib from a sit-down start, onto a sloping ledge that leads right. Finishing leftwards is **Grease Lightening**, *f7B+*.

㉓ Walker's Pulpit . . . . **HVD 4a**
From the grass bank traverse the steps left to the Pulpit, then exit awkwardly leftwards.

Pebble Mill

A fine buttress that is home to one of John Allen's classic pebble-pulling routes of the 1970s, *Pebble Mill*. There are some easier routes here too on the walls to the left.
Approach (see map on page 310) - The area is just to the north of the North Quarry and is most easily approached from above.

1 Broddle . . . . VS 4c
The left arete has a tricky mantelshelf start and soon eases.
FA. Dave Gregory 1964

2 Limmock. . . . . HVS 5b
The centre of the slab has a slippery, reachy start with no gear. The upper section is much easier and has runners.
FA. Dave Gregory (5' 4") 1964

3 Lino . . . . HVS 5a
Precarious moves up the green right arete on flaky holds.
FA. Dave Gregory 1964

4 The Birth of Liquid Desires . . HVS 5a
A minor line up the scooped slab left of the crack. There is no gear until the easy ground at the top.
FA. Clive Jones 1977

5 Wazzock . . . . S 4a
A pleasant crack left of the tall smooth slab has a tricky start.
FA. Dave Gregory 1964

6 Pebble Mill E5 6b
Layback the lower arete precariously on its left-hand side to a ledge on the right. Teeter up to better holds (the crux for shorties) and a romp to the top. Easier for the tall.
FA. John Allen 1976

7 Pebble Mill Traverse f7A+
A desperate thin traverse across the open face with great moves.

8 Pepper Mill . . . . f6C+
The *Pebble Mill* arete climbed on its right-hand side.

9 We Ain't Gonna Pay No Toll . . E5 6b
An underrated and contrasting right-hand start to *Pebble Mill*. Boulder up the wall to a break. Finger traverse this left onto the slab - *f6B* to here. Finish up *Pebble Mill* for the E5 bit.
FA. John Allen 1987

10 Dork Child. E1 5c
Between *Pebble Mill* and *Above and Beyond* is a tall slabby buttress. A boulder problem start - *f5+* - gains a ledge, continue up the wall above finishing just left of the arete.
FA. John Allen 1976

11 Above and Beyond the Kinaesthetic Barrier
.... E4 6b
A highly technical route up the arete. Use ancient bullet-marks to reach the first jugs then make some balancy moves to the top. The crux is the start but the top is scary and a mat is of limited use. Very-highball *f7A*. A direct start is *f7A+*.
FA. John Allen 1976

12 Samson f8A
Tough to climb and to grade. Swing out left to a big pocket then make a desperate move upwards to a still tricky finish. It can be led with a side-runner in *Goliath*, or a poor cam in the pocket.
FA. Jerry Moffatt 1997. With a poor cam in the slot and graded E9.

13 Goliath E4 6a
An unrelenting struggle up the wide crack. At least it is protectable nowadays by the biggest cams. The bold (crazy?) can layback the outer edge of the crack but that is rather avoiding the issue.
FA. Don Whillans 1958. Possibly the hardest route of its era.

14 David .... HVS 4c
The parallel-sided crack is best sprinted, passing a big threadable chockstone runner. A short and sweet route that is unfortunately over far too soon. Mild but just a little scary.

15 Sling Shot .... HVS 5b
Make a rising traverse up the ramp to reach *David* then climb the wide crack until a swinging hand-traverse leads around the arete to reach the top of *Goliath*.
FA. Chris Craggs 1984

16 Messiah E7 6c
The outrageous clean-cut arete. It is climbed by technical laybacking to reach holds and runners in the break (small cam) and a hard finish.
FA. Jerry Moffatt 1984

17 Messiah Traverse f7A
The crimpy wall rightwards from the arete.

18 Rollerwall f7C
A thin left-hand start to *Saul* via some old chipped holds. They were filled in some years ago but the cement has gradually eroded - harden your fingernails for this one.
FA. Ron Fawcett 1987

19 Saul .... VS 5b
The steep quarried slab has a neat tiptoe start trending right to a ledge and a mantelshelf. Step back left to an easier but slightly exposed finish.
FA. Dave Gregory 1964

David and Goliath
A famous pair of cracks bounded on either side by an impressive pair of aretes.
Approach (see map on page 310) - The area is just to the north of the North Quarry and is most easily approached from above.

Sheffield Area

Ladybower Area

Stanage

Burbage Valley

Millstone Area

Derwent Edges

Chatsworth Area

Southern Crags

The pumpy *Zeus* (E2 5b) - *this page* - in the North Quarry. Despite the reputation of Burbage South as being a cold northwest-facing crag this route and the nearby *Fox House Flake* have a much more southerly aspect and can be in condition throughout the year - in fact they are even a bit of a sun-trap. Further right the wall suffers from seepage.

North Quarry

A gloomy quarry with a few decent routes best done on high summer evenings. When the sun is flooding in *Fox House Flake* or *Zeus* will be memorable experiences and not greasy battles. The outer slab, including the classic *Millwheel Wall*, comes into condition more often. The often-wet wall at the back of the quarry is now home to a set of technical wall climbs that are rarely in condition.
Approach (see map on page 310) - Descend between or around either end of the quarries.

❶ **Great Flake Route** . . . . VD
A mini-expedition starting on up a tough chimney then a ramble along the crest of the flake with an optional belay on the way. The exit is loose. A direct start up a groove is a steep **VD**.

❷ **Zeus**. E2 5b
A surprisingly pumpy route up the parallel cracks in the smooth wall. Best laybacked rapidly to jugs and a tricky shelving exit.
Photo this page.
FA. Jack Street 1969. Originally called 'Tramlines'.

❸ **Fagus Sylvatica** E8 7a
The outrageously bold and technical arete is a "real beech".
FA. Miles Gibson 2002

❹ **Hades**. E1 5c
The slanting V-shaped groove gives a well-protected battle that is a complete nightmare if at all greasy, and it nearly always is.
FA. Gerry Rogan early 1960s

Descent

12m

David and Goliath

⑤ Fox House Flake . . . . . . 🔲🔲🔲 **VS 4b**
A pleasant diagonal crack leads, by a hand-traverse or tiptoeing,
to a steeper finale up the ledgy wall. Mild but often a bit green.
FA. Frank Burgess 1934

⑥ The Cock. . . . . 🔲🔲🔲 **VS 5a**
The cheeky groove on the right is steep and technical but soon
eases. Join and finish up *Fox House Flake*. The Cock is loose!
FA. Gerry Rogan early 1960s

⑦ Perched Block Route . . . 🔲🔲🔲 **HVS 4c**
Climb the groove past the block to a shelving ledge then step
right and climb the bitty groove and arete with care.
FA. Gerry Rogan early 1960s

The oft-damp wall just right has a neglected set of hard routes:

⑧ Stockbroker on the Woodpile
. . . . 🔲🔲🔲 **E5 6b**
Climb the crack with pegs. Move right then back left to finish.
FA. Paul Mitchell 1987

⑨ French Kiss . . . . 🔲🔲🔲 **E8 6b**
The blank wall is tricky and bold. Old peg and skyhooks protect.
FA. Gerry Rogan early 1960s

⑩ Inspiration Dedication 🔲🔲🔲 **E8 6b**
Bold moves up the wall lead to a hard rockover to gain a slot.
Easier and more protectable moves lead to the top.
FA. Pete Whittaker 2011

⑪ Psychosomatic Pigeon . . 🔲🔲 **E7 6b**
The vague groove on the right end of the wall.
FA. Pete Whittaker 2012

⑫ Shadows on the Wall 🔲🔲🔲 **E7 6b**
The arete and loose flake on the back wall.
FA. Ally Smith 2005

⑬ Coldest Crack . . . . 🔲🔲 **E2 5c**
In the back wall of the quarry is a thin curving crack, green for
50 weeks of most years. If you find it in condition, tick it pronto.
FA. Mick Fowler 1976

Descent

12m

South Quarry

⑭ Millwheel Wall . . . . 🔲🔲🔲 **E1 5b**
The blunt arete has a slippery start then climb the slab trending
rightwards, a good test of footwork, to better holds, the odd tiny
runner and a brisk mantelshelf finish. Stake belay.
FA. Len Millsom 1958

⑮ Dunkley's Eliminate . . . . 🔲 **VS 4c**
Mantelshelf onto the ledge from the 'Flintstone's spare-wheel'
then climb the well-positioned left arete which has good runners
and holds. Swing around left for an exposed finish - rather neat.

⑯ Pretzel Logic . . . . . . 🔲🔲🔲 **E3 6a**
A counter-diagonal to *MWW* is fingery and unprotected.
FA. Dave Jones 1979

⑰ Burssola . . . . 🔲🔲 **HVS 5b**
The thin crack in the shady north-facing wall is more stubborn
than it looks. Fortunately the gear is good.
FA. John Allen (solo) 1975

Sheffield Area
Ladybower Area
Stanage
Burbage Valley
Millstone Area
Derwent Edges
Chatsworth Area
Southern Crags

South Quarry

The Southern Quarry is as grim as its neighbour; it has a small collection of hard routes and a few lesser offerings. Most of the routes are only climbable after a dry spell. **Approach (see map on page 310) -** Descend between or around either end of the quarries.

❶ The Verdict . . . . 🔧🤜 ☐ **E2 6a**
The neglected V-shaped groove is a brutal but safe struggle.
FA. Ken Jones 1972

❷ The Old Bailey . . . . 🔆🔧 ☐ **HVS 5b**
The deep chockstoned and ferny groove has a tough exit. A good line that sees virtually no attention.

❸ Wizard Ridge . . . . 🔆 ☐
The fantastic arete remains a dream at present.

❹ The Simpering Savage . . 🔆🔧 ☐ **E5 6b**
A diagonal finger traversed to *The Old Bailey* and a possible stance. Continue across the wall (**5b**) to the top of *The Verdict*.
FA. Paul Mitchell 1981

❺ Poisoned Dwarf . . . . 🔆🔧👁 ☐ *f5*
Thin cracks used to give good pegging practice, now they have to be finger-jammed instead. More like **E1 5c** as a lead.

❻ The Dover and Ellis Chimney. 🔆 ☐ **E1 5b**
The highly historical cleft in the back corner of the quarry. Passing the wide section is the crux. Sandy and rarely done.
FA. Harry Dover, Gilbert Ellis 1932

❼ Silent Spring . . . . . . 🔆🔧👁 ☐ **E4 5c**
An exposed girdle of the Cioch (Gaelic for tit) Block.
1) 5c, 12m. Start in the dirty gully on the left and cross a thin green slab to a stance on the front (belay on a pre-placed rope).
2) 5c, 12m. Continue right and then down before traversing out to the arete and a fine finish. Don't trust the ancient bolts.
FA. Steve Bancroft, John Allen 1975

❽ Silent Scream . . . . . 🔆👁🔧 ☐ **E7 6c**
A lower version is technical and well named. Stay just above the lip of the roof until the right arete can be reached for a finish.
FA. Pete Whittaker 2009

❾ Off Spring . . . . 🔆�‖🔧 ☐ **E5 6b**
Exciting climbing in a dramatic position and much easier for the tall. From the arete (abseil in) traverse the parallel cracks on the northwest wall then move up and right to finish dramatically up the ramp. A great finish to *Silent Spring*. The lower part of the hanging arete is **Masters of the Universe, E6 6b**.
FA. Johnny Dawes 1985

❿ Captain Invincible . . 🔆🔧🔧 ☐ **E8 6c**
A free version of an old aid route up the awesome northwest face of the Cioch. Climb the technical arete then follow the thin parallel cracks out left to an easy finish up *Off Spring*. A bunch of 20+ year-old pegs protect. An astounding route!
Photo opposite.
FA. Sean Myles 1991

⓫ Captain Unclimbable . . . . . . 🔆 ☐
The amazing steep groove is the third of Burbage South's impossible projects.

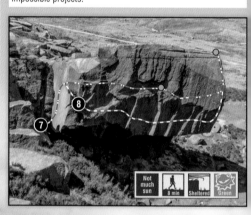

Descent

14m

Descent

North Quarry

TICKLIST
Burbage South Stoppers

A Ticklist to study and then probably studiously avoid.

- ☐ Messiah, E7 *(323)*
- ☐ Balance It Is, E7 *(316)*
- ☐ The Braille Trail, E7 *(316)*
- ☐ Silent Scream, E7 *(326)*
- ☐ Captain Invincible, E8 *(326)*
- ☐ Simba's Pride, E8 *(315)*
- ☐ Dynamics of Change, E9 *(317)*
- ☐ Equilibrium, E10 *(316)*
- ☐ Parthian Shot, E10 *(317)*

... and if you manage those then how about:

- ☐ Impossible Groove *(312)*
- ☐ Wizard Ridge *(326)*
- ☐ Captain Unclimbable *(326)*

Sheffield Area

Ladybower Area

Stanage

Burbage Valley

Millstone Area

Derwent Edges

Chatsworth Area

Southern Crags

Tom Randall on the rising crack of *Captain Invincible* (E8 6c) - *opposite* - in the South Quarry. Photo: Mike Hutton

Sheffield Area

Ladybower Area

Stanage

Burbage Valley

Millstone Area

Derwent Edges

Chatsworth Area

Southern Crags

Millstone Area

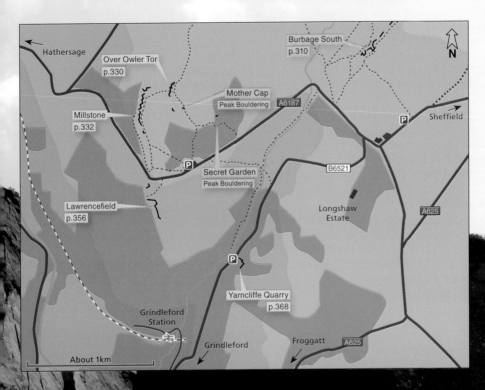

Hathersage

Over Owler Tor
p.330

Burbage South
p.310

N

Mother Cap
Peak Bouldering

A6187

Sheffield

Millstone
p.332

P

Secret Garden
Peak Bouldering

B6521

Lawrencefield
p.356

Longshaw
Estate

A625

P

Burbage Valley

Yarncliffe Quarry
p.368

Grindleford
Station

About 1km

Grindleford

Froggatt

A625

Sheffield Area

Ladybower Area

Stanage

Burbage Valley

Millstone Area

Derwent Edges

Chatsworth Area

Southern Crags

Mike Waters making short work of the classic jamming crack of *Dexterity* (E1 5b) - *page 338* - one of many of its genre on this great crag.

	No star	☆1	☆2	☆3
Mod to S	6	-	-	-
HS to HVS	5	5	-	-
E1 to E3	3	1	1	-
E4 and up	-	-	-	-

On the moor above and behind Millstone Quarry are some blocks that have been scrambled on for aeons; the higher one always has a few walkers taking in the view. Climbers have scratched around here for many years too, though more recently they have been used mainly for bouldering. There are several decent climbs worth calling in for though on the taller sections of Over Owler Tor. The block of Mother Cap and Mother's Pet Rock are used by boulderers only these days and are covered in the Peak Bouldering Rockfax.

Approach   See map on page 329
The outcrops are situated near the Surprise View, on the moor behind Millstone Quarry. Park at the large Surprise View car park then leave this northwards by any one of several narrow paths. These climb steeply though the woods and past the odd quarry before popping out onto the moor. Over Owler Tor is prominent just beyond Mother Cap.

Conditions
The elevated position means that the rocks catch all the weather that is going, it can be wild and windy up here. Most of the routes are on the northwest-facing side so tend to be green and shady, they are best visited after a dry spell.

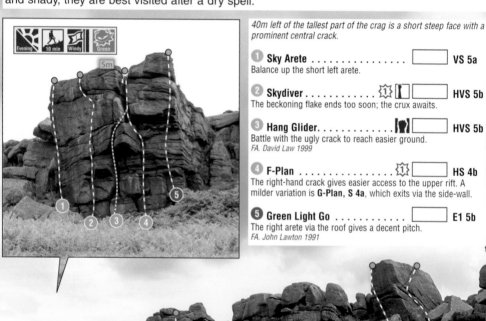

40m left of the tallest part of the crag is a short steep face with a prominent central crack.

❶ Sky Arete . . . .   VS 5a
Balance up the short left arete.

❷ Skydiver . . . . ☆1   HVS 5b
The beckoning flake ends too soon; the crux awaits.

❸ Hang Glider. . . . .   HVS 5b
Battle with the ugly crack to reach easier ground.
FA. David Law 1999

❹ F-Plan . . . . ☆1   HS 4b
The right-hand crack gives easier access to the upper rift. A milder variation is **G-Plan, S 4a**, which exits via the side-wall.

❺ Green Light Go E1 5b
The right arete via the roof gives a decent pitch.
FA. John Lawton 1991

6 Breaststroke . . . . **VD**
The tight rift in the right-side of a short buttress.

7 Elephantitis **E2 5c**
The left arete of the jutting block. Bold.
FA. John Lawton 1991

8 Zorro . . . . **VD**
The thin zig-zag cracks in the slabby face are pleasant.
FA. John Lawton 1991

The large block in front of the edge, known as The Ship, has a few good boulder problems. Most notable are:

9 Sailing **f6B**
A left to right traverse of the lip and a mantel.

10 Rod Stewart . . . . **f5+**
The arete facing the tallest buttress.

The wall under the high tower of rock has another short offering.

11 Really Exciting Flake . . . . **HS 4c**
From the block arete swing left to access the flake, then move up and right to climb the arete. A direct start is **5a**.

12 Brass Monkeys . . . . **S 3c**
The awkward narrow rift.

13 Brass Monkeys Chimney . . . . . . **Mod**
This is the easier cleft just right, to a leftward exit.

14 Three Men on a Rock . . . **HVS 5a**
The left arete leads to a short crack. No escaping left.

15 Aeroflot **E1 5b**
The fine right arete is the best route on the crag.

12m right is a short wall facing more to the west.

16 Balloon . . . . **HS 4a**
The rounded left arete is pleasant and bold too.

17 Goodyear . . . . **S 4a**
The centre of the face is worth a quick look. Big cams help.

To the right is a short arete with a couple of boulder problems.

18 Lil' Arete . . . . **f3+**
Layback the teeny arete.

19 Wafery Flake . . . . **f6A+**
The thin and brittle flakes to a mantel exit.

20 Plop . . . . **VS 4b**
The next taller arete gives a pleasant little pitch. Harder if you start on the left - **5a**.

21 Plip . . . . **VS 5a**
The reachy face just right finishing past a pocket.

Further right is the popular bouldering around Spider Crack - check out the Peak Bouldering Rockfax for details.

	No star	⭐	⭐⭐	⭐⭐⭐
Mod to S	7	4	-	-
HS to HVS	15	29	12	6
E1 to E3	2	16	13	11
E4 and up	4	9	14	13

Sheffield Area

Ladybower Area

Stanage

Burbage Valley

Millstone Area

Derwent Edges

Chatsworth Area

Southern Crags

Adam Bailles on the finest of Millstone's finger-cracks,
London Wall (E5 6a) - *page 351*. Photo: Mike Hutton

Quarries are usually depressing holes in the ground, but Millstone is the exception. With smooth walls, soaring grooves and inspiring crack-lines, it is the greatest of all the gritstone quarries. The cracks here span most widths from tips to fist, though luckily there are no dreaded off-widths. Many of the routes were originally done as aid climbs up spidery cracks, the repeated placing of pegs widened them enough to allow access to thin fingers and pointed toes and also to provide protection from wires. Fortunately the climbing here is not just about cracks, there are also many fine corners and aretes formed by the careful quarrying of the various bays. The section from *Green Death* to the Keyhole Caves could hardly have been better designed even if a climber had been in charge of the quarrying.

It is worth pointing out that some of the exits can be dangerous where weathering had started to erode the rock before it was exposed by the quarry-men. These 'chest-of-drawers' finishes require care; it is a good idea to place an extra runner or two below the top-out and ensure the second is on-the-ball. Wearing helmets here is a good idea too.

Approach   Also see map on page 329
There is an extensive Pay and Display car park (often with in-situ ice-cream van at weekends) just to the east of the Surprise View (a bend on the A625 with a sudden vista of the Hope Valley). Tracks lead out of the northwest corner of this over a ridge into the right-hand end of quarry.

Conditions
Although the quarry forms a series of bays it is often less sheltered than you might expect, the wind manages to sneak into even the deepest corners though some of the northern bays, and the Keyhole Caves, can be slightly less blowy. The sun arrives on most of the crag in the afternoon but the North Bay is shady until late afternoon in the summer and can be useful in hot weather. The walls dry quickly but tend to be green in winter.

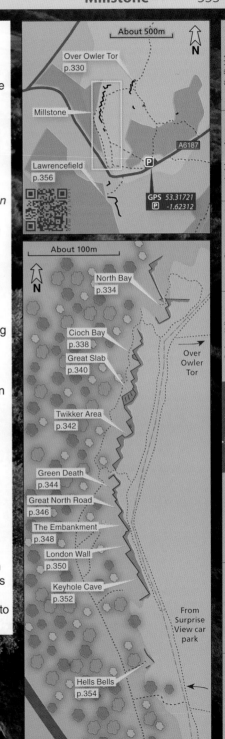

North Bay

For most of the year this is a gloomy spot at the left-hand extremity of the cliff. It only sees the sun late on in the summer although that makes it a good venue to escape from the heat. The routes include some excellent steep cracks and some more recent horrors.

Approach (see map on page 333) - The area can be reached by walking through the whole of the rest of the quarry. A speedier option is following the quarry-top fence and descending into the final bay.

① Brindle . . . .  VS 4c
The left-most route on the wall is neglected and grassy.

② Scrimsel . . . . VS 4c
The long crack. A decent line but crusty and rarely done.

③ Brimstone E2 5b
From beside the leaning blocks, climb the steep crack past plenty of nice fat wires. Low in the grade, but hard enough.
FFA. Henry Barber 1973

④ Satan's Slit . . . . HVS 5b
The leaning crack with a kink early on, is gained from the left and sprinted on jams and jugs, passing a niche. Steep and pumpy, it is often dirty and can feel hard for the grade.
FAA. John Loy 1964

⑤ Gates of Mordor E3 5c
The pod and leaning hand-crack give a withering pitch. The route swallows medium cams by the tonne and, although the initial groove is a grovel, the crux is right at the very top.
FA. Hank Pasquill 1969

⑥ Pin Prick E2 5c
The thin crack in the front of the pillar never gets done.

⑦ Hacklespur . . . . HVS 5b
Millstone's answer to *The Peapod* is worth doing. Although it doesn't have the cachet of Curbar's classic, it is just as awkward.
FAA. Alan Clarke 1960. FFA. John Loy (2nd man on the aided ascent) 1962

⑧ Cauldron Crack E3 5c
Climb the right side of the arete then swing left and follow the slanting, fingery crack to easier ground. Worthwhile though the start is both bold and a bit loose.
FFA. Mick Fowler 1976

Sheffield Area

Ladybower Area

Stanage

Burbage Valley

Millstone Area

Derwent Edges

Chatsworth Area

Southern Crags

Jon Fulwood on *Saville Street* (E3 6a) - *page 337* - in the North Bay at Millstone. Photo: Adam Long

Descent

20m

9 Estremo .... 🔲 HVS 5a
The wide, twisting crack is easier than it looks if you enjoy fat
fist-jamming. Pull over the roof and sprint up the tricky crusty
layback to finish.
FAA. Ted Howard early 1960s

10 Gimbals .... 🔲 HVS 5b
The long groove is climbed to the overhang. Pull through this
and climb the wall just right via shallow groove. Good value!
FA. Mick Fowler 1976

11 Mother's Pride ..... 🔲 E6 6c
A fierce finger-crack leads to a band of overhangs. Pull into the
steep leaning groove and finish up this. **London Pride, E5 6b,
5c,** climbed to the roof then took a hanging belay on the arete
before finishing up the slanting groove of *Perplexity.*
*FA. (London Pride) Mick Fowler 1976. FA. (as described) Mike Lea 2001.
The top wall was climbed as Which Way Up Robitho (FA. Paul Evans 1988).*

12 Perplexity .... 🔲 E6 6b
The steep arete is technical as far as a band of crusty rock.
Step right and climb the difficult slanting groove, and the
headwall. Holds were chipped off after the first ascent but it is
still climbable at the same grade. Some ancient bolts provide
much-needed protection.
FA. Johnny Dawes 1984. The top section was originally on London Pride.

13 Apoplexy .... 🔲 E7 6b
The thrilling direct finish via the impressive soaring upper arete.
FA. Tom Randall 2010

Descent

28m

14 Plexity . . . . HVS 5a
A class act with a big feel. The fine steep crack in the centre of
the wall leads through a series of bulges to a ledge out on the
right. Balance back left above the roof and sprint for the top.
FA. Joe Brown 1957

Next are three grassy climbs - more traffic would help.

15 Remembrance Day. . . . . VS 4c
Up the main groove at the back of the bay to ledges and a finish
up the groove above the grass ledge. Steep and worthwhile
climbing on jugs and jams with good gear along the way.
FA. Ted Howard 1960

16 Day Dream . . . . VS 4c
Climb the rib right of the main corner, then thin cracks and a
shallow groove to a ledge. Follow the continuation crack in the
wall to a loose finish. Often a bit green and grassy!
FA. John Loy early 1960s

17 Rainy Day. . . . . VS 4b
At the right side of the ledge is a crack in a groove. Climb this
to a ledge, then the continuation, past a couple of tiny grassy
ledges, to the final steep crack of *Day Dream*. Becoming
overgrown.
FA. Alan Clarke early 1960s

18 Commix E2 5c
A good line, pumpy but with decent gear. Avoid the lower groove
to a ledge, then follow its continuation until the thin crack on
the right can be reached. Up this to a ledge then finish up a
loose groove. Continuing up the main groove is the loose and
neglected **Southern Comfort, E3 5c**.
FA. John Loy (4 pegs) late 1950s. FFA. (Both ways) John Stevenson 1976

19 Top Loader E7 6c
The groove and hairline cracks to the left of *Saville Street* are
climbed until it is possible to trend right to reach the arete of
Saville Street. Step back left and make more hard moves to an
interesting finish. Pegs, bolts and some normal gear protect.
FA. Mike Lea 2001

20 Drifter E7 6c
Climb the arete to some pockets and gear. The arete above gives
a desperate sloping finish. Finish up the next route, or abseil off.
FA. Thomas de Gay 2000

21 Saville Street E3 6a
The superb but tough finger-crack in the right wall of the bay.
Gain the top of the pedestal awkwardly and climb the leaning
crack to crucial moves into a sloping niche. Exit steeply to easy
but broken ground. *Photo on page 335.*
FA. Reg Pillinger early 1960s. FFA. John Allen 1975

22 Soho Sally E1 5b
Climb the flake to ledges then follow the shallow groove above
(small gear) until it becomes necessary to swing onto the
exposed left arete. Care is required with the grassy finish.
FA. Geoff Birtles 1975

Cioch Bay

Sheffield Area
Ladybower Area
Stanage
Burbage Valley
Millstone Area
Derwent Edges
Chatsworth Area
Southern Crags

Descent

22m

12m

North Bay
down the slope

Sheffield Area

Ladybower Area

Stanage

Burbage Valley

Millstone Area

Derwent Edges

Chatsworth Area

Southern Crags

❶ February Fox . . . ☆ 🦶 ▯▮ 💗 ☐ **E1 5b**
The bold and reachy wall left of the arete.

❷ March Hare . . . . ☆ 💗 ☐ **E2 5b**
The square-cut arete is climbed on its left side and becomes
harrowing towards the top. Staying with the arete is best though
trending left is an easier option. Escape right or do *April Arete*.
FA. Gabe Regan 1975

❸ April Arete . . . . ☆ 💗 ☐ **HVS 4c**
The upper arete is gained from the right. Pleasant though poorly
protected, and featuring a huge chipped hold. The direct start up
the groove to the left of *February Fox* is an overgrown 6b.
FA. Alan Clarke early 1960s

❹ Dextrous Hare . . . . ☆ 🦶 ☐ **E3 5c**
The tenuous crack and tiny groove are approached on small flat
edges and entered by a bold layback. The crack right of the arete
offers a top pitch at an easier grade (5a).
FA. Martin Taylor 1976

❺ Dexterity . . . . ☆ 🤚 ✏️ ☐ **E1 5b**
Pumpy climbing up the crack cleaving the wall. Where it thins,
go direct, runners and holds keep appearing. Escaping out left
before the final section is more like a stiff HVS. From the ledge
select a way on/off. *Photo on page 328.*
FAA. Harold Drasdo 1957

❻ Cioch Corner . . . . 💗 ☐ **S 4a**
Climb the deep, greasy groove to the tip of the Cioch, and a
possible belay. Finish up the exposed arete above.
FA. Alan Clarke 1956

Cioch Bay

The main feature of the bay is the narrow tower of the Cioch leaning against its left side and, just left again, the steep classic jamming crack of *Dexterity*. The right wall has some pleasant offerings although the exits all need a careful approach; the top here is invariably loose.

Approach (see map on page 333) - The quickest access is to take the path above the quarry and descend just before the North Bay - tricky to locate on first acquaintance. Walking through the quarry takes a little longer but gives you a good look at the place.

18m

Great Slab

⑭

⑬

⑮

Sheffield Area

Ladybower Area

Stanage

Burbage Valley

Millstone Area

Derwent Edges

Chatsworth Area

Southern Crags

⑦ Mayday . . . . **HVS 5a**
Up the balancy arete of the Cioch (hard to start) to its tip, then finish up the exposed arete of *Cioch Corner*.
FA. Alan Clarke early 1960s

⑧ Supra Direct . . . . **HVS 5b**
The thin peg-scarred crack splitting the front of the Cioch proves tricky at the bulge. No escaping out right!
FA. Mike James 1959. FFA. (nearly) Pete Brayshaw 1975

⑨ The Hacker . . . . **VS 4c**
The short curving crack just to the right is a slight variation on the previous climb that soon eases. Finish up the exposed arete.

The easier routes to the right have some reasonable climbing, but protection can be sparse and the loose rock needs care.

⑩ Close Shave . . . . **S 4a**
Climb cracks right of the Cioch, trending left to reach the ledge and a belay. Finish up the deep groove at the back of the ledge or, better and more worthy of the star, up the arete.
FA. Alan Clarke 1956

⑪ Boomerang . . . . **S 4a**
Left of the main groove, follow the line of cracks and corners left then right to a ledge. Escape rightwards with great care.
FA. John Loy early 1960s

⑫ Brumal . . . . **VS 4c**
A direct line with some pleasant moves and a steep finale.
FA. John Loy early 1960s

In the main angle at the back of the bay are three abandoned lines offering a mixture of rock and grass.

⑬ Eartha . . . . **HS 4a**
Start just right of a wide crack and climb the groove to a ledge. Move right and climb the pleasant flake-crack up the slabby face.

⑭ Only Just **E2 5b**
Start up *Eartha* then head up the delicate and poorly-protected scoop to tricky final moves. Low in the grade when 100% dry.
FA. Ernie Marshall 1959

⑮ F.A.T.D. . . . . **HS 4a**
The right arete of the wall past a couple of heathery ledges.
FA. Steve C. 1968. The name reflects the bored nature of the FA team!

Great Slab

A fine sheet of quarried grit with a nice set of routes. *Great Slab* is one of the best lower grade routes in the quarry and there are a selection of harder climbs. The bay tends to be green after rain. The crusty walls up left and right see less action.

Approach (see map on page 333) - Walk through the quarry, up the slope left of *Crewcut* then round past the cave of *Lyons Corner House*.

On the left side of the bay are some unpopular routes. They start up the unsavoury grassy ramp. The belayer is best located at the bottom of this and out of the line of fire!

❶ The Pittsburgh Enigma . . **E4 5c**
The bold angular arete past a couple of old pegs.
FA. Paul Mitchell 1985

❷ Wuthering Crack . . . . . **HVS 5a**
The steep crack in the left wall of the bay leads strenuously past a huge suspect triangular block. The finish is loose.
FA. Alan Clarke, John Loy early 1960s.

❸ Evening Premiere . . **HVS 5a**
Take the thin left-trending crack to exit as for the last route. A direct finish isn't much harder or much more stable.
FA. Mick Fowler 1976

❹ Svelt . . . . **HVS 5a**
Low in the grade and well protected. The slippery slabby groove up the left edge of the slab gives good climbing to a ledge at its top. Continue up the left-hand of the two steep grooves. Care needed with the exit. The right-hand groove is harder and dirtier.
FA. Al Parker, Martin Boysen 1962

❺ The Snivelling Shits . **E5 6a**
The polished razor-edged iron bits (above a lurking flake) lead left then back right to the top of the slab. Escape via *Great Slab*. The only gear is a large cam above all difficulties. Stiff boots are a great help.
FA. Jonathan Lagoe late 1970s. Called Slideshow. It took over 20 years for his ascent to be credited. By then the name given by the second ascent party had stuck.

❻ Election Special **E3 6a**
This is a bit of an eliminate and requires distant side runners.
FA. Dominic Staniforth 1986

❼ The Moronic Chippings . . . . . **VS 4a**
A line of small polished and spaced chipped holds (shades of Yorkshire Grit) hopefully lead all the way up the slab, Finish up or down *Great Slab*.
FA. Bruce Burton, Martin Stokes 1961

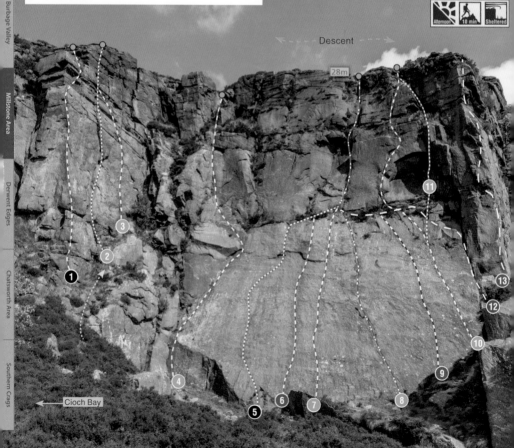

Descent

28m

Cioch Bay →

⑧ Great Slab .... 🔲 HS 4b
Climb the slippery crack which splits the right-hand side of the slab as it runs leftwards - poorly protected. Move back slightly right and then make a short traverse to a good ledge above the centre of the slab (possible belay). Climb the corner-crack to a ledge then finish direct with care. It is also possible to move right round the arete to a chimney with a loose exit.
FA. Alan Maskery 1952. FFA. Al Parker 1957

⑨ Sex Dwarves ...... 🔲 f6B+
The right edge of the slab has a series of tiny holds that are becoming ever more polished. Keep heading left to claim an E4 solo, or escape off right.
FA. Mark Millar 1982

⑩ Lorica .... 🔲 VS 4c
Climb the delicate thin crack near the right edge of the slab and the short-lived but gripping curving flake above which definitely looks detached! Finish up the short crack.

⑪ Bun Run .... 🔲 HVS 5a
Follow *Lorica* to the top of the slab then continue up the awkward groove directly above to a finish up the chimney.
FA. Al Evans 1969

⑫ Cake Walk .... 🔲 S 4a
A bit aimless though the easiest way up the face. Climb the easy crack on the right of the slab then traverse left to join (possible stance) and finish up *Great Slab*.

⑬ Windrete ...... 🔲 E2 5b
The impressive and well-named blowy arete has low gear (small wires) and mostly good holds. It proves to be bold and airy with some suspect rock.
FA. Al Evans 1969

⑭ Breeze Mugger . 🔲 E5 6b
Climb to a break (gear) then make hard moves up before moving left to a finish on the arete of *Windrete*.
FA. Paul Dearden 1990

⑮ Meeze Brugger . 🔲 E5 6b
Climb the wall first left then right. The hard bit is standing on the only good hold on the lower wall. Finish up suspect rock.
FA. Ron Fawcett 1984

⑯ Eros .... 🔲 E1 5b
Low in the grade and good, though some of the rock is a bit suspect. The steep crack has good jams and runners to a step left where a tricky finger-crack leads to a looser finish. The original finish was up the tottery wall above the prominent scar.
FFA. Paul Grayson 1969

Twikker Area

An imposing tall bay with the shallow cave of *Lyons Corner House* in its left wall. The area is more sheltered than other spots on the crag but it can be green, especially early in the year or after rain.

Approach (see map on page 333) - The area is at the top of the slope left of Green Death.

1 Lyons Corner House Direct . . 🔲 HVS 5a

An excellent and elegant pitch up the long arete, managing to avoid all the crucial sections on the regular route. The loss of a flake/hold has made the lower section harder and bolder; it is still a bit hollow but the positions on the upper arete are superb.

2 Lyons Corner House . . . . 🔲 HVS 5a

A fine expedition up the left edge of the bay, was originally done in three pitches, named after a famous London tearoom. A short groove (**4b**) leads into the cave. Head up the corner to the roof then traverse to the left arete and make difficult moves round to a narrow ledge. The leaning wall just to the left leads awkwardly to a rest and a finish up the superbly positioned final arete.
FAA. Kit Twyford, George Leaver 1957

3 Erb. . . . . 🔲 **E2 5c**

A fine varied pitch with a lot of good climbing and no nasty surprises along the way. Follow *Lyons Corner House* to the high ledge then trend right to reach and pass the central overlap awkwardly by finger-jamming and a tough mantelshelf. Finish up the wide gritty crack above.
FA. Alan Clarke early 1960s. FFA. Tom Proctor 1975

4 Twikker. . . . . 🔲 **E3 5c**

The right-hand side of the cave leads to the lip of the roof which is passed with difficulty (stepping in from the ledge on the right is taboo at the grade) to gain the upper slab. Pass the cave (occasional raven's nest) to the final crack which gives tenuous finger-jamming to a sandy exit. *Photo on page 355.*
FA. Dave Johnson 1956. FFA. Tom Proctor 1975

5 Lubric. . . . . 🔲 HVS 5b

From the cave trend up and right to the foot of the final smooth corner. This gives good climbing on the odd occasions when it isn't damp or full of grass!
FA. Alan Clarke early 1960s

30m

Great Slab

Sheffield Area | Ladybower Area | Stanage | Burbage Valley | Millstone Area | Derwent Edges | Chatsworth Area | Southern Crags

6 The Bed of Procrustes ☐☐☐☐ *f8A+*
A stunning boulder problem up tiny edges to reach the cave.
FA. Iain Farrar 2011

7 Pinstone Street . . . . ☐☐☐☐ E2 5c
The crack right of the corner turns mean (and a bit loose) at the overhang. Once past the bulges continue more easily stepping right at the ledge system to the final crack. Often grassy.
FA. Dave Johnson 1956. FFA. (well almost) Al Evans 1969

8 Diamond Groove . . . . ☐☐☐☐ HVS 5b
Start at a grass ledge under the centre of the wall and climb to a higher ledge. Move left to a groove which leads to a third ledge. Finish up the thin crack in the wall behind. Sadly the shady setting means it is almost always green and grubby.
FA. John Loy early 1960s

9 Flapjack . . . . ☐☐☐☐ VS 4b
Climb the crack on the left then move right and balance up the shallow groove. Pleasant but protection is lacking and it is often green. Finish up the prominent crack above.
FA. Jack Soper 1956

10 Neatfeet . . . . ☐☐☐☐ HVS 5a
Neat moves up the short-lived but bold arete to join the upper section of the previous climb, or finish up the arete.

11 SSS . . . . ☐☐☐☐ VS 4c
The stepped groove is poorly protected and often green. It leads to an exit by the finish of *Flapjack*.
FA. Jack Soper early 1960s

12 Winter's Grip . . . . ☐☐☐☐ E6 6b
Another of those gripping square-cut aretes. A couple of hand-placed pegs provide much needed protection.
FA. Neil Foster 1983

13 Keelhaul . . . . ☐☐☐☐ VS 4c
The hanging flake on the left wall of the groove is approached up a short corner and gives tricky but short-lived laybacking. Choose an exit; care required whichever way you go! Poor.
FA. John Loy early 1960s

14 Crusty Corner . . . . ☐☐☐☐ S 4a
The deep groove to the right is pretty overgrown nowadays.
FA. John Loy early 1960s

15 Quiddity . . . . ☐☐☐☐ HVS 5a
An impressive arete pitch. Fortunately there are more holds and runners than appearances suggest, though it is still bold! Small wires and a big reach both help.
FA. John Loy early 1960s

16 Billingsgate . . . . ☐☐☐☐ E1 5b
The open scoop gives nice technical climbing past lots of rather tired small-wire slots to a leftwards exit. The climb was once described as "being a bit like a well-protected *Green Death*". Well, it is a groove in a quarry.
FFA. Steve Chadwick 1969

Descent

Green Death
down the slope

Sheffield Area
Ladybower Valley
Stanage
Burbage Valley
Millstone Area
Derwent Edges
Chatsworth Area
Southern Crags

1 Stone Dri . . . . ☼ 🖼 ▯ ▭ **E2 6a**
The blank corner delicately past a perched flake to a taxing bridging sequence which is much easier for the tall.
FA. John Regan (1pt) 1976. FFA. Dave Humphries 1977

2 Crewcut . . . . ☼ 🖊 ▭ **VS 4c**
An intimidating layback up the imposing straight crack - fortunately it is easier than it looks, though the right wall is often a bit green and slippery. Threaded chockstones or large cams protect. Those heading Stateside might want to 'off-width' it just for the practice - a whole different ball-game at 5.9!
FA. Alan Clarke 1963

There are three routes starting from the ledge above Crewcut.

3 Yourolympus . . . . 🖼 ▭ **HVS 4c**
The grassy right-trending crack leads to ledges. From the highest of these head out to the arete for an airy finish.
FA. Dave Gregory 1969

4 Myolympus . . . . ▭ **HVS 5b**
Climb a flake to the middle of the wall then finish up the crack.
FA. Paul Grayson (1pt) 1969. FFA. Al Evans 1969

5 King Ellmore . . . . . . ☼ 🖼 🐾 ▭ **E6 6a**
The wall above right of *Myolympus*. Climb the flake, arrange wires, then head up the wall to a bold finale.
FA. Tom Randall 2012

6 Xanadu . . . . ☼ 🖼 ▭ **E1 5b**
A fine climb but it sees little attention.
1) **4c**, 20m. From part way up *Crewcut*, follow the ledge out right to reach the large corner and climb to the ledge above.
2) **5b**, 22m. The main angle gives an excellent pitch when clean, though it is often grassy, to just below the top. Finish by a wild hand-traverse out to the right arete.
FA. Keith Myhill, Al Evans 1969

7 Under Doctor's Orders . . ☼ 🖼 ▭ **E2 6a**
Follow the seam in the arete right of *Crewcut* (old peg) until it is possible to mantel out right, then reach the mid-way ledge.
FA. Keith Sharples 1987

The Bore Holes - These holes offer protection for some routes on these walls. They will take Tricams, Aliens or large nuts folded back on themselves.

Twikker Area
up the slope

Great North Road

Afternoon 8 min Sheltered

34m
20m

Sam Hamer *Edge Lane* (E5 5c) - *this page*. Photo: Mike Hutton

8 Jealous Pensioner .. 🎫📷❚❚ ⬜ **E4 5c**
The centre of the drilled wall gives an odd pitch with worrying stretches to and from the ledge. Ingenious use of the various bore holes for protection can make it reasonably safe.
FA. Jim Burton 1978

9 Xanadu Direct ..... 🎫🪝❚❚ ⬜ **E3 5c**
Weird and wonderful bridging up the blank corner. Shorties will have to shuffle, feet on one wall, hands on the other!
FA. Hank Pasquill 1974

10 Adios Amigo ...... 🎫🪝📷 ⬜ **E5 6b**
Climb the right wall of the corner on bore holes and small edges. Protection is placed in the holes.
FA. Mark Leach 1985

11 Great West Road ... 🎫📷🪚 ⬜ **E3 5b**
Fine climbing with two impressive and contrasting pitches.
1) E2 5b, 18m. Layback up the huge flake to a tiny ledge. The upper part is steeper and leads to a massive terrace. Escape or:
2) E3 5b, 16m. The upper arete is delicate and effectively unprotected. The ancient golo/bolt should not be trusted!
FAA. Dave Johnson 1957. FFA. Al Evans 1965

12 Edge Lane.......... Top 50 📷 ⬜ **E5 5c**
The magnificent scalloped arete is unprotected where it matters although gear can be fiddled in the half-height bore holes. Not for the faint of heart, because from the crux you will hit the ground, gear or not!
FA. Alan McHardy 1974

13 Green Death .... Top 50 📷 ⬜ **E5 5c**
The superb blank groove can be approached from a short way up *Edge Lane* by a tricky traverse (5c), a pile of stones or a *f6C* problem. The crucial upper section has an old cemented peg runner in the right wall, between the two cruxes. Finish using a tiny chipped hold. From the terrace continue up the easy corner, or abseil carefully from the chipped spike. *Photo this page.*
FA. Tom Proctor 1969

14 Green Death Superdirect. 🎫🪝 ⬜ **f7B**
Desperate smearing and bridging up the corner.

15 The Master's Edge .. Top 50 ❚❚ 📷 ⬜ **E7 6c**
One of the major routes of the 1980s up the soaring angular arete. A hard starting section enables the sanctuary of the bore holes to be reached (gear). Continue with rising anxiety to a final wild leap which is roughly twice as far off the ground as your last runner. There is a fixed belay on a bunch of pegs at the top. Climbed on the left-hand side is **Re-mastered Edge, E7 6c**.
FA. Ron Fawcett December 1983. FA. (Re-mastered Edge) Pete Whittaker

16 Pure Now .... 🎫📷 ⬜ **E9 6c**
The wall up and right of the runners on *The Master's Edge* gives a sustained, technical and deadly serious pitch.
FA. Tom Randall 2014

17 The Bad and the Beautiful 🎫📷 ⬜ **E6 6c**
A fine but desperate bold outing up the blank wall off the ledge.
FA. Mark Leech 1987

18 Great Arete .... 🎫📷 ⬜ **E5 5c**
The upper arete is delicate and serious. Start on the ledge and climb first on the right and then on the left. A low bunch of peg runners might just save your life, but you will fall a long way!
FA. Tom Proctor 1975

Green Death
The most impressive part of the quarry with a series of superb lines. From the old classic of *Crewcut*, through to the intense outings of *Green Death* and *Edge Lane*, and onto the fantastic line of *The Master's Edge*, there are routes here to inspire all. The rock gets afternoon sun and dries quickly, though it can be green in winter.
Approach (see map on page 333) - The area is on the far left of the first continuous section of the quarry, just beyond The Embankment.

Sheffield Area · Ladybower Area · Stanage · Burbage Valley · Millstone Area · Derwent Edges · Chatsworth Area · Southern Crags

Sheffield Area

Ladybower Area

Stanage

Burbage Valley

Millstone Area

Derwent Edges

Chatsworth Area

Southern Crags

Great Arete
- p.345

30m

20m

Green Death

Great North Road

In between the smooth sheet of the Embankment and the vertical aretes and corners of *Green Death* is a more broken section with the huge corner of *Great North Road*. This provides yet another of Millstone's classic ticks and one that gets a lot of ascents. Several of the other routes here are variations on the main corner, and just left again there is the amiable Diff of the *The Scoop*.
Approach (see map on page 333) - This is on the far left of the first continuous section of the quarry, just beyond the Embankment.

❶ Knightsbridge E2 5c
A fine thin crack which is one of Millstone's classic E2s with a crucial and fingery bulge near half-height. Most people start by scrambling up *Scoop Crack* to the mid-height ledge, though the steep and awkward lower corner crack is a good alternative and best done early in the year before the ferns take hold (**5b**).
FFA. Tom Proctor 1960s

❷ Scoop Crack . . . . VS 4b
A poor start leads to a better top pitch. Climb (or avoid) the grassy cracks in the broken arete to the big ledge and a stance. Take the blocky continuation in the left wall which eases with height, beware the loose finish. Mild at the grade.

❸ The Scoop. . . . . Diff
A worthwhile easy climb. The ramp trends right then steep rock is climbed left to the huge bivi-ledge and a stance. The juggy corner behind is followed all the way to the moor.

❹ Clock People . . . E6 6c
One the aid climbers missed; a hairline crack in the slab. Technical in the extreme but well protected where it matters.
FA. Ron Fawcett 1984

❺ Watling Street E3 5b
Start from the big ledge and climb the arete left of the central section of *Great North Road*. Mild but delicate and unprotected.
FAA. Len Millsom early 1960s

❻ Discovery . . . . HVS 5b
The cracked arete leads to a tiny ledge and the bold and easily avoidable crux up the blunt arete. *Scoop Crack* is a logical continuation.
FA. Nigel Berry 2010

❼ Detour E2 5c
Well-named; wandering but worthwhile! At least one stance will be needed along the way. Climb the steepening crack to the big ledge and belay. Traverse right to *GNR* and up this to just above the roof and a spectacular finish up the right arete.

❽ The Hunter House Road Toad E5 6b
The searing right-hand crack past a couple of pegs. Tough!
FA. Mark Pretty 1985

❾ Great North Road. . . . . . HVS 5a
The most popular route in the quarry, and amongst the best HVS routes in the Peak, up the magnificent long corner. It has a difficult central layback/bridging groove and tricky section to reach the final roof. It used to be split into three short pitches though one biggie is the norm nowadays.
FA. Peter Biven, Trevor Peck 1956. FFA. Joe Brown 1957

❿ By-Pass . . . . HVS 5a
Avoids the crux of *Great North Road*. Start up *GNR* but continue up the block-choked crack to the big ledge (**4b**). Traverse delicately rightwards into the corner and finish up *GNR*.
FA. John Loy 1963

⓫ Quality Street E5 6b
An eliminate based on the right arete of *GNR*! Struggle onto the hanging ramp, swing right and climb to the big ledge. Climb left into the short hanging groove then exit left - wild.
FA. Les Bonnington (as Blind Bat) 1968. FFA. Al Rouse, Phil Burke 1983

⓬ Deaf Dog . . . . HVS 5b
The flakes lead to the ledge. Seldom climbed.

⓭ Master Chef f7B
Tackle the fine scimitar shaped arete.

⓮ Technical Baiter. f5
The groove right of the curved arete. It has a very long descent for a boulder problem, unless you reverse it.

⓯ Technical Master f6B
The arete is a classic boulder problem and may be the shortest three star route in the Peak. Climbing it on the left-hand side is *f6C*. It has also been done one-handed!
FA. Keith Myhill late 1960s

The Embankment ▶

The Embankment

A superb sheet of rock, originally named after a similar but inferior feature in London. Once the place to learn to aid climb, it is now home of the finest set of finger-cracks in The Peak. If you don't like finger-jamming keep heading left.

Approach (see map on page 333) - The area is the unmistakable sheet of rock in the centre of the first continuous section of the quarry.

❶ Blind Bat. E4 5c
Bold climbing on the upper wall. A runner in *Embankment 1* is normal. Climb the wall leftwards on flat holds passing an ancient peg runner.
FA. Mick Fowler 1976. Despite the name the route covers little of the original aided Blind Bat which is actually taken by Quality Street - see previous page.

❷ Embankment 1. . . . . E2 5c
1) **VS 5a.** The crack and flake lead awkwardly past an ancient chunk of angle-iron (hands off) to the ledge. Often done on its own, though *Embankment 2* top pitch just to the right is worth a look as a way off the ledge.
2) **5c.** Climb the thin fingery crack to a steep exit.
FFA. John Allen 1975

❸ Elm Street. . . . . f7C+
The desperately thin peg scars give a fierce challenge which is usually done above a stack of mats.
FA. Adrian Berry 1994

❹ Who Wants The World . . E5 6a
The upper wall between the cracks is hard, serious and neglected.
FA. Gary Gibson 1981

Descent

14m

16m

Technical
Master - p.347

Great North Road

5 Embankment 2..... VS 4c

Worthwhile, though the second pitch is a bit of a let-down.
1) 4c. Climb the tough cracks, the left-hand one is tricky, the right-hand crack only gives painful finger-jamming at **E1 5c**.
2) 4b. Finish up the awkward groove to a loose exit.

6 Scritto's Republic .. E7 6c

A desperate vague seam between the proper cracks has both runners and holds in very short supply.
FA. Ron Fawcett 1982

7 Embankment 3....... E1 5b

1) 5b. An excellent finger-jamming pitch. Passing the tat (care, it is tied through an ancient peg/blob of rust) is the trickiest bit.
2) 5b. The thin crack in the upper wall, left of the groove, has hard moves (almost **5c**) low down.
FFA. Ed Drummond 1975

8 Time For Tea...... E3 5c

Low in the grade but a bit bold. Follow the crack to a poor rest below the blank upper section. Build a safety net then balance left to better holds. Either finish straight up or continue traversing to finish close to *Embankment 3* - both options are about the same grade and equally scary.
FA. Ed Drummond 1975

9 Tea for Two....... E4 6a

The direct finish to *Time for Tea* is bold, technical and poorly protected though at least there is a decent fall-out zone!
FA. Ian Riddington 1982

10 Time For Tea Original... E1 5b

From the poor rest below the blank upper section on *Time for Tea* traverse right to join and finish up *Embankment 4*. Only a couple of independent moves but still very worthwhile and probably better than *Embankment 4*.
FA. Ken Wilkinson 1974

11 Embankment 4........ E1 5b

The right-hand crack started from blocks has thin moves up the crack and a superb groove above to a shelving exit. Unlike the rest of the cracks here, this one isn't a toe and ankle wrecker!
FFA. Chris Addy 1975

12 Whitehall .... HVS 5b

The deep angle is straightforward (**4b**) to below the upper corner - belay. Above is good technical climbing when clean.
FFA. Keith Myhill 1969

13 Little Lotto Arete f5

The little arete past a lovely letter-box slot. Eliminate the letterbox at **f6A**, or climb it on its right-hand side at **f6C**.

14 Lotto E1 5c

Disjointed climbing though with some good moves. Easy ledges lead to an stance below a shallow groove (**4b**). Climb the groove with hard moves until forced round the arete. Step up then follow the big break back left to finish via the centre of the roof.
FA. John Loy early 1960s. FFA. Tom Proctor 1975

15 The Jasmine Corridor E6 6c

Climb the E1 crack until a wild and hard step left allows the slabby wall to be balanced up. Crux at the top, protected by all-too-short bolt studs hooked by wires.
FA. Tom Randall 2010

16 Lotto Direct....... E3 5c

A decent variation which avoids the right side of the arete by staying with the shallow groove - bold.

17 Seventies Style Wall ... f6B+

Thin crimps on the short wall.

Descent

24m

London Wall

Sheffield Area

Ladybower Area

Stanage

Burbage Valley

Millstone Area

Derwent Edges

Chatsworth Area

Southern Crags

1 Covent Garden . . . . 2★ ☐ **VS 4b**
Pleasant and mild at the grade, though the final arete is a bit on the airy side.
1) **4b**, 15m. A long groove leads via a couple of moves on its left arete to a stance in the corner on the right.
2) **4b**, 12m. Shuffle out left to gain the arete (a bit light on gear) and finish through the crusty bulges in a spectacular position.
FAA. Peter Biven, Trevor Peck 1956

2 Bond Street . . . . Top 50 ☐ **HVS 5a**
The near-perfect jamming crack has hard moves to enter and leave the prominent niche. It will swallow all the heavy metal protection you can afford (in both senses) to carry.

3 Monopoly . . . . . 2★ ☐ **E7 6b**
A blank wall with a combination of technical climbing and little in the way of protection. The upper section, linking good crimps by long reaches is the hardest and is VERY bold.
FA. Johnny Dawes 1983

4 Great Portland Street . . . Top 50 ☐ **HVS 5b**
A tough stopper mantelshelf guards access to the lovely hanging groove. This gives excellent and well-protected bridging.
FFA. Alan Clarke 1963

Afternoon | 8 min | Sheltered

26m
Section shared with Lotto - p.349
1
2
3
The Embankment

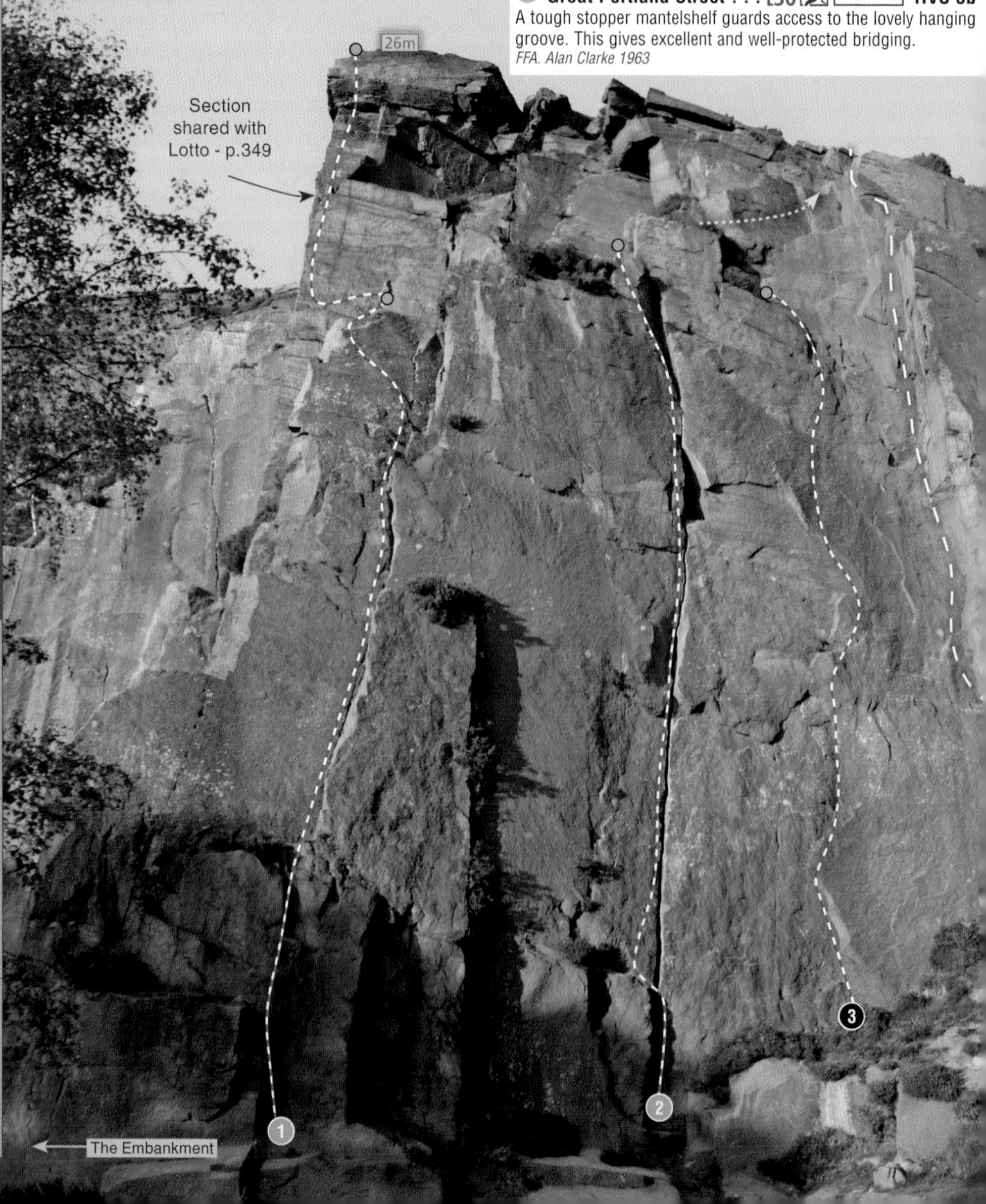

❺ White Wall ...... 🔲 E5 6b
The smooth wall left of the deep corner, linking ancient
peg-holes via hard moves. The crux is reaching and passing the
overlap, although the rest is no pushover.
FFA. Steve Bancroft 1976

❻ The Mall .... Top50 🔲 VS 4c
The sustained right-angled groove is quite hard at the grade,
though protection is excellent. Beware the dusty shelving top.
FAA. Pete Biven, Trevor Peck (at A3!) early 1950s. FFA. Joe Brown 1957

❼ London Wall .... Top50 🔲 E5 6a
One of the finest finger-cracks in the country sees many
attempts and many failures. The initial leaning fissure is as hard
as anything on the route (feels like 6b) although the leftwards
traverse is also taxing. Above this steady climbing leads to a
reasonable rest ledge before the breathtaking final crack where
many attempts flounder. An essential E5 tick.
Photo on page 332.
FAA. Trevor Peck 1956. FFA. John Allen 1975

❽ Lambeth Chimney .... 🔲 HS 4b
The shallow chimney on the right side of the wall leads to a
ledge. Step around the airy arete on the left to enter and finish
up a shallow groove. Can be green.

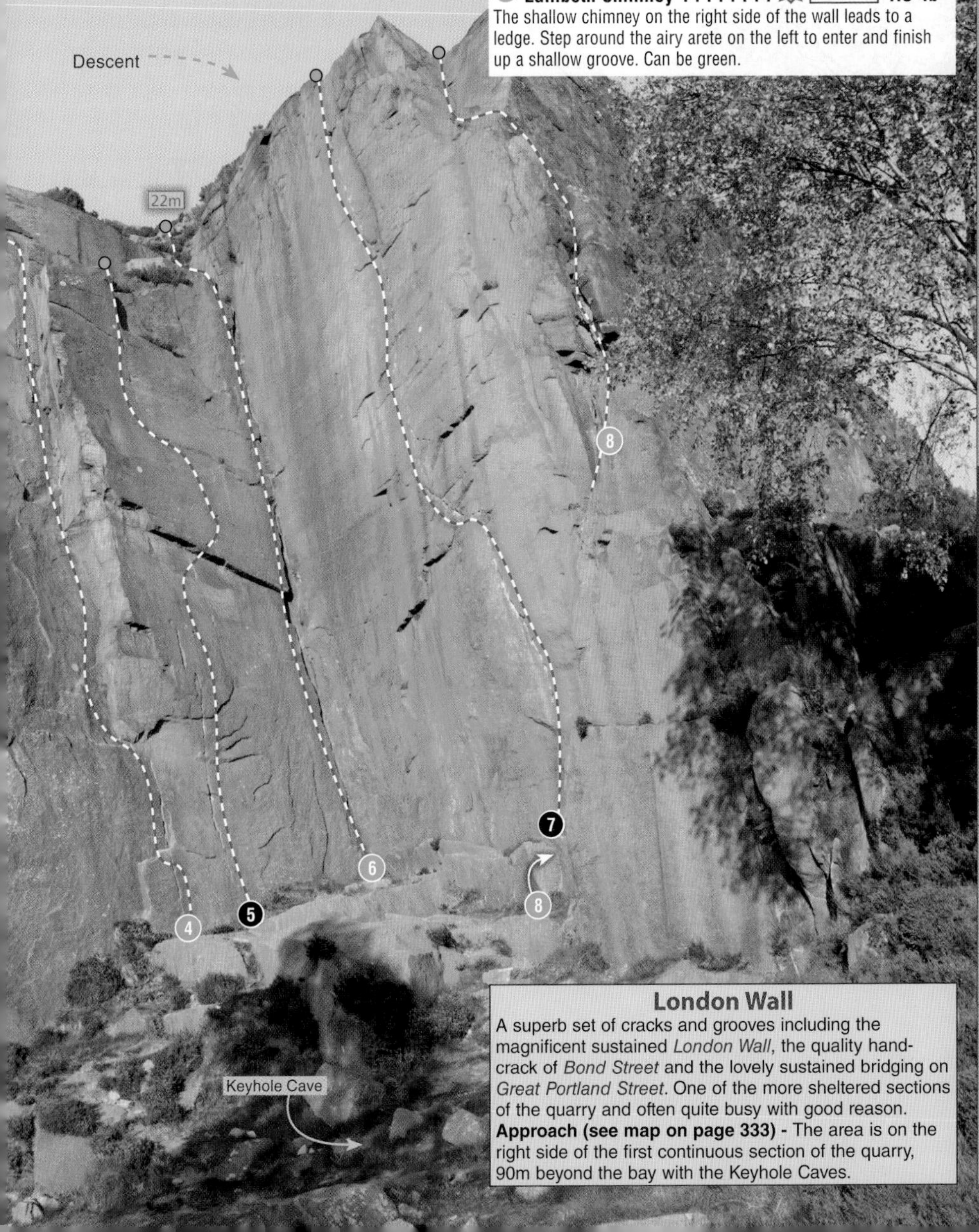

Descent

22m

Keyhole Cave

London Wall
A superb set of cracks and grooves including the
magnificent sustained *London Wall*, the quality hand-
crack of *Bond Street* and the lovely sustained bridging on
Great Portland Street. One of the more sheltered sections
of the quarry and often quite busy with good reason.
Approach (see map on page 333) - The area is on the
right side of the first continuous section of the quarry,
90m beyond the bay with the Keyhole Caves.

Keyhole Cave

A steep crack-riven wall with two wide red slots known for obvious reasons as the Keyhole Caves. The rock on the faces is good but that in the caves is sandy, unstable and horrid. *Regent Street* is one of the very best E2s in the Peak and it avoids the caves. *Coventry Street* and *Jermyn Street* are harder classics that do get involved with the red sandy stuff.

Fixed Belays - There are no fixed belays in the caves. If you just want to do any of the lower pitches you will need to fix a rope from the cliff-top beforehand. The only alternative is to finish up *Piccadilly Circus* at E2.

Approach (see map on page 333) - A track branches right from the main path to enter a wide bay.

Left of the Keyhole Wall is a long face of poor rock with a wide jagged crack in its right side. The routes here are mediocre.

❶ Petticoat Lane . . . . . ⛶ 📷 📋 ☐ **HVS 4c**
Follow the left-hand thin crack until it fades then move up and left to ledges. Trend right up the wall to finish with care.
FA. George Leaver 1956. Oddly one of the first routes in the quarry.

❷ Bow Street . . . . ⛶ 🎏 📋 ☐ **HVS 4c**
The right-hand thin crack is climbed to a narrow overlap. Pass this then move right into *Brixton Road*. Watch for snappy holds along the way.
FA. Frank Fitzgerald (A2) 1956. FFA. Alan McHardy 1967

❸ Brixton Road . . . . ⛶ 📋 ☐ **VD**
The best lower-grade route in the quarry - sadly it is not THAT good. Climb the wide crack to ledges then the groove and arete on the left to the unstable summit rubble-field. Helmets advised!

❹ Sky Walk . . . . ⛶ 📷 📋 ☐ **VS 4b**
A well-named trip traversing above the exposed lip of the Keyhole Cave. It is most easily reached via *Brixton Road* and protection is only adequate; watch for friable holds.
FA. John Loy early 1960s

❺ Adam Smith's Invisible Hand
. . . . ⛶ 🎏 ⚒ 📷 ☐ **E6 6b**
The fine left arete of the wall. Tat on the ancient rusty bolts and a peg round the arete are the only gear - bold. It is also possible to start round to the left at the same grade.
FA. Johnny Dawes 1984

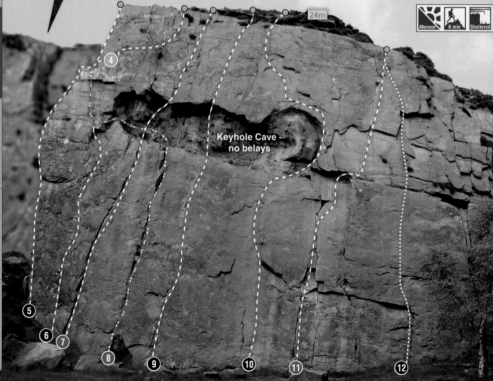

6 The Rack E5 6a
Follow the old bolt ladder on a series of sharp and rather snappy holds to the left edge of the cave. Side-runners protect.
FA. Loz Francombe 1982

7 Oxford Street E3 6b
The wide left-hand crack (a decent but stiff **HVS 5a** pitch) leads to the cave. A very hard move through the notch in the overhang (good gear but awkward to place) may allow you to access the easier upper wall.
FAA. Peter Biven 1956. FFA. Phil Burke 1969

8 Piccadilly Circus E2 5c
The middle finger-crack leads to the cave - worthwhile at solid **HVS 5b**. A tricky traverse left and technical wall gain a ledge on the arete. Trend rightwards more easily to finish.
FFA. Steve Bancroft 1976

9 Coventry Street E5 6b
A popular testpiece. Difficulties escalate to a hard final move - easier after a quick rest on the rope! The sandy roof above the cave gives a gripping struggle passing an ancient bong peg. The bottom section is often done on its own being hard but safe, though the belay spikes in the cave have now gone.
FA. Peter Biven 1956. FFA. Steve Bancroft, John Allen 1976

10 Jermyn Street E5 6a
A thin crack and shallow groove lead to the cave. Climb the right arete (small wires - tricky to place) then traverse the handrail out left (small cam), feet pedalling in the sand, to get established on the headwall with difficulty. Finish leftwards more easily.
FAA. Peter Biven, Trevor Peck 1956. FFA. Tom Proctor 1971

11 Regent Street E2 5c
Majestic! Climb steeply past the jammed block (technical crux?) then trend right to a shallow groove and ledges below the soaring final crack. This is best climbed quickly after placing high runners. A final short steep wall completes this gem. A harder direct start is possible at **E3 6a**, up the crack and groove to the right, and is worth a couple of stars.
FAA. Peter Biven, Trevor Peck 1956. FFA. Terry King 1968

12 Wall Street Crash . . . E5 6b
A good technical route with fingery moves on iron clumps. Now bolder due to the removal of the old aid bolts and their replacement with lower pegs. Finish up the steep ramp above.
FA. Johnny Dawes 1983

13 Shaftesbury Avenue . HVS 5b
The off-width crack at the right-hand side of the wall leads to a small overhang - big cams and big hams help. The wall above the overhang is much easier and the exit is loose.
FAA. Peter Biven, Trevor Peck 1956. FFA. Jim Campbell 1967

14 The Whore . . . . HVS 5b
Climb to the overhang and layback through it via a finger-crack to easier ground - awkward gear. Spoilt by a grotty exit.
FA. Jim Reading 1975

15 Gimcrack . . . . VS 4c
Good jamming leads up the wall left of the right-hand cave to a shallow right-facing groove. The exit from this requires care as a hugely unstable boulder-slope lurks above.
FA. Barry Ingle 1962

16 Happy Wanderer . . . . VS 5a
A tough crack leads to the cave then traverse left to escape.

17 Oriel . . . . VS 5a
The slanting jamming-crack has hard moves left to the cave. Step right and climb the slab to runners and an earth cornice.

20m

Sheffield Area
Ladybower Area
Stanage
Burbage Valley
Millstone Area
Derwent Edges
Chatsworth Area
Southern Crags

Hells Bells

A pleasant buttress with some mild offerings which are suitable for those who find the scale of the main quarry a bit intimidating - it is always popular.

Approach (see map on page 333) - This is the first piece of decent rock that you arrive at on the normal approach set to the right of the track.

① Bent Crack .... 🎯🎒📷 ☐ **HS 4c**
The kinked fissure tucked away just left of a shrubby groove.

② Butter-ess .... 🎯📷 ☐ **HVS 5b**
This is the prominent crack splitting the buttress on the left.

③ Crossways .... ☐ **HVD**
Amble across the ledges to the short awkward groove.

The next clutch of routes all finish on a clean ledge at 10m. There is an easy descent to the right, though the cliff top can be gained variously - the clean crack on the right is VD, and the arete on the right is HS 4b.

④ Flank Crack .... ☐ **VD**
The ferny groove on the left approached from the next route.

⑤ Chiming Cracks .... 🎯 ☐ **HS 4a**
On the left a pair of converging cracks and their continuation give pleasant and well-protected jamming.
FA. Alan Clarke c1960

⑥ Hells Bells .... 🎯📷 ☐ **HS 4b**
The left-hand groove is the best route here and a sample of what the rest of the quarry offers. Bridge and jam to the ledge.
FA. Alan Clarke 1963

⑦ Juniper .... 📷 ☐ **E1 5b**
The angular arete just right is bold and reachy. Side-runners lower the grade.

⑧ Midrift .... ☐ **VD**
The central groove is pleasantly mild. Another good introduction to the rock and the style of climbing at Millstone.

⑨ Giant's Steps .... ☐ **VD**
Yet another good starter; the groove up the giant steps.

⑩ Street Legal .... 🎯👤 ☐ **E2 5c**
Climb the smooth face on the right passing the Africa-shaped flake with difficulty.
FA. Paul Cropper 1978

⑪ Blood and Guts on Botty Street
.... 🎯👤📷 ☐ **E5 6b**
An extended boulder problem up the right-hand arete of the buttress is unprotected and precarious. Often done above mats.
FA. Allen Williams 1987

TICKLIST
Millstone Crackers
The quarrymen did us proud - welcome to the best set of cracks in the UK.

- [ ] The Mall, VS *(351)*
- [ ] Plexity, HVS *(337)*
- [ ] Bond Street, HVS *(350)*
- [ ] Dexterity E1, *(338)*
- [ ] Embankment 4, E1 *(349)*
- [ ] Regent Street, E2 *(353)*
- [ ] Knightsbridge, E2 *(347)*
- [ ] Time for Tea, E3 *(349)*
- [ ] Twikker, E3 *(342)*
- [ ] Saville Street, E3 *(337)*
- [ ] London Wall, E5 *(351)*

Dan Parkes finger-locking his way to glory on the upper crack of *Twikker* (E3 5c) - *page 342* - at Millstone.

Sheffield Area · Ladybower Area · Stanage · Burbage Valley · Millstone Area · Derwent Edges · Chatsworth Area · Southern Crags

	No star	⚑1	⚑2	⚑3
Mod to S	8	4	1	-
HS to HVS	7	16	1	3
E1 to E3	10	4	4	2
E4 and up	2	2	2	1

A hidden and sheltered quarry (named after the moor behind the old workings and called Laurencefield on some maps) has been visited by climbers for over sixty years. By the early 1970s climbing standards and protection had improved to the point that many of the early aid routes became excellent free climbs in a new route gold-rush not seen before or since.

Although playing second fiddle to nearby Millstone, Lawrencefield quarry remains very popular. With a good set of climbs, a selection of easier and immensely popular routes around Gingerbread Slab, and the hard classics on the steep smooth walls around the pool, there is something here for most tastes. The long right-hand side of the quarry used to be home to a reasonable selection of climbs but the vegetation continues to encroach and many are beyond recovery, apart from a small selection on the Red Wall.

Approach   Also see map on page 329

The quarry is situated near the Surprise View, on the opposite side of the road to Millstone Quarry. Park at the large Surprise View car park, cross the road and follow a narrow track towards the bend. Just before the bend follow a path down leftwards and through a gate. The quarry lies hidden from view but sandy paths lead rightwards down the slope past the end of the rocks into the main bay which is gradually filling with a sea of silver birch.

Conditions

The trees mean that the quarry is very well-sheltered and is ideal on cold or wild days. This fact is well known hence it does get crowded in such conditions. It can be midgy when humid and a real furnace on clear summer afternoons. Much of the rock gets very sandy in the summer and it doesn't dry very quickly after rain. Also in the summer the ants can be a pest, even if only in the casual way they wander up and down the blankest faces!

Side tabs: Sheffield Area · Ladybower Area · Stanage · Burbage Valley · Millstone Area · Derwent Edges · Chatsworth Area · Southern Crag

Map labels:
Millstone
Roadside Bay p.358
Surprise View
A6187
GPS 53.31721 -1.62312
Great Harry p.360
The Pool Wall p.362
Gingerbread Slab p.364
Stonemason's Buttress p.366
Red Wall p.367
About 100m
N

Sheffield Area

Ladybower Area

Stanage

Burbage Valley

Millstone Area

Derwent Edges

Chatsworth Area

Southern Crags

Chris Barr on the classic tester of *Boulevard* (E3 5c) - *page 362* - on the Pool Wall at Lawrencefield. Photo: Guy Van Greuning

Roadside Bay

Under the surprising bend, that gives the Surprise View its name, is a small quarried bay with a collection of short, steep cracks. The routes are not brilliant, but the bay is sheltered, close to the parking and quite often occupied by groups under instruction.

Approach (see map on page 356) - From the parking, cross the road and follow the narrow path towards the Surprise Bend. Just round this and past a rocky outcrop, hop over the wall and the crag is down and left.

Sheffield Area

Ladybower Area

Stanage

Burbage Valley

Millstone Area

Derwent Edges

Chatsworth Area

Southern Crags

1 Shallow Chimney . . VD
The rift round to the left of the arete gives tricky climbing which is awkward to protect and a bit loose.
FA. Eric Byne 1958. One of his first new routes.

2 Split Second Timing E1 5c
The technical wall just right is often a bit dirty.

3 Spec Arete E2 6a
The steep and reachy arete with a runner in the next route.
FA. Nicki Stokes 1976

4 Frustration E2 6a
This emigre from across the road is steep and tenuous. Its name stems from the difficulty of placing solid pegs back in the day.
FAA. Mike James 1956. FFA. John Allen 1976

5 Straight Crack . . . . VD
The sheaf of cracks eventually develop into a blocky groove.
FA. Eric Byne 1958

6 The Last Wet Wednesday . . . VS 4c
Climb the crack past a spike then make steep moves up the continuation to reach the easier grassy groove above.
FA. Dave Gregory 1989

7 Rocking Groove . . . . HVS 5b
The right-trending groove is sustained and a bit run-out.
FA. Fred Williams 1958

8 Redbits E2 5c
Steep, fingery work up the thin cracks splitting the smoothest part of the wall to a rest, then a tough finale.
FA. Pete Blackburn 1978

9 Slippery Wall . . . . HVS 5b
Curve right to the crack in the upper face and good jamming past a wobbly but safe block. The finish is tricky. It can be reached from the right by slightly easier climbing or direct at **5c**.

Evening | 4 min | Sheltered | Green

Another Last
Great Problem

10 Quantum Crack . . . . . . HVS 5b
The crack just left of the main angle has some useful slots and a short sharp crux just below good jamming.

11 Vaseline . . . . VD
Climb the steepening angle then escape right at the top. Cleaner than you might expect though awkward to protect.

12 Positively 4th Street . . . . VS 4c
The nail-scratched holds up the wall, then the blunt arete above.
FA. David Simmonite 1989

13 Grass Groove . . . . Diff
The left-trending crack/ramp is less grassy than it once was.

14 Proud Crack . . . . VD
Another left-trending crack leads to ledge then a Stygian cleft.

15 Brain Cells in Collision . . E3 5c
From the ledge and runners break right boldly and keep going.
FA. Paul Mitchell c1982

The wall to the right still remains unclimbed even though many notables have had a good look at it.

Sheffield Area
Ladybower Area
Stanage
Burbage Valley
Millstone Area
Derwent Edges
Chatsworth Area
Southern Crags

Descent

22m

The Pulpit

Great Harry

The walls and grooves to the left of the Pool have a fine set of middle grade routes that follow strong natural lines and are sheltered. *Three Tree Climb*, *Pulpit Groove* and *Great Harry* are thrilling outings. For something a little more taxing *Suspense* takes a trip above the water and getting on *Pool Wall* increases the likelihood of a ducking.
Approach (see map on page 356) - From the parking, cross the road and follow the narrow path towards the Surprise View. Go through a gate on the left then trend right to locate a path that descends round the left (looking in) extremity of the quarry.
Belays - There are stakes in place, and there is the odd boulder. Climbers have been asked to avoid belaying on the boundary fence.

TICKLIST
Lawrencefield Taster
The quarry is popular and has a good set of low to middle grade routes. Here is a sampler of the best.

☐ **Pulpit Groove, VD** *(361)*. Wandering but fun.

☐ **Three Tree Climb, HS** *(361)*. Excellent but treeless.

☐ **Great Harry, VS** *(361)*. Quite a butch pitch.

☐ **Excalibur, VS** *(362)*. A soaring line.

☐ **The Delectable Variation, VS** *(367)*. Looks unlikely.

Lots of sun | 5 min | Sheltered

Sheffield Area
Ladybower Area
Stanage
Burbage Valley
Millstone Area
Derwent Edges
Chatsworth Area
Southern Crags

❶ **Gregory's Slab**. . . . . ☐ **S 4a**
The short groove past a useful jutting flake. Often a bit grubby.
FA. Wilf White 1955

❷ **Summer Climb** . . . . ☐ **HS 4b**
The slabby groove has a short layback and a fun mantel.
FA. Albert Shutt 1956

❸ **Three Tree Climb**. . . . . ☐ **HS 4b**
A popular and pleasant line up the left arete of the quarry. A
strenuous juggy start and awkward groove lead to a ledge. A
grope around to the right should locate a good flake; a quick
layback reaches a pine stump on a ledge (popular belay spot)
then finish more easily out leftwards.
*FA. Albert Shutt 1952. After some over-exuberant pruning in about 2010
there is less than half a tree left now!*

❹ **Great Peter**. . . . . ☐ **E1 5b**
The thin seam splitting the wall is reached via a steep fingery
crack (5c - but easily avoided) and gives pleasantly delicate
moves. Protection is reasonable with enough small wires. Belay
by the tree stump and finish off upwards more easily.
FA. Peter Biven 1956. FFA. Clive Jones 1976

❺ **Pulpit Groove** . . . . ☐ **VD 4a**
An interesting and exposed expedition in three pitches. Climb
the short slippery crack (crux) to gain the base of the ramp and
follow this to a sitting stance on the Pulpit. Stride across the
gap and follow the exposed ramp to a large ledge and tree belay.
Finish out to the right for some rather nice exposure.
FA. Albert Shutt 1952

❻ **Great Harry** . . . . ☐ **VS 4c**
The steep angular corner is jammed and bridged to a stance
on the Pulpit. Continue up the wide and awkward corner crack
above to a tricky but well-protected exit up a short blank groove.
FA. Harry Hartley 1953

❼ **Suspense** . . . . ☐ **E2 5c**
Fine climbing with good rests and great positions. Climb the
right wall of the open corner on edges to the arete as for *Scoop
Connection*. Step around right to a small ledge and climb the
thin fingery cracks with difficulty to a final long reach.
FAA. Peter Biven 1956. FFA. John Allen 1975

❽ **Scoop Connection** . . . . . ☐ **E2 5b**
Mild but scary! Climb the slabby wall rightwards to an indifferent
set of small runners on the arete, then teeter left away from
these along the shelf to join and finish up *Pulpit Groove*.

❾ **Pool Wall** . . . . ☐ **E5 6b**
At low water, the direct start to *Suspense* is technical and bold.
Small wires and cams protect sparingly - remember to leave
room in the slots for your fingers. Above the crux, a bold sprint
leads to the crux of the regular route.
FA. Alan Clarke 1958. FFA. Roger Greatrick early 1980s

*The rest of the routes here are accessed from the far right-hand
side of the Pool via a quick mantel and ramble across the ledge.*

❿ **Cascara Crack** . . . . ☐ **HS 4b**
The tough and dirty wide crack behind where the mighty
sycamore once grew gives awkward moves to ledges. The steep
shallow groove just right gives a nice finish.
FA. Richard Brown 1953

⓫ **Lawrencefield Ordinary** . . . . . . ☐ **VD**
A wandering round trip that visits some interesting spots. From
the left end of the ledge behind the Pool, climb a groove then
head left up ledges and grooves towards the tree stance on
Pulpit Groove. Finish out right for maximum exposure.
FA. Albert Shutt 1952

⓬ **Austin's Variation** . . . . . ☐ **VS 4c**
The flake and corner above the start of the *Ordinary* (possible
belay below it) give a short and strenuous pitch.
FA. Allan Austin 1956

⓭ **S.A.E.** . . . . ☐ **HVS 5b**
Head up the steep corner that forms the left edge of the main wall.
*FFA. Don Morrison, Les Gillot, Alan Clarke 1964. Don had actually made the
first ascent eight years earlier with a single peg for aid.*

20m

*High Plains
Drifter - p.362*

High Plains Drifter - p.362

Sheffield Area
Ladybower Area
Stanage
Burbage Valley
Millstone Area
Derwent Edges
Chatsworth Area
Southern Crags

Sheffield Area

Ladybower Area

Stanage

Burbage Valley

Millstone Area

Derwent Edges

Chatsworth Area

Southern Crags

The Pool Wall

The most imposing face in the quarry is the tall wall behind the pool. Once an aid practice ground, it now has a fine collection of hard free routes. Several climbers have ended up in the weak mutton stew in the pool along with the dead sheep - not a pleasant thought; a belay on the starting ledge is a sensible idea.

Approach (see map on page 356) - The ledge is reached from the right over blocks, though at high tide this can be tricky.

①　Great Wall Traverse . . . .　　　　　　　HS 4a
The shelving ledges crossing the face give a bold trip to an escape up *Jughandle*. Not one for busy weekends or nervous types.
FA. Richard Brown 1953

②　High Plains Drifter . .　　　　　　　　　E4 6a
Wanders up the left-hand side of the wall. Climb a groove to steeper rock then pull right and back left (ancient peg) making long reaches to a narrow ledge on the left. Finish out right, steeply but on better holds.
FA. Jim Reading 1977

③　Boulevard . . . .　　　　　　　　E3 5c
The left-hand continuous crack system is tough. Start as for *H.P.D.* but move right to the crack. Protection is good and the holds keep appearing but the whole thing is quite hard work.
Photo on page 357.
FA. Peter Biven 1956. FFA. Ed Drummond 1975

④　Von Ryan's Express .　　　　　　　　　E6 6b
The gap had to be filled but the result never gets done. Start direct (or up *Billy Whizz*), arrange side-runners then gain a small ledge. Leave this and climb the wall left of *Billy Whizz* to finish.
FA. Tony Ryan 1985

⑤　Billy Whizz . . . .　Top 50　　　　　　　E2 5c
The central line on the wall is often well-chalked and high in the grade; short climbers with fat fingers may want to claim an E3. Climb to the base of the steeper rock (wires to the right) and sprint up a flake to a deep slot. Step left and climb the tough thin crack to a triangular hole which takes a big nut. A final couple of long reaches/powerful pulls gain the top.
Photo on page 22.
FA. Geoff Birtles 1975

⑥　High Street . . . .　　　　　　　　E4 6a
Amble up the slab then attack the right-hand crack system via a taxing start to a breather. Step right and follow the thin continuation strenuously though on good finger-locks. A start up the slab to the right is the bold **High Times, E5 6a**.
FA. Peter Biven 1956. FFA. Jim Reading 1975

⑦　Holy Grail . . . .　　　　　　　E4 5c
Neglected. Start up *Excalibur* and step left at the steepening and climb the blocky cracks. These may need cleaning beforehand.
FA. Jim Reading 1977

⑧　Excalibur . . . .　　　　　　　VS 4c
The long groove above the right side of the pool 'rising from the lake', can be greasy after damp weather. The start is probably the crux though the layback moves on the upper section feel tough; beware the final blocky corner - it is getting shorter!
FA. Peter Biven 1955

⑨　J.J.2 . . . .　　　　　E1 5b
The short-lived and dirty crack right of the layback of *Excalibur*.
FA. Nicky Stokes 1972. The JJ = Jealous Jelly, a dig at a chubby brother.

⑩　Jughandle/Pimpernel . . . .　　　　S 4a
Wander up the grassy giant's steps right of *Excalibur* then move out right to a sandy ledge and possible stance. The best finish is the short groove on the left but escape right is the easy option.
FA. Albert Shutt 1953

11 Louisette . . . . S 4a
Another overgrown one - the cracked arete would benefit from a bit of traffic. Originally the route was further right on the slab.
FA. Albert Shutt 1952

Access - tricky when the tide is in

Gingerbread Slab

Beyond the pool is the attractive and popular sheet of rock of Gingerbread Slab. This is good spot for a first crack at leading so it is often a bit crowded.

Approach (see map on page 356) - This is the obvious slab to the right of the pool

Descent - From the top of the slab, an awkward scramble leads to the cliff top, then head leftwards to join the approach path. It is possible to abseil from the decaying tree stumps on the ledge but this is not ideal. Best use nuts/cams and get the last man to walk round or use the more substantial tree above *Nova*.

❶ Once Pegged Wall . . . . . ☼ 🪝 ▢ **VS 5a**
The battered thin cracks in the left wall of the groove, moving onto the left arete to gain the top. Direct is a half-a-grade harder.
FAA. Don Morrison 1955

❷ Morning Glory . . . . 🪝 ▢ **E2 5c**
The line of old peg holes up the centre of the wall. A bit artificial, though less so than when pegs were used!
FA. Dominic Stainforth 1983

❸ Limpopo Groove . . . . ☼ ▢ **VS 4b**
The angular corner above the grey, green, greasy, waters has good gear, a tricky central section and a steep finale.
FA. Dave Gregory 1955. One of Dave's first new routes. In 2014 he climbed it once again, on his 80th birthday, with his son and granddaughter.

❹ Gingerbread . . . . ☼ ▢ **VS 4b**
The left arete of the slab has decent runners at half-height; so don't fall off the last moves!
FA. Albert Shutt 1952

❺ Everyman and His Dog . . . . . 🗺 ▢ **E1 5b**
An eliminate up the slab just right. Low in the grade but bold.

❻ Meringue . . . . ☼ 🗺 ▢ **HVS 5a**
The thin crack is delicate above half-height. The gear that is supposed to protect the final crucial moves is pretty poor.
FA. Albert Shutt 1953. FFA. John Fearon 1955

7 Eclair E1 5b
A tasty thin slab with tricky moves and minimal gear.

8 Vanilla Slice E1 5c
More thin slab climbing but this time a touch harder, although at least it has some (tiny) runners.

To the right are a trio of cracks that make good first leads. Abseil off (some of the stumps are not too solid) or scramble with care to the cliff top and descend well left, past the pool.

9 Snail Crack . . . . VD
The first continuous crack leads up steps to steeper moves and ledges on the left. Meander up easier rock to finish.
FA. Albert Shutt 1953

10 Nailsbane . . . . VD
This crack system leans to the left and is followed until it is possible to exit left as for the previous climb.
FA. Albert Shutt 1952

11 Bole Hill . . . . VD
A bit of a filler-in but it adds another easy pitch to the collection.
FA. Simon Jaques 1989

12 Chilly Days and Purple Acorns E1 5b
A fine dramatic finish to the previous route, up the headwall.
FA. Ian Loombe 1996

13 Tyrone . . . . VS 4c
Climb the crack to its end then the steep wall on good, spaced holds. Finish up the curving crack or easier, head right. Sandy.

14 Nova . . . . HS 4b
Climb either crack in the right-hand side of the slab (the right-hand one is easier) to a short jamming crack; up this to a tricky move onto a ledge and an awkward finish on flat holds.
FA. Don Morrison 1956

12m
A
12
9
10
11
13
14
Stonemason's Buttress - 70m

Sheffield Area
Ladybower Area
Stanage
Burbage Valley
Millstone Area
Derwent Edges
Chatsworth Area
Southern Crags

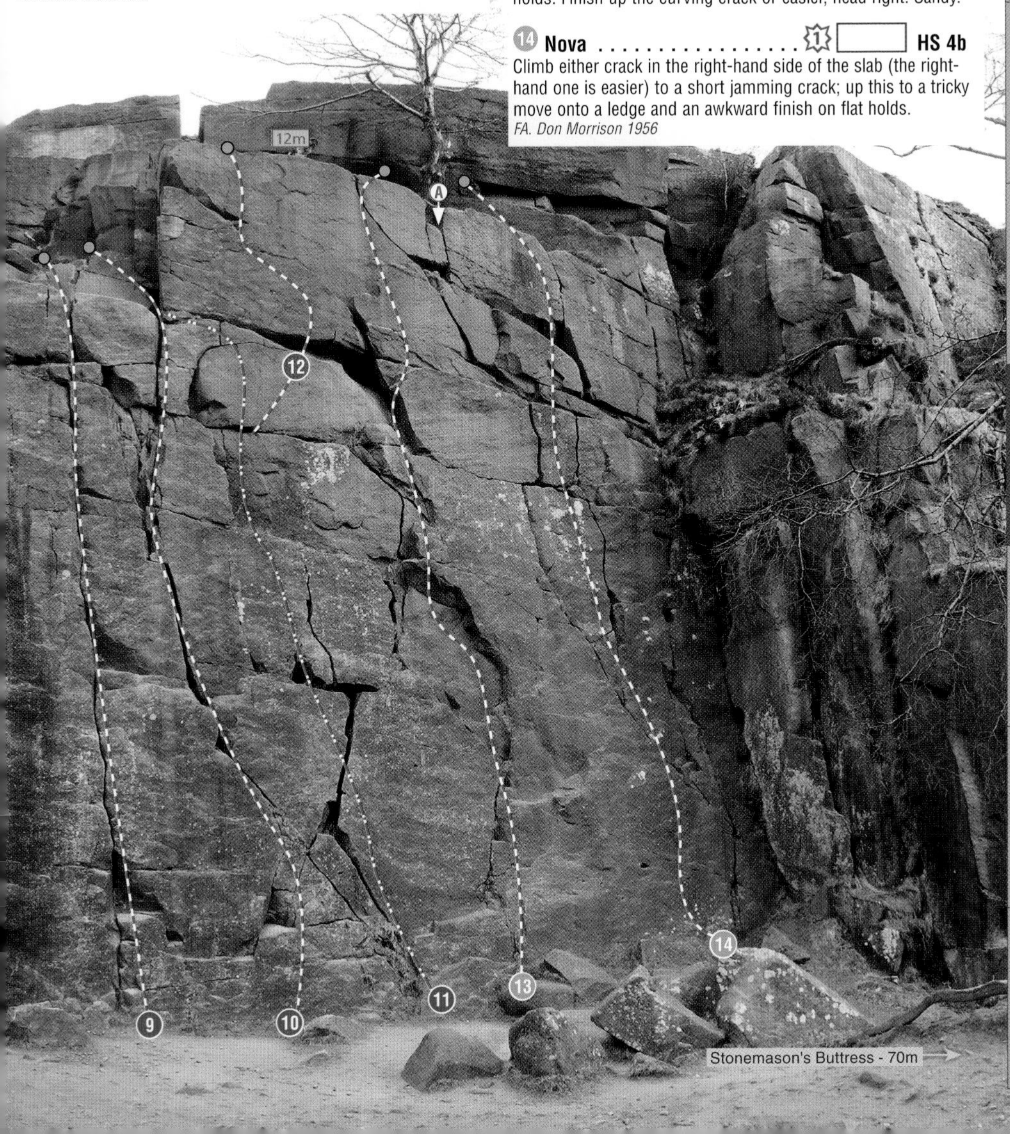

20m

6

5

4

Red Wall - 50m →

1

2

3

Stonemason's Buttress

The quarry continues rightwards from Gingerbread Slab but the quality deteriorates; there have been rockfalls and the vegetation has reclaimed much of the rock. Rising above a rocky pit with an occasional pool is a decent wall, though all the routes here could do with some traffic.
Approach (see map on page 356) - Continue through the trees for a couple of minutes to a tall buttress rising above a pit.

1 Stonemason's Climb . . . . . . VS 4b
The lower arete leads to the sculpted grooves above.
FA. Peter Rickus, Reg Pillinger 1953

2 Going for the One E2 5b
The wall left requires a leap to a single hold.
FA. Phil Baker, Adey Hubbard 1981

3 Blacksmith's Climb . . . . . . VS 4b
The main corner and continuation crack are worth a look.
FA. Reg Pillinger, Albert Shutt, Alan Clarke (2 pegs) 1956

4 Tuesday's Child . . . . VS 4b
Cracks to start and finish are linked by an arete and a couple of expansive bivi-type ledges.
FA. John Loy 1964

5 Vector . . . . HS 4b
A groove and crack lead to a ledge and short corner finish.
FA. Dave Gregory, Albert Shutt, Tom Collins 1955

6 Sinister Crack . . . . VS 4b
The crack high on the right approached from *Vector*.
FA. John Loy 1964

7 Rattus Norvegicus . . . . . [icons] **E5 6b**
Desperate climbing up the left side of Red Wall. Climb the steep wall rightwards (crux) then the hairline crack splitting the narrow roof and the upper face. Hard, poorly protected and never done.
FA. Gary Gibson 1981

8 Delectable Direct . . . . . . [icons] **E1 5c**
The thin crack in the centre of the wall gives excellent and well-protected climbing. It can be dirty after rain.
FA. Peter Biven 1956. FFA. Don Morrison 1964

9 Red Wall . . . . [icons] **VS 4c**
A worthwhile climb. Climb the lower wall rightwards and a short corner to a sandy ledge and possible belay. Finish up the corner groove on the right.
FA. Don Morrison 1956

10 Red Wall Variations . . . . . . [icons] **E1 5b**
The wall above the ledge by a desperate mantel or the thin crack just left offer much harder ways to reach the top.

11 The Delectable Variation [icons] **VS 4c**
Altogether a better way up the wall. Climb *Red Wall* to the sandy ledge/stance. Traverse the delicate wall on the left all the way to the arete, on a continuously surprising set of holds, for a superbly exposed finale.
FA. Don Morrison 1956

Red Wall
Continuing rightwards one section is well-worth a visit; a wall rising above a band of sandy red rock and with an arrow-straight corner-crack to its right. The rock on this wall is often sandy, especially after rain.
Approach (see map on page 356) - Continuing through the trees, Red Wall is opposite the point where the path heads up the slope away from the cliff.

12 Cordite Crack . . . . . [icons] **VS 4b**
The wide and intimidating layback crack is approached over ledges and best attacked with your bold head on, just blast it up. A couple of cam 'big guns' is a good idea, but stopping to place them can be problematic.
FA. Peter Biven 1955

13 Skyline . . . . [icons] **E3 5b**
The odd, blocky crack right on the arete
FFA. Daniel Lee 1981

14 Block Wall . . . . [icons] **E4 6b**
Attack the thin seam splitting the front face of the block.
FFA. Daniel Lee 1981

	No star	💠	💠💠	💠💠💠
Mod to S	4	1	-	-
HS to HVS	7	9	2	2
E1 to E3	1	3	-	-
E4 and up	-	2	-	1

A small sheltered quarry that has been popular for years because of its accessibility. If you arrive and there are more than a couple of outdoor centre/school minibuses parked in the gateway it is probably worth looking elsewhere for your sport, though it has to be said *Zapple* is often free. The quarry and nearby edge (not described here but worth a look if you are interested in unexplored jungle) are named after the millstones that used to be quarried here; an old name for them was querns and the corruption 'yarn'-cliffe (and also 'Wharn'-cliffe) indicates a location of this ancient industry.

Approach   Also see map on page 329

On the southern (uphill) side of the road that runs between Fox House and Grindleford is a large gated entrance, with parking for up to half a dozen carefully placed vehicles.
Note: avoid turning in the vicinity of the gate, the road is travelled by fast traffic. The nearest rock is only seconds away, just head through the gap right of the gate. The other good sector is up the track, on the right past the Council Tip. It is much safer to go down the hill and turn in the road that runs down to Grindleford station, only two minutes away.

Conditions

The quarry is very sheltered, partly because of its recessed position and partly because of the tree cover. It makes a good venue on cold windy days but can be unpleasantly midgy when the weather is humid. In high summer the large number of biting ants can be a bit off-putting. It is also almost always extremely sandy, especially after rain.

Ben Stainfield climbing *Latecomer* (HS 4b) while Sam James-Louwerse nears the top of *Ant's Crack* (S 4a) - *page 370* - in the first bay at Yarncliffe Quarry. Photo: Alan James

page 370

Sheffield Area

Ladybower Area

Stanage

Burbage Valley

Millstone Area

Derwent Edges

Chatsworth Area

Southern Crags

Erosion

When the quarry was first developed the initial bays had a good collection of climbs that largely used the recently exposed sharp-edged flakes for holds. Sadly the battering (through abseiling and repeated top-roping in unsuitable footwear) has led to the premature aging of most of these climbs, an indication of how rapidly good routes can be ruined by overuse. An added problem is that cliff-top erosion means that after rain the routes can be very sandy; polished holds and ball-bearing sand grains are not a good combination – care is required especially on the poorly protected faces. An attempt has been made to stabilise the cliff top, please keep off the netting that is there to let vegetation get established.

Ant's Slab

Entering the quarry, Ant's Slab is the first section you come to. This is the most popular part of the quarry and groups are common here, especially during the week. **Approach (see map on page 368)** - Go through the gate and head left.

Descent - For the routes on the main slabs please belay on the top and walk down the path leftwards to help preserve the crag-top edge.

❶ Ant's Arete . . . . **VS 4b**
The stepped left-hand arete of the quarry is very pleasant, and, although mild, is unprotected until above the crux.
FA. Nat Allen 1950

❷ Aphid's Wall **E1 5a**
Slabby wall climbing to the right of the arete. Poorly protected and the small rounded holds are often a bit sandy.
FA. Dave Gregory 1972

❸ Latecomer . . . . **HS 4b**
The long, thin crack is reached from the right and climbed passing a couple of angular niches. Finish direct or up right (a bit blocky). It can be started direct; a nice 5a problem.
Photo on page 369.
FA. Don Morrison 1964

❹ Soldier Ant **E3 5b**
Climb the narrow wall between the two cracks - without side-runners. Sketchy, slippery and unprotected! With easily placed side-runners it becomes a more enjoyable E1.
FA. Malcolm Salter 1978

❺ Ant's Crack . . . . **S 4a**
The wide crack in the centre of the slab is a good introduction to jamming. Usually a bit sandy and anty. *Photo on page 369.*
FA. Nat Allen 1950

❻ Ant's Wall . . . . **HS 4a**
Climb the steep slab and thin crack. Good holds and runners. Generally regarded as the best route on the slab.
FA. Dave Gregory 1972

❼ Formica Slab . . . . **HVS 4c**
More steep slab climbing to the left of the parallel cracks. Lacking in protection, just for a change.
FA. Dave Gregory 1972

❽ Angular Climb . . . . **HVD**
The parallel cracks in the right-hand side of the slab, starting up the right-hand one then stepping left. Originally it started up the thin left-hand crack at S 4a.

❾ Centipede . . . . **HVD**
The right-hand crack in its entirety, often a bit overgrown.

❿ Hidden Crack . . . . **VS 5a**
The thin diagonal crack in the left-hand side-wall runs out to the arete. Step back left along a ledge to find the once hidden crack and a steeper finish. Or finish up *Cardinal's Arete* at HS 4b.
FA. Dave Gregory 1971

⓫ Cardinal's Arete . . . . **VS 4c**
This undercut arete has a steep powerful start which sees many floundering. It can be bypassed on the left at **VS 4b**. The delicate finale can be avoided on the right.
FA. Don Chapman 1951

Cardinal's Slab

The tall fin of *Cardinal's Arete* and another clean, cracked slab of *Cardinal's Slab,* are just beyond the first area. **Approach (see map on page 368) -** Go through the gate and head left.

12 **Outdoor Centre Route** . . . . . . ▢ **VD**
The broken cracks are popular despite being loose and dirty!

13 **Cardinal's Slab** . . . . ▢ **VS 5a**
A long, thin crack up the left-hand edge of the slab, gives a pleasant pitch. Small wires are needed for protection.
FA. Dave Gregory 1972

14 **Hoey's Innominate** . . . . ▢ **HVS 5a**
A rather sketchy slab. Often green and has the odd creaky hold.
FA. Graham Hoey 1974. Claimed later as Threatened by Gary Gibson.

15 **Cardinal's Crack** . . . ▢ **VS 4b**
A wide crack in the slab leads to a big tree and loose finish. Quality finger-jamming or use the small holds on either side.
FA. Don Chapman 1950

16 **Chalked Up** . . . . ▢ **E1 5a**
A shallow groove and hairline crack in the centre of the next slab are easiest, as might be expected, when chalked up.
FA. Giles Barker 1978

17 **Griffin's Wall** . . . . ▢ **HS 4b**
The right-hand side of the slab. Green and rarely climbed.
FA. J.Willbourne 1952

To the right is a vertical arete with a series of steps right again.

18 **Sulu** . . . . ▢ **VS 5a**
The thin crack just left of the arete is steep as far as a good ledge. Continue on the left until forced right to finish. Nice.
FA. J.R.Barker 1971

19 **Rhythm of Cruelty** . . . . . ▢ **E4 5c**
Bold and precarious climbing up the right-hand side of the steep arete, as far as the ledge. Finish more easily.
FA. Phil Wilson 1979

20 **Capital Cracks** . . . . ▢ **VS 4c**
A crack 2m right of the arete leads to a ledge with difficulty. Step right and follow the continuation crack to the top.
FA. Dave Gregory 1971

21 **Pedestal Arete** . . . . ▢ **HS 4b**
Pleasant and with some good positions. Follow a series of giant steps out left to the arete. Finish as for *Sulu.*

Sheffield Area
Ladybower Area
Stanage
Burbage Valley
Millstone Area
Derwent Edges
Chatsworth Area
Southern Crags

Approach (see map on page 368) -

Zapple Area

Beyond the initial bays the routes are spread out, many are green and overgrown although there is the odd gem hidden amongst the shrubbery.
Approach (see map on page 368) - Go through the gate and head right up the track.
Descent - Abseil from one of the large trees above the wall is the easiest way off.

The next routes are on the vegetated wall right of Cardinal's Slab.

❶ Inverted Jigsaw . . . . 🧗 [   ] **E1 5b**
Well named! The cracks and creaky flakes require care.
FA. J.Barker 1971

❷ S.T.P. . . . . [   ] **VS 5a**
Follow the crack just left of the arete to a tree belay. The start is tricky. If you find it clean, get it done!
FA. W.Phillips 1971

Further right is the striking sharp-edged arete.

❸ Crème de la Crème . 🌀🧗🤙 [   ] **E6 6b**
The magnificent and unmistakable central arete of the quarry still sees few ascents. The boulder problem start on the left (*f7A+*) needs a lot of padding to be made safe. The upper section is a bit easier and needs small gear.
FA. Ron Fawcett 1977

❹ THEM! . . . . 🌀🧗🤚 [   ] **f7C+**
The right-hand side of the arete as far as the ledge. Using the old bolt head makes it more like *f7C* but arguably more fun!

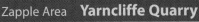

The last section has a steep wall split by a superb crack.

5 Fall Pipe . . . . **VS 4c**
The wall is split on the left by a long crack which gives good safe jamming and bridging when it is dry. Sadly it is often a bit green and greasy.
FA. Ted Howard 1964

6 Zapple Left-hand . . . . . . **HVS 5a**
The right-trending crack joins *Zapple* above its crux lower section giving easier access to the fine climbing above.

7 Zapple . . . . **HVS 5b**
The superb finger- and hand-crack that splits the centre of the wall is an essential Peak tick! The knuckle-cracking start is well protected and leads to easier but excellent climbing above.
FA. Pete Brown 1971

8 Trised Crack . . . . **VS 4c**
The flaky crack to the right gives slippery laybacking and is in need of a little TLC before it vanishes for ever!
FA. Don Cowan 1951

9 Stormfactor . . . . **HVS 5b**
Break left from near the top of *Trised Crack*. Another sadly neglected pitch.

10 Flaky Climb . . . . **VD**
Flaky in more ways than one! The exit is agricultural.
FA. Don Chapman 1952

11 The Spur . . . . **VS 4b**
The thinner crack to the right also has some botanical moments.

Sheffield Area | Ladybower Area | Stanage | Burbage Valley | Millstone Area | Derwent Edges | Chatsworth Area | Southern Crags

Tanya Meredith picks her way up the lonely wall climb of *Linden* (E6 6b) - *page 436* - on The Eliminate's Wall at Curbar. Although the easiest line on this section of the wall it is still a sustained, bold and technical outing. Photo: Mike Hutton

The Derwent Edges

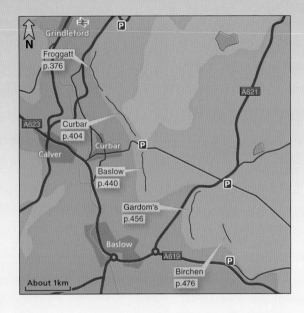

N

Grindleford

Froggatt
p.376

A621

A623

Curbar
p.404

Curbar

Calver

Baslow
p.440

Gardom's
p.456

Baslow

A619

About 1km

Birchen
p.476

Sheffield Area

Ladybower Area

Stanage

Burbage Valley

Millstone Area

Derwent Edges

Chatsworth Area

Southern Crags

	No star	⚝	⚝⚝	⚝⚝⚝
Mod to S	9	11	3	1
HS to HVS	7	27	7	8
E1 to E3	11	19	9	4
E4 and up	7	35	13	8

Froggatt is the second most popular of the Eastern Edges with good reason; the cliff is relatively low lying, escapes the worst of the weather, faces the afternoon sun, and has many neat slabby routes. There is high a concentration of quality here, in fact almost every route on the cliff is worthy of attention. Much of the cliff was quarried; abandoned millstones still lie where they were left when the industry collapsed. Odd that such great routes as *Green Gut*, *Brown's Eliminate* and the peerless *Great Slab* are as man-made the classics of Millstone. Although Froggatt is renowned for its superb slabs, it has a good collection of crack climbs too.

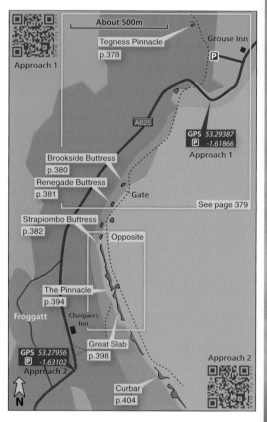

Approach   Also see map on page 375

There are two usual approaches:

1) From parking by the bend on the B6045 a short distance below the Grouse Inn. If this is full there is a National Trust car park a little way back up the road on the downhill side. Follow the hill-crest footpath to a stream and gate then onto the cliff, 15 to 20 minutes from the car. The first section of the main edge is 100m before the prominent bulk of Froggatt Pinnacle which protrudes above the line of the cliff.

2) From a small lay-by (up to 6 vehicles) on the bend below the Chequers Inn, walk back up the road past an old horse trough, then turn right and follow a steepening track straight up the hill to arrive, slightly sweaty, in front of *Downhill Racer*.

Conditions

Froggatt is low enough to escape the worst of the weather but high enough not to be bothered by the encroaching greenery that affects many gritstone cliffs. It is climbable all year if the weather is kind. A westerly aspect and the low angle of much of the cliff means that the afternoon winter sun warms the rock and makes it well worth a visit on clear winter days. On the odd occasion when an inversion fills the Derwent Valley with cloud, climbing here can be especially magical.

About 20m

N

Strapiombo Buttress
p.382

Sunset Slab
p.384

Hawk's Nest Crack
p.386

Terrace Crack
p.388

Tody's Wall
p.390

Pinnacle Boulders
Peak Bouldering

Three Pebble Slab
p.392

Turd Burgler Block
p.393

The Pinnacle
p.394

Downhill Racer
p.396

Great Slab
p.398

Brown's Eliminate
p.400

Chequers Buttress
p.402

Lower approach path

Sheffield Area

Ladybower Area

Stanage

Burbage Valley

Millstone Area

Derwent Edges

Chatsworth Area

Southern Crags

Duncan Campbell spending a moment to sort his feet out before
making the final committing moves on *Narcissus* (E6/*f7A*) - *page
394* - on the Pinnacle at Froggatt. Photo: Rob Greenwood

Fixed sling to aid descent

10m

Approach and descent

10m

Tegness Pinnacle

This pleasant pinnacle is tucked away in a small quarry, only minutes from the Froggatt parking. The *Original Route* is the most popular climb though they are all worth doing. Moonlight ascents, headstands and all the usual malarky have been practised here! There are another 20 or so short and poor routes in the quarry.

Approach - From the Grouse/Froggatt parking, head right through the wood and follow the track overlooking the valley until the quarry with its Pinnacle appears below. The easiest descent is just beyond the quarry.

❶ The Original Route . . . . 　　　 **Diff**
The arete facing the car park is the easiest way up (and down) the pinnacle. Belaying on the tiny summit is tricky and a thread in the summit blocks may be used to protect the escape.
FA. J.W.Puttrell, E.A.Baker late 1800s

❷ Rock the Casabah . . . . . 　　　 **E1 5b**
Climb the blunt cracked arete in the north-facing wall.
FA. S.Purdy 1988

❸ Thin Crack . . . . 　　　 **HVS 5b**
The thin crack is reached by a mantelshelf, then it and the arete are climbed in tandem. Can be green.
FA. Len Millsom 1962

❹ Silver Spoon . . . . 　　　 **E2 5c**
The narrow valley face is climbed mainly via the left arete, though the occasional 'lifting-a-fridge' move helps.
FA. Mick Fowler 1976

❺ Barrage . . . . 　　　 **E2 5c**
A technical and unprotected arete climbed on its right side.
FA. Mick Fowler 1976

❻ Pisa Cake . . . . 　　　 **E1 5b**
An eliminate squeezed up the wall just right of the arete starting via the wider of a pair of cracks.

❼ Pisa . . . . 　　　 **HVS 5a**
The right-hand crack leads to ledges, then trend left on good holds to the summit. Avoid the arete for the grade otherwise it is more like **VS 4c**.
FA. Len Millsom 1962

Downes' Buttress

Below the main crag-top path on the usual approach are some neglected buttresses. Most are overgrown, though the three routes around the deep groove of *Morty's Corner* are worth seeking out if you want some peace.

Approach - The crag is hidden in the trees about 80m before the gate above Brookside Buttress. Approach it down either side of the quarried bay. It can also be reached awkwardly from Brookside Buttress.

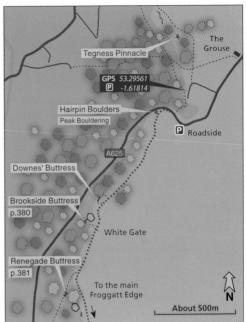

8 Slipper Slab . . . . ⬜ **HVS 5a**
Balance out to the arete (chipped?) and head up it direct on better holds.
FA. Wilf White 1954

9 Glass Slipper . . . . . ⬜ **f7A+**
The arete on its right-hand side to a rounded hold. From standing it is *f7A*.

10 Morty's Corner . . . . . ⬜ **HVS 5a**
The deep corner gives a good Curbaresque pitch with tough bridging and jamming.
FA. Joe (Morty) Smith 1957

11 Downes' Crack . . . . ⬜ **VS 5a**
Layback the thinning flake rapidly with hard moves to reach the ledge. An easier crack completes the route.
FA. Geoff Sutton 1957. Named for Bob Downes, killed in the Himalayas.

Not much sun | 12 min | Sheltered | Green

Afternoon | 12 min | Sheltered | Green

Brookside Buttress

The best of the buttresses passed on the approach is well hidden below the path but worth visiting for the fine arete of *Indoor Fisherman*.

Approach (see map on page 379) - At the gate on the main approach, turn right and follow a small stream downhill. Keep close to the right bank and after about 70m the buttress appears on your right.

❶ Neb Crack . . . . **VS 4c**
The crack on the left-hand side of the steep north wall.
FA. Nat Allen 1956

❷ Dick Van Dyke Goes Ballistic
. . . . **E7 6b**
Gain the shallow hanging groove in the wall from the base of *Neb Crack*. Sustained with a high crux and a bad landing.
FA. Dave Pegg (solo) 1994

❸ Indoor Fisherman **E4 6a**
The fine arete is one of the unsung gems of Froggatt. A tough start leads up flakes then a hard move gains a break and gear. From here pull up to gain and enjoy the rounded finish. Classic.
FA. Steve Bancroft 1977

4 Crooked Start . . . . S 4a HS 4b
Climb the wide cracks on the front face of the buttress. Head right at the top to the finish of *Tinsel's Tangle*.
FA. Wilf White 1956

5 Ghost of the Brook E4 6a
The finish up the wall has hard moves to gain a crack.
FA. Ben Heason 2002

6 Crooked Start Direct . . . . VS 4c
The shallow scoop and short leftwards traverse lead to the upper moves of *Tinsel's Tangle*.

7 Tinsel's Tangle . . . . S 4a
The arete on the right and the flake-crack above are pleasant, though can be green.
FA. Wilf White, Tinsel Allen 1956

8 Piledriver . . . . HVS 5b
On the side-wall, climb the thin crack and move left to finish direct (big cams). A direct start is **6a** but usually moss-bound.
FA. Al Evans 1977. FA. (Direct) by Steve Bancroft 1977

9 Brookside Crack . . . . VD
The short crack on the right-hand side of the face. Often dirty.
FA. Wilf White 1956

Renegade Buttress
This tiny lump of rock with a steep valley face is home to a couple of small routes with a big impact.
Approach (see map on page 379) - 100m after the white gate, locate a small track leading diagonally down right off the main track. 50m down here a steep block overhangs the path.

10 The Screaming Dream . . E7 6c
The desperate crack on the left-hand side sees few attempts and (far) fewer successes. It has been bouldered at **f8A** but the crack takes good gear so it is worth taking a rope.
FA. Mark Leach 1987

11 Renegade Master f7C+
The hanging arete starting from the left is usually bouldered above a stack of mats. It originally finished direct but most ascents slink right now. If leading it, the micro-wires are usually pre-placed which reduces the grade a bit from E8 to E7.
FA. Jerry Moffatt 1995

12 The Famous Chris Ellis . . E4 6a
Climb the right-hand side of the block and make a scary move onto the ledge.
FA. Paul Mitchell, Chris Ellis 1984

Strapiombo Buttress

A splendid buttress with two classic grit-ticks on an overhang theme though there is less quality in the lower grades. The front face gets the afternoon sun but *Strapiombante* faces north and can be cool in summer.

Approach (see map on page 376) - On the approach there is a bend after the gate, where a boulder on the left leans over the track. 90m after this, slant right towards the valley and the jutting overhangs of the Strapiombo Buttress should be apparent below.

❶ Strapiombante **E1 5b**
A fine micro-route, strenuous, with good gear to catch you if you blow the final moves. Trend right up the wall to a break (small cams) then back left to crux moves out left, or direct.
FA. Dave Brearly 1962

❷ Strapadictomy **E5 6b**
A real classic and rite of passage which is hard work but well protected. Climb the short arete to runners, then lean out (large wire in the flake) and layback onto the flake. About face, and finish briskly.
FA. John Allen 1976

❸ Cock Robin **E6 7a**
With gear in *Strapadictomy*, climb the wall to the lump in the roof. Now try and stand up (easier for the short) then finish up the slab. Loss of holds may have made it even harder.
FA. Robin Barker 1994

❹ Strappotente **E7 7a**
A bit of an eliminate. Head straight through the centre of the roof, place gear in the lip, then grovel and press for the top.
FA. Seb Grieve 1999

❺ Strapiombo **E1 5b**
The roof crack to the right is a battle. The use of knees, and loss of chunks of flesh, are pretty much par for the course.
FA. Don Whillans 1956

❻ Harrow **E6 6c**
Access and climb the jutting arete just right. Harrow...ing.
FA. Pete Whittaker 2009

❼ English Overhang . . . **VS 4c**
The wide crack right of the roof is an awkward struggle and a creaking flake doesn't help.
FA. Dave Gregory 1978

❽ Scarper's Triangle **E2 5b**
Climb left out of the capped corner and pull back onto the slab. Balance up this to a blind harrowing finishing crack. Originally and still often finished leftwards to *English Overhang* at **HVS 5a**.
FA. (Original) John Fearon 1957

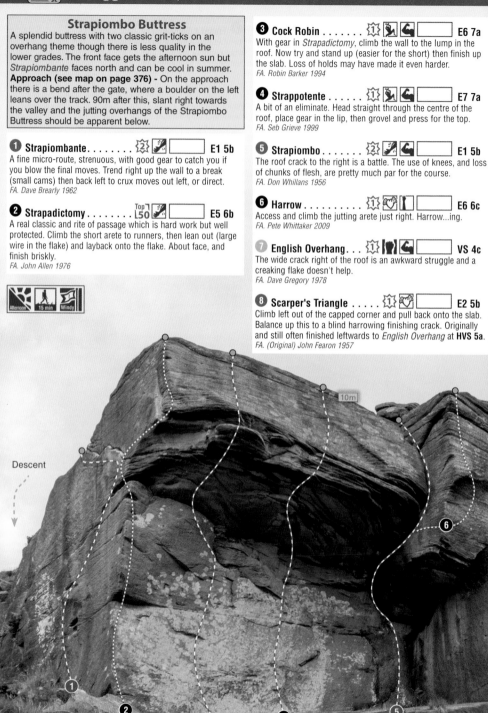

Descent

9 Scarpered . . . . **VS 4c**
The right arete on its right-hand side is bold but escapable.
FRA. Steve Clark 2002

10 Oss Nob **E4 6a**
Teeter warily up the scary left arete of the narrow slab.
FA. Colin Banton 1978

11 Left Flake Crack . . . . **S 4a**
The crack left of the jutting flake is awkward at half-height.
FA. J.W.Puttrell 1906

12 Right Flake Crack . . . . **HS 4b**
The right-hand crack is harder than it looks. Big gear helps.
FA. Wilf White 1949

13 Parallel Piped **E3 5c**
The reachy left arete of the smart slab, with gear in the low
break. Hard for the short. A fair intro to harder gritstone aretes.
FA. Graham Hoey 1986

14 Benign Lives **E7 6b**
The blank slab is lacking in pebbles and has thin moves high up.
Now usually climbed above a stack of well-placed mats at *f7A+*.
FA. Johnny Dawes 1984

15 Mild **E4 6b**
Step off the mid-height ledge as for *Benign Lives*. Move up
rightwards to the arete past a thin flake and a pocket.
FA. Julian Lines 1992

Sunset Slab - 90m ➞
bouldery scramble

Sheffield Area

Ladybower Area

Stanage

Burbage Valley

Millstone Area

Derwent Edges

Chatsworth Area

Southern Crags

❶ Science Friction. . . . ▨ ▧ ▨ [____] **E6 6a**
Very bold friction climbing up the arete left of *North Climb* with gear at just below half-height. Sadly the upper crux is avoidable.
FA. Mark Miller 1980

❷ Fatal Attraction . . . . ▧ ▨ [____] **E5 6a**
The narrow slab is an eliminate but the moves are engrossing enough once committed to the line.
FA. Darren Thomas 1989

❸ North Climb. . . . . ▨ [▪] [____] **HVD 4a**
The wide crack was a good effort for its day. Awkward and not too well protected, though a big chockstone is of some help.
FA. J.W.Puttrell 1906

❹ What's up Doc? . . . . ▨ [____] **E2 5a**
Climb the slab starting on the right then generally stay just right of *North Climb*. Can be made much harder if the easiest options are ignored.
FA. Graham Hulley 1990

❺ Sundowner . . . . ▨ ▧ ▨ [____] **E2 5a**
Friction climbing on poor pockets with a crux reach near the top. A side-runner on the right lowers the grade a couple of notches. The line here uses the Direct Start to *Sunset Slab* which makes for a logical and independent route.
FA. John Allen 1972

❻ Sunset Slab. . . . . ᵀᵒᵖ[50] ▧ [____] **HVS 4b**
THE route of the slab has long had a contentious grade, chiefly used to warn the uninitiated. With a good runner in the right place it would be nearer Hard Severe! From the initial crack, trend left across sloping ledges to a flake and teeter up this. The crux is a move higher than you might want. *Photo on page 387.*
FA. Joe Brown 1948

❼ Sunset Crack . . . . ▨2 ▨ [____] **HS 4b**
The awkward undercut crack has enough runners to make up for the previous two offerings! The initial bulge is the crux and the route has its fair share of sloping holds but, on the whole, it is pretty friendly at the grade.
FA. Len Chapman 1948

❽ Turret Crack . . . . ▨ [▪] [____] **HS 4b**
An awkward, blocky start to the crack in the edge of the face leads to a steepening just below the top.
FA. Don Chapman 1948

The block-choked gully just right offers an easy way down after the tricky initial slither under the chockstone.

❾ Slab and Crack . . . . ▨ [____] **Diff**
The narrow polished ramp in the right wall of the gully.
FA. Nat Allen 1948

❿ Ramp-Art . . . . ▧ ▨ [____] **E5 6a**
A route to nowhere! Gain the left trending mini-ramp on the wall and scoot along this to gain relief in the gully. Finish easily.
FA. Martin Veale 1986

Descent scramble

Sunset Slab
This is the first of many fine slabs at Froggatt. The routes up the cracks are very friendly but the others need a steady and confident approach as protection is minimal. To the right is a jutting prow with one of the best hard routes anywhere on Grit. **Approach (see map on page 376) -** On the main track there is a conspicuous left-hand bend by a jutting boulder. 200m after this head right to the cliff edge to locate the slab and an awkward descent just to its left (looking out).

12m

⑪

⑫

Evening | 15 min | Windy | Green

Hawk's Nest Crack

⑪ **Soul Doubt** . 🚫 📷 🔦 📷 📷 ☐ **E8 6c**
Indifferent low gear almost protects this hard and scary climb up the blank wall. Use the thin crack to reach the ramp and make some very hard moves on pebbles and a pocket to the top.
FA. Adrian Berry 2000

⑫ **Beau Geste** . Top 50 📷 🔦 📷 📷 ☐ **E7 6c**
The soaring arete is the classic hard route of the crag. Relatively easy climbing up the groove in the lower arete (micro-wires), and a worrying move right along the break, gain some much needed gear (cams). Back at the arete, make a desperate move to reach a thin crack on the left (crucial small wire, very hard to place) and sprint up the rest of the arete. Please don't stand on the pebble as there is only half of it left now! Three ropes are normally used to protect the line. *Photo this page.*
FA. Johnny Woodward 1982

Neil Kershaw squeezing the pebble on the magnificent *Beau Geste* (E7 6c) - *this page* - at Froggatt.
The photo illustrates the three rope system used to protect the climb. Photo: Adam Long

Sheffield Area

Ladybower Area

Stanage

Burbage Valley

Millstone Area

Derwent Edges

Chatsworth Area

Southern Crags

Hawk's Nest Crack

Past the soaring arete the oak trees shade a section of rock with some good vertical cracks and a slightly dingy cave; there are several fine climbs here. The whole area may be cooler in the summer (at least for the belayer) and the cave provides a decent shelter from the rain.
Approach (see map on page 376) - Descend as for *Sunset Slab* then follow the ledge around to the cave.

❶ Epiphany. . . . . 🔆 📷 [____] **E6 6b**
Climb the soaring arete on its left-hand side, with a detour left at half-height to place gear. A sustained and gripping pitch
FA. (Left start) Nick Dixon 1990s. FA. (As described) Ben Heason 1999

❷ Holly Groove . . . . 🔆 👊 [____] **VS 4c**
The slippery twin cracks in the groove - the holly has long gone. Start up the left one, step into the right for a couple of steep moves, then finish up a wide easy chimney.
FA. Slim Sorrell 1948

❸ Hawk's Nest Crack . . . . . 🔆 🔧 [____] **VS 4c**
A classic jamming crack that is a bit of a battle with a useful chockstone en-route where knees are usual. From the ledge finish over the exposed jutting flake on the left for an airy thrill.
FA. Joe Brown 1948

❹ Horizontal Pleasure . . . . 🔆 💪 [____] **E5 6b**
The wild roof. From under the roof span to the lip, slap for a break then move right to jugs. Finish direct; big cams needed.
FA. Andy Healy 1999

❺ Cave Crack Indirect . . . . 🔆 📷 [____] **HVS 5a**
For something a bit different, a teetery traverse right can be made which manages to sidestep the horrors of the roof crack.

❻ Rambeau . . . . 🔆 💪 👊 [____] **f7B**
A desperate left-hand start to *Cave Crack*. Possibly still easier than actually climbing *Cave Crack* though!

❼ Cave Crack . . . . . . 🔆 💪 👊 [____] **E3 5c**
A bruising battle for most. From a big thread, hand traverse the greasy flange and finger-jam the roof-crack. Once established on the front face things ease instantly. A VS from when grades were random, and upgraded (yet again) by popular demand!
FA. Joe Brown 1950

❽ Cave Crawl . . . . 🔆 🦎 [____] **HS 5a**
Unique and bizarre. Wriggle up into the greasy slot in the back left corner of the cave, then breast stoke toward *Swimmer's Chimney* and daylight. The route can also be descended by a downward slither (quietly) to spook people in the cave!
FA. Slim Sorrell 1948

❾ Cave Wall . . . . 🔆 📷 [____] **E3 5c**
Bold and precarious. From the right rib of the cave boulder up and right to a small ledge from where scary balance moves on the left lead to better holds and a rapid exit to the right.
FA. Don Whillans 1958

❿ Beau Brummel. . . . . 🔆 🪨 📷 [____] **E4 6a**
The right arete of the buttress with a harrowing leap for a sloping hold forming the crux. From above this move left to a finish over the roofs that cap the wall.
FA. Martin Veale (encouraged, spotted and followed by Chris Craggs) 1982

⓫ Swimmer's Chimney . . . . . . 🔆 [____] **S 4a**
The deep and ever-narrowing chimney slot is well named; you can flap but don't flounder!
FA. J.W.Puttrell 1890s

TICKLIST

Froggatt - The Slabs

Froggatt has long been known for its excellent set of slab routes - work your way up through the 10 below then you can consider yourself a slab-meister.

- ☐ **Slab Recess, Diff** *(397)*. Mild as they come.
- ☐ **Allen's Slab, S** *(397)*. Balancy and a little bold.
- ☐ **Sunset Slab, HVS** *(384)*. Pretty soft but don't slip.
- ☐ **Three Pebble Slab, HVS** *(392)*. Some neat padding.
- ☐ **Sundowner, E2** *(384)*. Trust your feet on this one.
- ☐ **Long John's Slab, E3** *(396)*. Boulder the start, then go.
- ☐ **Great Slab, E3** *(398)*. Loads of class and no runners.
- ☐ **Downhill Racer, E4** *(397)*. The crux is at a tricky height.
- ☐ **Artless/Hairless Heart, E5** *(399)*. Super-sustained.
- ☐ **Benign Lives, E7** *(383)*. Another real stopper.

Steve Cunnington on the final bold moves of *Sunset Slab* (HVS 4b) - *page 384* - miles from his runners at Froggatt.

Beau Brummel
- p.386

Terrace Crack

Two ancient quarried walls undercut by a section of soft red rock. The upper walls have some thin, hard climbing with sparse gear.
Approach (see map on page 376) - Move right from *Hawk's Nest Crack* or descend the gully to the left.

4 Skogul . . . . **S 4a**
Climb the wide crack to a ledge then the exposed arete, most easily reached from the left. It is nearer VS 4b when done direct.
FA. Joe Brown 1951

5 Mean Streak **E6 6b**
The wall right of the arete has low runners and gradually improving holds but is bold in the extreme. Sadly chipped.
FA. Dominic Lee 1981

6 The Gully Joke **E3 5c**
Climb the flake left of the steep crack, place runners on the right then teeter out left and climb the wall on small hidden holds.
FA. John Allen 1975

7 Terrace Crack . . . . **HS 4b**
The long blocky crack was once quarried and is unusual for the edge. It is juggy, well protected and low in the grade.
FA. Freda Rylett early 1940s

8 Bud **E7 6c**
The leaning left arete of the next slender buttress. Technical and bold to a nasty slap for a jug (micro-wires just right). A strange move enables you to stand on the jug and romp to the top.
FA. Andy Popp 1990s

9 Germination **E5 6a**
The right arete of the tower has concentrated difficulties.
FA. Iain Farrar late 1990s

1 Brightside **E2 5c**
Low in the grade. From halfway up *Swimmer's Chimney* squirm rightwards past the arete and climb the wall by a hard move, things then ease. A bouldery direct start up right side of the lower arete is **Better Dead Than Smeg, E6 6c**.
FA. Phil Burke 1980. FA. (BDTS) Stephen Fearn 1994

2 Greedy Pig **E5 6b**
The searing thin crack that forms a direct start to the last climb is fiercely technical and has gear which is hard to place.
FA. Paul Mitchell (with pre-placed runners, hence the name) 1981

3 Avalanche **E2 6a**
The groove on the right-hand side of the wall has a particularly hard pull over the roof.
FA. Daniel Lee 1981. The prophetically-named earlier version fell down.

Descent

Tody's Wall

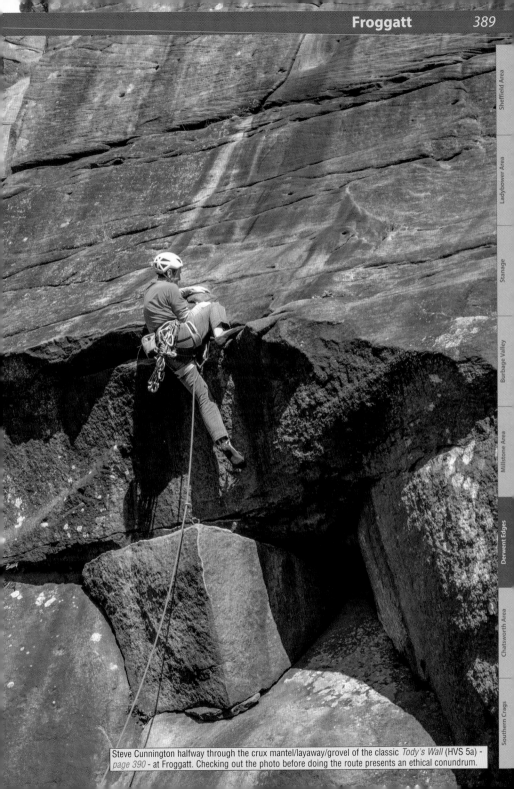

Sheffield Area

Ladybower Area

Stanage

Burbage Valley

Millstone Area

Derwent Edges

Chatsworth Area

Southern Crags

Steve Cunnington halfway through the crux mantel/layaway/grovel of the classic *Tody's Wall* (HVS 5a) - *page 390* - at Froggatt. Checking out the photo before doing the route presents an ethical conundrum.

❶ Nightshade E3 5c
The left arete of the slab is gained via a shallow groove in the left wall and climbed precariously and boldly. A more direct start is arguably better and definitely harder: **Kanji Class, E3 6a**.
FA. John Allen 1975. FA. (KC) Paul Mitchell 1993

❷ C.M.C. Slab . . . . HVS 5b
Keep as near as possible to the centre of the slab left of *Heather Wall*, with the odd runner in that route. It is a grade or two harder without these.
FA. Castle Mountaineering Club members 1970s

❸ Heather Wall . . . . HVD 3c
Mild at the grade and brilliant. An awkward start leads to a ledge then tackle the jamming crack up the shallow groove.
FA. Dick Brown late 1940s

❹ Grip E2 5c
Start up the green groove just right then continue up the arete (runners in *Heather Wall*) which manages to feel surprisingly independent once you get going!
FA. Gary Gibson 1978

❺ Ratbag E2 5b
A bold slab climb left of *Tody's* crack. It can be reached via *Grip* or *Tody's* itself. The final section is a gripper.
FA. John Allen 1974

❻ Tody's Wall . . . . HVS 5a
Mild for HVS but excellent. Grovel onto the jammed block, place a few cams and make the obvious move onto the slab - easier said than done. Finish up the slab and elegant crack above.
Photo on page 389.
FA. Joe Brown 1948

Afternoon 15 min Windy

Descent

18m

Terrace
Crack - p.388

Tody's Playground
Peak Bouldering

7 Motorcade E1 5a
Starting from a ledge up and right or the grotty corner below, climb the pocketed slab right of *Tody's* crack. Large low cams protect, but not really very adequately.
FA. D.Warriner 1969

8 Silver Crack .... HS 4b
The crack on the right-hand side of the slab is a widening thrash, recommended for those who feel like a punch-up.
FA. J.W.Puttrell 1890s

9 Silver Traverse .... HVD 4a
Traverse the crack/ledges to a finish on the right.
FA. Wilf White 1948

10 Silver Lining E5 5c
Bold and precarious arete climbing, even with the chockstone in *Silver Crack* threaded.
FA. Peter Beal 1986

8m

Descent

Three Pebble Slab →

11 Origin of Species ... E5 6a
A deceptive slab climb in a serious position; a sacrificial belayer might save you in the event of a fall, but no slinking off right towards the top. The route sees few ascents but is worthwhile if you are psyching up for the big *Great Slab* ticks.
FA. Gary Gibson 1978

12 Bollard Crack .... VS 4c
The kinked crack is a bit of a bollard. The star is awarded for people who prefer their climbing to have some character.
FA. Slim Sorrell 1948

Tody's Wall
One of the tallest sections of the edge and always busy because of many fine climbs across the grades. The classic *Tody's Wall* is a popular easy HVS tick and there is also the delightful *Heather Wall* providing a great intro to jamming. The tree cover gives shade in the summer although the upper sections are open to the elements.
Direct Approach (see map on page 376) - Follow the crag-top path almost as far as the Valkyrie Pinnacle. Head towards the edge before two prominent stones that once supported a bench and find an easy scramble descent down towards *Three Pebble Slab*. Alternatively descend down behind the Pinnacle and double back.

Sheffield Area

Ladybower Area

Stanage

Burbage Valley

Millstone Area

Derwent Edges

Chatsworth Area

Southern Crags

Three Pebble Slab

A neat slab with some great friction climbing and always popular. It includes one of the big ticks of the Peak. Generally the routes are lacking in gear and holds but if you enjoy slab climbing it is an essential spot.

Direct Approach (also see map on page 376) - Follow the crag-top path almost as far as the Pinnacle. Head towards the edge at two prominent stones that once supported a bench and find an easy but exposed scramble descent down right above *Three Pebble Slab*, or descend behind the Pinnacle and double back.

1 Soft Option . . . . **Diff**
The widening crack in the left-hand side of the slab gives a popular but poor and gritty little pitch. The tiny hanging groove just right is **Topomania, HS 4b**, another poor one.
FA. Dave Gregory 1960s

2 Two-sided Triangle . . . . . **HVS 5b**
A mini *Three Pebble* which has a harder move but is less satisfying. Climb the slab just to the right of the tiny groove.
FA. Gary Gibson 1978

3 Three Pebble Slab . . Top 50 **HVS 5a**
One of the classic Froggatt slabs which is always good fodder in the great grade debate. Climb to a hole (cam and small wire) rock up and right to a rest then pad to safety. Scary but mild.
FA. Joe Brown 1948

4 Four Pebble Slab . . . **E3 5c**
More then one pebble harder than its neighbour. Trend right up the steep lower wall via awkward ledges to runners then step left and burn rubber up the slab on barely adequate holds, avoiding the arete. A more direct start is a grade or so harder.
FA. John Allen 1972

5 Grey Slab . . . . **S 4b**
The lower wall leads steeply to the wide and oddly-named crack.
FA. Rucksack Club members early 1900s

6 Nanoq Slab **E1 5b**
The narrow slab to the right of the wide crack of *Grey Slab*. A grade harder if you avoid the arete completely - though artificial.
FA. Tom Metcalf 1990

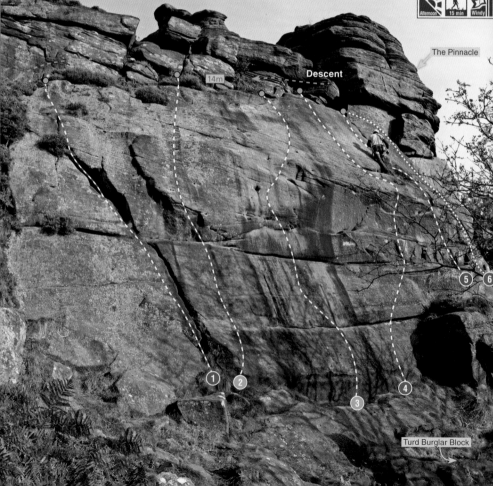

Turd Burglar Block

There is some good bouldering on the large blocks hidden a short distance below The Pinnacle.
Approach (also see map on page 376) - From below the Pinnacle, locate a path that heads steeply down to an innocuous looking block.

7 Heather in My Face . . . . . . 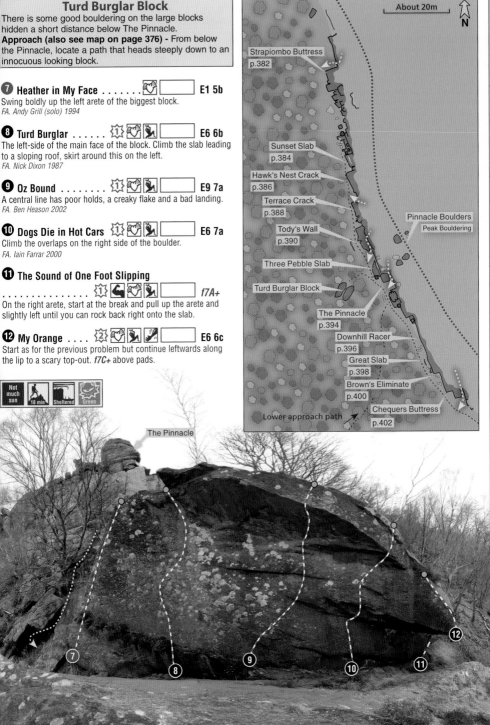 E1 5b
Swing boldly up the left arete of the biggest block.
FA. Andy Grill (solo) 1994

8 Turd Burglar E6 6b
The left-side of the main face of the block. Climb the slab leading to a sloping roof, skirt around this on the left.
FA. Nick Dixon 1987

9 Oz Bound E9 7a
A central line has poor holds, a creaky flake and a bad landing.
FA. Ben Heason 2002

10 Dogs Die in Hot Cars E6 7a
Climb the overlaps on the right side of the boulder.
FA. Iain Farrar 2000

11 The Sound of One Foot Slipping
. . . . f7A+
On the right arete, start at the break and pull up the arete and slightly left until you can rock back right onto the slab.

12 My Orange E6 6c
Start as for the previous problem but continue leftwards along the lip to a scary top-out. *f7C+ above pads.*

About 20m
N

Strapiombo Buttress
p.382

Sunset Slab
p.384

Hawk's Nest Crack
p.386

Terrace Crack
p.388

Tody's Wall
p.390

Three Pebble Slab

Turd Burglar Block

Pinnacle Boulders
Peak Bouldering

The Pinnacle
p.394

Downhill Racer
p.396

Great Slab
p.398

Brown's Eliminate
p.400

Chequers Buttress
p.402

Lower approach path

Not much sun | 18 min | Sheltered | Green

The Pinnacle

7   8   9   10   11   12

Sheffield Area
Ladybower Area
Stanage
Burbage Valley
Millstone Area
Derwent Edges
Chatsworth Area
Southern Crags

The Pinnacle

The unmistakable square bulk of Froggatt Pinnacle is home to one great classic and a set of only slightly less worthy offerings. Most of the harder routes are of a bouldery nature and don't reach the summit. For the other routes that do go all the way, the summit is equipped with a chunky abseil ring. Before the mid-1980s the usual escape from the summit involved a short abseil from the thread/hole on *Pinnacle Face*. An experienced climber from the Southwest did *Valkyrie* and assumed the jump from the summit to the main edge (Cook's Leap) was the normal way off. Once he was out of plaster he returned with a drill, a big bolt, a Primus stove and some lead, and placed the ugly lump of iron that is still used for the descent.

Direct Approach (see map on page 376) - Follow the crag-top path to the Valkyrie Pinnacle and scramble down the steep gully behind it.

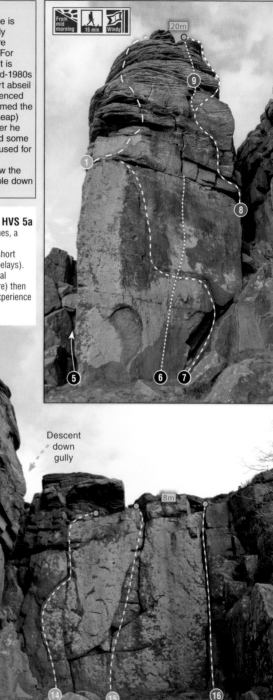

① Valkyrie . . . . 🔝50 🪢📷 ⬜ **HVS 5a**

A fine historic HVS which features two contrasting pitches, a mid-height stance and a belay on a proper summit.

1) 5a, 10m. The tricky, slanting, jamming crack, and a short traverse, lead to a small stance on the arete (awkward belays).

2) 5a, 10m. Step right, climb the wall (gear in the vertical crack) then move left (there is bizarre no-hands rest here) then mantelshelf to the easy upper slab. Enjoy the summit experience then abseil from the ring-bolt.

FA. Joe Brown, Wilf White 1949

Descent down gully

Sickle Buttress ➔

Sheffield Area

Ladybower Area

Stanage

Burbage Valley

Millstone Area

Derwent Edges

Chatsworth Area

Southern Crags

❼ Oedipus Ring Your Mother

. . . . **E4 6b**

A taxing traverse along the sloping finger-break, gains a shallow flake - a popular *f6B* to here. A committing long stretch and an ancient chipped hold (lest we forget) reaches the *Valkyrie* stance. There is also a direct start using another chipped hold which is *f6B+*, although easier than that for the tall.
FA. Tom Proctor 1968

The next routes start up the blocky gully behind the Pinnacle and are reached by a short scramble.

❽ Pinnacle Arete. **E2 5b**

Neglected but good. From the gully traverse left along the lowest break, pass the arete and pull up to gain a ledge. Climb the groove then step up and right to better holds and a sprint finish.
FA. Slim Sorrell 1948

❾ Birthday **E3 6a**

A direct finish to *Pinnacle Arete* from the ledge on the arete.
FA. Ben Heason 2001

The next routes start from the top of the gully behind the back of the Pinnacle.

❿ Chapman's Crack . . . . **VS 4c**

Traverse boldly left above the gully in a position of some exposure to reach and climb the short crack. The easiest way up the Pinnacle but often a bit green and not really all that easy.
FA. Len Chapman 1948

⓫ Route One . . . . **VS 5a**

The short northeast arete yields to a tough mantelshelf. An impressive route for its day and a viable way down for *Valkyrie* soloists who are technically proficient or have rubber legs.
FA. Henry Bishop 1912

⓬ Pinnacle Face . . . . **VS 5b**

From the top of the gully below the back arete, teeter right along sloping ledges (spotter advised) then climb the wall passing a useful and rather unusual hole.
FA. Gilbert Ellis 1947

⓭ My Newt **E1 5b**

The short and exposed arete on the right.
FA. Brian Rossiter 1990s

The short wall to the right of the Pinnacle has a trio of routes, one of which is very popular.

⓮ Truly Pathetic . . . . **HVS 5c**

The thin right-trending crack. A bit better than the name suggests.
FA. John Allen 1976

⓯ Diamond Crack . . . . **HS 4b**

The slanting crack gives a fine exercise in jamming - steep, strenuous and well protected, it was graded VD for many years. A popular route for logging your first flight time! Who said Joe Brown invented hand-jamming - check the FA date.
FA. Henry Bishop 1913

⓰ Corner Crack . . . . **VD**

A wide awkward start leads to easier things. Not great!

❷ Narcissus II **E5 6b**

Not a second pitch to *Narcissus* but a continuation above *Valkyrie's* start. Pull over and aim for the flared crack that leads to the top.
FA. Steve Bancroft 1979

❸ Pinnacle Traverse . . . . **f7A+**

Start low and work your way up and across a flake to the arete. Turn this and then pull up to reverse the *Oedipus* traverse.

❹ Neon Dust . . . . **f7C+**

The wall between the crack and arete is usually just done as a boulder problem before scuttling off left to the *Valkyrie* crack. The whole route is worth E6 and continues above on gradually improving finger-holds, easing to 6b after the start.
FA. (from the right) Ron Fawcett 1983. FA. (direct) Ron again 1986

❺ Narcissus **E6 6b**

The fine arete is increasingly taxing, and stays hard all the way. Usually now climbed above pads at *f7A*. *Photo on page 377.*
FA. Steve Bancroft 1978

❻ The Mint 400 . . . . **E6 6c**

Boulder up the wall to gain the break of *Oedipus* - *f7B+* to here. Next launch up the seemingly holdless wall above to gain the upper break. Escape left or right. A serious and technical undertaking which is an airy *f7B+* above pads.
FA. Ron Fawcett 1983. Direct start added at a later date.

Descent

10m

Sickle Buttress
This short wall has a compelling clean crack at its left-hand side and a popular Severe to its right.
Approach (see map on page 376) - The buttress is between the Pinnacle and the Downhill Racer area.

1 **Left Broken** . . . . **VS 5a**
Gain the wide crack awkwardly then romp on. Not popular!
FA. Slim Sorrel 1953

2 **Broken Crack** . . . . **VS 5a**
The lovely jamming-crack is best approached by a swift layback. If you think this HVS you need to smarten your jamming!
FA. Joe Brown 1948

3 **Sickle Buttress** . . . . **S 4a**
Climb the tough crack to polished ledges and follow them out to the right arete and an easier finish up a shallow groove.
FA. R.Davies 1945

4 **Sickle Buttress Direct** . . . **VS 4c**
Finish direct up the reachy centre wall instead of moving right. A **5a** bouldery start up the face just right is another option.
FA. Joe Brown 1948

5 **Performing Flea** . . **HVS 5a**
Up the arete and the wall above. Beware the bendy flake.
FA. Matt Boyer 1985. The old route, Sickle Buttress Arete, fell down.

6 **Sorrallion** . . . . **VD**
Climbs up most of the ledgy descent then an awkward little roof.

7 **Congestion Crack** . . . . . . **HS 4c**
The tight groove is trickier and better then it looks.
FA. Nat Allen 1948

8 **Long John's Slab** . . . **E3 5c**
From a lurking boulder, mantel onto a narrow ledge then use the old peg hole (6a for the short) to gain finger-holds and easier climbing. Soft, but unprotected. Pads help lower the grade. **Long John's Left-hand** is a different ball-game at **E6 6c**.
FA. Paul Grey (1 peg as a foothold) 1968. FFA. Al Rouse 1969

14m

Downhill Racer
One of the most popular areas at Froggatt with some great climbs in the lower grades and a famous blank slab. It is showing signs of wear and tear, and the whole area can be very busy at weekends.
Direct Approach (see map on page 376) - From the crag-top path descend the gully behind the Valkyrie Pinnacle and follow the lower path. Alternatively continue to the end of the crag and double back. The area is situated at the top of the Chequers Inn approach path for those coming up the hill.

9 Downhill Racer .... 🔲🅰️🔲 **E4 6a**
Climb the slab left of the shallow groove then step left and make a fierce, fingery mantelshelf to better holds and an uphill finger-traverse to ledges. One more scary move remains. A super-technical left-hand start is around *f7A+*.
FA. Pete Livesey 1977. "Cleaned with a wire brush with 6" nails for bristles".

10 Slab Recess Direct. ...... 🔲🔲 **HS 4c**
The shallow corner has an unhelpful set of sloping, slippery holds and great gear. The upper half is a doddle. Oddly there are easier 5b moves out there!
FA. Joe Brown 1948

11 Joe's Arete .... 🔲🔲🔲 *f6B*
The arete gives a nice problem layaway and mantel.

12 Thin Slab .... 🔲🔲🔲 *f7A+*
Smear up the blank slab.

13 Mono Seam. ...... 🔲🔲🔲 *f6C+*
From edges gain the two tiny pockets above, then the semi-circular flake and ledge. Just the right-hand pocket is *f7A*.

14 Joe's Slab. .... 🔲🔲🔲 *f5+*
The original and classic boulder problem mantelshelf is worth of a minute of your time. Polished.
FA. Joe Brown 1950s

15 Slab Pop. .... 🔲🔲🔲 *f6C*
An eliminate up the blank slab above the undercuts.

16 Slab Recess .... 🔲🔲 **Diff**
The best beginners' route on the cliff - much better led than top-roped. Climb the cracks on the right then move left to the ear-shaped flake. A mild layback leads into the final groove.
FA. Sandy Alton 1948

17 Gamma .... 🔲 **VD**
The blocky continuation to the start of the previous climb.
FA. Nat Allen 1951

18 Allen's Slab .... 🔲🔲🔲 **S 4a**
Popular but a bit bolder than you might be expecting. Start up *Gamma* but follow the diagonal crack out right to the left end of a heathery ledge. Balance right and finish up the juggy wall just left to the next crack (*Trapeze Direct*).
FA. Nat Allen 1951

19 Polyp Piece. .... 🔲🔲🔲🔲 **E7 6c**
Climb the blank slab on very poor footholds and undercuts direct to the traverse of *Allen's Slab*. Graded for a solo, it is about E5 with a side-runner in the diagonal crack of *Allen's Slab*.
FA. Nick Dixon 1987 (with a side-runner). FA. Ben Heason (solo) 2000

20 Swing. .... 🔲🔲 **E1 5a**
The right-hand side of the slab is graded for no side runners. At the ledge swing left then finish direct.

21 Trapeze Direct .... 🔲🔲🔲 **VS 4c**
The easy crack leads to a bulge split by a thin crack. Reach for a jug above, then heave away to easy ground. The route is rather unbalanced, low in the grade and a popular first VS lead.
FA. Wilf White 1948

22 Trapeze .... 🔲🔲 **VD**
A more satisfying variation. Follow *Trapeze Direct* to the bulge then swing right along a break to an open groove and climb this to the top.
FA. Rupert Davis 1945

23 Nursery Slab. .... 🔲 **Mod**
The well-named blocky cracks bounding the left edge of *Great Slab*. Used as a descent by the competent and low in the grade.
FA. J.W.Puttrell 1906

14m

Descent at the end of the crag

Great Slab →

Sheffield Area
Ladybower Area
Stanage
Burbage Valley
Millstone Area
Derwent Edges
Chatsworth Area
Southern Crags

Pinnacle Boulders
Peak Bouldering

Easy hidden approach

Sickle Buttress
p.396

Downhill Racer
p.396

Three Pebble Slab
p.392

Gully behind
Pinnacle approach

The Pinnacle
p.394

Approach from
lower parking

Great Slab

The finest gritstone slab in the Peak, with a great set of routes from Joe Brown's original *Great Slab* to the ultra-technical *Toy Boy*. Apart from the crack-line of *Synopsis* there is hardly a decent runner on the whole wall.

❶ Parting Hare . . . . . . 🎴 🪨 🧗 ⬜ **E3 5c**
A high girdle for the aficionado who has done everything else on the slab. Small cams and a stout second will both be useful.
FA. Nick Dixon 1983

❷ Heartless Hare . . . . 🎴 🧗 ⬜ **E5 5c**
The left-hand side of the slab is a bold undertaking passing a ledge then two tiny left-facing flakes. Often climbed with side-runners (as high as your conscience allows) at a friendlier **E3**.
FA. Steve Bancroft 1975

❸ Jugged Hare . . . . . . 🎴 🖼 🪨 ⬜ **E6 6a**
A right-hand finish to *Heartless Hare* using small holds to gain a thin break and a steep spooky finish. A distant side-runner is of little use. Chipped, filled-in and now gradually eroding.
FA. Johnny Dawes 1983

❹ Lonely Heart . . . . . . 🎴 🧗 🖼 ⬜ **E9 6c**
This might have been the last gap here? The crux is just below the break though the rest of it isn't much easier. Really bold!
FA. Ben Heason 2003

❺ Great Slab . . . . Top 50 ▯ 🖼 ⬜ **E3 5b**
Total class - not too hard but still unprotected and a touch precarious. Trend right up a delicate ramp to a ledge, 'piano-play' right on slippery footholds to a breather on a small ledge, then climb the steeper wall on flatties. Harder for the short.
FA. Joe Brown 1951

❻ Art Brut . . . . 🎴 🧗 🖼 ⬜ **E7 6b**
The direct finish above the start of *Great Slab* following a vague line about a metre left of *Hairless Heart*.
FA. Dave Thomas 1990s

❼ Hairless Heart . . . . Top 50 🖼 ⬜ **E5 5c**
The central line on the slab is quite superb. Follow *Great Slab* to its rest then friction up the slab to access the curving flake which is followed precariously to a rapid exit rightwards.
FA. John Allen 1975

18m

Nursery
Slab - p.397

Approach (see map on page 376) - Walk to the end of the crag and double back. The area is situated to the right of the top of the Chequers Inn approach path for those coming up the hill.

Great Slab

Brown's Eliminate
p.400

Chequers Buttress
p.402

Gully approach

8 Artless E5 6b

The right-trending ramp below the centre of the slab is gained awkwardly (if all else fails try a jump) and climbed via a hard dyno/slap or a harder rock-over. Move up and right to join and finish up *Great Slab* much more easily.
FA. John Allen 1976

9 Hairy Heart E6 6a

A more direct finish to *Great Slab*, after its crux climb the right-hand of the pair of overlaps. Low in the grade but don't slip!
FA. Mick Fowler 1975

10 Artless/Hairless Heart . . E5 6b

This combination, which also includes reversing the crux of *Great Slab* remains the finest slab route on grit - intense.
FA. John Allen 1975/76

11 Toy Boy . . . f7C+

The 'olds are so small, they are almost no 'olds at all! Progress depends on leaps between the micro-edges until you reach the finish of *Great Slab*. E7 without mats.
FA. Ron Fawcett 1986

12 Synopsis E2 5c

The once-pegged crack feels like a refugee from Millstone. The crux is at an awkward height off the ground, with tricky-to-place wires, just before the flat holds start to arrive and things ease.
FA. Nat Allen 1952. FFA. Steve Bancroft 1974

13 Beta . . . . VD

The long blocky corner is steep but mild, no beta required.
FA. Nat Allen 1951

14 Spine Chiller E4 5c

The left-hand arete of the block to the right of *Great Slab* is a scary and precarious prospect.
FA. Steve Bancroft 1984

15 Spinal Crack . . . . . . f5+

Struggle up the crack.

16 Spinal Tap . . . . f6C+

From jugs in the back, pull out and up the slanting crack.

17 Lankaster Bomber f7C

The reachy problem. The tall can knock off a couple of grades.

18m

Descent at the end of the crag

Nutty Land
- p.400

Brown's Eliminate

Sheffield Area
Ladybower Area
Stanage
Burbage Valley
Millstone Area
Derwent Edges
Chatsworth Area
Southern Crags

Brown's Eliminate

Some fine cracks here offer strenuous and well-protected climbing from Severe to E2, however the first routes around the jutting arete of *Brown's Eliminate* are more in keeping with the bold climbs elsewhere on the edge.
Approach (see map on page 376) - Follow the crag-top path to the end of the crag and double back.

1 Nutty Land E1 5c
Tackle the front face of the block. There is only one hard move but it is a bit of a teaser; a tricky mantelshelf.
FA. John Allen 1976

2 Flake Gully . . . . VD
Climb the gully behind the detached block then traverse left until the steep but juggy flake on the wall can be climbed.

3 Straight and Narrow E3 5c
The sharp arete on its left-hand side throughout. Bold moves to reach the runners on *Brown's Eliminate* then bolder again above.

4 Brown's Eliminate Direct E3 5c
Bolder and harder than the original, and with the same runners. The lower arete has a reachy sequence to the ledge, the upper section eases after initial tricky and precarious moves.

5 Armageddon . . . E3 5c
This would be a fine climb if it wasn't so escapable. Make a hard move to the ledge then continue direct past a couple of long reaches. Side-runners can be placed en route, making it **E2**.
FA. Alec Burns 1977

6 Brown's Eliminate . . Top 50 E2 5b
A bold and intimidating route which is often soloed, although there is gear just below half-height. From a couple of moves up the corner trend left to a ledge (cam runners down and left), step back right, then climb the wall on small flakes until things ease.
FA. Joe Brown 1948

7 Green Gut . . . . HS 4a
The fine groove is arguably the best line on the crag; it took a couple of days of digging before the first ascent was possible. The route is quite polished and a little awkward towards the top but protection is excellent throughout. *Photo on page 403.*
FA. Nat Allen 1948

8 Pedestal Crack . . . . HVS 5a
The long crack has a tricky layback move to reach a rest on the right then an awkward crack leads into the final short groove.
FA. Joe Brown 1948

9 Slide Show E6 6c
The roof approached from *Pedestal Crack* - bold and hard.
FA. Paul Mitchell (side-runners) 1988. FA. Ben Heason (without) 2003

10 Slingshot f8A
A well-known problem, but rarely climbed on account of the difficulty in protecting it. The first half is easier for the tall, the second easier for the short.
FA. Mo Overfield 2000. Top roped by Jerry Moffatt in 1988

⓫ Blind Vision . . . 🎯 ◼ ◼ ◼ ▢ **E9 7a**
Climb *Slingshot* but continue up the wall above and right. There is gear at the halfway ledge and some small wires above to protect the upper wall which is rumoured to be 'only 6c'.
FA. Adrian Berry 2003

⓬ Chequers Groove . . . 🎯 ◼ ◼ ▢ **f7C+**
An extended boulder problem right of *Sling Shot*, up the groove and overlaps.
FA. Jerry Moffatt 2000. Above a large gym mat.

⓭ The Big Crack . . . . 🎯 ◼ ▢ **E2 5b**
A compelling line with great climbing. Head steeply to a jug then pull on a couple of finger-jams gains good holds and the base of the wide upper crack. This proves to be awkward, although hidden holds out left help. Low in the grade but pretty pumpy.
FFA. John Syrett 1973. In 1955 the mighty Whillans used a machine nut for aid, the sharp-eyed may still spot it.

⓮ Hard Cheddar . . . . . 🎯 ◼ ◼ ▢ **E5 6b**
The thin seam/groove is hard on the left arm. Escape off right or pause before pressing on. *f6B+* above pads.
FA. Tom Proctor 1977

⓯ Circus. . . . . 🎯 ◼ ◼ ◼ ▢ **E7 6b**
Bold technical wall climbing continuing above *Hard Cheddar*. Originally done with side-runners at **E6**. The hardest moves are early on.
FA. Daniel Lee (with side-runners) 1982. Ben Heason (without) 2005

⓰ Stiff Cheese . . . . . . 🎯 ◼ ◼ ▢ **E2 5c**
A short and very stiff crack. You will probably get pumped trying to place gear, but do you have a choice?
FA. Steve Bancroft 1974

⓱ Beech Nut . . . . ◼ ◼ ▢ **E1 5c**
A nut that is hard to crack and easier to solo or boulder.
FA. Don Whillans, Nat Allen 1951

⓲ Chequers Crack . 🎯 ◼ ◼ ◼ ▢ **HVS 5c**
How can a 6m crack be this hard? One of the most frigged pitches in the Peak, despite its innocuous appearance. The crack leads to the break and an easier upper section on solid jams. For the competent it may be easier to solo than to faff with runners!
FA. Don Whillans 1951

⓳ Business Lunch . . . . 🎯 ◼ ▢ **f7C**
The roof and wall right of *Chequer's Crack*.
FA. John Allen 1984

⓴ Sole Power . . . . 🎯 ◼ ◼ ▢ **f7C**
The superb arete - high, but doable with plenty of normal pads. Climbed on its right-hand side is **Our Soles** also *f7C*.
FA. Jerry Moffatt 1983

㉑ Spock's Missing. . . . . 🎯 ◼ ◼ ▢ **E5 6b**
Climb the upper wall direct, with runners in *Chequers Crack* - or do it without at around **E6**.
FA. Ron Fawcett 1981

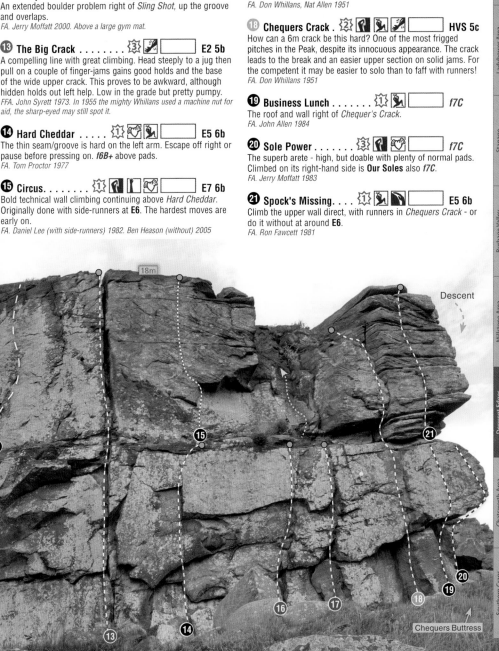

Descent

18m

Chequers Buttress

Sheffield Area · Ladybower Area · Stanage · Burbage Valley · Millstone Area · Derwent Edges · Chatsworth Area · Southern Crags

Chequers Buttress

Froggatt's final buttress is this tall undercut tower. The two famous *Chequers* routes provide contrasting challenges and further right are a trio of *Janker's* routes, which offer contorted fun and games, all courtesy of Baron Brown.
Approach (see map on page 376) - Follow the crag-top path to the end of the crag and double back.

❶ Bacteria Cafeteria . . . . 🗓🗺 ⬜ **E1 5b**
A direct line but inferior to its neighbours. Climb the bold wall left of the flake to the break, continue direct up cracks to finish.
FA. Gary Gibson 1979

❷ Chequers Climb . . . . 🗓🖊 ⬜ **VS 4c**
Devious but worthwhile - double ropes are sensible and may even be essential! Climb the ramp then traverse round the arete to access the upper section of *Chequers Crack* (p.401).
FA. Joe Brown 1949

❸ Chequers Buttress . . . . . ⎡Top⎤🏳 ⬜ **HVS 5a**
⎣50⎦
The final Froggatt classic and very photogenic. Climb the slippery ramp then the side-wall diagonally leftwards to a fat wire. Make a barn-door move left to the huge jug on the arete, then meander up this to a spectacular finish. Easier for the tall.
FA. John Gosling 1962

❹ Solomon's Crack . . . . 🗓 ⬜ **VD**
The awkward slanting ramp and upper corner feel very historical.
FA. J.W.Puttrell 1890

❺ Solomon's Variations . . . . . . 🖐 ⬜ **S 4a**
A direct start and finish are a grade harder and a lot less pleasant than the original. The wide rift right of the final corner is also a grovelly option.

❻ Janker's Crack . . . . . 🗓🎞🖐 ⬜ **HS 4b**
The first crack in the wall to the right is approached by a crack and jammed block and requires comedy moves to enter.
FA. Joe Brown 1948

❼ Janker's Groove . . . . 🗓🖐 ⬜ **VS 4c**
The right-hand of the grooves is approached from the previous climb and entered with difficulty and a bit of an udge. The direct start is *f6B+* and needs a fist-crunching jam. It was Whillans' barmy idea though apparently he never completed it.
FA. Joe Brown 1948

❽ Janker's End . . . . . . 🗓🗺🗡 ⬜ **VS 4c**
Climb into a short groove and rock out onto the arete. Finish with a bold move up the slab. It is also possible (more devious but historically correct) to start from *Janker's Crack*, though the ropework can cause issues.
FA. Joe Brown 1948

Descer

16m

From mid morning | 🚶 16 min | 🌬 Windy

Sole Power
- p.401

Claire Chipperfield eyeing up the next runner slot on *Green Gut* (HS 4a) - *page 400* - on the Brown's Eliminate area of Froggatt. It is one of the best and most popular lines on the crag. It is a lot cleaner now than it was back in 1948 when Nat Allen excavated it. Photo: Mark Watson

TICKLIST
Froggatt - The Cracks
Froggatt has its fine set of slab routes but it also has a stellar set of crack climbs across the grades. This list is a lot more tickable than the slab one for most climbers.

☐ **Heather Wall, HVD** *(390)*
Mild and beautiful.

☐ **North Climb, HVD** *(384)*
Always a right struggle.

☐ **Diamond Crack, HS** *(395)*
A proper jamming crack.

☐ **Green Gut, HS** *(400)*
The best line on the crag?

☐ **Terrace Crack, HS** *(388)*
Feels like a Millstone route.

☐ **Broken Crack, VS** *(396)*
Layback to get going.

☐ **Hawk's Nest Crack, VS** *(386)*
Avoiding knees is tricky.

☐ **Valkyrie, HVS** *(394)*
Only pitch one qualifies.

☐ **Pedestal Crack, HVS** *(400)*
Awkward and often damp.

☐ **Chequers Crack, HVS** *(401)*
So hard it is untrue.

☐ **Strapiombo, E1** *(382)*
Short but sapping.

☐ **The Big Crack, E2** *(401)*
Big crack, big feel.

☐ **Synopsis, E2** *(399)*
Finger-jamming delight.

☐ **Cave Crack, E3** *(386)*
The stopper in the list!

Sheffield Area
Ladybower Area
Stanage
Burbage Valley
Millstone Area
Derwent Edges
Chatsworth Area
Southern Crags

	No star	✹	✹✹	✹✹✹
Mod to S	23	15	1	-
HS to HVS	39	47	8	4
E1 to E3	16	38	19	3
E4 and up	6	30	18	15

Sheffield Area

Ladybower Area

Stanage

Burbage Valley

Millstone Area

Derwent Edges

Chatsworth Area

Southern Crags

Curbar the Taskmaster has long had a reputation for fierce routes at solid grades and with good reason. Everything here tends to be intimidating, strenuous and high in the grade - soft slabby stuff is a thin on the ground! Known as 'the Cloggy of Grit', many of the routes attack tough cracks up walls that are generally steeper than those found on the other edges. Despite the stiff grades Curbar holds a set of routes as fine as any on grit. Classics such as *The Peapod*, *L'Horla*, *Elder Crack*, *Right Eliminate*, *Moon Walk* and *Profit of Doom* should be on any serious grit climber's ticklist. There are few offerings for climbers looking for lower grade climbs but *P.M.C.1* is one and is probably the most popular climb on the crag.

Approach   Also see map on page 375

The edge overlooks the villages of Curbar and Calver. Above Curbar village is a Pay and Display car park just east of Curbar Gap. This car park can also be reached from a turning off the A625, just north of Gardom's. From here a short walk along the cliff top leads to the Eliminates Wall. There are a few free parking spots on the road below Curbar Gap but these are often full at weekends. The cliff can also be reached from Froggatt by heading south, gently uphill to the left end of the cliff, a couple of minutes away. The serious stuff of the business end is another ten minutes walk.

Conditions

Typical of the eastern edges: quick-drying, exposed to the afternoon sun but with the potential to be windy and cold in bad weather. Some of the hidden bays and smaller buttresses on the far left are green in winter and overgrown in summer.

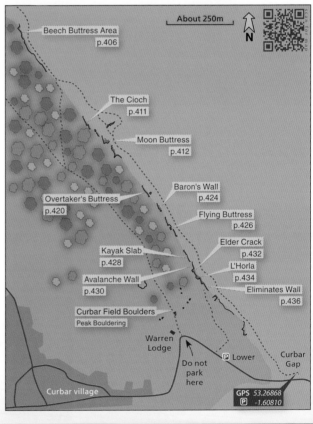

About 250m

N

Beech Buttress Area p.406

The Cioch p.411

Moon Buttress p.412

Baron's Wall p.424

Overtaker's Buttress p.420

Flying Buttress p.426

Elder Crack p.432

Kayak Slab p.428

L'Horla p.434

Avalanche Wall p.430

Eliminates Wall p.436

Curbar Field Boulders
Peak Bouldering

Warren Lodge

Do not park here

P Lower

Curbar Gap

GPS 53.26868
P -1.60810

Curbar village

Chris Fox soloing *Flying Buttress* (S 4a) - *page 426* - an example of one of the many hidden gems tucked away along the length Curbar. Photo: Chris Fox Collection

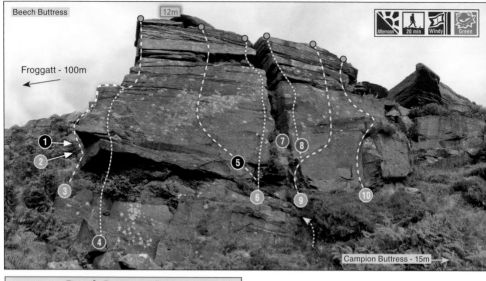

Beech Buttress

12m

Froggatt - 100m

Campion Buttress - 15m

Beech Buttress Area
The northern-most buttress on Curbar has a couple of attractive buttresses. The area can be green after rain.
Approach (see map on page 405) - Continue past Moon Buttress and 300m past a small wood on the crag top is a prominent buttress. Descend just before this and head right. This is just short of Froggatt.

❶ Marx's Wall **f7A**
On a shady side-wall, facing Froggatt. Make a sit start left of the *Angular Crack* - which is out of bounds. *f6B+* from standing.

❷ Angular Crack . . . . **VS 4c**
The wide crack and corner is dirty, damp and awkward.
FA. Joe Brown 1948

❸ Beech Buttress . . . . . . **VS 4b**
Balance boldy out to the arete and climb up its well-positioned valley face to a final tricky couple of moves.
FA. Wilf White 1948

❹ Beech Buttress Direct . . . **E1 5a**
A long reach and stiff pull gains the easier arete.
FA. Gary Gibson 1980

❺ Don't Slip Now **E5 6a**
The centre of the slab is precarious, hard and unprotected. The landing is especially unforgiving - well named!
FA. Phil Burke 1978

❻ Thought Cactus . . . . **HVS 5b**
The escapable left arete of the gully, usually with a side-runner.
FA. Gary Gibson 1981

❼ Beech Gully . . . . **Diff**
The awkward gully that splits the buttress has its moments.

❽ Sunday **E1 5b**
The right arete of the chimney, has a tricky start then eases.
FA. Doug Kerr 1983

❾ Amethyst . . . . **VS 4c**
Balance up the ramp to gain the centre of the wall and finish direct. Nearly a hidden gem.
FA. Clive Jones 1978

❿ Purple Quartz . . . . **HS 4b**
An inferior line using the rock to the right.

Campion Buttress

10m

Pillar Slab - 60m

Campion Buttress
15m to the right is a pit with a couple of worthwhile routes.

⓫ Campion Groove . . . . . . **S 4a**
Climb the wide corner-crack (big gear) to its top, then step right and balance up the pleasant ramp.
FA. Don Chapman 1948

⓬ Campion Wall . . . . . **VS 4c**
The fine finger-crack leads to ledges then step out right and climb the slab. The wall to the right provides a *f5+* start.
FA. Nat Allen 1948

Groans Buttress

This area is just left of Pillar Slab, at the top of a steep bank.

13 Storms of Biblical Proportions . . ⬜ **HVS 5b**
Tackles the juggy and reachy left arete of the buttress.
FA. Peter Stone 1997

14 Groans . . . . 🪧🪧📱⬜ **VS 5a**
The front face via a flake and a tricky little wall to a juggy finale.
FA. Clive Jones 1978

Pillar Slab
A small buttress with a few interesting climbs. The whole area can be green after rain and in summer deep bracken (ticks?) can make getting between the buttresses difficult.
Approach (see map on page 405) - Walk along the top of the edge to 150m before Froggatt, this is down and left.

15 Smiling Jenny . . . . ⬜ **HS 4b**
A short crack in a tiny groove, leading to heather fields above.
FA. Jacek Juszczyck 1986

16 Curbar Your Enthusiasm . 🎯🪧⬜ **f6A+**
The wall is worth a look.

17 Dive . . . . ⬜ **HS 4b**
A groove (or a shorter one to the right) leads to ledges where a crack in the wall accesses a higher ledge. Finish up the steep wall at the back of this.
FA. Clive Jones 1978

18 Port Wine . . . . 🎯🪧⬜ **VS 5a**
Climb the flat wall to a tricky rightward exit to easy ground.
FA. Mark Kemball 1978

19 Mad Era . . . . ⬜ **VS 4c**
A similar line just right of *Port Wine* leads to the ledge. Finish through the bulges above by a move out right.
FA. Steve Clark 2007

20 Leftism . . . . 🪧🎨⬜ **VS 5a**
The unremarkable left arete is a bit bold.

21 Pillar Slab . . . . 🎯🪧⬜ **VD**
A pleasant slab on the left has a tricky start. From the ledge escape right, or better finish up steeper juggy rock, with a dash of heather.

22 Dave's Unremarkable Arete. . . . ⬜ **HS 5a**
The short rounded arete is balancy.

Green Acres

This neat little face has some slab climbs that see occasional ascents and intervening cracks that could do with more traffic to keep the heather at bay. The place is worth a visit if you want a bit of peace and quiet.
Approach (see map on page 405) - Continue past Moon Buttress and 300m past a small wood on the crag top is a prominent buttress. Descend just before this and head left to immediately arrive at Green Acres.

① Happy Slapper. *f5*
A pockety problem just right - no slapping needed!

② Happy House. *f6B*
The blunt rib with a short flake. Highball.
FA. John Allen 1986

③ Short Buttress . . . .   **VS 4c**
The bulge and slanting crack is being reclaimed by nature.

④ Short Chimney. . . . .   **S 4a**
Struggle up the constricted left-hand side of the recess.

⑤ Short Crack . . . .   **HS 4b**
The right-hand variant is more awkward and better.

⑥ Blue Hawaii . . . .   *f6B+*
Gain the hanging arete with considerable difficulty.
FA. John Allen 1986

⑦ Green Acres . . . .   **HVS 5a**
Pull through the bulge and pad up the unprotected slab.
FA. Gary Gibson 1980

⑧ Short Slab. . . . .   **HVS 5a**
The right-hand side of the slab has sketchy moves at mid-height and little in the way of gear.
FA. Joe Brown 1950

⑨ Short Measure. . . . .   **Diff**
The crack on the right makes a reasonable first lead. The small tree runners are currently well pruned.

Beech Layback Area

The short walls here feature a jutting arete on the left and the quarried angular corner of *Beech Layback* to its right. This is a small collection of fairly unremarkable climbs; on the plus side, you will likely have the place to yourself.
Approach (see map on page 405) - The area is just to the right of *Green Acres*.

⑩ Black Silk on White Satin . . .   **HS 4c**
The juggy wall to a tricky finish.
FA. Roy Bennett 1997

⑪ The Arete . . . .   **S 4c**
A tricky couple of moves soon reach better holds.

⑫ The Art of White Hat Wearing
. . . .   *f7B*
The fine blank groove in the left wall of the corner.
FA. Andy Chrome 1992

⑬ Jimmy Hat *f7C*
Fingery wall climbing between the groove and the corner.

⑭ Beech Layback . . . .   **VS 5a**
A short-lived tussle that is safe but surprisingly hard work.
FA. Dick Brown 1953

⑮ Hanging Crack. . . . .   **VS 4b**
The flake-choked crack is quite steep.

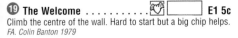

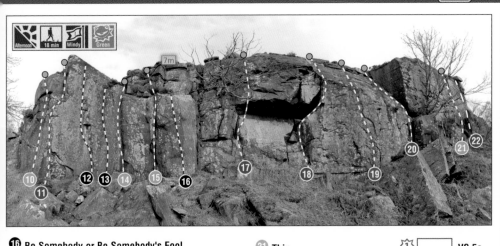

16 Be Somebody or Be Somebody's Fool
.... 🎲🧗 _f7A+_
The pillar just right.

17 Boa Crack .... 🧗 _VD_
The next crack has a huge tree blocking the exit.
FA. Nat Allen 1950

18 Reynard's Crack......... 🧗 _S 4b_
The slanting and narrowing crack. A crafty approach helps.
FA. Nat Allen 1950

19 The Welcome .... 🧗 _E1 5c_
Climb the centre of the wall. Hard to start but a big chip helps.
FA. Colin Banton 1979

20 Heron Wall .... 🧗 _VD_
The slabby groove that bounds the wall.
FA. Nat Allen 1950

Next a square buttress split by some thin cracks juts forward.

21 Thin .... 🎲 _VS 5a_
The parallel thin cracks are protected by tiny wires.

22 Slack Crack.............. _VD_
The crack on good jams and jugs to a tricky exit.

23 The Line .... 🎲🧗🧗 _HVS 5a_
A hidden gem tucked behind the encroaching oak. Climb to, and up, the finger-crack, then the short wall. Hard for the grade.

24 CB Variant .... 🧗 _S 3c_
Head across the crest of the floral flake, first as a hand-traverse then as a foot-traverse, to gain and finish up the grassy groove on the far left.

25 Triple-Bum-Drop ...... 🎲🧗 _E5 6a_
A bold outing up the right-hand side of the face.
FA. Ben Tetler 2008

26 Demolition Chimney.... 🧗🧗 _S 3c_
The short decaying rift on the right.

Up and left is a crack splitting the left-hand side of a short wall with four routes though only one of them sees any attention.

1 Twilight Crack . . . . VS 4c
This is the short-lived but pumpy crack. Worth seeking out.
FA. K.Brindley 1949

2 Deadbay Corner . . . . HS 4b
The groove on the left-hand side of the bay is a decent line. It is pity that it is often choked with shrubbery!

3 Deadbay Groove . . . E2 5c
The groove is awkward, sustained and often a bit damp, which doesn't help. At the break, monkey right to the top groove of *Deadbay Crack*, watch out for the odd loose hold near the top.
FA. Don Whillans 1954

4 Deadbay Groove Direct . . E3 6a
From the top of the initial groove, step left and steam up the wall above. A short-lived but quite intense piece of climbing.
FA. John Allen 1976

The Deadbay
This is a deep, shady pit with a small collection of taxing routes best visit early in the season after a dry spell.
Approach (see map on page 405) - Walk along the top of the edge until about 100m past some trees on the crag top. Scramble carefully down to the crag base.

5 Deadbay Crack E1 5b
The thin hand-crack, maybe with a quick layback too, gains the floral finishing groove that contains the odd loose hold. Short-lived but another pumpy number.
FA. Don Whillans 1952

6 Homicide E3 5c
The steep and sustained wall from the ledge on the right.
FA. Gabe Regan 1979. He called it Dead Bay Biz.

7 Deadbay Climb . . . . HVS 5a
Swing along the shrubby hand traverse then climb the steep, juggy final groove of *Deadbay Crack* taking care with the rock.
FA. Don Whillans 1951

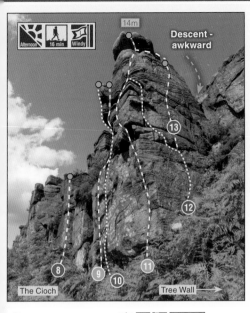

Descent - awkward

The Cioch

Tree Wall ➞

8 King of Crookrise . . . 🏴🏁📖 **E3 6a**
The short arete on the left; a neat little pitch with a hard top-out.
FA. Andy Barker 1991

9 Cioch Left-hand . 🏴📖✋🏁 **HVS 5a**
The left-hand crack leads to a hard exit. Use the flakes on the right to access the hanging chimney and an easier finish.
FA. Valkyrie members 1950

10 Flea Circus . . . . 🏴📖 **E2 5c**
Climb the second crack to the ledge then move left round the arete to access the hanging flake. Up this to a hard finish.
FA. Steve Bancroft 1975

11 Cioch Crack . . . . 🏴🏁📖📖 **HVS 5a**
A good physical pitch. Jam the widening crack on the right - tricky to start - to reach ledges. Squirm up the wide chimney/crack to easier ground then mantel between 'the paps', or escape off right for an easier time.
FA. Nat Allen 1950

12 Cioch Wall . . . . 🏴🏁📖 **S 4a**
Excellent but harrowing at the grade. Traverse the wall left and climb the crack right of the arete. Move left to the chimney/crack of *Cioch Crack* and escape right at its top.
FA. Nat Allen 1950

13 The Bear Hunter 🏴🏁📖📖 **E1 5b**
A direct line up the south-facing wall with a hard move to reach the short rounded crack and a bold-feeling finale.
FA. Bob Bradley 1981

To the right is a tricky descent then a wall with a series of cracks towards its right-hand side.

14 Big Friday . . . . 🏴🏁🏁 **f7C**
The left side of the wall is desperate and highball.
FA. Pete Robins 2009

15 Lithuania . . . . 🏴🏁📖 **E2 5c**
Boulder up to the hanging crack (the old left-hand finish to *Tree Wall*) from the left with difficulty.
FA. Falco Rech 1990

16 Tree Wall . . . . 🏴🏁 **HVS 5a**
The cracks trend to the right and are surprisingly hard work, leading to an awkward exit.
FA. Joe Brown 1954

17 Heather Wall . . . . 🏴🏁 **VS 5a**
The awkward crack leads to an easier tiny groove.
FA. Slim Sorrell 1950

18 Wall End . . . . 🏁 **VS 4c**
The final crack is trickier than it looks.

Cioch Top Boulders
Peak Bouldering
Moon Buttress - 50m
Approach and descent

The Cioch and Tree Wall
Just beyond Moon Buttress is the jutting buttress of The Cioch. Here are two areas with some varied and excellent climbing offering a good selection of rounded holds and tough jamming cracks. The area is usually quiet. In summer, deep bracken (ticks?) can make getting between the buttresses difficult.
Approach (see map on page 405) - Walk along the top of Curbar. Keep an eye out for Moon Buttress with its tall aretes and *Dog-leg Crack*. Continue for 90m to above the Cioch Area and descend just to its right.

Sheffield Area

Ladybower Area

Stanage

Burbage Valley

Millstone Area

Derwent Edges

Chatsworth Area

Southern Crags

Moon Buttress

Apollo Buttress

Hippo's Teeth Gully

p.416

1 **Downhill Gardener** . . . . . 🗝️ 🧗 ▢ *f7A+*
The short, curving arete on its left-hand side.

2 **Button Moon** . . . . 🗝️ ▢ *f5+*
The blunt flake on the wall to the right.

3 **Black Nix Wall** . . . . . 🗝️ 🧗 🎨 ▢ E1 5c
The technical wall just right of a short open corner, trending right via some thin flakes.
FA. Steve Bancroft (after Black Nick failed) 1976

4 **Mastiff Wall** . . . . 🗝️ 🖌️ ▢ VS 4c
Thin cracks have good holds and runners after a tricky start.
FA. Nat Allen 1964

5 **Camel Ticks** . . . . 🎨 ▢ E3 6a
A bold little problem up the thin groove and the wall to the left of the bulges tackled by *Rat Scabies*.
FA. Mike Hammil 1987

6 **Rat Scabies** . . . . 🗝️ 🧗 💪 ▢ E3 6b
A gruesome stopper mantelshelf move to pass the bulge is *f6B*. It eases above but take a rope since it is tricky to get off.
FA. Gabe Regan mid 1970s

7 **Bulldog Crack** . . . . 🗝️ 🔆 ▢ S 4b
The groove on the right has a tricky start (loose flake) and a stubborn upper section.
FA. K.Brindley 1950

8 **John's Arete** . . . . 🗝️ 🧗 ▢ E1 5b
A square, jutting arete and wall above are pleasantly technical but not something you would want to fall off.
FA. Steve Bancroft 1975

9 **Derwent Groove** . . . . 🖐️ ▢ S 4a
The open corner is awkward towards the top. A left-hand variation via a flake is usually cleaner and is a bit easier (HVD).
FA. Nat Allen 1950

10 **Cool Moon** . . . . 🗝️ 🧗 🖌️ 🎨 ▢ E7 6c
A bold climb up the thin flakes and sinuous cracks. The hard lower section has no gear but a side-runner in *Moon Walk* drops the grade a notch. Higher up, small cams protect.
FA. Daniel Lee (side-runners) 1981. FA. Ron Fawcett (without) 1981

Afternoon | 14 min | Windy

10m

Tree Wall - 50m

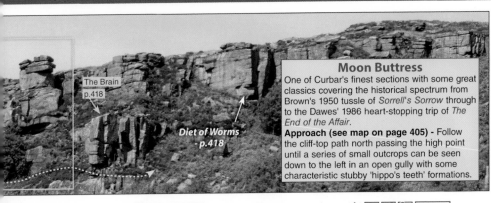

Moon Buttress

One of Curbar's finest sections with some great classics covering the historical spectrum from Brown's 1950 tussle of *Sorrell's Sorrow* through to the Dawes' 1986 heart-stopping trip of *The End of the Affair*.

Approach (see map on page 405) - Follow the cliff-top path north passing the high point until a series of small outcrops can be seen down to the left in an open gully with some characteristic stubby 'hippo's teeth' formations.

⑪ **Moon Walk** E4 6a
One of the finest grit experiences. A tricky start gains a flake in the arete. This leads to a break, which needs packing with cams, before the tasty finishing moves. Well worth attempting as a true ground-up, on-sight since commitment on the final moves will be rewarded with either success or flight-time.
FA. John Allen 1976

⑫ **Moon Crack** E5 6b
Moon Walk's tough twin. The thin bulging crack gives a fierce battle but with solid wires to protect. At the top of the crack, move right to the much easier slabby groove.
FA. John Allen (with one runner!) 1975

⑬ **Crack and Slab** . E7 6c
Climb *Moon Crack* to above its crux then gain the slab above by a wild mantelshelf. Hard smearing and a rounded finish might just gain the top of this particularly taxing trip.
FA. John Arran 1999

⑭ **Moon Madness** . E7 6c
The bulging rock to the right of *Moon Crack* is unprotected, reachy and the landing is particularly grim.
FA. Ron Fawcett 1987

⑮ **Sorrell's Sorrow** . . . . HVS 5a
The superb soaring central crack-line is compelling and hard work, but less so than you might be expecting. Big gear needed.
FA. Joe Brown 1950

⑯ **Mr Softee** E1 6a
Climb the bulges via a crack (hard for the short) to the break then head left past *Sorrell's Sorrow* to finish up the last section of *Moon Crack*. Only HVS after the technical start.
FA. John Allen 1973

The Brain p.418
Diet of Worms - p.418

Sheffield Area
Ladybower Area
Stanage
Burbage Valley
Millstone Area
Derwent Edges
Chatsworth Area
Southern Crags

17 The End of the Affair Top 50 **E8 6c**
The archetypal grit arete and one of grit's greatest hard routes.
The climbing is technical and ultra committing with good runners
at one-third height and the crux at the top. Don't fall off the last
move unless you have briefed your second man to leap from
the ledge in an attempt to shorten the fall - even then it is pretty
much touch and go! *Photos opposite, page 19 and on the cover.*
FA. Johnny Dawes 1986

18 Amphitheatre Crack . . . . **HVD 4a**
The wide crack in the south-facing wall is hard to enter (high wire
in the right rib) then eases rapidly.
FA. Valkyrie members 1950

19 Dirty Sanchez **E1 5c**
The shallow groove is a short-lived technical gem.

20 Glad Tidings . . . . **HVS 5a**
A stubborn crack leads to the ledge. Gain a ramp and finish up
left via a thin crack (the old left-hand finish to *Gladiator Buttress*).
FA. Colin Binks 2005

21 Gladiator Buttress . . . . . **VS 4c**
Climb the front arete to a big ledge then the crack just left of the
arete to a taxing exit - fortunately with good gear.

22 Hidden Pleasures. **E3 6a**
The thin cracks in the narrow tower, small wires protect.
FA. Andy Bailey 1984

23 Twin Crack . . . . **HS 4b**
The wide left-hand corner-crack using a subsidiary crack in the
left wall. Laybacking the whole thing feels like a reckless HVS 4c.

24 Straight Crack . . . . **VD**
Thrutch the widening right-hand corner-crack; awkward but safe.

25 Ulysses or Bust **E5 6b**
An attractive and unprotected arete. Layaway the right-hand
side usually above a rapidly diminishing stack of mats at *f7A+*.
Originally the route swapped sides - easier but bolder.
FA. Neil Foster 1984. Shortly before 'busting' himself on Ulysses.

26 The Unreachable Star **E3 6a**
The thin crack past an extended reach to a rounded exit. *f6A+*
above pads.
FA. Mark Stokes 1980

27 Dog-leg Crack . . . . **HVD 4a**
The jamming crack is a midget gem, pity it is so short.

28 The Dog's Hole **f6B**
The short wall just right is more involving than first appears.

Sheffield Area

Ladybower Area

Stanage

Burbage Valley

Millstone Area

Derwent Edges

Chatsworth Area

Southern Crags

Rob Greenwood fully committed on *The End of the Affair* (E8 6c) - *opposite* - the same move as the cover photo but with a very different approach to his footwork. Photo: Mike Hutton

Apollo Buttress

The main feature of central Curbar is the tall bulk of the Apollo Buttress with its impressive west face jutting out towards the valley. There is also a collection of lesser routes to either side of the main tower and further right, a series of smaller walls and buttresses scattered up and down the hillside.

Approach (see map on page 405) - Follow the cliff-top path to the 'Hippo's Teeth' gully and descend this turning left to locate the buttress.

1 Smiling Buttress *f8B*
The short face opposite *Dog-leg Crack* via the smiling hold. Highball with a bad landing and worth a big E grade.
FA. Tyler Landman 2013. No grade was offered.

2 Landlord's Out E3 6a
Climb the right arete of the front of the block via an overhang.
FA. Duncan Frisch 1995

3 Buckle's Sister HVD 4a
The left-hand crack is amenable enough.
FA. Nat Allen 1950

4 Buckle's Brother HVS 4c
The central crack is an exhausting thrash.
FA. Nat Allen 1950

5 Buckle's Crack HVS 4c
The right-hand crack is also a battle unless you dare layback it!
FA. Nat Allen 1950

6 Soyuz E2 5c
The cracks in the north-facing side-wall lead to a sloping shelf. Before you pump out, stretch awkwardly right and reach for the top, or go direct - rounded either way. *Photo on page 419.*
FA. John Allen 1972

7 Dark Entries E4 6a
Climb the bulges leftwards to a short crack then head right via long reaches to decent finishing holds at a flake.
FA. Ron Fawcett 1980

8 Forbidden Planet E5 6b
The fine flying arete on the right. Climb through the bulges with difficulty to the crucial roof. Undercut past this then sprint for the top either via the left arete or the harder face just right. A couple of large cams are pretty much essential.
FA. John Allen 1984

9 Apollo E2 5c
There is an unremarkable lower pitch to the right of *Two Pitch Route* that is usually ignored. Do this (**5a**) or start from a stance on the ledge left of the tower. Move out right then head through the imposing bulges via a short crack with one powerful move to reach easier ground.
FA. John Gosling (with a little tension) 1969

Descent

8m

18m

Afternoon   14 min   Windy

Moon Buttress

The next routes start down and right, directly below Apollo.

10 Two Pitch Route. . . . VS 5a
Climb the left-hand crack (loose blocks) to ledges then traverse right to pass the arete to a comfortable stance (**4c**). Finish up the tough crack to a superb juggy exit. A better combination is to start up the lower cracks of *The Beer Hunter* and continue up the second pitch as above, dubbed *Two Beers*.
FA. Joe Brown 1950

11 The League of Gentleman E6 6b
Climb the right edge of the lower wall. Continue over the big roof then climb the big bulges above to join *The Beer Hunter*.
FA. Pete Robins 1999

12 The Beer Hunter E3 6a
Usually started from the mid-height ledge. This is reached from the right (looking in). Climb the right arete of the buttress via a thin crack to a baffling move on a hidden pocket which gives access the front face. Keep right to finish. Starting up a crack below the upper arete is also possible.
FA. Steve Bancroft 1979

13 Combat les Pellicules. . . . . . HVS 5c
Hairy moves up the short arete on the lower buttress, first on the left then on the right.
FA. Bill McKee 1985

14 For the Good of the Cause E4 6b
Just left of *Big Rocker*, a hard start reaches pockets that are followed left to finish as for *Combat les Pellicules*.
FA. Andy Barker 1994

15 The Big Rocker . . . . HVS 5a
A complex line - two (or three) pitches is sensible. Climb a thin crack past a stump then a jutting rib. Move down and across right to a stance below the arete. Up the rounded rib then move along ledges to the far right arete. Climb the face just left of this then grope around the bulge to find 'the big rocker' and an exit.
FA. John Gosling 1966

The next three routes are by the northwest arete of Big Rocker.

16 Art of Japan f6C
The north facing side-wall via side-pulls is superb. Approach from the top of the crag. Coming in from the left is **The Arse of Japan**, *f7A+*.

17 Rocky Horror Show . E6 6b
The short and technical left arete above a rocky horror landing.
FA. Pete Robins 1999

18 Body Torque E3 5c
The left side of the west-facing wall with a hard lower section.
FA. Paul Mitchell 1981

19 The Vegas Years E1 5b
Basically climbs the right arete of the buttress with a jig right and left to pass the jutting capstone.
FA. John Allen 1999

Afternoon | 12 min | Windy

Descent

18m

6m

16m

The Brain →

The Brain

The lowest buttress of this complex area is seldom busy although *The Brain* gets lots of ascents. The *Diet of Worms* area is frequented by the hard-core.
Approach (see map on page 405) - Scramble across from under Apollo Buttress.

①　The Brain . . . . 　**VS 4c**
Climb the slabby lower wall trending right - bold - to the base of a groove (possible belay). Enter and climb the groove to a choice of finishes, direct is harder, stepping left onto the arete is more exposed - both are excellent.
FA. Slim Sorrell late 1940s

②　Mensa . . . . 　**E6 6b**
Climb the centre of the slab to reach the left-hand arete. Boldly finish up this using a blend of flair and subtlety.
FA. Neil Foster 1993. The lower part was Brain Variations, Andy Bailey 1983

③　Early Morning Day . . 　**f6B**
The right arete of the slab. High but a good landing.

④　Oblongata . . . . 　**HS 4b**
The open groove is precarious. Small wires protect.

⑤　Amphitheatre Chimney . . 　**HS 4b**
The continuation rift to *Oblongata* gives proper chimney graft.

⑥　Birthday Crack . . . . 　**VS 5a**
Thankfully the imposing fissure is easier than it looks.
FA. Valkyrie Club members 1950

⑦　Not Another Chimney . . . . . 　**S 4a**
This is the awkward widening rift on the right.

Up and right is a short but steep and imposing axe-edged arete.

⑧　King of the Swingers 　**E5 6c**
Climb the reachy wall left of the arete to a pocket (gear) then make a desperate long move left to finish.
FA. Ron Fawcett 1984

⑨　King Louis . . . . 　**E6 6c**
Start as for *King of the Swingers* to the runners, then make crucial moves up and right to a final mantel that has some ground-fall potential if your second is at all lax.
FA. Chris Wright 1999

⑩　Diet of Worms . . 　**E4 6a**
The arete is approached from the left. A tricky-to-place big cam protects the final difficult moves.
FA. Paul Mitchell (with pre-placed stacked Hexes!) 1978

⑪　Slackers . . . . 　**E6 6b**
The direct start is bold, dynamic and elegant, spotter(s) useful. The short may need to hand traverse the sloper under the roof.
FA. Robin Barker 1994

⑫　Birthday Groove . . . . 　**E1 5c**
The groove on the right is a pig to enter but eases above.
FA. Joe Brown 1950

⑬　Flake Crack . . . . 　**HS 4b**
Just right is a short wall split by a wide fissure - not on topo.

16m

Descent

Apollo Buttress

Overtaker's Buttress - 120m
along crag-top path

Martin Kocsis on the shady wall of *Soyuz* (E2 5c) - *page 416* -
on Apollo Buttress at Curbar. The route is a good bet for a first
Curbar E2, being pretty safe and short-lived. Photo: Mike Hutton

Sheffield Area

Ladybower Area

Stanage

Burbage Valley

Millstone Area

Derwent Edges

Chatsworth Area

Southern Crags

Fidget Area

Black and Tan

Potter's Wall

Overtaker's Buttress

Diddledum Wall - 40m →

Black and Tan

7m

Overtaker's Buttress and Potter's Wall

This disjointed section of the crag has the old classic of *Overtaker's Buttress*, the Johnny Dawes' despo of *White Lines*, and the excellent *Potter's Wall*. In amongst these are some other decent routes spread across the various formations though there no real central area of focus.

Approach (see map on page 405) - Follow the cliff-top path keeping an eye out for the prominent beak of *Fidget* which is perched above *Overtaker's Buttress*. Descend down a steep path about 50m before this which leads under *Potter's Wall*.

Black and Tan

To the left of the bulk of Overtaker's Buttress is a short wall with prominent twin cracks.

1 Black . . . . HVS 5b
The left-hand crack has a couple of thin moves.

2 Tan . . . . HVS 5b
The right-hand crack is more sustained.

The Brain - 120m
along crag-top path

12m

Black and Tan - 25m

Fidget Area

9m

6m

From mid morning | 15 min | Windy

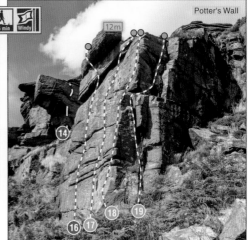

Potter's Wall

12m

Overtaker's Buttress

③ Overtaking on the Outside . . . . . [ ] **S 4a**
Balance up the low-relief protruding rib on the left.
FA. Steve Clarke 2003

④ Overtaking on the Inside . . . . . . [ ] **S 4a**
The groove just right using the thin crack as required.
FA. Steve Clarke 2003

⑤ Overtaker's Buttress . . . . ❄ [ ] **HVS 5b**
1) 4c, 10m. Reach the groove from the left and, at its top, traverse right below the overhangs to a ledge and stance.
2) 5b, 8m. Climb the tough wall right of the arete to finish.
FA. Don Chapman 1954

⑥ Overtaker's Direct . . ❄ 🦎 ✋ [ ] **E2 5b**
Climb direct to the groove on the original, then tackle the overhang above and left using some rather flexible flakes.
FA. Mike Simpkins 1970s

⑦ Snorter . . . . 🦎 🕷 [ ] **E4 6b**
The overhangs above the start of the *Overtaker's* traverse are tackled with great difficulty and a crucial small cam.
FA. Mike Lea 1999

⑧ White Lines. . . . . . . ❄ 🕷 🤚 [ ] **E7 6b**
The centre of the wall by a desperate mantelshelf then the overhangs above via a pocket. A brilliant sustained outing.
FA. Johnny Dawes 1984

⑨ Free Way . . . . ❄ [ ] **E5 6b**
Climb a seam on the right then the left side of the nose by a long stretch for distant pockets. Finish over the bulges above.
FA. Pete Robins 1999

Fidget Area
Up and right is a trio of buttresses including a huge jutting nose pointing out towards the valley, separated by a couple of wide chimneys.

⑩ Right Triplet Gully . . . . . ❄ 🧍 [ ] **VD**
Back and foot the deeply traditional cleft just left of the beak.

⑪ Lifeseeker. . . . . ❄ 🦎 🤚 [ ] **E4 6b**
The hanging flake on the right wall of the gully is reached by starting under the big roofs. *f6C* above pads.

⑫ Stretch Armstrong . . ❄ [ ] 🤚 [ ] **E6 6b**
Battle with the never-ending stacked roofs to the wild arete.
FA. Seb Greive 1998

⑬ Instant Karma . . . . ❄ 🦎 [ ] **E4 6b**
The imposing hanging arete is no place to ponder.
FA. Greg Lucas 1983

⑭ Fidget. . . . . ❄ 🕷 [ ] [ ] **E2 6b**
Climb the arete under the right edge of the nose then fidget left, stretch for the flake and go! It does take gear though is often done above pads at *f6B+*. There is a right-hand start at *f6C*.
FA. John Allen 1973

⑮ Rise of the Robots . . ❄ 🕷 [ ] [ ] **HVS 5c**
Extend-a-way up the wall. Short and sweet.
FA. Gary Gibson 1979

Potter's Wall
20m right of Overtaker's Buttress is a tall wall, with an oblong block on its top known as Potter's Wall.

⑯ Mad Hatter . . . . ❄ [ ] 🖐 [ ] **E2 5c**
Start up a groove on the left-hand side of the wall (or the harder wall to its right). Climb up and then left to the top break finishing with a desperate rounded mantel moves over the capping roof.
FA. John Gosling 1966

⑰ Potter's Wall . . . . . . ❄ [ ] 🤚 [ ] **HS 4b**
The discontinuous cracks up the right-hand edge of the buttress have decent holds but the upper part is a bit light on gear.

⑱ Circus of Dinosaurs . ❄ 🖐 🤚 [ ] **HVS 5b**
The arete of the wall on its left-hand side has some good moves. Avoiding holds (but not runners) in the previous route is tricky.
FA. Roy Bennett 1989

⑲ Grooved Arete . . . . ❄ [ ] **VS 4c**
Climb the shallow, stepped grove in the south-facing side-wall - good but short-lived. The hard move is well protected.
FA. Mike Simpkins 1966

← Potter's Wall - 40m

8m

Diddledum Wall to Lamebrain
A series of short walls and buttresses with a few decent routes scattered amongst them.
Approach (see map on page 405) - Follow the path north for 150m from the Kayak Area, then drop down before Quarry Wall and walk along under the face.

① **Sheep Pit Crack Left** . . . . . . | | *f5*
The roof taken directly to the crack. Starting from the right is the desperate **The Sheep Pit**, *f6B*.

② **Sheep Pit Crack Right** . . . . . | | *f5*
The steep crack on the right above a nasty landing.

❸ **Mark of Respect** . . . . . . | | **E4 6b**
Stretchy moves up the wall left of the gully.
FA. Neil Foster 1997

④ **Short Circuit** . . . . | | **HS 4b**
Tricky climbing through the niche in the right wall of the gully.
FA. David Simmonite 1989

⑤ **Diddledum Wall** . . . . | | **HVS 5a**
The tough little crack leads to a ledge and a rounded exit up the left arete. A direct finish is a precarious and bold **E2 5b**.
FA. Don Hadley late 1950s

⑥ **Honest John** . . . . | | **HVS 5a**
Starting right of the arete climb into the niche, move out left to pass the roof then traverse back right to a fine finish on the arete.
FA. Mike Simpkins 1966

⑦ **Little Layback** . . . . | | **S 4b**
The stubborn little angle left of the buttress.

⑧ **Mirror Image** . . . . | | **VS 4c**
Weave up the right arete of the buttress. Easier for the tall.

⑨ **The Scoop** . . . . . | | **E2 5b**
Up the scoopy feature - harrowing, though less so for the tall.
FA. John Gosling 1966

⑩ **Scoop Crack** . . . . | | **HVS 5a**
The tricky thin cracks.
FA. John Gosling 1966

⑪ **Alan's Crack** . . . . | | **VD**
Amble up the big steps. Trickier than it looks.

⑫ **Lamebrain** . . . . | | **E1 5b**
The centre of the face via a neat finger-crack - bomber wires. From a rest (big cam) finish rightwards on sloping holds.
FA. Steve Bancroft 1974

⑬ **Suspect Intellect** . . . . . . | | **HVS 5a**
Use the ramp and hole to access the front face and another useful hole. Finish up the arete to a rounded exit.
FA. Clive Jones 1978

⑭ **Allen's Climb** . . . . | | **Diff**
The gritty cracks in the side-wall have an awkward exit.
FA. John Gosling 1966

8m

Baron's Wall ►

Sheffield Area

Ladybower Area

Stanage

Burbage Valley

Millstone Area

Derwent Edges

Chatsworth Area

Southern Crags

Mark Watson making the crux stretch up the magnificent upper groove of *Profit of Doom* (E4 6b) - *page 431* - at Curbar. Photo: Chris Fox

Sheffield Area

Ladybower Area

Stanage

Burbage Valley

Millstone Area

Derwent Edges

Chatsworth Area

Southern Crags

❶ I Bet He Drinks Carling Black Label
. . . . **E6 6b**
The sketchy wall to a beckoning crack is desperate! *f7A* if you
can pad it properly.
FA. Andy Barker 1994

❷ The Squint Start. . . . . . . **HVS 5b**
An interesting and pumpy way for technical dunces to get at the
upper crack on *Baron's Wall* - don't expect it to be easy though!

❸ Tube of Foster's. **E4 6b**
This earlier version of *I Bet He Drinks...* climbs the blunt rib to
the ledge - move left to access the thin crack with difficulty to
finish. This can be padded at *f6C+* but it is still highball.
FA. Paul Mitchell (with distant side-runner) 1984

❹ Cartons and Curpets. **f6B**
The wall just right of the rib.

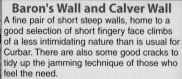

Baron's Wall and Calver Wall
A fine pair of short steep walls, home to a
good selection of short fingery face climbs
of a less intimidating nature than is usual for
Curbar. There are also some good cracks to
tidy up the jamming technique of those who
feel the need.
Approach (see map on page 405) - Follow
the cliff-top path north for 150m from the
Kayak Area, then descend down before
Quarry Wall and walk along under the face.

5 Smoke ont' Watter . . 🌟 E1 6a
A *f6A+* boulder problem start leads to a ledge. An awkward and scary move gains a thin hanging crack, leading to the top. It is still no pushover.
FA. Nicky Stokes 1976

6 Talon Man. . . . . 🌟 f6B
The wall past the side-pull.

7 Baron's Direct . . . . 🌟 f6A
Climb direct to the finishing crack of *Baron's Wall.*

8 Baron's Wall . . . . . . 🌟 HVS 5b
The right-hand crack is gained from the right. The start is problematic especially for the short. Leaning in from the arete on the right is a bit naughty.
FA. Joe (the Baron) Brown late 1950s

9 Blockhead. . . . . VS 5a
Climb past ledges and jam the groove to a steep finish using the crack on the right where needed.
FA. Dave Gregory 1978

10 Sweet Gene Vincent . . . . 🌟 HVS 5c
Take the wall right of *Blockhead* via a hard move to the break. Step left and climb the technical thin crack in the wall.
FA. Gary Gibson 1978

11 Saddy. . . . . 🌟 E2 5c
Exiting the thin crack is harder than it looks, the wires are tricky to place and the finish is pretty pumpy. It's good though!
FA. Steve Bancroft 1977

12 Wall Climb . . . . 🌟 VS 5a
The fine right-trending groove is sustained and awkward. Despite the good protection it is high in the grade.
FA. Joe Brown 1950

13 Top Secret . . . . 🌟 E1 5c
A bold start leads to the break, runners and a high crux.
FA. Gary Gibson 1981

14 Calver Chimney . . . . Diff
Usually a bit green though most of the best holds aren't!

15 Colossus. E2 5b
The right-hand arete of the chimney mostly on its left side.
FA. Gary Gibson 1981

16 Vaguely Great E1 5c
A filler though with some good moves up the wall and blind flake. A direct start is a bit harder.
FA. Colin Banton 1979

17 Calver Wall. . . . . 🌟 VS 5a
Climb the easy wall left of a tree to a ledge. Finish up the short but tricky crack by a layback move or two.

18 Brindle Crack . . . . 🌟 HS 4b
As for *Calver Wall* to the ledge but step right to reach and climb the right-hand branch of the crack. The shallow groove directly below is the reachy direct start - **5b**.

19 Polar Crack. . . . . 🌟 VS 4b
Start to the right of the tree and climb an awkward wide crack (huge cams help) to a ledge, finish up the steep right-hand crack in the upper wall.

20 Arctic Nose . . . . 🌟 HS 4a
Head up the arete (no gear) to the ledge then finish up the cracked arete. A finish to the right is easier, as is a start round the right arete using blocks.

Calver Wall ←
10m

Flying Buttress and Quarry Wall

Two small sections of ancient quarry - a jutting buttress with a couple of decent easier routes and a neglected wall composed of rather indifferent rock.

Approach (see map on page 405) - Follow the cliff-top path north for 150m from the Kayak Area, then descend down before Quarry Wall and walk along under the face.

From mid morning | 12 min | Windy

❶ The Wall **E2 6a**
The centre of wall; technical and a bit bold. A line just left is 5c.

❷ Betwixt **E1 5a**
The right-hand side of the wall is just a bit bold.

❸ The Corner . . . . **HVS 5b**
The blank corner is bridged. Technical but still low in the grade except for the short who might really struggle.
FA. Joe Brown 1955

❹ Eye Bigger than t'Ledges . . . **E4 6a**
Layback the arete then move out left for the high crux.
FA. Andy Barker 1985

❺ Flying Buttress . . . . **S 4a**
The left-hand side of the buttress via a groove and cracks. Finish using both cracks or it is a grade harder. *Photo on page 404.*

❻ Flying Buttress Right . . . . . . **S 4a**
The right-hand side of the buttress - the same comment applies.

❼ U.F.O. . . . . **S 4a**
A thin crack just right leads to a tight blocky groove in the arete.

10m

Kayak Slab →

❽ By George **E3 6b**
The technical hairline crack on the far left to a high crux.
FA. Keith Sharples 1984

❾ Culture Shock **E1 5c**
The crack and groove form a tricky little problem.
FA. Ian Riddington 1982

❿ Confidence Trick **E2 5c**
Climb past rickety blocks to the flaky upper wall; side-runners.
FA. John Russell 1985

⓫ Litreage . . . . **HVS 5c**
A tough little line just to the right.

⓬ Ling Crack . . . . **HS 4c**
A poor start leads to a short but action-packed crack. Big gear.
FA. Slim Sorrel 1949

⓭ Incestuous **E2 6a**
The tiny shallow groove gives a technical tussle.
FA. John Allen 1976

⓮ Cardinals Backbone II **E3 5c**
Climb the wall to the break then move left and follow the flakes with some trepidation.
FA. Nicky Stokes 1976

⓯ Superhands **E7 6c**
The wall gives a pitch with low runners and a high crux.
FA. Dominic Lee 2010

⓰ Vain **E3 5b**
Climb the bold arete, left then right - spooky but neat!
FA. John Allen (solo) 1976. He graded it HVS!

Curbar

Topping out on the most popular route on the crag in the evening sun, about as good as it gets - *P.M.C.1* (HS 4a) - *page 431* - Curbar.

Sheffield Area

Ladybower Area

Stanage

Burbage Valley

Millstone Area

Derwent Edges

Chatsworth Area

Southern Crags

TICKLIST
Curbar Crush

A great edge with a tough reputation and a ticklist to match. Very full-on in terms of quality and difficulty.

- **P.M.C. 1, HS** *(431)*. The most popular route on the crag.
- **The Brain, VS** *(418)*. Devious and interesting.
- **Avalanche Wall, HVS** *(430)*. It is a crack really.
- **Sorrell's Sorrow, HVS** *(413)*. Wide and intimidating.
- **The Peapod HVS,** *(436)*. Super-classic, hard for long legs.
- **L'Horla, E1** *(434)*. Short but action-packed.
- **Deadbay Crack, E1** *(410)*. A secretive slippery struggle.
- **Elder Crack, E2** *(432)*. A VS from years ago.
- **The Right Eliminate, E3** *(436)*. 5.10a about covers it.
- **Moon Walk, E4** *(413)*. Brilliant and bold, in a nice way.
- **Profit of Doom, E4** *(431)*. Great line, great moves.
- **Linden, E6** *(436)*. Bold despite the silly drilled holes.
- **White Lines, E7** *(421)*. Technical and sustained.
- **Slab and Crack, E8** *(430)*. Sketchy and bold.
- **The End of the Affair, E8** *(414)*. The arete of the world.
- **Knockin' on Heaven's Door, E9** *(432)*. Bolder than life.

Flying Buttress

7m

Kayak Slab

Sun and shade | 10 min | Windy

From mid morning | 10 min | Windy

3 Lepton . . . . 🎯🏴‍☠️🐾💚 ⬜ *f6C+*
The highball arete has a hard rounded and scary finish. Heading right is a bit easier, but not much!
FA. Al Rouse 1978

4 Lepton Wall . . . . 🎯 ⬜ *f6A+*
The wall is easier towards the top, hence less scary than its neighbour to the left.

5 Amy . . . . 🎯 ⬜ HS 4a
Hop onto the ramp and balance left to a short crack. Nice.
FA. Graham Iles 1989

The next trio of short slabs are always popular and a nice contrast to most of the other routes at this end of the crag.

6 Rapid . . . . 🏴 ⬜ E1 5c
The right-hand side of the slab immediately left of *Kayak*.
FA. Pete Robins 2000ish

7 Kayak . . . . 🎯🚪💚 ⬜ E1 5b
The left side of the slab trending right, harder for the short. The final break takes runners. A direct finish is a grade harder.
FA. Colin Mortlock 1964. FA. (Direct finish) Pete Robins 2000ish

1 Inch Crack. . . . . 🎯 ⬜ VS 4c
The left-hand crack is short, steep and wider than an inch.

2 Little Innominate . . . . . 🎯📐 ⬜ VS 5a
Classic Curbar, a tough nut to crack, being both narrower and harder then its neighbour
FA. Valkyrie Club members 1950

9m

Kayak Slab
A Curbar rarity, a set of slabs. It's not all good news though - the routes are technical and runners are in short supply. If you're feeling bold, step this way, but don't forget your life-jacket. As ever with short slabby grit, some of the grades are hotly disputed.
Approach (see map on page 405) - Walk along the top of the edge passing over the Eliminates Wall and descend easy ground.

Sheffield Area | Ladybower Area | Stanage | Burbage Valley | Millstone Area | Derwent Edges | Chatsworth Area | Southern Crags

8 Finger Distance . E3 6b
The pocketed centre of the slab is tenuous and unprotected. The right-hand start, using the big pocket, is easier but true technicians will ignore this and climb direct. *f6B+* above pads.
FA. Gary Gibson 1980

9 El Vino Collapso . . . E5 6a
Wobble up the right-hand side of the slab to a crucial stretch for distant jugs. Very highball *f6B+*.
FA. John Allen 1985

The next slab is high but easily paddable hence these are now almost always done above a stack of pads.

10 Canoe. . . . . f5+
The pocketed left-hand edge of the right-hand slab is a grade harder for the technically inept.
FA. Ed Drummond early 1970s

11 Stopper f6B
A thin slab with the final moves forming the stopper crux.
FA. Ron Fawcett 1987

12 White Water . . . . . . f7A+
The tiny but sustained and unprotected slab requires cunning.
FA. Johnny Dawes 1984

13 Done Years Ago E3 6a
Head right past the overlaps to the juggy arete. Often gritty.
FA. Johnny Dawes 1984

The angular corner round the arete is home to three cracking problems, the Corner is especially neat.

14 Neat. . . . . f5+

15 Curbar Corner f5
Has good wires so can be led at VS if required.

16 Little Stiffer. f6A

1 Million Dollar Bash . . . . 🖐️ 🔲 **E6 6b**
The left-hand side of the face requires commitment.
FA. Andy Popp 1997

2 Portrait of a Legend . . . . . . 🖐️ 🔲 **E4 6b**
Climb the fierce thin cracks in the left-hand side of the wall past
a deep break to a steeper finish.
*FA. John Allen 1987. Cleaned up by Chris Craggs and Martin Veale a couple
of years earlier, until they realised it was far too hard!*

3 Avalanche Wall . . . . 🔲 🔲 🔲 🔲 **HVS 5a**
A Curbar rarity - as in not too tough at the grade. Twin cracks
lead past blocks to steeper flaky cracks that are best tackled
rapidly. Protection is good and pressing on is the best idea.
FA. Joe Brown 1950

4 One Step Beyond . . . 🔲 🖐️ 🔲 🔲 **E6 6b**
From the base of *Avalanche Wall*, traverse the steep slab
rightwards passing a runner slot and crucial high step to an
easier finish just left of the far arete.
FA. Ron Fawcett 1980

5 Doctor Dolittle . . 🔲 🖐️ 🔲 🔲 🔲 **E10 7a**
A desperate outing. Start up *Slab and Crack* and traverse left into
One Step Beyond. Above the crux of this, break left and tackle
the headwall by more extremely tenuous moves.
FA. John Arran 2001. John graded the route H9 (Headpoint 9).

6 Slab and Crack . . . . 🔲 🖐️ 🔲 🔲 **E8 6c**
The centre of the steep slab is a Curbar testpiece, being both
technical and bold. Climb directly to the runner slot on *One
Step Beyond* then continue up the sustained thin crack above. A
microwire is useful in the crack but it is hard to place.
FA. Johnny Dawes 1986

7 Owl's Arete . . . . 🔲 🔲 **VS 4b**
The well-cracked arete is steep for a couple of moves in its
central section and protection is good. Sadly the upper section
is easier. The wide dirty rift in the left-hand angle of the next bay
is **Owl's Crack, VS 4c**.
FA. Slim Sorrell 1949

8 Little Chef . . . . 🔲 🔲 🔲 **E5 6b**
The thin flaky crack in the left-hand side of the recess is
normally dirty and sees little attention.
FA. Chris Plant 1987. Done earlier in 1987 by Mark Pretty with 1 peg.

Descent

16m

Avalanche Wall
A couple of mid-grade climbs and a trio of desperate
outings are the main draws of this once-quarried
bay. *P.M.C.1* is best easier climb here and *Avalanche
Wall* is as popular as any HVS route in the area. The
harder routes see less action though the class line of
Profit of Doom is popular with the hard core.
Approach (see map on page 405) - Walk along the
top of the edge passing over the Eliminates Wall and
descend easy ground, doubling back to this wall.

9 Predator E2 5c
The thin crack on the right is rather unsatisfying. The bulge is
the crux (knee-bar rest) and, although the ledges on the right are
difficult to avoid, you have to at least try!
FA. John Allen 1976

10 Argosy Crack . . . . . VS 4b
The wide crack in the corner is good practice for dirty American
off-widths and great at wrecking clothes old or new. The lower
crack is too wide and the upper chimney too narrow!
FA. Slim Sorrell late 1940s

11 P.M.C. 1 . . . . Top 50 HS 4a
The most popular route on the crag with some great positions.
The cracks to the right of the corner lead awkwardly and steeply
to a ledge. Trend right up the wall to a spike and a superb
exposed finish on sloping holds. A tiny left-hand finish is also
possible to extend the pleasure a bit. *Photo on page 427.*
FA. Bob Tomsett (Polaris Mountaineering Club) 1948

12 The Fall E6 6b
The big, brash, bold wall to the left of *Profit of Doom* looks
magnificent but sees few ascents. The rightward traverse is bold
as are the final moves up the dramatically positioned arete. It
needs a direct finish like no other line in the Peak!
FA. John Allen 1978

13 Profit of Doom . . . . . Top 50 E4 6b
The superb hanging groove in the arete is best approached
directly up the steep and awkward crack below it, although those
impatient individuals who can't wait to get at the main event,
often climb the wall to the left. Gear in the back of the groove is
hard to place (offsets?), especially for the short. Once suitably
protected bridge-a-way to glory making suitable use of the
left-hand arete. Many pre-place the gear in the groove on abseil
which reduces the commitment and possibly the grade.
Photo on page 423.
FA. John Allen 1975

22m

Afternoon | 10 min | Windy | Green

Rigid Digit - p.432

Elder Crack

Sheffield Area

Ladybower Area

Stanage

Burbage Valley

Millstone Area

Derwent Edges

Chatsworth Area

Southern Crags

1 Rigid Digit E5 6b
Climb the direct start to *Profit of Doom* to below the upper groove. Use a flake to start a sequence, heading up and right to access the other tantalising hanging groove (small wires) and a hard finishing sequence.
FA. Ron Fawcett 1980

2 Ramboid f7B
Make a chin-grinding mantel onto the triangular ledge.

3 Janus E7 6b
The long, shallow, leaning groove that forms the direct on *Rigid Digit* is arduous and superb as well as being one of the very best lines anywhere on grit. Small wires protect throughout but it is a good idea to place a solid runner early on to avoid them unzipping in the (inevitable?) event of a fall.
FA. Johnny Dawes 1986. He gave it E7 7a "the grooves looked like two sevens".

4 Elder Crack E2 5b
The imposing narrowing fissure is one of gritstone's great crack ticks. A brambly, blocky crack leads to the sentry-box. Runners can be placed deep in the crack (although not when wearing a helmet) but a large cam is a simpler modern method. Shin up the outside of the crack to a jug on the left arete then get established in the upper crack with difficulty. The wide upper crack is a little easier - just keep laybacking. Brilliant!
FA. Joe Brown 1950. Given VS - must have been more holds on it then!

5 The Elder Statesman ... XS 7b
Climb *Elder Crack* to the rest above the crux, then with a high runner, extemporise a way to gain the left-hand side of the arete. Finish more easily. Worth at least E2 7b! *Photo on page 27.*
FA. Steve McClure 2004

6 Knockin' on Heaven's Door
.... E9 6c
Well-named. Climb the steep wall initially up a shallow groove, then centrally with increasing apprehension to a final desperate sequence on ancient bullet marks. Originally done with a (hand) pre-placed peg runner by starting on the right. The direct start was added before it was finally soloed - high in the grade!
FA. Andy Pollitt 1988. Direct start added by Richie Patterson while repeating the route in 1996 and the whole route was renamed Born Slippy. Ben Tetler soloed the original line in 1999.

7 Keeper's Crack ...... VS 4b
The crack on the right is too wide for comfort although the upper section, behind the ledge, is easier. Another grovel that adds to Curbar's reputation. Huge cams lower the grip-factor considerably.
FA. Slim Sorrell 1949

8 Bill and Ben E4 6b
Climb the arete to ledges (**Ben, E4**) then the easier exposed continuation on the left (**Bill, E2 5c**). The lower arete has a high crux and there is not much in the way of gear on the upper one.
FA. Johnny Dawes 1984

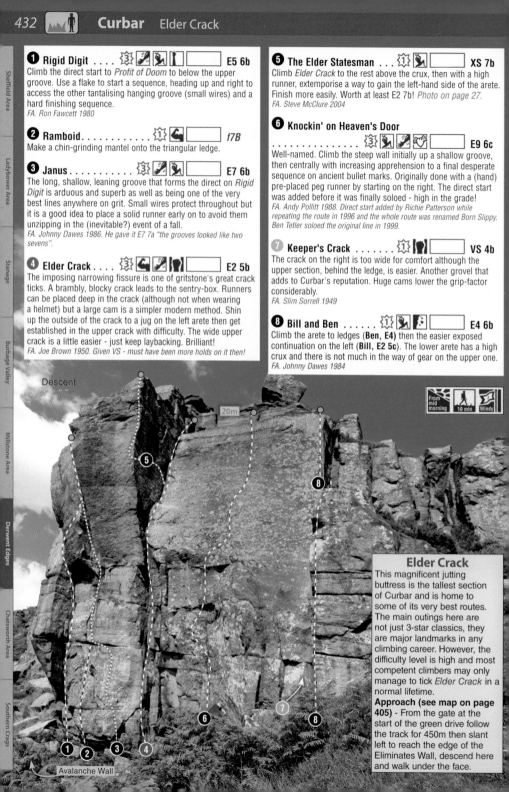

Descent

20m

Elder Crack
This magnificent jutting buttress is the tallest section of Curbar and is home to some of its very best routes. The main outings here are not just 3-star classics, they are major landmarks in any climbing career. However, the difficulty level is high and most competent climbers may only manage to tick *Elder Crack* in a normal lifetime.
Approach (see map on page 405) - From the gate at the start of the green drive follow the track for 450m then slant left to reach the edge of the Eliminates Wall, descend here and walk under the face.

Avalanche Wall

From mid morning | 10 min | Windy

Bel Ami

Slotted between two of Curbar's most imposing buttresses is a slightly more slabby wall with some lesser climbs. *Bel Ami* is good for its grade.

Approach (see map on page 405) - From the gate at the start of the green drive follow the track for 450m then slant left to reach the edge of the Eliminates Wall, descend here and walk under the face.

9 **Peter Rabbit** . . . . . . **HVS 4c**
Balance up and left from the polished ramp of the *Slab Route* to a tricky grassy exit. Escape leftwards.
FA. Al Evans 1988

10 **Slab Route** . . . . **S 4a**
Start below the centre of the slab and take the right-trending line of polished holds that steepen as they rise. Escape off right under the *Bel Ami* tower. Originally the route finished up the groove left of the tower (about **4b**) but this contains a suspect flake and is best avoided.
FA. Chuck Cook 1948

11 **Pretty Friend** . . . . **HVS 5a**
Climb the groove leftwards to join *Slab Route*. Cross the grass ledge and tackle the wall left of the arete of *Bel Ami* with a hard but slightly artificial move past the top break.
FA. Alan James 1984

12 **Bel Ami** . . . . **VS 4b**
The flake and narrowing crack (laybacking or jamming, it is your call) leads to ledges (possible stance). Continue up the crusty arete of the squat tower and a real summit tick.
FA. Wilf White late 1940s

13 **Green Crack** . . . . **HVS 5b**
Stride across the smelly toilet-pit then follow the curving flake out right to a poor rest and tricky moves to grasp the bounteous flutings. Making sure the ropes don't jam, finish easily.
FA. Joe Brown (some tension) 1957

14 **Minor 3** **E6 6b**
The arete on its left-hand side throughout. Just as far as the bulge is **Phone the Hallamshire** - a bold and reachy **E5 6a**.
FA. Pete Whittaker 2008. FA. (PtH) Ron Fawcett 1987

15 **Usurper** **E4 6a**
The crack just right of the arete leads to a non-rest at the overhang. Progress from here requires some sustained and painful jamming and usually stops most folks dead in their tracks, though the strong can layback straight through it.
Photo on page 1.
FA. Nicky Stokes 1977

20m

Descent under chockstone

Moonshine - p.434

L'Horla

Sheffield Area

Ladybower Area

Stanage

Burbage Valley

Millstone Area

Derwent Edges

Chatsworth Area

Southern Crags

L'Horla

The perfect introduction to Curbar, with three classic cracks - *Maupassant*, *L'Horla* and *Insanity*. All are short and high in the grade; how you perform on these will be a good pointer to how you are going to cope with the rest of the cliff; welcome to the 'Cloggy of The Peak'.
Approach (see map on page 405) - From the gate at the start of the green drive follow the track for 450m then slant left to reach the edge of the Eliminates Wall, descend here and walk under the impressive face.

1 Lardmaster E3 6a
The inevitable diagonal girdle though with some great climbing along the way. Link the initial crack *Usurper* (p.433) with the final jug of *L'Horla* approached from the wrong side.
FA. John Allen 1988

2 Spray Mane. f7B
From twin pockets, dyno to the break.

3 Sean's Arete . . . f7B
The arete climbed on its left. To the top break is *f7B+*.

4 Moonshine E5 6b
The thin bulging cracks on the right-hand side of the wall are gained from the right and are especially taxing where the initial crack fizzles out. Small cams and tiny wires are useful.
FA. Tim Leach 1980

5 Eclipse E6 6b
Start up *Moonshine*, pull over the roof and then continue up the slappy and well-positioned arete above and right.
FA. Pete Robins 1999

6 Maupassant . . . . Top 50 HVS 5a
Classic grit HVS. A jamming crack leads to a bridged rest, take a big breath and layback to glory. The big chockstone can be lassoed from below by cowboys.
FA. Don Whillans 1955

7 L'Horla . . . . Top 50 E1 5b
Classic grit E1. The leaning groove is awkward and insecure. At the bulge (high wire and/or big cam in the notch) leap onto the left arete and crank like a man possessed to finish or flounder with a flourish. Alternatively, ignore the photogenic jug dangle, and pull straight up into the groove. *Photo on page 439.*
FA. Joe Brown (some tension) 1957

8 Insanity E2 5c
Classic grit E2. Scuttle up the thin leaning crack by a tottering layback, especially where the side-wall disappears. Easier for the short-legged but always manages to feel a desperate struggle.
FA. Hugh Banner 1958

9 Committed E6 6b
Well-named. From part way up the bank cross the side-wall leftwards to a hard finish with the ground sweeping increasingly away helping to focus the mind. Might be only E5 for the very tall, and impossible for the very short without a run/bunk-up. A rope belayed from the right is sensible.
FA. Johnny Dawes 1984

The Toy Wall

A series of short problems on impeccable rock. As you might expect, most of the routes feel hard for the grade and, despite their diminutive size, many also manage to be bold. The occasional (tough) crack climb does give slight relief from bold technical face routes.

Approach (see map on page 405) - From the gate at the start of the green drive follow the track for 450m then slant left to reach the edge of the Eliminates Wall, descend here and walk under the face.

10 Tin Drum **E5 6b**
The thin crack on the left side of the wall is technical and bold. It has a high runner and some tough moves.
FA. Dominic Lee 1981

11 Be Bop Delux **E5 6b**
From the same start as *Tin Drum*, step out right and climb the wall with difficulty. It eases, eventually.
FA. Ron Fawcett 1984

12 The Toy **E1 5c**
The thin crack splitting the centre of the wall gives elegant, fingery climbing and really packs it in. The most popular route here and really rather hard for the grade.

13 Bok **E5 6b**
The wall between *The Toy* and *Plaything* is supposed to be protected by a solitary micro-wire!

14 Plaything **E2 5c**
The arete is another bold one. Start just left then trend right and beware the reachy finish and gritty footholds.
FA. Gary Gibson 1983

15 Pretty Face **E1 5b**
The narrow face right of the chimney on small finger-holds.
FA. Paul Mitchell 1975

16 October Crack . . . .   **VS 4c**
Steep parallel cracks give awkward or pleasant jamming depending on your outlook. A traditional Curbar Hard Severe - so enough said!
FA. Wilf White 1949

17 Shallow Chimney . . . .   **VD**
The eponymous rift is the easiest climb for miles and miles and even it has an awkward exit!

18 Grey Face . . . .   **VS 5a**
An oddly-named thin crack. Awkward though safe enough with fiddly gear and perhaps easier if you can keep moving.
FA. Dennis Gray 1964

19 Thirst for Glory **E1 5b**
A fairly unremarkable wall climb. Head first left then right to finish at a tiny crack. A dodgy spike and some wires protect.

20 Pale Complexion . . . .   **VS 4c**
The right arete of the wall on its left-hand side. Start up a crack (fiddly small wires) then follow the arete throughout.

Descent under chockstone

8m

Eliminates Wall

1 The Left Eliminate .. ⚡ E1 5c
The left-hand crack is short and 'ard. Maybe the same grade as *Toy*, but sees a lot less attention. Gaining the narrower upper section is especially difficult. If successful it is eyes right!
FA. Joe Brown 1951

2 The Zone .. ⚡ E9 6c
Climb the smooth wall left of *The Peapod* by desperately fingery climbing. Protected by a cluster of skyhooks.
FA. John Arran 1998

3 The Peapod......... Top ⚡ HVS 5b
Mega-classic. A short slippery crack leads to the base of the pod. Back and foot up this to a difficult exit. Arguments abound about the best way to face, we suggest left! The awkward upper crack leads to an easy chimney finish. *Photo on page 36.*
FA. Joe Brown 1951

4 Peas of Mind......... ⚡ E6 6a
The blunt right arete of *The Peapod* is sustained, unprotected and, except for the obvious method, inescapable!
FA. Dave Pegg 1994

5 The Shape of Things to Come
.... ⚡ E6 6b
A well-named impressive face climb between the two cracks. Passing a runner early on, climb the face on crimpy finger-holds to a tiny shallow groove. Wobble-a-way up this to easy ground.
FA. Phil Burke 1980

6 The Right Eliminate .... ⚡ E3 5c
Do this and *Great Slab* (in a pair of pumps!) on the same day to get a measure of the skill of the Master. An exhausting struggle on which upward progress is always too tenuous. The rotating chockstones that used to both help and hinder have now gone.
FA. Joe Brown 1951

7 Drummond Base ... ⚡ E8 6c
Climb the slim groove immediately left of *Linden*, crossing rightwards past another groove to finish up *Linden*.
FA. Johnny Dawes 2003

8 Linden .... ⚡ E6 6b
Brilliant face climbing, despite the drilled holds. Make a very hard move to leave the block and gain the dodgy flakes. Then sustained crimpy wall climbing gains better holds and a sprint for the top before you pump-out. Finish right or escape left.
Photo on page 374.
FA. Mick Fowler 1976. Climbed by Ed Drummond in 1973 with two skyhooks on wrist loops for aid. The tiny holes he drilled are still there.

9 The Grey Area ..... ⚡ E8 7a
Start as for *Linden*. From the nuts, climb diagonally right to gain *Hurricane* and some more gear. Continue direct.
FA. Charlie Woodburn 2003

Descent

The Toy Wall

The Eliminates Wall
The magnificent Eliminates Wall, one of the most intimidating bits of grit around, is home to arduous crack climbs from the 50s and desperate face climbs from the 70s, 80s and 90s. Apart from *The Peapod*, queues are unheard of!
Approach (see map on page 405) - From the gate at the start of the green drive follow the track for 450m then slant left to reach the edge of the Eliminates Wall, descend here.

10 Happy Heart E8 7a
Climb the incipient crack left of the shallow groove (low side-runners) and then the mighty bold wall above. An enigma that has had no known repeats in 25+ years.
FA. John Hart 1987

11 Hurricane E4 6a
Still a gripper but less so than when it was graded E2. Climb *Scroach* to below its jamming-crack then teeter left to gain a shallow ramp. Follow this into wilder and wilder territory until an escape can be made up *Linden*.
FA. Mick Fowler 1977

12 Scroach E2 5c
From the tip of the tombstone, make a baffling (6a until sussed?) step round left into the shallow groove which takes small wires that are tricky to place. The groove and steep jamming crack above lead to ledges. Traverse out left and climb the wall to finish.
FA. Ed Drummond 1975

13 Hercules E1 5a
The wide crack is a good warm-up for the *Eliminates* if you squirm it, and it might just make you change your plan for the day. The bold (reckless?) can layback it instead. A short continuation pitch (**VS 5a**) is available up and left.
FA. Chuck Cooke 1949

14 Alpha .... S 4b
The groove just right with a jutting tombstone is a bit of a contrast to most things hereabouts, though it still requires advanced gritstone 'udging' techniques by most. Keep to the right of the initial rib.
FA. Chuck Cook 1949

15 Twinkle Toes .... HS 4a
The left-hand crack - neat footwork helps.

16 The Severed Garden f6C
A taxing slab with a bad landing.

17 The Pugalist .... HS 4b
The right-hand crack is more of a fist-fight.

50m right is a recessed quarry with a blank back wall. The two most obvious lines here are twin fissures separated by the blank wall of the mighty Walk on By.

18 Quad Crack .... HVS 5a
The wide crack on the left.

19 Walk on By .... f7C+
The stunningly blank wall.
FA. Rob Gawthorpe 1980. He graded it E3 6c!

20 Quarry Climb .... S 4a
The other crack on the right.

From mid morning | 6 min | Windy

Little Rocker - 100m

Descent

The Quarry - 50m

Sidebar tabs: Sheffield Area | Ladybower Area | Stanage | Burbage Valley | Millstone Area | Derwent Edges | Chatsworth Area | Southern Crags

Little Rocker

A small buttress, the closest to the parking and directly above the lay-bys on to the road down to Curbar/Calver. There is a small section of routes here that are worth at least one quick visit especially if combined with the pleasant bouldering in the adjacent quarry.
Approach (see map on page 405) - From the Curbar Gap parking go through the gate and walk along for 100m or so then branch left to the cliff edge.

1 Late Start Gully . . . . Diff
The gully on the left to an awkward exit. A through-route is an even easier option.

2 Cheeky . . . . S 4a
The narrow sidewall of the jutting fin to a rightward exit.

3 Nosy . . . . HS 4b
The jutting arete has a couple of beefy pulls.

4 Nosy Gully . . . . Mod
Amble up the rift. Plenty of variations are available.

5 Rock and Roll . . . . VS 5a
The front face is gained from the left - tricky and scritty!
FA. Iain Mount 2007

6 Roadover . . . . S 4a
The right-slanting crack - nicer than it looks.

7 Rock On . . . . VS 4b
Layback the arete - don't forget your blinkers.

8 Little Rocker . . . . HVD 4a
The left-slanting crack is awkward, especially the start.

9 Thomas the Tanked . . . . f6A+
Layback the right arete on its right side..
FA. Steve Bancroft 2000

10 The Phat Controller . f6B+
The face just right is a bit harder than *Thomas* but finishes in the same place.

The Eliminates Wall - 100m

Little Quarry
Peak Bouldering

Sheffield Area

Ladybower Area

Stanage

Burbage Valley

Millstone Area

Derwent Edges

Chatsworth Area

Southern Crags

James Turnbull making the big move on *L'Horla* (E1 5b) - *page 434* - at Curbar. The big question here is whether to lunge for the jug, or do the less spectacular but arguably easier alternative method up the groove directly. Photo: Mike Hutton

	No star	🔲	🔲	🔲
Mod to S	28	12	2	-
HS to HVS	20	24	3	-
E1 to E3	6	14	-	-
E4 and up	-	5	-	1

Baslow is a quiet little backwater, lacking any of the great classics of its near neighbours. It has long been a neglected venue, mainly frequented by explorers looking for an escape from the busy cliffs further north. Despite this, Baslow is worthy of a visit for a little peace and quiet. The edge consists of a scattered set of buttresses, and the occasional small quarry, stretched out over more than a kilometre of hillside. The outlook is pleasant and in the autumn the slope below the cliff is loaded with bilberries. There a decent selection of low grade routes here, but awkward access along the base of the cliff (in places) and occasionally difficulties in locating solid belays above the cliff, plus a smattering of loose rock means that the place is not as ideal for beginners as it first appears.

Approach   Also see map on page 375

There is an extensive Pay and Display car park at Curbar Gap, and a some free lay-bys on the road that runs down to Curbar village. A good path runs along the top of the cliffs and most the buttresses are best reached from above because of the lack of a good path underneath. The cliff-top track splits right from the main track just beyond the gate and heads out to the jutting Bacchus Buttress with a walled-in view-point on its crest. The main path continues through a dip to reach the Flying Crag and then the Gullies Wall 100m further on. The Into the Woods routes are further south and beyond these, close to the main track is the Eagle Stone which is has rounded bouldering above a seasonal moat and soggy cow pats.

Conditions

The setting is typical of the Eastern Edges: quick-drying, exposed to the afternoon sun but affected by bad weather. Its relatively low altitude, and some tree cover encourages lichen growth so the rock can be green, especially in the winter.

Bouldering

There are several popular bouldering spots away from the main edge as well as some bouldering on the edge itself. This is covered fully in the Peak Bouldering Rockfax.

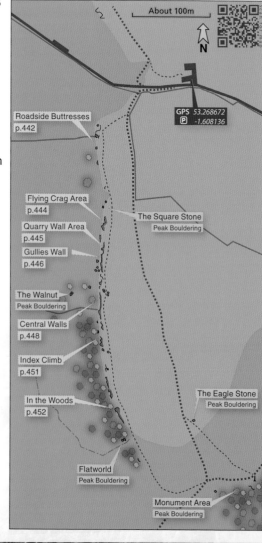

About 100m

N

Roadside Buttresses p.442

GPS 53.268672
Ⓟ -1.608136

Flying Crag Area p.444

The Square Stone
Peak Bouldering

Quarry Wall Area p.445

Gullies Wall p.446

The Walnut
Peak Bouldering

Central Walls p.448

Index Climb p.451

In the Woods p.452

The Eagle Stone
Peak Bouldering

Flatworld
Peak Bouldering

Monument Area
Peak Bouldering

Sheffield Area

Ladybower Area

Stanage

Burbage Valley

Millstone Area

Derwent Edges

Chatsworth Area

Southern Crags

Rob Greenwood enjoying some solitude whilst soloing on Baslow. The route is
Dick's Dilemma (HS 4b) - *page 444* - and is typical of the edge. Photo: Self Timer

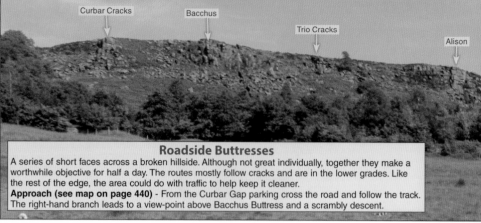

Roadside Buttresses

A series of short faces across a broken hillside. Although not great individually, together they make a worthwhile objective for half a day. The routes mostly follow cracks and are in the lower grades. Like the rest of the edge, the area could do with traffic to help keep it cleaner.
Approach (see map on page 440) - From the Curbar Gap parking cross the road and follow the track. The right-hand branch leads to a view-point above Bacchus Buttress and a scrambly descent.

Curbar Cracks
160m from the road is a small buttress which is worth a short visit despite its rather broken appearance.

❶ Corner Route . . . . VD 4a
Gain the crack on the left and finish up a short rib.

❷ Rib Route . . . . VD 3c
Follow the left-hand arete throughout.

❸ Curbar Cracks . . . . Diff
Awkward moves up the central crack lead to the upper corner.

❹ Cracked Wall . . . . HS 4a
Amble to a good finish up the thin crack in the final block.

Bacchus
50m right is a blocky buttress which has a stile to its right. The short routes here are generally better than they look.

❺ Rum and Pep . . . . S 4a
The left-hand chimney leads easily to a ledge then a tricky finish up the steep groove on the right.

❻ Bacchanalia E1 5c
Lower rib and hanging arete above.

❼ Mauvais Pas . . . . HVD 3c
Climb the central chimney then make the exposed 'mauvais pas' (crux for those who don't know) out right to a steep finish up the side-wall.

❽ Bitter . . . . VS 4b
The short leaning crack is awkward.
FA. David Boore 1965

❾ Shandy . . . . VD
The arete leads to a tricky wall and a finish up the groove.

Flying Crag
p.444

Quarry Wall
p.445

Gullies Wall
p.446

Central Wall
p.448

Trio Cracks

6m

Alison

8m

⑩
⑪
⑫

⑬
⑭
⑮

Trio Cracks
50m right is a steep buttress with a trio of worthwhile cracks.

⑩ **Left-hand Flake Crack...** **S 4a**
Good holds and good protection up the left-hand crack.

⑪ **Central Crack** .... **VS 5a**
The central fissure usually requires a bit of a tussle.

⑫ **Flake Crack.** .... **Diff**
Short-lived but on good flaky holds on the right.

Alison
70m right is a long stepped buttress with a short wall on its right. The easiest descent is on the right.

⑬ **Alison.** .... **S 4b**
From low on the left, a series of steps lead to tricky moves onto and off the final ledge.

⑭ **Death to Khomeini** ..... **VS 4b**
The narrow wall is quite bold, though with decent moves. A runner in the next route is a fair idea!

⑮ **Niched Wall** .... **S 4a**
Pleasant moves up the crack and the overlap.
FA. Wilf White mid 1950s

Sheffield Area
Ladybower Area
Stanage
Burbage Valley
Millstone Area
Derwent Edges
Chatsworth Area
Southern Craigs

Flying Crag Area

The most significant piece of rock at this end of the cliff is a north-facing wall capped on the right by a layer of disintegrating rock. The best routes are rather short and around the left edge of the buttress. Sadly they don't see much sunshine. A little further north is a lone buttress.

Approach (see map on page 440) - Continue along the cliff-top path for a 200m, past a dip, to a north-facing quarried wall.

There are a couple of routes on a narrow isolated buttress just to the north of Flying Crag.

1 Has Shaun Got False Teeth? **f6B**
A technical rib above a sloping landing. No right arete allowed.
FA. Neil Travers 1988

2 Dick's Dilemma . . . . **HS 4b**
Start just right of the arete and balance onto it. Above is easier. A harder start (**4c**) is just left of the arete. *Photo on page 441.*
FA. R.A. 'Dick' Brown 1951

3 Truancy **E1 6a**
The tricky wall past a small sloping triangular ledge.
FA. John Henry Bull 2000. Guess where he should have been!

4 Wasted Youth . . . . **HS 4b**
Make tricky moves past the initial bulge then continue more easily. Unprotected.
FA. 'Boris' Hannon 1981

5 Groove and Wall . . . . **VS 5a**
Start up an overhanging groove in the arete, then follow the left wall of the corner to finish as for *Wasted Youth*.
FA. Bruce Goodwin 1993

6 Flying Crag Groove . . . . **HS 4c**
Pleasant climbing up the open groove.

7 Don's Mantel **E2 5b**
The tricky and unprotected face does have a tough mantel.
FA. Don Morrison 1965

8 Flying Crag Crack . . . . **HVS 5a**
From a grim hollow power up the flaky crack.
FA. Wilf White 1951

9 Slanted and Enchanted . . **E6 6b**
The impressive side-wall. Pull on to the wall at an 'eye' in the break, rock left and follow holds to a scary last move.
FA. Mark Smith 1992

10 John Wilson . . . . . . **f6A+**
The double prow above a dodgy landing.

11 Flying Start **f6A**
Climb the groove - more awkward than it looks

12 The Flying Crag . . . . **HVS 5a**
Climb the crack in the front face then head left on crusty jugs.
FA. Eric Byne 1940

Quarry Wall Area

A couple of short walls, one natural and one quarried, with some small climbs and a bit of bouldering. The area is rarely visited.

Approach (see map on page 440) - Wander round in front of Flying Crag to the next bit of rock 20m to the south. The Quarry Wall is a little further on.

⑬ Laicifitra 1 . . . . **HVS 5a**
The left side of the face has bold precarious moves on the slab, especially if you avoid the left arete. There is a clue in the name.
FA. Dennis Grey 1965

⑭ Yarg Sinned **E1 5b**
Follows the centre of the face. Precarious and bold.
FA. Simon Triger 2007

⑮ Laicifitra 2 . . . . **S 4a**
An amenable finger-crack is less artificial than version 1.
FA. Dennis Grey 1965

⑯ Second-hand Goods . . . . . . **HS 4b**
The twin cracks merge to reach an unstable finish.
FA. David Simmonite 1989

⑰ Batu Motel . . . . **f7A+**
Fierce moves up the wall best done above pads.
FA. Paul Pepperday 1985

⑱ Quarry Wall. . . . . **HS 4c**
Worthwhile and on good holds, though often rather green; the initial slab is especially slippery.
FA. Dennis Gray 1965

⑲ Quarry Crack . . . . **S 4a**
The green groove has hidden holds on the left wall.
FA. Eric Byne 1940

⑳ Cold Diggerty . . **f6C+**
Climb rightwards up the left-hand side of the leaning side-wall.
FA. Ben Heason 2000

㉑ Hot Ziggerty . . . **f6C**
Starting from the boulder, climb the wall. *f7A* if started without the boulder.
FA. Dominic Lee 1982

㉒ Arise Sir Freddie! . . **f6B**
The main arete, on the left then on the right.
FA. David Norton 2005

㉓ Whatisit? . . . . **HVS 5b**
The front of the projecting rib is cleaner than most here. It gives a spooky little solo.
FA. Sam Sansom 1976

㉔ Hanging Slab . . . . **S 4a**
Up the shallow groove then step left onto the hanging slab.

㉕ The Groove . . . . **VD**
Continue up the groove and the easier slab above.

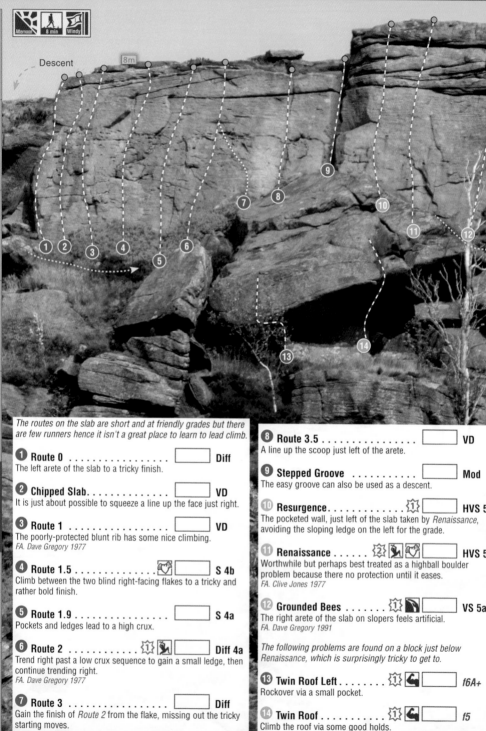

Descent

8m

The routes on the slab are short and at friendly grades but there are few runners hence it isn't a great place to learn to lead climb.

1 Route 0 . . . . `Diff`
The left arete of the slab to a tricky finish.

2 Chipped Slab. . . . . `VD`
It is just about possible to squeeze a line up the face just right.

3 Route 1 . . . . `VD`
The poorly-protected blunt rib has some nice climbing.
FA. Dave Gregory 1977

4 Route 1.5 . . . . `S 4b`
Climb between the two blind right-facing flakes to a tricky and rather bold finish.

5 Route 1.9 . . . . `S 4a`
Pockets and ledges lead to a high crux.

6 Route 2 . . . . `Diff 4a`
Trend right past a low crux sequence to gain a small ledge, then continue trending right.
FA. Dave Gregory 1977

7 Route 3 . . . . `Diff`
Gain the finish of *Route 2* from the flake, missing out the tricky starting moves.

8 Route 3.5 . . . . `VD`
A line up the scoop just left of the arete.

9 Stepped Groove . . . . `Mod`
The easy groove can also be used as a descent.

10 Resurgence. . . . . `HVS 5a`
The pocketed wall, just left of the slab taken by *Renaissance*, avoiding the sloping ledge on the left for the grade.

11 Renaissance . . . . . . `HVS 5b`
Worthwhile but perhaps best treated as a highball boulder problem because there no protection until it eases.
FA. Clive Jones 1977

12 Grounded Bees . . . . `VS 5a`
The right arete of the slab on slopers feels artificial.
FA. Dave Gregory 1991

The following problems are found on a block just below *Renaissance*, which is surprisingly tricky to get to.

13 Twin Roof Left . . . . `f6A+`
Rockover via a small pocket.

14 Twin Roof . . . . `f5`
Climb the roof via some good holds.

447

The grassy gully to the right - **Left-hand Gully, Mod** - *can be used as a descent though walking round is probably easier.*

15 Gully Wall . . . . Mod
The Easter Island Statue flakes passing the loose top block.
FA. Dave Gregory 1977

16 Gully Wall Variation . . . . VD 4a
Good holds lead to the same finish as *Gully Wall*.

17 Right Hand Gully . . . . Diff
This one has awkward moves past the narrows.

18 Shallow Rib . . . . VD
A delicate start leads to a steeper exit.
FA. Charles Darley 1978

19 Blocked Gully . . . . Mod
The slabby blocks in the gully.

20 Left-hand Tower . . . . S 4b
Originally a variation start to the next route. Direct up the initial arete has a 5b move but it can easily be avoided.

21 Broken Buttress . . . . VD
A 20m route on a 8m crag! Start at the boulders down the slope, climbing the right-hand pillar. Eventually the line crosses the path to the final slab which gives the crux, up the centre or the right edge.
FA. Charles Darley 1978

Gullies Wall
The most popular and nicest part of the cliff - a series of short slabby walls and cracks with an open aspect. This section of the crag wouldn't feel out of place tucked away somewhere on Burbage and consequently it is one of the few places at Baslow that you may see other parties.
Approach (see map on page 440) - The quickest approach is to follow the main track for 320m until just past a field corner on the left. The buttress is 80m away on the right.

The Rib - 25m

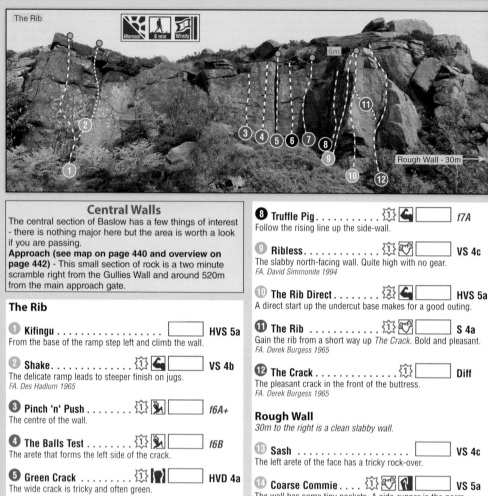

The Rib

Rough Wall - 30m →

Central Walls

The central section of Baslow has a few things of interest - there is nothing major here but the area is worth a look if you are passing.

Approach (see map on page 440 and overview on page 442) - This small section of rock is a two minute scramble right from the Gullies Wall and around 520m from the main approach gate.

The Rib

1 Kifingu . . . . **HVS 5a**
From the base of the ramp step left and climb the wall.

2 Shake . . . . **VS 4b**
The delicate ramp leads to steeper finish on jugs.
FA. Des Hadlum 1965

3 Pinch 'n' Push . . . . **f6A+**
The centre of the wall.

4 The Balls Test **f6B**
The arete that forms the left side of the crack.

5 Green Crack . . . . **HVD 4a**
The wide crack is tricky and often green.

6 The Ripper . . . . **f7A+**
The wall right of the crack, avoiding the arete of the crack.

7 Black Crack . . . . **Diff**
The short flake just right is a two move wonder.

8 Truffle Pig **f7A**
Follow the rising line up the side-wall.

9 Ribless . . . . **VS 4c**
The slabby north-facing wall. Quite high with no gear.
FA. David Simmonite 1994

10 The Rib Direct . . . . **HVS 5a**
A direct start up the undercut base makes for a good outing.

11 The Rib . . . . **S 4a**
Gain the rib from a short way up *The Crack*. Bold and pleasant.
FA. Derek Burgess 1965

12 The Crack . . . . **Diff**
The pleasant crack in the front of the buttress.
FA. Derek Burgess 1965

Rough Wall
30m to the right is a clean slabby wall.

13 Sash . . . . **VS 4c**
The left arete of the face has a tricky rock-over.

14 Coarse Commie . . . . **VS 5a**
The wall has some tiny pockets. A side-runner is the norm.

15 Rough Wall Climb . . . . **VS 4c**
The thin crack up the centre of the wall has nice moves but not much in the way of gear. *Photo opposite.*

Descent

Larceny - 20m →

16 **Jolly Rough.** . . . . VS 4c
The squeezed wall just right.

17 **Jolly Green Dwarf** . . . . . VS 5a
Trend left to the left arete of the slab. Bold and delicate.
FA. Pete Robertson 1982

18 **Mad Bilberries.** . . . . . f6A+
A touch of fine slabby padding. Short but quite intense.
FA. Chris King 1992

19 **Jolly Green Elephant** . . . f6B+
Climb the roof (crux) and arete left of *Pensioner's Bulge*.
FA. Michael Oliver 1993

20 **Pensioner's Bulge** . . . . . VS 5a
The bulge split by a stubborn thin crack. Save a bit for the exit.
FA. Don Whillans 1965. His last new route on Grit, aged 32.

21 **Gun Chimney.** . . . . HVD 4a
Easy work to a good thread then a tricky little exit left.
FA. J.W.Puttrell 1890

22 **Santa Claus Retreats** E1 5b
A short and mildly wild direct finish. Sporting stuff.
FA. Paul Mitchell 1985

23 **The Man with the Gritstone Gun.** HS 4b
Escaping right is also worthwhile, but harder than leftwards.

24 **Hair Conditioned Nightmare** . HVS 5a
Hug-a-way up the narrow buttress right of the chimney.

25 **Hair Conditioned Rightmare** . f5+
The arete above a ledge, climbed on its right-hand side. Just
about a boulder problem, if you jump onto the ledge.

TICKLIST
Baslow Bits and Bobs
Not much in the way of classics on Baslow but there is enough for a very pleasant day away from it all. We have been kind and left out the best route on the crag - the E7 *Grand Potato*.

☐ **Route 2, Diff** *(446)*
Pity it is so short.

☐ **The Cave Gully, VD** *(452)*
Grunt-tastic stuff.

☐ **Index Climb, S** *(451)*
Very nice, if you can find it.

☐ **Rough Wall Climb, VS** *(448)*
Neat and a bit bold.

☐ **Pensioner's Bulge, VS** *(449)*
Beefy Whillans' work.

☐ **Renaissance, HVS** *(446)*
Who needs runners?

☐ **Jam and Blast It, HVS** *(453)*
A hidden gem for jammers.

Claire Aspinall finishing the delightful *Rough Wall Climb* (VS 4c) - *opposite* - on the Central Wall section of Baslow. Photo: Mike Hutton

Gullies Wall
p.446

The Rib
p.448

Larceny Wall

Larceny Wall is situated directly above a curving drystone wall below the crag. The routes start past the stile.

26 Wall Groove . . . . ☐ **HS 4b**
A grubby lower section leads to a better crack and crux bulge.
FA. Derrick Burgess 1955

27 Larceny . . . . ☐ **HVS 5a**
The dubious lower wall is climbed past a ledge to a (slightly) more solid finish up thin cracks.
FA. Don Morrison late 1960s

28 Gary's Little Joke Book . . . . . ☐ **E2 6a**
The curving groove has tough moves at the top.
FA. Paul Pepperday 1982

29 Problem Wall . . . . ☐ **f5**
Boulder up the wall left of the thin crack.
FA. Graham Hoey 1976

30 Fingers Crack . . . . ☐ **VS 4b**
The narrowing crack to a leftward exit onto the ledge.
FA. Des Hadlum 1964

31 Cracked Fingers . . . . ☐ **HVS 5b**
The obvious continuation crack from the ledge.

32 Work the Wall . . . . ☐ **f6A**
Work out a way up the blank wall just to the right.
FA. Paul Pepperday 1985

33 Finger Wall . . . . ☐ **f5+**
The vague ramp on the face to the right, avoiding the arete.

Descent

12m

Index Climb - 200m

Larceny Wall

Afternoon   10 min   Windy

Rough Wall
p.448

Index Climb - 200m

Larceny Wall

Easily spotted
curving drystone wall

Sheffield Area

Ladybower Area

Stanage

Burbage Valley

Millstone Area

Derwent Edges

Chatsworth Area

Southern Crags

Descent

35

34

36

Buttresses either
side of easy descent

37

Index Climb
Approach (see map on page 440) - 200m right of
Larceny Wall a prominent lozenge-shaped block stands
near the edge of the cliff. Just beyond this is a buttress
hidden in the trees. It has one good route.

34 Index Climb. . . . . **S 4a**
Once considered the classic of the crag. From a useful tree at
the toe of the buttress climb a flake then move across and right
to a groove. Up this to a crucial exposed step out left to finish.
FA. Eric Byne 1940

35 Index Climb Direct . . . . **VS 4c**
The juggy finish over the overhang is a decent harder alternative.
FA. Don Morrison 1964

36 Heather Crack . . . . **HVD 4a**
The straight crack has some good jamming moves. A start from
the right is much easier - **Diff**.

To the right, past an easy descent, is another buttress.

37 Sewer-plumb. . . . . **VS 4c**
Bridge and jam the steep groove past the odd loose hold.

Sheffield Area | Ladybower Area | Stanage | Burbage Valley | Millstone Area | Derwent Edges | Chatsworth Area | Southern Crags

Afternoon | 20 min | Sheltered | Green

Descent

8m

Not much Sun | 20 min | Sheltered | Green

In the Woods

The crag leaves one of its best bits until last - a couple of well-sheltered buttresses, which are green after any unsettled weather because of the surrounding trees. The routes include two modern desperates and a reasonable selection of often rather grubby cracks.

Approach (see map on page 440) - Follow the cliff-top path south for 300m from the stone wall below the Central Buttresses to where a steep gully leads down under the rocks. This is almost due west of the Eagle Stone.

❸ Poppers **E5 6c**
A desperate route up the centre of buttress. Start below a short hanging arete and make hard moves to get a right hand on this then dyno for the large break - *f7A+* to here. With luck, small holds and chicken-heads will lead to the top. The finish is green.
FA. Richie Patterson 1994

❹ The Grand Potato **E7 6b**
Start under the right arete. The short will need a cheating stone to reach a slot in the roof, others will leap. Pull over to a poor break and finish up the tough arete. Very highball *f7A+*.
FA. Robin Barker 1993

❺ The Cave Gully . . . . **VD**
The hanging chimney gives a good old-fashioned struggle. The best footholds are on the right.

❻ Cave Rib **E1 5a**
Nice balance climbing up the rib right of the gully. Finish to the left, a direct finish is **E2 5c** and finishing rightwards is **E1 5b**.
FA. Steve Clark 2007

❼ Cave Climb Indirect . . . . **VS 4c**
Climb the wall to the hanging crack and a tricky exit left.

❶ Above and Beyond the Calisthenic Barrier
. . . . **HS 4b**
Just right of the cave, climb the tricky wall right then left via ledges. The finish above the last of these feels a little bold.
FA. Clive Jones 1977

❷ Left Hand Gully Buttress . . . . . . **VS 4b**
An awkward start leads to a perplexing finish. From a good side-pull reach a thin break then stretch for the top.

10m

8 **Cave Climb Direct** . . . 🔲 VS 5a
From the cave, storm the roof and the twin jamming cracks.

9 **Social Climber**. . . . . 🔲 HVS 5b
The pillar to the right is rather an artificial line, its difficulty
depends on how much use you make of the aretes.
FA. Graham Titterton 2003

*To the right are several vegetated cracks, which have all been
climbed in the past though they have become increasingly
neglected. Next is a smart jamming crack left of a steep groove.*

10 **Jam and Blast It** . . . . . . 🔲 E1 5b
Blast up the hanging left-hand crack. The route proves to be a
little hidden gem. Using the next route for a little help is a bit is
easier and some say more pleasant!
*FA. Charles Darley 1977. Charles wanted a new route so Dave Gregory
offered him one of his secret projects - he produced a mini-classic.*

11 **Corner Crack**. . . . . 🔲 VS 4c
Up the cracked groove to a tricky widening finish.

12 **Heather Wall**. . . . . 🔲 VD
Bridge up then traverse out right to access the crack in the face.

13 **Not Now John** . . . . 🔲 HVS 5c
A technical crux start leads to a ledge (awkward thread) and a
slabby finish needing a little care.
FA. Malc Taylor 1984

14 **I've Gotta Get On** . . . . 🔲 VS 5b
A right-hand variation on the previous climb - gritty.

15 **Capstone Chimney** . . . . . 🔲 VD
Interesting moves up the chimney, past the jammed boulder. Exit
inside the chockstone or outside at **VD**.
FA. J.W.Puttrell c1900

16 **Capstone Chimney Crack** . . . 🔲 S 4c
A hard start (often a bit green) leads to the delicate slabby face.

17 **Twin Cracks**. . . . . 🔲 VD
The trio of cracks. Nice enough though often a bit grubby. More
traffic would help.

Chatsworth Area

Sheffield Area

Ladybower Area

Stanage

Burbage Valley

Millstone Area

Derwent Edges

Chatsworth Area

Southern Crags

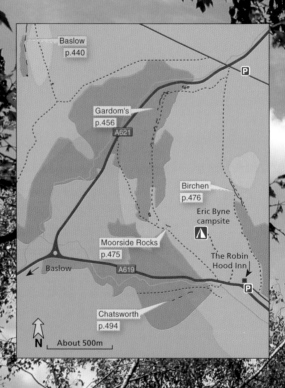

Baslow
p.440

Gardom's
p.456

A621

Birchen
p.476

Eric Byne
campsite

Moorside Rocks
p.475

Baslow

A619

The Robin
Hood Inn

Chatsworth
p.494

N

About 500m

Sheffield Area

Ladybower Area

Stanage

Burbage Valley

Millstone Area

Derwent Edges

Chatsworth Area

Southern Crags

Dave Vincent enjoying lovely conditions on *Apple Arete* (VS 4b) - *page 473* - at Gardom's. The southern end of the edge is a bit of a walk from the parking but has a good set of routes that are often cleaner than much of the rest of the cliff. This is the section of Gardom's where you are most likely to encounter other climbers.

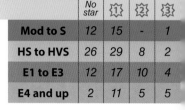

	No star	⚙	⚙⚙	⚙⚙⚙
Mod to S	12	15	-	1
HS to HVS	26	29	8	2
E1 to E3	12	17	10	4
E4 and up	2	11	5	5

Named after a blacksmith from the Chatsworth Estate, Gardom's is a neglected edge; except for the area around *Apple Buttress* it is unusual to see another team here. The classic *Moyer's Buttress* tops the hit list for visitors though and there are plenty of worthwhile offerings spread along the edge. Those who are prepared to pick and choose will be rewarded with some delightful and secluded routes. Gardom's has a quartet of fine routes in the E3 grade with *Sleeping Sickness*, *Stormbringer*, *Crocodile* and *Waterloo Sunset* offering a great day out for a suitably talented team. Travelling along the cliff base is tortuous in many areas, returning to the cliff top is often the best option when moving between buttresses. The neglected air of the cliff tends to add to the appeal for many some, making a nice change from the circus atmosphere at more popular venues.

Approach

The crag is hidden above the main A621 Sheffield to Baslow road. There is roadside parking by the minor cross roads above the crag. Although space is limited, parking is seldom a problem. Go through the gate then trend right across the moor (often wet) heading for the wood. Cross a couple of stiles and enter the trees. When you exit the trees the first buttresses are below and to the right.

Conditions

In humid weather it is unpleasant here; the tree cover gives an airless atmosphere, encouraging lichen growth and midges. Because of this, spring and autumn are the best times to visit, though by choosing carefully a winter's day here can be fun on the right bit of rock. Much of the crag faces in a northerly or northwesterly direction and these faces can often stay green long into the late spring. The tree-cover does offer shelter and the western aspect provides morning respite in hotter weather.

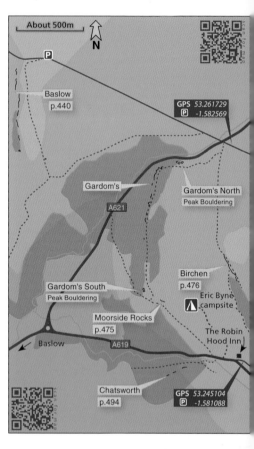

About 500m

N

P

Baslow
p.440

GPS 53.261729
P -1.582569

Gardom's

A621

Gardom's North
Peak Bouldering

Birchen
p.476

Gardom's South
Peak Bouldering

Eric Byne
campsite

Moorside Rocks
p.475

Baslow

A619

The Robin
Hood Inn

Chatsworth
p.494

GPS 53.245104
P -1.581088

Sheffield Area | Ladybower Area | Stanage | Burbage Valley | Millstone Area | Derwent Edges | Chatsworth Area | Southern Crags

Sheffield Area

Ladybower Area

Stanage

Burbage Valley

Millstone Area

Derwent Edges

Chatsworth Area

Southern Crags

Tom Randall puffing hard on the magnificent blunt arete climb of *Nah'han* (E8 6c) - *page 469* - at Gardom's. Over the years there have been countless 'last great problems' and even long lists of 'last great problems'. For some reason this arete seldom seemed to make these lists having been missed by many of the previous generation until Tom showed the way. And it truly is a great problem, but we suspect it won't be the 'last'. Photo: Mike Hutton

The left-hand side of the face has several neglected routes, which are currently very dirty and overgrown.

1 Black Wall Rt I . . . . [ ] **S 4a**
The wall right of the arete has a mantel start and awkward finish.

2 Black Wall Rt II . . . . [ ] [ ] **VS 5a**
A thin flake leads to a troublesome bulge, a tree, and a bigger flake to finish. Usually very dirty.

3 Promise . . . . [ ] **HVS 5a**
Interesting but devious and usually dirty. Traverse right to a ledge, move up, then traverse back left to a jammed flake. Finish up and left awkwardly - the tree helps. The direct version is the perfectly named **Green Wall, E4 6a**.
FA. Len Millsom 1960

4 Tsetse Fly . . . . [ ] [ ] [ ] **E1 5c**
Start below the hanging corner bounding the left edge of the big overhang. From a flake, gain a ledge where reachy moves access the corner. Finish out right up a thin crack.
FA. Mike Browell 1978

5 Narcolepsy . . . . [ ] [ ] [ ] **HVS 5a**
Use a thin flake and slopers to access a ledge - bold and tricky. At the roof, escape out right.
FA. Ernie Marshall 1976

6 Raging Insomnia . . . . . . [ ] [ ] **E3 6a**
Climb *Narcolepsy* to the roof, undercut left to better holds and a difficult move to gain the hanging arete. Finish more easily.
FA. Keith Sharples 1984

7 Mickey Finn . . . [ ] [ ] [ ] [ ] **E6 6b**
Start as for *Raging Insomnia* and tackle the stacked bulges direct. Superb, well protected and not TOO hard.
FA. Paul Mitchell 1990

8 Sleeping Sickness . . [ ] [ ] [ ] **E3 5c**
Climb the tough thin crack in the left wall of *Brown Crack* then traverse left below the roof to the front face and a reachy finish. The first of the quality E3 routes scattered along the edge.
Photo on page 465.
FA. John Allen 1975

9 Good Karma . . . . . . [ ] [ ] [ ] **E4 6b**
Short-lived but tenuous moves straight up the wall.
FA. Matt Boyer 1985

10 Brown Crack . . . . . . [ ] [ ] [ ] **S 4a**
The groove that bounds the right-hand side of the overhangs was the first route on the edge and remains a tricky struggle.
FA. J.W.Puttrell 1890

11 The Rattle . . . . [ ] **HVS 5a**
Mantle left out from under the roof heading left and then right via the meadows to the finishing flake.

12 Diamond Back . . . . [ ] **E2 5c**
The arete saves its crux until the end - a long reach on the right.
FA. Chris Craggs 1983

Descent

16m

Black Wall
The first section of Gardom's is not the best, facing northwest, with large damp overhangs and a neglected air. However there are a few things of interest and the wall is a good option in hot weather, providing the midges aren't out.
Approach (see map on page 461) - Follow the crag-top path past the bouldering area. Drop down the first gully after leaving the trees and head right under Overhang Buttress.

Descent

Overhang Buttress

Similar to its near neighbour, Overhang Buttress is often green, dirty and dank. In hot weather though it can offer some good climbs including *Spanish Fly*, *Four Horsemen* and *Vaya Con Dios*, the latter appealing to the more perverted gritstone gurus.

Approach (see map on page 461) - Follow the crag-top path past the bouldering area. Drop down the first gully after leaving the trees and head right.

⑬ Thunder . . . . **VS 4c**
The left line on the north wall. Head left via a couple of cracks, a niche and a corner. A finish out right is an exposed option.
FA. Ernie Marshall 1956

⑭ Four Horsemen **E2 5b**
Climb into the niche in the centre of the wall then continue direct to an awkward exit - excellent esoterica!
FA. Gary Gibson 1981

⑮ Lightning Wall . . . . **HVS 5a**
Devious and exciting. From *Four Horsemen's* niche, follow the descending break across the green wall, passing the arete awkwardly. Once established, finish delicately up the front face.
FA. Don Chapman 1951

⑯ The Igloo **E5 6b**
Pull over the overhang just left of the arete and climb the wall leftwards to finish as for *Four Horsemen*.
FA. John Allen 1986

⑰ Afro **f6B**
In the pit below a large overhang, climb the wall to the ledge

⑱ Spanish Fly **E7 6c**
The large roofs are tackled centrally (poor wires in the flakes in the roof, very hard to place) to gain the front face and a finish left up the wall. A stiff little problem of considerable quality, and usually done with pre-placed wires at **E6**.
FA. John Allen 1985

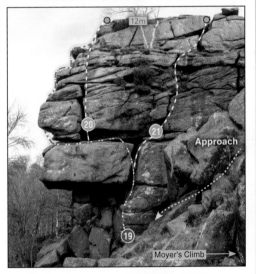

Approach

Moyer's Climb

⑲ Vaya Con Dios **E2 5c**
Gritstone weirdness at its best. Climb the crack in the south face to a horizontal break then squirm along this, passing the arete precariously. Stand up (hard!) and then finish easily.
FA. Allan Austin 1956

⑳ Overhang Buttress Ordinary . . . **VS 4b**
Intimidating and tricky. Start as for the previous route until it is possible to writhe into the vertical crack and finish easily. Passing the change in angle is a complete swine!
FA. Eric Byne 1934

㉑ Infirmary Groove . . . . **HS 4b**
Climb the initial crack then follow its awkward continuation rightwards up the wall on mostly good holds to a heathery exit.
FA. Ernie Marshall 1956

Sheffield Area | Ladybower Area | Stanage | Burbage Valley | Millstone Edge | Derwent Edges | Chatsworth Area | Southern Crags

Moyer's Climb

A small buttress with a green north face (home to a less well-known *Moyer's Climb*) and a south-facing wall with two fine cracks which always catch the sun.

Approach - Follow the crag-top path past the bouldering area. Drop down the first gully after leaving the trees and head left along the base of the crag. It can also be approached from Garden Face.

❶ Traction . . . . VS 4c
The centre of the face starting up a crack. Reachy and green.
FA. Ernie Marshall 1956

❷ Bloc Steno f6C
A problem up the hanging rib. Eliminating the right arete, climb the rib and groove as far as the overhang. *f6A* with the arete.

❸ Gardom's Gate . . . . VD
The tricky groove in the right arete is climbed to a ledge, where a traverse left leads around to a finish on the green wall.
FA. Keith Axon 1949

10m down and right is a square buttress.

❹ Corner Crack . . . . Diff
The gritty green angle on the left-hand side of the buttress.
FA. Dick Brown 1951

❺ Grey Crack . . . . VD
The short-lived crack in the right wall has its moments.

❻ Attraction . . . . HVS 5a
The blunt arete attracts lovers of green mantels.
FA. Ernie Marshall 1956

❼ Moyer's Climb . . . . . S 4a
From the left edge of the front face balance right to a rounded finish on the right arete. A touch bold and green.
FA. Clifford Moyer 1931

❽ Moyer's Variation . . . . . S 4b
The flaky centre of the face soon eases after an awkward start using undercuts.

❾ Cobweb Arete/Little Wanda . . E2 5c
The arete can be climbed on either side via a shared steep start. The rest is pleasant though rather artificial.
FA. (CA) Tim Beavis 1994. FA. (LW) Brian Rossiter 1999

❿ Nowanda . . . . HVS 5a
The first crack in the south-facing wall is worth seeking out by those in search of good jamming. Well protected and excellent.
FA. Ernie Marshall 1953

⓫ Landsick E1 5b
Take the right-hand crack to its end, then swing right with difficulty, pull-up to reach a flat hold and heathery ground.
FA. Peter Biven 1953

⓬ Landsickness E3 6a
Climb direct from the crack by a fierce couple of moves on really sloping holds. Harder than it appears initially.
FA. Ian Riddington 1981

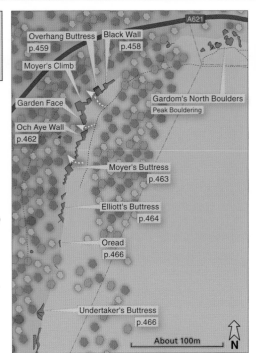

Garden Face

A popular blocky buttress that is split by several cracks and has a nice collection of easier climbs.

Approach - Follow the crag-top path past the bouldering area. Drop down the second gully after leaving the trees and head right along the base of the crag.

⑬ Cave Gully . . . . 🧍 ⬚ **Diff**
An exploratory trip through the dirty rift in the back of the gully.

⑭ Cave Gully Crack . . . 🔆📖🧗 ⬚ **HS 4b**
A tricky start leads to good jamming above - steep.

⑮ Chockstone Climb . . . . 🧍 ⬚ **HS 4a**
The smelly block-filled rift has a hard narrow exit - tough.

⑯ Garden Face Crack . . . . . 🔆🧗 ⬚ **VS 4b**
The continuous crack just left of the arete is tricky to enter (jig to the left) and is good above. Large gear helps but isn't essential.
FA. Clifford Moyer 1931

⑰ Garden Face Direct . 🔆🖐️🧗 ⬚ **VS 5a**
Start up GFC (or direct - **5b**) then move right onto the wall and climb it direct. Nice positions and moves but sadly a bit artificial.

⑱ Garden Face Indirect . . . . . . 🔆 ⬚ **Diff**
Just right of the arete, climb a short corner and the blocky continuation crack above. It gives steep climbing for the grade.
FA. J.W.Puttrell 1890

Overhang Buttress p.459

Black Wall p.458

Moyer's Climb

Garden Face

Gardom's North Boulders
Peak Bouldering

Och Aye Wall p.462

Moyer's Buttress p.463

Elliott's Buttress p.464

Oread p.466

Undertaker's Buttress p.466

About 100m N

A621

From mid morning | 12 min | Sheltered

16m

16m

Approach and descent

⑫ ⑰ ⑮ ⑯ ⑱ ⑬ ⑭

Och Aye Wall

⑨ ⑩ ⑪

Och Aye Wall

A smooth green slab that was quarried long ago. It has a trio of technical slabby wall climbs. To the right is a dank sidewall which gives shade in the summer but is best avoided at other times.

Approach (see map on page 461) - Follow the crag-top path past the bouldering area. Drop down the second gully after leaving the trees and head right along the base of the crag.

① Och Aye Wall Indirect . . . 〔icons〕 **VS 5a**
Just right of the arete, climb the wall on tiny polished holds to a ledge at 10m. Move to the centre of the wall to finish.

② Och Aye Wall Direct . 〔icons〕 **VS 5b**
The centre of the wall has a hard start, which is especially so for the short. Once the first runner arrives, it eases.
FA. Jack Macleod 1934

Moyer's Buttress

The best buttress on the crag is home to one of the Peak's most famous challenges - *Moyer's Buttress*. This brilliant route takes an unlikely line up the tall arete being strenuous and delicate by turns. *Stormbringer* and *Perfect Day* both take equally impressive lines to their easier companion. The side-wall is sheltered but the open front face can be green after rain.

Approach (see map on page 461) - The buttress is marked by a pair of large blocks on its rocky crest a few metres below the level of the path and 120m from where the path emerges from the trees. The path along the foot of the cliff from *Nowanda* is hard work.

③ Tartan Route . . . . . . 〔icons〕 **VS 5a**
Just out from the corner is another worthwhile line. Once again it has a hard start and a fluttery upper section.
FA. Ernie Marshall 1956

④ Capstone Gully . . . . 〔icons〕 **Mod**
The main angle to a tight exit. Better than it looks!

⑤ Slime Crack . . . . 〔icon〕 **HVS 5a**
The green crack in the wall is always a slippery struggle.

⑥ Fantasy . . . . 〔icon〕 **HVS 5b**
The right side of the wall moving left. Will probably need a clean.

⑦ Byne's Crack . . . . 〔icons〕 **S 4b**
A fine long groove gives an awkward pitch, large gear helps. At the top, escape off left or finish up the steep juggy rib.
FA. Eric Byne late 1940s

⑧ The Gritstone Treaty . 〔icons〕 **f7B**
Just left of the impressive leaning block of *Moyer's Buttress* is a diamond-shaped, undercut boulder. This high-ish problem tackles the left arete.

⑨ Mo's Problem . . . . . 〔icons〕 **f7A+**
The right arete needs some serious padding.

⑩ Cave Arete . . . . 〔icons〕 **HVS 5a**
Fight up the crack under the giant boulder to a good ledge, or bridge it if you are long-legged. Balance up the rib on the right in a fine position. A big contrast to the beefy goings-on below.
FA. Wilf White 1950

Approach and descent

20m

8 9

10

11

12

14

17

12

13

15

16

Elliott's Buttress - 60m

⑪ Stormbringer...... E3 6a
Another of the classic E3 routes at Gardom's. Climb the slabby arete to the right of the cave and lean out to reach a good jug. A gut-wrenching mantel gains the upper wall just right of the rib, which proves to be more delicate and bold.
FA. Pete Biven 1956. FFA. Dave Morgan 1976. Biven reached the mantelshelf using tension, though the moves were done free. The route then zig-zagged up the final buttress all the way out to Moyer's and back!

⑫ Moyer's Buttress...... Top 50 E1 5b
A major classic, originally led with a single thread-runner. Climb the cracked slab to the overhang then swing around the arete. The famous rocking block was removed in late 2013 - the crux is now a bit harder. Pull up and make difficult moves to get back on the front face. The upper slab is delicate though gear is adequate nowadays with modern technology.
FA. Peter Biven 1955. Alan Austin soloed the 2nd ascent a few years later.

⑬ Biven's Crack........ E1 5b
The long slanting crack is stormed on solid jams and jugs (once aided on wood wedges) to its end and a swinging escape right. A great pitch, worth seeking out.
FA. Pete Biven 1955. FFA. Jack Street 1966

⑭ Perfect Day....... E5 6b
A fine route with a crux that feels more committing than it should. Climb the previous route to the top of the crack - a good warm-up for what lies ahead. Attack the wall above, first left then right (good wires) to a desperate exit. Reaching the key hold is one thing, using it is another.
FA. Andy Parkin (as Solid Air, one nut for aid) 1976
FFA. Steve Bancroft 1979

⑮ Perfect Day Direct Start
.... f7B
The fingery wall - no jumping! Descend the crack on the left when you reach the jugs, or use this as an approach to the main route. With a jump at the start it is worth *f7A+*.

⑯ Keith's Corner Crack...... HS 4b
The short groove on the right is awkward. Finish up easy rock.
FA. Keith Axon 1949

⑰ The Enigma Variation... E3 5c
A small pumpy extension to *Biven's Crack* best done in one long pitch. Climb the wall left of the arete to a rounded exit.
FA. Keith Sharples 1983

Sheffield Area

Ladybower Area

Stanage

Burbage Valley

Millstone Area

Derwent Edges

Chatsworth Area

Southern Crags

Elliott's Buttress

The classic E1, *Eye of Faith*, makes a great second route of the day if you have come to do *Moyer's Buttress*. Both of the *Elliott* routes are also worth seeking out. Sadly the trees are getting ever closer, which has resulted in the lower section of the buttress often being green and damp.

Approach (see map on page 461) - Walk over the top of *Moyer's Buttress* (120m from where the path emerges from the trees) then drop down a gully and navigate through the undergrowth. If you are aiming for any of the buttresses further along the crag, return to the crag top path first.

① **Elliott's Buttress Indirect. . . .** 💠 ⬜ **VS 4b**
From 12m up the gully, jam along the green horizontal break onto the front of the buttress and access a ledge with difficulty. Climb the steep arete and wall on the left to finish. Airy.

② **Seventy One White Mice.** 💠 🔦 ⬜ **E2 6a**
Climb the thin crack to where a perplexing couple of pulls reach a deep break. Continue more easily up the wall.
FA. Gabe Regan 1981

③ **The Eye of Faith. . . .** 💠 🔦 ⬜ **E1 5c**
A fine route which is usually climbed by its original direct start, the easier (**HVS 5b**) left-hand version from the gully is equally worthwhile. Climb the groove to the roof, then traverse left to the finger-crack splitting the nose. Layback up to reach the crest of the buttress above. Finish up this, trending slightly right in a great position.
FA. Peter Biven 1956

④ **Rhythmic Itch . . . .** 💠 ⬜ **E1 5b**
Climb to the roof, move right, then stretch for the next break. Shuffle left then head directly up the easier wall. The described line avoids the old crux, the direct connection to *Elliott's*.
FA. Gary Gibson 1981

⑤ **Elliott's Buttress Direct . .** 💠 ⬜ **HS 4b**
Climb the groove that bounds the right-hand side of the buttress and the crack on the right to a good ledge. Move up and left to the crest of a huge flake and step onto a polished lump, before climbing the wall rightwards to the final crack. Excellent stuff.
FA. Frank Elliott 1934

⑥ **Jungle Arete . . . .** ⬜ **S 4b**
The flake and arete just across the gully give some good moves.

⑦ **Dead Tree Wall . . . .** 💠 ❤️ ⬜ **HS 4b**
The slabby face round to the right is climbed boldly leftwards to better holds and runners.

Oread 80m along crag-top path

 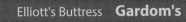

Sheffield Area

Ladybower Area

Stanage

Burbage Valley

Millstone Area

Derwent Edges

Chatsworth Area

Southern Crags

TICKLIST

Gardom's E3 Ticks

By some quirk Gardom's has a neat set of E3 routes. A great day out if you are up to the task. From north to south the best of these are:

☐ **Sleeping Sickness, E3** *(458)*
Devious and pumpy.

☐ **Stormbringer, E3** *(463)*
The mantel needs big shoulders.

☐ **Crocodile, E3** *(469)*
Bold and fingery on the upper wall.

☐ **Waterloo Sunset, E3** *(471)*
A neat and bold arete.

Dan Parkes not quite ready to drop off yet on *Sleeping Sickness* (E3 5c) - *page 458* - on Black Wall. This is the first of the four classic E3 ticks at Gardom's.

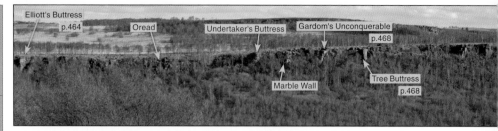

Elliott's Buttress p.464 · Oread · Undertaker's Buttress · Gardom's Unconquerable p.468 · Marble Wall · Tree Buttress p.468

Approach and descent — 14m — Afternoon · 15 min · Sheltered · Green — 22m — Approach and descent

Oread Buttress

A small, isolated buttress, halfway between the more conspicuous outcrops of *Moyer's Buttress* and *Undertaker's Buttress*. It has a couple of worthwhile climbs in a relatively sunny situation.
Approach - Best access is from the cliff-top path. The buttress is hidden just below the path, halfway between *Moyer's* and *Undertaker's Buttress*.

1 Nymph's Arete . . . . **VS 4c**
The wide left-hand crack is awkward. Step right onto the arete which leads to a steep finish. Usually a bit (or a lot) green.
FA. Ernie Marshall 1962

2 Oread . . . . **VS 4c**
The clean crack gives an excellent, well-protected pitch.
FA. Keith Axon 1949

3 Yellow Chimney . . . . **Mod**
The easy rift behind the tree.

Undertaker's Buttress

Another small, isolated buttress, most notable for its impressive jutting beak. Hidden in the trees, it is well-sheltered though often it is a bit green and dirty.
Approach - From the cliff top above *Moyer's Buttress*, pick out the beak of *Hearse Arete* which interrupts your view towards Chatsworth. The descent is just beyond the arete and involves doubling back under the face.

4 Blaze . . . . **VS 4c**
The wide crack and its thinner and trickier continuation.
FA. Gary Gibson 1981

5 Undertaker's Buttress . . . **VS 4c**
Start on the left and climb the 'coffin' crack to a chockstone, then move right and climb the wall (a bit bold) to a possible (sensible?) stance (**4c**). Climb to the roof then traverse round the arete rightwards to slopers and ashort finishing crack (**4b**).
FA. Joe Brown 1951

6 Hearse Arete **E1 5b**
A spectacular outing. Begin under the beak and climb onto a green ledge on the left with difficulty (crux?). Climb up and then trend right crossing the overhang on generally good holds. Thrilling and photogenic but manages to feel slightly artificial.
FA. Peter Biven (1 peg) 1956

Marble Wall

A very neglected section of the edge which is almost always green and dirty. The addition of a modern desperate might see it get a bit more attention.
Approach - From the cliff top above *Moyer's Buttress*, pick out the beak of *Hearse Arete*. The descent is just beyond the arete, at the bottom turn left under the wall.

7 Tales of the Black Widower . . . E5 6a
A technical challenge direct up the centre of the wall. Seldom in condition except after long dry spells. It may need a brush first.
FA. Simon Jones 1988

8 Marshall's Route . . . . HVS 5a
Start up *Black Widower* but break right along a line of holds to a crack. Follow the right-hand side of the wall above.
FA. Ernie Marshall 1963

9 White's Route . . . . HS 4b
Climb a crack to a flake then tackle the right side of the flake to reach a crack above - the left-hand side is harder - 5a. Follow the crack up some grassy ground to the top.
FA. Wilfred White 1950

10 Birthday Climb . . . . HVD
Right of the wall is a dirty, blocky corner and cleaner arete.

11 Pedestal Climb . . . . HS 4a
Scramble up onto a pedestal then pull awkwardly up left onto a ledge. Finish up a bold slab. Just about worth a star!

12 Selladore E8 7a
Follow *Pedestal Climb* but move right to the roof. Climb it directly with difficult moves to gain a good sloping ledge round the lip. Cunning heel work helps you gain the bold upper arete.
FA. Pete Whittaker 2012

13 Nursery Slab . . . . HVS 5a
Starting down and right, climb a short arete and gain the slab. Follow this and the steep narrow wall above - green.

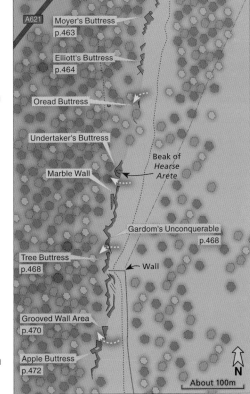

Afternoon | 15 min | Sheltered | Green

Photo taken in 2005, tree cover is now much worse

18m

Approach and descent

Gardom's Unconquerable

A fine steep face - an isolated anciently quarried section - which is almost impossible to view because of the trees. **Approach (see map on page 467) -** From above *Hearse Arete*, continue on the cliff-top path until 30m before the wall crossing the path. Double back right down a grassy gully and head right through trees to a quarried bay.

1 Bilberry Buttress . . . . . . VS 5a
Climb the boulder-problem rib on the left to a ledge, then follow the exposed arete to the top. The short may need to escape by stepping left just below the final move. The chimney of the next route gives an easier start, dropping the overall the grade to **4b**.

2 Bilberry Chimney . . . . HVD 4a
The wide awkward crack leads to ledges. Amble up the rift.

3 Stepped Crack . . . . Diff
The rising ramp-line gives an awkward low-grade climb to ledges above the *Unconquerable*. Exit right at the top.

4 Crottle E1 5b
A thin crack in the wall leads to steep juggy terrain. Avoiding *Bilberry Buttress* is tricky in places - just do your best.
FA. Chris Jackson 1983 Named after the lichen that covered the wall.

5 Gardom's Unconquerable VS 4c
The imposing corner-crack can be laybacked or thrutched, although hidden holds (and big cams) help. At the top, exit right up the wall. Hard work and high in the grade. The wall under the slanting groove up and left gives an extension at **E2 5c**.
FA. Joe Brown 1950

6 Whillans' Blind Variant . . E1 5b
From the ledge (belay) above *Gardom's Unconquerable* swing left below the overhangs to pass the arete, then finish rightwards up the wall. Only short but very intimidating - like its creator.
FA. Don Whillans 1951

Tree Buttress and Crocodile

A diverse section with some crack climbs plus a few harder challenges including a fine prow with contrasting side-walls. Shady in the summer but green for much of the rest of the year.
Approach (see map on page 467) - From above *Hearse Arete*, continue on the cliff-top path until 30m before the wall that crosses it. Double back right down a grassy gully and head left and follow the vague path under the crag until the buttress appears through the trees. Alternatively, drop down a path just beyond the stone wall.

7 Tree Buttress . . . . VS 4b
On the left-hand side of the bay climb to ledges, then move right almost to the big tree. Finish up the steep flaky crack on its left.

8 Midas Man E3 6a
The wall left of the tree, via a short crack and a long reach.
FA. Keith Sharples 1983

9 Tree Climb . . . . HS 4b
A good sharp-edged crack leads to the big tree. Continue up the steep crack and tree in tandem. Well named!

10 Tree Neighbour . . . . S 4a
From the tree, step right for some traditional chimney fun!
FA. David Penlington 1950

Next a scruffy crack with jutting flake offers an independent way to reach the ledge, though the options to left and right are better.

11 Third Time Lucky . . . . . . VS 4c
Climb the mini-*Inverted V*. The exit gives the tough crux.
FA. Nat Allen 1951 at the third attempt.

12 Gom Jabbar . . . E8 6c
The hanging right arete is unprotected, fingery and hard. A sensible side-runner stops a ground fall but not hitting the ledge.
FA. Simon Jones 1994

13 By-Pass Route . . . . HS 4b
Follow the ramp left to the ledge. The groove left of the corner is a little easier than it looks and has helpful chockstones.

14 Central Crack . . . . HVS 5b
The body-width crack splitting the roof is a really ugly customer. The groove at the back of the ledge is easier and more pleasant.
FA. Joe Brown 1956

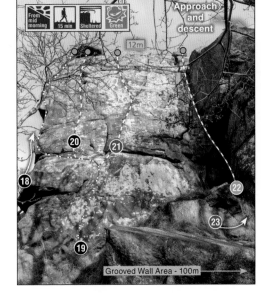

15 **Wall Finish** . . . . 🖼️ ⬜ **VS 4c**
A better finish to *Central Crack* up the flaky crack to the right.
FA. Joe Brown 1956

16 **Agadoo** . . . . 🖼️ ⬜ **E3 6b**
Boulder up to the hanging crack. The landing is poor.
FA. John Allen 1985

17 **Albert Spansworthy** . . . . ⚙️🟦⬜ **E5 6b**
Span right to a pocket (gear) then finish direct. Totally height
dependent - the E5 is for an 'average six footer'!
FA. Mark Turnbull 1998

18 **Nah'han** . . . . ⚙️🔲🟩 **E8 6c**
A superb line which slaps its wild way up the left-hand side of
the arete throughout into ever more serious territory.
Photo on page 457.
FA. Tom Randall 2013

19 **Make it Snappy** . . . . ⚙️🔲🟩⬜ **E6 6b**
The right side of the arete. From the ledges move up and left
around the arete to a black pocket. Hard moves up and right
reach better holds and an airy finish back on the right side.
FA. Neil Foster 1984

20 **Ecky Thump** . . . . ⚙️🔲🔲🟩⬜ **E6 6c**
The wall just right of the arete is bold, fingery and technical!
FA. Andy Popp 1995

21 **Crocodile** . . . . ⚙️🔲🟩⬜ **E3 5c**
A bold route; another of Gardom's fine E3 ticks. It is pushy in its
central part, the runners and holds are there, though both take
some finding, before moving left to finish. The even bolder direct
finish is **Old Croc, E4 6a**.
FA. Gabe Regan 1975 FA. Old Croc, Graham Parkes 2014

22 **Right-hand Crack** . . . . . . ⚙️🖼️⬜ **VS 4c**
The open groove on the right-hand edge of the wall with a useful
bonsai tree has its well-protected crux right at the top.
FA. Eric Byne 1940

23 **Red Sky Rib** . . . . ⚙️🔲⬜ **VD**
The rib around right is quite bold early on and leads to steeper
cracks above.

Grooved Wall Area

A couple of isolated buttresses with a classic E3 5c and a series of pleasant crack and groove climbs. The chunky oak in front of Grooved Wall offers shade in the summer but encourages humidity after rain.

Approach (see map on page 467) - Continue along the cliff-top path for 70m after the stone wall. A short distance before the tower of Apple Buttress, descend a gully which leads down between the two buttresses. Grooved Wall can also be reached from above Apple Buttress.

The Capillary Crack buttress is on the right-hand side (looking out) of the approach/descent gully, 20m left of Grooved Wall.

1 Soloman . . . . *f6A+*
The left edge of the steep wall.

2 A Fearful Orange . . . . . . *f6C+*
The short hanging crack starting matched on the big triangular hold. Leaning in higher is worth *f6A+*.

3 Two-Headed Boy *f6C*
The arete on its right-hand side, continuing out right along the shelf. Mantel to finish. On its left is **Neutral Milk Hotel**, *f6A*.

4 It's a Gas E1 5c
Ape across the break to reach a ledge. Finish up the groove.
FA. Tony Warwick 1990

5 Jumping Jack Flash . . . . HVS 5b
Access the hanging crack with difficulty and climb it with more!
FA. Ron Kenyon 1977

6 Broken Buttress . . . . VD
The central rift. A finish on the right is best.

7 Ladder Coins *f6B*
Follow crimps up the wall.

8 Gamorilla . . . . HVS 5a
Trend left to access the hanging groove, then up this and across the roof. Beware loose rock in the break below the roof.
FA. Gary Gibson 1981

9 Capillary Crack . . . . VS 4c
The thin crack and bulge give the best pitch on this buttress.
FA. Nat Allen 1951

Grooved Wall is the next bit of rock southwards. The first route is on the north-facing side-wall.

⑩ Whisky Wall . . . . S 3c
Climb the green groove to ledges then move out right to find better climbing and great positions on the arete.

⑪ Muswell Hillbillies E4 5c
An eliminate up the green unprotected slab down and right.
FA. Steve Bancroft 1986

⑫ Waterloo Sunset . . . E3 5c
The last of the classic Gardom's E3s is a bold arete climb which is often green. Start on the right and climb to a break where runners protect the moves up and left to easier ground. Oddly the route doesn't climb much like an arete.
FA. Martin Boysen 1977

The next clutch of routes are on the well-cracked triangular face that runs up right. They are all worth doing.

⑬ Finale Groove . . . . VS 5a
The oddly-named first crack in the face. The crux requires some beefy pinch-gripping then things ease. Large cams help.
FA. David Penlington 1951

⑭ Babylon's Finale . . . . VS 5a
Linking the two routes via the slanting crack is artificial but pleasant enough. Well protected.

⑮ Babylon's Groove . . . . VS 5a
Follow the right-hand branch of the Y-shaped crack to a tricky exit. Avoid the final chimney by using the crack on the left.
FA. Don Chapman 1951

⑯ Central Groove . . . . VS 4b
The continuous crack-line has tricky moves to reach the easy vegetated chimney above.
FA. Clifford Moyer 1934

⑰ Tree Groove . . . . VS 4b
Climb the pleasant groove until level with the tree, then move right awkwardly (large cam) into a narrow rift to finish. Escaping left into the chimney is a grade easier but feels like a cop-out.
FA. Clifford Moyer 1934

⑱ Tree Groove Direct . . . . VS 5a
Climb to the tree then continue up the wall. Tricky if the tree is used and trickier still if is avoided.
FA. Clifford Moyer 1934

⑲ Right-Hand Groove . . . . VS 4c
The penultimate crack gives vegetated bridging. The original and easier start was up the next crack.
FA. Clifford Moyer 1934

⑳ Spilt Crack . . . . VS 4b
Up the last crack in the face then move right to where a second crack splits the bulge and provides the meat of the route.
FA. Chris Craggs 1983. Only the finish was new.

16m

Grooved Wall

Not much sun | 15 min | Sheltered | Green

From mid morning | 20 min | Sheltered

The north face of Apple Buttress has a tiny collection of worthwhile routes that sadly are green after rain.

❶ Layback Crack . . . . **VS 5a**
The left-hand crack is short-lived and honest hard work! A slippery little monkey where 'cracking on' is essential.
FA. Wilf White 1950

❷ Flake Crack . . . . **HS 4b**
Better that it looks and with tricky moves at the nose - harder for the short who will struggle to reach past the crux. Only **HS** but harder than *Apple Arete* - which is a bit odd!
FA. Rupert Brooks 1934

❸ Twilight's Last Gleaming . . . **E2 5b**
Climb the slab to the left of *N.M.C. Crack* to a good ledge and then the rib on the left to the top. A green eliminate.
FA. J.Zonn 1989

❹ N.M.C. Crack . . . . **HVD 3c**
The fine stepped-groove in the north face of the buttress leads to a short crack and mini-summit. Polished and popular but still a very good tick with excellent protection.
FA. Frank Elliott (of Nottingham MC) 1930

❺ Apple Arete Direct . . **E4 5c**
The lower arete is very bold requiring unprotected, rounded and scary laybacking. More like a sensible **E1 5c** with side-runners.
FA. Gary Gibson 1980

16m

Descent

Approach and descent

Apple Buttress
One of the best bits of rock on the cliff with the classics of *N.M.C. Crack* and *Apple Arete*. The edge juts above the foliage and is a good bet for much of the year, plus the outward views are great. To the right is a short quarried slab with a pleasant collection of cracks and a couple of harder slab climbs.
Approach (see map on page 467) - Follow the crag-top path for about 150m past the wall. The tower of Apple Buttress will become visible. Descend the gully before this under Grooved Wall, or scramble down the gully south of Apple Buttress.

Pillar Wall - 300m

6 Apple Arete . . . . Top 50 VS 4b
The tall left-hand arete of the buttress is excellent and mild.
Climb the central crack and make a short traverse left to the
arete at the earliest opportunity. This is then followed throughout
with good runners in the breaks and lovely positions. The route
is very photogenic from either side. *Photo on page 454.*
FA. David Penlington 1952

7 Apple Crack . . . . VD
The wide crack in the buttress leads to a good ledge below the
summit, passing the jutting flake. The crack of *Giant's Staircase*
can be used to reach the summit, at a higher grade.

8 Apple Core E2 6a
The slab using the pinch on the lip and a side-runner.
FA. Malc Baxter 1990

9 Cider Apple . . . . HS 4a
From the right-hand side of the buttress move left past the arete
then climb the right edge of the slab to a large ledge. The short
arete on the final block offers an exposed extension.
FA. P.Knapp 1950

10 Giant's Staircase . . . . S 4a
The steep stepped crack in the side-wall leads to a short slippery
layback (crux), and then a final steep jamming crack leads on to
the summit. Belay with care on the narrow crest.
FA. Clifford Moyer 1931

11 Bitter . . . . VS 5a
The thin crack with a useful but flexible spike (nut either side or
a thin tape over it) is technical and slippery but nice and safe.
FA. Eric Finney 1960s

12 Master of Thought . . E2 5c
The steep slab is especially sketchy for the short. Side-runners
drop the grade a notch or two. Loss of a hold may have made
this a touch harder than it used to be.
FA. Gary Gibson 1979

13 Velvet Cracks . . . . VS 4b
The thin crack in the right side of the slab is pleasant and
popular despite being a bit of an eliminate. It is well protected.
FA. Ernie Marshall 1963

14 Apple Jack Cracks . . . . VD
Parallel jamming cracks splitting the centre of the slab can be
gained directly, though a balancy ledge traverse from the right
arete is also possible. Short, sweet and well protected.

15 Cydrax . . . . HVS 5b
A fingery slab leads, with a stretch, to a short finishing crack.
FA. Eric Finney 1957

16 Cider . . . . HVS 5a
The delicate right-hand arete of the wall is tricky, poorly
protected and high in the grade! Starting by laybacking out of
the pit on the right is a worthwhile **HVS 5b**.
FA. David Penlington 1950

17 Blenheim Gully . . . . . . VS 4c
The right-hand corner of the pit has a tricky undercut start, a
beefy wide crack and short unprotected wall to finish.
FA. David Penlington 1950

18 Blenheim Buttress E1 5a
Climb awkwardly to a ledge and loose flake then swing boldly
round left to the gully and back right a bit higher up. The creaky
flake should not be trusted for runners.

19 Blenheim E1 5a
The line up front of the buttress is a more direct version of the
previous climb and is another serious one. It is the last decent
route on this section of the edge - you can take our word for it!
FA. Don Morrison 1956

Pillar Wall

Beyond Apple Buttress is a neat wall tucked below the edge. It may be green early in the year although it cleans up when the weather improves.

Approach - From Apple Buttress, continue south. 80m after the trees finish and about 100m before a stone wall crosses the path, head right to locate the buttress.

❶ Charlotte Rampling **E6 6b**
Sustained and bold, with a poor landing. Start left of the ramp and make hard moves to reach it. Trend up left to the break then move left and make another hard and reachy move to the top.
FA. Johnny Dawes 1984

❷ Hired Goons **E8 6c**
The long awaited direct finish is as hard as expected.
FA. Will Atkinson 2013

❸ Left-hand Pillar Crack . . . **E1 5b**
An excellent crack requiring a subtle blend of laybacking and jamming. Plenty of gear if you can hang about to place it.
FA. Allan Austin 1956

❹ Right-hand Pillar Crack . . **HVS 5a**
Harder than it looks and not quite as good as its neighbour.
FA. Frank Elliott 1930

❺ Elliott's Crack . . . . **S 4a**
The steep and juggy crack to an exit on the right or better, and more in keeping, to the left.
FA. Frank Elliott 1930s

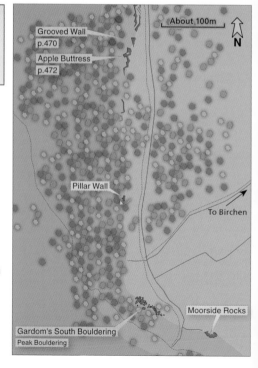

Grooved Wall p.470

Apple Buttress p.472

Pillar Wall

To Birchen

About 100m

N

Moorside Rocks

Gardom's South Bouldering
Peak Bouldering

Moorside Rocks

The southern extremity of Gardom's is a neat little outcrop. It looks a bit like a Dartmoor tor and features rounded rock, a number of desperate aretes and a lovely grassy base.

Approach (see map on page 456) - From Apple Buttress, head south and east for 800m; the crag soon appears on the left. The walk in from the Robin Hood Inn parking (see Birchen intro - page 477) is shorter than that from the north.

6 Short Arete *f6B*
The left arete.

7 Right Arete *f6C*
The right arete of the small block.

8 Choked Chimney . . . . VD 4b
The block-choked rift is surprisingly awkward to start and finish.
FA. Oread members late 1940s

9 Charlotte Dumpling . . E3 5c
Move out right from the crack using a small edge to make a high rock-over. *f6B* above pads. Eliminating the right side of the crack makes it *f7B*.
FA. Steve Bancroft 1986

10 Will's Dyno *f8A*
Gain the finish of *Charlotte Dumpling* via an impressive dyno.
FA. Will Atkinson 2013

11 Superbloc E8 6c
The huge rounded arete of the chimney is an impressive ground-up target above a decent stack of pads at *f8A+*.
FA. Miles Gibson 2003

12 Straight Chimney . . . . . . HVD 4a
A rectilinear rift giving interesting hard work. Often a bit green.
FA. Oread members late 1940s

13 Batter Patter . . . . *f6C+*
Climb the thin seam to an awkward leftwards exit onto the ledge.

14 Homeless E8 6c
Another rounded monstrosity with the usual sloping finale. The seam/groove in the centre of the face may be of help. *f6C* for just the start.
FA. Miles Gibson 2003

15 Brazil E6 6b
The earlier solution tackles the upper arete on its right side.
FA. Jon Read 2000

16 Moorside Crack . . . VS 5a
Udge and wriggle the tricky leaning and widening crack.
FA. Oread members late 1940s

17 Press Gang E3 5c
The centre of the domed buttress has the expected finish!
FA. Paul Mitchell 2003

18 Moorside Rib . . VS 5a
A mantel start reaches a ledge, then pad up the rib above. Short but technical to start and bold to finish.
FA. Oread members late 1940s

19 The Jackalope . . E3 6b
The hanging fissure gives a jamming/laybacking masterclass! Often done above mats at *f7A*.
FA. John Read 1985

20 Small Worlds E3 6a
Scale the front of the rib with a technical start, plus a rounded and reachy finish.
FA. Jon Read 2002

21 Pillar Chimney . . . . Diff
The last rift of any note gives a quick tick to get the tally up.

10m

Robin Hood Inn parking
10 mins

Sheffield Area · Ladybower Area · Stanage · Burbage Valley · Millstone Area · Derwent Edges · Chatsworth Area · Southern Crags

TICKLIST
The Best of Birchen
Birchen has a great selection of interesting climbs but few real classics. Working your way through the dozen routes in the ticklist below should ensure you visit all sections of the cliff. We could have added the tough classics of *Midshipman* and *Peaches* but that would have been a bit mean.

☐ The Promenade, D *(484)*
☐ Emma's Temptation, HVD *(479)*
☐ Trafalgar Wall, S *(485)*
☐ Powder Monkey Parade, S *(484)*
☐ Fo'c'sle Crack, S *(487)*
☐ Sail Buttress, HS *(482)*
☐ Porthole Direct, VS *(480)*
☐ The Crow's Nest, VS *(478)*
☐ Nelson's Nemesis, VS *(493)*
☐ Topsail, VS *(482)*
☐ Ratline, HVS *(482)*
☐ Orpheus Wall, HVS *(483)*

Lucie Sedlarova on the fine finishing slab of *Powder Monkey Parade* (S 4b) - *page 484* - on the Promenade area of Birchen. Photo: Chris Fox

Sheffield Area

Ladybower Area

Stanage

Burbage Valley

Millstone Area

Derwent Edges

Chatsworth Area

Southern Crags

	No star	☆	☆☆	☆☆☆
Mod to S	55	33	4	-
HS to HVS	16	37	7	1
E1 to E3	14	13	1	1
E4 and up	3	9	-	1

Birchen remains one of the most popular venues in the Peak due to its friendly atmosphere and good collection of low-grade routes. The place has always been a favourite with groups and this long-standing popularity has led to the wearing of many of the already rounded holds. Quite a number of the routes have slippery and awkward starts but get yourself going and things often ease rapidly with height. Summer weekends can be extremely busy, but if you leave the main section and head rightwards to the more secluded buttresses, you will probably find a bit of solitude.

The majority of routes at Birchen have names of a nautical nature linked to the monument on the cliff top, erected to celebrate Nelson's victory at the Battle of Trafalgar back in 1805.

Approach   Also see map on page 454

Birchen runs along the crest of the moor 3km east of Baslow village. The usual approach is from the National Trust car park by the Robin Hood Inn, though on busy days the field across the road is also available. Walk up the road to a stile on the left and a sandy track that leads to the rocks in 10 mins. Keeping left at the only fork leads straight to the main section of cliff, whereas heading right leads towards Kismet Buttress. It is also possible to approach from the Gardom's parking spot (see page 456).

Conditions

Birchen takes virtually no drainage and is probably the fast drying of all the Eastern Edges. It gets the afternoon sun, and has the usual potential to be windy and cold in bad weather.

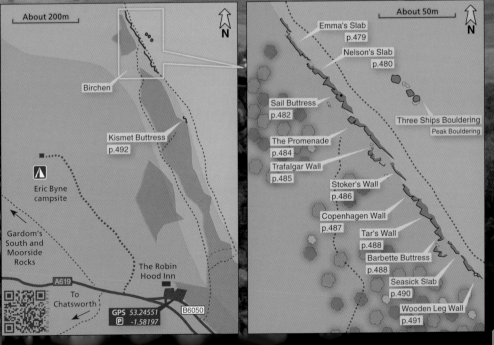

5m

60m from
The Gangplank

① ② ③

Sheffield Area

Ladybower Area

Stanage

Burbage Valley

Millstone Area

Derwent Edges

Chatsworth Area

Southern Crags

Far Left
The short walls at the left-hand extremity of the cliff are less popular than the rest of Birchen and so are a fair bet for a bit of solitude.

① Bosun's Nose . . . . S 4c
Up the left side of the wall and over the jutting nose - tricky.

② Bosun's Crack . . . . VD
The tiny angle gives mild jamming.

③ Bosun's Wall . . . . HVD 4a
The wall on the right to a tricky but avoidable last move.

5m

6m

⑤ ⑥ ⑦ ⑧ ⑨ ⑩ ⑪

Emma's Slab ➤

④ The Gangplank . . . . Mod
The isolated slab by pleasant balance climbing on polished holds. Experts can do it no-hands and in unsuitable footwear.

Up on the main edge the concentration of routes picks up.

⑤ Poop Crack f3
The teeny crack on the left. UK tech grade of 4a.

⑥ Handy Crack . . . . Diff
A chockstoned-crack gives a handy introduction to jamming.

⑦ Visitors Only . . . . HS 4a
The shallow left-facing groove has a few pleasant moves.

⑧ All Aboard . . . . Diff
The deeper central groove has an awkward start and exit.

⑨ Saltheart Foamfollower . . . HVS 5c
A thin crack in the smooth wall leads to a deep break which is tricky to attain a standing position in. More like **E1** if the aretes are avoided. From sitting it is **Howships Lacunae**, *f6C*.
FA. Bob Higginbotham 1980s

⑩ Poop Deck Crack . . . . S 4a
The awkward crack splitting the wall to a short V-groove.
FA. Reg Schofield early 1930s

⑪ The Pirate E2 6b
The wall and bulge are 'aaaard. Highball *f6B* to the second break.
FA. Daniel Warren 2005

Emma's Slab
The first section of the main part of the cliff is home to several worthwhile climbs, mostly cracks of one size or another. It is always popular. Many of the routes have become polished over the years though the quality of the best of the climbs continues to shine through.
Approach (see map on page 477) - Continue past all the main areas to the last substantial section of crag.

⑫ Dan's Arete f6C
The hanging left arete of the block.

⑬ Crow's Feet . . . . f5+
The hanging right arete of the block. UK tech grade of 5c.

⑭ Land Ho! . . . . HS 4c
Climb the tough crack right of the block then finish up the bold right-hand arete of the side-wall. The left arete is easier.

⑮ The Crow's Nest . . . . . . VS 4c
Start as for *Land Ho!* but at the top of the crack step onto the face on the right. Cross to the base of the slab and balance up this to a delicate final move which is tricky for the short.
FA. Frank Elliott late 1920s

⑯ Scrim Net f6A
The thin crack has a tough move or two to reach a large hole. Easier climbing above, or escape left.
FA. Richard Brown (2pts) 1951. FFA. Len Millsom 1963

17 Look-out Arete . . . . . S 4a
Climb the hard slippery groove into the base of the chimney of *The Funnel*. Bridge up until it is possible to swing onto the left arete, which is then followed in a fine position.
FA. Eric Byne 1956

18 The Funnel . . . . Diff
The deep chimney is gained via polished holds up the wall to the right (reachy) and is then climbed in traditional fashion. Fun.

19 Kiss Me Hardy . . . . HVD 4a
Skip up the right-hand wall as for *The Funnel* then try to make elegant progress up the awkward crack above and right using anything that works. The steep left arete is **The Dancer, E1 5c**.
FA. Eric Byne early 1930s

20 Kiss Me Arse f6C
The arete from a sitting start. *f6A* if you start standing.

21 Monocled Mono f6C
The centre of the wall.

22 Kiss Me Softly f6B
The right arete from a sitting start.

23 Victory Crack . . . . HS 4b
Climb onto the chock then move left to reach the narrow crack that splits the buttress left of the gully. Safe, but it is a fair test of crack technique and a good teaser for many a Stanage VS.
FA. Eric Byne, early 1930s

24 Victory Gully . . . . S 4a
Climb onto the chock then continue up the gully (more of a groove really) to a tricky final couple of moves.
FA. Eric Byne, early 1930s

25 Emma's Slab . . . . VS 4b
Climb onto the chock then stride out right and climb to, and on through, the capping roof via some pleasant moves.
FA. Ernie Marshall 1952

26 Roger the Cabin Boy II . . f6C
The arete from a sitting start.

27 Technical Genius f7A
Pull over the low roof. It is *f7A+* from a sitting start.
FA. Mark Katz 1997

28 Emma's Dilemma . . . . . S 4a
Worthwhile. Starting just right of a low overhang (4b?) climb the crack and groove to a steep safe finish up a crack.
FA. Eric Byne early 1930s

29 Emma Royd . . . . VS 4c
The slab, bulge and rib above. Artificial but pleasant enough.
FA. Colin Binks 1993

30 Emma's Temptation . HVD 4c
A route of two parts. Climb the tough slippery slab rightwards to a ledge. Step back left and take the nice thin crack to the top.
FA. Jack Macleod early 1930s

31 Emma's Delight . . . . HS 4b
Start just left of the right-hand edge of the slab and climb straight up the face to gain the final short crack.
FA. Dave Penlington 1952

32 Deluded . . . . VS 4c
Climb easy rock into a grassy niche then the steep awkward crack and short bulging wall above and left. Low in the grade.

33 Emma's Delusion . . . . S 4a
From the grassy niche take the bulging right-hand crack which is steep and awkward.

34 The Prow . . . . VS 4c
Pull over a small overhang to a ledge, then continue up a short wall to a second overhang which is well supplied with jugs.
FA. Chris Craggs 1993

35 Artificial . . . . VD
The rib on the right of the wall is gained from left or right.

36 Oak Gully . . . . Mod
The easy rift to the right behind the rowan tree.

The Crow's Nest Bouldering
Peak Bouldering

From mid morning | 10 min | Windy

Descent

12m

Descent

Nelson's Slab

Sheffield Area
Ladybower Area
Stanage
Burbage Valley
Millstone Area
Derwent Edges
Chatsworth Area
Southern Crags

1 The Bunk Ladder . . . . [ ] S 4a
The short flake and the ledgy side-wall above.

2 Captain's Prerogative . . . [1] [icon] [ ] HS 4b
The left edge of the slab has a hard start using a vague crack and polished holds. It eases a little above.

3 Captain's Bunk . . . . [1] [ ] HS 4b
The right-hand side of the slab is climbed via a trio of mantelshelves - the first is the crux, though the one to reach the ledge of the 'bunk' is not without interest.
FA. Chuck Cook 1951

4 Telescope Tunnel . . . . . [2] [icon] [ ] Mod
Bizarre but strangely attractive. Climb the easy chimney then move left to the claustrophobic slot. Squirm up this, then into the crag to reach easy ground on the other side of the face. A right-hand version is the similarly Stygian **Captain's Crawl, Diff.** The grades of both of these are nominal.

5 Porthole Buttress . . . . [1] [ ] S 4a
A bit of an expedition, best saved for quiet days. Climb the chimney to a cave and gain the ledge on the right. Follow this to its end then make tricky moves to access the slab further right again. Cross this to its right-hand edge then finish easily.

6 Porthole Direct . . . . [2] [ ] VS 4c
Start 1m right of the chimney and climb up into a shallow corner, passing the porthole, to a good ledge. Finish up the crucial leaning and narrowing crack on the left.
FA. Gilbert Ellis 1951

7 Captain Birdseye . . . . [ ] VS 4c
Climb the crack in the left-hand side of the gully to a cave and bridge past this. Step left then climb the overhang on the front of the buttress to finish.
FA. Chris Craggs 1993

8 Blind Eye . . . . [1] [ ] S 4b
A couple of tricky but well-protected moves. Climb up and left into the recess then exit irreversibly right (runner up and left) on good holds to reach the hanging slab. Finish direct.
FA. Gilbert Ellis 1952

Descent

12m

Emma's Slab

⑨ Dead Eye . . . . 🖼️ 🪝 ☐ **HVS 6a**
A lower exit pulls through the roof at the notch in the overhang to reach easy ground rapidly.
FA. John Allen 1986

⑩ Nelson's Slab Direct. . . . 🖼️ 🪝 ☐ *f6A*
Make a powerful pull through the roof.

⑪ Nelson's Slab . . . . 🖼️ 🪝 ☐ **HS 5a**
Start under the right-hand edge of the slab and make hard moves (4b for the strong) up and left via a polished niche (overhead gear) to gain the slab. Move 2m left then finish direct.
FA. Frank Burgess, early 1930s

⑫ Half Nelson . . . . 🖼️ 🪝 ☐ **VS 5a**
A more delicate right-hand finish to *Nelson's Slab*.
FA. Chris Craggs 1993

⑬ Left Ladder Chimney . . . . ☐ **VD**
The left-hand block-filled crevice is the better of the pair.

⑭ Right Ladder Chimney . . . . . . ☐ **HVD 4a**
The narrow right-hand slot is steeper, greener and harder.

Nelson's Slab

A couple of fine buttresses and an attractive hanging slab that is difficult to access ensure this particular bit of Birchen is always popular. The well-polished nature of the rock on the *Captain's* routes will keep you on your toes. The oddity of *Telescope Tunnel* is included for cavers who are up here having a rest day.

Approach (see map on page 477) - The area is 20m left of the conspicuous monument on top of the crag.

⑮ Midshipman . . . . . . 🖼️ 📕 🏴 ☐ **E2 6a**
From a jug, climb leftwards to a thin crack then continue up the centre of the wall until under the capping overhang. A long reach from jams and a rounded exit overcome the final roof. Great climbing which is well protected throughout.
FA. (Finishing on the right) Len Millsom 1963
FA. (direct) Gary Gibson 1982. He renamed the whole thing Plain Sailing.

⑯ Cold Compass . . . . 🖼️ 🪝 ☐ **E2 6b**
Start from a large sloping block. Pull powerfully over the roof using a flake and pocket high on the right, then follow the direct line to a hard exit. A pre-placed cam up and left is sensible to protect the start unless you want to bounce.
FA. Gary Gibson 1980

12m

Sail Buttress

Sail Buttress - p.482

Sail Buttress

With a steep north-facing wall and an attractive valley face, Sail Buttress is a fine lump of rock that is home to some of the best routes on the edge. A classic day out is assured if you tick all of the starred climbs here. The area is always very popular. To the right is the leaning face with *Orpheus Wall*, which is topped by the conspicuous monument that celebrates Nelson's victory at Trafalgar. Climbers are asked not to use it as an anchor.

Approach (see map on page 477) - The area is right under the conspicuous monument on top of the crag.

1 **Sail Buttress** . . . . 🌟🪓⬜ **HS 4b**
A slippery classic. Start below the steep arete and climb up and right to a good ledge. Use the deep horizontal crack to aid a shuffling traverse out to the left to gain the final easier slab.
FA. Bert Smith 1934

2 **Roger the Cabin Boy I** . . . 🌟⬜ **VS 4c**
A bolder feeling finish to *Sail Buttress* up the groove and slab.
FA. Paul Hornbrook 1997. The first of two routes with this name to be claimed on Birchen.

3 **Ratline** . . . . 🌟⬜ **HVS 5b**
Often started via *Sail Buttress*, the direct start up the thin crack left of *Sail Chimney* improves the overall experience. Climb the crack, move left to the ledge then step up and right again to reach a good flake. Climb through the bulge by a bold high step to reach the upper slab.
FA. Len Millsom 1963

4 **Amazing Grace** . . . . ⬜ **E2 6a**
The steep and reachy wall right of *Ratline* with a jig right at two-thirds height. Avoiding the opposite wall is tricky!
FA. Wim Verhoeven 1998

5 **Sail Chimney** . . . . 🌟⬜ **S 4a**
An ancient classic. Climb the initial awkward and polished groove then continue directly up the chimney. Back and foot technique is best though squirming up the back also works.
FA. Eric Byne early 1930s

6 **Topsail** . . . . 🌟⬜ **VS 4c**
A classic and low in the grade - except for the short! Approach the overhang via a crack and groove (thread) and power through the bulge via a flake. The slab above is much easier. The cam slot in the roof has become dramatically enlarged by people sitting on the gear and grinding the rock. It is tough love but if you are resting on the gear maybe the route is too hard for you.
FA. David Penlington 1951

7 **Marie's Gone to Canada** . . . . ⬜ **E1 5c**
An eliminate up the rib and roof to the right.

8 **Monument Chimney Crack** . . . 🌟⬜ **VD**
Climb into the chimney/groove from the left via a short polished ramp then climb the steep, juggy crack on the left of the main groove. The first move is awkward.

Nelson's Slab

9 Monument Chimney . . . . ☆1 ☐ **Diff**
Start on the left and climb the slab rightwards as for *Monument Chimney Crack* to enter the neat open groove. Bridge up this to the monument. A direct start is harder and less pleasant.
FA. Henry Bishop, early 1910s

10 Pillar Wall . . . . ☐ **S 4a**
Climb an awkward groove directly below the main corner then the centre of the wall on the right on spaced holds. Often green.
FA. David Penlington 1951

11 The Bow . . . . ☆1 ☐ **S 4a**
The arete is gained from the left and is then followed on its right-hand side. The direct start up the steep lower arete is a nice **5b** as long as your blinkers don't get in the way.

12 Orpheus Wall . . . . ☆2 ☐ **HVS 5c**
Climb the thin crack just right of the arete to reach the leaning wall and a horizontal slot. Good cams here protect the bewildering moves to jugs (hint - it is all about what you do with your legs). Make a prompt exit to easy ground. Almost E1, the route is one of the most frigged in the Peak and sadly the runner placements are suffering because of this.
FA. Joe Brown 1950

13 Peaches . . . . . . ☆3 ☐ **E4 6b**
An excellent and arduous route that feels like it is on the wrong cliff. Climb the technical slab until the rock leans. Battle on to the prominent hollow where final desperate moves leftwards gain easy ground. Intense!
FA. Gary Gibson 1980

14 Monument Gully . . . . ☆1 ☐ **VD**
Climb the short slab into the chimney. Continue to a roof and exit awkwardly leftwards to gain a slab and an easy finish.
FA. Henry Bishop, early 1910s

15 Book Sniffer . . . . ☐ **E6 6b**
Tackle the short bulges right of the gully by strenuous undercutting. Serious, with poor protection and missing holds.
FA. Paul Mitchell 2001

16 Monument Gully Buttress ☆1 ☐ **HVS 5b**
The arete has tough moves to stand on the beak at half-height. A huge jug on the ledge is helpful.
FA. Ken Wright 1951

17 The Keel . . . . ☆1 ☐ **HVS 5b**
The wall a couple of metres right of the arete has hard moves to get established in the midway break and then eases dramatically.

18 Naughty Nauticals . . . . ☐ **E2 6b**
Reach the flake on the lip of the overhang (small wires) then make the crux moves to gain the slab. Naughtical but neat.
FA. John Allen 1985

10m

Descent

The Promenade ▶

Sheffield Area
Ladybower Area
Stanage
Burbage Valley
Millstone Area
Derwent Edges
Chatsworth Area
Southern Crags

The Promenade to Trafalgar Wall

One of the most popular beginners' areas on grit with the fine clean (and slippery) slab of *The Promenade*, although it is not a good first lead since protection is poor. The classic of *Powder Monkey Parade* is also worth a go though the polished start up *Hollybush Gully* is an unholy struggle for most. On the right is a fine clean slab set above an undercut base and split centrally by a prominent wide crack. All the routes are worth doing though many have disproportionately tough starts. As elsewhere on the cliff, polished holds are a problem. In amongst this are some desperate boulder problems tackling the undercut bulging starts.

Approach (see map on page 477) - The area is just left of the point where the approach path arrives at the crag.

❶ Cutting Corners . . . . 🔲🔲 **S 4a**
Traverse out to the arete, a short wide crack and a slabby finish.

❷ The Promenade . . . . ✩2 ◣ **Diff**
A good introduction to grit though the initial slab is unprotected. Climb the left-hand edge of the slab to its crest then traverse right to the continuation beyond the cleft. Some consideration for protecting nervous seconds is sensible.

❸ Promenade Direct . . ✩1 ◣ 🥾 **HVD 4a**
Follow the balancy centre of the slab - unprotected and polished, to easy rock above. Finish right up the short bold arete.

❹ Promarete. . . . . ✩1 ◣ **f6A**
A technical left-hand start to the next climb.

❺ The Chain . . . . ✩1 🔧 **S 4a**
Climb the right arete of the slab directly (**5a**) using very polished holds or tough undercutting from below the roof on the right. From ledges, climb the middle of the face out to the right.
FA. David Penlington 1951

❻ Gritstone Megamix . . ✩1 🔧 ◣ **f7A**
The highball roof is superb! Small pockets in the roof allow a flake to be reached. Once above the bulges, the rest is easy. There is a left-hand variation at a slightly harder **f7A+**.
FA. John Allen 1984

❼ HMS Daring . . . . . . ✩1 🔧 ◣ **f7B+**
The left-hand side of the hanging arete is even harder - a real wrestling match. The right-hand side is harder again.
FA. Bob Smith 2009

❽ Thing on a Spring . . . . . ✩1 🔲 **f7A**
Bounce and extend-a-way up the left wall of the gully.

❾ Hollybush Gully . . . . ✩1 ◣ **VD 4b**
The gully with a jammed boulder at 3m is a fight. The technical grade is a guesstimate - how else do you grade struggles? The upper part is easy romping.

❿ Anchor Traverse. . . . . . . ✩1 🪝 **HS 4b**
A pleasant counter to the ever-popular *Powder Monkey Parade*. From atop the chock, head left to the arete, step around this and ascend the pleasant front face. The crux is the section shared with *Hollybush Gully*, though the traverse is a bit bold.
FA. David Penlington 1952

⓫ Floating Anarchy . . . . . . ◣ ◣ **HVS 5a**
A direct finish up the wall above the middle of the traverse using the big rounded pocket to get started.
FA. A.Payne 1984

⓬ Powder Monkey Parade . ✩2 ◣ **S 4b**
From the chock move right onto the arete, swing round the corner (4b, but harder for the short who will have to dangle), then teeter out right and finish up the well-positioned slab. Nice.
Photo on page 454.
FA. David Penlington 1951

Descent

12m

Sail Buttress

The bulges under Powder Monkey have a quintet of tough probems. Mats and spotters are the norm for these.

13 Oarsman Arete . . . . *f6B+*
The right side of the hanging arete. *f6C* from sitting.

14 Oarsman. . . . . *f6B+*
The thin crack in the slab provides technical moves.
FA. Mark Stokes 1984

15 'Oar 'Ouse. *f7A*
A right-facing layaway might get you started - but then again...

16 Hornblower. *f6C*
Just left of the blunt nose is climbed left and right.
FA. 'An unknown youth' 1952

17 Obstructive Pensioner . . *f7A+*
Use the flakes above the nose and slopers on the left. A right-hand version is of a similar grade.
FA. Nick Jennings 2000

18 Jumpers for Trousers . . . *f7C+*
Climb through the notch right of the arete if you can.
FA. Ben Bransby 2009

19 Hangover . . . . **HVS 5b**
Bridge the cleft then traverse the break leftwards, passing the arete with difficulty to an easier finish over the bulge on the left.

20 Admiral's Progress. . . . . . . **Diff**
Progressing up the wide V-chimney is straightforward.

21 Polaris Exit . . . . **Diff**
A more interesting finish to *Admiral's Progress* moving left past a large block to reach a short chimney. Finish up this.

22 Bulbous Bow . . . . *f5+*
The undercut arete is climbed rapidly on its right side and has a couple of technical moves before easing off.
FA. Chris Craggs 1993

23 Hammock . . . . **VS 5b**
Tricky moves up the wall left of the crack lead to romping.

24 Camperdown Crawl . . . . **HS 4c**
Good climbing up the thin crack and wall above. For the technically proficient a problem start is available on the right at a tough and rounded *f5+*.
FA. Eric Byne 1951

25 Barnacle Bulge . . . . **HS 4c**
The thin crack and groove in tandem (climbing just the right-hand fissure is 5a) lead into the base of the wide crack. From here move 2m right and climb directly up the slab more easily.
FA. Stan Moore 1950

26 Trafalgar Crack . . . . **VD 4a**
A nice route rather spoilt by overuse. From a polished block, climb shelving and unhelpful rock to gain the centre of the ramp that runs up left into the main crack. Finish up this.
FA. Eric Byne early 1930s

27 Trafalgar Wall . . . . **S 4b**
Access the lowest point of the ramp with difficulty, then climb the delicate slab above. Friends provide adequate protection but beware the final rounded moves. Quite a bit harder (and scarier) for the short, or in less than perfect conditions. A start up the right arete is **The Defiance Variation** - a bouldery *f5*.

28 The Long Promenade . . . **HS 4b**
A pleasant girdle of this section of the crag from *The Promenade* to *Trafalgar Wall* taking the obvious line. Probably best soloed to avoid cutting across teams on the proper climbs. Not marked on the topo, but you shouldn't get lost.

12m   Descent

Stoker's Wall

Sheffield Area
Ladybower Area
Stanage
Burbage Valley
Millstone Area
Derwent Edges
Chatsworth Area
Southern Crags

Sail Buttress
p.482

Trafalgar Wall
p.485

Stoker's Wall

Copenhagen Wall

Tar's Wall
p.488

Barbette Buttress
p.489

Seasick Slab
p.490

Wooden Leg Wall
p.491

The Promenade
p.484

Approach

Stoker's Wall

A short wall split by a series of cracks and with a bunch of low grade climbs. The area provides a good area for knocking off a heap of routes or maybe instructing in the basics of gritstone climbing away from the busy areas further left.

Approach (see map on page 477) - The wall is just right of the point where the approach path arrives at the crag.

❶ Bell Bottom Arete . . . . **S 4a**
At the left-hand edge of the wall, gain a hanging groove and then climb the crack in the arete. Short-lived but pretty steep.

❷ Sailor's Crack . . . . . **S 4b**
Climb the overhanging crack, just right of the arete, on solid jams to a tricky exit. Another steep one that packs a punch.

❸ Sailor's Problem . . . . **VD**
The short wall and deep groove are straightforward.

❹ Whatknot? . . . . **S 4b**
The left-hand side of the left-hand wall.

❺ Reef Knot . . . . **S 4b**
The centre of the face has nice moves passing the overlap (hidden footholds) leading to a rounded finish.
FA. Richard Brown 1951

❻ Sheetbend . . . . **S 4b**
The right-hand side gives more of the same.

❼ Nautical Crack . . . . **VD**
The two parallel cracks lead to an inverted-V slot with a block in its base. A tricky couple of moves complete the climb.

❽ Heave Ho . . . . **S 4a**
Heave over the bulge and scuttle up the short slab above.

❾ Yo-Ho Crack . . . . **VD**
The crack in a shallow corner is approached via a shallow groove and proves to be well protected and very pleasant.
FA. Reg Schofield early 1930s

❿ Rum Wall . . . . **VD**
Polished holds lead to thin left-trending cracks above.

⓫ Stoker's Break . . . . **VD**
The short wall leads to ledges at the foot of a slanting ramp, just to the right of a burgeoning tree. Continue up the thin crack.
FA. E.J.Clegg 1951

⓬ Stoker's Hole . . . . **HS 4a**
From a block, climb to a ledge then make delicate moves just left of a pale streak, using the half-hidden foothold.
FA. Colin Binks 1993

⓭ Stoked . . . . **S 4a**
Mantelshelf onto a ledge just right of the streak and follow the thin crack to a tricky couple of moves just below the top.
FA. Chuck White 1951

⓮ Stoker's Wall . . . . **Diff**
Climb the face just to the left of an easy crack, close to the right-hand edge of the wall.

From mid morning | 15 min | Windy

Descent

6m

Trafalgar Wall

Copenhagen Wall

The low, undercut face of Copenhagen Wall is taller than it used to be - erosion of the ground in front of the block has made all the routes a little longer and harder. The landings are good though and the wall has few runners hence the routes are usually bouldered or soloed. To the right the recess of The Fo'c'sle has some longer amenable offerings.

Approach (see map on page 477) - The wall is just right of the point where the approach path arrives at the crag.

15 Scandiwall . . . . *f3+*
Follow the good holds up the wall. UK tech grade of 4b.

16 Copenhagen Corner . . . . *f3+*
Start on the side-wall to the left of the arete and climb the centre of this using a thin flake. UK tech grade of 4b.
FA. David Penlington 1952

17 Scandiarete . . . . *f5+*
A technical tease. Start on the right, a good pocket around left will be found to be of use. UK tech grade of 5c.

18 Dane's Delight *f5*
The wall 2m right of the arete is hard to start if you are tall and harder still if you are short. If you can actually do the start, one more pull remains. UK tech grade of 5b.

19 Dane's Disgust *f5*
Start at a boulder embedded in the ground and climb the face passing the right-hand end of an elongated pocket at half-height to a rounded finish. UK tech grade of 5b.

20 Carlsberg Export *f6B*
An eliminate up the blankest part of the face. Holds are taboo!
FA. (from the left) Simon Triger 2001. FA. (direct) Simon Hunter 2001

21 Mermaid *f7C*
From a jug on a block under the roof, pull over and traverse left. Finishing direct after this start is **MP3, f7B**.

22 Copenhagen Wall . . . . **VS 5a**
Start just left of a pink block jammed below the overhang. Using a pocket and flake, reach the first break then trend right on better holds to a finish up the right edge of the wall.
FA. Norman Kershaw 1951

23 Wonderful Copenhagen . . *f4+*
Balance up onto the pinkish block from the right then trend left up the wall on sloping holds to finish left of *Copenhagen Wall*. UK tech grade of 5a.

24 Mast Gully Ridge . . . . . . **VD**
Climb the left arete of the gully on its right-hand side using shelving holds. A start on the left is **4b**.

*To the right is the amiable rift of **Mast Gully, Easy** which makes a useful descent or a super-soft but rather green climb.*

25 Mast Gully Wall . . . . **VD 4b**
The right wall has a hard start on sloping holds or bridge it. From the cave move right onto the front face for a good finish.

26 Mast Gully Crack . . . . . . **HS 4b**
Climb the crack in the right wall of the gully to a niche, then jam the continuation crack above.

27 Mast Gully Buttress . . **VS 5a**
Start just right of the gully and climb boldly rightwards to pass the bulge; continue more easily. Especially hard for the short.
FA. Gilbert Ellis 1950

To the right is the deep V-cleft known as The Fo'c'sle - pronounced "fox-sill" - a raised bit of a ship up the front.

28 Fo'c'sle Wall . . . . . . **VS 4c**
Climb the difficult right-trending crack to good pockets and a finish directly up the wall.
FA. David Penlington 1952

29 Fo'c'sle Crack . . . . **S 4b**
The straight crack and shallow groove just left of the back of the main groove has good holds - apart from at the start.
FA. Reg Schofield early 1930s

30 Fo'c'sle Chimney . . . . **VD**
The main angle of the recess is climbed direct.

31 Fo'c'sle Arete . . . . **VS 5b**
The right arete of the recess is reached from the left; a pocket up and left is useful. Once established it eases. A direct start is a decent and powerful *f5+* problem.

Descent

From mid morning — 15 min — Windy

Sheffield Area

Ladybower Area

Stanage

Burbage Valley

Millstone Area

Derwent Edges

Chatsworth Area

Southern Crags

Tar's Wall to Barbette Buttress

To the right of the Fo'c'sle area is series of short slabby walls and grooves ending at a prominent flying prow resting on a large block. This is another good area for beginners that fancy getting on with climbing without too many eyes on them, as it is invariably quieter than the areas to the left.

Approach (see map on page 477) - The area is a couple of minutes right of the point where the approach path arrives at the crag.

1 Broadside . . . . *f6A+*

Using the arete make a long reach right for a hidden pocket and a tricky layback move reaches the slanting shallow groove.
FA. (from left) G.Warren 1988. FA. (direct) Graham Parkes 1993

2 The Brigand . . . . . . *f7C+*

The desperate right-hand side of the face.
FA. Mark Katz 1997

3 The Buccaneer. *f7A*

Gain the sloping pocket from the edge out right.

4 Cave Gully . . . . VD

The groove above the cave recess is climbed by some stretchy bridging moves. Green and awkward to protect.

5 Ta Very Much . . . . HS 4c

Climb the right wall of the gully by a few decent moves using a pocket and small flake. Keep left for the best effect.
FA. Chris Craggs 1993

6 Tar's Arete . . . . VD 4a

Approach the arete steeply from the left (or direct - harder) using well-glossed holds then follow it with pleasant situations.

7 Ta Ta For Now . . . . HS 5a

Start at a pointed spike below the bulges, pull through the overhang (4c for the strong-of-arm?) and climb the slab above.
FA. Chris Craggs 1993

8 Tar's Crack . . . . VD

The steep crack is awkward to enter, bridging works best.

9 Tar's Wall . . . . HVD 4b

A problem start gains the easier slab above.

10 Sodomy *f6C*

Traverse the lip left, finishing without using the crack/arete.

11 Tar's Traverse . . . . Diff

A mild rising traverse across the hanging Tar's Slab, from the gully on the far right, to a finish on the arete to the left.

12 Tar's Climb . . . . Mod

The right-hand arete of the wall on slopers.

13 Tar's Gully . . . . Diff

Easily up the gully then the crack, escape right at the top.

Descent (scramble)

9m

Fo'c'sle Crack - p.487

Copenhagen Wall

14 Pig Head . . . . 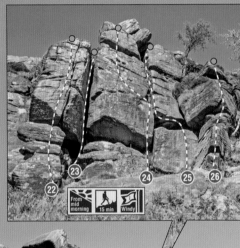 **S 4c**
The right-hand arete of the gully is a bit of a grunt to start.
FA. Ken Holton 1982

15 Pigtail . . . . **S 4a**
Climb a left-slanting groove to easy ground.
FA. Dick Brown 1951

16 Wavedance . . . . **f4+**
Start at a small jug and climb the wall direct using slopers to an overgrown exit. Nicely technical. UK tech grade of 5a.

17 Prow Wall . . . . **Mod**
Climb the blunt arete to the left of the gully to a steeper crack.

18 Prow Gully . . . . **Mod**
Vegetated peregrinations up the groove in the angle.

19 Barbette Arete . . . . **S 4b**
The short left edge of the jutting prow.

20 Barbette Crack . . . . . **HS 4b**
Climb the thin crack to its end, then swing left and continue boldly to a reachy and shelving exit. A loose flake has to be used (carefully) for the final move.

21 Barbette Wall . . . . **S 4a**
The left-hand wall of the jutting prow is climbed on an unusual set of pockets.
FA. David Penlington 1951

22 Barbette Buttress . . . . **S 4b**
Start from the supporting block and climb the front face of the prow via the thin crack and some holds on the left.

23 Cannonball Crack . . . . **S 3c**
The V-shaped groove right of the prow is wedged and wriggled. Awkward to protect without 'big guns'.
FA. Eric Byne early 1930s

24 Cannonball Wall . . . . **VD**
Mantelshelf onto a block, step left and climb the pocketed face. A direct start is **5a**, if you can reach the first of the holds.

25 Gunner's Gangway . . . . **Diff**
Start on the right to reach the ledge at the start of the previous climb and continue up the widening crack.

26 Lieutenant's Ladder . . . . **Diff**
The blocky ridge has a tricky little bulge.

Descent

Seasick Slab

Seasick Slab

Up and right of the prow of Barbette Buttress is a short clean wall of lovely rock above a level grassy platform. This has a number of bouldery little routes and a pleasant picnicking area. It is usually quiet here.

Approach (see map on page 477) - Scramble rightwards for a few minutes from the point where the approach path arrives at the crag to locate a small slab.

1 Midge's Manoeuvre E2 6a
The centre of the narrow pillar is gained from the slab on the right and followed to a grasping exit.
FA. Simon Triger 2001

2 Middy's Manoeuvre . . . . HS 4c
The left-hand crack is precarious though fat fists do help. Good practice for many a Curbar tussle.

3 Midway E1 6b
The bulging wall is tough - pass the overhang if you can.

4 Torpedo Tube . . . . HVD 4a
The central crack is a constricted struggle. Talented climbers can bridge the outside at a higher grade.

5 Flataback E1 6a
The technical wall to the right originally started up the previous climb but now is done direct.
FA. Quentin Fisher early 1980s

6 Das Boot . . . . VS 5a
A poorer right-hand version keeps close to the edge of the wall. Avoiding the crack of the next route is tricky.

7 Gunner's Groove . . . . Diff
The awkward right-hand crack soon eases although some of the footholds are well polished.

8 Seasick Arete . . . . f4+
Follow the square arete to a ledge. The final move is the crux. UK tech grade of 5a.
FA. Ernie Marshall 1951

9 Seasick Slab . . . . f3+
A mantelshelf just to the right reaches the ledge. UK tech grade of 4b.

10 Seasick Steve . . . . f6A+
Start with a side-pull for your left hand and climb directly to a sloping top-out.

From mid morning | 15 min | Windy

6m

Descent

← Barbette Buttress

Wooden Leg Wall - 30m →

Sail Buttress
p.482

Trafalgar Wall
p.485

Stoker's Wall
p.486

Copenhagen Wall
p.487

Tar's Wall
p.488

Barbette Buttress
p.489

Seasick Slab

Wooden Leg Wall

The Promenade
p.484

Approach

Sheffield Area

Ladybower Area

Stanage

Burbage Valley

Millstone Area

Derwent Edges

Chatsworth Area

Southern Crags

Wooden Leg Wall

A few interesting routes in an out-of-the-way setting. The place gets a bit overgrown with bracken in the height of summer but is fine at all other times. The routes on the flanks are generally the easier ones; the central bulges are tackled by the harder offerings.

Approach (see map on page 477) - This is the right-most piece of rock in this area. Scramble rightwards for five minutes from the point where the approach path arrives at the crag.

⑪ Cabin Fever. . . . . HVD 4a
The shallow groove and the arete of the narrow block above.
FA. Doug Kerr 2000

⑫ Moby Dick. . . . . S 4a
Bypass the edge of the overhang using a flake. It can be started by traversing from away on the right, but this doesn't add much.
FA. George Sutton 1951

⑬ Old Codger . . . . VS 4c
Cross the bulges at the left edge of the overhang utilising a finger-flake. Finish more easily.

⑭ Bold Codger E2 6a
The gap succumbs to a bold and technical approach.
FA. Graham Hoey 2009

⑮ Wooden Leg Wall . . . . . HVS 5c
Climb the central bulge by some taxing moves (good small wires up and right) to reach easy ground.
FA. Dick Brown (2pts) 1951. FFA. Len Pearson 1963

⑯ Owd Gadgee E2 6a
Climb the bulges trending right with a desperate mantelshelf onto the sloping ledge on the arete. A pre-placed runner in the previous climb lowers the grade.
FA. Colin Binks (side-runner) 1993. FA. John Allen (without) 1993

⑰ Stoker's Crack . . . . S 4b
Follow the flake-crack in a short hanging groove and then the delicate open corner above.

⑱ Knick Knack E1 5b
The thin cracks in the south-facing wall lead to hard moves leftward and an exit via the arete.
FA. R.Sheriff 1990

⑲ Stoker's Saunter . . . . VD
Climb the corner right of the arete then traverse left under the roof to join and finish as for *Stoker's Crack* - the crux.

⑳ Matelot's Meander. . . . . S 4a
The green and balancy slab to the right of the main angle.

From mid morning | 15 min | Windy | Green

Kismet Buttress ——▶
140m via crag-top path

Descent

8m

Kismet Buttress

Birchen's last gasp is not a bad effort. Sheltered and usually quiet, the place is worth a couple of hours if only to tick the stars. *Nelson's Nemesis* is especially worth calling in for if you are passing by on the way home, and there are several other offerings of interest.

Approach (see map on page 477) - From the main crag go up to the cliff-top path. Turn right (south) and walk above the other areas to the next substantial piece of rock about 200m away. It can also be reached directly and more quickly by taking the right-hand branch on the approach path. Follow this to a junction and turn left along the crag-top path that leads to the crag.

On the left is a short steep wall with a few bouldery-type routes.

1 Implosion . . . .🔦☐ *f5+*
Climb the face left of the thin central crack to bubbly pockets above the break; a long reach gains the top. UK tech grade 5c.
FA. A.Russell 1989

2 Explosion . . . . 🔦🪃☐ *f4+*
The central crack-line is strenuous. It can be protected but it is awkward and it is best to just blast up it. UK tech grade of 5a.
FA. Trevor Baugh 1952

3 Blast Hole Wall . . . . 🔦🔦☐ *f5*
Gain the prominent floral pocket via a long reach from a hole. Stand up with difficulty and finish easily. UK tech grade of 5b.

4 Cor Limey . . . . ☐ **VD**
The slabby arete to the right of the grassy gully has a high crux.
FA. Doug Kerr 2004

5 Powder Keg . . . . ☐ **S 4a**
The short and tricky corner/groove leads to pastoral ramblings.

6 Fuse . . . . 🔦🔦🔦☐ **VS 5a**
Climb the narrow slab passing a small roof with difficulty. Finish up the side of the prow above for extra interest.

7 Gun-cotton Groove . . . . . 🔦🔦☐ **VD**
The grassy crack and shallow groove is a good beginners' climb, as it is well protected. One or two of the blocks wobble.

8 Cook's Rib . . . . 🔦🔦☐ **E1 5c**
Climb the square-fronted buttress direct with the crux passing the low bulge by a fingery stretch. Using either arete lowers the grade a bit, not a bad effort for an ancient Severe.

9 Horatio's Direct . . . . 🔦🔦☐ **VS 4c**
Climb the thin crack in a shallow corner (fiddly small wires) then layback up the easier continuation corner. The route stays a bit greasy long after rain.

10 Horatio's Horror . . . . 🔦☐ **HS 4a**
The main groove is taken on excellent jams to the overhang and an awkward rest. Ape leftward (the tall can bridge it) to gain a square-cut groove. Up this to finish.
FA. Keith Axon 1949

Wooden Leg Wall
140m via crag-top path

Descent

11 Heavy Cruiser E1 6a
The short-lived but tough roof is climbed left of centre.
FA. Paul Mitchell 2002

12 Nelson's Nemesis . . . . VS 4b
Climb the main corner to the roof as for *Horatio's Horror* then traverse right, with a crucial foot change on a shiny 'button', to reach the base of the continuation crack. Up this to a ledge and an exit on the left on huge holds.
FA. Keith Axon 1949

13 Tom's Arete E5 6b
The bold arete is climbed on its right-hand side to the roof, which is crossed with difficulty and little in the way of gear.
FA. Paul Mitchell 2002

14 Victory Vice . . . . VD
The deep, narrowing chimney is hard work but quite safe despite the rattling chockstone - try not to get stuck in it.

15 For Queen and Country . . . . . HVS 4c
A devious oddity climbing first the right then the left aretes of the chimney to finish up a shallow groove.
FA. Izzy Stewart 2001

16 Device . . . . HVS 4c
The buttress is climbed via a mantelshelf, a thin crack and a tricky shelving exit. The gear is not really very reassuring.
Ernie Marshall 1963

17 Gunpowder Gully Arete . . S 3c
Climb the left arete of the deep gully and finish under a large perched flake. Unprotected so care needed.

18 Gunpowder Gully . . . . Diff
The gully behind the block gives steep but easy bridging.

19 Sea Dog Slab . . . . VD
The front face of the block is climbed diagonally from its bottom left corner and is a bit too steep to be a real slab.

20 Sailor's Chute . . . . HVD 4a
Round the corner is this narrowing leaning rift - it is fun!

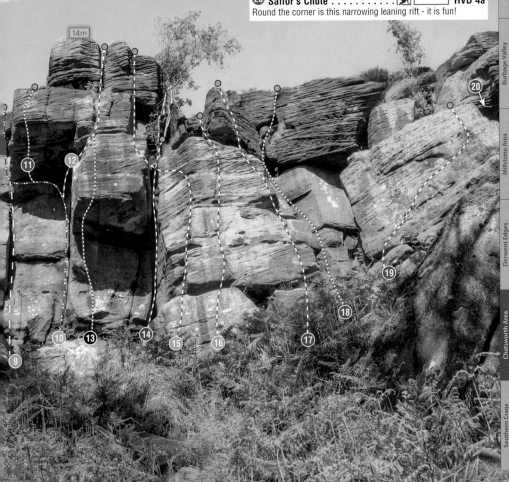

Sheffield Area

Ladybower Area

Stanage

Burbage Valley

Millstone Area

Derwent Edges

Chatsworth Area

Southern Crags

	No star	☆	☆☆	☆☆☆
Mod to S	10	8	4	-
HS to HVS	8	7	3	-
E1 to E3	9	7	5	3
E4 and up	1	3	1	-

Retiring and evermore neglected despite our best efforts, Chatsworth is the Cinderella of the Eastern Edges. It faces northwest and only receives sun on summer afternoons. It might be expected that the proximity of the A619 with its never-ending stream of traffic would spoil the cliff, but the thick tree cover muffles the noise. The slope below the cliff is overgrown by the start of the summer, making navigation along the foot of the cliff tricky. Also large trees growing close to the cliff face have encouraged lichen growth in recent years. Despite these negative aspects, under the right conditions climbing here is pleasant as the main buttresses escape the worst of the vegetation. The best routes here are the equal of any on grit, and any true gritstoner will one day have to bite the bullet and throw themselves at the likes of *Vibrio*, *Emerald Crack*, *Pearls* and the intimidating battle of *Sentinel Crack*. If you like to climb away from the crowds it is worth putting Chatsworth on your list. It is possible to have the place pretty much to yourself, and from the top of the buttresses the crowds on nearby Birchen are visible.

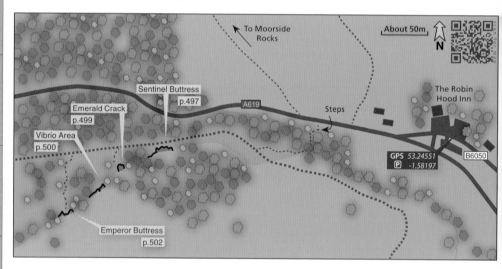

Approach   Also see map on page 454

There is parking by the Robin Hood Inn. Walk down the road for 150m to a discreet stile on the opposite side of the road. Cross this and follow steps down to a footbridge. Once across the river, head right over marshy ground to reach a well-made track that runs rightwards to the crag; less than 10 minutes from the parking. The buttresses further to the right are reached along an indistinct track that weaves up and down across the slope or directly via vague paths from the main track. This is no fun once the bracken is neck-high!

Conditions

A neglected edge, which can be green and midgy; best enjoyed on late spring evenings. After rain it is worth avoiding, though after a dry spell, especially in spring and autumn, the place becomes worth a visit. In the heat of summer it can make a good cool venue.

Tom Dixon making the crucial thuggish moves around the lip on the beast that is *Sentinel Crack* (E3 5c) - *page 497* - at Chatsworth. Photo Mike Watson.

TICKLIST

Chatsworth Choice Cuts

What does the Cinderella of the Peak have to offer? Well more than you might expect, though a bit of dabbing about and a dry spell will both help.

- ☐ **Emperor Flake Climb, VD** *(502)*. Excellent stuff.
- ☐ **Empress Crack, S** *(502)*. Steep for the grade.
- ☐ **Prince's Crack, HS** *(502)*. A great line.
- ☐ **Emperor Crack, VS** *(502)*. The best of its grade.
- ☐ **Mort Wall, HVS** *(496)*. Short and elegant.
- ☐ **Puppet Crack, HVS** *(497)*. Jiggery pokery?
- ☐ **Vibrio, E1** *(500)*. Full-on for the grade.
- ☐ **Lichen, E2** *(497)*. Super-rounded.
- ☐ **Pearls, E2** *(499)*. Strings you along.
- ☐ **Emerald Crack, E3** *(499)*. A grand finale.
- ☐ **Sentinel Crack, E3** *(497)*. The one true beast.

Sheffield Area
Ladybower Area
Stanage
Burbage Valley
Millstone Area
Derwent Edges
Chatsworth Area
Southern Crags

Mort Wall

The first walls have a small set of pleasant though often green routes generally in the lower grades. *Mort Wall* is a good first HVS being short and safe. If you feel a little underwhelmed by the look of the place just walk another 30 seconds to eyeball *Sentinel Crack*, then head back to *Mort Wall*!

Approach (see map on page 494) - This is the first piece of rock on the left on the approach.

1 Sidewinder . . . . 🔅 ◥ ☐ **HVS 5b**
The rounded arete of the buttress has its moments.
FA. Paul Harrison 1984

2 Mort Wall . . . . 🔅 ☐ **HVS 5a**
Climb the centre of the wall, with a tricky start via a niche. Low in the grade and with good gear throughout.
FA. Colin Mortlock 1958

3 Slip Arete . . . . 🔅 ▦ ◥ ☐ **E2 5b**
The arete climbed by a series of balancy moves. Elegant, unprotected and more than a grade harder for the short.
FA. Gabe Regan 1975

4 Strangler's Groove . . . . 🔅 ☐ **S 4a**
The groove is pleasant and well protected to an awkward exit.
FA. Don Chapman 1951

5 Strangler's Crack . . . . . . 🔅 🔨 ☐ **HVD**
A thin finger-crack and then the arete and short wall above.
FA. Don Chapman 1951

6 Throttled Groove . . . . 🔅 ☐ **S 4b**
The deep angular groove gives pleasant climbing with good gear.
FA. Don Chapman 1951

7 Dumper . . . . 🔅 ▯ ☐ **E1 5b**
Traverse right from the deep corner to access the cracks in the centre of the side-wall and haul up these to the crowning pine.

8 Jumpers . . . . 🔅 ▯ ☐ **E3 6a**
Jump your way up the spaced jugs on the leaning prow - the landing is shocking. Finish up a crack on the right - steep!
FA. Bill Briggs 1976

9 Where Next, Colombus? . . . ☐ **E2 5c**
Starting up the cracks right of *Jumpers* misses out the leaping fun but not the arduous final crack.
FA. Paul Pepperday 1985

Descent

10m

10m

Sentinel Buttress

The imposing buttress that looks out over the collapsing bridge. *Sentinel Crack* is the one to do, if you feel you are up to it, most of the others here are mere diversions! **Approach (see map on page 494)** - The buttress leans out over the approach path in a rather confrontational way just beyond *Mort Wall* - it is impossible to miss.

10 Leaper . . . . **VS 5b**
The rounded and undercut arete of the main buttress is awkward to access and much easier above.

11 Choked Crack . . . . **Diff**
The juggy, gritty cracks in the centre of the slab.

12 Choked Chimney . . . . **VD**
Bridge the main angle to a blocking boulder. Exit left.

13 Puppet Crack. . . . . . **HVS 5b**
The leaning crack has a reachy start from the right then gives glorious jamming to a final wide grovel. Good value at the grade.
FA. Joe Brown (with a little aid from the rope) 1951

14 Sentinel Crack . . **E3 5c**
An awesome roof-crack; a desperate struggle for most. Climb an awkward groove to a poor rest and then undercut out left. The struggle to finger-jam past the lip is memorable and will leave its mark one way or another. Once past the lip easy jamming remains, if you have any steam left. E2? I don't think so.
Photos on page 15 and 495.
FA. Don Whillans 1959. Runnerless, or so the stories go!

15 Sentinel Buttress . . . **E3 5c**
Bold feeling but still a bit of a cop out! At the roof scuttle right and escape around the arete to a belay in the gully.
FA. Mick Fowler 1977

16 Sentinel Groove. . . . **E6 6c**
The elegant and obviously desperate blank groove.
FA. Johnny Dawes 2003

17 No One Here Gets Out Alive . **E6 6c**
Climb the blunt arete in its entirety - without side-runners.
FA. Pat King 2002. Previously claimed in two parts with side-runners.

18 Cave Climb . . . . **Diff**
The wide crack with chockstones is a bit of a battle to a tight, spider-ridden, subterranean exit. Not one for chubby types.
FA. Eric Byne 1928

19 Wrinkled Nose. . . . . **VS 4b**
Traverse the wide break out to the arete then climb this on the right, then on the left - pleasant. The tough direct start via the thin flake is **Shy Boy** a highball *f7A*.
FA. Colin Winfield c1970

20 Cave Crack . . . . **S 4b**
Wriggle up the awkward slanting crack (crux - avoidable on the right if you are really flummoxed) to its easier continuation.
FA. Eric Byne 1920s

21 Pretty Vacant. **E1 5a**
The centre of the slab is pleasantly bold when clean.
FA. John Stevenson 1978

22 Monk's Park **E1 5c**
The left arete of the gully eases with height.
FA. Alpha Club members 1963

23 Lichen **E2 5b**
1) 5a, 2) 5b, 3) 5b. A great girdle, tough and well-named, following the right-to-left line in three short pitches. Lots of sloping holds and a superb exposed finale. High in the grade(s).
Start up *Sloping Crack* - see next page.
FA. Keith Myhill, Bill Haley, J.Crown 1971

High Step
- p.498

Descent

Emerald Crack - 50m

Evening | 8 min | Sheltered | Green

Sheffield Area
Ladybower Area
Stanage
Burbage Valley
Millstone Area
Derwent Edges
Chatsworth Area
Southern Crags

Photo from 2005

8m

Descent

Spiral Route

High Step to Spiral Route

Right of *Sentinel Crack* are some pleasant climbs but sadly they are rarely in prime condition. Even after a dry spell a bit of gentle cleaning may be required.
Approach (see map on page 494) - Scramble rightwards up the bank from *Sentinel Buttress*.

1 Sloping Crack . . . . **VD**
The slanting crack/groove is quite awkward. It is also used by the start of *Lichen* - previous page.
FA. Eric Byne 1928

2 Do You Wanna? . . . . **HVS 5a**
The blunt arete is delicate.

3 Tree Crack . . . . **VD**
The wide and treeless crack to a heathery exit.
FA. Eric Byne 1928

4 Cadenza **E3 5c**
Climb the rounded arete by unprotected friction moves until it is possible/necessary to escape out right.
FA. Mark Turnbull 1991

5 High Step **E1 5a**
The centre of the slabby wall features the eponymous move, then move left and back right to finish. Starred for when clean.
FA. Ernie Marshall 1959

6 Price . . . . **HVS 5a**
Climb the blunt arete on the right-hand side of the wall to a niche out left, then the wall above on big green slopers.
FA. Eric Price 1959

10m

Emerald Crack - 50m →

7 Spiral Route . . . . **VS 5a**
From the right gain a heathery ledge on the arete, move up to a bigger ledge then shuffle right to a tricky finish up the cracked slab. A direct finish up the left side of the arete is a dirty **E1**.

8 The Morning After **E1 5b**
Climb left of the porthole to a bold finish up the curving arete.

9 Three Pebble Slob **E1 5c**
Head right of the porthole to access the crucial upper slab.
FA. Chris Craggs 1990

16m

Evening | 8 min | Sheltered

Descent

⑲

⑪

⑱

⑩

⑭

⑫

⑯ ⑰

⑬ ⑮

Vibrio - 40m →

← Sentinel Buttress - 50m

Emerald Crack

This tall buttress is home to the classic struggle of *Emerald Crack* and the excellent face climb of *Pearls*. There are some easier cracks here, though these are generally both green and awkward!

Approach (see map on page 494) - Head right along a vague undulating track from below the *High Step* slab for 50m, or continue down the main track for 70m to locate a narrow path on the left that leads straight up to the buttress past a big boulder - overgrown in high summer.

⑩ The Clasp . . . . 🔟🗺️🪨☐ **E3 5b**
The left arete is usually green and may leave you grasping.
FA. Martin Boysen 1978

⑪ Emily . . . . 🪨🧗☐ **HVS 5a**
A route to nowhere pumps along the mid-height break.
FA. Ian Milne 1991

⑫ Left Twin Crack . . . . . . 🔟🧗☐ **S 4a**
The wide, straight crack is a trad grit battle with all that entails.
FA. Eric Byne early 1930s

⑬ Emerald Crack . . . . . 🔟🗺️🧗☐ **E3 6a**
The superb leaning crack is quite steady up to two-thirds height, and then it starts to turn mean. Long reaches, thin jams and a tricky exit all add up to make an arduous but high-quality outing.
FA. Joe Brown (1pt) 1957. FFA. Jim Campbell 1967

⑭ Esmerelda . . . . 🪨🧗☐ **f6A**
A neat fingery traverse along the lowest break from right to left.

⑮ Diamond Life . . . . 🔟🗺️☐ **E5 6b**
The soaring right arete on its left then its right-hand side has a bold and rounded finale.
FA. Andy Elliott 1987

⑯ Pearls . . . . 🔟🧗☐ **E2 5c**
A great route that strings you along, with every move a little harder than the last one! Cracks in the side-wall lead to small runners from where thin moves reach the crest, leaving only a tough rounded mantelshelf to glory.
FA. Keith Myhill 1971

⑰ Double Cave Climb . . . . . . 🧗☐ **VD 4a**
The two-stepped floral groove on the right-hand side of the face leads to a chockstoned exit. Traditional with a capital T! Subterranean variations are available if you really must.

⑱ Capstone Chimey . . . . 🧗☐ **VD 4a**
Another one of those esoteric rifts. At the capstone, burrow inwards or exit to the right - awkward.

⑲ The Arete . . . . ☐ **VS 4c**
From the base of the chimney climb the short arete on the right.

Emerald Crack - 40m

Oak Tree Climb →

Vibrio Area

Continuing along the crag from *Emerald Crack* another fine buttress appears out of the undergrowth with a characteristic mid-height overhang. *Vibrio* is the one to do here though the *Direct* is also well worth the effort.
Approach (see map on page 494) - Head right along a rough undulating track from below the *Pearls* slab for 40m, or continue down the main track from Sentinel Buttress for 100m to locate a narrow path on the left that leads up to the buttress - overgrown in summer.

1 High in the Thin Cold Air. . . . . . VS 4c
An out-of-the-way and short-lived arete up and left.
FA. Chris Craggs 1990

2 Step Buttress. . . . . HVD
Wandering but quite worthwhile. Climb the steps up the left-hand side of the front face then move over to the wide crack in the side-wall above the grass ledge. The groove to the left gives and easier option for crack-a-phobes.

3 Good Vibrations. E2 5c
The left arete of the buttress has a boulder-problem start (6a?) up a short wall, some crusty rock and a spectacular finale. Climb the upper section on the left via the crack then head to the right to finish out in space as for *Vibrio*.
FA. Chris Craggs 1990

4 Vibrio. E1 5b
Climb the centre of the buttress to a tricky and butch roof (knees?) which enables you to reach holds and runners in a thin slot. Make a technical and worrying traverse out to the left arete and better holds. Exciting, varied and good value.
Photo on page 503.
FA. Black and Tans Club members 1963

5 Vibrio Direct E2 6a
The true finish is short, sharp and well protected but still manages to feel scary. Head slightly right from the runner slot precariously on holds that invariably disappoint.
FA. Keith Myhill (one point of aid) 1971. FFA. John Allen 1976

6 Twisted Reach E4 6b
Climb the tiny groove in the right hand edge of the buttress via a roof crack, a pocket and an extended reach or two. The flakes to the left of the arete have also been climbed at around **E6 6c**.
FA. Bob Berzins 1979

7 Step Buttress Crack . . . . VD
The short wide crack high on the right to a tufty exit.

8 Mark Pretty. . . . . VD
Take the short arete on the right to a reach for the stumpy ledge.
FA. Ben Moon 1985

9 Broken Buttress Climb . . VS 4b
The next (broken) buttress. Trend left on good (loose?) holds and climb steeply to a ledge and tree belay. Climb onto a jutting block/ledge on the right and shuffle right again to finish up the exposed arete. Just about worth a star.

The next routes are in the oak trees just right of *Vibrio Buttress*.

⑩ Noser . . . . 🔟 🪣 ☐ **VS 4c**
Just above the path, a groove leads to a roof, then the ledge on
the left is accessed awkwardly. Continue up the short wall.
FA. Don Chapman 1952

⑪ Thin Air . . . . 🪨 🪣 ☐ **HVS 5a**
As for *Noser* but move right at the roof to the thin fingery crack.
FA. John Woodhouse 1975

The next routes start from a grassy mid-height ledge reached by
a grotty *Diff* scramble direct, or more easily from the right.

⑫ The Zig-zag Finish . . 🔟 🪓 🅱 ☐ **HS 4b**
Originally a spicy left-hand finish to the next climb, it weaves via
a niche and the kinked cracks.
FA. Don Chapman 1952

⑬ Oak Tree Climb . . . . 👐 ☐ **S 4a**
Enter the hanging crack with a bit of a struggle.

⑭ Shut Your Mouth . . . . . . 🪓 🪣 ☐ **E2 5c**
Horizontal jamming leads out to the hanging right arete.
FA. Mark Turnbull 1993

⑮ O'Reilly's Staircase . . . . 🔟 ☐ **S 4a**
Some decent moves weaving up the grooves just right of the big
tree - which gets in the way a bit. Going direct is a bit harder
FA. Harry Pretty 1949

⑯ Caylpso Crack . . . . ☐ **HVD 4a**
The right-facing groove to a tricky exit.
FA. David Penlington 1949

Oak Tree Climb

A neglected set of routes on a neglected crag - a
place for peace and quiet, plus moss and grass!
Approach (see map on page 494) - These are the
buttresses just right of *Vibrio*, though the large oak
trees manage to camouflage them well.

Sheffield Area · Ladybower Area · Stanage · Burbage Valley · Millstone Area · Derwent Edges · Chatsworth Area · Southern Crags

Descent

14m

The Royal
Seat

Emperor Buttress
The final buttress has some pleasant, if grunty, low and mid-grade climbs that follow great lines, plus the popular problem of *Desperot*. A good place to escape the crowds, though be warned it can be terminally green after rain.
Approach (see map on page 494) - Follow a small path from below *Vibrio* Buttress for about 70m through the trees. This path can be almost completely overgrown in the summer.

❶ Emperor Flake Climb . . . . . . 🔲 **VD**
Climb the left arete of the buttress, then follow flaky cracks on the left-hand wall as they lead back right to an exposed finish out on the airy arete - lovely positions. A direct finish up the centre of the side-wall is a bold **VS 4c**.
FA. Eric Byne 1940. FA. (Direct Finish) Al Evans 1990

❷ Emperor Crack . . . . 🔲 **VS 4c**
The long crack in the left-hand side of the face is hard work where it splits the roof. A classic struggle, though a sneaky layback/bridging sequence can help get past the hardest section.
FA. Eric Byne 1930s

❸ The Tyrant . . . . 🔲 **E2 5c**
From a short distance up *Emperor Crack,* move right and climb the left-hand side of the central face. A bit of an eliminate.
FA. Geoff Hornby 1993

❹ Desperot . . . . 🔲 **f7A+**
Bizarrely, one of the most popular routes on the cliff and well named too. If successful, escape rightwards along the break.
FA. Ben Moon 1991. Initially unnamed, Desperot has become the norm.

❺ Despot . . . . . . 🔲 **E1 5c**
From a short way up *Empress Crack,* follow the low break out onto the wall. Make a hard move to the next break then climb the face by more tricky moves. For those who can't manage the crux moves, traversing the next break up is easier - **5b**.
FA. Tim Leach 1977

❻ Empress Crack . . . . 🔲 **S 4b**
The long crack on the right-hand side of the wall is enjoyable. It gives bridging and jamming with a tough crux and steep finish.
FA. Eric Byne early 1930s

❼ Princess Crack . . . . 🔲 **Diff**
The short blocky crack leads to the 'Royal Seat'. The easiest escape is back the way you came!
FA. Eric Byne 1940

❽ Prince's Crack . . . . 🔲 **HS 4b**
From a roofed-in alcove, move left to access the 'Royal Seat' then finish up the steep groove behind. A compelling line.
FA. Eric Byne early 1930s

❾ Up the Establishment . . . 🔲 **E1 5b**
Bomb up the slanting flake to reach the arete with difficulty. Once established, climb the left-hand side of it by neat moves with nicely exposed positions.
FA. Chris Craggs 1990

❿ Anarchist's Arete . . . . . . 🔲 **VS 4c**
Climb the groove on the right then teeter left along the break - tricky for the short - to an exposed finish up the cracked arete.
FA. Don Chapman 1951

⓫ Emperor's Struggle . . . . 🔲 **S 4a**
The final corner crack is a bit of an awkward thrash despite the generally good holds
FA. Eric Byne early 1930s

Sheffield Area

Ladybower Area

Stanage

Burbage Valley

Millstone Area

Derwent Edges

Chatsworth Area

Southern Crags

Graham Parkes and Dave Vincent on the classic pumpy route of *Vibrio* (E1 5b) - *page 500* - Chatsworth.

Southern Crags

Sheffield Area
Ladybower Area
Stanage
Burbage Valley
Millstone Area
Derwent Edges
Chatsworth Area
Southern Crags

Rowsley

B5057

A6

A632

Alport

Stanton
-in-the-
Peak

Youlgreave

B5056

Two Dales

Ashover

Robin Hood's Stride
p.506

Cratcliffe
p.510

Birchover

Darley Bridge

Turningstone Edge
p.536

Elton

Winster

Matlock

A5012

Matlock
Bath

A615

Grangemill

Cromford

Duke's Quarry
p.542

Brassington

Black Rocks
p.520

Crich

Wirksworth

A6

N

Shining Cliff
p.543

About 1km

B5036

B5035

Sheffield Area

Ladybower Area

Stanage

Burbage Valley

Millstone Area

Derwent Edges

Chatsworth Area

Southern Crags

Steve Cunnington makes the last few delicate moves on the ancient classic of *Birch Tree Wall Direct* (VS 5a) - *page 532* - which follows a superb curving line across the West Face of the Black Rocks of Cromford. Ivan Waller won't have had many runners on the first ascent back in 1924.

	No star	⚙	⚙	⚙
Mod to S	4	1	1	-
HS to HVS	3	3	1	-
E1 to E3	-	1	-	-
E4 and up	-	1	-	2

Largely neglected by climbers but very popular with boulderers, the Stride (or Mock Beggars' Hall as it is also known) has a nice selection of mainly ancient routes in a fantastic sylvan setting. It is a prime spot for chilling, picnicking, taking in the surroundings and doing a few routes. The fact that the twin pinnacles can be bagged adds something a little different to the venue. We have described a neat selection of routes here, enough to have a very pleasant day out in a superb corner of the Peak, especially if you manage *Kaluza Klein*! Bring the kids and a picnic, and make a decent day of it.

Approach   Also see map on page 504

The crag is situated in the central Peak, 5km south of Bakewell. There are two approaches.
1) Park by the side of the B5056 Bakewell to Winster road opposite a wide farm entrance. Cross the road and follow the gravel track that leads to the farm but keep left up the hill heading towards the rocky towers of Robin Hood's Stride that are up on the left.
2) On the minor road that runs from Alport to Elton there is some limited verge-side parking by a stile in view of Robin Hood's Stride. Follow the collapsed wall towards the Stride - a flat 5 minutes from the car.

Conditions

Robin Hood's Stride is low lying with routes facing in most directions. The place can be green after rain, and the less travelled routes can be lichenous.

Bouldering

The area contains some of the best and most popular bouldering in the Peak District, with the added attraction of more great problems at the nearby Cratcliffe Tor; consult the Rockfax Peak Bouldering guidebook for a detailed look at the area.

Wiz Fineron taking the air from *Kaluza Klein* (E7 6c) - *page 508*. This striking arete is arguably the most popular route at Robin Hood's Stride although the bouldering sees much more attention. It also isn't very typical of the rest of the climbing being bold, hard and scary whilst most of the other routes are shorter, pleasant and at a friendly grade.
Photo: Owen Hughes/Calum Muskett

- *page 508*

Sheffield Area

Ladybower Area

Stanage

Burbage Valley

Millstone Area

Derwent Edges

Chatsworth Area

Southern Crags

Kaluza Klein
These is a huge boulder hidden in the trees overlooking the lower approach path - see map. There is one major classic here.

❶ Kaluza Klein . E7 6c

Gain the arete from the left and teeter up with increasing apprehension. Hard for the tall and much harder for the short.
Photo on page 507.
FA. Johnny Dawes 1986

Kaluza Klein

The Weasel Pinnacle
The smaller northern tower is 'w'easily distinguished from its big brother. It has routes on all sides. These are listed left to right (anticlockwise) starting with the shortest face.

❷ Letter Route . . . . Diff

The short side via scoured footholds, mega-flutings and elegant carved 'S'. Also the way down - a consideration for beginners.
FRA. J.W.Puttrell 1890. Others had gone before.

❸ West Arete . . . . HS 4c

The fluted arete.

❹ Stonnis Wall . . . . HVS 5b

The south face is green, gritty, precarious and unprotected.
FA. Reg Schofield 1936

❺ Long Climb . . . . VS 4c

Start from a ledge and climb the valley face, tricky to start, to good jamming up the runnels. Not really very long is it?
FA. J.W.Puttrell 1890. Moderately astounding for the day!

❻ Crucifix . . . . HS 4c

The northwest arete via a quick layback. Short and unprotected.

The next routes are on the ridge below the Weasel.

❼ Straight Crack . . . . S 4b

The wide fissure is green, awkward and neglected.

❽ Big Al Qaeda f7B

The excellent hard arete requires some cunning footwork.

❾ Nobody Knows f6B

The wall just left of the arete. Enter the scoop and finish over the bulge on good holds.

❿ Muscle Crack . . . . . S 4b

The wide crack has a useful jug on the left - thank goodness.
FA. Henry Bishop 1907

Inaccessible Pinnacle

The bigger southerly tower has more to offer featuring some fine climbs. Descent is via the *Short Climb* and the runnels on the top can be used to protect this. Alternatively, throw a rope over the top and anchor one end, or do a 'seesaw' abseil. The routes are listed left to right (anticlockwise) from the wide crack on the north side, down and left of the Pinnacle.

⑪ Pinnacle Chimney . . . . [ ] **Mod**
Amble up the rift. As mild as a really mild thing.

⑫ Crack and Furrow . . . . 🔯 [ ] **S 4b**
Gain the hanging crack by bridging in from the left, or via a fierce 5b pull. Up the cracks to the ledge then move out right and plough up the furrow to the top.
FA. Henry Bishop 1907

⑬ Boulder Climb . . . . 🔯 [✊] [ ] **HS 4c**
Access the top of the boulder via the funnel-shaped crack on the left (a bit despo really) then climb a short wall and traverse out towards the arete. Finish back left up the fine flutes. Excellent.
FA. Owen Glynne Jones 1897. Originally called Shoulder Route, which gives the game away - crafty beggars!

⑭ Path of the Righteous Man
. . . . 🔯 🏞️ 🧗 [ ] **E7 6c**
The arete to the right of the huge boulder.
FA. Sam Whittaker 1998

⑮ Byne's Traverse . . . . 🔯 🪓 [ ] **HVS 5b**
A delicate ramp and groove lead to the break. Hand traverse this leftwards (no footholds) to the arete and an easier finish.
FA. Eric Byne 1930

⑯ Old Hat . . . . 🔯 🧗 📏 [ ] **HVS 5c**
The flaky arete leads to a long rounded reach then easy ground.

⑰ Short Climb . . . . [ ] **VD**
Use the boulders to access the short crack and a tricky top-out.

	No star	{1}	{2}	{3}
Mod to S	5	3	-	-
HS to HVS	2	10	2	1
E1 to E3	2	2	6	5
E4 and up	1	3	5	4

Cratcliffe Tor is in an extremely rural setting with a view out over tranquil farmland rather than distant moors. It is home to a small but superb set of climbs. The main event are the sheer walls of *Owl Gully*. Here the many breaks offer fine pumpy climbs often traversing out of the gully into impressive positions on the exposed faces. The breaks usually offer plenty of protection, though being fit enough to hang on and place it is crucial. Around the corner from the gully is the dramatic tall face tackled centrally by *Suicide Wall*. The recent felling of the trees that used to shroud the face have revealed it in all its glory - surely the finest wall in all Gritdom?

Located south of the main edges, and lacking much in the way of quality climbs in the lower grades, it is seldom busy, though the area is popular as a bouldering venue.

Approach   Also see map on page 504

The crag is situated in the central Peak, 5km south of Bakewell. There are two approaches.

1) Park by the side of the B5056 Bakewell to Winster road opposite a wide farm entrance. Cross the road and follow the gravel track that leads to the farm but keep left up the hill heading towards the rocky towers of Robin Hood's Stride. Near the top of the track is a stile in the wall on the right. Cross this then turn right to locate a path leading through the trees to the foot of the cliff. **Do not try to reach the Tor via the farm**.

2) On the minor road that runs from Alport to Elton there is some limited verge-side parking by a stile in view of Robin Hood's Stride. Follow the collapsed wall towards the Stride then bear left towards the cliff which lies hidden in the trees beyond the corner of the next field.

Conditions

Cratcliffe is low lying and south facing; one of the best-sheltered gritstone cliffs in this book. Although the place can be green after rain, the cliff is often in better condition than you might expect and is climbable throughout the year; autumn days here can be especially enthralling.

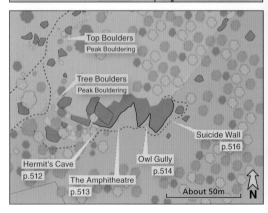

Bouldering

The area contains some of the best bouldering in the Peak. The main areas of interest are on the boulders around Cratcliffe Tor; consult the Rockfax Peak Bouldering guidebook for a detailed look at the area.

Sheffield Area

Ladybower Area

Stanage

Burbage Valley

Millstone Area

Derwent Edges

Chatsworth Area

Southern Crags

TICKLIST
Cratcliffe Crackers

This is only a small ticklist but the quality is extremely high - the standard of the climbing is pretty high too.

☐ **Suicide Wall, HVS** *(517)*. Peerless quality on this magnificent wall.

☐ **Fern Hill, E2** *(514)*. A technical start leads to wonderful climbing on the sheer face.

☐ **Mordaunt, E2** *(518)*. The best girdle on grit.

☐ **Five Finger Exercise, E2** *(515)*. The start is tricky but the flying flake is the real business.

☐ **Escape/Boot Hill, E3** *(514)*. Elegant balance climbing up a lovely blunt arete.

☐ **Requiem, E3** *(516)*. Another route where 'magnificent' is the only suitable adjective.

Char Williams committed to the dramatic finishing flake of *Five Finger Exercise* (E2 5c) - *page 515*. Photo: Adam Long

Hermit's Cave and The Amphitheatre

The first section is dominated by a huge yew tree, next to a dark cave. The walls here offer some short steep pitches on two levels. They can be green and overgrown although the fine prow of *Tom Thumb* is usually clean. **Approach (see map on page 510)** - The crag can be seen from the lower parking place and guessed at from the upper one. The Hermit's Cave is the arrival point.

① The Nemesis Exit . . . . . . ⬜⬜⬜ **HVS 5b**
The crack that splits the overhang above the cave starts off on perfect jams but gradually widens to fist size and then widens a bit more. The moss adds a touch of spice. Walk off leftwards.
FA. Vin Ridgeway 1951

② Hermitage Groove . . . . ⬜ **S 5a**
The green tree-capped groove is a battle. Walk off left or head up and right to finish up **Hermitage Chimney - Mod** see below.

③ Hermitage Crack . . . . ⬜⬜ **VS 5a**
The tricky curving crack is hard to access via a good flake and was a great effort for its day; the exit can be mossy. Walk off left. A jamming start just right is a beefy 5a.
FA. J.W.Puttrell 1901

The next three routes start from the ledge above the previous climbs. This is best reached by walking in from the left passing under the superb boulder traverse of **Jerry's Traverse**, *f7A+.*

④ Reticent Mass Murderer . ⬜⬜⬜ **E4 6b**
Short but exquisite. From the ledge above the cave invent a way up the narrow leaning crack. Fat fingers or thin hands make things just a little easier and protection is perfect.
FA. John Allen 1976

⑤ Genocide . . . . ⬜⬜⬜⬜ **E6 6c**
The thin flake on the right leads to absurd extending moves up the short wall above. Only the talented will succeed, though the tall have a bit of an advantage!
FA. Jerry Moffatt 1983

⑥ Hermitage Chimney . . . . ⬜ **Mod**
The short-lived angular rift on the right of the *Genocide* wall.

Back at ground level the next routes are based around the jutting prow and the rounded buttress to its right.

⑦ Tom Thumb . . . . ⬜⬜⬜ **E2 5c**
A thin crack in a shallow groove leads to a ledge on *The Giant's Staircase* - stance? Climb up left to a ledge then lean back right to enter the spectacular, but short lived, jamming crack. Once round the roof (try to get your left hand in the highest jam) finish easily. A real battle for most and watch the rope-drag!
FA. Tom Proctor 1971

⑧ Enigma Variations . . . . ⬜⬜⬜⬜ **E5 6a**
The direct extension to *Tom Thumb* goes where you really don't want to go! Wild!
FA. Steve Allen 1988

⑨ The Giant's Staircase . . . . . . ⬜⬜ **HVS 5a**
An odd route consisting of a series of mantels between stance-sized ledges. Trend right up the lower wall then left via polished steps to a final difficult grovel onto the last ledge. Walk off left, or better finish via the left-hand version of **Hermitage Chimney Left, HS 4b**, which is the shallow groove to its left.
FA. Fred Pigott 1922

The next routes are on the rounded pillar just to the right.

⑩ No Peru . . . . ⬜⬜⬜ **E4 6a**
The disjointed grooves in the left arete of the pillar give some good moves, but it may need gardening before an ascent.
FA. John Allen 1984

⑪ Bean Stalk . . . . ⬜⬜⬜⬜ **E2 5c**
The rounded arete provides an excellent little route now the cloaking birch has been pruned. Approach the rib via a wide diagonal crack. Above this there is one fierce pull (small wires) before it eases to fine climbing up the rib.
FA. Mike Hardwick 1976

Sheffield Area | Ladybower Area | Stanage | Burbage Valley | Millstone Area | Derwent Edges | Chatsworth Area | Southern Crags

⑫ Amphitheatre Crack . . . . [ ] **Mod**
The easiest climb on the cliff and the normal descent. The enclosed groove leads to the open space of the Amphitheatre; finish up the back right-hand corner. A great scramble for kids.

⑬ Bramble Groove . . . . [ ] **VS 4b**
The groove breaking left from the last route has some vegetated struggling - the steep crack on the right is the best option - leading to a tough finale up the short leaning crack.
FA. J.Milward 1947

⑭ Bramley's Traverse . . . . [ ] **HS 4b**
Follow the wide 'udgy' crack right of *Bramble Groove* to the ledge below its finish, then make an exposed traverse out left above *Tom Thumb* to a short groove just around the corner.
FA. Henry Bishop and six others with the initials R, A, M, L, E and Y 1907

Lots of sun | 10 min | Sheltered | Green

⑮ Oblique Chimney . . . . [ ] **VD**
A diagonal scramble through impressive terrain to an awkward exit up the wide slanting fissure. Backstroke works best.

⑯ Darren Hawkins' Invisible Neck . [ ] **E4 5c**
The undercut arete eases once you are established.
FA. Malcolm Taylor, Darren Hawkins 1986

⑰ Elliott's Unconquerable . . [ ] **HVS 5a**
A short-lived but pleasant piece of jamming with a tricky undercut start then good climbing above.

⑱ Mephistopheles Exit . . . . [ ] **HVS 5a**
Heading out left from the top of the crack, this variation extends the fun a bit with some great positions.
FA. Vin Ridgeway 1951

⑲ Elliott's Right-hand . . . . [ ] **E1 5c**
The flake and wall to the right of *Elliott's* main crack has thin moves to reach the wide crack above but soon eases.
FA. Chris Hunter 1977

Descent - - - →

The Hermit's ave behind the big yew tree

Owl Gully →

The short chimney in the back right-hand corner of The Amphitheatre offers a convenient descent route.

⑳ Hey Turkey Neck . . . . [ ] **E2 5c**
This is the pocketed wall right of the upper section of *Weston's Chimney* - see below. Not marked on topo.
FA. John Allen 1985

㉑ Weston's Chimney . . . . [ ] **VD**
Down and right, climb the manky red/green and slippery chimney to the Amphitheatre and a belay, then off-width the narrow extension in the right wall. Not marked on topo.
FA. Owen Glynne Jones 1897

Sheffield Area | Ladybower Area | Stanage | Burbage Valley | Millstone Area | Derwent Edges | Chatsworth Area | Southern Crags

The Amphitheatre

20m

❶ Escape/Boot Hill . . . 　　　　　　　　E3 5c

A magnificent arete climb, low in the grade but exciting all the same. Climb the greasy chimney and monkey along the break to the arete. Follow this with crucial moves on the left side (the very tall can teeter up the front) to reach a fat fluting and the final blank wall with its superb hidden jug.

FA. Geoff Sutton 1951. Rediscovered by Tom Proctor in 1971

❷ The Groove . . . . 　　　　　　　　E9 7b

The blanktastic groove in the wall was lusted after for generations. Now it gives one of the hardest around, with highly technical moves and some worrying situations. Layback the edge of the groove to the break, then continue as it fizzles out to a finish up the rib and eventually exit via *Fern Hill*.

FA. James Pearson 2008

❸ Nutcracker . . . . 　　　　　　　　E2 5c

Launch out left and hand traverse out to the arete and a rest. Climb the steep slab (as for the long reach method of *Escape/Boot Hill*) to the roof then exit rightwards as for *Fern Hill*. The short will find the start 6a and the slab on the front impossible.

FA. Vin Ridgeway 1951

❹ Fern Hill Indirect . . . 　　　　　　　　E4 5c

Superb. Consider placing a runner in the start of the regular route to avoid a massive pendulum if you muff the crux moves. Follow the diagonal crack, as for *Nutcracker*, out to a poor rest. Then climb a shallow groove and the crack that runs back to the right to reach the pumpy crux of *Fern Hill*. Follow this to the top. The start is 6a for the short.

FA. Ron Fawcett 1976

❺ Fern Hill . . . . 　Top 50　　　　E2 5c

Magnificent climbing up the diagonal cracks in the left wall of *Owl Gully*. Start by a thin horizontal crack and swing left. Make some hard moves past where it splits, then continue along the rising juggy diagonal to the arete and a good rest. Step back right and pull over the roof finishing with a steep mantel.

FA. Keith Myhill (one point of aid) 1971. FFA. Tom Proctor, soon after.

Sheffield Area | Ladybower Area | Stanage | Burbage Valley | Millstone Area | Derwent Edges | Chatsworth Area | Southern Crags

22m

Bower Route 1 - p.516

The Bower

Suicide Wall

Owl Gully

The impressive sheer walls that flank either side of the deep rift of *Owl Gully* contain some of the finest routes on grit. The left-hand wall gets more sun and tends to stay cleaner than the other sections of the cliff. Although slightly overshadowed by its neighbour, the right wall would rank as the best wall of the cliff on most other Peak crags. The splendid *Five Finger Exercise* is particularly impressive, giving great climbing on a line that looks so unlikely. The right-hand wall is often greener than the *Fern Hill* side as it gets sun later in the day. **Approach (see map on page 510)** - Scramble down and right from the Hermit's Cave until below the huge gash of *Owl Gully*.

Afternoon | 10 min | Sheltered

6 Owl Gully . . . . VD
The deep cleft is a half-decent low-grade route climbed awkwardly on glossy holds to a substantial chockstone and an exit to the right. An exit to the left is a bit harder/steeper.
FA. J.W.Puttrell 1890

The next two routes start from a stance part way up Owl Gully.

7 Tiger Traverse E2 5b
A pumpy little number that swings along the rounded break halfway up the wall - keep your eye open for the foothold. Escape up and out right at the end of the traverse.
FA. Peter Harding (with the high chockstone threaded) 1951

8 Nettle Wine E4 6b
Safe technical climbing up the left side of the wall with a spectacular finish. From a little way along *Tiger Traverse* (or from *FFE*) climb the wall to the next break, shimmy right then gain the tiny flakes and use them to scale the final blank wall.
FA. John Hart 1978

9 Five Finger Exercise . . . . Top 50 E2 5c
A superb route up the right wall of the gully with a wild finale that trips many a suitor. Pull right over a narrow overlap and climb the wall on small sharp holds (looks harder than it is) then continue to ledges. Fill the horizontal break with runners then swing around the rib and power up the hanging flake. Only the weak are spurned, though the timid may have a hard time too.
Photo on page 511.
FA. Andy Edgar 1976

10 Liquid Assets E4 6b
Traverse out the square arete (high runners) and climb to the edge of the huge overhang and then up the crimpy wall above. Step out right to reach the upper arete and finish up this.
FA. John Allen 1987

Sheffield Area

Ladyworth Area

Stanage

Burbage Valley

Millstone Area

Derwent Edges

Chatsworth Area

Southern Crags

1 Bower Route 1 . . . . 🔄 [____] **HS 4b**
A short but pleasant pitch that is the easiest way to access
the Bower and which was the first route to tickle the edges of
this fine face. From a flake make a precarious move right to a
polished ledge which leads to a slabby groove and follow this to
the Bower. Escape is by abseil unless you are proficient at HVS.
FA. Fred Pigott 1922

2 Direct Start . . . . 🔄 [____] **VS 4c**
Oddly indirect. Start as for *Bower Route 1* but jam the angular
corner to the roof then traverse rapidly out right to the sanctuary
of the Bower and the mighty oak. Escape by abseil is the easiest,
or maybe the only option.
FA. David Cox 1935

3 Requiem . . . . 🔄 [icons] [____] **E3 6a**
A superb outing up the left-hand side of the biggest face on
the cliff. The crux moves are fierce but can be avoided by
some scary monkey business in the upper branches of the oak
reducing the grade to E2 5c, but not detracting from the quality.
1) 5a, 10m. Climb an overhanging crack with a large jutting
block straight into the Bower - easier than it looks.
2) 6a, 16m. Head up the desperate crack springing from the
right-hand edge of the Bower to a deep horizontal break (or
reach the same place from the tip of the tree). Swing left along
the break then climb flutings to the final roof, which is passed
spectacularly on superb holds. Glory, glory!
FA. Paul Nunn (2pts) 1970. FFA. John Allen 1975

4 The Long Distance Runnel 🔄 [icons] [____] **E5 6c**
From the Bower, climb *Requiem* to the top of the crack, then
climb to and up the shallow runnel, finishing direct.
FA. Neil Foster (after Chris Craggs pointed out the line) 1996

Descent down
The Amphitheatre

28m

The
Bower

Owl Gully

Descent

Side panel tabs: Sheffield Area · Ladybower Area · Stanage · Burbage Valley · Millstone Area · Derwent Edges · Chatsworth Area · Southern Crags

5 Suicide Wall . . . . Top 50 HVS 5b
A stunning classic following an impressive line of cracks up the steep wall. Climb the tough crack, past the tree stump, and jam onwards to an optional stance in the Bower. Move out right and climb the wall on finger holds then a crack to a niche. Layback the crack on the left to the final overhang and finish with gusto.
FA. Peter Harding 1946

6 Suicide Wall Direct . E1 5c
The cave can be avoided by climbing the thin crack branching right to give a fine direct and very long pitch.

7 Oak Tree Chimney . . . . VD
The wood-filled wift. Usually avoided by scrambling round.

Starting from the ledge up and right of the foot of Suicide Wall are several worthwhile routes.

8 Stihl Life. E5 6a
A recent discovery (since the trees were cleared) up the wall past the wide porthole. A link into *Savage Messiah* is logical.
FA. Dominic Lee 2010

9 Sepulchrave . . . . HVS 5a
Excellent climbing up the diagonal cracks in the wall. A good jamming crack is climbed to the break. Follow the continuation leftwards until it is possible to step up and follow another crack back to the right. The finish lies up the daunting wide crack which is a little easier than it appears from below.
FA. Paul Nunn 1970

10 Savage Messiah E2 5c
A direct on *Sepulchrave* with only a short independent section but with some memorable moves! Climb *Sepulchrave's* crack then continue directly to enter the large porthole by awkward undercutting and a precarious high step. Finish up *Sepulchrave*.
FA. Rob Burwood 1975

11 Stretch Limo . . . E5 6b
The right arete of the Suicide Wall face gives a neglected pitch. Start just right of the crack taken by *Sepulchrave* and follow the arete throughout. Claimed earlier its the right-hand side at E2.
FA. Andy Cave 2001

12 North Climb. . . . . S 4a
A nail-scratched groove leads to bulges then traverse left to finish up the airy arete. Pleasant.
FA. J.W.Puttrell 1890

13 Niche Direct . . . . VS 4c
Just right an awkward crack gains the niche. Pull right over the roof to finish.
FA. Mike Hardwick 1976

The last route described here is on a vertical wall 15m right of North Climb, above the approach path to the Sepulchrave ledge and just beyond a tricky descent.

14 Jimmy's Crack. . . . . HVS 5b
The thin cracks zig-zagging up the wall lead to a tree. Finish up the wall behind - harder than it looks!
FA. Chris Hunter (aka Jimmy) 1977

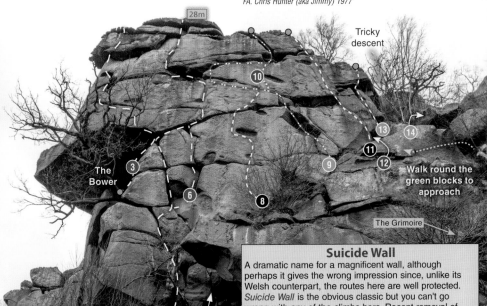

Tricky descent

The Bower

Walk round the green blocks to approach

The Grimoire

28m

Suicide Wall
A dramatic name for a magnificent wall, although perhaps it gives the wrong impression since, unlike its Welsh counterpart, the routes here are well protected. *Suicide Wall* is the obvious classic but you can't go wrong with any of the climbs here. Recent removal of trees along the base of the wall has improved conditions. All the routes are superbly exposed, on wonderful clean rock formations with perfect cracks, big pockets, juggy flutings and blank faces.
Approach (see map on page 510) - Scramble down and right from the Hermit's Cave until below the huge gash of *Owl Gully*. Head round the corner to find this fine wall.

Sheffield Area · Ladybower Area · Stanage · Burbage Valley · Millstone Area · Derwent Edges · Chatsworth Area · Southern Crags

Suicide Wall

The Grimoire

The removal of the trees revealed the boulder/buttress below and right of the soaring face of *Suicide Wall*. A couple of easier new routes have been added and the older desperates have been opened up.

Approach (see map on page 510) - Scramble down and right from the Hermit's Cave and head round the corner under *Suicide Wall*, then down and right again.

① Whose Line is it Anyway? . . . 🔾 [ ] **HVS 5a**
Start under the overhang at the base of the buttress below *North Climb*. Climb leftwards to reach the base of a left-trending ramp, then head out left on good holds to a small bulging overhang. Take this direct using a flake and finish up the fluted block.
FA. Gabe Mazur 2011

② Rocky's Revival . . . . 🔾 [ ] **VS 4c**
Start as for *Whose Line is it Anyway* and follow the ramp to its end. Tackle the face at the end of the ramp via the finger-crack and finish up the short off-width above the sliver birch.
FA. B.Levey 2011

Round right and up the slope is a short sharp arete above a bit of a drop. The routes here can be highballed by the brave/ talented/reckless (delete all that do not apply).

③ Chess Boxer . . . . . . 🔾 🔾 🔾 [ ] **E6 6c**
Tackle the technical left side of *Grimoire* arete. The landing has been improved, making a solo more feasible at *f7A+*.
FA. Dan Honeyman 2004

④ Grimoire . . . . 🔾 🔾 🔾 [ ] **E6 6c**
The right side of arete gives a committing highball. Hard moves over the bottom bulge and a sketchy high foot move on the wall above combine to make a short but memorable trip.
FA. Martin Veale 1997

The Girdles

There are three excellent girdles (well two girdles and a bit of a spiral) that make their different ways across this majestic bit of rock. Only one of them gets done very often, but we have included all three on one composite topo so you can see where they go. A good half-day (!) outing could be had by starting with *Renaissance*, descend via the Amphitheatre, following *Trick or Treat* to the right-hand end of the crag and then nip down the descent and take *Mordaunt* back the other way. **The Cratcliffe Super-Girdle, E3**, in 10 pitches.

⑤ Trick or Treat . . . . 🔾 🔾 [ ] **E3 5c**
The hardest of the trio, a solid seconder is required.
1) 5c, 18m. Start via *Boot Hill* to the arete then continue along the break (*Fern Hill Indirect*) to a belay down the gully a bit.
2) 5c, 15m. Traverse right, crossing *Five Finger Exercise* and follow the break round the arete and under the roof to a belay in the Bower.
3) 5c, 18m. Move out right along the break as far as junction with *Savage Messiah* then follow the fingery flake diagonally right to a finish up the arete.
FA. John Allen, Paul Williams 1985

⑥ Renaissance . . . . . . 🔾 🔾 🔾 [ ] **E2 6a**
A wandering route with some quality climbing.
1) 6a, 10m. Climb the thin hanging crack and its wider continuation until the Bower can be reached by a short traverse.
2) 5c, 15m. Climb to the giant roof then follow the strenuous hand-traverse out left to the arete. Step left and climb *Five Finger Exercise* to below its crux flake then traverse left to a belay in *Owl Gully*. Problematic rope-work on this pitch.
3) 5c, 10m. Climb the steep diagonal crack to the right edge of the *Fern Hill* ledge and an awkward exit
FA. Brian Rossiter, Chris Craggs, Nigel Baker (alts) 1985

⑦ Mordaunt . . . . 🔾 🔾 [ ] **E2 5b**
A magnificent girdle covering impressive territory at a sustained but amenable grade. The best of its genre on grit!
1) 5b, 28m. Follow *Sepulchrave* to the end of its traverse and continue to *Suicide Wall*. Follow the same line then swing down to join *Requiem* above its crux and take the wide crack around the arete to a belay on the ledge on *Five Finger Exercise*.
2) 5b, 10m. Mantel down off the ledge then reverse *Tiger Traverse* to a stance in Owl Gully.
3) 5b, 10m. From the gully follow the crack of *Renaissance* but continue out to the arete and a move up to small stance.
4) 5b, 12m. Traverse below the roof to round the arete and continue into *Weston's Chimney* - the logical line, or finish up *Boot Hill* for a better finale
FA. Paul Nunn and team 1970. A little aid might have been used.

⑤ Start

⑥ Start

Suicide Wall - p.517

Suicide Wall - p.517

⑦ Start

to mid afternoon | 10 min | Sheltered

Sheffield Area
Ladybower Area
Stanage
Burbage Valley
Millstone Area
Derwent Edges
Chatsworth Area
Southern Area
Cratcliffe Crags

	No star	🟊	🟊🟊	🟊🟊🟊
Mod to S	13	6	3	2
HS to HVS	5	7	5	5
E1 to E3	5	10	6	1
E4 and up	3	17	8	5

Black Rocks is a fine but often neglected cliff. It sits proudly on a hill above Cromford and not far from the limestone crags of High Tor, Willersley and Wild Cat. The cliff has a reasonable selection of lower grade climbs, some good mid-grade routes and a whole bunch of the really hard stuff up the bald and blank aretes, slabs and walls. It is somewhat lacking in the lower extreme grades but there is the ultra-classic sideways shuffler of *Promontory Traverse* as some compensation.

The rock is very even-textured gritstone, almost devoid of big pebbles and often smoother than elsewhere. This gives climbing that is often strenuous, precarious and rounded in the extreme, with many flaring breaks and sloping holds. Getting your hands on a full set of cams, including some big ones, is a good idea before a visit.

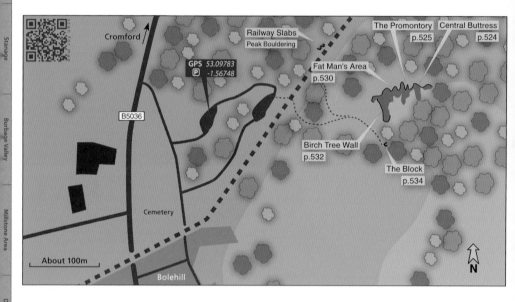

Approach   Also see map on page 504

The crag is 1km south of Cromford, which is 3km south of Matlock. From lights on the A6 turn south into Cromford and follow the B5036 uphill, forking left onto a minor road after 1.3km. Two left turns lead into the Black Rocks parking (Pay and Display), the upper is (a bit) nearer the rocks and sometimes has an ice cream van in-situ.

Conditions

The crag overlooks the Derwent Valley and the Matlock area. Much of the cliff faces north and tends to be green and unpleasant after poor weather and all winter. In contrast the west-facing *Birch Tree Wall* dries quickly and is in condition for much of the year. The position on top of a hill means that it is exposed to the wind. Some of the harder routes are not climbed that often and may need a gentle brushing before an ascent.

TICKLIST
Black Rocks
Historic Classics
A bit of a neglected crag which is odd as the quality of the climbing is exceptional - as long as you visit after a dry spell. Unusually for grit most of these routes can easily be done in a couple of pitches. Here is a neat selection of climbs from the first half of the last century.

☐ **Central Buttress, HVD** *(524)*
Not especially central but wanders up the buttress in an intriguing way.

☐ **Stonnis Crack, HS** *(529)*
A real gem of a crack and an astounding ascent for 1900.

☐ **Sand Buttress, VS** *(529)*
A magnificent line that sneaks up an imposing buttress. 1922, amazing!

☐ **Queen's Parlour Slab, VS** *(523)*
Mild but bold and quite spooky out on the final slab.

☐ **Birch Tree Wall Direct, VS** *(532)*
The initial crack is a teaser, the rest just traditional grit roundedness.

☐ **Lean Man's Climb, VS** *(529)*
The initial green layback is always tough, the top crack a bit less so.

☐ **Lean Man's Superdirect, VS** *(530)*
Two excellent and taxing pitches.

☐ **Promontory Traverse, E1** *(526)*
The crag's 'last great problem' in the 1940s with much extreme rounded weirdness along the way.

Steve Cunnington makes the final steep moves of the superb *Sand Buttress* (VS 4c) - *page 529* - an impressive ascent for 1920 at Black Rocks.

Sheffield Area | Ladybower Area | Stanage | Burbage Valley | Millstone Area | Derwent Edges | Chatsworth Area | Southern Crags

Queen's Parlour

The far left-hand end of the crag has some nice lower grade routes, a couple of which are popular with groups hence the trashed state of the cliff base. The place was popular way back, at the height of the polluting Industrial Revolution - it must have been cleaner than it is now!
Approach (see map on page 520) - Undulate left to a clearing under the face.

The left-hand side of the crag runs into a gully that makes a useful descent from all the routes in this area.

❶ East Crack. . . . . S 3c
Start on the left below a left-facing groove high on the crag. Climb a grotty crack, or the harder slab to its left. Continue until it is possible to traverse to the wide final crack - knee jams and big gear help.
FA. John Laycock 1913

❷ Mental Pygmy E3 6a
Climb to the beckoning roof-crack high on the buttress and battle up this to a perplexing exit. Tiny but taxing and often dirty.
FA. Steve Bancroft 1976

❸ New Year Buttress . . . . HVD
An indifferent vegetated start up the groove (or a *f3+* boulder problem just left) leads to better climbing with an exposed final pull into the scoop right of the prow on jugs.

← - - - - Descent

Central Buttress ➤

Queen's Parlour p.524 | Central Buttress p.525 | The Promontory | Stonnis Buttress p.528 | Lean Man's Climb p.528 | Fat Man's Area p.530

4 Queen's Parlour Slab   VS 4b
This ancient classic can feel bit bold. Climb the easy slab until
the projecting buttress to the right can be reached by a short
traverse. Balance up this to a final sketchy move (large gear or
thread) or sneak off right if you are too short.
FA. Bernard Simmonds 1939

5 Queen's Parlour Gully . . . . . .   VD
The gully left of the big overhangs is a good intro to climbing,
but it is polished and hard when damp. Pass either side of
the block (easier to the right) to reach the chimney - stance?
Continue up the chimney, big chipped holds, to a choice of exits.
FA. J.W.Puttrell 1890

6 Original Route . . . .   HVD 3c
Start as for *Queen's Parlour Gully* (or more direct - a grubby **4b**)
and slant right - more big chipped holds - to a possible stance
below the chimney. Climb a recess then take the awkward
through-route. Sneak off left or, alternatively, finish up the hard
and polished crack springing from the recess - more like **4c**.
FA. J.W.Puttrell 1890

7 Queen's Parlour Chimney . . .   HS 4b
Follow *Original Route* but back-and-foot the exposed outer
part of the chimney to ledges and a right-slanting exit. An
astoundingly wild ascent for its day and still very intimidating.
FA. J.W.Puttrell 1890

8 DynoMight .   E7 6b
The bold arete on its right-hand side via a couple of dynos,
linked by a couple of mantels. Poor protection.
FA. James Pearson 2003

*The next routes are on the left-hand side of the wide, open and
vegetated gully which runs up to steeper rock above.*

9 Pine Tree Gully . . . .   Diff
The pine-less rift in the left-hand side of the wide gully improves
with height. Back-and-footing is one way of doing it.
FA. John Laycock 1913

10 The Raunge . . . .   HS 4b
Scramble up *Pine Tree Gully* then climb the crack in the side-wall
of the gully, traversing the horizontal break. Awkward and poorly
protected but quite hard to fall out of!

11 Moonchild E7 6c
The pale wall is climbed on not very much.
FA. Toby Bentham 2006

12 Birch Tree Climb . . . .   HVD
The slot in the high buttress is approached direct then threaded.
FA. John Laycock 1913

8m to ledge

The next routes are on the gloomy right wall of the open gully.

13 Green Crack . . . .   HVS 5a
The well-named crack high in the right-hand wall of the gully;
short lived but hard work. Sadly it is almost always dirty.
FA. Tony Moulam 1945

14 Black Crack . . . .   VS 4c
The cleaner right-hand crack gives good jamming or laybacking.
Well protected and excellent when dry - a fine physical pitch.
FA. George Bower 1923

Sheffield Area / Ladybower Area / Stanage / Burbage Valley / Millstone Area / Derwent Edges / Chatsworth Area / Southern Crags

❶ Central Buttress . . . . 🎲 🔲 ⬜ **HVD 3c**

A classic outing up the tallest buttress on the cliff and a good spot to practice multi-pitch climbing. Start left of the buttress, on a block amongst grassy ledges. Traverse right along the break to the front face and climb polished holds to the notch by the pinnacle (a quick ascent is the norm) and a stance on a big boulder. A more direct version up the flake-crack is an option as is a green stomach-traverse from the base of *Central Chimney*. Continue up the centre of the slab to steeper ground then traverse left at one of two levels to a short jamming crack - the final section of *Black Crack*.
FA. Morley Wood 1923

❷ Central Buttress Direct . . 🎲 ⬜ **E1 5a**

The front face of the lower buttress is balancy, reachy and green. It feels bold despite the runners in the break, and a long reach is a great asset. Another great effort for its day.
FA. Bernard Simmonds 1938

Central Buttress

The attractive slabby face of Central Buttress with the tooth of the Stonnis Pinnacle is home to a classic VD and some good but neglected crack climbs. A quick ascent (and descent) of the Pinnacle is straightforward at VD thanks to the chipped holds, and the ancient trick of leaping from its summit back to the main face is no longer required.
Approach (see map on page 520) - From the West Face, walk left until just past the towering Promontory.

❸ Central Buttress Chimney 🎲 ⬜ **VS 4c**

The narrowing-chimney is grassy to start and hard at the blocked exit. Step left to join and finish up *Central Buttress*.
FA. Bernard Simmonds 1938

Stonnis Pinnacle

25m

❹ Soft Rush . . . . 🎲 ⬜ **E6 6a**

The overhanging pillar right of the chimney.
FA. Jon Fullwood 2011

❺ Blind Man's Crack . . . . . 🎲 ⬜ **HVD 4a**

A awkward groove in the right-hand wall of *Central Buttress* which is tricky to start and (a bit) easier above. A direct finish up the wall and crack above the final ledge is **VS 5a**.
FA. Henry Bishop 1913

❻ Blind Man's Buttress . . . 🎲 ⬜ **HVD 4a**

Traverse the break out left from the gully to *Blind Man's Crack* then teeter back right to access the edge of the slab. Climb this - often green - to ledges then finish up the crack on the left.
FA. J.Cotterill 1925

❼ Left Promontory Gully. . . . . . . ⬜ **Diff 3a**

The deeply-recessed gully left of the Promontory gives easy scrambling through garbage thrown in from above to a harder exit on the right up a short, steep, slippery corner. Much used as a way down, though it is easier and safer to walk round!

Not much sun | 8 min | Sheltered | Green

Queen's Parlour

The Promontory

The huge jutting prow of the Promontory is one of the tallest buttresses on grit and has a interesting set of climbs; the oddity of *Promontory Traverse* is a 'must-do' and it is worth a quick look at *Meshuga* before shaking your head and walking away, suitably stunned. The gloomy northeast-facing side-wall of the Promontory has some good routes though they tend to be green and lichenous for most of the year; when dry there is some fine steep climbing on rounded holds and flaring breaks to be had here.

Approach (see map on page 520) - From the west face, walk left to the towering Promontory.

8 Rope Trick . . . . 🕙🗹 ☐ **E2 5c**

Traverse the lowest break to the arete by strenuous jamming and no footholds. Lassoing the spike on *Promontory Traverse* alleviates the need to place runners on the crucial part of the route and is more like **E1 5c**. Pull onto the ledge on the nose awkwardly, to a possible belay. The best way on is by the exposed and awkward *Easy Exit* up the crest of the buttress.
FA. Roy Leeming 1969

9 Vikings in a Sea of Sweat . . . 🗟 ☐ **E2 5c**

A rarely repeated route up the breaks in the wall above the start of the traverse of *Rope Trick*.
FA. John Allen 1986

10 Longships . . . . . 🕙🗏🗹🗟 ☐ **E2 5c**

Low in the grade for lanky jamming aficionados, others will find it desperate. Traverse the break to where it becomes double, then climb the reachy wall and rounded wall to a finish up the wall right of *Promontory Traverse*; or escape off left.
FA. Gary Gibson 1981

11 Firebird . . . . 🕙🗟 ☐ **E2 5c**

Start along the central break until it is possible to climb up to the spike on *Prom Traverse*, then finish up the pumpy layback flake and short finger-crack above.
FA. Dave Humphries 1977

12 The Bounder . . . . ☐ **E1 7a**

With a pre-flicked rope over the spike, leap the void, latch and climb past the poor pocket then choose a route up the wall.
FA. Johnny Dawes 1996. Well named, OK the grade is a bit odd!

Routes 13, 15 and 18 described on next page

The Spike

13 Prominent Tory Reverse . 〈23〉 ▨ ▭ **E2 5c**
A counterpoint to the classic traverse gives an alternative view of the buttress with some harrowing positions along the way. See previous page for topo of pitch 1.
1) 5c, 15m. Traverse the highest break out to the spike and make a hard move to reach the belay out on the nose.
2) 5c, 15m. Continue at the same level (delicate) via the very rounded break to easy ground: a scary pitch to follow.
FA. Chris Craggs, Colin Binks (alts) 1992

14 Meshuga. . . ⌜Top⌝ ▯ ▨ ✎ ▱ ▭ **E9 6c**
        ⌞50⌟
A major route following the blunt overhanging prow, up the front face of the Promontory, above an evil landing. It gives sustained, dynamic and blind moves between some reasonably positive holds and some unreasonably sloping ones. Start beneath the pocket on the front face. Once above this, a nasty slap around the arete for a hidden dish leads to the famous knee-move - not needed unless you've got long inflexible legs. A final worrying stretch for the break (hard for the short) gains protection and easier ground.
FA. Seb Grieve 1997

15 Easy Exit. . . . . 〈1〉 ▨ ▱ **E1 5b**
The direct escape from the stance on the nose gives a short pitch in an astounding position.
FA. Peter Harding 1949

16 A Day at the Prom . . 〈1〉 ▨ ▨ ▭ **E4 6b**
The beckoning crack is gained by a wild flop/dyno from the other side of the gully (pre-placed, pre-clipped gear), then sprint up the crack to easier ground. Still awaits a clean lead, go and have a look to see why - gulp.
FA. John Allen 1988

17 Kitkat . . . . 〈1〉 ▨ ▯ ▭ **E3 6a**
Teeter across the green shelf to reach *Promontory Traverse* then climb the side-wall, by a series of long reaches linking rounded holds, to a final grasping exit. Typical gritstone requiring large cams to protect.
FA. Charles French 1991

18 Promontory Traverse . . . 〈3〉 ▨ ▭ **E1 5b**
A classic graunch; well protected and quite bizarre though not too difficult for those used to gritstone weirdness.
1) 5b, 14m. Traverse the lowest break to a vertical slot and wriggle up this with difficulty. Shuffle out to the arete (harassing for the short) to a fine stance and awkward belays.
2) 5b, 14m. Roll off the ledge and use a tiny pocket to lunge for the spike. Continue left then pull up onto a short ramp back to the cliff top. This is the original line. The break in the north wall is sometimes followed all the way to the gully by mistake.
FA. Peter Harding 1945

19 Twisted Smile . . . . . 〈1〉 ▨ ▯ ▭ **E1 5b**
From the start of *Promontory Traverse,* climb up the wall to the contorted mouth, then finish direct.
FA. Sean Golden 1977

20 Right Promontory Gully . . . . . . ▭ **Mod**
The deep rift over a series of big boulders. A mild scramble but surprisingly clean and a decent intro to climbing for the timid.

Stonnis Buttress
p.528

Meshuga - p.526

The hanging flake, tough mantel and green slab in the right wall of the gully combine to give **Silicosis - E2 5c**.

1 Stonnis Arete Variations .... VD 4a
1) 4a, 14m. Start round to the left and climb easy rock to the base of a steep slab formed by a huge leaning block on the *Stonnis Arete*. Climb this (crux - hollow holds) to a stance and belay on a ledge over to the right on the other side of the ridge.
2) 12m. Head up the easy-angled groove below the ridge (big gear) to a steep and wide crack, just above the final easy groove.

2 Stonnis Arete .... HVD 4a
A fine climb but very polished in places. Climb the front of the buttress, first right up a slippery groove then left up a short V-chimney. Traverse left past a sharp rib and round the arete to climb the steep slab formed by a huge block to good ledges at the base of a slabby arete, or go direct up a wide crack - awkward and **HS 4b**. Step onto the ridge then 'a cheval' or hand traverse this (poor protection) to the final easy walls and a finish up a short groove.
FA. Henry Bishop 1900

3 The Eighth Fold E6 6c
The roof and hanging rib. Small gear can be placed in the thin slot out right from the start of *Ladykiller Peak*.
FA. Jon Fullwood 2011

4 Ladykiller Peak E3 6b
The tough hanging flake leads to the stump and a delicate finish.
FA. Andy Barker 1992

Stonnis Buttress to Lean Man's Climb
More typical Black Rocks fare; good beefy Orange Spot cracks interspersed with desperate blank walls and rounded aretes. There is less in the way of easier stuff though the Stonnis routes are worth a look.
Approach (see map on page 520) - From the West Face walk left to an open bay.

The Promontory p.525

Descent down the gully - awkward

28m

Descent

5 Fireworks for the Blind E4 6a
The scoopy green slab left of the crack has a few useful and well-spaced holds, and no runners.
FA. Paul Mitchell 1986

6 Stonnis Crack . . . . 🔲🔲 **HS 4b**
This fine crack was left out of the earliest guides as it was thought to be unjustifiably dangerous! Now it gives pleasant climbing to an awkward and rapid exit left. Much harder if you can't jam, but then it would be wouldn't it?
FA. J.W.Puttrell 1900

7 Discombobulator . . . . . . 🔲🔲 **E5 6c**
Climb the hanging scoop above *Stonnis Crack* rightwards with great difficulty to flutings (a big cam gets in the way a bit) then crimp through the bulges above to easy ground on *Sand Buttress*.
FA. Andy Barker 1986

8 Caught Smiling . 🔲🔲🔲🔲 **E6 7a**
Leap from the boulder to a sloper and use a sandy pocket to climb the prow above. A far distant side-runner in *Stonnis Crack* gives little in the way of comfort.
FA. Richard Heap 1998

9 Sand Buttress . . . . 🔲🔲 **VS 4c**
Excellent steep climbing up the imposing buttress. Tackle the steepening crack left of the deep gully to its end then hand traverse out left to a ledge. Climb more steep cracks to another ledge then finish though the bulge directly above. A tougher finish is to traverse back to the right arete and finish up the awkward undercut groove there - **HVS 5b**. *Photo on page 521.*
FA. Fred Pigott 1920

10 Untoward . . . . 🔲🔲 **E5 6b**
The disappearing crack above the start of *Sand Buttress* leads to desperate moves up the arete and an easier finish.
FA. Johnny Dawes 1986

11 Sand Gully . . . . 🔲🔲 **Diff**
A grubby route up the rift, with a choice of lines - sandy and often littered with bottles and cans hurled from the cliff top by escapees from t'City - pillocks! An odd right-hand exit creeps along a ledge below the cliff top - **HVD 4a**.
FA. J.W.Puttrell 1890

12 Camel Hot . . . . . 🔲🔲🔲🔲 **E6 6b**
Good small cams protect the hanging arete which features hard slapping (or a jump) to a sloping break and then tricky laybacking up the fine arete. It will usually need cleaning, or a proper summer, to be in condition. Low in the grade.
FA. Johnny Shephard 1986

13 The Indirect Start . . . . . . 🔲🔲 **E2 6a**
The baffling leaning corner runs out at an impossible wall, so escape right to *Lean Man's Climb*; a tough cookie.
FA. John Allen 1976

14 Lean Man's Climb . . 🔲🔲🔲 **VS 5a**
Tackle the awkward and slippery elephant's-ear layback (crux?) to good ledges; belay. Climb the wall leftwards following the superb zig-zag crack into a final steep groove.
FA. Fred Pigott 1920 .FA. (the flake start) Eric Byne 1933

15 Feeding the Pony . . . 🔲🔲🔲 **E8 6c**
The desperate slab right of *Lean Man's* has great moves - four of them at 6c in a row. Originally done with a big hex side-runner at E7 and said to be easier for the tall.
FA. Mike Weeks 1990s. FA. Ben Heason (without side-runner) 2000s

Fat Men
- this way

Sheffield Area
Ladybower Area
Stanage
Burbage Valley
Millstone Area
Derwent Edges
Chatsworth Area
Southern Crags

1 The Superstitious Start.. 🎲 🦎 ☐ **HVS 5b**
From inside the grungy gully, start up the crack of *Lean Man's Superdirect* to a runner. Cross the left wall above the bulges to a hanging crack and mantelshelf finale.
FA. Peter Harding Friday 13th May 1949

2 Lean Man's Superdirect . 🎲 🦎 ☐ **VS 5a**
1) 5a, 10m. Excellent. Climb the steep, green and awkward groove in the left wall of *Fat Man's Chimney* to a good stance.
2) 5a, 10m. The steep cracks above lead to a ledge on the left and a technical finish back right. Full value for the grade with both pitches being upgraded from 4c by popular demand.
FA. Alf Bridge 1930. Left unrecorded for 15 years due to its difficulty.

3 Fat Man's Chimney .... 🎲 🚶 ☐ **Diff**
The squeezy green rift has a traditional grade and is fun for the fuller of figure - just grunt and go.
FA. J.W.Puttrell 1890

4 Branch Chimney .... ☐ **Mod**
The easier rift branching right from the base of *Fat Man's* also makes a useful way down.

The arete and side-wall above Fat Man's Chimney have a couple of routes. The easiest way up here is via Branch Chimney.

5 Cider Frenzy .... 🧡 🗡 ☐ **E3 6a**
The hanging arete is a less attractive proposition than it looks from below being both bold and bald.
FA. Johnny Shepherd 1987

Lean Man's Climb
p.529

Fat Man's Area
Obviously named in a time when political correctness didn't exist - a deep green rift with several routes in and around it plus a short slab with harder offerings just to the right. *Lean Man's Climb* is the only route here that sees much action. The area can be very green.
Approach (see map on page 520) - From the West Face walk left for 90m.

6 Lean Man's Eliminate... 🎲 ☐ **VS 4c**
This is the well-positioned crack high on the side-wall, starting via the upper section of *Fat Man's Chimney*, or the tricky slab to its right. Finish leftwards using a good pocket and a long reach.
FA. Peter Harding 1945

7 Gomorrah .... 🗡 ☐ **E1 6a**
Tenuous but well-protected climbing, up the slim groove right of the arete which gives a short-lived tussle.
FA. Tony Moulam 1973

8 The Sprain .... 🎲 🗡 🧡 ☐ **E2 5b**
Access the hanging ramp from the block and climb the pocketed wall above. Small cam protection in the thin crack.

9 Liquid Abs .... 🎲 🗡 🧡 🗡 ☐ **E5 6b**
Gain the good pocket then move left and climb the wall on a poor set of holds and with little for your feet.
FA. Andy Barker 1986

10 Badmotorfinger . 🎲 🗡 🧡 🗡 ☐ **E5 6c**
Make a desperate dyno to the mono in the wall, then step slightly left and finish, still with considerable difficulty.
FA. Mark Turnbull 1994

Fat Men - this way

Finale Wall

A series of bold or very bold faces split by arduous wide cracks. Few of the routes see many ascents; they are either too scary or too much like hard work.
Approach (see map on page 520) - From the West Face walk left under the block that is home to *Gaia*, and just round the corner.

⑪ Twin Cracks. . . . . ☐ **VD**
The twin cracks in the groove, reached via steep corner.

⑫ Curtain Call. . . . . ☐ **E1 5b**
Climb a flake to the base of a slab then follow the polished (and chipped) pockets up its centre until holds lead up and left.

⑬ Finale Wall Direct . . . . . ☐ **E2 5b**
From the upper slab stride boldly out right - exposed - and climb the pockets to the top. Not too hard, but very fluttery!

⑭ Cybertron Mission . . . . . ☐ **E6 6b**
The bald, blunt, bold arete from the big flake - scary!
FA. Rob Mirfin 1994

⑮ Lawyer's Chimney . . . . . **HVD**
The left chimney, finish rightwards by floundering onto the slab or direct **HS 4b**. The next route provides a continuation.
FA. Henry Bishop 1913

⑯ Chancery Slab . . . . ☐ **VS 4c**
The polished flutes and pockets up the short face above the col between the west and north faces.
FA. Morley Wood 1923

⑰ Our Kid. . . . . ☐ **E4 5c**
Bridge the gap then bail right to access the hanging slab. Climb this rightwards, then centrally and with no gear!
FA. John Allen 1989

⑱ Slanted and Enchanted . . ☐ **E6 6b**
From runners on the jammed stone, bridge out and swing left to gain pockets, the arete and a sketchy finish.
FA. Mark Turnbull 1994

⑲ Jammed Stone Chimney . . . . ☐ **VS 5a**
The chimney with the eponymous block is pretty much the expected battle, at half-height and again at the top.
FA. Henry Bishop 1913

Birch Tree Wall

1 Curved Crack . . . . ▨ ⬛ ☐ **HS 4b**
The awkward kinked and polished crack has a tricky exit.
FA. Fred Pigott 1920

2 Kra S'Haon . . . . ☐ **VS 4b**
The crack below the huge block of *Gaia* is a route to nowhere.
The reverse journey is *Noah's Ark* at the same grade.
FA. Dave Humphries 1977

3 Gaia . . . . . . ⌜Top⌐ ⬛ ⬛ ⬛ ⬛ ☐ **E8 6c**
⌞50⌟
The stunning hanging groove; brilliant but only for the bold.
The technical crux is getting into the groove but is well
protected (easier for the tall). Superb moves above this gain
a psychologically draining rest point at the top of the groove
where even breathing feels precarious! Slopers out right lead
to the psycho-crux pull onto the arete with a high kick for a
toe-hook, much gusto and a strong will to live.
Photo on page 38.
FA. Johnny Dawes 1986

4 Harder Faster . . ▨2 ⬛ ⬛ ⬛ ☐ **E9 7a**
Gaia's direct finish is harder than its parent and from this one
you will definitely hit the ground - have no doubts.
FA. Charlie Woodburn 2000

5 Through the K-hole . ▨1 ⬛ ⬛ ☐ **E7 6b**
Start as for *Curving Arete* but swing round onto the outer face
as soon as possible and layback above the huge drop. Good
climbing but slightly artificial.
FA. Michael Garton 2001

6 Curving Arete . . . . ▨3 ⬛ ☐ **E5 6b**
Hop onto the undercut arete with great difficulty and then
layback to easier ground. Unprotected.
FA. Derek Bolger 1976

7 Birch Tree Wall Variations . . . ▨ ☐ **HVS 5a**
The left-hand crack leads steeply to a poor rest. Follow the
pumpy lowest crack out left to finish passing a useful tree, or
easier (**4c**) step up and foot traverse along the same crack.
FA. Ivan Waller 1929

8 Birch Tree Wall . . . . ⌜Top⌐ ☐ **VS 4c**
⌞50⌟
1) 4c, 10m. Climb the thin and polished left-hand crack then
move awkwardly right to a blocky groove leading to a stance.
2) 4c, 10m. Traverse the rounded breaks out left to easy ground.
A high tree makes a useful belay for timid seconds.
FA. Jack London 1928.

9 Birch Tree Wall Direct . . ▨3 ⬛ ☐ **VS 5a**
Climb the thin hand-crack into the blocky groove, then follow the
original route throughout - a fine varied pitch.
Photo on page 505.
FA. Ivan Waller 1928

Finale Wall

10 Birch Tree Wall Eliminate 🔲 **E4 6a**
From *Birch Tree Wall* move right, bounce for the break then step back left and undercut for the top. Hard for the short.
FA. Derek Bolger 1978

11 Demon Rib **E3 5c**
The elegant rib is reachy and the landing is poor until the flakes are reached (small cam). Finish up the easier upper arete.
FA. Peter Harding (shoulder for aid) 1949. An astounding ascent for the day although there was a grassy base then.

12 Lone Tree Groove . . . . . . **VS 5a**
The neat slanting groove is a swine to enter. Climb steeply to its base and then improvise; if all else fails try it on your back.
FA. Ivan Waller 1928

13 Lone Tree Gully . . . . **S 4a**
The deep groove gives steep awkward bridging past bulges.
FA. Fred Pigott 1920

14 Pseudonym **E5 6b**
An unprotected rockover gains the slab (easier for the short) then move up to the break (easier for the tall). Continue up the rounded arete above, gained from around the corner.
FA. Nick Plishko 1977

15 Black Book Jon **E7 6c**
Climb the blunt rib on the wall to a sloping shelf (this is **Non Stick Vicar**, *f7B+*). Crozzley slopers lead leftwards to join *Fun Traverse* at its crux, but without its side-runners.
FA. Pete Whittaker 2014

16 The Devil is in the Details **E7 7a**
The indirect finish to *Pseudonym*, up the wall above the break by "the biggest dyno on a gritstone route".
FA. 'Tall' Tom Briggs 2003

17 Fun Traverse **E4 6b**
Hilarious - the pocketed traverse line is followed leftwards with difficulty, passing a useless set of rounded holes. Big cams help.
FA. Dave Humphries 1977

18 South Gully . . . . **HVD 4a**
The final cleft in the cliff is polished and awkward. Heading left at half-height is **South Gully Rib, HS 4b.**
FA. John Laycock 1913

19 South Corner . . . . **HVS 4c**
Up the chimney until the flake on the right can be reached. Swing round on this to a harrowing exit. Odd!
FA. Dave Humphries 1977

20 Bad Hair Day **E4 6b**
The old boulder problem up the arete (*f6B*) to the flakes and a breather. Continue via a solitary good hold to a rounded exit.
FA. Percy Bishton 1998

21 The Runnel **E3 6b**
Balance up the slanting groove to a rounded exit. Unprotected but can be highballed at *f6C*.

22 Slab End . . . . **Diff**
The left-hand chipped and sandy staircase just around the corner. The right-hand version is **VD** and has a tricky exit.

Birch Tree Wall

The attractive west-facing walls are the first to be reached and are arguably the cliff's finest feature. A good introduction to Black Rocks with some great classics like *Lone Tree Gully* and the excellent *Birch Tree Wall* and its variations. Also there is the awe-inspiring line of *Gaia*.
Approach (see map on page 520) - Cross the railway line and scramble up the scree to the face.

Sheffield Area | Ladybower Area | Stanage | Burbage Valley | Millstone Area | Derwent Edges | Chatsworth Area | Southern Crags

1 Diagonal . . . . ☐ **S 5a**
The short slanting crack on the left is harder than it looks.

2 Shredded Feet . . . . ☐ **f7A**
The rounded break is hand-traversed at the limit of friction all
the way to a finish up *Golden Days*. It is more like 6c except on
cool and crisp days. Worth E3 if you place gear.
FA. John Allen 1976

3 Small Things . . . . . . ☐ **E6 6c**
Make a big jump to the flake below the bulge - *f7B*. Step left to
flakes (gear) and make a massive dyno for the top.
FA. Thomas de Gay 2001

4 Golden Days . . . ☐ **E3 6a**
The thin flake in the blunt nose has a huge reach (wire) and then
a sprint for the rounded top. A midget gem - *f6B+* above pads.
FA. John Allen 1976

Birch Tree Wall

*The four slab routes are now always done above pads and
spotters although all of them were originally soloed and given
hefty E Grades.*

5 Jumping on a Beetle ☐ **f7B**
Round in the shade. Mantel onto the gutter - hard - then step left
and make a delicate step up to the arete. E6 as a solo.
FA. Johnny Dawes 1994

6 The Angel's Share . . ☐ **f7C**
A desperate route up the centre of the slab with weird moves.
Lack of holds on the blank slab require several rockovers with
timed momentum from the previous rockover to make progress
- ultimate Dawes. E8 as a solo. *Photo opposite.*
FA. Johnny Dawes 1994

7 Velvet Silence . . . . . ☐ **f7A+**
The original route on this slab, just within bouldering height.
Make a tough mantel onto the gutter and teeter right to the blunt
arete which is used to gain the top. There isn't a single pebble
on the whole slab. E6 as a solo.
FA. Gabe Regan 1987 Onsighted by Johnny Dawes.

8 Make it Slappy . . . . ☐ **f7B+**
Round in the recess climb the hanging left arete to a grasping
exit on to the slab. E6 as a solo.
FA. Simon Hunter 1994

9 Tree Crack . . . . ☐ **HVS 5b**
This wide crack is a bit of a hump until you can reach the stump.

10 Damp . . . . ☐ **S 4b**
The greasy angle to an awkward exit.

11 Dry . . . . ☐ **S 4a**
The slabby rib with an overlap is the end of everything.

The Block

Behind the right-hand edge of the cliff, directly beyond the approach gully and tucked away in a little wooded valley, is the retiring buttress of The Block. This is home to a bunch of hard routes and a couple of easier ones.
It is rarely busy, and the trees offer shade, though it can be green here after wet weather.
Approach (see map on page 520) - From *Birch Tree Wall*, walk right and up into the open gully.

Pete Whittaker making the tenuous final moves on *The Angel's Share* (**f7C** or E8) - *opposite* - on The Block at Black Rocks. Although quite high, the landing from this slab is good if well padded and these routes now see a lot more traffic than they used to. They are very highball though and can only be considered boulder problems in the modern idiom. Photo: Mike Hutton

Sheffield Area

Ladybower Area

Stanage

Burbage Valley

Millstone Area

Derwent Edges

Chatsworth Area

Southern Crags

	No star	☆	☆☆	☆☆☆
Mod to S	3	2	2	-
HS to HVS	5	7	4	-
E1 to E3	2	6	6	-
E4 and up	-	3	4	-

Hidden, neglected, and rarely visited, Turningstone Edge has always kept its delights camouflaged under a green cloak. The slope below the cliff is smothered in rhododendrons and this invasive species has taken quite a hold on the cliff too. Concerted efforts by keen locals have cleared sections of the cliff face and its base, making the place worth a visit. A pair of secateurs might be an addition to your normal rack to help keep the shrubs in check.

Approach   Also see map on page 504

There is roadside parking opposite a farm where a track (footpath sign) heads towards the trees. Follow this to a beech copse with a stone wall around it. Walk straight through this (the footpath jigs away right) and follow a narrow trod across the field and straight into the woods. A hundred metres or so into here is a clearing where the local kids build dens and campfires; continue in the same direction to arrive at the top of the cliff where a scramble down a narrow gully reaches its base, towards its centre.

Conditions

The buttresses face east and only receive sun in the morning. The area is best avoided after damp weather though it also makes a good retreat on hot summer days as it is almost always shady. It is also very sheltered from westerly winds.

Map showing Kelstedge, Chesterfield, B6036, A632, Ashover, Bradley Edge (Peak Bouldering), Turningstone Edge, Holstone Gate Road, Copse, Cocking Tor. About 500m. N. GPS 53.15221 / -1.49513

Cocking Tor

A minor edge just south of Turningstone Edge which has a couple of good routes and a bit of bouldering. It is northeast facing, so shady in the afternoon. The buttress juts from the hill and dries rapidly.

Approach - From the copse on the main approach, follow the edge of the field to the right and continue into the woods until you reach a path that runs rightwards to the top of the crag. Wrestle your way down to the base.

❶ **Both Sides Now** . . . . 　　　　　 **E4 6a**
The bulges and arete on its left-hand side has a bold finish.
FA. Jon Fullwood 2008

❷ **Jelly Tot** . . . . 　　　　 **f6A+**
The short lower arete. Just left is *f6A+* as well.
FA. John Allen 1976

❸ **Jelly Ache** . . . . 　　　　 **E3 5c**
The jutting prow gives a great climb with a high crux. The start is a *f5* problem to the break.
FA. John Allen 1976

❹ **Cyclops' Eye** . . . . . . 　　　　 **E2 5c**
Climb the centre of the wall past the 'eye'.
FA. Tom Proctor 1974

Sheffield Area | Ladybower Area | Stanage | Burbage Valley | Millstone Area | Derwent Edges | Chatsworth Area | Southern Crags

Graham Parkes above the sea of rhododendrons on the excellent *Overton Arete* (HVS 5b) - *page 541* - Turningstone Edge.

Sheffield Area

Ladybower Area

Stanage

Burbage Valley

Millstone Area

Derwent Edges

Chatsworth Area

Southern Crags

Approach and descent

Happy Landings to Amber Buttress

An imposing roof and a couple of arete/groove combos provide a good range of routes. There are another half a dozen or so climbs further left but they are normally inaccessible without advanced jungle warfare tactics. **Approach (see map on page 536)** - At the bottom of the approach gully turn right (looking out) and scramble under some steep imposing grooves and down a short slippery slab.

1 Second Chance . . . . 🎯🔳☐ **E3 6a**
A Tom Proctor special, bold and strenuous. Start on the boulders below the left end of the roof and climb the right-trending break through the roof. Move right and then up the right side of the next overhang to the ledge. A second pitch heads through the roof via a flake and then up the arete above.
FA. Tom Proctor 1977

2 Calling the Grit . . . . 🎯🔳☐ **E4 6b**
The first weakness in the big roof right of *Second Chance*. From a thin black flake and tricky gear use poor pinches to gain the lip and easier moves into *Second Chance*.
FA. Jon Fullwood 2008

3 Happy Landings . . . . 🎯☐ **E2 5b**
Start under the centre of roof and follow the flake out right to access a ledge - a dangle, heel-hooks and pulling on rhododendron stumps are the norm. The slabby wall above is easier but reachy and often a bit damp and dirty.
FA. Len Millsom 1963

4 National Power . . . . 🎯🔳🔳☐ **E4 6a**
Follow the *Happy Landings* break to halfway. A long stretch leads to holds above the lip. Power up to a good ledge and finish direct. Big cams will be found useful/essential.
FA. Mark Turnbull 1994

Approach

Descent/escape tricky scramble

Approach

Approach and descent

⑤ Finger Bang . . . f7A+

The roof/prow is followed to a finish on the ledge. Descend either by traversing or jumping. Highball but a padded landing in the bushes.

⑥ Jay Walker . . . . VS 4c

Climb the corner to the roof and traverse airily out left to access the ledge on *Happy Landings*. Finish awkwardly as for that route.
FA. Len Millsom 1963

⑦ Depressed Arete E1 5b

Climb straight into the corner of **Happy Crack** (an **HS 4b** that comes in from the right) then move out right along the break to the arete, and up to ledge. Take the nose right and back left to an exposed and grubby finish (micro-cams useful).
FA. Andy Lewandowski 2009

⑧ Cave Chimney Direct . . . VS 4c

Climb out of the cave by heading up the left wall then bridging past the scary jammed blocks hanging in the jaws above. An intimidating exercise which is harder for the short of leg.
FA. Tom Proctor 1970s

⑨ Cave Route . . . . S 4a

Avoid the main challenge by heading easily into the cliff then burrowing skywards (various lines) to a rat-hole of an exit. Heading right after the initial easy section offers a devious but easy way to the cliff top (**Mod**). This is also a useful descent always assuming you can locate it from above.

⑩ A Clash of Kings E6 6b

The acute angled prow is started on the left then climbed direct with an increasing feeling of urgency.
FA. Kyle Rance 2013

⑪ Twilight Slab . . . HVS 5a

A blunt arete leads to a hanging slab. Teeter up this to a tricky exit, a bit better protected that it first appears.
FA. Barrie Dixon 1975

⑫ Rhody Groove . . . . VD

The angular corner with a substantial tree is a bit rubbish really - but at least it is a good line. From the ledge at its top either escape right, or left and down - reversing *Cave Route*, or struggle up the short wide crack - **S 4b**.

⑬ Amber Buttress . . . . . . HVS 5a

A fine climb up the side-wall. Head steeply to the short flake, place decent gear here then commit to moves round right to access a ledge. Head up the bold slab to a ledge and a finish up a short arete.
FA. Barrie Dixon 1975

⑭ Amber Arete . . . . VS 4c

A 'near classic' up the arete. Climb steeply up the arete to a short slab and head warily up this - be aware of the possibility of dirt which has washed down from the ledge above. Finish as for the last route.
FA. Barrie Dixon 1975

⑮ Amberration . . . . . . HVS 5c

The side-wall right of the arete (and left of the descent gully) gives a decent pitch with fingery but well-protected climbing. A late discovery rescued, at least temporarily from the clutches of the rhoddies.
FA. Andy Lewandowski 2009

Awkward belays on the ledge

Descent scramble

6m

12m

Plum Groove to Overton Arete

Approach (see map on page 536) - At the bottom of the Descent Gully turn left (looking out) to arrive at a short wide wall. The routes here now terminate at the undercut ledge as the roof and wall above are inaccessible due to a huge rhody cornice. Beyond this the path undulates past three steep jutting buttresses, all of which have worthwhile routes.

① Plum Bob . . . . HS 4c
The left arete of the wall to a tricky exit onto the ledge.
FA. Tom Proctor 1975

② Plumb-Line . . . . S 4a
Reachy moves up the juggy wall 3m right of the arete.
FA. Tony Kartawick 1991

③ Burn before Listening . . . HVS 5b
Just right again is this snappy eliminate.
FA. Nick Taylor 2009

④ The Diagonal Line . . . . . S 4b
The overlap that crosses the previous climb is worth doing.

⑤ Plum Groove . . . . HVD 4a
The shrubby groove in the centre of the wall to an awkward exit.
FA. Tom Proctor 1975

⑥ Damson . . . . HS 4c
Climb the neat right arete of the groove. No jam(ming) required.

⑦ Stump Route . . . . VS 4c
An awkward start past the overlap leads to better holds.
FA. Tony Kartawick 1991

To the right the base of the cliff becomes severely undercut.

⑧ Bent Line . . . . VS 5a
Access the wall awkwardly from a block, climb to a break then shuffle right until it is possible to finish direct.
FA. Tom Proctor 1975

⑨ Umbongo E1 5c
From under the roof pull onto the wall to the upper break then move strenuously right to a nice finish on the arete. A direct finish as for *Bent Line* is an easier option.
FA. Paul Williams 1985

⑩ River of Life . . . f7C+
A fine but arduous problem across the roof on flat side-pulls.
FA. James Pearson c2010

⑪ Right Between the Eyes . E5 6b
The left-hand wall of the deep groove is climbed initially via a tough rib (side-runner) then between the 'eye' pockets, first left then right to finish direct.
FA. Jon Fullwood 2008

⑫ Vee Variant . . . . VS 4c
Climb into the cleft then make a tricky start to traverse the left wall to reach a fine finish out on the arete.
FA. Tom Proctor 1975

Sheffield Area | Ladybower Area | Stanage | Burbage Valley | Millstone Area | Derwent Edges | Chatsworth Area | Southern Crags

13 Vee Chimney . . . . S 4a
The imposing rift is better than it looks. For an easier time, don't get too involved with the damp depths of the chimney.
FA. Tom Proctor 1975

14 Hello Sailor. E2 5c
The jutting arete is a tough direct start to *Sail Arete*. Finishing up the left-hand side of the upper arete is a harder option.
FA. Mark Turnbull 1993

15 Car Boot Sale . . . . VS 4b
An awkward start leads to decent crimpy moves up the slab above about 3m right of the arete. Keeping left is harder - **5a**.

16 Sail Arete . . . . S 4b
A fine exposed diagonal climb that can be a bit dusty. Cams for the horizontals might be found useful. Finish up the lovely arete with a tricky last move.
FA. Barrie Dixon 1975

17 Sail by Date E3 6a
Technical climbing up the right-hand side of the slab, via a crucial mantel/rockover. The rhododendrons are encroaching once again.
FA. Mark Turnbull 1993

Next is the imposing face of the Sugar Loaf Buttress.

18 Rainy Day Blues E3 5c
A fine intimidating line through the roof and up the soaring arete above. The starting roof is powerful, reachy and a bit bold to a rest ledge. Move right to the upper arete which is very exposed.
FA. Tom Proctor 1975

19 Baker's Groove E1 5b
The central crack is a fine butch pitch, though the upper part is often a bit dirty. The initial wall and roof are powerful, a start on the right is easiest. Once established a good rest is available before a tough move to access the final easy slab.
FA. Len Millsom 1963. A solid VS from the 60s though a convenient tree eased the access over the initial roof.

20 Fall From Grace. E2 5c
The right-hand side of the face is a decent pitch, sadly the upper slab is often dirty making the exit tough to impossible.
FA. Jim Lawrenson 1991

21 Buns Out of the Oven . . . . HS 4b
Climb the huge groove just right until above the roof then traverse left to avoid the jungle above. An intimidating pitch.

To the right is Overton Buttress, it has a good set of climbs.

22 Waiting for Tony E1 5b
An interesting eliminate up the narrow wall left of the arete.
FA. Mark Danson 1992

23 Overton Arete . . . . . HVS 5b
The smart arete is most often climbed following its right-hand side to start, and left to finish - excellent. It is also possible to start on the left and finish on the right - **E1**. *Photo on page 537.*
FA. Tom Proctor 1975

24 Hugo de Vries E1 5b
The flaky seams right of the arete give a fine balancy pitch with a rockover to reach the niche. Finish leftwards.
FA. Mark Turnbull 1993

25 Overton Wall . . . . VS 4c
Balance straight up the slabby face to the niche, step right and then finish direct - steep.
FA. Barrie Dixon 1975

Further right is Secret Buttress which has some good bouldering. The easiest approach is to return to the top of the crag-top path and tunnel through rhododendrons until you reach a large boulder - the Turning Stone. Secret Buttress lies below.

Sheffield Area

Ladybower Area

Stanage

Burbage Valley

Millstone Area

Derwent Edges

Chatsworth Area

Southern Crags

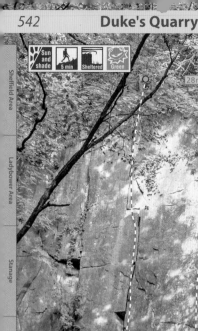

28m

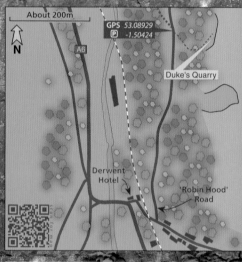

Sheffield Area

Ladybower Area

Stanage

Burbage Valley

Millstone Area

Derwent Edges

Chatsworth Area

Southern Crags

There are a lot of abandoned quarries around Matlock and most of them are pretty grotty. Duke's Quarry is one of these though it does have a couple of outstanding lines - *Great Crack* in particular is worth a look after a dry spell. It is well sheltered from any bad weather.

Approach   Also see map on page 504

Follow the A6 to a bridge over the river and turn off by the Derwent Hotel towards Crich. After 100m turn left along a minor road to Robin Hood/ Holloway. After about 400m pull onto a muddy parking area on the left where a track leaves the minor road. Cross the road and head up the footpath into the quarry. No access problems.

❶ Great Crack . . . . Top 50   **HVS 5a**
The superb soaring crack in the left-hand side of the main wall. The start is often damp and the whole thing can be a bit greasy - when bone-dry it might just be VS.
FA. Tom Proctor 1975

❷ Dharma **E7 6c**
This is the withering wall to the right of *Great Crack*. It has some peg runners and gives great fingery technical wall climbing when it is clean - which isn't very often.
FA. Johnny Dawes 1986

	No star	☆	☆☆	☆☆☆
Mod to S	-	3	-	-
HS to HVS	-	2	2	-
E1 to E3	3	3	5	-
E4 and up	-	2	-	3

A sheltered and secluded crag in the southern Peak with a small but decent selection of climbs. Well worth a visit if you are in the area and fancy somewhere a little different. The climbs tend to be steep and are fairly well spread through the grades. There are several worthwhile crack climbs here plus some bold aretes.

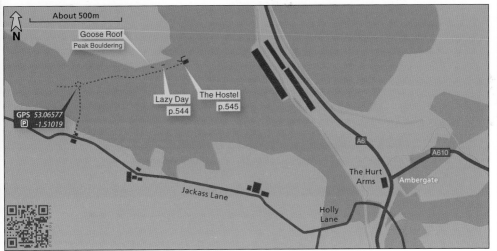

Approach   Also see map on page 504

The crag is reached from the superbly named Jackass Lane which is accessed from the A6 just south of Ambergate. From The Hurt Arms (another great name) in Ambergate, drive south for 200m and turn west by a church onto Holly Lane. Follow this over the river, then turn left and continue along Jackass Lane for about 2km to a gated track on the right, just past a fancy stone house with unfeasibly large chimneys. Drive up the rough track (shut the gate) to parking at an open area in the trees 250m from the gate. From the muddy parking, follow the track to the right as it descends gently for about 500m (less than 10 minutes) passing the odd bits of rock hidden in the trees away to the left. Eventually the tall walls and buttresses of the Lazy Day area appear on the left, a short scramble from the path. Just beyond this is the rather incongruous hostel and its associated walls.

Conditions

A neglected edge, which can be green and midgy; best enjoyed on late spring evenings after a dry spell. The surrounding trees means that the whole place is exceptionally sheltered and may even be worth a look on damp days as the foliage will keep the worst of the rain off.

Sheffield Area

Ladybower Area

Stanage

Burbage Valley

Millstone Area

Derwent Edges

Chatsworth Area

Southern Crags

Lazy Day

The first significant buttress is one of the last two sections of rock reached on the approach. It presents a decent wall with trees that shade the area in summer. In winter the place can be sunny and pleasant.
Approach (see map on page 543) - Walk down the track until Lazy Days appears on the left.

1 Brian . . . . [   ] **E2 5b**
Steady climbing leads to tricky moves to access the left arete.

2 Positively Pointless . . . . [   ] **E3 5c**
A direct finish to *Brian* gives a short but bold pitch.
FA. Chris Plant 1981

3 That's Cool by Me . . [   ] **E6 6b**
Tackle the taxing hanging groove (tiny wires) to a high crux.
FA. Andy Chrome 1997

4 Concrete Parachute . . . . [   ] **E3 6a**
The surprisingly tough blank, right-facing corner. Gear is tricky.
FA. Chris Plant 1984

5 Lazy Day. . . . . [   ] **E5 5c**
The fine jutting pillar is the best route on the cliff, though sadly the ancient bolts that protect it turn the whole thing into a bit of a worry-fest. The final roof is quite tough but at least this section has some proper runners.
FFA. Graham Hoey 1997

6 Fryday . . . . [   ] **E6 6b**
The right side of the arete has insecure moves to the first gear - a hand-placed bolt at half-height. Move onto the left side at the jug below the overlap to place good gear, then finish back on the right, with hard moves between small crimps and slopers.
FA. Matt Fry 2010

7 Plumber's Corner. . .  **VS 4c**
The vertical angle gives a fine pitch reminiscent of Millstone's *The Mall*, though with the odd loose hold. At the top of the corner, make a long and delicate traverse away right until a usually dirty exit presents itself.
FA. Ted Wells, Len Pearson et al 1970s

8 Plumber's Direct . . . . . . [   ] **E1 5c**
A stubborn left-hand finish is often dirty.

9 Farewell to Arms . . . . . . [   ] **E1 5b**
The fine crack right of the corner gives a great pitch which can be reasonably well protected with tiny wires. Trend right to finish. A direct finish is a grade harder - E2 5c.
FA. Pete Clarke 1989 Direct Finish Graham Parkes 2006

10 Visually Stunning Underpants
. . . . [   ] **E5 6b**
The tenuous line up the centre of the wall has one very sticky move then eases rapidly. Gear is tiny wires and an old peg.
FA. Matt Szabo 1987

11 Bramble Crack. . . . . [   ] **HVS 5b**
A good solid crack-climb mostly on locking jams though with trickier moves at two-thirds height.
FA. Ted Wells, Len Pearson et al 1970s

12 Blackberry . . . . [   ] **E3 6b**
The next seam is finger-tip thin, and highly technical too. The usually dirty finish provides the cherry on the cake.
FA. Ted Wells, Len Pearson et al 1970s

The Hostel

The final walls are behind the actual hostel. Some of these are given the bouldering treatment these days. Be wary of tricky exits onto mulch-covered ledges - care required.

13 Curving Crack . . . . **VS 4c**
The twisting fissure is a bit too wide for comfort for most; holds on the walls help a bit.

14 Flyaway **E1 5b**
The shallow open groove gives a nice pumpy pitch.
FA. Malc Taylor 1984

15 Marathon Man **E3 6a**
The wall left of the arete via crucial moves onto the flexi-flake and a reachy finish up the blunt rib above.
FA. Pete Clarke 1988

16 The Bat House . . . . **HVD**
The atmospheric cleft narrows with height to a tricky exit. A claustrophobic inner exit (at about **HS**) is an option for deviants and other dark variations exist.

17 Pillar Chimney . . . . **VD**
The narrower rift in the right wall of the big chimney is awkward to start, and to finish, but worthwhile as well.

18 The Man from Delmonte . **HVS 5b**
The rounded arete on the left, then the right, to an easier finish.
FA. John Gilthorpe 1986

19 Unidentified Flying Object **E2 5c**
The attractive shallow grooves in the face lead to a crucial stretch for green ledges. Once established, finish easily.
FA. Bob Hassell 1981

20 S.H.A.D.O. **E1 5c**
The bouldery wall left of the arete.
FA. Matt Szabo 1987

21 Wet with Sweat **E2 5c**
The arete through the gap is precarious and gear is lacking.
FA. Howard Tingle 1981

22 Black Corner . . . . . . **S 4a**
The big imposing corner gives a fine physical pitch.

To the right are more routes though they are generally overgrown and neglected although there is one notable route.

23 My Kai **E8 6c**
A compelling line that links the boulder problem (usually chalked) of **Moo Cow**, *f7A+* with the finish of **Gecko Blaster**, E7 6c which traverses in from the arete on the right.
FA. Tom Randall 2013

Side tabs: Ingleborough Area · Giggleswick Area · Malham and Gordale · Arncliffe to Kilnsey · Loup Scar and Troller's Gill · South Cumbria · Lancashire

Ingleborough Area

Giggleswick Area

Malham and Gordale

Arncliffe to Kinsey

Loup Scar and Troller's Gill

South Cumbria

Lancashire

Sheffield Area · Ladybower Area · Stanage · Burbage Valley · Millstone Area · Derwent Edges · Chatsworth Area · Southern Crags

Sheffield Area · Ladybower Area · Stanage · Burbage Valley · Millstone Area · Derwent Edges · Chatsworth Area · Southern Crags

Sheffield Area — Ladybower Area — Stanage — Burbage Valley — Millstone Area — Derwent Edges — Chatsworth Area — Southern Crags

Sheffield Area · Ladybower Area · Stanage · Burbage Valley · Millstone Area · Derwent Edges · Chatsworth Area · Southern Crags

Sheffield Area • Ladybower Area • Stanage • Burbage Valley • Millstone Area • Derwent Edges • Chatsworth Area • Southern Crags

Sheffield Area • Ladybower Area • Stanage • Burbage Valley • Millstone Area • Derwent Edges • Chatsworth Area • Southern Crags

Stars Grade Route . . . . *Photo*. **Page**

Crag Index

Sheffield Area · Ladybower Area · Stanage · Burbage Valley · Millstone Area · Derwent Edges · Chatsworth Area · Southern Crags

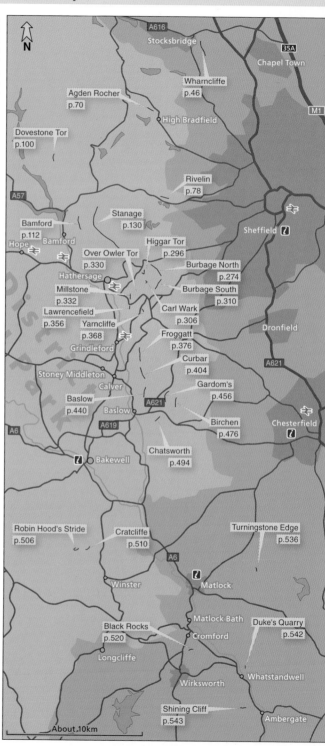